Trademark and Copyright Litigation: Forms and Practice

Trademark and Copyright Litigation: Forms and Practice

Volume 1: From Case Assessment through Electronic Discovery

Mark V.B. Partridge and Phillip Barengolts

OXFORD
UNIVERSITY PRESS

Oxford University Press, Inc., publishes works that further Oxford University's objective of excellence in research, scholarship, and education.

Oxford   New York
Auckland   Cape Town   Dar es Salaam   Hong Kong   Karachi   Kuala Lumpur   Madrid   Melbourne
Mexico City   Nairobi   New Delhi   Shanghai   Taipei   Toronto

With offices in
Argentina   Austria   Brazil   Chile   Czech Republic   France   Greece   Guatemala   Hungary   Italy
Japan   Poland   Portugal   Singapore   South Korea   Switzerland   Thailand   Turkey   Ukraine
Vietnam

Published by Oxford University Press, Inc.
198 Madison Avenue, New York, New York 10016

Oxford is a registered trademark of Oxford University Press
Oxford University Press is a registered trademark of Oxford University Press, Inc.

Library of Congress Cataloging-in-Publication Data

Partridge, Mark V. B.
 Trademark and copyright litigation : forms and analysis / Mark V.B. Partridge, Phillip Barengolts.
  p. cm.
 Includes bibliographical references and index.
 ISBN 978-0-19-973493-1 (hardback : alk. paper)
 ISBN 978-0-19-979582-6 (cd-rom)
 1. Intellectual property—United States—Trial practice.
 I. Barengolts, Phillip. II. Title.
 KF2983.P37 2011
 346.7304'820269—dc22   2010044256

1 2 3 4 5 6 7 8 9

Printed in the United States of America on acid-free paper

Note to Readers
This publication is designed to provide accurate and authoritative information in regard to the subject matter covered. It is based upon sources believed to be accurate and reliable and is intended to be current as of the time it was written. It is sold with the understanding that the publisher is not engaged in rendering legal, accounting, or other professional services. If legal advice or other expert assistance is required, the services of a competent professional person should be sought. Also, to confirm that the information has not been affected or changed by recent developments, traditional legal research techniques should be used, including checking primary sources where appropriate.

(Based on the Declaration of Principles jointly adopted by a Committee of the
American Bar Association and a Committee of Publishers and Associations.)

Contents

Preface

This book grows out of years of experience with trademark and copyright litigation, as sifted through an LLM course taught by the authors at The John Marshall Law School in Chicago. Our students are eager for the "real thing." As a result, we share with them actual materials that we and others have used in trademark and copyright litigation in federal courts around the country. There are plenty of how-to books available on litigation, but we have not found any built around actual samples of the materials filed in court in trademark and copyright cases. Our purpose in our course, and in this book, is to give those real world examples, supported with the kind of commentary and advice you might get from discussing your case with an experienced litigator. We seek to give the "what and how" of litigation, as we have experienced it in our practices.

The forms appearing in this book are taken from actual cases. In many instances they are public records on file in court. In others, the forms are internal memos, working outlines, or letters with clients or opposing counsel. We've gathered samples that we think will be useful to both novice and experienced litigators in preparing and litigating cases in this field. These are not intended as perfect examples of how things are done, only real ones. In many cases, we've changed the documents to preserve confidentiality, protect the innocent, or save the guilty from embarrassment, but all of the forms are "the real thing"—prepared and used in the course of actual disputes.

CHAPTER

1

Case Assessment

A. Preliminary Considerations

The first step in addressing an infringement problem is to identify the client's goals. Does the client seek money, or will it be satisfied with an injunction to halt the infringement? Is the client concerned about an encroachment on its rights, or does it seek to stop or inhibit competition? Is the client responding to a particular wrong, or does it recognize the importance of a general enforcement effort to deter others from infringing conduct? Does the client need to take action to preserve the scope of its trademark rights?

It is important that you help your client shape realistic goals; otherwise, your efforts are destined to fail. To shape and evaluate these goals, you should weigh the risks of litigation against the risks of taking less aggressive action—or taking no action at all.

One risk of litigation is the potential to substitute a financial problem for a legal one. Litigation is expensive and unpredictable. Cost estimates are possible, but the process is akin to trying to build a house while someone else is trying to tear it down. The needs of the case will constantly change depending on the actions taken by your opponent. You and your client should consider whether the legal problem justifies the cost. Can you afford to win? A second risk of litigation is the potential effect of a loss. If you pursue a weak case, will a loss damage your rights against others? Is your trademark at risk of being held generic? Will your copyright be held invalid? Would it be better to begin with stronger cases or weaker opponents?

Not taking action presents different risks. Trademark rights can be lost or weakened through a failure to enforce them—a failure to take action against one infringer may reduce your ability to prevent more damaging infringements in the future. Also, your client's failure to take action may foster a reputation in its industry, making it a target for other encroachments.

Trademark and copyright owners should take a strategic approach to the protection of their rights. Rather than merely reacting to particular infringements when they rise to a level sufficient to inflict competitive damage, it is desirable to investigate and identify potential problems at an early stage and formulate a plan for challenging the infringements before they become major problems. One approach is to take on the easy cases first, building a record of successful enforcement through publicly available consent judgments and settlements. Another approach is to pursue a prominent test case where a solid victory will create precedent to deter other infringers. Either way, the favored approach is to develop a consistent proactive plan rather than a reactive response that varies from case to case.

B. Investigation

Before determining a course of action, it is important to fully investigate the situation. A complete understanding of the client's problem will help you determine the best plan for a particular situation. Moreover, the obligations imposed by Rule 11 of the Federal Rules of Civil Procedure require that the attorney have a good faith basis for the allegations presented in a complaint. Courts have imposed sanctions where attorneys have relied solely on the representations of their clients and failed to make an independent investigation of the facts alleged in a complaint.

The initial investigation of the case should be guided by an evaluation of the matters typically at issue. Investigations of trademark rights involve significantly more issues surrounding protectability, and we focus primarily on those issues below, touching on copyright matters when appropriate.

Protectability. The existence of protectable rights is an essential element of any infringement action. Is the term, device, or work at issue capable of being protected? Protectability may not be immediately apparent when encountering a term in an unfamiliar industry, with product configuration, or with a work of unknown origin. An investigation will need to address whether the term is generic, descriptive, or arbitrary in the particular industry to determine the scope of protection available or whether product configuration is functional and incapable of protection. If the term or device is capable of protection, is it inherently distinctive? If the term or device is not inherently distinctive, has the client made sufficient use of it to create secondary meaning? Is a work sufficiently creative to have protection under the Copyright Act? If the work is older, did the owner follow the formalities of renewal under the prior versions of the Copyright Act to maintain protection? Is the chain of title in the work properly documented, especially if the work is one allegedly made for hire?

Priority. Before filing a claim of trademark infringement, it is essential to confirm that the rights a client seeks to protect were acquired prior to the alleged defendant's. First adoption is not necessarily sufficient. Priority can be established through federal application date for a trademark, use analogous to trademark use, or technical trademark use in commerce.

Strength of mark. Once prior rights are confirmed, you must turn to the key issue of likelihood of confusion, which involves balancing various factors. Strength refers to the source-indicating power of a mark shown through distinctiveness, use, advertising, and public awareness.

Similarity of marks. In an infringement action, to evaluate the similarity of the marks, you must consider the marks as they appear to the consuming public. Thus, the context in which the client uses the mark, including on packaging or advertising, is important.

Channels of trade. Are the products sold through the same outlets? Is one strictly an institutional product, while the other is sold only to retailers? Likelihood of confusion is increased if the products are sold through the same channels of trade. Confusion may be avoided if the channels are unrelated.

Nature of purchase. This factor involves consideration of the cost of the goods involved, the method of purchase, and the characteristics of the purchaser. Confusion is more likely for inexpensive items, purchased on impulse by ordinary consumers, rather than for expensive items purchased after careful deliberation by professional purchasers.

Actual confusion. Although hard to obtain, evidence of actual confusion is the best evidence of a likelihood of confusion. Such evidence can include misdirected communications, returned product, incorrect attribution in the media, and comments from competitors or customers. If a client is experiencing actual confusion, it is essential to document and preserve the evidence at the earliest possible moment in the contemplation of an enforcement action.

Intent. While bad intent is in the mind of the defendant, a client may possess circumstantial evidence that supports a finding of the defendant's intent to trade on the client's goodwill. Has there been past contact between the parties? Are they direct competitors in a narrow field? Did they previously have a contractual relationship?

Licensing. After considering the information that supports a finding of prior rights and the likelihood of confusion, you should also assess the potential defenses that may be raised against a client's claims. If the client licenses the trademark, does it exercise quality control? If not, its marks may be at jeopardy to a claim of naked licensing, i.e., licensing without quality control, which can result in an abandonment of rights. The naked licensing defense is rarely successful, but it can significantly cloud the issues, reducing your chances for quick relief or a favorable settlement. By investigating the potential problem early, the client may be in a position to mend its ways before the matter becomes a problem.

Ownership. In these times of frequent corporate acquisitions, reorganizations, and transfers to holding companies, you should determine that your client is the correct owner of the rights at issue. Mistakes over title are not likely to determine the final merits of the case, but disputes over title can again reduce your chances of quick relief or a favorable settlement.

Genericide. Before bringing suit, you should question your client on whether their mark is at risk of being deemed a generic term. This is particularly important in specialized fields, such as medical products or computer technology. The client may have marketing studies that bear on this issue. Misuse of the mark in advertising and promotional materials may also be a problem. The client may want to change its marketing strategies before bringing suit.

Laches and acquiescence. How long has your client known of the potential infringement? Undue delay in bringing action may prevent you from obtaining a preliminary injunction or damages.

C. Sources of Information

There are a variety of sources of information for your prelitigation investigations.

Witnesses. It is useful to begin your case analysis with interviews of the persons immediately concerned about the problem. What do they see as the problem? Why do they want you to take action? How would they explain the matter to the judge or jury? In the typical consumer products company, the brand manager is likely to be the person immediately concerned about the problem and will be a source of evidence throughout the case. In a smaller company, perhaps the president will be the one most concerned about the problem. Regardless of who brings the problem to your attention, your task will be easier if you have the support of the persons most concerned with the problem. Based on their concerns, you can shape the client's claims and engage in further investigations of the issues. After all, these persons likely will be your key witnesses. Cases often flounder when attorneys pursue a case theory that is not fully supported by the persons directly involved with the products at issue.

Client's records. An initial review of the relevant documents held by your client is important. Smoking guns often cool and become insignificant if uncovered early in the investigation. At a minimum, you can avoid shaping a case that is contradicted by your own documents and can develop a favorable spin for those documents that seem damaging. The failure to uncover problem documents early is akin to climbing out on the limb of a large tree, then handing your opponent a saw. In addition to marketing documents relating to the products at issue, you should review the following categories of documents:

Registration files. Especially in the trademark context, look particularly for positions taken by the client during prosecution that may limit its rights. The copyright registration process often is straightforward, however, in some cases a client may have exchanges with the copyright office that would be discoverable.

Trademark and Work development. The selection and adoption of a mark, as well as the discussions surrounding that selection and adoption, often play a central role in trademark litigation. Contracts involved in the development of a work, e.g., employee contracts and agreements with independent contractors for works made for hire often are crucial in establishing copyright ownership. Joint authorship issues also should be reviewed. If facing a copyright infringement claim, review of any and all materials used in the creation of the work.

Licensing. Proper licensing may strengthen you client's rights, but improper licensing may weaken the strength of the mark or result in an abandonment of rights. Rights in a work may be divided in numerous ways, so careful analysis of any licenses in the work, especially one transferring rights to or from the other side in a dispute, is essential.

Market research. Look for brand awareness studies that confirm the strength of the mark at issue, advertising and focus group studies that may provide evidence of actual confusion, brand studies that may bear on genericness.

In the copyright context, market analysis should focus on the potential for implicating the transformative work doctrine in fair use.

Sales. In addition to sales data, field sales reports may include instances of actual confusion or reports of product disparagement by your opponent. Sales of a work will be relevant to the actual damages calculation if infringement is found.

Litigation. Look for past decisions affecting the brand or work, contrary positions taken in other litigation, settlement agreements that limit the scope of your client's rights, prior adverse testimony.

Trademark search. Commercial search reports will include registration, application, and common-law use information that can help you evaluate priority, the extent of third-party use, and the scope of your client's rights. Copyright searches also are available, including through the Copyright Office's personnel.

Dun & Bradstreet reports. Public reports used for credit checks will help you correctly identify the defendant and evaluate the potential for damages. Such reports may also provide information and admissions on the nature of the defendant's business and its first use of the name at issue.

Online information. In the twenty-first century, the other side's website will usually provide you with information useful for evaluating the similarity of the products, marks, and channels of trade, as well as the identity of officers and other relevant witnesses. A simple search on an Internet search engine can provide you with information about the defendant's business, first use of the offending mark, and media accounts of the a product, service, or work, as well as information on the fame of a mark and the extent of third-party use or similar marks. Social networks such as LinkedIn and Facebook also can provide valuable information about an opponent's officers and company. Industry-specific websites, newsgroups, and blogs often also are available over the Internet. For more in-depth information, news searching services, such as Nexis, can uncover harder to find and historic materials.

Government filings. Official records will help you correctly identify the defendant in your pleadings and may also provide admissions by the defendant that help you prove some of the elements of your claims. Some of the places you may want to check are The Patent and Trademark Office; Secretary of State for the defendant's state of incorporation and/or residence; Securities and Exchange Commission; Food and Drug Administration; Bureau of Alcohol, Tobacco, Firearms, and Explosives; and others.

Investigators. You should consider using paralegals or outside investigators to obtain information about the potential defendant, particularly in counterfeiting or gray market goods cases where information about the defendant is not available through public sources. Investigators often obtain information by posing as potential customers. As long as the investigators do not interact with the other side in a manner beyond that of an ordinary consumer, e.g., cause the defendant to commit an infringement it would not otherwise commit or inquire about intent, the use of a subterfuge to obtain information will not harm your case or the evidence obtained. Courts in most jurisdictions also have found that pretext investigations in this context do not violate an attorney's obligations under the rules of professional ethics.

Surveys. The use of survey evidence has become common at trial in trademark infringement cases. You can also use a survey to evaluate the likelihood of succeeding in a potential action or as a tool to drive settlement discussions. You can use attorney-designed and supervised surveys both to evaluate the merits of a potential case as well as in negotiations with opponents to induce settlement. Although you would need to have a survey conducted by an independent expert for use at trial, the attorney-designed survey is substantially cheaper and can be a very effective tool to show your opponent the kind of evidence that you would be able to present if the case goes to trial.

D. Identification of the Claims

Having gathered the necessary information for a full understanding of the problem, your attention should turn next to the identification of the legal claims that may be pursued. In addition to traditional trademark infringement, the problem may give rise to other claims, based on the principles of trademark law, including trade dress, product configuration, counterfeiting, gray market, false advertising, and dilution. There may be state law claims for unfair competition, based on the same acts that give rise to federal claims under the Federal Trademark Act (the Lanham Act). Where domain names are involved, consider cybersquatting claims under the Anti-Cybersquatting Consumer Protection Act. Where logos or trade dress are involved, there may also be claims for copyright infringement. The use of a person's identity may raise right of publicity claims. The choice of claims can affect the available remedies and the defenses at issue.

If material that may be protected by copyright is involved, typically, only a copyright infringement claim will be permitted because of the Copyright Act's preemption clause. That is, the Copyright Act preempts all state laws that provide rights equivalent to rights granted under the Act. Thus, tort claims that purport to protect a work from copying or breach of contract claims based upon the unauthorized distribution of a work will not be heard by a court because such claims should be brought under the Copyright Act. Also, copyright protection is only offered for a limited time and courts are wary of extending protection to works once they have fallen into the public domain under another theory, such as trademark. *See Dastar Corp. v. Twentieth Century Fox Film Corp.*, 539 U.S. 23 (2003). Breach of contract claims, however, may lie where the contract protects the use of material beyond what copyright may protect.

E. Initiating the Objection

The decision to contact your opponent before filing suit arises in every case. The decision is a strategic one: which course will lead most directly to the desired result at the cheapest cost? There is no legal obligation to contact your opponent before filing suit. Moreover, your opponent's complaint to the court that the case was brought without warning will probably fall on deaf ears. Judges know that an attorney may have many good and sufficient reasons to file suit without first notifying the defendant. Thus, the failure to give prior warning is not likely to have any adverse effects on the merits of your client's claims.

In some circumstances, an initial contact by phone or written demand may be the best course of action to resolve a case quickly. Can your client build on an existing relationship to resolve the matter short of litigation? Sometimes it is easier to resolve a dispute before the litigators get involved. Once you file the complaint, compromise may become more difficult as your opponent consults outside counsel and positions harden. The value of in-house settlement negotiations, or even negotiations between outside counsel for the parties, must be balanced against the risk of litigating in a distant foreign jurisdiction because threatening litigation may permit your opponent to bring a declaratory judgment action in its home forum. A compromise is to file a complaint at the same time that you make your demand, but refrain from service if your opponent agrees to negotiate a prompt settlement.

F. Available Relief

Your selection of forum will partly be controlled by the desired relief. In federal court, the relief available for violation of trademark rights includes an injunction, actual damages, disgorgement of profits, up to treble damages in exceptional cases, attorney's fees, product recall, corrective advertising, the use of a disclaimer, and destruction of infringing materials. If a trademark counterfeiting claim is asserted, statutory damages and up to treble damages may be available. Cybersquatting claims also permit recover of statutory damages. Relief available in federal court actions for copyright infringement includes an injunction, actual damages, statutory damages, attorneys' fees, costs, and destruction of A wider range of options is available through settlement or mediation. A private resolution can make creative use of licensing, assignment of rights, label modifications, phase-out periods, and other business arrangements. At the Trademark Trial and Appeal Board (TTAB), relief is limited to refusal or cancellation of registration. No monetary relief is available. In proceedings under the UDRP, relief is limited to transfer or cancellation of the domain name at issue.

G. Considerations for Litigation

Once you decide to proceed with litigation, there are a number of additional questions to address.

1. Who do we sue?

In addition to the corporate defendant, should you include individual officers in the complaint? When dealing with a small counterfeiter, you will generally include the individual principals in the complaint; otherwise, the value of any injunction may evaporate as the principals form new operations to continue their illegal activities. You may also want to consider the benefit of including suppliers, retailers, or distributors as defendants. When dealing with private label problems, for example, clients are often reluctant to sue their own customers. Such problems can be handled effectively by suing the supplier.

2. Where should we sue?

This question goes beyond the formal requirements of personal jurisdiction and venue. There is a wide divergence between the federal courts in terms of local practice. Virginia is known for its "rocket docket." Illinois has a special mediation program for the Lanham Act. Some districts have a docket backlog that may delay summary judgment decisions and trial. The Northern District of California has an early neutral evaluation procedure to help resolve disputes. In choosing between courts, you will want to supplement your own research with the advice of knowledgeable local counsel. You may find that the most helpful local counsel is not necessarily an intellectual property lawyer but rather someone familiar with the local courts.

3. What procedures should we pursue?

The client's goals may demand that you seek immediate relief. That relief could come in the form of an ex parte temporary restraining order (TRO), a TRO with notice, or a motion for preliminary injunction. A TRO is most likely to be granted in counterfeiting situations. Both a TRO and a preliminary injunction will be difficult to obtain if the plaintiff has known of the infringing conduct for a substantial period of time.

4. Should we ask for a jury?

Aside from the usual David and Goliath considerations, a jury demand may affect pretrial aspects of a case. A judge may be more reluctant to grant summary judgment if there is a jury demand but more willing to become involved in settlement efforts.

5. What about insurance?

As a plaintiff, there is nothing you can do about insurance coverage, right? Wrong. The possibility of insurance coverage may improve your ability to recover monetary relief. Conversely, it may also result in a vigorous, insurance-funded defense. You can draft your complaint in a way that increases or decreases the likelihood that there will be coverage under the advertising injury clause of a typical general comprehensive liability policy.

I. Trademark Litigation

The principal source of civil trademark law in the United States is the Lanham Act, 15 U.S.C. §§ 1051–1141, a federal trademark statute that provides for the registration of trademarks and for the protection of registered and unregistered trademarks. Individual states also provide protection for trademarks by statute or common law. Federal courts have original jurisdiction over civil actions for trademark infringement arising under the federal statute. Claims may also be brought in state courts.

The principal interest of U.S. trademark law is to protect the public from deception in the marketplace. The secondary interest is to protect the trademark owner's rights in the value of the trademark as a designation of source.

The definition of a trademark under U.S. law is broad. A mark is any device that serves as an indication of source. In addition to words or logos, a trademark may be a sound, color, slogan, product configuration, or smell. To serve as an indication of source, a device must be inherently distinctive (i.e., immediately recognized by consumers as a designation of source) or must acquire distinctiveness or "secondary meaning" through use (i.e., come to be recognized as a designation of source). Secondary meaning is proved through circumstantial evidence such as length and amount of use, media recognition, and survey evidence.

There are four basic classifications of trademarks: generic, descriptive, suggestive, and arbitrary. Generic terms are never protected. Descriptive terms (such as names and geographic places) can be protected only after they acquire secondary meaning. Suggestive terms (such as MUSTANG for cars or COPPERTONE for suntan lotion) are protected upon use in commerce. Arbitrary terms (such as KODAK or EXXON) are deemed to be inherently distinctive and can also be protected upon use.

Trademark rights in the United States arise from use, not from registration. Registration is beneficial, however, to increase the scope of protection. For example, upon registration, the registrant receives nationwide constructive use back to the date of application. After five years, a registered mark may become incontestable so that it can no longer be challenged as descriptive.

The test for trademark infringement is whether the junior user's use of a mark is likely to create confusion with the senior user's use of its mark. Likelihood of confusion is determined by considering various factors including the strength of the plaintiff's mark, the similarity of the marks, the similarity of the goods or services involved, the similarity of the channels of trade, the nature of the purchase and purchaser, evidence of actual confusion, and the intent of the defendant. None of these factors are determinative. Infringement is not determined by an in-court side-by-side comparison of the marks but must be based on the marks as they are encountered in the marketplace.

The strength of a mark refers to its level of distinctiveness and recognition. A highly distinctive, well-known mark is entitled to a broader scope of protection than a descriptive mark. The marks and goods need not be identical to establish infringement. The use of confusingly similar marks for related goods or services may be sufficient to create a likelihood of confusion. Evidence of actual confusion and bad intent are not required to establish infringement. The courts recognize that evidence of actual confusion is difficult to obtain. When found, however, actual confusion is deemed to be the best evidence of a likelihood of confusion. Since the test for infringement involves deception of the public, lack of bad intent is not a defense. Intent to infringe, however, will raise a presumption of a likelihood of confusion. Evidence used to prove infringement typically consists of direct testimony on the relevant factors, as well as survey evidence regarding the reaction of relevant purchasers.

Although trademark law prohibits uses that create a likelihood of confusion regarding the source of the goods, it does permit some uses. Permissible uses include parody, comparative advertising, and indications of compatibility or descriptive use.

The trademark owner initiates a claim for infringement by filing a complaint in state or federal court. (The general public does not have standing to sue for trademark infringement.) If the trademark owner seeks damages, a jury may hear the case; otherwise, a judge will hear the case.

The relief available for trademark infringement includes injunctive relief, destruction of the infringing marks, and monetary damages. Monetary relief may include actual damages, lost profits, or an award of the infringer's profits. Attorney's fees may be awarded in extraordinary cases, such as cases of willful infringement. Under federal law, the awards for infringement constitute compensation, not a penalty, although punitive damages may be available under state law.

Preliminary injunctive relief for trademark infringement is available upon consideration of the following factors: likelihood of success on the merits; threat of immediate, irreparable injury; the balance of hardship between the parties; and the public interest. Summary judgment prior to trial may be granted if there are no material disputes of fact, and one party is entitled to judgment as a matter of law.

The final decision of the trial court can be appealed to the court of appeals for review of legal error or clearly erroneous findings of fact. A final appeal to the Supreme Court is possible but is usually granted only to resolve conflicts between the lower courts over interpretation of the federal statute.

The Lanham Act also provides causes of action against trademark counterfeiting, dilution of a trademark, and cybersquatting. Counterfeiting occurs when someone uses a spurious mark that is identical with or substantially indistinguishable from a registered mark. The relief available for counterfeiting includes an ex parte seizure of goods and records, lost profits, treble damages, prejudgment interest, statutory damages and attorney's fees.

Dilution statutes protect the trademark owner's interest in the value of its famous mark by providing injunctive relief against tarnishment of the mark or blurring of the distinctiveness of the mark. Damages are available for willful violations. The fame of a mark is determined by considering various factors: the length of use, the amount of sales and advertising, public recognition, and the absence of similar marks used by third parties. Tarnishment occurs when the defendant associates the plaintiff's mark with unsavory goods or activities. Blurring of the distinctiveness of a mark is generally found when a unique and well-known mark is used for unrelated goods or services, thereby reducing the public's association of the mark with the plaintiff. A likelihood of confusion regarding the source or sponsorship of the defendant's goods or services is not an element of a dilution claim. Protection against dilution is also available under the statutes of various states.

Cybersquatting protects a trademark owner from attempted hijacking of domain names that are identical or confusingly similar to the protected mark if the defendant "has a bad faith intent to profit" from the use of the protected trademark. http://blog.pattishall.com/category/cybersquatting/ - _ftn1

A. Distinctiveness: The Starting Point for Trademark Protection

The concepts surrounding distinctiveness began to emerge in the case law of the early twentieth century. In 1917, for example, the Sixth Circuit considered a trade dress infringement case involving the packaging for fly paper.[1] This case is significant for its recognition of the rationale for such protection:

> Wherever, then, the first user has through a particular trade dress, as here, *so identified his product as to indicate that it is his*, every principle of fair dealing, fair competition, forbids any subsequent user of the same product to adopt any part of the first user's dress without otherwise effectively distinguishing his dress from that of the first user.

How are we to know when a plaintiff has "so identified" his product so as to earn protection? It is through the combination of "details for the very purpose of denoting the origin of his product." Those details may be unremarkable when segregated, but when aggregated, they create trade dress that identifies the product as his. "[I]t is through such distinctive characteristics, considered in a unitary way, that the first user and the public can be protected against confusion and deception as to his product."

---

1. O. & W. Thum Co. v. Dickinson, 245 F. 609, 611 (6th Cir. 1917).

In this language, we see the beginning of the principle that "distinctive" trade dress may serve to identify the source of the product. The perspective of the consumer is implied but not directly identified. The public's perception appears more clearly in the language of a 1933 case involving the mark DOBBS for hats.[2] The court notes that efforts to distinguish one mark from another in the marketplace "will largely depend upon the connotations which the public has become habituated to attach to the plaintiff's use of the name." The name has come to mean more than just a name; it has taken on a new meaning:

> Since this name *has acquired its secondary meaning* largely by advertising, that fact and the content of such advertising will indicate the association of ideas which attaches in the public mind to the name.

The defendant's mark is an infringement because it evoked "[p]recisely the same images" in the public mind as the plaintiff's.

How do we decide if the trade dress or trademark is distinctive? In 1925, a case arose over the use of the mark GOLD MEDAL for flour.[3] The court recognized that the right to protection may vary according to the type of mark:

> To take another view of the matter, the degree of exclusiveness of appropriation accorded to the originator of a trade-name often varies with the kind of name he originates. If the name or mark be truly arbitrary, strange, and fanciful, it is more specially and peculiarly significant and suggestive of one man's goods, than when it is frequently used by many and in many differing kinds of business .... The phrase "Gold Medal" is distinctly not in the same class of original, arbitrary, or fanciful words as "Kodak" and "Aunt Jemima." It is a laudatory phrase, suggestive of merit, recognized by some organization of authority awarding a prize. It is only allied to some particular business or person by insistent, persistent advertising.

The court identified an important distinction in trademark law that has become more sharply cleaved over time: the distinction between terms that are inherently distinctive—that is, terms that immediately identify source— and terms that are not and only acquire distinctiveness through advertising or other persistent use. In other words, they acquire a "secondary meaning."

The implication of these early cases and others like them is that mere adoption and use of a device is not enough. One's mere attempt to identify a product as his own is not sufficient in itself. The evidence should show that

---

2. Hat Corp. of Am. v. D.L. Davis Corp., 4 F. Supp. 613, 622 (D. Conn. 1933).
3. Fr. Milling Co. v. Washburn-Crosby Co., 7 F.2d 304, 305 (2d Cir. 1925).

the attempt successfully makes that impression on the public mind. Justice Frankfurter commented on this "psychological function" of trademarks in 1942, stating: "Whatever the means employed, the aim is the same—to convey through the mark, in the minds of potential customers, the desirability of the commodity upon which it appears. Once this is attained, the trade-mark owner has something of value."[4]

An important corollary is also suggested by Justice Frankfurter's language. If the mark or trade dress conveys nothing to the public mind, the owner has nothing of value. A device may perhaps serve as an indication of source in the public mind immediately, because the device is "original, arbitrary, or fanciful," or it may only do so after "insistent, persistent advertising." The important issue is the factual question of the effect of the device on the public mind. Over time, however, there has been a tendency to shift attention from that important issue and instead focus on whether the device fits into one analytical category or the other.

B. The Love of Categories

The Second Circuit provided the classic statement on the categories of distinctiveness in a case involving the mark SAFARI for clothing.[5] The court stated:

> The cases, and in some instances the Lanham Act, identify four different categories of terms with respect to trademark protection. Arrayed in an ascending order which roughly reflects their eligibility to trademark status and the degree of protection accorded, these classes are (1) generic, (2) descriptive, (3) suggestive, and (4) arbitrary or fanciful.

In the lengthy explanation that follows in the case, there is little mention of the relationship of the categories to the perspective of the public. The public is given a passing nod in mentioning that a generic term cannot be protected regardless of "what success it has achieved in securing public identification." The case leaves the impression that the critical question is the identification of the correct category. If that Holy Grail is known, all else is revealed.

The Fifth Circuit did a better job of connecting the test to the public mind in *Chevron Chemical Co. v. Voluntary Purchasing Groups, Inc.*,[6] the leading case on the application of the categories of distinctiveness to trade dress.

---

4. Mishawaka Rubber & Woolen Mfg. Co. v. S.S. Kresge Co., 316 U.S. 203, 205 (1942).
5. Abercrombie & Fitch Co. v. Hunting World, Inc., 537 F.2d 4, 7 (2d Cir. 1976).
6. 659 F.2d 695 (Former 5th Cir. 1981).

Deciding a dispute over the trade dress for agricultural chemicals, the court recognizes the public's place in the equation, stating:

> The purpose of a trademark is to enable consumers to distinguish between similar goods or services supplied from different sources. Some words and phrases are patently distinctive and, therefore, qualify facially for legal protection . . . . However, descriptive terms, geographical place names, and family surnames are not inherently distinctive and do not alone identify any particular company's product. They were not protected as trademarks unless they had acquired distinctiveness through extensive use by a single supplier, *so that the public would recognize them as identifying the source of the product.* This consumer identification is known as "secondary meaning."

TWO PESOS

In *Two Pesos, Inc. v. Taco Cabana, Inc.,*[7] the Supreme Court considered the protection of trade dress in the décor of Mexican restaurants. The case arose from a special verdict after a jury trial in which the jury found that the plaintiff's trade dress was inherently distinctive but lacked secondary meaning. The trade dress at issue was defined as:

> a festive eating atmosphere having interior dining and patio areas decorated with artifacts, bright colors, paintings and murals. The patio includes interior and exterior areas with the interior patio capable of being sealed off from the outside patio by overhead garage doors. The stepped exterior of the building is a festive and vivid color scheme using top border paint and neon stripes. Bright awnings and umbrellas continue the theme.

The Supreme Court endorsed the categories of descriptiveness set out in *Abercrombie*. Finding no basis in the Lanham Act for treating trade dress any differently from trademark, the Court held that inherently distinctive trade dress was entitled to protection without a showing of secondary meaning:

> The Fifth Circuit was quite right in *Chevron*, and in this case, to follow the *Abercrombie* classifications consistently and to inquire whether trade dress for which protection is claimed under § 43(a) is inherently distinctive. If it is, it is capable of identifying products or services as coming from a specific source and secondary meaning is not required. This is the rule generally applicable to trademarks, and the protection of trademarks and trade dress under § 43(a) serves the same statutory purpose of preventing deception and unfair competition. There is no persuasive reason to apply different analysis to the two.

---

7. 505 U.S. 763 (1992).

The Court's decision in *Two Pesos* confirms the general rule for distinctiveness and establishes that the rule applies to trade dress as well as trademarks.

C. Likelihood of Confusion: Trademark Law's Key Principle for Infringement

Likelihood of confusion is the key term of art in trademark law. All trademark infringement cases turn on this issue. Yet the words alone hold little content.

D. Background

In 1944, the likelihood of confusion concept entered federal statutory law. Today, Section 32 of the Lanham Act[8] provides a cause of action against any person who shall:

use in commerce any reproduction, counterfeit, copy, or colorable imitation of a registered mark in connection with the sale, offering for sale, distribution, or advertising of any goods or services on or in connection with which such use is likely to cause confusion, or to cause mistake, or to deceive.

Similar protection of *un*registered marks arose under Section 43(a) of the Lanham Act. While the original statute did not clearly encompass the use of a mark that is likely to cause confusion, Section 43(a) developed into a provision that covered infringement of unregistered marks and trade dress in effectively the same manner as Section 32 covered registered marks. With the Trademark Law Revision Act of 1987, Section 43(a)(1)(A) was revised and provided explicit protection for the likelihood of confusion consistent with the then-developed case law and now states:

Any person who, on or in connection with any goods or services, or any container for goods, uses in commerce any word, term, name, symbol, or device, or an combination thereof . . . which is likely to cause confusion, or to cause mistake, or to deceive as to the affiliation, connection, or association of such person with another person, or as to the origin, sponsorship, or approval of his or her goods, services, or commercial activities by another person . . . shall be liable in a civil action by any such person who believes that he or she is or is likely to be damaged by such act.

---

8. 15 U.S.C. § 1141(1).

With that amendment, the protection recognized by the courts for unregistered marks and trade dress became explicit. The current version of Section 43(a) provides a comprehensive standard for interpreting likelihood of confusion.

E. Types of Confusion

Generally, there are three types of confusion: actual, source, and sponsorship. Actual confusion occurs when a person mistakes one product or service for that of another because of similar names or packaging. For example, persons familiar with PINE-SOL cleaner who encounter PINE-SOLL cleaner in a similar package are likely to mistake it for the national brand.

Source confusion occurs when a person believes that two products come from the same source or are manufactured by the same company. Persons familiar with the Morton's Steakhouse restaurant chain would not mistake MORTON'S frozen dinners for the popular restaurant, but they are likely to believe that the frozen dinners are manufactured by the restaurant.

Sponsorship confusion occurs when a person is likely to believe that the second product is authorized, sponsored, or approved by the original company. When a person sees a Chicago CUBS logo on a baseball hat, she does not mistake the hat for a baseball team, nor does she think that the baseball team has entered into the hat business. She does, however, think that the hat is authorized or sponsored by the baseball team.

Each of these three types of confusion is actionable. In each case, the basis for trademark protection is to prevent deception of the public. The public's interest is primary; the trademark owner's interest is secondary. In other words, the trademark owner's rights are protected so that the public is not deceived, and the scope of the trademark owner's rights are (or should be) exactly equal to the scope of rights necessary to prevent deception of the public.

F. The Subjects and Objects of Confusion

Since trademark infringement arose as a species of unfair competition, it was initially thought that the confusion could only be created by a competitor. The early cases now seem quaint, but at the time, it was not so obvious that principles of unfair competition could be extended to situations where there was no competition between the parties. In 1917, for example, the Second Circuit asserted in *Aunt Jemima Mills Co. v. Rigney & Co.*,[9] where the district

---

9. 247 F. 407 (1917).

court had decided that use of the mark AUNT JEMIMA'S for pancake syrup did not infringe the plaintiff's rights in the same mark for flour:

> It is said that even a technical trade-mark may be appropriated by any one in any market for goods not in competition with those of the prior user. This was the view of the court below in saying that no one wanting syrup could possibly be made to take flour. But we think that goods, though different, may be so related as to fall within the mischief which equity should prevent. Syrup and flour are both food products, and food products commonly used together. Obviously the public, or a large part of it, seeing this trade-mark on a syrup, would conclude that it was made by the complainant. Perhaps they might not do so, if it were used for flatirons. In this way the complainant's reputation is put in the hands of the defendants. It will enable them to get the benefit of the complainant's reputation and advertisement. These we think are property rights which should be protected in equity.

Thus, since the early case law recognized that a broad range of goods or services can result in a likelihood of confusion, it should be no surprise when a modern tribunal finds confusion between the use of the same mark on shoes and hair care products.[10]

For similar reasons, it was also argued in early unfair competition cases that the victim of the confusion must be engaged in business, thereby excluding protection to charitable institutions. As late as 1975, this notion was still noted favorably by the First Circuit in *DeCosta v. Columbia Broadcasting System, Inc.*[11] (denying protection on other grounds to the creator of the Paladin persona as charitable entertainment for children):

> We hesitate to take the step of offering common law unfair competition protection to eleemosynary individuals. Whether legislatures are better equipped than courts to deal with this problem, we cannot clearly say, but in our posture of doubt would prefer to see expansion of protection come from that source.

The trademark laws are not designed to prevent all persons from being confused. Likelihood of confusion is determined on the basis of a "reasonably prudent consumer" and depends on the circumstances. When expert buyers are involved, the standard becomes the "reasonably prudent expert buyer." When children are involved, the standard is "reasonably prudent child" because the courts generally rule that children are less discerning than adults and more likely to be confused. When there are mixed buyer classes, the Third Circuit has held that "the standard of care to be exercised by the

---

10.   Helene Curtis Indus. Inc. v. Suave Shoe Corp., 13 U.S.P.Q. 2d 1618 (T.T.A.B. 1989).
11.   520 F.2d 499 (1st Cir. 1975).

reasonably prudent purchaser will be equal to that of the least sophisticated consumer."

G. When Does Confusion Occur?

Initially, the only relevant confusion involved the purchase of the parties' goods. Section 32(1) of the Lanham Act only proscribed likelihood of confusion, mistake, or deception of "purchasers as to the source of origin of such goods and services." In 1962, however, Congress amended the Act to delete the quoted portion from the section.[12] Now, it is clear that relevant confusion can involve any person, consumer, prospective consumer, end user, or even an uninvolved onlooker. The result is a much expanded confusion test encompassing nonpurchasers.

Confusion that occurs *after* the initial purchase is referred to as "post-sale confusion." The injury derives in part from the fact that post-sale nonpurchasers may be prospective purchasers, with the confusion potentially affecting their future purchasing decisions. As stated in *Lois Sportswear, U.S.A., Inc., v. Levi Strauss & Co.*,[13] "[t]he confusion the Act seeks to prevent in this context is that a consumer seeing [appellant's] familiar stitching pattern will associate the jeans with appellee and that association will influence his buying decisions." Thus, even if the street corner retailer explains to a purchaser that the cheap ROLEX watch is a counterfeit, the retailer will still be liable because people who observe the purchaser wearing the counterfeit or who receive the watch as a gift are likely to be confused into believing it is the real thing.[14] The direct purchaser, furthermore, might sell it to an unknowing third party without explaining that it is counterfeit.

The recognition of prepurchase confusion was slower to develop. Perhaps the earliest case was *Grotrian, Hefferich, Schulz, Th. Steinweg Nachf. v. Steinway & Sons*,[15] where the Second Circuit declined in 1975 to hold "that actual or potential confusion at the time of purchase necessarily must be demonstrated to establish trademark infringement." The court explained that the harm at issue was not that someone would be confused when she bought the piano. Rather, that harm arose because the "Grotrian-Steinweg" name

---

12. 15 U.S.C. § 1114(1) (amended 1962).
13. 799 F.2d 867, 872–73 (2d Cir. 1986).
14. *See, e.g.,* U.S. v. Hon. 904 F.2d 803 (2d Cir. 1990), *cert. denied,* 498; U.S. 1069 (1991) (jury could consider likelihood of confusion of general public, not just purchasing public); U.S. v. Yamin, 868 F.2d 130, 133 (5th Cir.), *cert. denied,* 492; U.S. 924 (1989) (no error where jury was instructed to find liability if general public, not just potential purchasers, likely to be confused); U.S. v. Torkington, 812 F.2d 1347, 1352–53 (11th Cir. 1987) (likelihood of confusion encompasses post-sale confusion).
15. 523 F.2d 1331, 1341–42 (2d Cir. 1975).

would attract potential customers based on the Steinway reputation. Later, in *Mobil Oil Corp. v. Pegasus Petroleum Corp.*,[16] the Second Circuit found the defendant's use of its name would infringe Mobil's use of a flying horse logo because "potential purchasers would be misled into an initial interest" in the defendant's products, even if they learned the truth before the sale was consummated. The court therefore held that "such initial confusion works a sufficient trademark injury."

Recent decisions have embraced the notion of prepurchase confusion by calling it "initial interest" confusion. In *Dr. Seuss Enter. v. Penguin Books USA, Inc.*, the Ninth Circuit recognized in 1997 that the use of another's trademark in a manner calculated "to capture initial consumer attention, even though no actual sale is finally completed as a result of the confusion, may be still an infringement."[17]

H. Where Does Confusion Occur?

Most U.S. laws only apply to conduct within the United States, but its trademark law is unique. While U.S. law recognizes that trademark rights are territorial, confusion occurring outside of the United States may be actionable under U.S. law.[18] This is a departure from the norm. The U.S. Copyright Laws, for example, generally have no extraterritorial application.[19]

The test for extraterritorial application of the federal trademark laws involves three issues: (1) there must be some effect on American foreign commerce, (2) the effect must be sufficiently great to present a cognizable injury to plaintiffs under the federal statute, and (3) the interests of American foreign commerce must be sufficiently strong in relation to those of other nations to justify an assertion of extraterritorial authority.[20]

Most extraterritorial application cases require confusion within the United States. In *Steele v. Bulova Watch Co.*,[21] the Supreme Court held in 1952 that the U.S. trademark laws applied when a U.S. citizen used the BULOVA mark in Mexico. In *Bulova*, there was some evidence of confusion within the United States because some of the watches came back into Texas. Not all extraterritorial application cases require confusion within the United States, however. In *Reebok Int'l, Ltd. v. Marnatech Enter. Inc.*,[22] the Ninth Circuit found that the U.S. trademark laws applied in a case where actual

16.   818 F.2d 254, 257–58 (2d Cir 1987).
17.   109 F.3d 1394, 1405 (9th Cir. 1997).
18.   *See* Steele v. Bulova Watch Co., 344 U.S. 280 (1952).
19.   Reebok Int'l, Ltd. v. Marnatech Enter., Inc., 970 F.2d 552 (9th Cir. 1992).
20.   344 U.S. 280 (1952).
21.   *Id.*
22.   970 F.2d 552 (9th Cir. 1992).

consumer sales of the infringing products may have occurred only in Mexico. The Second Circuit held in *Vanity Fair Mills v. T. Eaton Co.* that the Lanham Act "should not be given extraterritorial application against foreign citizens acting under presumably valid trademarks in a foreign country."[23] A similar result was reached in *Totalplan Corporation of America v. Colborne,*[24] where the Second Circuit refused to apply the Lanham Act to the distribution of cameras in Japan.

I. How Much Confusion is Enough?

The United States Supreme Court has recognized that the junior user does not have an obligation to avoid all possibility of confusion. Instead, the junior user has the obligation "to use every reasonable means to prevent confusion."[25] The Third Circuit has gone beyond the boundaries of that rule and held that the standard for infringement when the defendant enters a new field occupied by an established business should be the "possibility of confusion," rather than the traditional standard of likelihood of confusion.[26] It has since retreated from that position, confirming that the standard for determining trademark infringement under the Lanham Act is likelihood of confusion and cannot be lowered to a "possibility of confusion."[27] Likelihood of confusion is thus firmly established as the controlling principle for trademark infringement.

Surveys are often used to show that prospective purchasers are likely to be confused, but what percentage of confusion is sufficient to demonstrate a likelihood of confusion? In *James Burroughs, Ltd. v. Sign of the Beefeater, Inc.*,[28] the Court of Appeals for the Seventh Circuit rejected the district court's characterization of 15 percent confusion as "small," stating:

> We cannot agree that 15% is "small." Though the percentage of likely confusion required may vary from case to case, we cannot consider 15%, in the context of this case, involving the entire restaurant-going community, to be *de minimus.*

Thus, the court concluded that a 15 percent rate of confusion "evidences a likelihood of confusion, deception or mistake regarding the sponsorship of [defendant's] services sufficient on this record to establish Distiller's right

23.   234 F.2d 633(2d Cir. 1956).
24.   14 F.3d 824 (2d Cir. 1994).
25.   Kellogg Co. v. Nat'l Biscuit Co., 305 U.S. 111 (1938).
26.   Merchant & Evans, Inc. v. Roosevelt Bldg. Prods. Co., 963 F.2d 628, 637–38 (3d Cir. 1992); Country Floors, Inc. v. Gepner, 930 F.2d 1056 (3d Cir. 1991).
27.   A&H Sportswear, Inc. v. Victoria Secret Stores, Inc., 166 F.3d 197 (3d Cir. 1999)(en banc).
28.   540 F.2d 266, 279 (7th Cir. 1976).

to relief." In contrast, in *Henri's Food Products Co., Inc. v. Kraft, Inc.,*[29] the Seventh Circuit held that the district court was correct in holding that a 7.6 percent rate of confusion weighs against a finding of infringement.

Typically, survey researchers and courts recognize that survey results include a "noise" level (or level of meaningless responses) of about 5 percent Accordingly, a level of confusion below 10 percent is at risk of being dismissed as de minimus, while 15 percent to 20 percent or more is usually deemed to be solid evidence in support of a finding of likelihood of confusion.

J. What Factors are Considered?

All of the federal courts apply multifactor tests as guidelines in assessing the likelihood of confusion occurring. One of the first to set forth such a test was the Second Circuit in *Polaroid Corp. v. Polarad Electronics Corp.*, in 1961[30]:

> Where the products are different, the prior owner's chance of success is a function of many variables: the strength of his mark, the degree of similarity between the two marks, the proximity of the products, the likelihood that the prior owner will bridge the gap, actual confusion, and the reciprocal of defendant's good faith in adopting its own mark, the quality of defendant's product, and the sophistication of the buyers. Even this extensive catalogue does not exhaust the possibilities—the court may have to take still other variables into account.

The Second Circuit now applies that test in competing goods cases as well.[31]

The other circuits utilize similar factor tests: for example, the First Circuit, *Boston Athletic Assn. v. Sullivan*[32]; the Third Circuit, *Ford Motor Co. v Summit Motor Products, Inc.*[33] (listing ten relevant factors); the Seventh Circuit, *Schwinn Bicycle Co. v. Ross Bicycles, Inc.*[34] (referring to the factors as "digits" of confusion); and the Eleventh Circuit, *ConAgra, Inc. v. Singleton.*[35] Some courts use the factors listed in Section 729 of the Restatement of Torts (1938), for example, the Tenth Circuit, *Beer Nuts, Inc. v. Clover Club Foods Co.*[36]

---

29.   220 U.S.P.Q. 386 (7th Cir. 1983).
30.   287 F.2d 492, 495 (2d Cir. 1961).
31.   Thompson Med. Co. Inc. v. Pfizer, Inc., 753 F.2d 208, 214 (2d Cir. 1985).
32.   867 F.2d 22, 29 (1st Cir. 1989).
33.   930 F.2d 277, 293 (3rd Cir. 1991).
34.   870 F.2d 1176, 1185 (7th Cir. 1989).
35.   743 F.2d 1508, 1514 (11th Cir. 1984).
36.   805 F.2d 920, 925 (10th Cir. 1986).

Perhaps the most comprehensive list of factors appears in the 1973 case, *In re E. I. Du Pont de Nemours & Co.*[37]:

(1) The similarity or dissimilarity of the marks in their entireties as to appearance, sound, connotation, and commercial impression.

(2) The similarity or dissimilarity and nature of the goods or services as described in an application or registration or in connection with which a prior mark is in use.

(3) The similarity or dissimilarity of established, likely-to-continue trade channels.

(4) The conditions under which and buyers to whom sales are made, i.e., "impulse" vs. careful, sophisticated purchasing.

(5) The fame of the prior mark (sales, advertising, length of use).

(6) The number and nature of similar marks in use on similar goods.

(7) The nature and extent of any actual confusion.

(8) The length of time during and conditions under which there has been concurrent use without evidence of actual confusion.

(9) The variety of goods on which a mark is or is not used (house mark, "family" mark, product mark).

(10) The market interface between applicant and the owner of a prior mark:

    (a) a mere "consent" to register or use

    (b) agreement provisions designed to preclude confusion, i.e., limitations on continued use of the marks by each party

    (c) assignment of mark, application, registration and good will of the related business

    (d) laches and estoppel attributable to owner of prior mark and indicative of lack of confusion

(11) The extent to which applicant has a right to exclude others from use of its mark on its goods.

(12) The extent of potential confusion, i.e., whether de minimus or substantial.

(13) Any other established fact probative of the effect of use.

The *Du Pont* factors continue to provide a useful and comprehensive checklist for proof of likelihood of confusion.

It must be remembered that the factor tests are only aids that must be weighed in determining the ultimate issue of likelihood of confusion. The analysis of confusion is a question of fact, not a mechanical process or calculation. There is no precise mathematical formula. The factor tests are helpful guidelines, not "hoops a district court need jump through." It is erroneous to

---

37. 476 F.2d 1357, 1361 (C.C.P.A. 1973).

engage in a "pedantic" application of the factors without consideration of the totality of circumstances. Ultimately, we are concerned only about whether in fact the public will be deceived by the defendant's conduct.

II. Copyright Litigation

A. The First Step

Generally, a plaintiff must own a copyright registration in order to file a copyright infringement suit. While some courts have held that merely filing an application to register one's copyright in a work is sufficient to grant jurisdiction to the federal courts to hear a claim, having a copyright registration for the work at issue guarantees that your client will not be thrown out of court for failing to satisfy this technical requirement of the Copyright Act.

B. Understanding Substantial Similarity and Scope of Protection

Reported copyright decisions often reflect a misunderstanding of "substantial similarity" and "scope of protection." The proper application of these key principles can help you shape a copyright infringement case to your best advantage.

C. Substantial Similarity

To prove infringement, the plaintiff must show that the defendant copied elements of a work that are original.[38] The *Feist* test for infringement established by the Supreme Court involves two separate inquiries. First, did the defendant actually copy the plaintiff's work? Second, were the copied elements protected expression and sufficiently important to be actionable? In other words, did the copying constitute infringement? The term "substantial similarity" is used by the courts for both inquiries but has a different meaning in each instance.

The first prong of the infringement test—actual copying—can be established by showing access to the work and substantial similarity. Here, substantial similarity means that the works are in fact sufficiently similar to support a conclusion that one was actually copied from the other. This involves a

---

38.   *See* Feist Publ'n, Inc., v. Rural Tel. Service Co., 499 U.S. 340 (1991).

relatively low threshold: substantial similarity for the purpose of showing actual copying involves a comparison of the works in their entirety, including protectable and unprotected elements.

The second prong of the infringement test also involves a showing of "substantial similarity," but the meaning is very different. Here, the question is limited to similarities of protected expression. The bar is higher, requiring a showing that the defendant copied a substantial amount of protectable expression.

Problems can arise in litigation when the wrong definition of "substantial similarity" is used. For example, if the court uses the first definition for the second prong of the infringement analysis, the defendant suffers. The court may incorrectly find infringement based on the works as a whole, without determining if the copying involves protectable expression. In the same vein, if the court applies the second definition to evaluate the question of actual copying, the failure to consider the works as a whole may disadvantage the plaintiff.

Recognizing the confusion caused by the use of the same term for two different tests, some courts have suggested a distinction between probative or factual similarity on the one hand and substantial or legal similarity on the other.[39] According to this line of cases, the first prong involves probative similarity: whether as a matter of fact, the similarities show actual copying. Under the second prong, the inquiry into substantial similarity is primarily a legal conclusion: whether there are substantial similarities of protected expression sufficient to support a finding of infringement.

Although helpful, the distinction between probative similarity and substantial similarity is not widely stated in reported decisions. Since few courts have a regular docket of copyright infringement matters, litigators should ensure that the court is fully informed about the different definitions of substantial similarity arising in a copyright infringement action, particularly when the difference may have an effect on the client's position.

D. Scope of Protection

A second area of confusion involves the scope of protection afforded protectable expression in copyright infringement actions. Not all works are entitled to the same level of protection. This issue is particularly important when the works involve a compilation of otherwise unprotectable elements.

The constitutional requirement of originality precludes protection for facts, and the copyright statute precludes protection of "any idea, procedure,

---

39. *See, e.g.,* Repp v. Webber, 132 F.3d 882, 889 (2d Cir. 1997) (noting the considerable confusion caused by the use of the term "substantial similarity" for two different tests).

process, system, method of operation, concept, principle or discovery."[40] Nevertheless, the "selection, coordination or arrangement" of such unprotectable elements may be entitled to protection if the selection and arrangement has a minimal degree of creativity.

The scope of protection granted to a compilation of unprotectable elements is less than the protection afforded to elements protectable in their own right. It is sometimes said that compilations and factual works are only entitled to "thin" protection, but what does this mean?

According to the Second Circuit, one of the most experienced courts in dealing with copyright issues, a compilation is not infringed if the defendant's work differs in more than a "trivial degree" from the plaintiff's work.[41]

In other courts, the "thin" protection afforded compilations means no relief unless the works are "virtually identical."[42]

In practice, the "trivial difference" test and the "virtually identical" standard have the same result. The plaintiff's burden is higher when seeking protection for compilations of unprotectable elements, and the defendant may escape liability if the works differ by more than a trivial degree. If the plaintiff's work involves elements protectable in their own right, there will be a lower test for infringement. In such cases, the defendant will be liable if the works are found to be substantially similar, as that term is understood in the second prong of the infringement test discussed above.

In the abstract world of copyright litigation, the formulation of the tests applied by the court to determine infringement can have a major impact on the outcome of the case. Much may turn on whether the judge or jury is asked to determine if works are substantially similar as a whole or only with respect to protectable elements. Likewise, the results may differ if the fact finder is instructed to determine that the works are virtually identical rather than substantially similar. An understanding of these different tests is important for successful litigation.

E. The Key Dimensions of the Fair Use Defense

A principal defense in copyright litigation is the fair use exception to copyright found in Section 107 of the Copyright Statute.[43] When evaluating the

---

40. 17 U.S.C. § 102(b).
41. Kregos v. Associated Press, 937 F.2d 700, 710 (2d Cir. 1991). *See also* Harbor Software, Inc. v. Applied Systems, Inc., 936 F. Supp. 167, 171 (S.D.N.Y. 1996) (applying the "trivial difference" test to computer screen displays which were compilations of factual information).
42. *See,* for example, Mitek Holdings Inc. v. Arce Eng'g Co., 89 F.3d 1548, 1554 (11th Cir. 1996); Apple Computer Inc. v. Microsoft Corp. 35 F.3d 1435, 1446 (9th Cir. 1994).
43. 17 U.S.C. § 107.

statutory factors, the key dimensions or aspects of the factual inquiry appear to be transformation, commercial use, and market value.

The fair use exception permits reproduction of copyrighted material "for purposes such as criticism, comment, news reporting, teaching (including multiple copies for classroom use), scholarship, or research."[44] This list of purposes is not exhaustive but merely illustrative of the types of uses that may be deemed fair use.

The fair use doctrine involves a mixed question of law and fact, based on a set of statutory factors. These factors stated in Section 107 are

(1) The purpose and character of the use, including whether such use is of a commercial nature or is for nonprofit educational purposes
(2) The nature of the copyrighted work
(3) The amount and substantiality of the portion used in relation to the copyrighted work as a whole
(4) The effect of the use upon the potential market for or value of the copyrighted work

None of these factors is deemed determinative and must be balanced together in making the analysis. Generally, the most critical evidence addresses three key dimensions or aspects of the fair use inquiry: transformation, commercial use, and market value.

Most fair use questions can be resolved by focusing your litigation strategy on these factual issues.

(1) *Transformation.* The first dimension involves the character of the use: whether the work is transformative or merely supersedes the original. A work is transformative if it adds something new to the original. Although such transformation is not absolutely necessary for a finding of fair use, it does further the purpose of the Copyright Laws and weighs in favor of a finding of fair use.

(2) *Commercial Use.* The second key dimension is the purpose of the use: whether the defendant intended to profit from the use without proper payment. Again, this factor is not conclusive. Although most of the statutory examples of fair use typically involve some profit motive, the lack of commercial purpose favors a finding of fair use.

(3) *Market Value.* The third key dimension is the effect on the value of the original: whether the defendant's work will impair the market value of the original work. Any use that supplants the market for the original is unlikely to be considered a fair use.

---

44. *Id.*

CHAPTER
2

Cease and Desist Demands

I. Threats of Litigation

Clients and attorneys often want to enhance the recognition of their rights and reputations for enforcement through out-of-court publicity. Litigators should recognize, however, that threats of litigation and press releases can give rise to counterclaims.

Imagine you have filed suit against a website operator who republishes your client's copyrighted fashion photographs. Other infringers dot the Internet, so your client wants to send warning letters to potential defendants and issue press releases about the case to industry publications. What are the risks? Should you intervene to control or prevent this campaign?

There is certainly cause for concern. For example, Hewlett-Packard filed counterclaims for contractual interference, unfair competition, and injurious falsehood against Computer Aid, Inc. and its attorneys for statements made in a press release about the initial lawsuit. The court permitted the claims to go to the jury. *Computer Aid, Inc. v. Hewlett-Packard*, 56 F.Supp. 2d 526 (E.D. Pa. June 15, 1999).

A. Guidelines

DirectTV sent out tens of thousands of demand letters alleging the recipients had accessed its satellite television signal illegally and would be sued if they did not quickly settle DirectTV's claims. One of the recipients, Rod Sosa, filed a class action lawsuit on behalf of the recipients of the letters who reached settlements with DirectTV, claiming that DIRECTV violated the Racketeer Influenced and Corrupt Organizations Act (RICO). The court found that the cease and desist letters were immune from action because of the Noerr-Pennington doctrine. See *Sosa v. DIRECTTV, Inc.*, 437 F.3d 923 (9th Cir. 2006).

The Noerr-Pennington doctrine originated as a rule in antitrust cases that relied upon the right to petition embodied in the Constitution, but the doctrine has transcended its roots to encompass a wide range of the law. The doctrine provides immunity from any liability arising out of a party's filing and maintaining any civil lawsuit and can be overcome only upon a showing that the lawsuit is a mere "sham," i.e., both (1) objectively baseless and (2) intended as an anticompetitive weapon. See *Prof'l Real Estate Investors, Inc. v. Columbia Pictures, Inc.*, 508 U.S. 49, 60–61 (1993). In most jurisdictions, this immunity extends to prelitigation acts, such as sending cease and desist letters in an effort to settle claims. For example, *Sosa* found that "the Noerr-Pennington doctrine stands for a generic rule of statutory construction, applicable to any statutory interpretation that could implicate the rights protected by the Petition Clause." 437 F.3d at 931; but see *Cardtoons, L.C. v. Major League Baseball Players Ass'n*, 208 F.3d 885 (10th Cir. 2000) (en banc) (finding that cease and desist letters are communications between two private parties and therefore do not implicate the constitutional right to petition).

In *Sosa*, the Ninth Circuit decided that "prelitigation communications demanding settlement of legal claims must be afforded *Noerr-Pennington* protection . . ." (437 F.3d at 942) because to find otherwise "would render the entire litigation process more onerous, imposing a substantial burden on a party's ability to seek redress from the courts." 437 F.3d at 936. The Ninth Circuit further stated that "extending immunity to private presuit demand letters protects the same interests that the Supreme Court has identified as implicated in the Petition Clause's protection of private litigation . . ." *Id.*

The privilege has also been extended to postfiling publicity about a lawsuit. In *Aircapital Cablevision, Inc. v. Starlink Commc'ns Grp.*, 634 F. Supp. 316 (D. Kan. 1986), one of the Plaintiffs, Multimedia Cablevision, issued press releases and threatened suits against customers of Defendant Starlink. The press releases implied that Starlink customers were "pirates" and were "stealing" from cable companies. Although the lawsuit and publicity caused Starlink to lose business and customers and Multimedia admittedly hoped to put Starlink out of business, the court found no liability as a matter of law. The court stated (634 F. Supp. at 326):

> Clearly, Multimedia was engaging in bully-type conduct and undoubtedly Starlink's business was hurt as a result. Although Multimedia would have been better advised to have refrained from making such comments, this short-lived publicity and its indirect threats against Starlink's customers were incidental to the lawsuit. Therefore, the publicity is also protected by the Noerr-Pennington doctrine.

B. Maintaining Control

Some courts have held that even one cease and desist letter threatening litigation creates a sufficient controversy to establish jurisdiction such that the recipient can file an action in its home court under the Declaratory Judgment Act. A client may not anticipate facing suit in a potentially distant and unfamiliar court, so advising the client of this possibility prior to sending the letter is a necessity. Furthermore, you as the attorney would lose the initiative in being forced to file an answer and counterclaim, being forced to tell your side of the story only in response to the declaratory judgment plaintiff's version of events. Might a softer approach work better in your situation? Depending on the circumstances and the adverse party, you should consider calling the potential defendant to invite them to discuss a compromise of your client's claims. While making a call rather than sending a cease and desist letter does not guarantee that the potential defendant will refrain from filing a declaratory judgment action, this softer approach may result in a more receptive opponent who believes your client's desire to reach an amicable resolution.

FORM 2.1

Example Demand Letter Involving Infringing Domain Name
(Trademark Infringement, Dilution, Cybersquatting)

Dear Mr. Dxxxxxxx:

We are counsel to Acme International Incorporated ("Acme"). Our client administers and licenses its member financial institutions and merchants to participate in the ACME payment card program.

As you undoubtedly know, our client has used and advertised the ACME name and mark throughout the United States and abroad for many years. Acme is the owner of numerous federal registrations for ACME, including Reg. Nos. xxxxxxxxx and xxxxxxxxx, and operates on Internet site at <www.Acme. com>. Our client has also used the mark WORLD ACME for many years and owns federal registrations for that mark, including Reg. No. xxxxxxxxx. In light of its fame and celebrity, these ACME marks have become exceedingly valuable assets of our client.

It has come to our attention that you or your company are the registrant of the domain name www.worldAcmeoffers.com ("the Infringing Domain Name"), which is used for a commercial site providing links to various credit-related services, including sites unrelated to Acme. It is evident that the Infringing Domain Name is confusingly similar to our client's famous marks, and is likely to cause confusion, mistake or deception among Internet users. The addition of "offers" only increases the likelihood of confusion by suggesting a site run or authorized by our client.

Your use of the Infringing Domain Name violates the terms of your domain name registration agreement and constitutes trademark infringement, dilution, and cybersquatting in violation of the laws of various countries, including the Trademark Act of the United States. See 15 U.S.C. §§ 1114, 1125(a), (c), and (d). The remedies available for cybersquatting under U.S. law include injunctive relief and statutory damages up to $100,000.00 per domain name. 15 U.S.C. § 1117(d).

Proper use of the ACME marks is a matter of great concern to our client. Therefore, we hereby demand that you confirm to us, no later than December 31, 2010, that you will:

1. Refrain from any and all unauthorized use of ACME or WORLD ACME alone or in combination with other matter, as a domain name, trade name, or trademark for your website or business, including but not limited to www.worldAcmeoffers.com;

2. Transfer to Acme or its designated representative the Infringing Domain Name and any other domain name(s) containing ACME, WORLD ACME, or any other confusingly similar terms.

To comply with this demand, you need simply respond to this letter with your consent to these terms. We will then provide you with the information necessary to complete the transfer of the Infringing Domain Name to our client.

Unless you comply with Acme's demands, we will recommend that Acme pursue all available legal and equitable remedies to obtain the maximum penalties imposed by law against you, including an injunction, damages, costs, and attorneys' fees.

Nothing in this letter shall be deemed a waiver of any rights or remedies of Acme, all of which are expressly reserved.

Very truly yours,

FORM 2.2

Example Demand Letter Involving Infringing Use of a Trademark (Trademark Infringement, Dilution, Unfair Competition)

Dear Mr. Smith:

We are trademark litigation counsel for ABC Company ("ABC"). As you are aware, ABC owns the mark XYZ for its [GOODS/SERVICES] ("XYZ Marks"). ABC has invested substantial sums in advertising, promoting, and maintaining the XYZ Marks, which are extensively registered throughout the world. ABC owns, among others, U.S. Registration No. _____ for XYZ. As a result, it has acquired immensely valuable goodwill in its XYZ Marks, along with widespread fame and public recognition. ABC regards infringing uses of its name and marks very seriously, as they damage its goodwill and deceive the public.

We have recently become aware that you are promoting a [IDENTIFY PRODUCT] under the trademark "[INFRINGING MARK]". A copy of [PACKAGING/WEB PAGE/ADVERTISING] showing your use of "[INFRINGING MARK]" is attached for your reference. Your actions are likely to mislead the public into thinking, falsely, that you or your company are somehow affiliated with or authorized by ABC and its XYZ [GOODS/SERVICES]. This constitutes willful trademark infringement, dilution, and unfair competition, subjecting you to a potential civil action for an injunction, damages, an accounting of your profits, and recovery of our client's costs and attorneys' fees.

Therefore, we request that you immediately:

(1) cease and desist from all further use of the term [INFRINGING MARK];
(2) cease and desist from use of any other marks, trade names, or domain names consisting of XYZ, or variations thereof, in whole or in part; and
(3) represent and warrant that you have not registered, and will not apply to register, any other marks, trade names, or domain names consisting of XYZ, or variations thereof or consisting of any other trademark of ABC.

Please confirm that you will comply with the above requests no later than December 31, 2010. If we do not have your complete cooperation in this matter, ABC has authorized us to take appropriate legal action to compel your compliance.

Sincerely,

Copyright Demand

We are copyright counsel for Acme Works. As you know, Acme Works publishes "Acme Works Manual" in connection with its Acme brand construction products, and owns all copyright in the content of this publication. Attached hereto as Exhibit A are excerpts from this publication.

We recently learned that, without Acme Works' authorization, your company misappropriated several of Acme Works' photographs and drawings from the "Acme Works Manual" and published them in the instruction manual for your own "Widget" brand construction products. Attached hereto as Exhibit B is a copy of your Widget instruction manual showing this unauthorized duplication.

Your blatant copying of Acme's photographs and drawings constitutes willful copyright infringement under the United States Copyright Act. Accordingly, Acme demands that your company:

(a) immediately and permanently cease and desist from publishing Acme's copyrighted materials, including but not limited to the photographs and drawings shown in Exhibit B; and
(b) enter into a written agreement confirming the terms on which this matter has been resolved.

Acme is willing to resolve this matter amicably. To do so, however, we must receive your written assurance within two weeks that you will comply with these terms. Unless and until we confirm that this matter is resolved, Acme reserves its right to take whatever action it deems appropriate without further notice.

CHAPTER
3

Selecting a Forum, Jurisdiction and Venue

Selecting the appropriate forum in which to bring your case could be as important as selecting the claims to allege. Your client will have many choices in selecting an appropriate forum for its complaint, including selecting no forum at all: that is, attempting to resolve its claim with the infringer through direct negotiations between business personnel, counsel, or before a private mediator.

I. Available Forums for Trademark and Unfair Competition Disputes

Depending on the types of claims that a client may be able to assert, actions involving trademark infringement, unfair competition, false advertising, or domain name disputes may be heard in the following forums:

- Federal court
- State court
- Foreign courts
- The Trademark Trial and Appeal Board of the Patent and Trademark Office
- Under the Uniform Dispute Resolution Policy administered by the World Intellectual Property Organization, the National Arbitration Forum, and others
- Request the intervention of U.S. Customs and Border Protection
- the International Trade Commission
- the National Advertising Division of the Council of Better Business Bureaus
- Private mediation or arbitration

The decision of the appropriate forum for a particular case will involve numerous considerations that must be discussed with the client in light of its goals and the law of each jurisdiction. Two of those considerations that often weigh heavily on the ultimate decision are available remedies and cost. Most actions involving trademark and unfair competition claims are brought in federal court, but in some circumstances, there may be a preferable forum to meet the client's goals.

State courts have concurrent jurisdiction over trademark claims, although in pleading such claims, one must be careful not to permit the other side simply to remove the case to federal court. Since a plaintiff can choose whether to plead claims under the Lanham Act or solely under state law, it can determine whether or not its claim will proceed in state court. The federal courts' familiarity with trademark claims and the state courts' lack of that familiarity could play into a decision on where to proceed. Some attorneys may also prefer to proceed in state court because of a procedural advantage or their significant experience in trying cases before those courts. Of course, to keep a case in state court, a plaintiff may have to forego some remedies available under the Lanham Act.

In some cases, it may be preferable to seek enforcement in a foreign jurisdiction. While foreign courts may be less predictable for U.S.-based businesses, the reality of today's marketplace provides enormous opportunities for even the smallest companies to sell their products worldwide. Where an infringement occurs in multiple countries, there may be a tactical or cost advantage to taking action outside of the United States. In such circumstances, an attorney should confer with trustworthy foreign counsel who is familiar with the courts of such foreign countries.

If an infringer also has applied to register a trademark or owns a trademark registration for an allegedly infringing mark, it may be more cost effective for a claimant to proceed before the Trademark Trial and Appeal Board (the TTAB) in an inter partes proceeding. The TTAB can only hear claims about the registrability of a trademark, and no monetary remedies are available. Moreover, a determination that a mark is not registrable does not mean that a defendant is prohibited from using that same mark. Despite these limitations on available remedies, many claimants prefer to proceed first in the TTAB because of the relative speed and low cost of such actions, as well as the ability to take discovery of the other side.

If the primary object of a dispute is a domain name, a very low cost and fast approach to obtaining the domain name is to proceed under the UDRP, a dispute resolution policy incorporated into most domain name registration agreements. While the only available remedy in UDRP proceedings is the transfer of the allegedly infringing domain name, most such proceedings are decided within six months and cost under $10,000 to prosecute.

A trademark owner facing the importation of infringing goods may choose to ask for the help of U.S. Customs and Border Protection (Customs), provided, however, that the trademark owner must record the federal registration for its trademark with Customs. *See* 15 U.S.C. § 1124. Given Customs' current priorities, it may be preferable to proceed directly before the International Trade Commission (ITC) through a "Section 337" action under 19 U.S.C. § 1337, especially if multiple parties are importing the infringing goods. The ITC has the authority to issue in rem exclusion orders but has suggested that it may accept a disclaimer remedy to allow the infringing goods to come into the United States. *See In re Certain Agricultural Tractors*, 44 U.S.P.Q.2d 1385, 1399–1400 (ITC 1997). Section 337 investigations proceed quickly as compared to federal litigation. When an investigation is instituted, the ITC sets a target date for completing the investigation, generally within one year from when the investigation is published in the *Federal Register*. This expedited process results in accelerated discovery, with responses to discovery requests typically required in 10 days rather than 30.

Restrictions on discovery that apply in federal court, such as limits on the number of interrogatories, often do not apply in the ITC, resulting in discovery that is simultaneously more accelerated and broader than federal litigation. Therefore, the costs in an ITC proceeding have the potential to mount quickly. In rare circumstances, a decision of the ITC may also be overturned by the president. *See In re Certain Alkaline Batteries*, Inv. No. 337-TA-165.

The National Advertising Division of the Council of Better Business Bureaus (NAD) provides a forum for its advertiser participants to mediate disputes over national advertisements. Challenges before the NAD generally are inexpensive to mount, and decisions are quick, usually within three months of an initial challenge. Monetary remedies are not available, and the NAD cannot issue orders; but, instead, compliance with an order is voluntary.

Parties can also choose to have disputes arbitrated under the rules of one of the many arbitration providers, such as the American Arbitration Association. Arbitration is final, binding, and practically unappealable. *See* 9 U.S.C. § 1 et seq. The rules and procedures of any particular arbitration forum should be researched carefully before choosing because each provider has its own rules and procedures that may or may not benefit a client's position. For example, most arbitration providers do not permit third-party discovery, while discovery between the parties may be unlimited in scope.

Finally, parties can choose private mediation through a mediator in the field—usually an experienced practitioner. Such mediation can lead to settlements crafted by the parties and guided by knowledgeable neutrals. Of course, both parties must agree to participate and abide by the decision, which apart from a settlement agreement at the end of the process, is not binding. One of the primary benefits of such a process is the low cost and ability to manage the outcome.

A. Subject Matter Jurisdiction

Federal courts have original jurisdiction over claims brought under the Lanham Act. *See* 15 U.S.C. § 1121 ("The district and territorial courts of the United States shall have original jurisdiction, [and] the courts of appeal of the United States (other than the United States Court of Appeals for the Federal Circuit) [and the United States Court of Appeals for the District of Columbia] shall have appellate jurisdiction, of all actions arising under this Act."). Specifically, "the district courts . . . have original jurisdiction of any civil action arising under any Act of Congress relating to . . . trademarks [and] . . ." 28 U.S.C. § 1338(a).

As a practical matter, it is often useful to also allege, where possible, diversity jurisdiction under 28 U.S.C. § 1332 in case the Lanham Act claims are dismissed. Assuming the amount in controversy exceeds $75,000—and given the nature of valuation of the goodwill in a trademark, such an allegation is not far-fetched—and the parties are citizens of different states, such an allegation should be relatively easy to assert.

State claims that arise from a common nucleus of operative facts may be brought under the doctrine of 28 U.S.C. § 1338(b), which states that "The district courts shall have original jurisdiction of any civil action asserting a claim of unfair competition when joined with a substantial and related claim under the . . . trademark laws."

In certain cases, infringements abroad may be addressed through the U.S. courts. *See Fun-Damental Too v. Gemmy Indus. Corp.*, 111 F.3d 993 (2d Cir. 1997). In particular, where the defendant's conduct has a substantial effect on U.S. commerce, the defendant is a U.S. citizen, and there is no conflict with trademark rights established under foreign law, the U.S. courts may exercise jurisdiction. *Id.* at 1006.

Foreign plaintiffs that own trademark rights in the United States can assert those rights just as easily as U.S.-based parties. However, where a company has used a mark abroad, and the mark has gained notoriety in the United States, but the mark has not been used there, that company may find it difficult to protect its rights in the United States. *Compare Grupo Gigante S.A. de C.V. v. Dallo & Co.*, 391 F.3d 1088, 1098 (9th Cir. 2004) (vacating lower court summary judgment for junior U.S. user of identical mark for supermarkets where consumers in Southern California were familiar with senior user's mark used exclusively in Mexico) *with ITC Ltd. v. Punghini Inc.*, 482 F.3d 135 (2d Cir. 2007) (expressly rejecting applicability of famous marks doctrine in federal trademark infringement cases); *see also Bayer Consumer Care AG v. Belmora LLC*, 90 U.S.P.Q.2d 1587 (TTAB 2009) (finding that under U.S. law, there is no protection for marks used abroad, even if they are famous here but permitting Bayer to proceed upon a claim of misrepresentation under Section 14(3) of the Lanham Act).

B. Personal Jurisdiction Generally

The personal jurisdiction analysis in trademark cases follows traditional principles. First, the court looks to see if a potential defendant is subject to general personal jurisdiction. General jurisdiction permits a court to exercise personal jurisdiction over a defendant when the defendant has "systematic and continuous" contacts in the forum state. *See Helicopteros Nacionales de Colombia, S.A. v. Hall*, 466 U.S. 408, 414–16, (1984). The most typical example of activities sufficient to enable a court to exercise general jurisdiction over a defendant are incorporation or domicile in the forum state. If there is no general jurisdiction over a defendant, the court determines if there is specific jurisdiction, which permits a court to exercise personal jurisdiction over a defendant where the defendant has sufficient "minimum contacts" with the forum such that exercise of jurisdiction will not offend "traditional notions of fair play and substantial justice." *Int'l Shoe Co. v. Washington*, 326 U.S. 310 (1945).

Federal courts generally only have the authority to assert jurisdiction over a defendant to the extent permitted by their home state's long-arm statute. Fed. R. Civ. P. 4(k)(1)(A); *see, e.g., Klump v. Duffus*, 71 F.3d 1368, 1371 (7th Cir. 1995). The Illinois long-arm statute, like many others, authorizes the exercise of personal jurisdiction to the extent allowed under due process. 735 ILCS 5/2-209(c) ("A court may also exercise jurisdiction on any other basis now or herafter permitted by the Illinois Constitution and the Constitution of the United States"). Because "there is no operative difference between the limits imposed by the Illinois Constitution and the federal limitations on personal jurisdiction," one due process analysis suffices. *Hyatt Int'l Corp. v. Coco*, 302 F.3d 707, 715 (7th Cir. 2002).

To have "minimum contacts" sufficient to establish specific jurisdiction, the defendant must have "purposefully availed itself of the privilege of conducting activities within the forum state, thus invoking the benefits and protections of its laws," such that the defendant should "reasonably anticipate being haled into court there." *Burger King Corp. v. Rudzewicz*, 471 U.S. 462, 475 (1985); *World-Wide Volkswagen Corp. v. Woodson*, 444 U.S. 286 (1980).

II. Effects Test: Calder and Indianapolis Colts

Generally, conducting business, e.g., offering to sell goods or services bearing an infringing mark, in a forum state is sufficient to establish jurisdiction in that state if the alleged acts arise out of those contacts. *See, e.g., QRM Publ. Co., Inc. v. Reed*, 230 U.S.P.Q. 217 (S.D.N.Y. 1986) (15 of 300 subscribers to allegedly infringing newsletter resided in New York, which was sufficient for the court to exercise personal jurisdiction over the defendant); *but see Taurus Int'l Inc. v. Titan Wheel Int'l Inc.*, 892 F. Supp. 79, 82 (S.D.N.Y. 1995) (sending of quarterly report advising investors of intention to use an allegedly infringing mark without offer of goods/services or solicitation of customers insufficient to establish jurisdiction under New York long-arm statute). Although the effects of confusion may be felt in the trademark owner's home forum, trademark infringement often occurs in a distant location. To provide trademark owners with potential relief in the face of such infringement, the courts adopted the "effects test" (also known as the "effects doctrine") for determining whether the defendant has sufficient contacts with the forum to warrant exercise of personal jurisdiction. *See, e.g., Indianapolis Colts, Inc. v. Metro Baltimore Football Club Ltd.* 34 F.3d 410 (7th Cir. 1994). There, plaintiff Indianapolis Colts, a National Football League franchise, sued defendant Baltimore Colts, a Canadian Football League franchise, for trademark infringement in federal court in Indiana. The defendant moved to dismiss for lack of personal jurisdiction because, it claimed, the only contact it had with Indiana was a plan for nationwide broadcast of games on cable television. The district court denied the motion to dismiss, and the Seventh Circuit affirmed, relying on the "effects test." "If the [plaintiff's] trademarks are impaired," the court reasoned, "the injury will be felt mainly in Indiana. By choosing a name that might be found to be confusingly similar to that of the Indianapolis Colts, the defendants assumed the risk of injuring valuable property located in Indiana." *Id.* at 411. On the basis of this trademark injury, the Seventh Circuit held that personal jurisdiction was properly exercised.

The court also stated that it "need not rest on so austere a conception of the basis of personal jurisdiction." The court noted that in *Calder v. Jones*, 465 U.S. 783 (1984), which inaugurated the "effects test," as well in cases following *Calder* that involved intellectual property, the defendants had "done more than brought about an injury to an interest located in a particular state." Defendants planned national broadcasts that were that something more, the court found, but declined to hold "whether the addition is indispensible." *Id.* at 412. In a subsequent decision, the Seventh Circuit went even further, indicating that the "something more" was not required. *Janmark, Inc. v. Reidy*, 132 F.3d 1200 (7th Cir. 1997); *see also Ford Motor Co. v. GreatDomains.com Inc.*, 61 U.S.P.Q.2d *1718 (E.D. Mich. 2001) (defendants' intentional—rather than negligent—registration of allegedly infringing domain names were sufficient to confer jurisdiction). Most other jurisdictions require that activity be directed at the putative forum state before exercising personal jurisdiction where the harm will be felt in that state. *See, e.g., Revell v. Lidov*, 317 F.3d 467 (5th Cir. 2002) (posting article on the Internet that criticizes Texas citizen not sufficient to confer jurisdiction in Texas over author of article).

III. Personal Jurisdiction in Web Site Cases

Generally, the analysis relevant to determining whether a court may have jurisdiction over a potential defendant who uses a trademark on the Internet follows the traditional principles described above. *See, e.g., CompuServe, Inc. v. Patterson*, 89 F.3d 1257 (6th Cir. 1996) (finding jurisdiction proper in Ohio where Texas-based defendant sold products through plaintiff's Ohio-based computer service, including to customers in Ohio but had never personally entered Ohio). In order to facilitate this analysis, however, one court developed a sliding scale test dependent on a website's interactivity. *Zippo Mfg. Co. v. Zippo Dot Com*, 952 F. Supp. 1119 (W.D. Pa. 1997). In now familiar language, the court stated:

> [T]he likelihood that personal jurisdiction can be constitutionally exercised is directly proportionate to the nature and quality of commercial activity that an

entity conducts over the Internet. This sliding scale is consistent with well developed personal jurisdiction principles. At one end of the spectrum are situations where a defendant clearly does business over the Internet. If the defendant enters into contracts with residents of a foreign jurisdiction that involve the knowing and repeated transmission of computer files over the Internet, personal jurisdiction is proper. At the opposite end are situations where a defendant has simply posted information on an Internet Website which is accessible to users in foreign jurisdictions. A passive Website that does little more than make information available to those who are interested in it is not grounds for the exercise personal jurisdiction. The middle ground is occupied by interactive Websites where a user can exchange information with the host computer. In these cases, the exercise of jurisdiction is determined by examining the level of interactivity and commercial nature of the exchange of information that occurs on the Website.

Zippo, 952 F. Supp. at 1124 (citations omitted). This test has been widely adopted. *See, e.g., Intercon, Inc. v. Bell Atl. Internet Solutions, Inc.*, 205 F.3d 1244 (10th Cir. 2000); *Mink v. AAAA Dev. LLC*, 190 F.3d 333, 337 (5th Cir. 1999); *Cybersell, Inc. v. Cybersell, Inc.*, 130 F.3d 414, 419–20 (9th Cir.1997).

Courts will exercise personal jurisdiction over a defendant who operates an infringing website depending on which end of the sliding scale of interactivity it falls. On one end of the scale are passive websites that do nothing more than provide information about products or services. Courts will not exercise jurisdiction over defendants who operate such passive websites. *See, e.g., Pebble Beach Co. v. Caddy*, 453 F.3d 1151 (9th Cir. 2006) (declining to exercise jurisdiction over UK bed and breakfast that operated a website that used plaintiff's name but merely advertised the bed and breakfast); *see also Jennings v. AC Hydraulic A/S*, 383 F.3d 546 (7th Cir. 2004); *Quck Techs. v. Sage Grp. PLC*, 313 F.3d 338 (5th Cir. 2002).

On the other end are websites through which defendants "conduct business," which typically consists of selling products through the website. *See, e.g., George S. May Int'l Co. v. Xcentric Ventures, L.L.C.*, 409 F. Supp. 2d 1052, 1059 (N.D. Ill. 2006) (defendant was conducting business through its website by soliciting and collecting donations online, by selling books, by allowing users to post comments, and by posting replies to user comments on its site); *Rainy Day Books, Inc. v. Rainy Day Books & Cafe, LLC*, 186 F. Supp. 2d 1158, 1165–66 (D. Kan. 2002) (finding jurisdiction because defendant's website provides information about the bookstore, upcoming events, store, and book reviews, permits a user to subscribe to a mailing list or to obtain information regarding gift certificates, permits an Internet user to purchase books through a third-party provider); *Euromarket Designs, Inc. v. Crate & Barrel Ltd.*, 96 F. Supp. 2d 824, 837–38 (N.D. Ill. 2000) (defendant was conducting business by allowing users to browse through its catalog and place online orders through its website).

With respect to the middle ground of interactive websites, the more interactive and commercial the defendant's website, and the more it targets the potential forum state, the more likely it is that a court will exercise personal jurisdiction over the defendant. *See Public Int'l, Ltd. v. Burke/Triolo, Inc.*, 121 F. Supp. 2d 1178, 1183 (N.D. Ill. 2000) (defendant's website that allowed users to fill out and submit a request for a catalog online and advertised national listing of clients on the website (including Illinois clients) was interactive enough to render jurisdiction proper); *GTE New Media Services Inc. v. Ameritech Corp.*, 44 F. Supp. 2d 313, 315 (D.D.C. 1999) (jurisdiction proper where defendants operated Internet Yellow Pages sites that were dependant on advertising revenue, depended on the number of users accessing the site, directed users to their site through other sites, and derived profit from DC related activities); *LFG, LLC. v. Zapata Corp.* 78 F. Supp. 2d 731, 734 (N.D. Ill. 1999) (defendant's portal website that allowed users to sign up for its mailing list and provided contact information to users was interactive enough to render jurisdiction proper, given that defendant's success hinged on the number of users interacting with [the website]); *but see Berthold Types Ltd. v. European Mikrograf Corp.*, 102 F. Supp. 2d 928, 930 (N.D. Ill. 2000) (defendant's website that provided product information to users, allowed users to download, print and send in a services agreement, but did not allow users to purchase products or otherwise engage in commercial transactions online was not interactive enough to render jurisdiction proper).

IV. Rule 4(K)(2) of the Federal Rules of Civil Procedure

For claims arising under federal law, if a foreign defendant is not amendable to service of process under any state's long-arm statute, Rule 4(k)(2) of the Federal Rules of Civil Procedure allows the federal court to exercise personal jurisdiction over a defendant based on the defendant's contacts with the United States as a whole. Fed. R. Civ. P. 4(k)(2) ("If the exercise of jurisdiction is consistent with the Constitution and laws of the United States, serving a summons or filing a waiver of service is also effective, with respect to claims arising under federal law, to establish personal jurisdiction over the person of any defendant who is not subject to the jurisdiction of the courts of general jurisdiction of any state.").

In *ISI Int'l, Inc. v. Borden Ladner Gervais LLP*, 256 F.3d 548 (7th Cir.2001), the Seventh Circuit adopted the following burden-shifting framework that has been adopted in other circuits as well.

A defendant who wants to preclude use of Rule 4(k)(2) has only to name some other state in which the suit could proceed. Naming a more appropriate state would amount to a consent to personal jurisdiction there (personal jurisdiction, unlike federal subject-matter jurisdiction, is waivable). If, however, the defendant contends that he cannot be sued in the forum state and refuses to identify any other where suit is possible, then the federal court is entitled to use Rule 4(k)(2).

Id. at 552; *see also Adams v. Unione Mediterranea Di Sicurta*, 364 F.3d 646, 651 (5th Cir. 2004); *Mwani v. Bin Laden*, 417 F.3d 1, 11 (D.C. Cir. 2005).

V. In Rem Jurisdiction Under the Anticybersquatting Consumer Protection Act

The Anticybersquatting Consumer Protection Act (ACPA) provides in rem jurisdiction over an Internet domain name when personal jurisdiction cannot be obtained over the registrant, or the registrant cannot be located. 15 U.S.C. § 1125(d). The remedies in such actions are limited to forfeiture or cancellation of the domain name or the transfer of the domain name to the owner of the mark. 15 U.S.C. § 1125(d)(2)(D)(i). The Fourth Circuit, however, concluded that the ACPA "authorizes in rem actions for certain federal infringement and dilution claims." *Harrods Ltd. v. Sixty Internet Domain Names*, 302 F.3d 214, 228 (4th Cir. 2002). While the Fourth Circuit therefore overturned the district court's dismissal of the infringement and dilution claims, because it affirmed the district court's transfer of the domain names under the ACPA, it advised that the district court need not consider these claims further. *Id.* at 232.

VI. Venue

Under 28 U.S.C. § 1319(b),

[a] civil action wherein jurisdiction is not founded solely on diversity of citizenship may, except as otherwise provided by law, be brought only in (1) a judicial district where any defendant resides, if all defendants reside in the same State; (2) a judicial district in which a substantial part of the events or omissions giving rise to the claim occurred, or a substantial part of property that is the subject of the action is situated;or (3) a judicial district in which any defendant may be found, if there is no district in which the action may otherwise be brought.

In trademark infringement actions, allegedly infringing activity may occur in many locations and, arguably, venue may be proper in all of them.

However, a federal court has discretion to transfer a civil action for "the convenience of the parties and witnesses" under 28 U.S.C. § 1404(a). Thus, it is usually prudent to choose a venue where a substantial amount of evidence and witnesses, especially third-party materials, are located. For example, when pursuing an action against a corporation, that corporate defendant "shall be deemed to reside in any judicial district in which it is subject to personal jurisdiction at the time the action is commenced. In a State which has more than one judicial district and in which a defendant that is a corporation is subject to personal jurisdiction at the time an action is commenced, such corporation shall be deemed to reside in any district in that State within which its contacts would be sufficient to subject it to personal jurisdiction if that district were a separate State, and, if there is no such district, the corporation shall be deemed to reside in the district within which it has the most significant contacts." 28 U.S.C. § 1319(c).

To transfer the venue under 28 U.S.C. § 1404(a), a party must show that

- The transferee court must be a court where the action "might have been brought" originally
- Transferring the case will enhance the convenience of the parties and the witnesses and be in the interest of justice

Courts typically evaluate the following factors when determining whether convenience will be enhanced:

- The convenience of the parties
- The convenience of the material witnesses
- The availability of process to compel the presence of witnesses
- The cost of obtaining the presence of witnesses
- The relative ease of access to sources of proof
- Calendar congestion
- Where the events in issue took place
- The interests of justice in general.

See, e.g., The Willowbrook Found. Inc. v. Visiting Nurse Ass'n Inc., 87 F. Supp. 2d 629, 636 (N.D. Miss. 2000); *Sassy, Inc. v. Berry*, 406 F. Supp. 2d 874, 875 (N.D. Ill. 2005).

VII. Bringing a Copyright Claim in Federal Court

Federal courts have exclusive jurisidiction over claims arising under the Copyright Act. *See* 28 U.S.C. § 1338(a) ("The district courts shall have original jurisdiction of any civil action arising under any Act of Congress relating to . . . copyrights . . . Such jurisdiction shall be exclusive of the courts of the states in . . . copyright cases."). An action "arises under" the Copyright Act if: "(1) [T]he complaint is for a remedy expressly granted by the Act, e.g., a suit for infringement or for the statutory royalties for record reproduction . . .;" or (2) "[T]he complaint . . . asserts a claim requiring construction of the Act . . . ." *Bassett v. Mashantucket Pequot Tribe,* 204 F.3d 343, 349 (2d Cir. 2000) quoting *T.B. Harms Co. v. Eliscu,* 339 F.2d 823, 828 (2d Cir. 1964); *see also Scholastic Entm't, Inc. v. Fox Entm't Grp. Inc.,* 336 F.3d 982, 985–86 (9th Cir. 2003). Because federal courts have exclusive jurisdiction over claims arising under the Copyright Act, failing to sufficiently plead allegations that give the courts jurisdiction will destroy any claim the plaintiff may have in some circumstances because they will not be able to assert claims that implicate the Copyright Act in any other court. Of course, should a federal court determine that it does not have jurisdiction because a claim does not arise under the Copyright Act, by necessary implication, the claim must involve some other violation, usually a breach of contract, as was the case in *Bassett.*

Although ownership of a copyright in a work begins when the work is fixed in a tangible medium of expression, in order to bring an action for infringement of a work originating in the United States, the work must be registered with the Copyright Office.[1] Works originating from another country may not need to be registered for a suit to be brought, provided that they originate from a country that is a member of the Berne Convention for the Protection of Literary and Artistic Works, but registration confers benefits generally that favor registration, especially given the low cost. If a registration has not yet been obtained, but an application has been properly submitted to the Copyright Office, most jurisdictions permit a plaintiff to proceed with a suit while the application is pending; however, some jurisdictions view the registration requirement as absolute and will dismiss a claim that is not based on a registration (or a denied application to register). *Compare Apple Barrel Prod., Inc. v. Beard,* 730 F.2d 384, 386 (5th Cir.1984) (plaintiff must only show that it paid the fee, deposited the work, and the Copyright Office received the application); *La Resolana Architects, PA v. Clay Realtors Angel Fire,* 416 F.3d 1195, 1200–01 (10th Cir. 2005) ("[O]nly upon registration or refusal to register is a copyright holder entitled to sue for copyright infringement under § 411.").

A practical consideration in deciding when to file suit, i.e., after filing an application or after issuance (or rejection) of registration is the availability of statutory remedies, including statutory damages and attorneys' fees.

---

1. *See* 17 U.S.C. § 411(a) ("Except for an action brought for a violation of the rights of the author under section 106A(a), and subject to the provisions of subsection (b), no civil action for infringement of the copyright in any United States work shall be instituted until preregistration or registration of the copyright claim has been made in accordance with this title.").

Such remedies only are available for infringements that occur after registration. Thus, if a client mostly seeks damages from its copyright claim, it may be worthwhile to wait until a registration issues to file suit.

VIII. Opinions Evaluating Different Forums

Below are sample opinions evaluating different forums in connection with various types of claims available under the Lanham Act.

FORM A –

MEMORANDUM REGARDING A POTENTIAL FALSE
ADVERTISING CLAIM

In the Sixth Circuit, a statement that is deemed to be commercial speech may be subject to a false advertising claim under the Lanham Act, but most circuits have adopted the test articulated in *Gordon & Breach Science Publishers v. Am. Inst. of Physics*, 859 F. Supp. 1521 (S.D.N.Y. 1994), which states that:

> In order for representations to constitute "commercial advertising or promotion" . . . they must be: (1) commercial speech; (2) by a defendant who is in commercial competition with plaintiff; (3) for the purpose of influencing consumer to buy defendant's goods or services. While the representations need not be made in a 'classic advertising campaign,' but may consists instead of more informal types of 'promotion,' the representation (4) must be disseminated sufficiently to the relevant purchasing public to constitute 'advertising' or 'promotion' within that industry.

859 F. Supp. at 1535–36. Even if more than mere commercial speech is required for a statement to constitute advertising or promotion, if the distribution of the statement is to a limited number of customer but in a relatively small market, or there is proof of further dissemination in the market, even through in-person discussion, it may be sufficiently disseminated to constitute advertising or promotion.

C. Analysis

The Lanham Act gives no definition for "commercial advertising or promotion." In fact, based on the legislative history, it seems that Congress specifically avoided providing any guidance on the subject, other than to make clear that Section 43(a) of the Lanham Act covered only commercial speech as that term is defined by the Supreme Court. Thus, what constitutes commercial advertising or promotion has been left to be defined by the courts, even though the literal definitions are quite broad and would effectively make Section 43(a) a federal law of business disparagement.

D. Legislative History

The legislative history of the Lanham Act provides no direct indication regarding the meaning of advertising or promotion in Section 43(a)(1)(B). *See, e.g., H & R Indus., Inc. v. Kirshner,* 899 F. Supp. 995, 1006 (E.D.N.Y. 1995) ("There is no clear definition of . . . promotion for purposes of the Lanham Act.").

1. The U.S.T.A. Review Commission Report

The 1989 amendments that added the language were based on an U.S.T.A. Review Commission report. *See* The United States Trademark Association Trademark Review Commission Report and Recommendations to USTA President and Board of Directors, 77 T.M.R. 375 (1987). This report itself did not include the phrasing "commercial advertising or promotion." Its proposed Section 43(a) stated: "Any person who, in commerce, shall use in connection with any goods or services . . . (2) by use of . . . a false or misleading description or representation . . . misrepresents the nature, characteristics, or qualities of his or another person's goods . . ." The plain intent of this draft, as stated in the Commission's Report was to clarify that "Section 43(a) is a broadly remedial section which extends deeply into false advertising." 77. T.M.R. at 430. Thus, it was meant to provide relief for a plaintiff "whose business is being injured by clearly false and disparaging representations about its products."[2] *Id.* The Commission obviously recognized that such language would "impinge on state laws of trade libel and product disparagement." *Id.*

2. Senate and House Reports

Both the Senate's and House's first drafts of the bill introducing the amendments used the same language as the Commission. Again, the discussion of this section focused on clarifying that Section 43(a) applied to representations about another's products as much as one's own. In the first Senate Debate, discussion of Section 43(a)'s false advertising provision was limited.

---

2. Ostensibly, this particular change to Section 43(a) was meant to overrule the 7th Circuit decision in *Bernard Food Indus. v. Dietence Co.,* 415 F.2d 1279 (7th Cir. 1970), which held that Section 43(a) only applied to representations about one's own product and nothing more.

As one Senator Grassley put it, " . . . section 43 . . . is essentially used to protect against unfair competition," but he went on, "The changes, however, will only codify the law laid down by our Federal courts." 10 Gilson VI-395.

It is only in the subsequent House version of the bill that the "commercial advertising or promotion" language appears. This language was inserted because "[t]o avoid legitimate constitutional challenge . . . the reach of the section specifically extends only to false and misleading speech that is encompassed within the 'commercial speech' doctrine of the United States Supreme Court.' Statement of Rep. Kastenmeier. Senator DeConcinni agreed with the insertion of this language 'only to eliminate any possibility that the section might be applied to political speech.' Statement of Sen. DeConcinni."

E. Definitions

The definition of advertising is "the action of calling something to the attention of the public." Webster's Third New International Dictionary, p. 31 (1981). On the other hand, the definition of advertise is "to make known to (someone): give notice to." *Id.* In the marketing world, anything that draws attention to a brand, product, or service is "advertising." Burns, Jean W., *Confused Jurisprudence: False Advertising Under The Lanham Act*, 79 B.U.L. Rev. 807, 846 (1999) (citations omitted).

The definition of promotion is "the act of setting up or furthering a business enterprise or active furtherance of sale of merchandise through advertising or other publicity." Webster's Third New International Dictionary, p. 1815 (1981). As one commentator has observed, "promotion" in the Act appears to apply to any formal or informal communications that encourages sales. Burns, 79 B.U.L. Rev. at 846.

F. Case Law

With regard to level of advertising or promotion, "the statute itself contains no requirement concerning the amount or type of advertising or promotion necessary to sustain a lawsuit." Burns, 79 B.U.L. Rev. at 847.

1. Sixth Circuit Law Regarding Advertising and Promotion Under the Lanham Act

In *Semco, Inc. v. Amcast, Inc.*, 52 F.3d 108 (6th Cir. 1995), the Sixth Circuit declined to define the phrase "commercial advertising and promotion." *Id.* at 112 ("We shrink from attempting to divine the true meaning of 'commercial advertising and promotion' because of the contradictory legislative history concerning that language."). There, the defendant had been granted summary judgment on plaintiff's Lanham Act claim because defendant's article, published in an industry magazine, written by its president and allegedly touting its own goods, did not constitute advertising or promotion according to the district court. Plaintiff appealed, and the Sixth Circuit reversed and remanded because it found that defendant's article did constitute commercial speech. Although defendant subsequently used copies of the article in promotional materials, plaintiff only challenged the publishing of misrepresentations about defendant's goods in the article itself. *Semco*, 52 F.3d at 110.

The Sixth Circuit, in referencing the alternative definitions of "commercial advertising or promotion" in the legislative history, and throughout the rest of the opinion, implicitly adopted the notion that Section 43(a)(1)(B) encompasses all commercial speech. Though the question before the Court was whether the article constituted commercial advertising or promotion under the Lanham Act, the Court, after declining to define "commercial advertising or promotion," explicitly and consistently referred to "commercial speech" to conduct its analysis. Specifically, the Court stated that: "A company's admission that the speech in question is advertising may strongly indicate that it is commercial, but the company's refusal to admit that does not convince us that it is not *commercial speech*." *Semco*, 52 F.3d at 113 (emphasis added). Furthermore, the Sixth Circuit's holding was "that the alleged misrepresentations . . . represent *commercial speech* and are actionable under the Lanham Act." *Semco*, 52 F.3d at 114 (emphasis added).

As noted in *Semco*, "the core definition of 'commercial speech' is that speech 'which does no more than propose a commercial transaction.'" *Id.* quoting *Virginia State Bd. of Pharmacy v. Virginia Citizens Consumer Counsel, Inc.*, 425 U.S. 748, 762 (1976). Defendant was clearly soliciting business in sending materials to the potential customer.

In *Balance Dynamics Corp. v. Schmitt Indus. Inc.* 204 F.3d 683 (6th Cir. 2000), the plaintiff sued the defendant for sending a letter, signed by defendant's president, to 3200 customers or potential customers that stated that plaintiff's product had come under scrutiny by the EPA, along with an allegedly false statement in a cartoon sent to 2500 customers. One of plaintiff's customers faxed the letter to plaintiff and plaintiff sued. The lower court granted defendant judgment as a matter of law on plaintiff's Lanham Act claim for literally false advertising because it found the statements not to be literally false, and plaintiff offered no evidence of customer reaction to the advertisements. *See Balance Dynamics Corp. v. Schmitt Indus.*, 1997 U.S. Dist. LEXIS 17253 (E.D. Mich. 1997). Even though the statements were in letters, there was no discussion of whether the statements and letters constituted advertising or promotion under the Lanham Act.

The Sixth Circuit found that granting of judgment as a matter of law was error by the lower court and vacated the judgment. Of some note is the Sixth Circuit's discussion about recovery of damages to goodwill if all the plaintiff has proof of is the literal falsity of the statement. First, the Court stated that "most of the circuits have ruled that when a statement is literally false, a plaintiff need not demonstrate actual customer deception in order to obtain relief under the Lanham Act." *Balance Dynamics*, 204 F.3d at 693. In this discussion, the Court noted that plaintiff could not recover such damages without evidence that its goodwill was harmed or that customers were actually deceived. *Id.* at 694. It went on to state there was no evidence of a "decrease in the price of [plaintiff's] product." *Id.* Arguably, this permits a recovery of damage to goodwill if the advertisement is literally false, and there is proof of a price drop.

In *Herman Miller, Inc. v. Palazetti Imports and Exports, Inc.*, 270 F.3d 298 (6th Cir. 2001), however, the Sixth Circuit stated that:

> An isolated statement, even if false, does not give rise to a Lanham Act claim and provide a basis for pursuing suit in federal court. Rather, the Sixth Circuit has held that the Lanham Act reaches to cases where the information was distributed sufficiently to constitute 'commercial advertising' and that the potential deception of a single customer is not actionable.

In *Cincinnati Sub-Zero Prods. Inc. v. Augustine Med. Inc.*, 800 F. Supp. 1549 (S.D. Ohio 1992), the court granted a preliminary injunction to plaintiff on its false advertising claim. Here, the vice president of one of defendant's dealers, distributed to some current customers a notice that contained allegedly false statements concerning plaintiff's products and defendant's director of marketing sent a letter to plaintiff's customers making allegedly false statement concerning defendant's own products. *Id.* at 1553. There was also evidence that defendant disseminated other advertisements as part of "defendants' overall mission to market the [product]." *Id.* at 1554.

Given this precedent, it is arguable that, in the Sixth Circuit, Section 43(a)(1)(B) extends to all commercial speech and therefore defendant's statements.

2. Circuit Decisions Explaining Commercial Advertising or Promotion

a. Favorable Circuit Decisions

i). Ninth Circuit

In *Coastal Abstract Service, Inc. v. First Am. Title Ins. Co.*, 173 F.3d 725 (9th Cir. 1999), the Ninth Circuit held that dissemination of statements to one of three members of a market was sufficient to uphold a jury's finding of false advertising under the Lanham Act. This case centered around three statements made by defendant to a large customer of the parties' refinancing products. These statements were made in the course of the customer's refinancing efforts that involved both parties.

While two of the statements were found to be statements of opinion, and therefore, not actionable under the Lanham Act, the third statement that plaintiff was not paying its bills, which appeared in a report based on an investigation of the conduct of plaintiff, was found to be a violation of the Lanham Act by a jury and upheld by the Ninth Circuit. *Coastal*, 173 F.3d at 729–30.

Defendant asked the Court to overturn the jury verdict because the statement was not "commercial advertising or promotion" as a matter of law. The Ninth Circuit adopted the formulation of *Gordon & Breach Science Publishers v. Am. Inst. of Physics*, 859 F. Supp. 1521 (S.D.N.Y. 1994), which stated that:

> In order for representations to constitute "commercial advertising or promotion" . . . they must be: (1) commercial speech; (2) by a defendant who is in commercial competition with plaintiff; (3) for the purpose of influencing consumer to buy defendant's goods or services. While the representations need not be made in a 'classic advertising campaign,' but may consists instead of more informal types of 'promotion,' the representation (4) must be disseminated sufficiently to the relevant purchasing public to constitute 'advertising' or 'promotion' within that industry.

Coastal, 173 F.3d at 735 quoting *Gordon & Breach*, 859 F. Supp. at 1535–36. The Ninth Circuit also cited approvingly to the language in *Seven-Up Co. v. Coca-Cola Co.*, 86 F.3d 1379, 1386 (5th Cir. 1996), which states that "where the potential purchasers in the market are relatively limited in number, even a single promotional presentation to an individual purchaser may be enough to trigger the protections of the [Lanham] Act."

Coastal argued that the evidence showed that there were only two or three institutions that performed nationwide refinancing operations like those of the customer, such that the statements to that one customer were sufficiently disseminated to constitute promotion. *Coastal*, 173 F.3d at 735. The district court and Ninth Circuit agreed. Specifically, the Ninth Circuit approved the district court's jury instruction and found the jury's verdict on that instruction to be supported by substantial evidence. The jury instruction stated:

> To establish the existence of a "commercial promotion" . . . plaintiff has the burden of establishing that the "relevant purchasing public" to which plaintiff was marketing its services consisted only of customers operating nationwide programs for the refinance of residential mortgages. If you find that the relevant purchasing public to which plaintiff was marketing its services included any institutional lender or other purchaser of escrow services, you must find against plaintiff.

Id.

ii). Eighth Circuit

In *Porous Media Corp. v. Pall Corp.*, 173 F.3d 1109 (8th Cir. 1999), the Eighth Circuit upheld a jury finding of false advertising by defendant. The defendant sent an "Alert" that contained allegedly false statements to five companies, and information from the Alert circulated more widely in the industry. *Id.* at 1114. The Court noted two relevant markets. The first relevant market for the products at issue was a market with a "small number of high volume participants," where "three companies produce seventy percent of all [products]." *Id.* Of the six largest companies in that market, three—all of whom were plaintiff's customers—received the Alert. *Id.* The second market also consisted of a "small number of large volume vendors," and participants in the markets overlapped. *Id.* Once again, three of the six largest participants received the allegedly false Alert. *Id.*

On appeal, defendant contented that the Alert was neither commercial speech nor an advertisement or promotion under the Lanham Act because it was not disseminated sufficiently. In discussing the commercial speech doctrine, the Court stated that "[The Alert] was an advertisement because it 'proposed' a commercial transaction." *Id.* at 1120, quoting *Cincinnati v. Discovery Network*, 507 U.S. 410, 423 (1993). The court, in addressing the dissemination issue further stated that "To be 'commercial advertising or promotion' under the Act, one's statements must be 'disseminated sufficiently to the relevant purchasing public . . . within that industry." *Id.* at 1121, quoting *Seven-Up*, 86 F.3d at 1384. The Court upheld the jury's finding on liability because the relevant purchasing public was found to be a small number of companies for the products, and that liability was also based on the sending of information "derived" from the Alert to other companies, the distribution of the information in the market, and discussions of the information by defendant with other customers. *Id.* at fn. 9 ("Because [defendant's] broader post-Alert communications were themselves causally connected to the Alert, the jury could reasonably conclude that the injuries inflicted by the post-Alert communications occurred 'as a result of' the Alert itself.").

iii). Fifth Circuit

In *Seven-Up Co. v. Coca-Cola Co.*, 86 F.3d 1379 (5th Cir. 1996), the Fifth Circuit affirmed the district court's grant of judgment as a matter of law that defendant did not commit false advertising under the Lanham Act because there was insufficient evidence for the jury to draw the causal inference that bottlers had switched from 7-UP to Sprite as a result of Coca-Cola's false and misleading promotional presentation. Coca-Cola had made the presentation to 11 bottlers, only 2 in full, out of a potential market of 74, and 5 later switched. The jury also found that the presentation was false and misleading, although that issue was not raised on appeal. It should be noted that the Fifth Circuit affirmed the magistrate judge's denial of permanent injunctive relief, despite the jury's falsity finding, because Seven-Up failed to show irreparable harm. *Id.* at 1390 (there was no evidence that the presentation had been used in years, and the statistical date there was of questionable significance at the time of the lower court and appellate decisions).

Coca-Cola, in its appeal, argued that the presentation was not disseminated sufficiently to the "public" to constitute advertising under the Lanham Act, and that the Act did not apply to "materials given in individual, face-to-face business meetings with a few local bottlers." *Id.* at 1384. The Fifth Circuit adopted the definition of "advertising or promotion" articulated in *Gordon & Breach, supra,* and stated that Coca-Cola's proposition did not have support in the case law. The Court distinguished *Am. Needle & Novelty, Inc. v. Drew Pearson Mktg. Inc.*, 820 F. Supp. 1072 (N.D. Ill. 1993), because there a single, private letter was sent to a nonconsuming licensor.

The Court went on to state that "for purposes of the Lanham Act's definition of 'commercial advertising or promotion,' both the required level of circulation and the relevant 'consuming' or 'purchasing' public addressed by the dissemination of false information will vary according to the specifics of the industry." *Seven-Up*, 86 F.3d at 1385. Thus, "where the potential purchasers in the market are relatively limited in number, even a single promotional presentation to an individual purchaser may be enough to trigger the protections of the Act." *Id.* at 1386. The Court further explained that the use of the presentation materials during negotiations with representatives of the bottlers were not merely isolated, individual statements of opinion by a single sales representative to a single customer, but the materials were specifically developed and designed by Coca-Cola to target these independent bottlers and convince them, based on sales statistics, to switch to Coca-Cola's product. *Id.* The presentation, although only shown to two bottlers in full, was "a far cry form the individualized comments held by some courts to fall outside the meaning of commercial advertising or promotion under the Act." *Id.*

b. Unfavorable Circuit Decisions

i). Second Circuit

In the most recent decision on point, the Second Circuit in *Fashion Boutique of Short Hills, Inc. v. Fendi USA, Inc.*, 314 F.3d 48 (2d Cir. 2002), affirmed the judgment of the district court that systematic, reactive comments by sales clerks at defendant's store that were allegedly disparaging to plaintiff's store were not false advertising under the Lanham Act. Plaintiff here based its Lanham Act claim on allegations that employees at defendants' stores made misrepresentations to some customers, and those customers relayed the misrepresentations to other of plaintiff's customers. *Id.* at 53. Plaintiff attempted to elicit evidence of the misrepresentations by sending investigators to the defendant's store and by submitting the declarations of 40 of plaintiff's customers. *Id.*

The evidence showed that in none of the alleged conversations did defendant's clerks initiate the discussions of plaintiff's store. *Id.* The evidence amounted to defendant's clerks reacting to comments by customers by stating that plaintiff's store carried an "inferior, 'department store' line of products" and that plaintiff's store sold "fake or bogus" merchandise. *Id.* at 54. The district court granted summary judgment to defendant on plaintiff's Lanham Act claim because the "Lanham Act is violated when defendants proactively pursue customer contacts and disparage plaintiff's goods or services," and because there was insufficient dissemination of the statements as required by the *Gordon & Breach* test in so far as there were only "a dozen admissible comments within a purchasing public universe consisting of thousands of customers." *Id.* at 55.

The Second Circuit thoroughly analyzed the statutory language in reviewing the district court's decision. It ended up adopting the first, third, and fourth elements of the *Gordon & Breach* test as its own (omitting the necessity for the parties to be in competition). In adopting the test, the Second Circuit found that "advertising is generally understood to consist of widespread communication through print or broadcast media," but that "promotion may take other forms of publicity used in the relevant industry, such as displays at trade shows and *sales presentations to buyers.*" *Id.* at 57 citing *Seven-Up*, 86 F.3d at 1386 (emphasis added). The Second Circuit criticized the Seventh Circuit's decision in *First Health Grp. Corp. v. BCE Emergis Corp.*, 269 F.3d 800, 803 (7th Cir. 2001), which limited the scope of Lanham Act false advertising claims to "a form of promotion to anonymous recipients, as distinguished from face-to-face communication . . . [and] a subset of persuasion [that relies on] dissemination of prefabricated promotional material," because the Seventh Circuit did not define the term "promotion" in any meaningful way. *Fendi*, 314 F.3d at 57. Nevertheless, it stated that the Lanham Act does not extend to all commercial speech because advertising and promotion connote activity designed to disseminate information to the public. *Id.*

> Thus, the touchstone of . . . 'commercial advertising or promotion' under the Lanham Act is that the contested representations are part of an organized campaign to penetrate the relevant market. Proof of widespread dissemination within the relevant industry is a normal concomitant of meeting this requirement. Thus, businesses harmed by isolated disparaging statements do not seek have redress under the Lanham Act . . . .

Id.

In assessing plaintiff's Lanham Act claim under its standard, the Court noted that there was no evidence to suggest that statements by the plaintiff's clerks were part of an organized campaign to enter the marketplace, and the clerks' statements were not widely enough disseminated—"twenty-seven oral statements . . . in a marketplace of thousands of customers." *Id.* at 58.

ii). Tenth Circuit

In *Sports Unlimited, Inc. v. Lankford Enter. Inc.*, 275 F.3d 996 (10th Cir. 2002), the Court upheld the district court's summary judgment ruling against plaintiff on its claim of false advertising. The district court had found insufficient distribution of a reference sheet that allegedly contained false and misleading statements about plaintiff. *See also Proctor & Gamble Co. v. Haugen*, 222 F.3d 1262 (10th Cir. 2000) (adopting *Gordon & Beach* test and declining to address issue of "commercial advertising or promotion" because there was a genuine issue of material fact and "a difficult factual determination" of the distribution of statements alleging plaintiff's affiliation with Satan). The statements were in the form of notes on the sheet regarding unfavorable comments by certain of plaintiff's customers. *Id.* at 999. Defendant admitted to distributing the sheet to two persons, who were both connected to one project, while plaintiff had found seven recipients of the sheet, all of which were alleged to have obtained the sheet from defendant. *Id.* The judge below had found that distribution to even all seven of the alleged recipients would not amount to "advertising or promotion in the industry" where plaintiff made at least 150 bids a year. *Id.* at 1003.

The Tenth Circuit upheld the lower court's ruling in part because "plaintiff failed to show evidence of sufficient communications with any prospective customers or persons . . . who might have influence over prospective customers." *Id.* at 1004. Likewise, plaintiff could only put forth evidence that the sheet was distributed to the aforementioned two individuals on the one project and that they were already unhappy with plaintiff's performance on the project. *Id.* Plaintiff's other documents were only surmise and conjecture according to the Court. *Id.* Thus, the court found that distribution to two persons on the same project did not amount to commercial advertising or promotion.

iii). Seventh Circuit

In *First Health, supra,* the Seventh Circuit affirmed the lower court's ruling but criticized it for treating commercial advertising or promoting as coextensive with commercial speech. 269 F.3d at 803. The Seventh Circuit noted that the statement there at issue, whether a company was a "PPO" or not, was made in the context of negotiations between hospitals and a health care provider among business executives and lawyers, and that such negotiations were not advertising or promotion under the Act. *Id.*

The Seventh Circuit specifically went on to define advertising as "a form of promotion to anonymous recipients, as distinguished from face-to-face communication . . . a person-to-person pitch by an account executive is not [advertising]." *Id.* at 803–04. Nevertheless, the Court went on to state that because the lower court did not inquire whether any of defendant's endeavors "entailed promotional material disseminated to anonymous recipients," it would assume that some of the materials were in fact promotional. *Id.* at 804. Despite this assumption, the Court found that plaintiff had not established that any of the statements made were false or misleading. Thus, the Court only held that the statements were not false or misleading, in part because plaintiff did not show any evidence that it would likely be damaged by the statements, which the Court stated was necessary under Section 43(a)(1)(B). *Id.* at 805–06.

3. Other Helpful, Relevant Case Law From District Courts

The case that articulates the generally accepted test for determining commercial advertising and promotion is *Gordon & Breach Science Publishers v. Am. Inst. of Physics*, 859 F. Supp. 1521 (S.D.N.Y. 1994). This case involved two journal publishers where the defendant ran articles, allegedly containing false comparisons of the cost effectiveness of such journals, ranked plaintiff's journal as one of the least cost effective and distributed the results to librarians. Plaintiff further alleged that the publishing of the articles was part of a continuous advertising and promotional campaign against plaintiff that included distribution of preprints of the articles, issuance of a press release, publication of a letter to the editor, and repetition of the false results of defendant's surveys in electronic mailings to librarians. *Id.* at 1526–27.

Defendant moved to dismiss on, among other grounds, the fact that none of its statements constituted advertising or promotion. The court articulated its oft-cited test and moved to a consideration of whether the articles were commercial speech. It determined that the articles themselves were not nor was the letter to the editor. Nevertheless, the court noted that the distribution of preprint and published articles to librarians constituted "activities explicitly promotional in nature: distribution of survey results favoring defendants' products to an audience that represents the core consumers of those products." *Id.* at 1544. Thus, the Court let these claims stand.

In *Goldsmith v. Polygram Diversified Ventures*, 37 U.S.P.Q.2d 1321 (S.D.N.Y. 1995), the district court granted defendant's motion to dismiss because the complaint did not allege sufficient dissemination. *Id.* at 1326. Here, the defendant, through its attorney, sent a single letter to the would-be publisher of plaintiff's book in which it was stated that plaintiff did not have rights in the photographs to be included in plaintiff's book. *Id.* at 1322. This letter was sent in order to prevent competition between plaintiff's soon-to-be published book about the 1994 Woodstock festival and defendant's book on the same subject. Because of the letter, plans for publication of plaintiff's book were discontinued, and plaintiff could not obtain another publisher.

In distinguishing *Mobius Mgmt. Systems, Inc. v. Fourth Dimension Software, Inc.*, 880 F. Supp. 1005 (S.D.N.Y. 1994), the Court noted that in that case, the relevant market was small and that the letter in that case had been sent to the ultimate consumer of the product who could have tainted the goodwill of the plaintiff with other purchasers. *Goldsmith*, 37 U.S.P.Q.2d at 1326. The court then stated that a single letter to a publisher could not constitute advertising or promotion and stated that whatever claims plaintiff had, they were best pursued under state law. *Id.* "A single communication without any allegation that it was part of a pattern or campaign to penetrate more of the relevant market is insufficient" to constitute "advertising or promotion." *Id.* at 1326.

In *Avon Products, Inc. v. S.C. Johnson & Son, Inc.*, 984 F. Supp. 768 (S.D.N.Y. 1997), the Court found that defendant's counterclaim was commercial advertising or promotion but not literally false even though the allegedly false statements were only found in "100 lists" while the potential customers numbered in the millions. *Id.* at 795. The court did note that "dissemination to a single customer is generally not sufficient. However, where the relevant purchasing public is very small, misrepresentations, though few in number, which reach a significant portion of the purchasing public are actionable." *Id.* (citations omitted).

The Court concluded that plaintiff's lists were advertising or promotion because (1) The lists had limited but significant distribution because they appeared in disparate locations across the country over a decade; (2) In addition, some of plaintiff's managers encouraged sales representatives to use the lists in promoting its products; (3) Plaintiff had produced other promotional materials advertising the product as a repellent (the allegedly false statement at issue); (4) At least 7 percent, and possibly as much as 32 percent, of the population that purchased plaintiff's product to use as an insect repellent had been influenced by a source related to plaintiff to believe that the product was an effective insect repellent. "This evidence of [plaintiff's] dissemination of information about [the product's] repellency power, in the context of a business that relies exclusively upon promotion by its sales representatives, constitutes advertising and promotion under the Lanham Act." *Id.* at 795–96.

In *Ultra-Temp Corp. v. Advanced Vacuum Systems, Inc.*, 27 F. Supp. 2d 86 (D. Mass. 1998), the court granted summary judgment to defendant on plaintiff's Lanham Act claim for damages. Here, the parties were in competition but at some point were discussing a license for defendant to use plaintiff's patented product. At that same time, defendant was negotiating a potential sale to a customer. *Id.* at 88. During the negotiations with the customer, defendant represented in a letter that it in fact had a license for the patented technology, when it had not. It was uncontested that the letter was not disseminated further than the one customer. *Id.*

Defendant contended that the admittedly false representation was an "isolated, aberrant statement that was not disseminated sufficiently to the relevant purchasing public." *Id.* at 92. The two parties disagreed about the size of the relevant market, but the Court did not even address the issue. It went on to simply determine that defendant's letter was not "advertising" or "promotion" because they "contemplate something more in the realm of public dissemination than what is involved in the case at bar, a single, discrete misrepresentation to one potential customer that did not ultimately become a term or condition of the parties' written contract." *Id.* at 95.

In *Am. Needle & Novelty, Inc. v. Pearson Mktg. Inc.*, 820 F. Supp. 1072 (N.D. Ill. 1993), the Court dismissed plaintiff's Lanham Act claim because of insufficient dissemination of the relevant statements, which alleged that plaintiff's license was terminated and that were contained in one letter to a nonconsuming licensor. Here, the Court found that "the September 17th letter was an isolated individualized written statement about [plaintiff's] alleged breach of the Agreement; that letter is at the opposite pole of clearly definable media advertising containing specific verifiable or disprovable statements and given wide distribution in commerce." *Id.* at 1078. The judge did not find plaintiff's claim that, in the industry, the effect of the letter would be the same as defendant having gone to a trade show and made the same statements to retailers.

In *Med. Graphics Corp. v. SensorMedics Corp.*, 872 F. Supp. 643 (D. Minn. 1994), the Court denied plaintiff's motion for preliminary injunction. Plaintiff's claim for false advertising was based on the contention that defendant had falsely represented to customers and potential customers that plaintiff was having trouble with the FDA. *Id.* at 645. The allegations were based, in part, on a chart that showed plaintiff's cost per test to be higher than defendant's. This chart had been attached to a letter from one of defendant's salespeople to a potential customer. Defendant stated that the chart was not meant for distribution and that its sales personnel were directed not to distribute the chart. *Id.* at 647. Defendant further contended that none of its statements constituted commercial advertising or promotion.

In analyzing the *Gordon & Breach* factors, the court determined that market was large, although that was not contested by the plaintiff, and that the statements were made to one potential customer, and therefore, defendant's actions did not constitute advertising or promotion. *Id.* at 650.

In *The Garland Co. Inc. v. Ecology Roof Systems Corp.*, 895 F. Supp. 274 (D. Kan. 1995), the Court granted defendant's motion to dismiss. Here, plaintiff and defendant were competitors in the roofing business and, in particular, for a roofing project with the Lawrence School District. During the competition, defendant allegedly sent a letter to one of the bidding contractors that purported to compare the physical characteristics of the parties' materials and that the letter contained false statements. Plaintiff stated that the contractor provided the letter to the school district and, as a result, defendant won the contract. *Id.* at 275.

The Court noted that the "plain meaning of the term 'advertising' carries with it a public dissemination component," but "the same conclusion is less obvious with regard to the term 'promotion.'" *Id.* at 276. The Court explained that the term "carries with it the idea of an organized campaign or, perhaps, communications to a number of potential customers and it appears to be an unlikely term for Congress to have employed if it had intended to include isolated communications with the Act's purview." *Id.* It went on to find that the purchasing public involved was "large, certainly nationwide in scope, and the communication in question is purely isolated, directed at one contractor on one job." *Id.* at 279.

In *Kansas Bankers Surety Co. v. Bahr Consultants, Inc.*, 69 F. Supp. 2d 1004 (E.D. Tenn. 1999), the Court granted summary judgment to defendant on plaintiff's Lanham Act claim. The claims arose out of defendant's allegedly false and misleading statements to five banks concerning plaintiff's employment policies. *Id.* at 1006. The court summarized the facts as being that defendant provided erroneous information concerning particular coverage policies of plaintiff to two banks—the other allegedly false statements to the other three banks consisted of question marks next to dollar figures of policy quotes. The court found those not to be false or misleading statements. *Id.* at 1010.

In analyzing the claim, the Court stated that it would only address prongs 2 and 3 of the *Gordon & Breach* test—that the parties were not in competition and that the statements did not influence the consumers. It concluded that the fact that defendant was a consultant not trying to promote his services over plaintiff's and that therefore his erroneous statements could not have been aimed at influencing the client to purchase the competing products or services. *Id.* at 1013–14.

In *BellSouth Adver. & Pub. Corp. v. Lambert Pub.*, 45 F. Supp. 2d 1316 (S.D. Ala. 1999), the Court denied both parties' motions for preliminary injunction. The majority of the discussion focused on the fact that plaintiff could not show that defendant's statements were false. In the specific discussion concerning representations of defendant's salespeople during one-on-one presentations to potential customers, the Court found that such presentations were clearly within the reach of the Lanham Act because they included visuals that displayed the allegedly false information and that such visuals were advertisements for purposes of the Lanham Act. *Id.* at 1323. Again, though, there was no evidence that the visuals were actually false, and this case had no discussion of dissemination. On the other hand, a statement made by one salesperson, who subsequently was fired, to the effect that plaintiff was going out of the yellow pages business was brushed off as a foolish remark, and the Court stated: "Generally, a statement made by an individual salesperson to an individual potential customer is not actionable." *Id.* at 1324.

In *Pearson Indus. Inc. v. Pet Friendly, Inc.*, 33 F. Supp. 2d 1322 (M.D. Ala. 1999), the Court granted plaintiff's motion for preliminary injunction on its

Lanham Act claims, including for false advertising. Here, defendant sent out cease and desist letter to competitors falsely claiming that it would obtain a trademark registration for its pet products and that they were infringing defendant's trademark rights. *Id.* at 1323–24. After sending these letters, defendant's vice president gave them to the director of sales and marketing, who testified by affidavit that he was instructed to use them as a sales and marketing tool and as "show and tell" devices in customer presentations. *Id.* at 1324. The statements in the letters were subsequently repeated to various buyers from retail chains. *Id.* The court found that use of the letters in sales pitches constituted commercial advertising or promotion. *Id.* at 1325.

In *Nat'l Artists Mgmt. Co., Inc. v. Weaving*, 769 F. Supp. 1224 (S.D.N.Y. 1991), the Court found that there was federal question jurisdiction under the Lanham Act. Here, the case was about theater-booking agents. The defendant was a former employee of plaintiff and, with her husband, sought to form a competing company despite her noncompete clause. In preparing to set up her new business, defendant made disparaging remarks about plaintiff's business during conversations with friends and colleagues, which she argued were not promotion or advertising under the Lanham Act. The court, though, determined that in the context of the theater-booking industry, which it termed "small and closely interconnected," services are promoted by word of mouth, and information spread through a network of telephone contacts, and that defendant's "advertising campaign" was quite effective. *Id.* at 1235. The Court also noted that defendant's husband had initiated some of the conversations rather than simply responding to inquiries about her termination.

In *Derby Indus. Inc. v. Chestnut Ridge Foam, Inc.*, 202 F. Supp. 2d 818 (N.D. Ind. 2002), the Court found that a prison mattress manufacturer who distributed a video to seven potential customers could be found liable under the Lanham Act. The videotape at issue showed a test of the competing mattresses. *Id.* at 820. The defendant made the tape at the request of a customer, subsequently distributed to seven entities, two of whom had been defendant's long-time customers, and stated that it had no plans to further distribute the tape. *Id.* After one of plaintiff's customers obtained the tape and expressed confusion over whether plaintiff's mattress met industry standards, plaintiff filed the complaint.

The Court described the industry at issue as "a highly specialized market consisting of a considerably smaller number of end-users than a product that is used by the general consuming public . . ." *Id.* at 822. The Court stated the inquiry as being whether the tape was used as promotional material to entice anonymous recipients to purchase the mattresses and that advertising was a subset of persuasion that refers to the dissemination of prefabricated promotional material. *Id.* citing *Zurich Ins. Co. v. Amcor Sunclipse*, 241 F.3d 605 (7th Cir. 2001). The Court, therefore, found that since defendant had admitted to distributing the tape to potential customers, "the tape constituted prefabricated promotional material intended for the purpose of generating sales and therefore constituted commercial advertising." *Id.* at 823. The Court, though, denied the plaintiff's preliminary injunction request because the plaintiff could not, at that time, show that the statements made by defendant were false.

In *Republic Tobacco v. North Atl. Trading Co.*, 1999 U.S. Dist. Lexis 6098 (N.D. Ill. 1998), the Court permitted a 43(a) claim to pass a motion to dismiss where the relevant purchasing public was middlemen in the sale of "roll your own ('RYO')" cigarettes. The disparaging remarks here at issue involved statements that plaintiff's incentive programs violated the law. These statements were made in a letter to a customer of plaintiff's products, in a conversation between defendant's CEO and five nationwide distributors of plaintiff's products during a meeting, and in letters to defendant's customers, many of whom were also plaintiff's customers. *Id.* at *6–9. The Court stated: '[W] hether North Atlantic's statements constituted advertising or promotion depends on how Republic and North Atlantic's industry advertises or promotes RYO cigarette papers and on the size of their relevant purchasing public.' *Id.* at *23."

The Court found that plaintiff's allegations were based on statements made on a number of occasions to middlemen who were the relevant purchasing public, which was enough to state a Lanham Act claim. *Id.* at *24.

In *Mobius Mgmt. Systems, Inc. v. Fourth Dimension Software, Inc.*, 880 F. Supp. 1005 (S.D.N.Y. 1995), the Court determined that one letter containing false representations comparing the parties' products and sent to a potential customer, who was about to purchase plaintiff's product, amounted to false advertising. The representations in the letter also violated a previous settlement agreement between the parties.

In analyzing the facts under the *Gordon & Beach* factors, the Court found that plaintiff met the first three easily. The Court stated that "the primary concern of Congress in requiring 'commercial advertising or promotion' was to ensure that" the Lanham Act did not reach protected speech, but that "only promotional representations that are directed at the purchasing public can be reached." *Id.* at 1020. The Court found that the common strand in the cases that denied relief was that the false advertising had not reached the consumers at issue. *Id.* The market was small such that tainting the goodwill of plaintiff with one customer could easily affect another purchaser's view, and the court found that the functional market was just the one customer. *Id.* at 1020–21. Finally, the Court found that the letter constituted advertising or promotion under the Lanham Act because it was presented directly to the customer, who was known to be in the market for the product and the letter was expressly designed to discourage the customer from purchasing plaintiff's product. *Id.* at 1021.

In *Johnson Controls, Inc. v. Exide Corp.*, 152 F. Supp. 2d 1075 (N.D. Ill. 2001) (J. Shadur), defendant moved to dismiss plaintiff's Lanham Act claims, and the Court granted the motion. Plaintiff's claims were based on a couple representations, but only one was analyzed under the commercial advertising or promotion doctrine. Specifically, defendant's representations to Sears in negotiating a battery supply contract with Sears. *Id.* at 1080–81. The Court stated: "Numerous courts have held . . . that misrepresentations made to a single customer in the context of negotiating a transaction cannot constitute 'advertising' or 'promotion' in the statutory sense." *Id.* at 1081–82.

The Court distinguished *Seven-Up* by stating that plaintiff presented no evidence that this case had a similar small industry and negating plaintiff's claims that Sears represented five rather than one customer. *Id.* at 1082.

In *Synygy, Inc. v. Scott-Levin, Inc.*, 51 F. Supp. 2d 570 (E.D. Pa. 1999), the Court granted summary judgment to defendant because defendant's allegedly misleading statements in e-mails and a slide shown at a presentation were not actionable under the Lanham Act. One of the statements in an e-mail was analyzed under the advertising or promotion section of the Lanham Act. The Court stated that the oral statement, which was described in the e-mail put into evidence, did not meet the definition of commercial advertising or promotion because "it was isolated, individualized, informal and oral." *Id.* at 576–77.

In *Schmidt, Long & Assoc. v. Aetna U.S. Healthcare, Inc.*, 2001 WL 856946 (E.D. Pa. 2001), the Court found a triable issue of fact on defendant's counterclaim for false advertising because the parties agreed that the relevant purchasing public was the pool of self-funded medical plan customers. *Id.* at *11. Although not stated in the case, presumably the issue raised was whether this relevant public was large or small and whether plaintiff's statement went to a sufficient number of this relevant public.

In *Florida Breckenridge Inc. v. Solvay Pharm. Inc.*, 47 U.S.P.Q.2d 1491 (S.D. Fla. 1998), the Court found that oral representations made during phone calls to customers regarding a comparison of the parties' products were commercial advertising or promotion with the industry. The Court found that these phone calls were "an integral part of [the] advertising campaign." *Id.* at 1497. This finding was based on an affidavit that stated that phone calls were an integral part of the sales process in the prescription drug industry. *Id.* The Court, though, found that the statements were not false or misleading. *Id.* at 1500–01.

In *Wehrenberg v. Moviefone, Inc.*, 73 F. Supp. 2d 1044 (E.D. Mo. 1999), the Court found that defendant's incorrect statements in its electronic movie listing system of movie times at plaintiff's movie theaters were not actionable under the Lanham Act.

FORM B –
Memorandum on Choice of Forum for Potential
Copyright Misuse Action

This memo outlines certain considerations for a potential suit by our client against the potential defendant based on warnings on audiobooks that they are for personal use and not intended for library circulation. Specifically, we conducted preliminary research into the state of the law in potential forums such as Ohio, Illinois, and California with respect to claims for unfair competition and copyright misuse based on this conduct. We considered these forums because of the client's location, the location of its attorneys, and the recent copyright misuse decision in California.

G. Copyright Misuse

The doctrine of copyright misuse "prevents copyright holders from leveraging their limited monopoly to allow them control of areas outside the monopoly." *Assessment Tech. of Wisconsin LLC v. WIREdata Inc.*, 350 F.3d 640, 68 U.S.P.Q.2d 1953, 1957 (7th Cir. 2003). Parties typically raise copyright misuse as a defense to a copyright infringement action, though one court recently has acknowledged it as an independent cause of action. *See Apple Inc. v. PsyStar Corp.*, Case No. 08cv3251 (N.D. Cal. Feb. 6, 2009). In this matter, a potential defendant is attempting to leverage its copyright in its audiobooks to control matters beyond the rights granted by its copyright, namely, by abrogating the first sale doctrine and imposing downstream conditions on the resale of its audiobooks.

1. Sixth Circuit

Based on our research, the Sixth Circuit has yet to consider whether copyright misuse may be raised as a defense. *See Nat'l Football League v. Rondor Inc.*, 840 F. Supp. 1160, 30 U.S.P.Q.2d 1941, 1946 (N.D. Ohio 1993) (noting that the Sixth Circuit has neither adopted nor rejected the defense of copyright misuse, but finding that the National Football League did not misuse its copyrights where it "blacked out" its copyrighted broadcasts in markets where home football games did not sell out; copyright law permits "such limited license"). Although the Sixth Circuit has not affirmatively acknowledged this defense, the leading copyright treatise indicates that, unless a circuit holds otherwise, "it should be presumed that copyright owners may not, through the vehicle of a contract, magnify their rights beyond those sanctioned by the Copyright Act." Nimmer § 13.09[A][2][b] at 13–299.

2. Seventh Circuit

The Seventh Circuit has effectively adopted the defense of copyright misuse in dicta. *See WIREdata*, 68 U.S.P.Q. at 1957. It did not decide whether the defense applied in that case but suggested that the doctrine of copyright misuse would prevent an owner of a copyright in a compilation of data, which is thinly protected, from leveraging that copyright via a license agreement to prevent distribution of the underlying data itself, which is not protected by copyright. The Seventh Circuit has not addressed whether a party can assert copyright misuse as a cause of action.

3. Ninth Circuit

The Ninth Circuit has adopted the copyright misuse doctrine as a defense. *See Practice Mgmt. Info. Corp. v. Am. Med. Ass'n*, 121 F.3d 516, 45 U.S.P.Q.2d 1780, 1784–85 (9th Cir. 1997) (finding that plaintiff, American Medical Association, misused its copyright when it granted license to the Health Care Financing Administration (HCFA) to use its copyrighted medical procedure code, on condition that the HCFA not use any other system of procedure nomenclature). One district court in the Ninth Circuit also has recognized copyright misuse as an independent claim, at least where copyright infringement has been asserted against the party raising it as a defense. *See Apple Inc. v. PsyStar Corp.*, Case No. 08cv3251 (N.D. Cal. Feb. 6, 2009).

This claim may not be available, however, when copyright infringement has not been asserted.

See Altera Corp. v. Clear Logic Inc., 424 F.3d 1079, 76 U.S.P.Q.2d 1265, 1273–74 (9th Cir. 2005) (rejecting copyright misuse where there has been no allegation of infringement); *but see Ticketmaster LLC v. RMG Tech. Inc.*, 536 F. Supp. 2d 1191, 1199 (C.D. Cal. 2008) (copyright misuse "does not support an independent claim for damages" but suggesting that it may be proper where no copyright infringement claims has been asserted). Some courts have also suggested that the defense may be limited to instances where the alleged misuse frustrates the goal of the Copyright Act—i.e., that it restrains creative expression. *See Metro-Goldwyn-Mayer Studios Inc. v. Grokster Ltd.*, 81 U.S.P.Q.2d 1461, 1481–84 (C.D. Cal. 2006) (rejecting defense and noting that "the existing case law teaches that the misuse defense applies when a copyright holder leverages its copyright to restrain creative activity.").

4. Recommendation

Based on our research so far, the Seventh Circuit appears to be the most desirable forum from the perspective of legal precedent. Although the Ninth Circuit has the most developed case law regarding copyright misuse, at least some of that law is not advantageous to our client. The Sixth Circuit offers a relatively clean slate, which creates uncertainty. However, from a practical perspective, the risk of facing a motion to transfer increases with suit in both Illinois or California, depending on the extent of the parties' sales in those forums.

IX. Letter to Client on Choice of Forum

Dear Client:

Further to our discussions, we recommend that you file suit against the potential defendant in federal district court rather than wait for the outcome of the currently pending proceeding. A federal lawsuit will pressure the defendant to cease its unlawful use of the mark as part of a settlement agreement or, absent settlement, will give you access to broader relief in federal court than is available from the Trademark Trial and Appeal Board (e.g., enjoining the defendant's use of the mark in the United States). Because the state of the law is uncertain with respect to foreign marks, you should carefully consider where to file a potential suit.

H. Potential Forums

• *Central District of California*

We recommend filing suit in the U.S. District Court for the Central District of California, primarily because the Ninth Circuit offers the most favorable case law. The Ninth Circuit is the only circuit court that has recognized the "famous marks" exception to the territoriality principle of trademark law, which could be a crucial theory for success in a potential suit. *See Grupo Gigante S.A. de C.V. v. Dallo & Co.*, 391 F.3d 1088, 1098 (9th Cir. 2004). *But see ITC Ltd. v. Punghini Inc.*, 482 F.3d 135 (2d Cir. 2007) (expressly rejecting applicability of famous marks doctrine in federal trademark infringement cases). Under the famous marks doctrine, a foreign mark that has not been used in the United States still may be entitled to protection if it has acquired secondary meaning and "a substantial percentage of consumers in the relevant American market is familiar with the foreign mark." *Grupo Gigante*, 391 F.3d at 1098. To succeed under this claim, you likely should conduct a survey to establish the requisite familiarity of your mark by consumers where the defendant sells its infringing product.

Filing suit in California, however, probably will require you to fight a motion to transfer venue. While there is some risk that a court might transfer this action to another forum, we believe that the benefits of proceeding in the Ninth Circuit outweigh the risk of losing a motion to transfer, which, of course, would not substantively bar your available relief.

• *Eastern District of Virginia*

You could also file suit in the U.S. District Court for the Eastern District of Virginia, where the defendant is located. Although filing suit in Virginia will negate any venue objections, Fourth Circuit law with respect to foreign marks is less certain. The Fourth Circuit has some favorable precedent as to when use of a foreign mark entitles the foreign mark holder to protection in the United States, which is based on a broad interpretation of when a foreign mark is "used in commerce" for purposes of establishing U.S. rights. *See Int'l Bancorp, LLC v. Societe des Bain de Mer et du Cercle des Etrangers a Monaco,* 329 F.3d 359 (4th Cir. 2003). The Fourth Circuit has not yet squarely addressed the famous marks doctrine, but it has signaled that it may not be receptive to it. *See id.* at 389 n.9 (Motz, J., dissenting) (stating that the viability of the famous marks doctrine is uncertain); *Maruti.com v. Maruti Udyog Ltd.,* 447 F. Supp. 2d 494, 500 (D. Md. 2006) (refusing to apply the famous marks doctrine because the Fourth Circuit has never recognized it). Thus, while Virginia is also a suitable forum, it is less desirable than California.

I. Conclusion

Because the applicable law is still developing, we recommend proceeding in the forum that is most likely to accept your strongest argument, which is California. Of course, there are other theories of infringement you can argue (e.g., rights based on analogous use, violation of state law); we highlight only the most viable theories. We can provide a more developed analysis if you are interested.

CHAPTER

4

Complaint, Answer, Counterclaims

When drafting complaints, answers, and counterclaims, it important to consider the intended audience and desired effect of the pleading. Federal Rules require only notice pleading, rather than detailed statement of facts, so barebones pleading may be sufficient to get the case on file. But the client's purpose and expectations may dictate a different approach.

Consider several possible audiences when drafting pleadings:

- The Client—what are the desires and goals of the client? A simple pleading may be best when the client desires to open a dialogue for settlement with the opponent when initial contacts are unsuccessful. A simple pleading may also be best as a means of reducing cost and limiting the scope of discovery.
- The Opponent—what effect do you want from your opponent? A simple pleading may be useful in bringing the matter to the attention of higher management. Yet once litigation is filed, the matter will soon be turned over to outside counsel for aggressive advocacy. A detailed narrative in the complaint may help the opponent better understand the risks it faces.
- The Court—what response do you want from the court? Obviously you want the court to see the merits of the claims and side with your client if possible. A neutral, simple pleading may do little to achieve this effect, while a complaint containing specific exhibit and examples may prove very persuasive. A short complaint with effective examples may have a better effect than a long complaint that goes unread. Another response usually desired is to establish your credibility as an advocate. Carefully drafted pleadings that avoid careless mistakes or overstated claims and invective can help achieve this goal.
- Opposing Counsel—consider the reaction of opposing counsel as well. Do the pleadings give them ammunition for discovery? Do they demonstrate care in preparation, knowledge of the relevant law, and a full understanding of the facts?
- The media—pleadings are public records, now readily available online in most jurisdictions. Pleadings involving well-known parties or interesting issues are likely to by publicized by trade or general media. If your client wants to tell its story, a narrative pleading may be most effective.

This chapter provides examples of actual pleadings used in various cases. Some are simple and straightforward. Others provide more detailed narrative. As always, the use of these models should be adapted to the specific needs and goals of the particular dispute.

4.1 Complaint for Trademark Infringement

This is a classic trademark infringement complaint based on ownership of a federal registration. The simple complaint clearly states all necessary elements of the claim without elaboration:

- use of a trademark on goods or services in commerce;
- registration of the trademark in connection with the goods and/or services; and
- use of a designation that is likely to cause confusion between the designation and the registered trademark.

United States District Court
Northern District of Illinois
Eastern Division

THOUGHTWORKS, INC.,	)	
Plaintiff,	)	Civil Action No.
	)	COMPLAINT FOR TRADEMARK
V		INFRINGEMENT AND UNFAIR
		COMPETITION
BEN JOHNSON, doing business as	)	
THOUGHTWERKS		
Defendant	)	

1. Plaintiff, ThoughtWorks, Inc., is an Illinois corporation with its principal place of business in Chicago, Illinois.
2. Defendant, Ben Johnson, is a citizen of Erehwon, and is doing business as ThoughtWerks throughout the United States over the Internet.
3. This Court has jurisdiction by virtue of the facts that (i) this is a civil action under the United States Trademark Act (15 U.S.C. § 1051, et seq.), jurisdiction being conferred in accordance with 15 U.S.C. § 1121 and 28 U.S.C. § 1338(a); and (ii) this is a civil action in which plaintiff and defendant are citizens of different states and the value of the matters in controversy exceeds seventy-five thousand dollars ($75,000) exclusive of interest and costs, jurisdiction being expressly conferred under 28 U.S.C. § 1332(a). This Court also has pendent jurisdiction over all related claims herein in accordance with 28 U.S.C. § 1338(b).

Count I
Trademark Infringement

4. ThoughtWorks is engaged in the business of computer software development and consulting.

5. Since long prior to the acts of defendant, ThoughtWorks has sold many millions of dollars of its goods and services under the THOUGHT WORKS mark and has spent millions of dollars to advertise and promote that trademark.

6. As a result of its sales, advertising and use, the THOUGHTWORKS mark has come to represent a valuable goodwill owned by ThoughtWorks.

7. ThoughtWorks owns the following United States Trademark registrations for its THOUGHTWORKS mark for use in connection with the identified goods.

Trademark	Registration Number	Goods/Services
ThoughtWorks	1,866,548	Business consulting services.
ThoughtWorks	2,013,630	Software development and computer hardware and software consulting services.
ThoughtWorks	2,361,539	Computer software design for others and computer hardware and software consulting services.

Said registrations are valid and subsisting, and in accordance with Section 7(b) of the United States Trademark Act (15 U.S.C. §1057(b)), are prima facie evidence of ThoughtWorks' ownership of the marks, the validity of the marks, and its exclusive right to use the mark in connection with the above identified goods and services.

Reg. No. 1,866,548 is incontestable and in accordance with Section 33(b) of the United States Trademark Act (15 U.S. C. §1115(b)), is conclusive evidence of ThoughtWorks' ownership of the mark, the validity of the mark, and its exclusive right to use the mark in connection with the above identified goods and services.

8. Defendant recently began using the mark THOUGHTWERKS and the Internet domain name "thoughtwerks.com" to advertise, market, and sell computer software and development services over the Internet in competition with ThoughtWorks.

9. Defendant's use of the THOUGHTWERKS mark and domain name is likely to cause confusion, mistake, or deception with ThoughtWorks or its goods and services offered under the THOUGHTWORKS trademark, or to result in the belief by purchasers and others that defendant

or its products and services are connected with, sponsored by, or approved by ThoughtWorks.

10. Defendant's use of the THOUGHTWERKS mark and domain name is without ThoughtWorks' authorization or consent.
11. ThoughtWorks has written to defendant asking that it cease and desist from using the THOUGHTWERKS mark and domain name, but defendant has refused to respond.
12. Defendant's use of the THOUGHTWERKS mark and domain name trademarks constitutes infringement of registered trademarks in violation of Section 32 of the United States Trademark Act (15 U.S.C. § 1114(1)).
13. Upon information and belief, defendant's acts have been willful, intentional, or in reckless disregard of, ThoughtWorks' rights.
14. Defendant acts are greatly and irreparably damaging to ThoughtWorks and will continue to damage ThoughtWorks until enjoined by this Court; wherefore, ThoughtWorks is without adequate remedy at law.

Count II
Unfair Competition

15. ThoughtWorks realleges paragraphs 1 through 14 of Count I.
16. Defendant's acts tend falsely to represent defendant and its products and services as being affiliated, connected or associated with, or sponsored or approved by, ThoughtWorks in violation of Section 43(a) of the United States Trademark Act (15 U.S.C. § 1125(a)).
17. Defendant's acts constitute unfair competition with ThoughtWorks and result in defendant's unjust enrichment under the common law of the State of Illinois and elsewhere.
18. Defendant's aforesaid activities constitute unfair business practices in violation of the Unfair Trade Practices Act of the State of Illinois.

WHEREFORE, ThoughtWorks prays that:

1. Defendant and its officers, agents, servants, employees, attorneys, and all others in active concert and participation with any of them, be individually and collectively, preliminarily and permanently, enjoined from:
   a. using the THOUGHTWERKS mark or domain name, or any other name or mark which includes such mark, or is otherwise likely to cause confusion with ThoughtWorks' use of its trademark;
   b. doing any other act or thing likely to confuse, mislead, or deceive others into believing that defendant or its products or services,

emanate from, or are connected with, sponsored by or approved by, ThoughtWorks;

c. Defendant be required to pay to ThoughtWorks:

d. in accordance with 15 U.S.C. § 1117(a), an award of the greater of treble the actual damages suffered by ThoughtWorks, or the wrongful profits enjoyed by defendant, as a result of its aforesaid unfair competition, as well as an award of ThoughtWorks' costs and attorney's fees;

and

e. in accordance with the common law of unfair competition of the State of Illinois, ThoughtWorks' actual damages, as well as punitive damages in a sum sufficient to deter further acts of unfair competition.

2. Defendant is required to transfer to ThoughtWorks the domain name registration for thoughtwerks.com.

3. ThoughtWorks have such other and further relief as the Court deems just.

Respectfully submitted,

4.2 Complaint for Trademark Infringement

This is another example of a similar infringement claim that directly states the elements of the case. The jurisdiction paragraphs mirror those stated in the complaint above (4.1) and are omitted.

United States District Court
For the Northern District of Texas

Booher CONSULTANTS, INC.,	)	CIVIL ACTION No.
	)	COMPLAINT FOR:
Plaintiff,	)	
	)	
v.	)	(1) VIOLATION OF SECTION 32 OF THE LANHAM ACT; AND
	)	
JOHN GALT,	)	(2) VIOLATION OF SECTION 43(A) OF THE LANHAM ACT
Defendant.	)	

Complaint

Jurisdiction and Venue

[Paragraph 1 and 2 intentionally omitted]

Parties

3. Plaintiff, Booher Consultants, Inc., is a Texas corporation located in Grapevine, Texas (referred to hereafter as "Booher").
4. Defendant, John Galt, is a resident of Atlantis (referred to hereafter as "Galt") and is doing business throughout the United States and in this judicial district by selling the products and services that give rise to this complaint.

Facts

5. Booher is a global consulting business that works with organizations to increase profitability and market share through effective communication. Booher's founder and CEO, Dianna Booher, is a widely known expert on communication and productivity, popular keynote speaker and seminar leader, and author of more than 40 books, including the books entitled YOUR SIGNATURE LIFE and YOUR SIGNATURE WORK.
6. For many years and long prior to the acts of Galt alleged in this Complaint, Booher has used the distinctive name and mark YOUR SIGNATURE LIFE in connection with books, keynote speaking programs and other products, publications and services offered throughout the United States and abroad.
7. The mark YOUR SIGNATURE LIFE has been prominently displayed as the name and mark of Booher's products and services since 2002.
8. Booher owns the federal trademark registration for the mark YOUR SIGNATURE LIFE, Reg. No. 2,820,039, issued March 2, 2004, in Class 35 for "business consulting services in the field of business writing, technical writing, grammar, oral presentations, customer services, interpersonal skills, listening, conflict resolution, meetings, gender communication differences, and personal productivity," showing first use on June 9, 2002, and filed on May 8, 2003.
9. Booher's registration for the mark YOUR SIGNATURE LIFE is valid and subsisting, and in accordance with §1057(b) of the United States Trademark Act, is prima facie evidence of Booher's ownership of the mark, the validity of the mark, and its exclusive right to use the mark in connection with the above identified services.

10. Booher's services and products offered under the mark YOUR SIGNATURE LIFE have been widely sold and advertised throughout the United States and abroad.

11. By virtue of its long use and registration, the mark YOUR SIGNATURE LIFE represents valuable trademark rights owned by Booher.

12. As a result of Booher's long use, advertising and promotion, YOUR SIGNATURE LIFE mark is strongly associated with Booher and represents an extremely valuable goodwill owned by Booher throughout the United States and abroad.

13. Long subsequent to Booher's adoption, use and registration of YOUR SIGNATURE LIFE mark, Galt adopted the name and mark DESIGNING YOUR SIGNATURE LIFE ("the Infringing Mark") for books, publications, seminars, keynote speaking programs and related products and services in competition with Booher.

14. Galt's use of the Infringing Mark is without Booher's consent.

15. Booher has demanded that Galt cease use of the Infringing Mark, but Galt has refused to comply.

16. On information and belief, Galt's actions have been and continue to be committed intentionally with full knowledge of Booher's prior rights and of the fact that such actions are likely to cause further confusion, mistake or deception, and in a deliberate attempt to trade on Booher's goodwill.

17. Galt's acts are greatly and irreparably damaging to Booher and will continue to damage Booher until enjoined by this Court; Booher is therefore without adequate remedy at law.

Count I
Trademark Infringement

18. Booher realleges paragraphs 1 through 17, as if fully set forth herein.

19. Galt's use of the Infringing Mark is likely to continue to cause confusion, mistake or deception as to the source, origin, sponsorship or approval of Galt's products and services in that purchasers and others are likely to believe Booher authorizes or controls Galt's products and services or that Galt is associated with or related to Booher and its YOUR SIGNATURE LIFE products and services.

20. Galt's use of the Infringing Mark constitutes trademark infringement in violation of the Trademark Laws of the United States, 15 U.S.C. § 1114.

21. On information and belief, Galt's wrongful use of the Infringing Mark is deliberate, intentional and willful attempts to injure Booher's business, to trade on Booher's business reputation, and to confuse or deceive purchasers.

Count II
Unfair Competition

22. Booher realleges paragraphs 1 through 21 as if fully set forth herein.
23. Galt's use of the Infringing Mark constitutes unfair competition in violation of the Trademark Laws of the United States, 15 U.S.C. § 1135(a), and the laws of the various states, including Texas.

WHEREFORE, Booher demands the following relief:

That Galt, and all persons acting in concert or participating with her, be preliminarily and permanently enjoined from:

a. using DESIGNING YOUR SIGNATURE LIFE ("the Infringing Mark") in connection with goods and services related to Booher's business;
b. registering or maintaining any registration of the Infringing Mark, or any other names, words, designations or symbols consisting of, incorporating in whole or part, or otherwise similar to YOUR SIGNATURE LIFE mark ("Booher's mark");
c. using the Infringing Mark or any other names, words, designations or symbols consisting of, incorporating in whole or part, or otherwise similar to Booher's mark;
d. otherwise infringing Booher's mark;

That Galt be ordered to account for and pay Booher all profits realized by Galt by reason of the unlawful acts as set forth in this Complaint. 15 U.S.C. § 1117(a).

That the Court award Booher three times the damages suffered by reason of the intentional, unlawful acts of Galt as set forth in this Complaint. 15 U.S.C. § 1117(a).

That Galt be ordered to pay Booher punitive or exemplary damages as provided by law.

That Galt be required to file with this Court and serve on the undersigned counsel for Booher within thirty (30) days after the entry of judgment a written report under oath setting forth in detail the manner in which Galt has complied with the injunction ordered by this Court. 15 U.S.C § 1116.

That Galt be ordered to pay to Booher the costs of this action and reasonable attorneys' fees. 15 U.S.C. § 1117(a).

That Booher shall have such other relief as this Court may deem just and proper.

Respectfully submitted,

4.3 Complaint for Trademark Infringement

This complainant provides more detailed narrative than those above to explain a more unusual case of misrepresentation and infringement involving a website and use of metatags.

United States District Court
Northern District of Illinois
Eastern Division

CADILLAC MACHINERY CO., INC.	)	
and RANDALL PUBLISHING, INC.	)	
		Civil Action No. 04 C 3927
Plaintiffs,	)	
v.	)	Hon. Rebecca Pallmeyer
R. P. MACHINE ENTERPRISES, INC. and	)	Magistrate Judge Bobrick
TRAFFIC-POWER.COM	)	
Defendants	)	

Amended Complaint for Unfair Competition, Trademark Infringement, Deceptive Trade Practices, and Declaratory Judgment

Jurisdiction and Parties

1. Plaintiff Cadillac Machinery Co., Inc. ("Cadillac Machinery") is an Illinois corporation with its principal place of business at 1401 Lunt Avenue, Elk Grove, Illinois 60007.
2. Plaintiff Randall Publishing, Inc. ("Randall") is an Illinois corporation with its principal place of business at 1425 Lunt Avenue, Elk Grove, Illinois 60007. Randall and Cadillac are sister companies under common ownership and control.
3. Defendant R. P. Machine Enterprises, Inc. ("RP") is a New York corporation located at 325 Miller Avenue, Statesville, North Carolina.
4. Defendant Traffic-Power.com ("Traffic-Power") is a business entity located at 4850 W. Flamingo Road, Las Vegas, Nevada. On information

and belief, Traffic-Power is a Nevada corporation or a proprietorship owned and controlled by Matthew A. Marlon, a Nevada resident.

5. RP is doing business in Illinois through the purchase of machinery from and the sale of machinery to customers located in Illinois and through an interactive Internet website. Traffic-Power is doing business in Illinois through the sale of search engine optimization services to customers located in Illinois and through an interactive Internet website.

6. This Court's jurisdiction arises: (i) from the fact that this is an action brought under the Trademark Laws of the United States, 15 U.S.C. §§ 1051–1127, jurisdiction conferred by 15 U.S.C. § 1121 and 28 U.S.C. §§ 1331 and 1338; and (ii) by virtue of the fact that certain claims are joined with substantial and related claims under the Trademark Laws of the United States, 15 U.S.C. §§ 1051–1127, jurisdiction conferred by 28 U.S.C. § 1338(b) and 28 U.S.C. § 1367(a). Venue is proper in this judicial district pursuant to 28 U.S.C. § 1391(b).

Facts

Plaintiff

7. Cadillac Machinery was founded over 50 years ago and is the world's leading supplier of quality reconditioned second-hand gear manufacturing equipment.

8. For many years and long prior to the acts of RP alleged in this Complaint, Cadillac Machinery has used the name and mark CADILLAC MACHINERY in connection with its business throughout the United States and abroad.

9. By virtue of its use for over 50 years, Cadillac Machinery owns valuable common-law trademark rights in its CADILLAC MACHINERY name and mark.

10. Cadillac Machinery also operates an Internet website at the domain name <www.cadillacmachinery.com> on which Cadillac Machinery advertises, promotes, and sells products and services under the CADILLAC MACHINERY mark.

11. Cadillac Machinery has sold many millions of dollars worth of products under the CADILLAC MACHINERY mark throughout the United States and abroad, including the State of Illinois, and Cadillac Machinery has spent many thousands of dollars to advertise and promote that name and mark throughout the United States and abroad.

12. By virtue of Cadillac Machinery's long use, advertising and promotion, the CADILLAC MACHINERY mark is distinctive and possesses

a secondary meaning signifying Cadillac Machinery and represents an extremely valuable goodwill owned by Cadillac Machinery throughout the United States.

13. Randall is the publisher of the magazine "Gear Technology: The Journal of Gear Manufacturing," the leading publication of the gear manufacturing industry distributed every two months to thousands of readers throughout the United States and abroad. The magazine is available for free to qualified members of the gear manufacturing industry located in the United States and is available to others on a paid subscription basis. Randall has also published an electronic version of GEAR TECHNOLOGY magazine since January 2003. Randall receives a substantial portion of its revenue from paid advertising that appears in the GEAR TECHNOLOGY magazine.

14. Randall has used the name and mark GEAR TECHNOLOGY in connection with its magazine in commerce continuously since at least 1984, and has engaged in extensive advertising and promotion for its magazine bearing the GEAR TECHNOLOGY mark.

15. Randall also operates an Internet website at the domain name www.geartechnology.com on which Randall advertises, promotes, and sells its magazine and related services using the GEAR TECHNOLOGY mark.

16. By virtue of 20 years of use, advertising and promotion, Randall owns valuable common-law trademark rights in its GEAR TECHNOLOGY mark for magazines.

17. Randall also owns a federal registration issued by the United States Patent and Trademark Office for the mark GEAR TECHNOLOGY: THE JOURNAL OF GEAR MANUFACTURING for "magazines regarding the design, manufacture, testing or processing of gears," Reg. No. 1,368,889, issued November 5, 1985. The registration is incontestable and constitutes "conclusive evidence of the validity of the registered mark and of the registration of the mark, of the registrant's ownership of the mark, and of the registrant's exclusive right to use the registered mark in commerce on or in connection with the goods . . . specified in the registration" in accordance with 15 U.S.C. § 1115(a). The registration includes a disclaimer of exclusive rights in the words "Gear Technology" apart from the mark as shown in the registration. In accordance with 15 U.S.C. § 1056, that disclaimer shall not be deemed to prejudice or affect Randall's rights arising in the disclaimed matter.

18. By virtue of Randall's long use, advertising and promotion, the mark GEAR TECHNOLOGY is distinctive and possesses secondary meaning signifying Randall's magazine and now represents an extremely valuable goodwill owned by Randall throughout the United States.

Defendant

19. RP sells reconditioned second-hand gear manufacturing equipment in competition with Cadillac Machinery, and has an Internet website at <www.rpmachine.com> (the "RP website"). Traffic-Power acted on RP's behalf to optimize the performance of the RP website through the use of key words and metatags.

20. Through the RP website, RP uses deceptive methods and false or misleading statements to mislead consumers searching the Internet for Cadillac Machinery and to create confusion about the relationship between Cadillac Machinery and RP, including, but not limited to the following:

i.   (a) To attract customers who are searching for Cadillac Machinery, RP makes deceptive, repeated and gratuitous use of the CADILLAC MACHINERY mark on the RP website. The more often a term appears on a website, the more likely the website will be highly placed in a search for that term on the Internet. The RP website contains so many uses of the CADILLAC MACHINERY mark that it is the first of about 21,600 results in a Google search for "CADILLAC MACHINERY." A copy of the first page of these Google search results is attached as Exhibit A.

ii. (b) Upon arriving at the RP website, the customer views a webpage with the following heading in very large print: "Cadillac Machinery at Rpmachine.com." Four additional pages bear the headings: "Cadillac Machinery Information Available on Rpmachine.com," "Cadillac Machinery Sources Available on Rpmachine.com" and "Cadillac Machinery Sources Available Through Rpmachine. com. See Exhibit B. The text on the site furthers the false and misleading impression that Cadillac Machinery is related to RP, can be found at RP, sources its product from RP or is otherwise related to RP, when in fact RP is not the source of Cadillac Machinery products and is not related to or affiliated with Cadillac Machinery. The false and misleading statements include, but are not limited to, the following statements on the RP website:

a) "Cadillac machinery information presented at Rpmachine.com."
b) "Cadillac machinery sources by clicking above."
c) "Find cadillac machinery on Rpmachine.com."
d) "Cadillac machinery sources at Rpmachine.com."
e) "Cadillac machinery related phases are on Rmachine.com."
f) "Look for cadillac machinery on Rpmachine.com."
g) "Cadillac machinery is related to Rpmachinery.com."

iii. (c) RP also makes deceptive, repeated and gratuitous use of the CADILLAC MACHINERY mark in the metatags of the RP websites.

Metatags are hidden computer codes used to direct consumer Internet traffic to a website by obtaining placement for it in Internet search results. The metatags are invisible to viewers of the website but are read by search engines seeking the hidden terms. The more often a term is used in the metatags, the more likely the website will be found in an Internet search for that term. The RP website includes at least 15 invisible references in the metatags to the CADILLAC MACHINERY name and mark.

21. RP makes deceptive, repeated and gratuitous use of the CADILLAC MACHINERY mark in the text and metatags of the RP website, with full knowledge of Cadillac Machinery's prior use and ownership of that mark.

22. On information and belief, RP has made infringing use of Cadillac Machinery's mark for the purpose of trading on Cadillac Machinery's goodwill in that mark.

23. All of RP's uses of the CADILLAC MACHINERY marks are without Cadillac Machinery's authorization, permission, consent or license.

24. On May 13, 2004, counsel for Cadillac Machinery sent a letter of objection to RP regarding the use of the CADILLAC MACHINERY name and mark on the RP website. RP's counsel responded on May 20, 2004, stating that RP has "ceased and desisted from" the acts complained of in the May 13th letter.

25. In a subsequent letter dated June 4, 2004, new counsel for RP asserted that the use of "Cadillac machinery" on the RP website is "entirely proper" either because it was done by RP's agent without RP's knowledge, or because it merely refers to the CADILLAC mark of another company or because RP and Cadillac Machinery at one time owned equipment together as a joint venture. These inherently inconsistent reasons are not a justification or defense to RP's false and misleading statements or its misuse of the CADILLAC MACHINERY name and mark.

26. Despite Cadillac Machinery's objections and RP's assertion that it removed references to "Cadillac Machinery" from the RP website, the misuse has continued.

27. RP also has infringed the plaintiffs' rights by making false and deceptive use of GEAR TECHNOLOGY in the content and metatags of the RP website in an attempt to redirect Internet users seeking Randall's GEAR TECHNOLOGY magazine and website. RP's deceptive and misleading use of GEAR TECHNOLOGY includes but is not limited to the following:

i. (a) Deceptive, repeated and gratuitous use of the GEAR TECHNOLOGY mark on the RP website so that the RP website is one of the highest listed search results for GEAR TECHNOLOGY.

ii. (b) Repeated references on the RP website that create a false connection between the GEAR TECHNOLOGY mark and RP, including the false and misleading statement that "Gear technology is related to Rpmachinery.com."

    iii. (c) Deceptive, repeated and gratuitous use of the GEAR TECH-NOLOGY mark in the metatags for the RP website.

28. RP makes deceptive, repeated and gratuitous use of the GEAR TECHNOLOGY mark in the text and metatags of the RP site with full knowledge of Randall's prior use and ownership of that mark.

29. RP's repeated and gratuitous use of the GEAR TECHNOLOGY mark is not made fairly and in good faith only to describe the goods and services of RP, but on information and belief is done for the purpose of trading on Randall's goodwill to redirect Internet users to the RP website for commercial gain.

30. RP's use of GEAR TECHNOLOGY is without Randall's authorization, permission, consent or license.

31. On information and belief and based on the specific accusations of RP, Traffic-Power actively participated in the selection and use of the CADILLAC MACHINERY and GEAR TECHNOLOGY marks in violation of Plaintiffs rights and is jointly and severally liable to Plaintiff for that conduct.

Count I
False Designation in Violation of Federal Law

32. Plaintiff realleges paragraphs 1 though 31.

33. Defendants' unauthorized use of the CADILLAC MACHINERY and GEAR TECHNOLOGY marks in connection with the RP website is likely to cause confusion, mistake and public deception regarding the affiliation, connection or association between RP, its products and its website, and Plaintiffs, or as to the origin, sponsorship or approval of RP, its products and its website, by Plaintiffs.

34. On information and belief, Defendants' conduct is deliberately intended to misdirect and divert to RP customers seeking Plaintiffs and their goods and services sold under the CADILLAC MACHINERY and GEAR TECHNOLOGY marks.

35. Defendants' unauthorized use of the CADILLAC MACHINERY and GEAR TECHNOLOGY marks constitutes the improper use of names or false designations of origin in violation of the Trademark Laws of the United States, 15 U.S.C. § 1125(a)(1)(A).

36. Defendants' acts are greatly and irreparably damaging to Plaintiffs and will continue to damage Plaintiffs until enjoined by this Court; wherefore Plaintiffs are without an adequate remedy at law.

Count II
False Representations in Violation of
Federal Law

37. Plaintiffs reallege paragraphs 1 through 31.
38. The false and misleading statements included on the RP website misrepresent the nature, characteristics, and qualities of RP's goods, services, and commercial activities.
39. On information and belief, Defendants' use of those false and misleading statements is deliberately intended to deceive the public and to injure Plaintiffs' business and reputation.
40. Defendants' use of false and misleading statements on its website constitutes the use of false or misleading representations of fact in commercial advertising and promotion in violation of the Trademark Laws of the United States, 15 U.S.C. § 1125(a)(1)(B).
41. Defendants' acts are greatly and irreparably damaging to Plaintiffs and will continue to damage Plaintiffs until enjoined by this Court; wherefore Plaintiffs are without an adequate remedy at law.

Count III
Trademark Infringement

42. Plaintiffs reallege paragraphs 1 through 31.
43. Defendants' unauthorized use of GEAR TECHNOLOGY constitutes use in commerce of a colorable imitation of Randall's federally registered GEAR TECHNOLOGY mark which is likely to cause confusion, mistake, or deception between RP and its products and website, and Randall and its GEAR TECHNOLOGY magazine and website.
44. Defendants' conduct violates the Trademark Laws of the United States, 15 U.S.C. § 1114.
45. Defendants' acts are greatly and irreparably damaging to Randall and will continue to damage Randall until enjoined by this Court; wherefore Randall is without an adequate remedy at law.

Count IV
Unfair Competition and Unjust Enrichment
Under Common Law

46. Plaintiffs reallege the allegations of paragraphs 1 through 31.

47. As a result of its unauthorized use of the CADILLAC MACHINERY and GEAR TECHNOLOGY marks, Defendants have, on information and belief, intended to cause, and are likely to continue to cause confusion, mistake or public deception.

48. On information and belief, Defendants have offered products and services in commerce with knowledge of the falsity and misleading effect of the designations used on this RP website, in violation of the common law of the several states, including the common law of the State of Illinois.

49. Defendants' aforesaid acts of unfair competition result in unjust enrichment under the common law of several states, including the common law of the State of Illinois.

50. Defendants' acts are greatly and irreparably damaging to Plaintiffs and will continue to damage Plaintiffs until enjoined by this Court; wherefore Plaintiffs are without an adequate remedy at law.

Count V
Deceptive Trade and Business Practices
in Violation of Illinois Law

51. Plaintiffs reallege the allegations of paragraphs 1 through 31.

52. On information and belief, Defendants' knowingly offered RP products, and services in commerce with knowledge of the falsity and misleading effect of the designations and statements used on the RP website.

53. Defendants' aforesaid deceptive acts constitute deceptive trade practices in violation of the Illinois Uniform Deceptive Trade Practices Act, 815 ILCS §§ 510/1, et. seq.

54. Defendants' aforesaid deceptive acts constitute consumer fraud and deceptive business practices in violation of the Illinois Consumer Fraud and Deceptive Business Practices Act, 815 ILCS §§ 505/1, et. seq.

55. Defendants' acts are greatly and irreparably damaging to Plaintiffs and will continue to damage Plaintiffs until enjoined by this Court; wherefore Plaintiffs are without an adequate remedy at law.

Count VI
Request for Declaratory Judgement

56. On May 20, 2004, Michael Goldstein, the President of Cadillac Machinery, filed a complaint with the Machinery Dealers National

Association for violation of the Association's Code of Ethics based on the misuse of the CADILLAC MACHINERY name and mark. A copy of that letter is attached is Exhibit C (the "MDNA complaint").

57. Between May 21 and May 27, 2004, Mr. Goldstein sent letters to seven other companies whose names and marks also are used on the RP website. The recipients of the letters are advertisers in "Gear Technology: The Journal of Gear Manufacturing," which is published by Randall. The purpose of the letters was to inform the recipients that the RP website included false and misleading references to the CADILLAC MACHINERY name and mark regarding the relationship between Cadillac Machinery and RP. The letters also informed the recipients that the RP website also included statements made about the recipients' respective companies. Copies of the letters are attached as Exhibit D (the "OEM letters").

58. On June 4, 2004, counsel for RP sent counsel for Cadillac Machinery a demand letter, asserting in part that Cadillac Machinery's statements "suggest that [RP] is somehow making improper use of the name of several original equipment manufacturers," and that "Such statements are false and misleading and constitute violations of the Lanham Act as well as North Carolina's Unfair Competition and Deceptive Trade Practices Act." RP further demanded that Cadillac Machinery "immediately cease and desist making any further statements or sending any further correspondence that even remotely suggests that [RP] has made any improper use of any name or trademark of any original equipment manufacturer." A copy of the letter is attached as Exhibit E.

59. Cadillac Machinery did not make any false or misleading statement of fact regarding RP's use of any name or trademark of any original equipment manufacturer in the MDNA complaint or the OEM letters.

60. Cadillac Machinery did not distribute the MDNA complaint or OEM letters in North Carolina.

61. The MDNA complaint does not violate the Lanham Act or the North Carolina Unfair Competition and Deceptive Trade Practices Act.

62. The OEM letters do not violate the Lanham Act or the North Carolina Unfair Competition and Deceptive Trade Practices Act.

63. As a result of RP's demand, Cadillac Machinery has a reasonable belief that it may be sued by RP based on the MDNA complaint or the OEM letters and an actual controversy exists between the parties; wherefore, Cadillac Machinery is entitled to a declaration of rights pursuant to 28 U.S.C. § 2201.

WHEREFORE, Plaintiffs pray for a judgment:

1. Preliminarily and permanently enjoining and restraining Defendants their officers, agents, employees, subcontractors, attorneys, representatives, and all others acting in concert and participation with any of them from:

    i.   (a) using the CADILLAC MACHINERY and GEAR TECHNOLOGY marks, or any other colorable imitation of those marks in a manner that is likely to confuse, mislead or deceive others into believing that RP or its products, emanate from, or are connected with, sponsored by or approved by Cadillac Machinery or Randall;

    ii.   (b) using any other trademarks owned by Cadillac Machinery or Randall or any other colorable imitation of such marks, or any other mark in a manner that is likely to confuse, mislead or deceive others into believing that RP or its products emanate from, or are connected with, sponsored by or approved by Cadillac Machinery or Randall;

    iii. (c) making any false or misleading description or representation, including, without limitation, stating or implying that RP's goods and services are in any way affiliated or associated with, authorized, endorsed or sponsored by Cadillac Machinery or Randall;

    iv.   (d) doing any other act or thing likely to induce the belief that RP's business, products or services are in any way connected with Cadillac Machinery's business, products or services, Randall's business, products and services, or are sponsored or approved by Cadillac Machinery or Randall; and

    v.   (e) making any other use of the CADILLAC MACHINERY or GEAR TECHNOLOGY marks.

2. Directing Defendants, within 15 days, to:

    i.   (e) cause all Internet search engines, websites, cached files, cross references or "similar page" files to delete and remove all references connecting RP and any names, words, designations, or symbols confusingly similar to the CADILLAC MACHINERY or GEAR TECHNOLOGY marks or any other Cadillac Machinery or Randall trademarks, and to remove all cached information containing such references;

    ii.   (f) account for and pay over to Cadillac Machinery and Randall all profits derived by RP from its acts complained of herein, enhanced as the Court deems just, together with prejudgment interest, in accordance with 15 U.S.C. § 1117 and applicable state law;

    iii. (g) pay to Cadillac Machinery and Randall all damages Cadillac Machinery and Randall have suffered as a result of the acts of Defendants complained of herein, together with prejudgment interest, and a sum equal to three times the damages for any Lanham Act violation, in accordance with 15 U.S.C. § 1117 and applicable state law;

    iv. (h) pay to Cadillac Machinery and Randall the costs and its attorneys' fees in connection with this action, in accordance with 15 U.S.C. § 1117, 815 ILCS § 510/3, and 815 ILCS § 505/10a;

    v. (i) file with this Court and serve on counsel for Cadillac Machinery and Randall within thirty (30) days after entry of an injunction issued by this Court, a sworn written statement as provided in 15 U.S.C. § 1116(a); and

    vi. (j) pay Cadillac Machinery and Randall one thousand dollars ($2500.00) for each day it fails to comply with any of the obligations imposed under this Section.

3. Declaring that:

    i. (j) the MDNA complaint is not a violation of the Lanham Act, the North Carolina Unfair Competition and Deceptive Trade Practices Act, or any federal or state law;

    ii. (k) the OEM letters do not violate the Lanham Act, the North Carolina Unfair Competition and Deceptive Trade Practices Act, or any other federal or state law; and

    iii. (l) the MDNA complaint and the OEM letters do not constitute defamation or libel.

4. Awarding Cadillac Machinery such further relief as this Court deems just and equitable.

Respectfully submitted,

Chapter 4.4–Complaint for False Advertising

This complaint presents a Lanham Act claim for false advertising based upon the purchase of a competitor's trademarks as keywords and use of those trademarks in potentially misleading sponsored links in Internet search results. The law surrounding the use of competitors' trademarks as keywords to trigger advertising in Internet search results currently is in flux. *See, e.g., Hearts on Fire Co. LLC v. Blue Nile, Inc.*, 603 F. Supp. 2d 274 (D. Mass. 2009); *J.G. Wentworth, SSC Ltd. v. Settlement Funding LLC*, 2007 U.S. Dist. Lexis 288 (E.D. Pa. Jan. 4, 2007). This complaint follows the format required in the Southern/Eastern District of New York.

United States District Court for the Eastern District of New York

ARG HOME APPLIANCES CORPORATION	))	Civil Action No. _____
Plaintiff,	)	ECF Case
v.	)	
AJ CORP.	)	
Defendant.	)	

Complaint

Plaintiff, by and for its complaint, states:

Parties and Jurisdiction

1. Plaintiff brings this case under § 43(a) of the Lanham Act, 15 U.S.C. § 1125(a), for false advertising and unfair competition, and under New York common law and § 349(a) of the New York General Business Laws for unfair and deceptive business practices. Plaintiff seeks injunctive and monetary relief from the deceptive Internet advertising practices of AJ Corp.
2. Plaintiff, ARGARG Home Appliances Corporation ("ARG"), is a Delaware corporation with its principal place of business in California.

On information and belief, Defendant, AJ Corp.is a New York corporation with its principal place of business in Brooklyn, New York.

This Court has jurisdiction over the subject matter of Plaintiff's claims in this action because (1) certain claims arise under the Trademark Act of 1946, as amended, 15 U.S.C. §§ 1051, et seq. (the Lanham Act), jurisdiction being conferred in accordance with 15 U.S.C. § 1121 and 28 U.S.C. § 1338(a); (2) the claims of this action arise between diverse parties and the amount in controversy exceeds $75,000, exclusive of interest and costs, jurisdiction being conferred in accordance with 28 U.S.C. § 1332(a); (3) certain claims are joined with a substantial and related claim arising under the Trademark Laws of the United States, jurisdiction being conferred in accordance with 28 U.S.C. §1338(b); and (4) certain claims are so related to claims within such original jurisdiction that they form part of the same case or controversy, supplemental jurisdiction being conferred in accordance with 28 U.S.C. § 1367(a).

Venue is proper in this Court under 28 U.S.C. § 1391(a).

ARG and the ARG Trademarks

For many years, and long prior to the acts of Defendant complained of herein, ARG, at substantial expense, has distributed, advertised, and sold kitchen appliances in commerce throughout the United States under the ARGARG trademarks.

ARG owns United States trademark registrations for its ARGARG mark, including the following:

Mark	Reg. No.	Reg. Date	Goods/Services
ARG	100000	10/10/1910	Various kitchen appliances
ARG	200000	11/11/1911	Other kitchen appliances

These registrations are valid, subsisting, and incontestable in accordance with 15 U.S.C. §§ 1064 and 1115(b), and are conclusive evidence of ARG's exclusive right to use the ARG trademark in connection with the registered goods. 15 U.S.C. § 1115(b).

ARG has sold millions of dollars worth of kitchen appliances bearing the ARGARG trademarks in the United States and has spent millions of dollars advertising these kitchen appliances.

As a result of the aforesaid extensive sales, promotion, and advertising, the ARGARG trademarks represent extraordinarily valuable goodwill in the United States.

Defendant's Infringing Activities

Defendant is a retailer of kitchen appliances that advertises and sells kitchen appliances on the Internet through its website located at the domain name <www.aj.com>.

Defendant is not, and never has been, an ARG-authorized dealer for ARG appliances. On information and belief, Defendant does not currently sell ARG appliances.

On information and belief, Defendant has purchased the trademark ARG as an Internet keyword, or part of Internet keywords, for Internet search engines such as Google. Thus, consumers searching the Internet for "Arg," "Arg Appliances," "Arg Stove," "Arg Oven," and/or "Arg Dishwasher" are presented with search results showing Defendant as a "sponsored link," with a hyperlink to Defendant's website. *See* Exhibit A attached hereto (printouts of results fARG searches on Google). Several of Defendant's "sponsored links" specifically state "Arg Appliances" in the heading.

Moreover, consumers searching the Internet for "ARG Appliances" or "ARG Refrigerators" through Google are presented with search results showing Defendant as a "sponsored link," with a hyperlink to Defendant's website. *See* Exhibit B attached hereto (print-outs of results for ARG searches on Google). Defendant's "sponsored links" specifically state "ARG Appliances" or "ARG Refrigerator" in the heading.

On information and belief, Defendant writes its own "sponsored link" advertisements, including the "title" or "headline" of the advertisement. *See* Exhibit C attached hereto (excerpts from Google, Inc.'s AdWord Policy).

Consumers who arrive at Defendant's website through these "sponsored" hyperlinks cannot find the ARG appliances they are seeking but rather are presented with competitors' products that Defendant promotes and sells.

On information and belief, Defendant uses and has used the ARG trademarks in connection with Internet "sponsored link" advertisements and website links in a deliberate attempt to trade upon the goodwill and reputation of the ARGARG marks, to deceive consumers, to engage in a "bait and switch" of competitors' products in place of the ARG products consumers are seeking, and to give Defendant's website a notoriety it would not otherwise have.

Count I: False Advertising and Unfair Competition Under Federal Law

ARG realleges paragraphs 1 through 18, as if fully set forth herein.

Defendant's acts are likely to cause confusion, mistake, or deception, in that consumers or others are likely to believe that Defendant or its products or services are sponsored by, or connected or affiliated with, ARG and/or its ARG products.

Defendant's acts have likely injured and are likely to continue injuring ARG by creating "initial interest" confusion to deceptively capture the initial attention of consumers searching for ARG products, but thereafter directing them to the purchase of competitive products.

Through its unauthorized use of the ARGARG marks, Defendant is engaging in unfair competition, which likely has caused and will cause confusion, mistake or deception, in violation of 15 U.S.C. § 1125.

Defendant's "sponsored links" that specifically use ARGARG in the headlines constitute false and misleading advertising under 15 U.S.C. § 1125, in that Defendant advertises, but does not actually sell, ARGARG appliances.

Defendant's actions greatly and irreparably damage ARG, and will continue to damage ARG unless restrained by this Court; wherefore, ARG is without an adequate remedy at law.

Count II: Unfair and Deceptive Business Practices Under New York Statutory and Common Law

ARG realleges paragraphs 1 through 18, 20, and 21 as if fully set forth herein.

Defendant's use of the ARGARG trademarks is materially misleading in that it directs consumers to its own website, only to engage in a "bait and switch" by offering competitors' products instead of the ARGARG products desired by the consumers. Such inappropriate use of the ARGARG trademarks capitalizes on the goodwill of those trademarks to the detriment of ARG and consumers.

Defendant's aforesaid acts constitute an unfair and deceptive business practice in violation of Section 349(a) of the New York General Business Laws, and unfair competition in violation of the common law of the various states, including New York.

Defendant's actions greatly and irreparably damage ARG, and will continue to damage ARG unless restrained by this Court; wherefore, ARG is without an adequate remedy at law.

Prayer for Relief

WHEREFORE, ARG prays that:

Defendant, its officers, agents, servants, employees, and attorneys, its successors and assigns, and all others in active concert or participation with it or them, be permanently enjoined from:

using the ARGmarks in its advertising, or as Internet search terms and keywords; and performing any other acts which are likely to lead consumers or others to believe that Defendant, its website, or its products or services are, in any way affiliated with, or licensed, sponsored, approved, or authorized by, ARG.

Defendant, and all others holding by, through or under Defendant, be required, jointly and severally, to:

account for and pay over to ARG all profits derived by Defendant from its acts of false advertising, unfair competition, and deceptive business practices;

pay over to ARG all damages suffered by reason of Defendant's false advertising, unfair competition, and deceptive business practices;

pay to ARG three times the damages suffered by reason of the intentional and unlawful acts of Defendant;

pay to ARG exemplary damages under the common law of New York in an amount sufficient to punish Defendant and to deter Defendant and others similarly situated from engaging in Defendant's fraudulent, malicious, and oppressive acts; and

pay to ARG the costs of this action, together with its reasonable attorneys' fees.

Defendant is required to file with this Court and serve on the undersigned counsel for ARG within thirty (30) days after the entry of judgment a written report under oath setting forth in detail the manner in which Defendant has complied with the injunction ordered by this Court.

Defendant is required to deliver up to the Court, for destruction or other disposition, all labels, signs, prints, packages, wrappers, receptacles, and advertisements bearing the ARGARG trademarks and all plates, molds, matrices, and other means of making the same; and

ARG has such other and further relief as this Court deems just and equitable.

Dated: August ___, 2005   Respectfully submitted,

4.4 Complaint for Cybersquatting

This complaint presents a claim under the Lanham Act for cybersquatting, in addition to traditional trademark infringment. In 1999, Congress passed the Anticybersquatting Consumer Protection Act (ACPA), which establishes liability where: 1) a defendant "has a bad faith intent to profit" from the use of a protected trademark; and 2) the defendant registers, traffics in, or uses a domain name that is identical or confusingly similar to the protected mark. 15 U.S.C. § 1125(d).

United States District Court
District Court of Colorado

LAURA STACK,	)	CIVIL ACTION No.
	)	COMPLAINT FOR:
Plaintiff,	)	
v.	)	(1) VIOLATION OF SECTION 32 OF THE LANHAM ACT;
KAREN SMITH	)	(2) VIOLATION OF SECTION 43(A)) OF THE LANHAM
	)	
ACT; and	)	(3)VIOLATION OF THE
	)	ANTICYBERSQUATTING
Defendant	)	CONSUMER PROTECTION ACT

Complaint Jurisdiction and Venue

1. This Court has jurisdiction by virtue of the fact that: (i) this is a civil action under the United States Trademark Act (15 U.S.C. § 1051, et seq.), jurisdiction being conferred in accordance with 15 U.S.C. § 1121 and 28 U.S.C. § 1338(a); and (ii) this is a civil action in which the parties are citizens of different states and the value of the matters in controversy exceeds seventy-five thousand dollars ($75,000) exclusive of interest and costs, jurisdiction being expressly conferred under 28 U.S.C. § 1332(a).

2. Venue is proper in this judicial district pursuant to 28 U.S.C. § 1391(c).

Parties

3. Plaintiff Laura Stack, is a resident of Highlands Ranch, Colorado (referred to hereafter as "Stack") and is doing business as "The Productivity Pro."

4. Defendant Karen Smith, on information and belief, is a resident of Cloud City (referred to hereafter as Smith") and is doing business as "Time's Up."

Facts

5. Stack is an author, speaker, consultant and internationally known expert on productivity and time management.
6. For many years and long prior to the acts of Defendants alleged in this Complaint, Stack has used the distinctive name and mark THE PRODUCTIVITY PRO in connection with her products and services offered throughout the United States and abroad.
7. The name and mark THE PRODUCTIVITY PRO has been prominently displayed as the name of Stack's business, as the brand name of her products and services, and as the name of Stack's website, <www.productivitypro.com>, since 2000.
8. Defendant provides seminars, coaching, training and related services and products in competition with Stack using the name TIME'S UP at a website located at <www.thetimesup.com>.
9. Stack owns the federal trademark registration for the service mark THE PRODUCTIVITY PRO, Reg. No. 2532266, in Class 41 for "educational and entertainment services, namely, providing motivational and educational speakers," with the mark's date of first use and first use in commerce on December 21, 2000, and registration issued on January 22, 2002.
10. Said registration is valid and subsisting, and in accordance with § 1057(b) of the United States Trademark Act, is prima facie evidence of Stack's ownership of the mark, the validity of the mark, and its exclusive right to use the mark in connection with the above identified services.
11. Stack has sold many thousands of dollars worth of services and products under THE PRODUCTIVITY PRO mark, and has invested thousands of dollars to promote and distribute materials bearing that mark throughout the United States and abroad.
12. By virtue of its long use and registration, THE PRODUCTIVITY PRO mark represents valuable trademark rights owned by Stack.
13. As a result of Stack's long use, advertising and promotion, THE PRODUCTIVITY PRO mark is strongly associated with Stack and represents an extremely valuable goodwill owned by Stack throughout the United States and abroad.
14. Long subsequent to Stack's adoption, use and registration of THE PRODUCTIVITY PRO mark and the <www.productivitypro.com> domain name, Defendant acquired a registration for the domain name <www.productivitypros.com> ("the infringing domain name"), the plural form of Stack's domain name, and began using that domain name in commerce to divert Internet users to Defendant's <www.thetimesup.com> website.

15. Defendant's infringing domain name is confusingly similar to Stack's mark and domain name.
16. Defendant's use of the infringing domain name is likely to mislead Internet users seeking Stack's services to Defendant's website.
17. On information and belief, Defendants do not have any intellectual property rights in <www.productivitypros.com> or any other terms identical or similar to the Stack's THE PRODUCTIVITY PRO mark.
18. On information and belief, Defendant is deliberately using the domain name <www.productivitypros.com> to attract and divert Internet users to Defendant's website for the purpose of commercial gain based on a likelihood of confusion as to the source, sponsorship, affiliation or endorsement, with Stack and her mark and domain name.
19. Defendant's use of the infringing domain name is without Stack's consent.
20. Stack has demanded that Defendant cease use of the infringing domain name, but Defendant has refused to comply.
21. On information and belief, Defendant's actions have been and continue to be committed intentionally with full knowledge of Stack's prior rights and the fact that such actions are likely to cause further confusion, mistake or deception, and in a deliberate attempt to trade on Stack's goodwill.
22. Defendant's acts are greatly and irreparably damaging to Stack and will continue to damage Stack until enjoined by this Court; wherefore, Stack is without adequate remedy at law.

Count I
Trademark Infringement

23. Stack realleges paragraphs 1 through 22, as if fully set forth herein.
24. Defendant's use of the infringing domain name is likely to continue to cause confusion, mistake, or deception as to the source, origin, sponsorship or approval of Defendants' services in that purchasers and others are likely to believe Stack authorizes or controls Defendant's website and services or that Defendant is associated with or related to Stack.
25. Defendant's use of the infringing domain name constitutes trademark infringement in violation of the Trademark Laws of the United States, 15 U.S.C. § 1114.
26. On information and belief, Defendant's wrongful use of the infringing domain name is deliberate, intentional and willful attempts to injure Stack's business, to trade on Stack's business reputation, and to confuse or deceive purchasers.

Count II
Unfair Competition

27. Stack realleged paragraphs 1 through 26 as if fully set forth herein.
28. Defendant's use of the infringing domain name constitutes unfair competition in violation of the Trademark Laws of the United States, 15 U.S.C. § 1135(a), and the laws of the various states, including Colorado.

Count III
Cybersquatting

29. Stack realleges paragraphs 1 through 28, as if fully set forth herein.
30. On information and belief, Defendant is using the infringing domain name with the bad faith intent to profit from their confusing similarity to, and dilutive effect on, Stack's mark.
31. Defendant's use of the infringing domain name constitutes cybersquatting in violation of the Anticybersquatting Consumer Protection Act, 15 U.S.C. § 1125(d).

WHEREFORE, Stack demands the following relief:

That Defendants, and all persons acting in concert or participating with them, be preliminarily and permanently enjoined from:

a. using <www.productivitypros.com> ("the infringing domain name") in connection with goods and services related to Stack's business;

b. registering or maintaining any registration of the infringing domain name, or any other names, words, designations or symbols consisting of, incorporating in whole or part, or otherwise similar to THE PRODUCTIVITY PRO mark ("Stack's mark");

c. using the infringing domain name or any other names, words, designations or symbols consisting of, incorporating in whole or part, or otherwise similar to Stack's mark;

d. using any names, words, designations, or symbols consisting of, incorporating in whole or part, or otherwise similar to Stack's mark anywhere on any website or websites of Defendant;

e. using any names, words, designations or symbols consisting of, incorporating in whole or part, or otherwise similar to Stack's mark in any buried code, metatags, search terms, keywords, key terms, hits generating pages, or any other devices used, intended, or likely to cause any website or websites of Defendant to be listed by any

Internet search engines in response to any searches that include any terms identical with or confusingly similar to Stack's mark;

f. otherwise infringing Stack's mark;

g. making any description or representation stating or implying that defendant's goods or services, domain names, or website is in any way affiliated, associated, authorized, sponsored, endorsed or otherwise connected with Stack;

That Defendants be ordered to disclose to the Court and Stack all other domain name registrations owned by Defendant in order to permit the Court and Stack to consider whether any such other registrations should be subject to relief in this matter.

That Defendant, and all persons acting in concert or participating in conjunction with her, be ordered to transfer their registration in <www.productivitypros.com > and any other registrations as may be determined by the Court as appropriate herein for relief. (15 U.S.C. § 1125(d)(1)(C).)

That Defendant be ordered to pay statutory damages in the amount of $100,000 per domain name. (15 U.S.C. § 1117(d).)

That Defendant be ordered to account for and pay Stack all profits realized by Defendant by reason of the unlawful acts as set forth in this Complaint. (15 U.S.C. §§ 1117(a).)

That the Court award Stack three times the damages suffered by reason of the intentional, unlawful acts of Defendant as set forth in this Complaint. (15 U.S.C. §§ 1117(a).)

That Defendant be ordered to pay Stack punitive or exemplary damages as provided by law.

That Defendant be required to file with this Court and serve on the undersigned counsel for Stack within thirty (30) days after the entry of judgment a written report under oath setting forth in detail the manner in which Defendant has complied with the injunction ordered by this Court. (15 U.S.C § 1116.)

That Defendant be ordered to pay to Stack the costs of this action and reasonable attorneys' fees. (15 U.S.C. §§ 1117(a).)

That Stack shall have such other relief as this Court may deem just and proper.

Respectfully submitted,

4.5 Complaint for Declaratory Judgment

This complaint addresses a dispute over the ownership of copyrighted works and seeks a declaration from the court regarding existence of a contract between the parties. In trademark and copyright disputes, actions for declaratory judgment often are brought seeking a determination of non-infringement in response to threats by a rightsholder. Recent case law has liberalized the standard upon which a court may exercise jurisdiction in the context of a declaratory judgment action, but the courts nevertheless retain their discretion to accept a case or not.

In the United States District Court
For the Northern District of Illinois
Eastern Division

NEW SVE, INC., A CORPORATION,	)	
	)	
Plaintiff,	)	Civil Action No.
v.	)	
UNIVERSAL HOME ENTERTAINMENT	)	
PRODUCTIONS, LLC	)	
Defendant.	)	

Complaint for Declaratory Judgment
and Injunctive Relief

1. Plaintiff is New SVE, Inc. ("SVE"), an Illinois corporation located in Chicago.
2. Defendant is Universal Home Entertainment Productions, LLC, ("Universal"), located in Universal City, California. On information and belief, Universal is a limited liability corporation organized under the laws of California.
3. This Court has jurisdiction over this action by virtue of the fact that this is a civil action between citizens of different states in which the value of the amount in controversy exceeds seventy-five thousand dollars ($75,000.00), exclusive of interest and costs, jurisdiction being conferred in accordance with 28 U.S.C. § 1332. SVE seeks a declaration of the parties rights pursuant to 28 U.S.C. § 2201.
4. For many years, Plaintiff, through itself or its predecessors in interest, has engaged in the publication and sale of videos and related works in the educational market.

5. Among the works owned and marketed by Plaintiff are "Curious George," "Curious George Goes to the Hospital," and "The Making of Curious George" (the "SVE Works").

6. SVE reproduces, distributes and sells the SVE Works to schools and libraries ("the educational market") and has authorized other parties to exploit the SVE works in markets other than the educational market.

7. Universal is engaged in the production and marketing of motion pictures.

8. On information and belief, Universal plans to distribute a motion picture based on the story and character Curious George.

9. In early 2003, Universal contacted SVE about acquiring SVE's rights in the SVE works.

10. The parties discussed possible terms for an assignment of rights in the SVE works from SVE to Universal.

11. In June, 2003, Universal solicited SVE to submit written offers for the sale of the SVE works to Universal. SVE made an offer to transfer the rights in the SVE works to Universal with a license back. Universal stated that "Universal will agree to accept your offer" subject to further review, approval and definition of various material terms. Universal's purported acceptance was contingent upon review and approval of the chain of title, but that review and approval was never completed. Universal's purported acceptance did not match the term of the license back contained in SVE's offer, since SVE sought a 10-year minimum term (meaning that the term would be at least 10 years and potentially longer); whereas Universal limited the proposed term to 10 years only. Universal's purported acceptance was also contingent on further definition of the territory, scope and royalty for the license back of rights to SVE. Universal's understanding of these material terms did not agree with SVE's understanding and expectation.

12. The parties did not reach final agreement on the material terms of the proposed transactions, and at no time was there a binding agreement between SVE and Universal for the transfer of the SVE works to Universal.

13. One of the obstacles to a proposed transfer of rights was the fact that the SVE works were under contract with another party and SVE was not free to transfer all rights in the SVE Works to Universal.

14. In August, 2003, Universal and SVE again discussed the situation. SVE explained to Universal that it was negotiating a potential settlement that would terminate the restrictions on the SVE Works. UAV asked what would happen if SVE received a more favorable offer from another party. SVE explained that SVE would then be free to negotiate with Universal or others for a more favorable deal involving the SVE Works.

15. In late September 2003, SVE received an offer from another party to acquire rights in the SVE Works and other works.

16. On October 2, 2003, SVE advised Universal that it had received a favorable offer from another party and would pursue that offer unless Universal was prepared to make a more competitive offer.

17. On October 3, 2003, SVE received a response from Nancy Eagle, Senior Vice President of Legal Affairs for Universal, stating: "I want to reiterate that our companies have already reached an agreement for the purchase of the three (3) stop-motion animated projects entitled 'Curious George,' 'Curious George Goes To The Hospital' and 'The Making of Curious George'[the SVE Works]. Any agreement that you enter into with a third party regarding those rights will be in breach of our agreement."

18. SVE and Universal never reached an agreement for the purchase of the SVE Works. There has been no offer and acceptance of the material terms necessary for the sale of rights in the SVE Works and there has been no exchange of consideration.

19. Universal's allegations of breach of contract constitute improper threats of litigation and create a reasonable apprehension on the part of SVE that it will be sued for breach of contract because it intends to enter into an agreement with a third party regarding rights in the SVE Works.

20. SVE is entitled to a declaration of rights pursuant to 28 U.S.C. § 2201 due to Universal's improper threats of litigation.

21. Universal's allegations of breach of contract interfere with SVE's reasonable expectation of a favorable business advantage involving the SVE Works.

22. SVE will be immediately and irreparably harmed if Universal is not enjoined from asserting improper claims of breach of contract; wherefore, SVE is without adequate remedy at law.

WHEREFORE, SVE prays for relief as follows:

a. A declaration that there is no agreement between SVE and Universal involving transfer of the SVE Works and that SVE is entitled to enter into transactions with third parties without interference or restriction by Universal.

b. Universal is preliminarily and permanently enjoined from asserting the existence of any agreement between SVE and Universal regarding the SVE Works or from interfering with any transactions between SVE and third parties regarding the SVE Works.

c. SVE is entitled to the cost related to this action, including reasonable attorney's fees, if available, and to such further relief as this Court deems just and fair.

Date: _____, 2003 Respectfully Submitted,

4.6 Answer and Counterclaim— This form presents a simple answer to a declaratory judgment complaint for non-infringement and a counterclaim for trademark infringement. United States District Court Southern District of New York

	:
BABECO CHEMICALS CORP.,	:
	:
Plaintiff,	: Civ. Action No.:
v.	: **ECF Case**
OZARK AG and OZARK CORPORATION.	: **ANSWER AND COUNTERCLAIMS**
	: **OF DEFENDANTS OZARK AG**
Defendants.	: **AND OZARK CORPORATION**
	:
	: **ECF Filed**

Defendants Ozark Aktiengesellschaft ("Ozark AG") and Ozark Corporation (collectively, "Ozark") submit the following answer, affirmative defenses and counterclaims in response to the complaint ("Complaint") of Plaintiff, Babeco Chemicals Corp. ("Babeco"):

Answer
Parties

1. Admitted.
2. Ozark admits that Ozark AG is a joint stock company organized under the laws of Germany and having a place of business in Berlin, Germany.
3. Ozark admits that Ozark Corporation is a Delaware corporation with a place of business at 123 Ozark Drive, Chicago, Illinois 60035. Ozark admits that Ozark Corporation is registered to do business in the state and county of New York as an active foreign corporation. Ozark denies the remaining allegations in Paragraph 3.

Jurisdiction and Venue

4. Ozark admits that Babeco brought this action under the Declaratory Judgment Act, 28 U.S.C. §§ 2201–2202, and the Lanham Act, 15 U.S.C. § 1051, *et seq.*, and New York statutory and common law. Ozark denies the remaining allegations of Paragraph 4.
5. Ozark admits that Babeco brought this action under the Declaratory Judgment Act, 28 U.S.C. §§ 2201–2202, and the Lanham Act, 15 U.S.C. § 1051, *et seq.*, and New York statutory and common law. Ozark denies the remaining allegations of Paragraph 5.
6. Ozark admits that this Court possesses specific personal jurisdiction over Ozark Corporation and Ozark AG for purposes of this action only. Ozark also admits that Ozark Corporation is registered to do business in the State of New York and transacts business in the State of New York. Ozark denies the remaining allegations in Paragraph 6.
7. Ozark admits that venue is proper in the United States District Court for the Southern District of New York and that Ozark Corporation resides in this district for venue purposes under 28 U.S.C. § 1391(c). Ozark denies the remaining allegations of Paragraph 7.

General Allegations

Background of Plaintiff's Business

8. Ozark is without knowledge or information sufficient to form a belief as to the truth of the allegations in Paragraph 8, and therefore denies them.
9. Ozark is without knowledge or information sufficient to form a belief as to the truth of the allegations in Paragraph 9, and therefore denies them.
10. Ozark is without knowledge or information sufficient to form a belief as to the truth of the allegations in Paragraph 10, and therefore denies them.
11. Ozark admits that Babeco is listed as the owner of U.S. Trademark Application Serial No. 99/999,999 in the United States Patent and Trademark Office's Trademark Applications and Registrations Retrieval (TARR) system. Ozark also admits that the record for this application on the TARR system indicates that the application is to register the mark PORFIRON for "herbicides for agricultural use" in International Class 5. Ozark is without knowledge or information sufficient to form a belief as to the truth of the remaining allegations of Paragraph 11, and therefore denies them.

12. Ozark is without knowledge or information sufficient to form a belief as to the truth of the allegations in the first sentence of Paragraph 12, and therefore denies them. Ozark denies the remaining allegations of Paragraph 12.

Background on Defendants

13. Ozark admits that Ozark AG is a global enterprise that, together with its subsidiaries and affiliates, specializes in the fields of chemicals and high-tech materials.
14. Ozark admits that it produces and sells a fungicide product under the brand name PORLIRON and that the famous OZARK name and trademark appears on the label of the product. Ozark admits that its PORLIRON product is marketed and sold to control fungus growth on crops. Ozark denies the remaining allegations of Paragraph 14.
15. Admitted.
16. Denied.

Defendants Oppose Babeco's Trademark Application

17. Ozark admits that Ozark AG filed a Notice of Opposition with the Trademark Trial and Appeal Board ("TTAB") requesting that Babeco's Application Serial No. 99/999,999 be refused registration. Ozark admits that Ozark AG alleged that Babeco's PORFIRON mark so resembles the Ozark PORLIRON mark as to cause confusion, mistake, and deception, and that Ozark AG will be damaged by Babeco's registration of the PORFIRON mark for the goods identified in the application. Ozark further admits that a document purporting to be Ozark AG's June 29, 2009 Notice of Opposition is attached to Plaintiff's Complaint as Exhibit 1. Ozark denies the remaining allegations of Paragraph 17.
18. Denied.
19. Ozark admits that, as of the date of the filing of Plaintiff's Complaint, Ozark had not instituted a civil action in federal or state court against Babeco, but Ozark denies the remaining allegations of Paragraph 19.
20. Denied.
21. Denied.
22. Ozark is without knowledge or information sufficient to form a belief as to the truth of the allegations in Paragraph 22, and therefore denies them.

First Claim for Relief

23. Ozark repeats and reasserts its responses to Paragraphs 1 through 22 of the Complaint as if fully set forth herein.
24. Denied.
25. Denied.

Affirmative Defense

Plaintiff has failed to effectuate service of process on Ozark AG.

Counterclaim

Defendants/Counterclaim Plaintiffs, Ozark Aktiengesellschaft ("Ozark AG") and Ozark Corporation (collectively, "Ozark") bring the following counterclaim against Plaintiff/Counterclaim Defendant, Plaintiff, Babeco Chemicals Corp. ("Babeco"):

Parties

1. Defendant/Counterclaim Plaintiff Ozark AG is a joint stock company organized under the laws of Germany and having a place of business in Berlin, Germany.
2. Defendant/Counterclaim Plaintiff Ozark Corporation is a Delaware corporation with a place of business at 123 Ozark Drive, Chicago, Illinois 60035.
3. Plaintiff/Counterclaim Defendant Babeco is a New York Corporation with its principal place of business at One Babeco Lane, New York, New York 11000.

Jurisdiction and Venue

4. The Court has jurisdiction under 28 U.S.C. §§ 1331 and 1338 and 15 U.S.C. § 1121 because this counterclaim arises under the Lanham Act, 15 U.S.C. §§ 1051, *et seq.* Jurisdiction for the New York state common

law claims is conferred under 28 U.S.C. § 1338(b) in accordance with the principles of supplemental jurisdiction pursuant to 28 U.S.C. § 1367(a). Personal jurisdiction over Babeco exists because it has consented to jurisdiction.

5. Venue is proper in this district under 28 U.S.C. § 1391(b) because Babeco has consented to personal jurisdiction in this district and, therefore, is deemed to reside here for purposes of venue. *See* 28 U.S.C. § 1391(b) and (c).

Ozark's Porliron Trademark and Products

6. Ozark AG and its predecessors, subsidiaries, and affiliates have for many years been engaged in the manufacture, distribution, advertising and sale of products in fields of chemicals and high-tech materials.

7. Ozark Corporation and its parent and affiliates are global leaders in crop protection.

8. Since at least as early as May 7, 2001, Ozark has continuously used the trademark PORLIRON in commerce throughout the United States in connection with the advertising, promotion and sale of fungicides.

9. Ozark markets and sells PORLIRON fungicide for agricultural use.

10. Ozark AG owns U.S. Registration No. 9,500,000 for PORLIRON for "fungicides for agricultural use" in International Class 5. The application that matured into this registration was filed on May 1, 2001, and the registration issued on April 15, 2002.

11. By virtue of extensive sales, advertising and promotion of the PORLIRON products, Ozark AG has built up and now owns valuable goodwill symbolized by its PORLIRON trademark.

Babeco's Infringing Porfiron Mark and Product

12. On information and belief, Babeco began using the PORFIRON trademark in U.S. commerce in March 2009 for herbicides.

13. Babeco markets and sells PORFIRON herbicide for agricultural use.

14. Ozark acquired rights in the PORLIRON mark prior to Babeco's first use of its PORFIRON mark.

15. On information and belief, Babeco was aware of Ozark's use of the PORLIRON mark prior to Babeco's commencing use of the PORFIRON mark.

Likely Confusion Between the Marks

16. PORLIRON and PORFIRON are used on closely related goods and are marketed for use in connection with overlapping crops.
17. On information and belief, PORLIRON and PORFIRON are distributed to and used by the same class of consumers and distributed through the same channels of trade.

Count I
Trademark Infringement

18. Ozark re-alleges paragraphs 1–17, as if fully set forth herein.
19. Babeco's aforementioned use of the PORFIRON trademark is likely to cause confusion, mistake or deception as to the source of origin, sponsorship or approval of Babeco's goods in that purchasers and others are likely to believe that Babeco's goods are Ozark's goods, or are in some way legitimately connected with, licensed or approved by the Ozark.
20. On information and belief, Babeco's use of the PORFIRON trademark constitutes a deliberate, intentional and willful attempt to trade upon Ozark's goodwill in its PORLIRON trademark.
21. Babeco's acts constitute trademark infringement in violation of Section 32 of the Lanham Act, 15 U.S.C. § 1114, and the common law of the State of New York.
22. Babeco's acts greatly and irreparably damage Ozark and will continue to so damage Ozark unless restrained by this Court; wherefore, Ozark is without an adequate remedy at law.

Count II
Unfair Competition

23. Ozark re-alleges Paragraphs 1–17 and 19–20, as if fully set forth herein.
24. Babeco's acts constitute unfair competition in violation of Section 43(a) of the Lanham Act, 15 U.S.C. § 1125, and the common law of the State of New York.
25. Babeco's acts greatly and irreparably damage Ozark and will continue to so damage Ozark unless restrained by this Court; wherefore, Ozark is without an adequate remedy at law.

WHEREFORE, Ozark prays that:

A. Babeco, its agents, servants, employees, and attorneys, successors and assigns, and all others in active concert or participation with Babeco, be enjoined and restrained during the pendency of this action, and permanently thereafter, from using the designation PORFIRON, or any other designation or mark confusingly similar thereto, in connection with herbicides or fungicides and other related products for agricultural use.

B. Babeco, and all others holding by, through or under Babeco, be required, jointly and severally, to:

1. account for and pay over to Ozark all of Babeco's profits and Ozark's damages from Babeco's acts of trademark infringement and unfair competition in accordance with 15 U.S.C. § 1117(a) and the laws of New York, and Ozark asks that these amounts be trebled in accordance with 15 U.S.C. § 1117(a) and the laws of New York;

2. pay to Ozark the costs of this action, together with reasonable attorneys' fees and disbursements, in accordance with 15 U.S.C. § 1117(a);

3. deliver up for destruction all of Babeco's labels, signs, prints, packages, wrappers, receptacles, and advertisements for products bearing the PORFIRON trademark, and all plates, molds, matrices, and other means of making the same, in its possession, in accordance with 15 U.S.C. § 1118; and

4. file with the Court and serve on Ozark an affidavit setting forth in detail the manner and form in which defendants have complied with the terms of the injunction, in accordance with 15 U.S.C. § 1116.

C. Ozark have such other and further relief as this Court deems just.

4.7 Answer and Affirmative Defense of Fair Use

This answer includes a simple allegation regarding the fair use of a term alleged to likely cause confusion. Liberal pleading standards permit simple allegations that simply give notice to the other side about the defenses claimed.

In the United States District Court for the
Northern District of Illinois Eastern Division

UNISTRAW INTERNATIONAL LTD.,	)	
and	)	Civil Action No. 08CV1751
UNISTRAW PATENT HOLDINGS LTD.,	)	
and	)	Judge Dow
UNISTRAW ASSET HOLDING LTD.,	)	Magistrate Judge Mason
Plaintiff,	)	
vs.	)	
FELFOLDI EDESSEGGYARTO KFT.	)	
Defendant.	)	

Defendant's First Amended Answer and
Affirmative Defenses to <u>Plaintiffs' Complaint</u>

Defendant Felföldi Édességgyártó és Szolgáltató Korlátolt Felelösségu Társaság (hereinafter referred to as "Felföldi"), by undersigned counsel, hereby answers the Complaint of Plaintiffs Unistraw International Ltd., Unistraw Patent Holdings Ltd., and Unistraw Asset Holding Ltd (collectively, "Plaintiff"), and asserts its Affirmative Defenses, as follows:

Jurisdiction and Venue

1. This is an action for trademark infringement and unfair competition brought under the Lanham Act, 15 U.S.C. §§ 1114(b) *et. seq.* 1125(a) and for unfair competition and deceptive trade practices brought under the statutory and common law of the State of Illinois. Jurisdiction is predicated upon 28 U.S.C. §§ 1331, 1338(a) and (b). Venue is proper under 28 U.S.C. § 1391 (b) and (d).

ANSWER: Felföldi admits that Plaintiff purports to bring an action for trademark infringement and unfair competition under the Lanham Act and deceptive trade practices under the statutory and common law of the State of Illinois. Felföldi admits that jurisdiction is predicated on 28 U.S.C. §§ 1331, 1338 (a) and (b). Felföldi admits that venue is proper under 28 U.S.C. § 1391 (b) and (d).

Parties

2. Unistraw International Ltd. is an Australian company with its principal place of business at 36–42 Chippen Street, Chippendale, NSW 2008 Australia.

ANSWER: Felföldi is without knowledge or information sufficient to form a belief as to the truth of the allegations of Paragraph 2 and therefore denies the same.

3. Unistraw Patent Holdings Ltd., a wholly owned subsidiary of Unistraw International Ltd., is a Malaysian company with its principal place of business at U0195, Jalan Merdeka 87007 Federal Territory of Labuan Malaysia.

ANSWER: Felföldi is without knowledge or information sufficient to form a belief as to the truth of the allegations of Paragraph 3 and therefore denies the same.

4. Unistraw Asset Holding Ltd., a wholly owned subsidiary of Unistraw International Ltd., is an Australian company with its principal place of business at 36–42 Chippen Street, Chippendale, NSW 2008 Australia.

ANSWER: Felföldi is without knowledge or information sufficient to form a belief as to the truth of the allegations of Paragraph 4 and therefore denies the same.

5. Unistraw is the exclusive owner of certain individual trademark rights, an overall trade dress and each separate element of the trade dress for the packaging used on its drinking straw product.

ANSWER: Felföldi admits that the records of the United States Patent and Trademark Office identify Unistraw Patent Holdings Ltd. as the owner of record of a number of registered trademarks, but denies the remainder of Paragraph 5.

6. Plaintiff's SIPAHH products are manufactured and sold by its licensee, The Jel Sert Company (hereinafter, "Jel Sert"), in the Northern District of Illinois and throughout the United States.

ANSWER: Felföldi is without knowledge or information sufficient to form a belief as to the truth of the allegations of Paragraph 6 and therefore denies the same.

7. Jel Sert is an Illinois corporation having its principal place of business at Route 59 & Conde Street, West Chicago, Illinois 60185.

ANSWER: Felföldi is without knowledge or information sufficient to form a belief as to the truth of the allegations of Paragraph 7 and therefore denies the same.

8. Defendant is a Hungarian company with its principal place of business at 4030 Debrecen, Dioszegi ut Keleti Ipartelep 6, Hungary.

ANSWER: Felföldi admits the allegations of Paragraph 8.

9. Defendant has advertised and offered for sale, to businesses that are located in this District or do business in this District, a substantially similar

drinking straw to that of Unistraw, which employs a packaging, a trade dress and numerous trademark elements that are confusingly similar to those of Unistraw.

ANSWER: Felföldi denies that the product referred to in Paragraph 9 (the "Quick Milk Product") is "substantially similar" to any product of Plaintiff, or that the packaging or trade dress of the Quick Milk Product is confusingly similar to any valid trademark or trade dress rights owned by Plaintiff. Felföldi admits the remaining allegations of Paragraph 9.

10. Upon information and belief, Defendant will continue to advertise or offer for sale confusingly similar drinking straws to business that are located in this District or do business in this District.

ANSWER: Felföldi denies that any drinking straws that it offers are "confusingly similar" to any valid trademark or trade dress rights owned by Plaintiff. Felföldi admits the remaining allegations of Paragraph 10.

11. After a reasonable opportunity for further investigation or discovery, there is likely to be evidentiary support that Defendant's infringing products have been advertised and offered for sale in this District.

ANSWER: Felföldi denies that any drinking straws that it offers are "infringing" any valid trademark or trade dress rights owned by Plaintiff. Felföldi admits the remaining allegations of Paragraph 11.

Plaintiff's Ownership of Trademarks Relating to Its Sipahh Products

12. Unistraw is the owner of United States Trademark Registration No. 3,344,462 (attached Exhibit A) for the design mark SIPAHH for drinking straws containing flavoring for beverages.

ANSWER: Felföldi admits that the records of the United States Patent and Trademark Office identify Unistraw Patent Holdings Ltd. as the owner of record of U.S. Trademark Registration No. 3,344,462. Felföldi is without knowledge or information sufficient to form a belief as to the truth of the remaining allegations of Paragraph 12 and therefore denies the same.

13. Unistraw is the owner of United States Trademark Registration No. 3,073,732 (attached Exhibit B) for the word marks SIPAHH for drinking straws containing flavoring for beverages.

ANSWER: Felföldi admits that the records of the United States Patent and Trademark Office identify Unistraw Patent Holdings Ltd. as the owner of record of U.S. Trademark Registration No. 3,073,732. Felföldi is without knowledge or information sufficient to form a belief as to the truth of the remaining allegations of Paragraph 13 and therefore denies the same.

14. Unistraw is the owner of United States Trademark Application No. 77/428,175 (attached Exhibit C) for a logo design of a drinking straw for flavoring beverages.

ANSWER: Felföldi objects to Paragraph 14 on the grounds that a pending trademark application confers no legal rights or presumptions, and is therefore irrelevant as a matter of law. Subject to and without waiving this objection, Felföldi admits that the records of the United States Patent and Trademark Office identify Unistraw Patent Holdings Ltd. as the owner of record of U.S. Trademark Application Serial No. 77/428,175. Felföldi is without knowledge or information sufficient to form a belief as to the truth of the remaining allegations of Paragraph 14 and therefore denies the same.

15. Unistraw is the owner of the United States Trademark Application Serial No. 77/425,176 (attached Exhibit D) for the design of Unistraw's cow mascot, named "Mort Thort", as used on the packaging and advertisements for SIPAHH drinking straw products.

ANSWER: Felföldi objects to Paragraph 15 on the grounds that a pending trademark application confers no legal rights or presumptions, and is therefore irrelevant as a matter of law. Felföldi admits that the records of the United States Patent and Trademark Office identify Unistraw Patent Holdings Ltd. as the owner of record of U.S. Trademark Application Serial No. 77/425,176. Felföldi is without knowledge or information sufficient to form a belief as to the truth of the remaining allegations of Paragraph 15 and therefore denies the same.

16. Since their introduction, Unistraw's clear drinking straws products, having its unique trade dress and design, have enjoyed great success in the marketplace. Unistraw's straws have appeared in the 2005 innovation showcase at ANUGA, the world's largest international food and beverage fair; won the Sweetie 2006 Product of the show award at the ISM Trade Show in Cologne, the largest confectionary and biscuit trade show in the world; won the 2006 Food Industry Innovation Award from the Australian Institute of Food Science and Technology; and won the Retailers Choice Award for the Beverage Category at the Food Marketing Institute Show in 2006.

ANSWER: Felföldi denies that Plaintiff's "clear drinking straws products" have a "unique trade dress and design." Felföldi is without knowledge or information sufficient to form a belief as to the truth of the remaining allegations of Paragraph 16 and therefore denies the same.

17. Plaintiff's U.S. license has expended over $1.625 million in advertising and promotional activities relating to its SIPAHH products.

ANSWER: Felföldi is without knowledge or information sufficient to form a belief as to the truth of the allegations of Paragraph 17 and therefore denies the same.

18. Since the inception of the SIPAHH products, Plaintiff's advertising and promotional activities have included the use of the Mort Thort cow design in promoting its products.

ANSWER: Felföldi is without knowledge or information sufficient to form a belief as to the truth of the allegations of Paragraph 18 and therefore denies the same.

19. SIPAHH products utilize "flavor granules (known as pellets or beads)" called "UniBeads" to dispense flavor to beverages.

ANSWER: Felföldi is without knowledge or information sufficient to form a belief as to the truth of the allegations of Paragraph 19 and therefore denies the same.

20. The SIPAHH mark is nonfunctional and distinctive; and has acquired strong secondary meaning with the relevant consuming public. The SIPAHH mark, shape, design and packaging, including the cow design are recognized as an indicator of high quality products from a single source.

ANSWER: Felföldi denies the allegations of Paragraph 20.

21. Plaintiff maintains an active Internet website from which Illinois residents of this District may learn about the SIPAHH products.

ANSWER: Felföldi is without knowledge or information sufficient to form a belief as to the truth of the allegations of Paragraph 21 and therefore denies the same.

22. Jel Sert maintains an active Internet website from which Illinois residents of this District may purchase SIPAHH products.

ANSWER: Felföldi is without knowledge or information sufficient to form a belief as to the truth of the allegations of Paragraph 22 and therefore denies the same.

Defendant's Tortious Acts

23. Defendant has advertised and offered for sale products with a confusingly similar trade dress.

ANSWER: Felföldi denies the allegations of Paragraph 23.

24. Defendant has advertised and offered for sale products under the confusingly similar name SIPPER.

ANSWER: Felföldi denies the allegations of Paragraph 24.

25. Defendant's clear drinking straw products prominently showcase a confusingly similar cow design to that of Unistraw's Mort Thort in promoting its product (attached Exhibit E).

ANSWER: Felföldi admits that certain packaging for its straw products contains a picture of a cow, but denies the remaining allegations of Paragraph 25.

26. Defendant's clear drinking straw products have a confusingly similar shape to Plaintiff's product.

ANSWER: Felföldi denies the allegations of Paragraph 26.

27. Defendant's clear drinking straw products promote confusingly similar straw design, having a clear straw containing flavor crystals.

ANSWER: Felföldi denies the allegations of Paragraph 27.

28. Defendant's use of the confusingly similar trade dress is not authorized by Plaintiff.

ANSWER: Felföldi denies any trade dress used on or in connection with its products is "confusingly similar" to any valid trademark or trade dress owned by Plaintiff. Felföldi admits that Plaintiff has not authorized Felföldi to use any particular trade dress, but denies that any such authorization from Plaintiff is required.

29. Defendant's use of the confusingly similar name SIPPER is not authorized by Plaintiff.

ANSWER: Felföldi denies that "sipper" is confusingly similar to any valid trademark owned by Unistraw. Felföldi admits that Plaintiff has not authorized Felföldi to use "sipper," but denies that any such authorization from Plaintiff is required.

30. Defendant's use of the confusingly similar cow is not authorized by Plaintiff.

ANSWER: Felföldi denies that the cow design that it uses is confusingly similar to any valid trademark owned by Plaintiff. Felföldi admits that Plaintiff has not authorized Felföldi to use a picture of a cow, but denies that any such authorization from Plaintiff is required.

31. Defendant's use of the confusingly similar shape is not authorized by Plaintiff.

ANSWER: Felföldi denies that the shape of its Quick Milk Product is confusingly similar to any valid trademark or trade dress rights owned by Plaintiff. Felföldi admits that Plaintiff has not authorized Felföldi to use the shape of the Quick Milk Product, but denies that any such authorization from Plaintiff is required.

32. Defendant's use of the confusingly similar flavor crystals is not authorized by Plaintiff.

ANSWER: Felföldi denies that the flavor crystals used in its Quick Milk Product are confusingly similar to any valid trademark or trade dress rights owned by Plaintiff. Felföldi admits that Plaintiff has not authorized Felföldi to use the flavor crystals used in the Quick Milk product, but denies that any such authorization is required.

33. In September of 2007, Defendant advertised and offered for sale its clear drinking straw products at the National Candy Confectionary Show in Chicago, Illinois.

ANSWER: Felföldi admits the allegations of Paragraph 33.

34. Defendant is actively seeking distributors to distribute its clear drinking straw products in the United States, including in this District.

ANSWER: Felföldi admits the allegations of Paragraph 34.

35. Defendant's clear drinking straw products tout "patent pending"; however there is no record of any current U.S. patent application pending for this product.

ANSWER: Felföldi admits that the packaging for the Quick Milk Product states "patent pending." To the extent this paragraph alleges that Felföldi is falsely representing the status of patent applications relating to the Quick Milk Product, Felföldi denies the same.

Count I
Trade Dress and Trademark Infringement

36. Paragraphs 1–35 are incorporated herein by reference.
ANSWER: Felföldi realleges its answers to Paragraphs 1 through 35 herein by reference.

37. Defendant's unauthorized use in commerce of a confusingly similar trade dress, a confusingly similar cow design and mark confusingly similar to the SIPAHH mark in connection with the offering for sale and advertising of Defendant's products has caused, and is likely to cause, confusion and mistake or deception as to origin, sponsorship or approval of Defendant's products in violation of Unistraw's rights under 15 U.S.C. §§ 1051 and 1125(a).
ANSWER: Felföldi denies the allegations of Paragraph 37.

38. After a reasonable opportunity for further investigation or discovery, there is likely to be evidentiary support to show that there has been actual confusion by the public caused by Defendant's unauthorized and willfully infringing use of Unistraw's trademarks and trade dress, individually and in combination, for the exact same type of goods.
ANSWER: Felföldi denies the allegations of Paragraph 38.

39. After a reasonable opportunity for further investigation or discovery, there is likely to be evidentiary support to show the conduct by Defendant alleged herein was willful and intentional.
ANSWER: Felföldi denies the allegations of Paragraph 39.

40. Unless enjoined by this Court, Defendant will continue to do the acts complained of herein all to the irreparable harm of Unistraw. Unistraw has no adequate remedy at law.
ANSWER: Felföldi denies the allegations of Paragraph 40.

Count II
Unfair Competition and Deceptive
Trade Dress Practices

41. Paragraphs 1–40 are incorporated hereby be reference.
ANSWER: Felföldi realleges its answers to Paragraphs 1 through 40 herein by reference.

42. The aforesaid acts of Defendant constitute unfair competition and deceptive trade practices under Federal law (15 U.S.C. § 1051 et seq), and the common law of the State of Illinois.

ANSWER: Felföldi denies the allegations of Paragraph 42.

43. By reason of Defendant's acts as alleged above, Unistraw has suffered and will continue to suffer damage and injury to its business, reputation and good will; and will sustain serious loss of revenues and profits in an indeterminate amount.

ANSWER: Felföldi denies the allegations of Paragraph 43.

44. After a reasonable opportunity for further investigation or discovery, there is likely to be evidentiary support to show the conduct by Defendant alleged herein was willful and intentional.

ANSWER: Felföldi denies the allegations of Paragraph 44.

45. Unless enjoined by this Court, Defendant will continue to do the acts complained of herein all to the irreparable harm of Unistraw. Unistraw has no adequate remedy at law.

ANSWER: Felföldi denies the allegations of Paragraph 45.

Count III
Illinois Consumer Fraud and Deceptive
Business Practices

46. Paragraphs 1–45 are incorporated herein by reference.

ANSWER: Felföldi realleges its answers to Paragraphs 1 through 45 herein by reference.

47. The aforesaid acts of Defendant constitute deceptive trade practices in violation of the Illinois Uniform Deceptive Trade Practices Act, III. Rev. Stat. Ch. 815 ILCS § 505 *et seq.*, and the Illinois Consumer Fraud and Deceptive Business Practices Act, 815 ILCS 510/2 *et seq.*

ANSWER: Felföldi denies the allegations of Paragraph 47.

48. By reason of Defendant's acts as alleged above, Unistraw has suffered and will continue to suffer damage and injury to its business, reputation and good will; and will sustain serious loss of revenues and profits in an indeterminate amount.

ANSWER: Felföldi denies the allegations of Paragraph 48.

49. After a reasonable opportunity for further investigation or discovery, there is likely to be evidentiary support to show the conduct by Defendant's alleged herein was willful and intentional.

ANSWER: Felföldi denies the allegations of Paragraph 49.

50. Unless enjoined by this Court, Defendant's will continue to do the acts complained of herein all to the irreparable harm of Unistraw. Unistraw has no adequate remedy at law.

ANSWER: Felföldi denies the allegations of Paragraph 50.

Affirmative Defenses

First Affirmative Defense

Felföldi's use of the term "sipper" on its Quick Milk Product is fair use under 15 U.S.C. § 1115(b)(4).

Second Affirmative Defense

Plaintiff's claims relating to all elements of the trade dress of the Quick Milk Product other than the word "sipper" are barred because Felföldi began using these elements prior to Plaintiff's use of its claimed trade dress.

Third Affirmative Defense

The straw design and flavor crystals that Plaintiff uses are functional and therefore entitled to no protection as trademarks or trade dress.

WHEREFORE, Felföldi prays for judgment as follows:

1. That Plaintiff take nothing by way of its Complaint;
2. That Felföldi recovers reasonable attorneys' fees;
3. That Felföldi recovers costs of suit; and
4. For such other and further relief as the Court may deem just and proper.

4.8 Complaint for Trademark Infringement

The final complaint in this chapter involves a complicated dispute for trademark infringement. The complainant and answer take a detailed narrative approach to pleading, attempting to tell a persuasive story about the dispute.

In the United States District Court for the
Northern District of Georgia Atlanta Division

SUNAMERICA CORPORATION (formerly)	)	
SUN LIFE GROUP OF AMERICA,	)	
INC.), a Delaware corporation,	)	
and SUN LIFE INSURANCE COMPANY	)	
OF AMERICA, INC., a Maryland	)	
Corporation	)	
	)	
Plaintiffs,	)	CIVIL ACTION FILE
v.	)	NO. 1:89-CV -1315-JTC
SUN LIFE ASSURANCE COMPANY OF	)	
CANADA, a Canadian corporation,	)	
and SUN LIFE ASSURANCE COMPANY	)	
OF CANADA (U.S.), a Delaware	)	
corporation,	)	
Defendants.	)	

Complaint

COME NOW plaintiffs SunAmerica Corporation formerly known as Sun Life Group of America, Inc. ("SunAmerica"), and Sun Life Insurance Company of America, Inc. ("Sun Life America") and for their Complaint allege as follows:

Jurisdiction and Venue

1. This is an action at law and in equity for unfair competition, cancellation of federally registered service marks, trademark and service mark infringement, false advertising, and unfair and deceptive trade practices arising under the Federal Trademark Act of 1946, 60 Stat. 427, 15 U.S.C. § 1050 et *seq.*; the Georgia Uniform Deceptive Trade Practices Act, O.C.G.A. § 10-1-370 et *seq.*; the Georgia false advertising statute, O.C.G.A. § 10-1-421; the Georgia fraudulent misappropriation statute, O.C.G.A. § 23-2-55; and the common law.

2. This Court has jurisdiction of the subject matter of this action under § 39 of the Trademark Act of 1946, 15 U.S.C. § 1121, and under 28 U.S.C. § 1331.

3. Venue is proper in this district and division pursuant to 28 U.S.C. § 1391 because the defendants reside in this district and the acts hereafter complained of occurred and are occurring in the Northern District of Georgia and in interstate commerce.

The Parties

4. Plaintiff SunAmerica is a Delaware corporation with a place of business at 260 Peachtree Street, N.W., Atlanta, Georgia 30303. SunAmerica is an insurance holding company which, until May 2, 1989, did business under the corporate name "Sun Life Group of America, Inc." ("SLG America").

5. Plaintiff Sun Life America is a Maryland corporation with a principal place of business at 260 Peachtree Street Atlanta, Georgia 30303. Sun Life America is a wholly owned subsidiary of SunAmerica. Sun Life America markets and sells life insurance products and annuities to consumers throughout the United States except for the States of New York and Wyoming.

6. Defendant Sun Life Assurance Company of Canada ("Sun Life Canada") is a Canadian corporation registered to do business in Georgia and is subject to the jurisdiction of this Court. Its United States headquarters is located at One Sun Life Executive Park, Wellesley Hills, Massachusetts. Its registered agent for service of process in Georgia is Gavin Dubuiddom, 41 Perimeter Center, N.E., Suite 350, Atlanta, Georgia 30346. Sun Life Canada markets and sells individual and group life and health insurance products and annuities within the United States pursuant to a Michigan branch trust arrangement used by Canadian insurance companies.

7. Defendant Sun Life Assurance Company of Canada (U.S.) ("Sun Life Canada (U.S.)") is a Delaware corporation with its principal place of business at One Sun Life Executive Park, Wellesley Hills, Massachusetts. Sun Life Canada (U.S.) is a wholly owned subsidiary of Sun Life Canada. Sun Life Canada (U.S.) is registered to do business in Georgia and is subject to the jurisdiction of this Court. Its registered agent for service of process is Daniel A. Sullivan, 2 Peachtree Street, N.W., Atlanta, Georgia 30383. Sun Life Canada (U.S.) markets and sells life insurance and annuity products and group pension contracts.

Factual Background

8. Since at least as early as 1916, Sun Life Canada and Sun Life America simultaneously have used the terms "Sun" and "Sun Life" as part of their corporate names and trademarks and service marks in connection with the marketing and sale of their respective life insurance and annuity products in the United States. Sun Life America and Sun Life Canada are separate and independent companies that are wholly unrelated to each other. Although they both have sold life insurance, annuity and financial services products through the same or similar channels of trade in overlapping geographical areas for many years, their respective usages of "Canada" or "America" along with the sales methods used in the past by the insurance industry and the regulatory restrictions on the business activities of companies and agents in that industry have served to distinguish the two companies and their products and to reduce or mitigate any likelihood of public confusion resulting from their simultaneous usage of "Sun" and "Sun Life" for closely related products and services.

9. On information and belief, from 1916 through the present, Sun Life Canada has operated in the United States under a Michigan branch trust arrangement pursuant to which Sun Life Canada's assets in the United States are held in trust by the Michigan Insurance Commissioner. In 1970, Sun Life Canada formed a wholly owned U.S. subsidiary named Sun Life Assurance Company of Canada (U.S.) ("Sun Life Canada (U.S.)") and also began marketing and selling life insurance and annuity products and group pension contracts in the United States through that entity. Sun Life America and Sun Life Canada (U.S.) are separate and independent companies that are wholly unrelated to each other.

10. Sun Life America initially was authorized to sell life insurance products in Maryland. On information and belief, Sun Life Canada initially was authorized to sell life insurance products in Michigan, and Sun Life Canada (U.S.) initially was authorized to sell life insurance products in Massachusetts. As Sun Life America and Sun Life Canada and Sun Life Canada (U.S.) expanded their operations and applied for authorization to do business in additional states, neither of the parties objected to the other's obtaining qualification to sell life insurance products in any state. In some instances, however, state insurance commissioners would inquire whether the first company authorized to do business in the state objected to the issuance of a certificate of authority to sell insurance products to an unrelated company whose name included "Sun" or "Sun Life." In response to such inquiries, the

consistent practice of both parties was to consent to the authorization of the applying company to do business in the state under its full corporate name which included "America" or "Canada" as a distinguishing element.

11. Sun Life America now has policyholders throughout the United States and is qualified with the state insurance commissioners of all but two states to sell insurance under the name "Sun Life Insurance Company of America, Inc." On information and belief defendants are also qualified to sell life insurance throughout virtually the entire United States under the name Sun Life Assurance Company of Canada and/or Sun Life Assurance Company of Canada (U.S.), but neither defendant is qualified to sell insurance in any state under a corporate name which does not include the word "Canada."

12. By virtue of long-standing concurrent use of names and marks including the terms "Sun" and "Sun Life" in conjunction with identifying geographical modifiers, both parties are entitled pursuant to 15 U.S.C. §§ 1115(b)(5) and 1051 (note) (sections 33(b) and 49 of the Lanham Act) and the common law to continue such concurrent usage.

13. Plaintiffs and Defendants have generally refrained from objecting to use by the other of any corporate names, trademarks, or service marks including "Sun" or "Sun Life" as long as the identifying modifier "America" or "Canada" was used in immediate proximity to the term "Sun." However, in 1979 when Sun Life America's parent holding company was formed as "Sun Life Group, Inc.," Sun Life Canada objected to Sun Life Group, Inc.'s unmodified use of "Sun Life Group" based on the assertion that such usage would cause public confusion. Sun Life Canada also objected to the use of a stylized "S" logo by Sun Life Group, Inc. and Sun Life America as a service mark for life insurance underwriting services based on Sun Life Canada's use of a dissimilar "S" logo which it had adopted for use only in connection with mutual fund investment services. (A copy of a federal registration certificate depicting that mark is attached hereto as Exhibit A.) Sun Life Canada was not then using any "S" logo in connection with life insurance underwriting services, but rather was using a "tree of life" logo for such services. (A copy of a federal registration certificate depicting that mark is attached hereto as Exhibit B.)

14. On May 30, 1980, Sun Life Group, Inc. and Sun Life Canada on behalf of themselves and their affiliates executed a Settlement Agreement resolving both of the above-described service mark disputes. Both parties agreed not to use "Sun Life Group" without the modifier "of Canada" or "of America," thereby reflecting their belief that their respective uses of "Canada" and "America" served to distinguish them and their affiliates. Thereafter, pursuant to the said Agreement,

Sun Life Group, Inc. changed its corporate name to Sun Life Group of America, Inc. ("SLG America"). Sun Life Canada also consented to the use and registration of SLG America's stylized "S" logo, as amended, for life insurance services, which is the subject of Registration No. 1,218,580 issued by the U.S. Patent and Trademark Office on November 30, 1982. (A copy of which is attached hereto as Exhibit C.)

15. During late 1981 through 1982, the parties expressed objections to and entered into negotiations regarding their respective usages of "Sun" and "Sun Life" in advertising and promotional materials for their goods and services. This dispute centered around Sun Life Canada's objection to SLG America's usage of "Sun Life" in stylized lettering allegedly similar to the typeface of Sun Life Canada's federally registered mark SUN LIFE OF CANADA (Registration No. 1,614,060) for life insurance underwriting and the provision of annuities, and SLG America's objection to Sun Life Canada (U.S.)'s use of "U.S." and "Sun Life (U.S.)" which imparted a false impression to the public regarding Sun Life Canada's identity and geographical origin and created an essentially identical impression to Sun Life America's use of "America." The parties reached no resolution of those disputes.

16. The life insurance industry's methods of product distribution have undergone significant changes in recent years. In the past, life insurance products primarily were sold through face-to-face contact with purchasers either by home service agents employed by life insurance companies who contacted consumers in their homes or by locally based representatives of independent insurance agencies. Consumers generally purchased life insurance products based on their personal contacts with and trust and confidence in those agents in conjunction with the reputation of the underwriting company. Further, such personal contacts between purchasers and agents provided an opportunity for any confusion created by concurrent use of "Sun" and "Sun Life" to be dispelled or explained. However, the life insurance and annuity products of both parties are increasingly being sold through less personal trade channels including through broker dealers, financial planners, financial institutions, investment firms, independent agents, and direct mail marketing. As a result, consumers are now more likely to rely on brand names as a means of distinguishing and purchasing life insurance and annuity products.

17. During recent years, life insurance companies have expanded into the broader financial services field. Many life insurance companies, including both of the parties, currently sell annuities and other investment oriented products. Life insurance companies and their affiliates also

are beginning to provide a wide range of other financial and money management services.

18. As a result of the recent expansion of life insurance companies into the broader financial services market and their changing methods of product distribution, it is increasingly important for the parties to this action to preserve their separate identities in order to enable the public to distinguish the source of their respective products and services.

19. In recent years, as the defendants have expanded their U.S. operations and lines of products and services, they have progressively reduced their use of identifying terminology incorporating the term "Canada" and have begun using names and marks which include no geographic identification or which incorporate the term "U.S." The use of such terminology fails to clearly identify and distinguish Sun Life Canada and its affiliates and their products and services and inhibits the public's ability to distinguish them from SunAmerica and its affiliates and their products and services. Defendants' said actions and practices undermine plaintiffs' efforts to maintain an identity separate and apart from that of defendants while retaining the good will which plaintiffs have established for their names and marks including "Sun" and "Sun Life" and constitute false descriptions, false representations, and false designations of origin including geographical origin and unfair competition and infringe plaintiffs' trademark and service mark rights by creating actual confusion and a likelihood of confusion between the parties and their products and services.

20. The actions by defendants which misrepresent defendants' identity and create a likelihood of public confusion regarding the relationship between the parties and their affiliates and their respective goods and services include, inter alia: (1) the use of "Sun Life (U.S.)" without the prominent use of the identifying modifier "of Canada" as part of or immediately adjacent to that name; (2) the adoption and use of a sunburst "S" mark, often used in conjunction with names including the term "Sun" or "Sun Life" for life insurance, annuities, and financial management services that is confusingly similar to SunAmerica's federally registered stylized "S" mark for life insurance underwriting services (a copy of defendants' application to federally register the sunburst "S" mark is attached hereto as Exhibit D); (3) a decline in the prominence and use of identifying and distinguishing nomenclature including the term "Canada" and increasing use of references to "U.S." on defendants' sales, advertising, and promotional materials; and (4) the adoption and usage of a series of trademarks and service marks which include the term "Sun" or "Sun Life" without incorporating the identifying modifier "Canada."

21. Defendants' foregoing practices demonstrate an intentional pattern of advertising and promotional methods and activities which misrepresent and misdescribe defendants and their products and the geographical origin thereof and which are creating and are likely to create confusion, deception, and mistake by the public regarding the origin and source of the parties' respective goods and services. Defendants said practices inhibit the public's ability to distinguish the parties and their goods and services by means of public recognition of the parties' long-standing usage of the identifying nomenclature "America" or "Canada" and by reason of plaintiffs' use of its stylized "S" logo service mark. Plaintiffs have objected to defendants' foregoing misrepresentations and infringing activities which create public confusion and reduce consumers' ability to distinguish the parties and their respective goods and services. To date, however, defendants have refused to discontinue their misrepresentations and infringing activities and to take necessary steps to reduce or eliminate the likelihood of public confusion resulting therefrom.

22. In contrast to defendants' actions, plaintiffs have consistently attempted to reduce or eliminate the likelihood of public confusion caused by defendants by prominent use of the geographical term "America" or the equivalent geographical designations "U.S." or "U.S.A." on all printed materials, advertisements, and other literature. Plaintiffs also have opposed defendants' November 6, 1986 application to federally register a sunburst "S" mark for underwriting life insurance and financial management services. That opposition is based on SLG America's prior usage of and common law rights in and its ownership of incontestable Registration No. 1,218,580 for its stylized "S" mark for life insurance underwriting services. The subject opposition proceeding (No. 76,045), currently is pending before the Trademark Trial and Appeal Board.

    In order to further distinguish SLG America, Sun Life America and other related companies from defendants and to reinforce the public's association of Sun Life America with designations denoting a United States origin including "America," plaintiffs' parent company Kaufman and Broad, Inc. (now Broad Inc.) in 1988 acquired from the former SunAmerica Corporation, a subsidiary of Chemical Banking Corporation, at great expense, all rights, title and interest in and to the corporate names, trade names and service marks, "SunAmerica" and "SunAmerica Corporation" for use in connection with insurance and financial services together with the good will of the business associated therewith.

23. As a result of the said transaction, Broad Inc. acquired from the former SunAmerica Corporation ownership of the following service

mark registrations issued by the United States Patent and Trademark Office:

Mark	Registration Number	Services
SUNAMERICA	1,126,452	Insurance and financial services, acceptance of reinsurance premiums, acceptance of specific risks, investigation and settlement of claims; financial services—namely, personal loans and financing the purchases of others; consulting agency services in the fields of personal loans and financing the purchases of others—Class 36
SUNAMERICA	1,055,824	Insurance and financial services, acceptance of reinsurance premiums, acceptance of specific risks, investigation and settlement of claims; financial services—namely, personal loans and financing the purchases of others; consulting agency services in the fields of personal loans and financing the purchases of others—Class 102
"S" LOGO	854,632	Financial services—namely personal loans, and consumer financing - Class 102

Copies of the aforesaid regulations are annexed as Exhibits E, F, and G hereto.

24. As of May 2, 1989 the corporate name of Sun Life Group of America, Inc. was changed to SunAmerica Corporation (plaintiff herein). Plaintiffs have now begun use of the "SunAmerica" name and mark in place of the designation "Sun Life Group of America" in advertising and printed materials. Such materials which relate to the life insurance and annuity products and financial services of Sun Life America, will identify Sun Life America as "a SunAmerica Company" thereby further reinforcing the public's recognition of the element "America" in conjunction with "Sun" and "Sun Life" as identifications of plaintiffs and of the services of Sun Life America and as a term which distinguishes plaintiffs and their services from defendants' identification with the term "Canada."

25. Plaintiffs' expenditures in excess of a million dollars in acquiring and initiating use of the SunAmerica name and mark were occasioned and necessitated in large part by the deliberate encroachment

of defendants on the names, marks, symbols and designations used by plaintiffs including defendants' adoption and extensive use of the "Sunburst S" logo, the "Sun Financial" name and mark, and their use of the name "Sun Life" alone or in conjunction with the designations "U.S." and "U.S.A."

26. Plaintiffs' acquisition and adoption at great expense of the SunAmerica name and mark evidences and is part of a continuing good faith effort by plaintiffs and their ultimate parent to clearly distinguish plaintiffs and the products and services of Sun Life America by use of the designation "America" and variations thereof, in the face of continuing and deliberate encroachment on plaintiffs' identity by defendants and despite defendants' complete disregard for the likelihood of public confusion created by such progressive encroachment. By contrast with plaintiffs' good faith efforts to maintain and reinforce the distinction between plaintiffs and defendants, defendants are continuing to progressively encroach on plaintiffs' rights rather than taking good faith steps to prevent public confusion regarding the parties and their respective products and services.

27. Defendants' activities complained of herein constitute false representations, false descriptions, and false designations of origin, including geographical origin, of defendants' products and services which are causing and, unless enjoined by this Court, will continue to cause a likelihood of confusion and deception of members of the consuming public, and injury to plaintiffs' goodwill and reputation for which plaintiffs have no adequate remedy at law.

Count I
Federal Unfair Competition

28. Plaintiffs repeat and incorporate by reference all of the allegations set forth in paragraphs 1 through 29 above as if fully set forth herein.

29. Defendants' foregoing activities in connection with the advertising, marketing, and sale of their goods and services in interstate commerce constitute false designations of origin, false descriptions and false representations regarding the source, authorization, sponsorship, and origin, including geographical origin, of defendant's products and services and are calculated to cause confusion and mistake and to deceive consumers and the public as to the true identity, affiliation, connection, source, origin, authorization, and sponsorship of the parties and their respective products and services in violation of 15 U.S.C. § 1125(a).

30. Defendants' acts of unfair competition are causing and are likely to cause substantial injury to the public and to plaintiffs, and plaintiffs

are entitled to injunctive relief and to recover damages, costs, and reasonable attorneys' fees pursuant to 15 U.S.C. §§ 1125(a), 1116, and 1117.

Count II
Federal Service Mark Infringement

31. Plaintiffs repeat and incorporate by reference all of the allegations set forth in paragraphs 1 through 32 above as if fully set forth herein.
32. Defendants' aforesaid use in interstate commerce of their "Sunburst S" logo particularly in conjunction with names including "Sun" and "Sun Life" without the identifying modifier "Canada" is causing and is likely to continue to cause confusion, mistake, and deception of the public regarding defendants' identity and regarding the existence of a connection or affiliation between defendants and plaintiffs and between their products and services and concerning the source, origin or sponsorship of defendants' products and services and infringes the rights of SunAmerica in its federally registered stylized "S" logo in violation of 15 U.S.C. § 1051 et seg., and more particularly 15 U.S.C. § 1114(1).
33. Defendants' infringing conduct is causing and is likely to cause substantial injury to the public and to SunAmerica, and plaintiffs are entitled to injunctive relief and to recover damages, costs, and reasonable attorneys' fees pursuant to 15 U.S.C. §§ 1114, 1116, and 1117.

Count III
Cancellation of Sun Financial Group Mark

34. Plaintiffs repeat and incorporate by reference all of the allegations set forth in paragraphs 1 through 35 above as if fully set forth herein.

    Since at least as early as September 1985, plaintiffs have used SUN FINANCIAL SERVICES and variations thereof to advertise, identify, and promote their products and services. By virtue of extensive usage by plaintiffs of the SUN FINANCIAL SERVICES trade name and mark and variations thereof in printed materials and in oral communications with the public, the term "Sun Financial" has become identified with plaintiffs as a symbol of the source and origin of plaintiffs' products and services.
35. Despite plaintiffs' prior usage of SUN FINANCIAL SERVICES to identify and advertise their products and services, defendants thereafter

began using the confusingly similar name SUN FINANCIAL GROUP, frequently without use of the distinguishing term "Canada," to identify and advertise products and services of the same type as those for which Plaintiffs' SUN FINANCIAL SERVICES mark is used. Plaintiff is the prior user of the term "SUN FINANCIAL" in the financial services field and Defendants' usage of SUN FINANCIAL GROUP creates a likelihood of confusion, mistake and deception regarding the source, origin, and sponsorship of the products and services of both parties.

On April 21, 1987, defendants obtained federal Registration No. 1,437,498 from the U.S. Patent and Trademark Office for the mark SUN FINANCIAL GROUP for "underwriting life insurance and financial management services" based on a claimed April 30, 1986 date of first use. Pursuant to § 2(d) of the Lanham Act, 15 U.S.C. § 1052(d), defendant's said registration should be canceled on the ground that defendant's SUN FINANCIAL GROUP mark so resembles SUN FINANCIAL SERVICES, which was previously used as a mark and trade name in the United States by plaintiff for similar products and services and not abandoned, as to be likely when applied to the products and services of defendant, to cause confusion, or to cause mistake or to deceive.

36. Defendants have used the SUN FINANCIAL GROUP mark so as to misrepresent the source and origin of their products and services in connection with which the mark is used by failing and refusing to use the mark only in conjunction with the adjacent identifying modifier "Canada" and the federal registration for that mark also should be canceled pursuant to §14(c) of the Lanham Act, 15 U.S.C. § 1064(c).

37. As an alternative to cancellation of the SUN FINANCIAL GROUP registered mark, plaintiffs pray that this Court use its equitable powers to require defendants to use that mark only in conjunction with the prominent and adjacent use of the term "Canada" in order to clearly inform the public of the identity of the company to which such usage refers and to enter appropriate injunctive relief directing the modifications of the registration in accordance with such requirement.

Count IV
Cancellation of Defendant's Registrations for
Service Marks Incorporating "Sun" or "Sun Life"

38. Plaintiffs repeat and incorporate by reference all of the allegations set forth in paragraphs 1 through 41 above as if fully set forth herein.

39. Defendants have obtained federal registrations for the following service marks incorporating the elements "Sun" or "Sun Life":

Mark	Registration Number	Services
SUN ULTRATERM	1,433,237	Underwriting life insurance
SUN EXECUMASTER	1,391,865	Issuing interest-sensitive whole life insurance policies
SUN INTEREST MASTER-Q	1,364,872	Issuing interest sensitive whole life insurance policies
SUN INTERESTMASTER	1,333,608	Issuing Interest sensitive whole life insurance policies
SUN PENSIONMASTER	1,335,888	Issuing universal life insurance policies
SUNPLAN 2	1,273,865	Annuities underwriting
SUN LIFEMASTER	1,272,133	Underwriting life insurance
SUN FUND	916,514	Services in issuing and administering equity- based variable insurance and equity contracts and for segregated fund investment services
SUNPLAN	1,151,906	Annuities underwriting, brokerage, and administration
SUN FUND (and Design)	920,910	Services in issuing and administering equity- based variable insurance and annuity contracts and for segregated fund investment services
FOLLOW THE SUN FOR LIFE	830,778	Underwriting of individual and group life, health, accident and disability insurance protection

40. Defendants have used the above listed marks so as to misrepresent the source or origin of their goods and services in connection with which the marks are used by failing and refusing to make prominent use of the geographical term "Canada" immediately adjacent to such marks. By reason of defendant's said misuse of its registered marks, plaintiff submits that those registrations should be canceled pursuant to § 14(c) of the Lanham Act, 15 U.S.C. § 1064(c).

41. As an alternative to cancellation of the above listed registrations, plaintiffs pray that this Court use its equitable powers to compel defendants only to use the subject marks if identifying language prominently including the term "Canada" is used immediately adjacent thereto.

Count V
Damages for Corrective Advertising
and Remedial Actions

42. Plaintiffs repeat and incorporate by reference all of the allegations set forth in paragraphs 1 through 45 above as if fully set forth herein.
43. Defendants have knowingly and deliberately encroached on the separate identity of plaintiffs and have pursued a pattern of use and advertising of "Sun," "Sun Life," and the "Sunburst S" logo designed to diminish or eliminate the prominent use of distinguishing elements which have historically differentiated the parties, and especially the term "Canada," with reckless disregard for the resulting confusion of the public and injury to plaintiffs and their separate identity.
44. Defendants' knowing, willful, and deliberate acts of unfair competition have inhibited plaintiffs' efforts to distinguish themselves and the products and services of Sun Life America from defendants and their products and services. Because Defendants have encroached on and undermined the distinguishing value of plaintiffs' names and marks and the good will associated therewith, plaintiffs have been and will be required to expend significant time, effort, and money on corrective efforts and advertising in order to maintain the good will of plaintiffs' marks and in attempting to counteract defendants' efforts to blur the distinction between the parties and their products and services. Plaintiffs are, therefore, entitled pursuant to 15 U.S.C. §§ 1125(c) and 1117 to recover the costs of corrective advertising and other remedial steps which have been and will be necessary to educate the public as to the differences between the parties and to dispel the public confusion caused by defendants' knowing, willful, and deliberate acts of unfair competition and to maintain the separate good will associated with plaintiffs' names and marks.

Count VI
Common Law Trademark Infringement,
Common Law and Statutory Unfair Competition

45. Plaintiffs repeat and incorporate by reference all of the allegations set forth in paragraphs 1 through 48 above as if fully set forth herein.
46. Defendants have engaged in the foregoing activities with full knowledge of plaintiffs' use of and common law and statutory rights to use "Sun" and "Sun Life," and of SunAmerica's federally registered stylized "S" logo and, on information and belief, with prior knowledge of plaintiffs' SUN FINANCIAL SERVICES name and mark without regard to the likelihood of confusion of the public created thereby.

47. Defendants have engaged in the foregoing activities in a manner calculated to misdescribe and misrepresent their identity and origin and that of their products and services and to falsely imply an association, connection or affiliation with plaintiffs and plaintiffs' products and services with knowledge that confusion and deception of the public would inevitably result from such activities.

    The aforesaid conduct of defendants violates O.C.G.A. § 232-55 and constitutes unfair competition and common law trademark infringement which have created and will continue to create a likelihood of confusion to the irreparable injury of plaintiffs unless restrained by this Court and plaintiffs have no adequate remedy at law therefor.

Count VII
Deceptive Trade Practices

48. Plaintiffs repeat and incorporate by reference all of the allegations set forth in paragraphs 1 through 52 above as if fully set forth herein.
49. By reason of the acts set forth above, defendants have engaged in deceptive trade practices within the meaning of the Georgia Uniform Deceptive Trade Practices Act, O.C.G.A. § 10-1-370. et sec. by: (1) passing off and contributing to the passing off of defendants' products and services as those of plaintiffs; (2) causing likelihood of confusion or misunderstanding as to the source, origin or sponsorship of the parties' respective products or services; (3) causing likelihood of confusion or of misunderstanding as to the affiliation, connection or association of defendants and their affiliates or their products or services with plaintiffs and the products and services of plaintiffs; (4) using deceptive representations or designations of origin including geographical origin in connection with their products or services; (5) representing that defendants' products and services have the sponsorship or approval of plaintiffs which they do not have or that defendants have an affiliation or connection with plaintiffs that they do not have; and (6) engaging in other conduct which similarly creates a likelihood of confusion or of misunderstanding of the public.
50. Defendants' deceptive practices are causing and are likely to cause substantial injury to the public and to plaintiffs, and plaintiffs are entitled to injunctive relief pursuant to O.C.G.A. § 10-1-373(a). Plaintiff is also entitled to an award of costs and of attorneys fees pursuant to O.C.G.A. § 10-1-373(b)(2) because defendants have acted willfully with knowledge of the likelihood of confusion, mistake and deception of the public created by defendants' aforesaid actions and practices.

Count VIII
False Advertising

51. Plaintiffs repeat and incorporate by reference all of the allegations set forth in paragraphs 1 through 55 above as if fully set forth herein.

    Defendants' aforesaid acts constitute false and fraudulent advertising within the meaning of O.C.G.A. § 10-1-422.

52. Defendants' false advertising is injurious to plaintiffs, and plaintiffs are entitled to injunctive relief pursuant to 0.C.G.A. § 10-1-423.

WHEREFORE, plaintiffs pray:

1. That defendants, their agents, servants, employees, attorneys, and those persons in active concert or participation with them be permanently enjoined and restrained from:

    (a) Using the designation "Sun Life U.S." or any other United States geographical descriptions, such as "U.S.," "U.S.A.," "United States of America," or "America" in conjunction with the term "Sun" or "Sun Life" except for the use of "U.S." as part of the complete corporate name "Sun Life Assurance Company of Canada (U.S.)":

    (b) Using any trademarks, service marks, trade names, or product names consisting of or including "Sun" or "Sun Life" in connection with the advertising, marketing, or sale of their products and services unless the term "Canada" is prominently used immediately adjacent to any such use of "Sun" or "Sun Life";

    (c) Using its sunburst "S" logo or any logo confusingly similar to plaintiffs' stylized "S" logo in connection with the advertising, marketing or sale of their products and services;

    (d) Expressly, or by implication, representing to the public that defendants or their affiliates are identical to, connected or affiliated with, or endorsed or sponsored by plaintiffs;

    (e) Representing by words or conduct that any products or services provided, offered for sale, sold, advertised, or rendered by defendants or their affiliates are those of plaintiffs or their affiliates or are authorized, sponsored, approved or endorsed by, or otherwise connected with plaintiffs or their affiliates or from passing off their goods and services as those of plaintiffs or their affiliates;

    (f) Making any express or implied false representations, false descriptions or false designations of origin, including geographical origin of defendants or of the products or services of defendants;

    (g) Engaging in any conduct that will cause, or is likely to cause, confusion, mistake or misunderstanding as to the origin, source, affiliation, connection or association of defendants and their affiliates or their products and services or as to any connection or association thereof with plaintiffs or the products or services of plaintiffs; or

(h) Otherwise engaging in misrepresentations or deceptive trade practices or infringing upon plaintiffs' trade name, service mark, and trademark rights as described herein and from otherwise unfairly competing with plaintiffs in any manner whatsoever.

2. That defendants' federal registrations for the service marks SUN FINANCIAL GROUP, SUN ULTRATERM, SUN EXECUMASTER, SUN INTEREST MASTER-Q, SUN INTERESTMASTER, SUN PENSIONMASTER, SUNPLAN 2, SUN LIFEMASTER, SUN FUND, SUNPLAN, SUN FUND (and Design), and FOLLOW THE SUN FOR LIFE marks be canceled, or alternatively, that defendants and their affiliates be required to use identifying language including the term "Canada" in a prominent manner immediately adjacent to all uses of such names and marks including the term "Sun."

3. That judgment be entered in favor of plaintiffs for all damages, expenses and costs sustained by them on account of defendants' trademark and service mark infringement, unfair competition, false representations, false descriptions and false designations of the origin of their products and services, and other deceptive trade practices, including but not limited to the costs of corrective advertising and other remedial steps.

4. That plaintiffs are able to recover their costs of this suit including reasonable attorneys' fees and expenses.

That Plaintiffs Have Such other and Further Relief as this Court May Deem Just and Proper In the United States District Court For the Northern District of Georgia Atlanta Division

U.S.D.C.

SUNAMERICA CORPORATION (formerly *SUN* LIFE GROUP OF AMERICA, INC.), a Delaware corporation, and SUN LIFE INSURANCE COMPANY OF AMERICA, INC., a Maryland corporation, Plaintiffs and Counterdefendants,

---

(Continued)

v.

SUN LIFE ASSURANCE COMPANY OF
CANADA, a Canadian corporation, and *SUN* LIFE ASSURANCE
COMPANY
OF CANADA (U.S.), a Delaware
corporation,
Defendants and
Counterclaimants.

Answer and Counterclaim Qf Defendants
Sun Life Assurance Company of Canada and
Sun Life Assurance Company of Canada (U.S.)

Defendants Sun Life Assurance Company of Canada ("Sun Life") and Sun Life Assurance Company of Canada (U.S.) ("Sun Life (U.S.)"), by their undersigned counsel, answer the Complaint herein and counterclaim against plaintiffs as follows (the paragraphs of the Answer are numbered to correspond with those of the Complaint):

"Jurisdiction And Venue"

1. Defendants deny the allegations of this paragraph, except that they admit that plaintiffs purport to bring this action at law and in equity under the Federal Trademark Act of 1946, 60 Stat. 427, 15 U.S.C. § 1050 *et seq.*; the Georgia Uniform Deceptive Trade Practices Act, O.C.G.A. § 10-1-370 *et seq.*; the Georgia false advertising statute, O.C.G.A. § 10-1-421; the Georgia fraudulent misappropriation statute, O.C.G.A. § 23-2-55; and the common law.
2. Defendants deny the allegations of this paragraph, except that they admit that plaintiffs purport to invoke the jurisdiction of this Court under § 39 of the Trademark Act of 1946, 15 U.S.C. § 1121, and under 28 U.S.C. § 1331.
3. Defendants deny the allegations of this paragraph, except that they admit that, for purposes of this lawsuit, venue is proper in this district and this division pursuant to 28 U.S.C. § 1391.

"The Parties"

4. Defendants are without knowledge or information sufficient to form a belief as to the truth of the allegations of this paragraph.

5. Defendants are without knowledge or information sufficient to form a belief as to the truth of the allegations of this paragraph.
6. Defendants admit the allegations of the first, second, and fourth sentences and deny the allegations of the third sentence of this paragraph.
7. Defendants admit the allegations of this paragraph.

"Factual Background"

8. Defendants are without knowledge or information sufficient to form a belief as to the truth of the allegations of the first sentence of this paragraph, except that they admit that, since at least 1895, the words "Sun" and "Life" have appeared in Sun Life's corporate name and in certain service marks and trade names used in connection with the marketing and sale of its life insurance and annuity products in the United States. Defendants admit the allegations of the second sentence of this paragraph. Defendants are without knowledge or information sufficient to form a belief as to the truth of the allegations of the third sentence of this paragraph, except that they admit that Sun Life's usages of its name and service marks have served to distinguish the two companies and their products and to reduce or mitigate any likelihood of public confusion.
9. Defendants deny the allegations of the first sentence of this paragraph, except that they admit that from 1895 through the present, Sun Life has operated in the United States under a Michigan branch trust arrangement. Defendants admit the allegations of the third sentence of this paragraph and deny the allegations of the second sentence of this paragraph, except that they admit that Sun Life formed a wholly owned U.S. subsidiary named Sun Life Assurance Company of Canada (U.S.) in 1970 and thereafter began marketing and selling life insurance and annuity products and group pension contracts in the United States through that entity.
10. Defendants are without knowledge or information sufficient to form a belief as to the truth of the allegations of the first sentence of this paragraph. Inasmuch as use of the word "initially" in the second sentence of this paragraph is vague, confusing, and uncertain as to the period or periods of time to which it purports to refer, defendants are without knowledge or information sufficient to form a belief as to the truth of the allegations of the second sentence of this paragraph. Defendants are also without knowledge or information sufficient to form a belief as to the truth of the allegations of the third, fourth and fifth sentences of this paragraph, except that they admit that in some instances a state insurance commissioner did inquire whether the party first authorized

to do business in the state objected to the issuance of such a certificate of authority to a second company whose name included "Sun" or "Sun Life" and that in some instances the party first authorized consented to the issuance of such a certificate to the applying company.

11. Defendants are without knowledge or information sufficient to form a belief as to the truth of the allegations of the first sentence of this paragraph. Defendants deny the allegations of the second sentence of this paragraph, except that they admit that they are authorized to sell life insurance under the name Sun Life Assurance Company of Canada and/or Sun Life Assurance Company of Canada (U.S.) in every state in the United States and the District of Columbia (except New York, where Sun Life Insurance and Annuity Company of New York, a wholly-owned subsidiary of Sun Life (U.S.), is authorized to sell life insurance), and that they have never applied for such authorization under any other corporate names, and defendants further aver that they are entitled to use names and marks that do not include the word Canada in connection with their sales of insurance in all such states.

12. Defendants are without knowledge or information sufficient to form a belief as to the truth of the allegations of this paragraph, except that they admit that they are entitled, pursuant to both the Lanham Act and common law, to continue usage of all their names and marks, and except that they deny that plaintiffs are entitled to continue usage of any of their names or marks that include the terms "Sun" or "Sun Life" pursuant to 15 U.S.C. §§ 1115(b)(5) or 1051 (note) (sections 33(b) and 49(sic) of the Lanham Act).

13. Defendants deny the allegations of the first sentence of this paragraph, except that they admit that plaintiffs refrained for many years from objecting to defendants' use of their names and service marks including "Sun" or "Sun Life," regardless of whether the modifier "Canada" was used in immediate proximity to the term "Sun" or not. Defendants deny the allegations of the second sentence of this paragraph, except that they are without information sufficient to form a belief as to the truth of the allegation that the parent holding company of Sun Life Insurance Company of America, Inc. was formed in 1979 as "Sun Life Group, Inc." ("SLG") and except that they admit that Sun Life objected to SLG's use of "Sun Life Group" on grounds set forth in documents provided to plaintiffs, to which plaintiffs are referred for the contents thereof. Defendants deny the allegations of the third sentence of this paragraph, except that they admit that Sun Life objected to SLG's use of a stylized "S" logo on grounds set forth in documents provided to plaintiffs, to which plaintiffs are referred for the contents thereof, and that Exhibit A to the Complaint is a copy of the United States Patent Office certificate for a stylized "S" logo registered by Sun Life for

mutual fund investment services in U.S. Class 102. Defendants admit the allegations of the fourth sentence of this paragraph, except that they deny that in 1979 the logo attached as Exhibit B to the complaint was the mark primarily used by Sun Life in connection with life insurance underwriting services, and defendants aver that in 1979 Sun Life was using an "S" logo in connection with mutual fund investment services.

14. Defendants deny the allegations of this paragraph, except that they admit that on May 30, 1980, SLG and Sun Life executed a written Settlement Agreement, to which plaintiffs are referred for the provisions thereof, and that Exhibit C to the Complaint is a copy of the United States Patent and Trademark Office certificate for a stylized "S" logo registered by Sun. Life Group of America, Inc. ("SLGA") for life insurance underwriting services in U.S. Class 102, and except that defendants are without knowledge or information sufficient to form a belief as to the truth of the allegation that thereafter, pursuant to the said Agreement, Sun Life Group, Inc. changed its corporate name to Sun Life Group of America, Inc.

15. Defendants deny the allegations of this paragraph, except that they admit that in late 1981 and 1982 defendants objected to SLGA's usage of "Sun Life" in stylized lettering similar to the typographically fanciful design of Sun Life's federally registered mark "Sun Life of Canada" on grounds set forth in documents provided to plaintiffs, to which plaintiffs are referred for the contents thereof, that the parties negotiated but reached no agreement concerning this objection, that SLGA objected in writing on June 16, 1982 and July 20, 1982 to defendant Sun Life (U.S.)'s usage of "Sun Life (U.S.)," to which writings plaintiffs are referred for the contents thereof, and that Sun Life (U.S.) refused to discontinue its usage of "Sun Life (U.S.)."

16. Defendants are without knowledge or information sufficient to form a belief as to the truth of the allegations of this paragraph, except that they admit that there have been changes over the years in the product distribution methods utilized by some life insurance companies.

17. Defendants are without knowledge or information sufficient to form a belief as to the truth of the allegations of this paragraph, except that they admit that defendants operate in the field of financial services and currently sell annuities and other investment-oriented products.

18. Defendants are without knowledge or information sufficient to form a belief as to the truth of the allegations of this paragraph.

19. Defendants deny the allegations of this paragraph, except that they admit that they have used and obtained federal service mark registrations for marks which include no geographic identification and that Sun Life (U.S.) has used names which incorporate the term "U.S."

20. Defendants deny the allegations of this paragraph, except that they admit that a copy of defendants' application for federal registration of their sunburst "S" mark is attached as Exhibit D to the Complaint.

21. Defendants deny the allegations of this paragraph.

22. Defendants deny the allegations of this paragraph, except that they admit that plaintiffs have objected to defendants' usage of certain of their names and marks and that defendants have continued to use their names and marks.

23. Defendants deny the allegations of this paragraph, except that they admit that SLGA filed an opposition to defendants' November 6, 1986, application for federal registration of their sunburst HS" mark for underwriting life insurance and financial management services, to which opposition plaintiffs are referred for the alleged basis thereof, and that said opposition proceeding (No. 76,045) is currently pending before the Trademark Trial and Appeal Board, and defendants further aver that said opposition proceeding has been stayed pending resolution of this action.

24. Defendants are without knowledge or information sufficient to form a belief as to the truth of the allegations of this paragraph.

25. Defendants are without knowledge or information sufficient to form a belief as to the truth of the allegations of this paragraph.

26. Defendants are without knowledge or information sufficient to form a belief as to the truth of the allegations of this paragraph.

27. Defendants deny the allegations of this paragraph.

28. Defendants deny the allegations of this paragraph.

29. Defendants deny the allegations of this paragraph. *"Count I"*

"Federal Unfair Competition"

30. Def Defendants repeat and incorporate by reference all of the answers set forth in paragraphs 1 through 29 above as if fully set forth herein.

31. Defendants deny the allegations of this paragraph.

32. Defendants deny the allegations of this paragraph. *"Count II"*

"Federal Service Mark Infringement"

33. Defendants repeat and incorporate by reference all of the answers set forth in paragraphs 1 through 32 above as if fully set forth herein.

34. Defendants deny the allegations of this paragraph.

35. Defendants deny the allegations of this paragraph. *"Count III"*

"Cancellation Of Sun Financial Group Mark"

36. Defendants repeat and incorporate by reference all of the answers set forth in paragraphs 1 through 35 above as if fully set forth herein.
37. Defendants are without knowledge or information sufficient to form a belief as to the truth of the allegations of the first sentence of this paragraph and deny the allegations of the second sentence of this paragraph.
38. Defendants deny the allegations of this paragraph, except that they are without knowledge or information sufficient to form a belief as to the truth of the allegation that plaintiff is the first user of the term "Sun Financial" in the financial services field.
39. Defendants admit the allegations of the first sentence and deny the allegations of the second sentence of this paragraph.
40. Defendants deny the allegations of this paragraph.
41. While no answer is required to the prayer for relief set forth in this paragraph, defendants aver that no basis exists in law or equity for the relief requested therein.

"Count IV"
"Cancellation of Defendant's Registrations for Service darts Incorporating 'Sun' or 'Sun Life'"

42. Defendants repeat and incorporate by reference all of the answers set forth in paragraphs 1 through 41 above as if fully set forth herein.
43. Defendants admit the allegations of this paragraph.
44. Defendants deny the allegations of this paragraph.
45. While no answer is required to the prayer for relief set forth in this paragraph, defendants aver that no basis exists in law or equity for the relief requested therein.

"Count V"
"Damages for Corrective Advertising and Remedial Actions"

46. Defendants repeat and incorporate by reference all of the answers set forth in paragraphs11 through 45 above as if fully set forth herein.
47. Defendants deny the allegations of this paragraph.
48. Defendants deny the allegations of this paragraph. "*Count VI*"

"Common Law Trademark Infringement, Common Law and Statutory Unfair Competition"

49. Defendants repeat and incorporate by reference all of the answers set forth in paragraphs 1 through 48 above as if fully set forth herein.
50. Defendants deny the allegations of this paragraph.
51. Defendants deny the allegations of this paragraph.
52. Defendants deny the allegations of this paragraph.

"Count VII"
"Deceptive Trade Practices"

53. Defendants repeat and incorporate by reference all of the answers set forth in paragraphs 1 through 52 above as if fully set forth herein.
54. Defendants deny the allegations of this paragraph.
55. Defendants deny the allegations of this paragraph.

"Count VIII"
"False Advertising"

56. Defendants repeat and incorporate by reference all of the answers set forth in paragraphs 1 through 55 above as if fully set forth herein.
57. Defendants deny the allegations of this paragraph.
58. Defendants deny the allegations of this paragraph.
59. Except as expressly admitted, defendants deny each and every remaining allegation in the Complaint.

First Affirmative Defense

The Complaint fails to state a claim upon which relief can be granted.

Second Affirmative Defense

The claims asserted in the Complaint are barred, in whole or in part, by the applicable statute of limitations.

Third Affirmative Defense

The claims asserted in the Complaint are barred, in whole or in part, by the doctrine of laches.

Fourth Affirmative, Defense

Plaintiffs have acquiesced in defendants' usage of their names and marks and are therefore barred from asserting any claims based on such usage.

Fifth Affirmative Defense

Plaintiffs are estopped from asserting some or all of the claims alleged in the Complaint.

Sixth Affirmative Defense

Plaintiffs have waived some or all of the claims alleged in the Complaint.

Seventh Affirmative Defense

Plaintiffs come to this Court with unclean hands and are not entitled to any relief.

Eighth Affirmative Defense

Certain of the claims alleged in the Complaint are asserted in violation of, and are barred by, the Settlement Agreement of May 30, 1980, between Sun Life and SLG.

Ninth Affirmative Defense

Plaintiffs have released defendants from some of the claims alleged in the Compliant.

Tenth Affirmative Defense

On information and belief, plaintiffs have abandoned the stylized "S" logo the alleged rights to which defendants are claimed in Count II of the Complaint to have infringed.

WHEREFORE, defendants pray that plaintiffs take nothing by their Complaint herein, that judgment be entered for defendants and against plaintiffs on each count of the Complaint, that defendants be awarded their attorneys' and experts' fees and costs incurred herein, as well as the costs of suit herein, and that defendants be granted such other and further relief from the Complaint as the Court deems just and proper.

Counterclaim

COME NOW counterclaimants Sun Life Assurance Company of Canada and Sun Life Assurance Company of Canada (U.S.) and for their Counterclaims against counterdefendants SunAmerica Corporation and Sun Life Insurance Company of America, Inc. allege as follows:

Jurisdiction and Venue

1. Counterclaimants assert these counterclaims at law and in equity for unfair competition, breach of contract, service mark infringement, false advertising, unfair and deceptive trade practices, and cancellation of a federally registered service mark under the Federal Trademark Act of 1946 (the "Lanham Act"), 60 Stat. 427, 15 U.S.C. § 1050 et sec., the Georgia Uniform Deceptive Trade Practices Act, O.C.G.A. § 10-1-370 et. *sec.*, the Georgia false advertising statute, O.C.G.A. § 10-1-421 *et seq.*, the Georgia fraudulent misappropriation statute, O.C.G.A. § 23-2-55 *et seq.*, and the common law.

2. This Court has ancillary jurisdiction pursuant to Rule 13, Fed. R. Civ. P., by virtue of the Complaint filed herein by counterdefendants SunAmerica Corporation and Sun Life Insurance Company of America, Inc. This Court also has jurisdiction under sections 37 and 39 of the Lanham Act, 15 U.S.C. § 1119 and § 1121; under 28 U.S.C. § 1331; under 28 U.S.C. § 1332(a); and under 28 U.S.C. § 1338(a) and (b). Venue is proper in this District under 28 U.S.C. § 1391.

The Parties

3. Counterclaimant Sun Life Assurance Company of Canada ("Sun Life") is a Canadian corporation which is authorized to do business in every

state of the United States (except New York) and in the District of Columbia and which has done business in the United States continuously since 1895. Its principal place of business in the United States is located at One Sun Life Executive Park, Wellesley Hills, Massachusetts. Sun Life also transacts business in all of the Canadian provinces and territories, Great Britain, Ireland, Hong Kong, Puerto Rico, the Virgin Islands, Bermuda, and the Philippines. Sun Life markets and sells individual and group life and health insurance products and annuities throughout the United States (except in New York).

4. Counterclaimant Sun Life Assurance Company of Canada (U.S.) ("Sun Life (U.S.)") is a Delaware corporation which is authorized to do business in all states of the United States except New York and Vermont. Sun Life (U.S.) was incorporated in 1970 and has done business in the United States continuously since 1973. Its principal place of business is located at One Sun Life Executive Park, Wellesley Hills, Massachusetts. Sun Life (U.S.) markets and sells life insurance and individual and group annuity products throughout the United States (except in New York and Vermont). Sun Life (U.S.) has a wholly-owned subsidiary, Sun Life Insurance and Annuity Company of New York, which issues individual fixed and combination fixed/variable annuity contracts and group life and long-term disability insurance in New York. Other wholly-owned subsidiaries of Sun Life (U.S.) include Massachusetts Financial Services Company, a registered investment adviser, Sun Investment Services Company, a registered broker-dealer and investment adviser, Sun Benefit Services Company, Inc. which offers claims, administrative and pension brokerage services and distributes disability income products, The New London Trust Company, a bank, and Massachusetts Casualty Insurance Company, which offers individual disability income insurance. Sun Life and Sun Life (U.S.) have over 38,000 licensed agents in the United States.

5. Counterdefendant SunAmerica Corporation ("SunAmerica"), a plaintiff in this action, is a Delaware corporation which currently has its principal place of business in Atlanta, Georgia but which has announced that it will move its principal place of business within the next nine months to Los Angeles, California. Until recently, SunAmerica did business under the corporate name "Sun Life Group of America, Inc." Prior to that, it did business under the corporate name "Sun Life Group, Inc." and, prior to that, under the corporate name "Sun Life Holding Company." SunAmerica is the same corporation as the corporation previously named "Sun Life Group of America, Inc.," "Sun Life Group, Inc.," and "Sun Life Holding Company." The name "SunAmerica" is accordingly hereinafter used, as appropriate, to refer to that corporation, not only during the period that it has been named "SunAmerica Corporation," but also during the prior periods when it was named

"Sun Life Holding Company," "Sun Life Group, Inc." and "Sun Life Group of America, Inc." SunAmerica is a wholly owned subsidiary of Broad Inc., a California corporation having its principal place of business in Los Angeles, California. Upon information and belief, SunAmerica is a holding company which does not itself market or sell any products or services and which has never done so.

6. Counterdefendant Sun Life Insurance Company of America, Inc. ("SLIA") is a Maryland corporation having its principal place of business in Atlanta, Georgia. SLIA is a wholly-owned subsidiary of SunAmerica, which is in turn a wholly owned subsidiary of Broad Inc. SLIA markets and sells annuities and life insurance products.

Factual Background

7. Sun Life was chartered in Canada in 1865 and began operations in the United States in 1895. Sun Life has operated continuously in the United States under the name Sun Life Assurance Company of Canada since 1895. Neither of the counterdefendants used any "Sun Life" name or mark in the United States until 1916 at the earliest, when SLIA began to use the name Sun Life Insurance Company of America. Sun Life is thus the prior user of "Sun Life" in the United States by at least 21 years.

8. Sun Life (U.S.) was incorporated as a wholly-owned subsidiary of Sun Life in 1970 and began doing business in the United States in 1973. Thereafter, Sun Life (U.S.) adopted and has used "Sun Life of Canada (U.S.)" and "Sun Life (U.S.)" as names and marks to identify the company and the products and services it provides. Counterdefendants have been aware of Sun Life (U.S.)'s use of these names and marks for many years and have acquiesced in its use thereof.

9. In addition to being the prior user of "Sun Life" names and marks in the United States by at least 21 years, Sun Life expanded its business in the United States much more rapidly than did SLIA, both in terms of the number of states in which the respective companies were authorized to sell insurance and in terms of the volume of the business done by the respective companies in the United States. Indeed, the corporation now named SunAmerica was not even created until 1978 and has never been authorized to sell, and has never sold, insurance or any other product in any state. Moreover, SLIA -was, in comparison to Sun Life, a latecomer both in obtaining state authorizations and in expanding the size of its operations in the United States. Historically, Sun Life on a consolidated basis has been authorized to sell life insurance in a greater number of states than SLIA, has had greater annual net premiums in the United States than SLIA, has had greater total assets in the United States than SLIA, and has at all times had assets under

management which exceeded by many times the assets under management by SLIA.

10. In 1971, SLIA was acquired by Kaufman & Broad, Inc. In 1978, Kaufman & Broad created a wholly owned subsidiary to serve as a holding company for SLIA and other companies, which subsidiary (referred to herein as "SunAmerica") was initially named "Sun Life Holding Company" and was subsequently renamed "Sun Life Group, Inc.," "Sun Life Group of America, Inc.," and, finally, "SunAmerica Corporation."

11. Under the ownership of Kaufman & Broad, SunAmerica adopted a two-fold strategy to emulate and imitate Sun Life and Sun Life (U.S.). First, well after Sun Life and Sun Life (U.S.) had expanded from their traditional insurance business into a broader range of financial services and products (including for example mutual funds), SunAmerica followed suit with a similar program of expansion into the broader financial services market. Second, SunAmerica adopted and began using corporate names and marks that closely resembled and, on information and belief, were designed to trade on the established names, marks and goodwill of the older, larger, and more established Sun Life and Sun Life (U.S.).

12. SunAmerica has followed, or announced plans to follow, virtually every step Sun Life and Sun Life (U.S.) have taken to expand beyond the traditional insurance business and into the broader financial services market. For example, after Sun Life (U.S.) formed a New York subsidiary (Sun Life (New York)) in order to participate in the important New York financial services market, SunAmerica followed suit by acquiring a New York company (Capitol Life Insurance Company of New York), which is now a SunAmerica subsidiary. Similarly, after Sun Life (U.S.) acquired a major mutual fund company in order to enter that part of the financial services market, SunAmerica acquired two broker-dealer networks, both of which sell mutual funds, and announced its intention to acquire a mutual fund management firm. And not long after Sun Life (U.S.) acquired a bank, SunAmerica announced that it too was in the market for a bank or similar depository institution.

13. Since at least 1978, SunAmerica has also repeatedly adopted and used names and marks in a manner calculated falsely to suggest for the products and services of its subsidiaries an association, connection or affiliation with Sun Life and Sun Life (U.S.). In 1978, for example, SunAmerica began using in advertising and promotional materials, as well as on its letterhead, the name "Sun Life Group," together with a stylized "S" mark that closely resembled the stylized "S" mark for which Sun Life had obtained a federal registration and which a wholly owned subsidiary of Sun Life was then using.

14. Sun Life protested to SunAmerica in 1978 that its "S" mark was strikingly similar to Sun Life's federally registered "S" mark and that SunAmerica's use of "Sun Life Group" could also cause confusion among the public because of its similarity to Sun Life's name and Sun Life's Group Division in particular.

15. As a result of Sun Life's protest, negotiations between the parties ensued. SunAmerica ceased use of its "S" mark depicted in paragraph 13 above and adopted instead a different stylized "S" mark, which Sun Life did not regard as confusingly similar to its stylized "S" mark. A copy of SunAmerica's revised "S" mark, which is lined for the colors brown and gold, is attached as Exhibit C to the Complaint and is hereinafter referred to as SunAmerica's "second 'S' mark."

16. As a result of the negotiations undertaken in response to Sun Life's protest, Sun Life and SunAmerica entered into a written Settlement Agreement on May 30, 1980. In that Agreement, Sun Life agreed, inter alia, not to oppose SunAmerica's application for federal registration of its second "S" mark, and SunAmerica agreed, inter alia, to cease using "Sun Life Group" standing alone as its name or as a service mark. Sun Life also released SunAmerica from all claims based on SunAmerica's prior use of "Sun Life Group." Accordingly, none of the counts of this Counterclaim is, or should be deemed to be, based thereon.

17. In 1981, little more than a year after the May 30, 1980, Settlement Agreement had been executed, however, SunAmerica embarked on yet another attempt to trade on Sun Life's established name and mark. Specifically, SunAmerica began publishing in 1981 a promotional piece which bore the heading shown below:

Sun Life *OVUM* is moving ahead
The typeface in which the words "SUN LIFE" appear in the above heading is virtually identical to the typographically fanciful design in which the words "SUN LIFE" appear in Sun Life's service mark "SUN LIFE OF CANADA," for which Sun Life had previously obtained a federal service mark registration and which it had been using and was using extensively at the time.

18. Once again, Sun Life protested in 1981 and 1982 this blatant attempt by SunAmerica to trade on the Sun Life name and mark. Once again, as a result of Sun Life's protest, negotiations between the parties ensued. Although no agreement was reached as a result of those negotiations, SunAmerica elected not to risk litigation and ceased its imitation of the typographically fanciful design in which the words SUN LIFE appear in Sun Life's registered mark.

19. In response to Sun Life's protests concerning this imitation, however, SunAmerica also lodged the following complaint with Sun Life. In a

letter dated June 16, 1982, SunAmerica complained of Sun Life (U.S.)'s use of the name "Sun Life (U.S.)," claiming that it was confusingly similar to "Sun Life Group of America" and demanding that Sun Life (U.S.) cease using "Sun Life (U.S.)." This was the first occasion on which SunAmerica had ever protested Sun Life (U.S.)'s use of "Sun Life (U.S.)," even though Sun Life (U.S.) had been using it for many years and even though, upon information and belief, SunAmerica had been well aware of such usage for many years.

20. Sun Life (U.S.) responded to this protest in July 1982 by expressing surprise that SunAmerica was raising the issue at that late date, by disagreeing that "Sun Life (U.S.)" was likely to cause any confusion, and by refusing the demand that Sun Life (U.S.) cease usage of "Sun Life (U.S.)."

21. Thereafter, Sun Life (U.S.) continued its usage of "Sun Life (U.S.)" continuously to the present, and SunAmerica never again protested or sought to prevent such usage until some six years later in correspondence that immediately preceded the filing of the Complaint in this action.

22. On the contrary, more than five years later, in 1987, with full knowledge that Sun Life (U.S.) had been using "Sun Life (U.S.)" for many years and that SunAmerica had acquiesced in such usage, SunAmerica began yet another of its campaigns to trade on the goodwill of the names and marks of Sun Life and Sun Life (U.S.). Specifically, in 1987 SunAmerica began referring to itself in advertisements, promotional materials and otherwise as "Sun Life U.S.A." As alleged in Count I below, moreover, Sun Life (U.S.) has protested SunAmerica's usage of "Sun Life U.S.A.," but SunAmerica has refused to discontinue such usage.

23. Contrary to the fantasy image of themselves that they seek to portray in the Complaint as companies that have "consistently attempted to reduce or eliminate the likelihood of public confusion" (Complaint ¶ 23), counterdefendants have in fact consistently attempted to do just the opposite. Contrary to the suggestion in the Complaint, moreover, that Sun Life and Sun Life (U.S.) have sought to pass themselves off as affiliates of, or somehow related to, the much smaller and less well-known SunAmerica and SLIA, Sun Life and Sun Life (U.S.) have in fact consistently attempted to do just the opposite protect their own valuable names and marks, and the goodwill they represent, from SunAmerica's repeated attempts to misappropriate them.

24. Unlike SunAmerica, moreover, Sun Life and Sun Life (U.S.) have consistently followed the logical policy of choosing, adopting and developing marks related to their corporate names, which all include the word "Sun" or "Sun" imagery. In keeping with this policy, Sun Life and Sun Life (U.S.) have obtained federal registration of no fewer than

15 service marks containing the word "Sun" or "Sun" imagery since 1967. These registered marks include the following:

Mark	Registration No.	Date of Registration
*SUN LIFE OF CANADA plus design	830,779	June 20, 1967
*FOLLOW THE *SUN* FOR LIFE	830,778	June 20, 1967
*SUN FUND	916,514	July 13, 1971
**SUN* FUND plus design	920,910	September 21, 1971
*"S" logo (with sun design)	946,041	October 24, 1972
*SUNPLAN	1,151,906	April 21, 1981
*SUN LIFE OF CANADA (stylized)	1,164,060	August 4, 1981
SUN LIFEMASTER	1,272,133	March 27, 1984
SUNPLAN 2	1,273,865	April 10, 1984
SUN INTERESTMASTER	1,333,608	April 30, 1985
SUN PENSIONMASTER	1,335,888	May 14, 1985
SUN INTERESTMASTER-Q	1,364 872	October 8, 1985
SUN EXECUMASTER	1,391,865	April 29, 1986
SUN ULTRATERM	1,433,237	March 17, 1987
SUN FINANCIAL GROUP	1,437,498	April 21, 1987

The registrations of those marks preceded by an * in the above listing have become incontestable pursuant to Section 15 of the Lanham Act, 15 U.S.C. § 1065. The registrations listed above demonstrate, that Sun Life and Sun Life (U.S.) have developed, used, and registered an entire family of "Sun" marks in the United States. Neither SunAmerica nor SLIA opposed registration of any of these "Sun" marks of Sun Life and Sun Life (U.S.).

25. On information and belief, neither SunAmerica nor SLIA has obtained registration of a single mark containing the word "Sun," nor have they made any effort to develop or use a family of "Sun" marks to identify their products and services. On the contrary, the only two federally registered "Sun" marks which either of them claims the right to use– the "SunAmerica" marks—were allegedly purchased by their parent corporation, Broad Inc., from a third party only months before they filed their Complaint in this action. Two of the only three other registrations owned by SunAmerica are for marks (ISL and Design, and USL and Design) that are entirely unrelated to the word "Sun" or to "Sun" imagery, and the third, SunAmerica's second "S" logo *(see* Ex. C to the Complaint) likewise is totally unrelated to "Sun" imagery or to the word "Sun" (aside from the fact that the word "Sun" begins with an "S").

Count I

Federal Unfair Competition

26. Counterclaimants repeat and incorporate by reference all of the allegations set forth in paragraphs 1 through 24 above as if fully set forth herein.

27. Sun Life (U.S.) has used the name and mark "Sun Life (U.S.)" for many years to identify itself and the products and services it provides. This name accurately describes Sun Life Assurance Company of Canada (U.S.), a United States company operating entirely in the United States, and its wholly owned subsidiaries, which include a major mutual fund company, a bank, an underwriter of disability income insurance, a registered broker-dealer and investment advisor, a company providing claims, administrative and pension brokerage services and distributing disability income products, and a New York life insurance and annuity company, each of which has operated since its inception entirely in the United States, and none of which does any business in Canada.

28. Sun Life (U.S.) began to use "Sun Life (U.S.)" long before SunAmerica or SLIA began to use "Sun Life U.S.A." By reason of the extensive and continuous use by Sun Life (U.S.) of the "Sun Life (U.S.)" name and mark in printed materials distributed to the public and in oral communications to the public, "Sun Life (U.S.)" has become identified with_Sun Life Assurance Company of Canada (U.S.) as a symbol of the company and of the source and origin of its products and services.

29. Despite their knowledge of the prior usage of "Sun Life (U.S.)" by Sun Life (U.S.) to identify itself and its products and services, SunAmerica and SLIA thereafter began using the confusingly similar name and mark "Sun Life U.S.A." to identify SunAmerica and its subsidiaries and to advertise their products and services of the same type as those identified by the mark "Sun Life (U.S.)." Sun Life (U.S.) is the prior user of "Sun Life (U.S.)" in the fields of financial and insurance services, and usage by SunAmerica and SLIA of "Sun Life U.S.A." creates a likelihood of confusion, mistake, and deception regarding the source, origin, and sponsorship of the products and services of both parties.

30. Counterdefendants have engaged in the foregoing activities in a manner calculated to misdescribe and misrepresent their identity and origin and that of their products and services and to falsely imply an association, connection, or affiliation with Sun Life (U.S.) and Sun Life (U.S.)'s products and services with knowledge that confusion and deception of the public inevitably would result from such activities.

31. The foregoing activities of counterdefendants in connection with the advertising, marketing, and sale of their products and services in interstate commerce constitute false designations of origin, false descriptions, and false representations regarding the source, authorization, and sponsorship of their products and services, and are calculated to cause confusion and mistake and to deceive consumers and the public as to the true identity, affiliation, origin, and sponsorship of the parties and their respective products and services in violation of section 43(a) of the Lanham Act, 15 U.S.C. § 1125(a).

32. Counterdefendants' acts of unfair competition are causing and are likely to continue to cause substantial injury to the public and to counterclaimants Sun Life and Sun Life (U.S.), and counterclaimants are entitled to injunctive relief and to recover damages, costs, and reasonable attorneys' fees pursuant to sections 34, 35, and 43(a) of the Lanham Act, 15 U.S.C. §§ 1116, 1117, and 1125(a).

Count II

Breach of Contract

33. Counterclaimants repeat and incorporate by reference all of the allegations set forth in paragraphs 1 through 31 above as if fully set forth herein.

34. As alleged in paragraph 16, Sun Life and SunAmerica entered into a written Settlement Agreement on May 30, 1980. The Agreement was made by these parties on behalf of themselves and their "allied, associated and affiliated companies." Sun Life (U.S.) is and was at the time an affiliated company of Sun Life. SLIA is and was at the time an affiliated company of SunAmerica. Accordingly, the Agreement is binding on both SunAmerica and SLIA.

35. The Agreement arose out of the objections raised by counterclaimants in 1978 to SunAmerica's use of its first "S" mark and the name "Sun Life Group," as described in paragraphs 13–16 above.

36. Paragraph 15 of that Agreement provides:

"15. The Parties shall forever refrain and forebear from commencing, instituting, prosecuting, or participating in, either as a named or unnamed party, any lawsuit, action or other proceeding against any of the par ties hereinabove released, based on any claim or cause of action hereinabove released *or based on the use of any service mark and/or corporate name herein consented to and agree that this Agreement may be pleaded az a full and complete defense to, and may be used as a basis for an injunction against any such action, lawsuit or other prose-cuted or attempted by anyone."* (Emphasis added).

37. Insofar as the claims asserted by plaintiffs in this action are based, in part, on SunAmerica's use of the mark and/or name "Sun Life Group of America," they fall within the category of claims that are barred by paragraph 15 of the Agreement.

38. SunAmerica and SLIA are "Parties" to the Agreement, or successors or assigns of parties within the meaning of paragraph 19 of the Agreement, which provides:

"19. This Agreement shall bind and inure to the benefit of the parties and their respective successors and assigns."

39. The action commenced by the filing of the Complaint herein is a "lawsuit action or other proceeding" within the meaning of those words in paragraph 15 of the Agreement.

40. Paragraph 13 of the Agreement releases Sun Life and its allied, associated and affiliated companies from certain claims and causes of action defined therein. Sun Life and Sun Life (U.S.) are therefore "parties hereinabove released" within the meaning of those words in paragraph 15 of the Agreement.

41. In paragraph 13 of the Agreement, Sun Life "consents to" the use by SunAmerica of "Sun Life Group of America" as a corporate name and/or service mark. "Sun Life Group of America" is therefore a "service mark and/or corporate name herein consented to" within the meaning of those words in paragraph 15 of the Agreement.

42. The action commenced by the filing of the Complaint herein is an action based, in part, on the use by SunAmerica of the name and mark "Sun Life Group of America." The claims asserted in Counts I, V, VI, and VII of the Complaint against Sun Life (U.S.)'s use of "Sun Life (U.S.)" are, for example, based in whole or in part on SunAmerica's use of "Sun Life Group of America," and the claims asserted *in* Count IV for cancellation of defendants' federal registrations for marks incorporating "Sun" or "Sun Life" are likewise based in whole or in part on SunAmerica's use of "Sun Life Group of America."

43. When Sun Life entered into the Agreement of May 30, 1980 and thereby "consented to" SunAmerica's use of "Sun Life Group of America," it did so on the understanding, as reflected in paragraph 15 of the Agreement, that SunAmerica could not thereafter assert its use of "Sun Life Group of America" as a basis for challenging the validity or use of names or marks that Sun Life or Sun Life (U.S.) was using at the time. The names and marks that Sun Life and/or Sun Life (U.S.) were using at the time, the use and validity of which SunAmerica has nevertheless

challenged in the Complaint on the basis of its use of "Sun Life Group of America," are: "Sun Life (U.S.)," "Sun Fund," "Sun Fund" (plus design), "SunPlan," and "Follow The Sun For Life."

44. Inasmuch as the Complaint challenges the validity and use by Sun Life and Sun Life (U.S.) of the foregoing names and marks on the basis of SunAmerica's use of "Sun Life Group of America," counterdefendants have, by filing the Complaint, breached paragraph 15 of the May 30, 1980, Agreement to the irreparable injury of Sun Life and Sun Life (U.S.). Said breach of the Agreement has damaged, is damaging, and, unless enjoined, will continue to damage counterclaimants Sun Life and Sun Life (U.S.).

45. Paragraph 15 of the Agreement provides that the Agreement "may be pleaded as a full and complete defense to, and may be used as a basis for an injunction against any such action, lawsuit or other proceeding" which is filed in violation of said paragraph 15 of the Agreement. In addition to recovering their damages and costs resulting from said breach of the Agreement, counterclaimants are accordingly entitled to an injunction against further prosecution of the Complaint in this action insofar as it asserts claims in violation of paragraph 15 of the Agreement.

46. Paragraph 11 of the Agreement provides:

"11. In the event of litigation resulting from a breach of the terms of this Agreement, the prevailing party shall be entitled to recover reasonable attorneys' fees incurred in the prosecution of such litigation."

47. The Complaint and the Counterclaim in this action constitute "litigation resulting from a breach of the terms of this Agreement" within the meaning of those words in paragraph 11 thereof. Accordingly, after prevailing in this litigation, counterclaimants will also be entitled to recover their reasonable attorneys' fees incurred in the prosecution of the litigation.

Count III

Cancellation of Federally Registered Service mark

48. Sun Life and Sun Life (U.S.) repeat and incorporate by reference all of the allegations set forth in paragraphs 1 through 46 above as if fully set forth herein.

49. SunAmerica has obtained federal registration of its stylized "S" service mark as federal registration no. 1,218,580. The stylized "S" mark

registered as federal registration no. 1,218,580 is lined for the colors brown and gold. SunAmerica's registration of its stylized "S" mark is accordingly limited to the mark depicted in the colors brown and gold.

50. SunAmerica has abandoned the stylized "S" logo registered as federal registration no. 1,218,580 by failing to use the mark as registered.

51. SunAmerica had abandoned, and on information and belief, knew it had abandoned, the stylized "S" logo registered as federal registration no. 1,218,580 when SunAmerica filed the affidavit under section 15 of the Lanham Act, 15 U.S.C. § 1065, required to obtain the incontestable right to use the stylized "S" logo registered as federal registration no. 1,218,580. On information and belief, SunAmerica therefore obtained certification of the incontestable right to use this mark by fraud.

52. SunAmerica and SLIA have knowingly and willfully affixed the federal registration symbol, a letter "R" within a circle, to depictions of their stylized "S" mark in colors other than brown and gold, despite the fact that SunAmerica's registration of the stylized "S" mark is limited to the colors brown and gold, in a deliberate effort to mislead and deceive the public, consumers, and persons considering registration or use of a stylized "S" mark, in violation of section 29 of the Lanham Act, 15 U.S.C. § 1111.

53. Pursuant to section 14(c) of the Lanham Act, 15 U.S.C. § 1064(c), SunAmerica's federal registration no. 1,218,580 should be cancelled on the grounds of abandonment, fraud, misrepresentation and misuse.

Common Law Service Mark Infringement
Common Law and Statutory Unfair Competition

54. Counterclaimants repeat and incorporate by reference all of the allegations set forth in paragraphs 1 through 52 above as if fully set forth herein.

55. Counterdefendants have engaged in the foregoing activities in a manner calculated to misdescribe and misrepresent their identity and origin and that of their products and services and to falsely imply an association, connection, or affiliation with Sun Life (U.S.) and Sun Life (U.S.)'s products and services with knowledge that confusion and deception of the public inevitably would result from such activities.

56. The conduct of counterdefendants herein described violates O.C.G.A. § 23-2-55 as an attempt to encroach on the business of Sun Life and Sun Life (U.S.) with intent to deceive and mislead the public and constitutes fraud, unfair competition and common-law service mark infringement. Such conduct, for which counterclaimants have no

adequate remedy at law, has created and will continue to create a likelihood of confusion to the injury of Sun Life and Sun Life (U.S.) unless restrained by this Court.

Deceptive Trade Practices

57. Counterclaimants repeat and incorporate by reference all of the allegations set forth in paragraphs 1 through 55 above as if fully set forth herein.
58. Counterdefendants have engaged in deceptive trade practices in violation of the Georgia Uniform Deceptive Trade Practices Act, O.C.G.A. § 10-1-370 et seq., by the conduct described above. Through such conduct counterdefendants have passed off their products and services as those of Sun Life and Sun Life (U.S.); have caused likelihood of confusion or misunderstanding as to the source, sponsorship, or approval of those products and services; have caused likelihood of confusion or misunderstanding as to the affiliation, connection, or association of SunAmerica and SLIA with Sun Life and Sun Life (U.S.); have represented that counterdefendants' products and services have the sponsorship or approval of counterclaimants which they do not have or that counterdefendants have an affiliation or connection with counterclaimants that they do not have; and have engaged in conduct which
59. similarly creates a likelihood of confusion or of misunderstanding of the public.
60. The deceptive practices of counterdefendants are causing and will continue to cause substantial injury to counterclaimants Sun Life and Sun Life (U.S.), and counterclaimants are accordingly entitled to injunctive relief under O.C.G.A. § 10-1-373(a). Counterclaimants are entitled also to an award of costs and attorneys' fees under O.C.G.A. § 10-1-373(b)(2), because the conduct complained of was willful, counterdefendants having known it to be deceptive.

Count VI

False Advertising

61. Counterclaimants repeat and incorporate by reference all of the allegations set forth in paragraphs 1 through 58 above as if fully set forth herein.

62. Counterdefendants have engaged in false or fraudulent advertising in violation of O.C.G.A. §§ 10-1-421 and 10-1-423 by reason of the acts set forth above.

63. Counterclaimants have been injured and will continue to be injured by the false advertising of counterdefendants and are entitled to injunctive relief under O.C.G.A. § 10-1-423.

WHEREFORE, Sun Life and Sun Life *(U.S.)* respectfully request that this Court enter judgment in their favor and grant them the following relief:

A. Cancellation of SunAmerica's federal registration of its stylized "S" service mark, registration no. 1,218,580.

B. A permanent injunction enjoining SunAmerica, SLIA, their affiliates, associates, agents, employees, servants, and those in active concert or participation with them, from:
   1. Using the names or marks "Sun Life U.S.A.," "Sun Life U.S.," "Sun U.S.A.," or "Sun U.S." in any oral, written, or audiovisual communication to the public;
   2. Instituting or prosecuting any lawsuit, action, or other proceeding against Sun Life or Sun. Life (U.S.) based in whole or in part on their use of the service mark or name "Sun Life Group of America" in violation of the Agreement of May 30, 1980, between the parties, including but not limited to the continued prosecution by counterdefendants of the claims asserted in the Complaint herein in violation of said Agreement;
   3. Using the federal registration symbol or any version or imitation thereof in conjunction with any trade name, trademark, or service mark as to which no federal registration has issued;
   4. Asserting or in any way representing, either expressly or by implication, in any advertising or promotional materials or in any oral, written, or audiovisual communication to the pUblic, that SunAmerica, SLIA, their affiliates, or their products and services are in any way connected or affiliated with, or authorized, sponsored, or endorsed by, Sun Life, Sun Life (U.S.) or their affiliates; and
   5. Passing off or attempting to pass off their products and services as those of Sun Life, Sun Life (U.S.) or their affiliates.

C. Damages in an amount to be determined.

D. An award of costs, expenses, and attorneys' fees incurred by Sun Life and Sun Life (U.S.) in defending against the Complaint herein and in prosecuting this Counterclaim.

E. A declaration that this is an "exceptional case" and an award of attorneys' fees pursuant to Section 35 of the Lanham Act, 15 U.S.C. § 1117, on account of the willful, wanton, and persistently irresponsible conduct of SunAmerica and SLIA.

F. An award of attorneys' fees and costs pursuant to O.C.G.A. § 10-1-373(b)(2).

G. Such further and additional relief as the Court deems just and proper.

CHAPTER

5

Preliminary Injunction and TRO

The harm in trademark cases often is irreparable because it is harm to the goodwill in a brand, an intangible asset that is difficult to give a monetary value. Clients recognize this and often want immediate action to protect their brands. The Lanham Act provides for such relief.

The most common manner for counsel to obtain expedited relief is to seek a temporary restraining order (TRO) or a preliminary injunction. In trademark cases, these types of motions are routinely granted where the merits, at the initial stage of litigation, warrant preservation of the status quo. In counterfeiting cases, this is especially important because of the potential harm to the public. Both of these types of motions can, and often do, result in minitrials with live witnesses and evidence, although under standards that are more lax than at trial on the merits, given the usually short amount of time the parties have to prepare for hearings on such motions.

Examples of situations requiring immediate relief include counterfeiting, the introduction of an allegedly infringing marketing campaign, potential divulgence of trade secrets, potential publication of a work that will harm the reputation of a client, and potential release of an infringing product that could overwhelm the market for the senior user's/plaintiff's products.

Application for Temporary Restraining Order, Expedited Discovery, Seizure of Counterfeit Goods and Recall

United States District Court Central District of California Western Division

NEW BEVERAGE, INC., a North Carolina corporation, and SUI CORPORATION, a Delaware corporation, Plaintiffs, vs. STASH SAFE WORLD, a California corporation, and DAVID KONG, an individual, Defendants.	Case No. APPLICATION FOR TEMPORARY RESTRAINING ORDER, ORDER FOR EXPEDITED DISCOVERY, INCLUDING A REQUEST FOR ENTRY ONTO DEFENDANTS' PREMISES FOR INSPECTION AND A RECALL, AND ORDER TO SHOW CAUSE RE PRELIMINARY INJUNCTION

In accordance with Section 32 of the Lanham Act, 15 U.S.C. §§ 1114, Rule 65 of the Federal Rules of Civil Procedure and Central District of California Local Rule 65, Plaintiff, New Beverage Inc. ("NBI"), and SUI Corporation ("SUI") SUI(SUINBI and SUI hereinafter collectively referred to as "Plaintiffs"), move this Court for a temporary restraining order and request a hearing on the entry of a preliminary injunction against Defendants, Stash Safe World and David Kong (collectively, "Defendants"), in the form of the proposed Order attached hereto. This order will stop the manufacture, advertising, and sale of:

A. Defendants' infringing SUIbottle safe products; and
B. Defendants' infringing can safe products.

Plaintiffs seek immediate relief because, before the matter can be fully heard and adjudicated, immediate and irreparable injury, loss, and damage will result to Plaintiffs in the form of:

A. confusion in the marketplace as to the source of Defendants' bottle safes and can safes bearing SUIPlaintiffs' trademarks;
B. tarnishment of NBI's business reputation and tarnishment and dilution of the famous NBI trademarks;
C. harm to the goodwill Plaintiffs have in the federally registered NBI and SUI trademarks;
D. SUISUIunfair competition with Plaintiffs.

Plaintiffs further support this motion through the specific facts recited in the memorandum of law, declarations, and exhibits submitted herewith, and the complaint filed in this action. Plaintiffs are likely to succeed on the merits in showing that:

A. Defendants are infringing the SUINBI and SUI marks in connection with the manufacture, advertising and sale of their can safe and bottle safe products;
B. Defendants' aforesaid acts are diluting and tarnishing the NBI marks and are tarnishing NBI's business reputation; and
C. Defendants unfairly compete with Plaintiffs.

In addition, Plaintiffs allege that:

A. immediate and irreparable injury will occur if Defendants are not restrained from these acts;
B. the harm to Plaintiffs of denying the order outweighs any harm to Defendants' legitimate interests; and
C. harm to the public interest will occur if Defendants are not restrained.

In particular, Plaintiffs request that the Court temporarily restrain and enjoin Stash Safe World and David Kong and their agents, servants, employees, officers, attorneys, successors and assigns and all persons in active concert or participation with them, from:

A. manufacturing, distributing, selling, offering for sale, holding for sale, advertising, hiding or destroying products consisting of bottle safes, can safes or any other concealment devices bearing the NBI trademarks, SUIany colorable imitations thereof, or any other trademark owned by Plaintiffs (hereinafter, "Infringing Safes");
B. doing any other act or thing likely to confuse, mislead or deceive members of the public that the Infringing Safes emanate from Plaintiffs or are connected with, licensed, sponsored or approved by Plaintiffs;
C. destroying, moving, concealing, distributing or otherwise disposing of any documents, equipment, machinery or things relating to the manufacturing, sale, distribution, advertising or promotion of the Infringing Safes, including documents and equipment relating to Defendants' manufacture of the Infringing Safes, the identity of other sources or manufacturers of the Infringing Safes, Defendants' distribution, sale, advertising and promotion of the Infringing Safes and documents relating to Defendants' purchase or receipt of bottles, cans, labels or packaging bearing the SUIPlaintiffs' marks; such documents shall consist of any writings, correspondence, notes, books, electronically stored information, e-mail messages, memoranda, invoices, purchase orders, receipts, pamphlets, reports, account books,

rolodex information, calendars, photographs, slides, videotapes, films, drawings, sketches, illustrative materials, magnetic recording tapes, computer records or data, websites, microfilm and other storage means by which information is retained in retrievable form, and all other materials whether printed, typewritten, handwritten, recorded or reproduced by any process and whether in final or draft form; and such machinery consists of any article of production by which the Infringing Safes are made, altered, fashioned or put into final form;

D. contacting, or having someone else contact, any other sources, importers, sellers, manufacturers or distributors of bottle safes or can safes bearing the SUI Plaintiffs' trademarks, or any source of Defendants' bottles, cans, labels or other components of the Infringing Safes bearing the SUI Plaintiffs' trademarks until further order of this Court;

E. assisting, aiding or abetting any other person or business entity in engaging in any of the activities prohibited in subparagraphs (a) through (d) above; and

F. to stop the spread of the Infringing Safes and to effectuate the Court's order, Plaintiffs also request this Court for an order that Defendants recall the Infringing Safes from their customers, by written notice sent via United States mail within seven (7) days from the date Defendants are ordered to comply with Plaintiffs' request, instructing Defendants' customers not to sell the Infringing Safes, indicating that Defendants will refund to them the cost of the Infringing Safes, requiring them to return the Infringing Safes to Defendants' location at Defendants' expense, and an order that requires the Defendants to execute a declaration confirming this recall.

In accordance with Section 34 of the Lanham Act, 15 U.S.C. § 1116(a), and Rule 65 of the Federal Rules of Civil Procedure, Plaintiffs further move this Court to enter a preliminary injunction upon the expiration of the temporary restraining order to supersede the previously entered temporary restraining order and that the scope and terms of said preliminary injunction be the same as those of this previously entered temporary restraining order.

Plaintiffs also move this Court, in accordance with Rules 26, 30, and 34 of the Federal Rules of Civil Procedure, to permit Plaintiffs to take expedited discovery from Defendants in anticipation of any preliminary injunction hearing with regard to, among other things, its manufacture, distribution and sale of Infringing Safes and other sources for the Infringing Safes, and to require Defendants to:

A. pursuant to the notices attached hereto as Exhibit "A," within seven (7) days after the date they have been ordered to comply, produce for entry, inspection, inventorying and photographing, the areas of Defendants' premises where they manufacture, sell or store the Infringing Safes for the purpose of inventorying the Infringing Safes, and Defendants shall provide access to and passwords for Defendants' computers, computer databases, files and hard drives used to store information pertaining to their business for the purpose of allowing the inspection and copying of any electronically stored information relating to the Infringing Safes;

B. produce documents and things responsive to the document requests, attached hereto as Exhibit "B," and produce the requested materials within ten (10) days after the date Defendants have been ordered to comply and have received Plaintiffs' documents requests;

C. produce Rule 30(b)(6) designees of Stash Safe World, Inc., as directed in Plaintiffs' deposition notice, attached hereto as Exhibit "C," beginning on a date fourteen (14) days after Defendants have been ordered to comply and have received Plaintiffs' notice;

D. produce David Kong as directed in Plaintiffs' deposition notice, attached hereto as Exhibit "D," beginning on a date fourteen (14) days after Defendants have been ordered to comply and have received Plaintiffs' notice; and

E. respond to any supplemental interrogatories, document requests or deposition notices from Plaintiffs within ten (10) days of service.

Plaintiffs request this expedited discovery in addition to any other discovery available under the Federal Rules of Civil Procedure and Local Rules of the United States District Court for the Central District of California. Plaintiffs also request that they be allowed to serve expedited discovery upon any persons that Plaintiffs discover are acting in concert with Defendants, including, but not limited to, any other manufacturers or sources for the Infringing Safes.

Based on the evidence presented to this Court, Plaintiffs respectfully submit that they have shown good cause for the immediate relief requested under Central District of California Local Rule 65 through this Application for Temporary Restraining Order, Order for Expedited Discovery and a Recall, and Request for a Preliminary Injunction.

III. Memorandum of Points and Authorities

A. Introduction

This action follows an extensive investigation conducted by Plaintiffs, during which the Defendants relocated, and recently added to their distribution network, and expanded their infringing business operations into retail drug paraphernalia channels. Plaintiffs seek an immediate injunction to stop the irreparable harm caused by Defendants' marketing and sale of the following products:

- bottle and can safes bearing NBI's famous NBI trademarks (the "NBINBI marks"); and

- bottle safes bearing SUISUI's federally registered SUISUI trademarks (the "SUISUI marks"; the NBINBI marks and the SUISUI marks are referred to herein, collectively, as the "Plaintiffs' marks").

Defendants' bottle and can safes frequently are used to conceal illicit narcotics. Indeed, the newest catalog that the Defendants have issued in connection with the recent expansion of their operations underscores the relationship between these products and the drug culture and confirms their utility to the drug trade. The bottle safes have unidentified liquids in them that are not Plaintiffs' authorized beverages. Consumers may mistakenly ingest these liquids. The can safes have sharp edges that can cut consumers.

Plaintiffs also seek a recall to stop the distribution of these unauthorized products. Finally, Plaintiffs request this immediate order to allow for expedited discovery, including the inspection of Defendants' premises, to prevent Defendants and their agents from destroying evidence relating to their illegal conduct and to prepare for the preliminary injunction hearing.

B. Statement of Facts

1. NBI's Trademarks and Products

NBI is engaged in the manufacture and marketing of beverages and related products throughout the United States and the world. *See* Declaration of Trademark CounselIn-house Trademark Counsel ("Trademark CounselTrademark Counsel Decl."), ¶¶ 3, 6 and 13. NBI has adopted and made continuous use of the NBI marks and variations on these marks in connection with the manufacture, sale and advertising of soft drinks and purified drinking water. Trademark Counsel Decl., ¶ 4. NBI has registered the NBI marks for soft drinks and for drinking water (the "NBI products") in the United States Patent and Trademark Office. Trademark Counsel Decl., ¶ 5.

The NBI products have a reputation for quality maintained through a strict quality control program. *See* Declaration of Consumer Experience DirectorDirector of Consumer Experience ("Consumer Experience Director Decl."), ¶¶ 4–5. NBI licenses the NBI marks for a wide variety of products. Trademark Counsel Decl., ¶ 6. This licensing program is subject to stringent quality control requirements. Trademark Counsel Decl., ¶¶ 7–8. NBI does not license the NBI marks for use on bottle safes, can safes or other concealment devices. Trademark Counsel Decl., ¶ 9.

3. SUI's Trademarks and Products

SUI is a wholly owned subsidiary of NBI and is engaged in the manufacture and marketing of beverages and related products throughout the United States. Trademark Counsel Decl., ¶¶ 17–18. SUI has registered its SUISUI trademarks for soft drinks (the "SUI products") in the United States Patent and Trademark Office. Trademark Counsel Decl., ¶ 19.

The SUI products have a reputation for quality maintained through a strict quality control program. Consumer Experience Director Decl., ¶ ¶ 14–15. SUI does not license the SUISUI marks for use on bottle safes or can safes or other concealment devices. Trademark Counsel Decl., ¶ 20.

a) Defendants' Actions

After an extensive investigation that included multiple purchases of Infringing Safes to confirm that Defendants were significant distributors and to confirm their changes in location and business associates, Plaintiffs determined that Defendants are in the business of manufacturing, marketing and selling bottle safes and can safes created from other companies' original packaging that bear the other companies' trademarks. *See* Declaration of Private Investigator ("Investigator Decl."), ¶ ¶ 3–16; *see also* Defendants' catalog, attached to the Investigator Decl. as Exhibits 3 and 10. As part of their business, Defendants manufacture, advertise and sell bottle safes and can safes that bear the Plaintiffs' marks which are manufactured from the Plaintiffs' actual products and packaging ("Infringing Bottle Safes" and "Infringing Can Safes," respectively, collectively referred to herein as "Infringing Safes"). Investigator Decl., ¶ ¶ 5–16. Defendants distribute and sell the Infringing Safes to wholesale distributors and directly to consumers at its Los Angeles warehouse. Investigator Decl., ¶ ¶ 8–9, 11 and 14–16. More recently, Defendants have promoted the Infringing Safes to retailers and consumers of pipes, grinders and other specialized drug paraphernalia and equipment. *See* Investigator Decl., Exhibit 3.

The Infringing Safes are manufactured by converting Plaintiffs' genuine products into diversionary concealment devices that contain hidden compartments. *See* Declaration of Product Analyst ("Product Analyst Decl."), ¶ ¶ 6, 7, 10, 11, and 16–19. They are outwardly identical to Plaintiffs' products. *See* Product Analyst Decl., ¶ ¶ 7, 11, and 19. Even when handled, the Infringing Safes are indistinguishable from the legitimate products in appearance and weight. Product Analyst Decl., ¶ ¶ 5-7, 10–11, and 19.

The Infringing Safes contain information about NBI, including a telephone number at which to contact NBI, but contain no references to Defendants nor to the fact that the Infringing Safes are not authorized by NBI. Product Analyst Decl., ¶ ¶ 8 and 20–22. Consumers who encounter the Infringing Safes, especially those consumers who encounter them post-sale, are therefore likely to mistakenly believe that these products are authorized by NBI. Consumer Experience Director Decl., ¶ 17.

The modification process for the Infringing Bottle Safes includes the use of unidentified liquids that simulate the look of Plaintiffs' legitimate soft drinks and drinking water, but that, upon closer inspection, contain a pungent odor and other properties that are not consistent with Plaintiffs' legitimate soft drinks and water. Product Analyst Decl., ¶¶ 8 and 20–22. Consumers who imbibe the liquids are likely to be alarmed at their vile taste and blame Plaintiffs. Consumer Experience Director Decl., ¶ 19.

The modification process for the Infringing Can Safes creates sharp edges where the Infringing Can Safe lid screws into the can body. Product Analyst Decl., ¶ 12. These sharp edges can cut people who use the products. *Id.* As part of Plaintiffs' quality control procedures, all cans undergo a thorough rinsing process to guard against contamination and ensure product safety. Product Analyst Decl., ¶ 13. The Infringing Can Safes do not go through this quality control process to sterilize them during the modification process. *Id.*

C. Law Enforcement Concern With the Infringing Safes

Defendants' Infringing Safes are associated with the use and concealment of illicit narcotics. *See* DEA Factsheet, "Drug Paraphernalia: Tools of the Illegal Drug Trade" <www.dea.gov/concern/paraphernaliafact.html> attached hereto as Exhibit "F." The Defendants' recent expansion into new distribution channels confirms and exploits this association by promoting the Infringing Safes alongside pipes, grinders and other specialized drug paraphernalia and equipment. *See* catalog attached to Investigator Decl. as Exhibit "3." California and the United States Drug Enforcement Agency recognize that drug users often employ these devices to conceal their possession of illegal drugs and have identified such devices and other products as illegal drug paraphernalia. *See* CAL. HEALTH & SAFETY CODE § 11014.5 ("drug paraphernalia" defined to include "Containers and other objects designed for use or marketed for use in storing or concealing controlled substances.") and Exhibit F; *see also* 21 U.S.C. § 863(d) (defining "drug paraphernalia" to include products designed or intended for "concealing" controlled substances). California prohibits the sale of drug paraphernalia, including bottle and can safes intended for use as storage or concealment of controlled substances. *See* CAL. HEALTH & SAFETY CODE § 11364.7 (sale of drug paraphernalia is misdemeanor).

Additionally, Defendants' Infringing Safes are commonly referred to as "stash bottles" or "stash cans." "Stash" refers to the fact that these products are used to hide illicit narcotics. *See* MERRIAM WEBSTER'S COLLEGIATE DICTIONARY 1148, (10th ed. 1999), attached hereto as Exhibit "G." Such stash bottles and stash cans of the type sold by Defendants are a concern to law enforcement authorities because they are used to conceal illicit narcotics. *See* Exhibit "F."

Like law enforcement, the public also recognizes concealment devices like the Infringing Safes as tools of the illicit drug trade. *See* articles attached hereto as Exhibit "H."

Defendants' sales of Infringing Safes damage Plaintiffs' goodwill in Plaintiffs' marks. Consumer Experience Director Decl., ¶¶ 16–18 and 20–21. Defendants' conduct also damages Plaintiffs' business reputations. *Id.*

D. Argument

1. Introduction

NBI has obtained temporary restraining orders against infringing bottle and can safes in this jurisdiction as well as others.

2. A Temporary Restraining Order and Recall are Necessary

Courts routinely grant requests for temporary restraining orders under the Lanham Act to stop infringement and dilution of federally registered marks. *See, e.g., Nova Wines, Inc. v. Adler Fels Winery, LLC*, 467 F. Supp. 2d 965, 972 (N.D. Cal. 2006); *Paisa, Inc. v. N & G Auto*, 928 F. Supp. 1004 (C.D. Cal. 1996); *see also Anheuser-Busch, Inc. v. Andy's Sportswear, Inc.*, 40 U.S.P.Q.2d 1542, 1996 U.S. Dist. Lexis 15583 (N.D. Cal. 1996).

A temporary restraining order is the only adequate way to protect the public from the danger posed by Defendants' Infringing Safes and the scourge that such stash products have become to the public, law enforcement, and Plaintiffs.

Plaintiffs also are entitled to an order that Defendants immediately recall their Infringing Safes. "The imposition of a recall requirement is well within the district court's broad powers as a court of equity." *Behnam*, 45 U.S.P.Q.2d 1078, 1094, 1997 U.S. Dist. Lexis 15927 at *56–57 (S.D.N.Y. 1997) *quoting Perfect Fit Indus. Inc. v. Acme Quilting Co., Inc.*, 646 F.2d 800, 805 (2d Cir. 1981). As noted in *Behnam*, Defendants "need only write a letter to [their] . . . customers and pay the cost of the return for customers who comply." *Behnam*, 45 U.S.P.Q.2d at 1094, 1997 U.S. Dist. Lexis 15927 at *57; *see also Andy's Sportswear*, 40 U.S.P.Q.2d 1542, 1996 U.S. Dist. Lexis 15583 (recall granted pending preliminary injunction hearing). A recall would quickly stop any more of Defendants' Infringing Safes from reaching consumers.

E. Plaintiffs Are Entitled to Expedited Discovery, Including an Inspection

Plaintiffs request that this Court enter an order authorizing expedited discovery and an inspection of Defendants' premises. This Court has broad power to permit expedited discovery in this case. Moreover, such discovery is routinely granted in actions involving infringement and unfair competition. *See, e.g., Behnam*, 45 U.S.P.Q.2d at 1094, 1997 U.S. Dist. Lexis 15927 at *58.

Plaintiffs must quickly determine the scope of Defendants' activities to protect the public and Plaintiffs' goodwill. *See NEA Enter. Inc. v. Am. Horse Enter., Inc.*, 211 U.S.P.Q. 109, 111, 1980 U.S. Dist. Lexis 16910 at *8 (N.D. Cal. 1980) (inspection granted).

F. Plaintiffs are Entitled to a Preliminary Injunction

Plaintiffs are entitled to a preliminary injunction because they can demonstrate (1) a combination of probable success on the merits and the possibility of irreparable injury, or (2) the existence of serious questions going to the merits and the balance of the hardships tips sharply in their favor. *GOTO.com. Inc. v. Walt Disney Co.*, 202 F.3d 1199, 1204–05 (9th Cir. 2000); *see also Paisa*, 928 F. Supp. at 1007. "These formulations are not different tests but represent two points on a sliding scale in which the degree of irreparable harm increases as the probability of success on the merits decreases." *Dr. Seuss Enters., L.P. v. Penguin Books USA, Inc.*, 109 F.3d 1394, 1396–97 n.1 (9th Cir. 1997) (citation omitted).

NBI, as well as other trademark owners, have obtained injunctions against the sale of bottle and can safes bearing the trademark owners' marks. *See, e.g., Anheuser-Busch, Inc. v. Meenahan*, Civil Action No. 93-5652 WDK (C.D. Cal. 1994) (Judgment for Permanent Injunction attached hereto as Exhibit I); *Sahni, supra*; *Coca-Cola Co. v. Menendez*, Civil Action File No. 3-93-0989 (M.D. Tenn. 1994) (Agreed Final Judgment and Permanent Injunction attached hereto as Exhibit J). The facts of this case are nearly identical to the cases cited above.

In a prior case similar to this one, the Northern District of Georgia granted a permanent injunction prohibiting defendants from manufacturing, advertising, distributing and selling bottle safes and can safes bearing the NBI marks. The court found that defendants' use of the NBI marks on such safes was likely to cause confusion because "consumers will mistakenly believe either that NBI is the source of defendants' Infringing Safes or that NBI authorized them." Additionally, the court found that defendants' bottle safes and can safes bearing NBI marks caused dilution because, like Defendants, the defendant "use[d] the NBI marks on goods commonly associated with the concealment of illicit narcotics." *Id.* at *12. Thus, Plaintiffs also are entitled to a preliminary injunction here.

a) Plaintiffs Have a Substantial Likelihood of Succeeding on the Merits of Their Claims

i) Trademark Infringement and Unfair Competition Under Federal and California Law

Plaintiffs will prevail on their trademark infringement and unfair competition claims under both federal and California law because Defendants have used Plaintiffs' marks in commerce without Plaintiffs' consent, and Defendants' use of those marks is likely to deceive, cause confusion, or result in mistake by consumers.

IV. Plaintiffs' Marks

A. The NBINBI marks

NBI's incontestable registrations for the NBI marks (Reg. Nos. XXX,XXX; and Y,YYY,YYY) constitute conclusive evidence of the validity of these marks and NBI's exclusive right to use them. 15 U.S.C. §§ 1065 and 1115(b). The other registrations for the NBI marks constitute *prima facie* evidence of the validity of the NBI marks covered by them and of NBI's ownership of and exclusive right to use these marks for the listed goods. 15 U.S.C. § 1057(b).

The NBI marks are famous and entitled to the widest scope of protection. Consumer Experience Director Decl., ¶ 3; *See James Burrough Ltd. v. Sign of the Beefeater, Inc.*, 540 F.2d 266, 276 (7th Cir. 1976) (famous marks have a wide scope of protection).

B. The SUI Marks

SUI's registrations for the SUI marks are valid and subsisting, and constitute prima facie evidence of the validity of the SUI marks covered by them and of SUI's ownership of and exclusive right to use these marks for the listed goods. 15 U.S.C § 1057(b).

V. Defendants' Conduct

A. Defendants' Infringing Safes

Defendants violate the Lanham Act through their use of the NBI and SUI marks in connection with the manufacture, marketing and sale of bottle safes and through their use of the NBI marks in connection with the manufacture, marketing and sale of can safes. 15 U.S.C. § 1114(1)(a). The Infringing Safes are made from Plaintiffs' actual products and look like Plaintiffs' products because the Infringing Safes are meant to dupe people into believing that they are Plaintiffs' actual products.

B. Defendants' Infringing Safes are Likely to Confuse Consumers

To establish their federal and state trademark infringement and unfair competition claims, Plaintiffs also can show a likelihood of confusion stemming from Defendants' use of Plaintiffs' marks. 15 U.S.C. §§ 1114, 1125; CAL. BUS. & PROF. CODE § 14320; *see also Malaytex USA, Inc. v. Colonial Surgical Supply, Inc.*, 44 U.S.P.Q.2d 1291 (C.D. Cal. 1997). Likelihood of confusion depends upon the determination of the following factors: (1) the similarity of the marks, (2) the relatedness of the two companies' goods, (3) the marketing channel used, (4) the strength of plaintiff's marks, (5) defendants' intent in selecting their marks, (6) evidence of actual confusion, (7) the likelihood of expansion into other markets, and (8) the degree of care likely to be exercised by purchasers. *GOTO.com, Inc.*, 202 F.3d at 1205; *AMF Inc. v. Sleekcraft Boats*, 599 F.2d 341, 348–49 (9th Cir. 1979). In recent cases involving bottle safes and can safes bearing NBI marks, the Central District of California found a likelihood of confusion. *See also Rolex Watch, U.S.A., Inc. v. Michel Co.*, 179 F.3d 704, 707 (9th Cir. 1999) (upholding an injunction against the sale of reconditioned watches under the mark ROLEX because these watches contained non-ROLEX parts).

Furthermore, Defendants are not merely reselling Plaintiffs' genuine product, but are creating wholly new products from Plaintiffs' packaging and selling them as Infringing Safes. *See, e.g., Davidoff & CIE, SA v. PLD Int'l Corp.*, 263 F.3d 1297 (11th Cir. 2001) (defendant's etching off of batch codes from Davidoff's fragrance bottles created a materially different product and constituted infringement warranting injunctive relief).

Likelihood of confusion exists not only among those who directly purchase Defendants' Infringing Safes, but also among anyone who encounters the products post-sale. *See also Rolex*, 179 F.3d at 707; *Karl Storz Endoscopy-Am., Inc. v. Surgical Techs., Inc.*, 285 F.3d 848, 854 (9th Cir. 2002) (post-sale confusion is as harmful as confusion at time of sale); *H-D Michigan, Inc. v. Biker's Dream, Inc.*, 48 U.S.P.Q.2d 1108, 1111, 1998 U.S. Dist. Lexis 17259 at *9 (C.D. Cal. 1998) (citation omitted). Here, anyone who encounters the Infringing Safes post-sale in households, schools, businesses, or anywhere else, is likely to believe that the Infringing Safes are manufactured or authorized by Plaintiffs.

Defendants' marketing of the Infringing Safes also creates a likelihood of confusion among purchasers who are likely to believe that Plaintiffs license or otherwise authorize these products. NBI licenses the use of the NBI marks for a variety of goods. Consumers could therefore mistakenly assume that NBI has begun producing bottle safes and can safes, or licensing the NBI marks to the producers of these products. *See Gucci Am. Inc. v. Action Activewear, Inc.*, 759 F. Supp. 1060, 1064 (S.D.N.Y. 1991). Even remotely connected products may create confusion as to sponsorship by the trademark owner. *E. Remy Martin & Co., S.A. v. Shaw-Ross Int'l Imports, Inc.*, 756 F.2d 1525, 1530 (11th Cir. 1985). This is especially so given Defendants' obvious intent to trade off of the Plaintiffs' marks.

1. Defendants' Infringing Safes Dilute Plaintiffs' Famous Marks

The Infringing Safes are likely to dilute the famous NBI trademarks. To prove a violation of the Federal Trademark Dilution law, as amended by the Trademark Dilution Revision Act, Plaintiffs must show that 1) the NBI marks are famous because they are widely recognized by the general consuming public of the

United States; 2) Defendants commenced using the NBI marks in commerce after the NBI marks became famous; and 3) Defendants' use of the NBINBI marks and MUG marks is likely to cause dilution by blurring or dilution by tarnishment of the NBINBI marks and MUG marks. 15 U.S.C. § 1125(c); *Nike, Inc. v. Nikepal Int'l, Inc.*, 2007 U.S. Dist. Lexis 66686 at *14–15 (E.D. Cal. Sept. 18, 2007). The test for dilution is similar under California law. *Nike*, 2007 U.S. Dist. Lexis 66686 at *15 n. 7 *citing Jada Toys, Inc. v. Mattel, Inc.*, 496 F.3d 974 (9th Cir. 2007); *Panavision v. Toeppen*, 141 F.3d 1316, 1324 (9th Cir. 1998); CAL. BUS. & PROF. CODE § 14330; *see also H-D Michigan v. Bikers Dream*, 48 U.S.P.Q.2d at 1112, 1998 U.S. Dist. Lexis 17259 at *13 (citation omitted) ("Under California's anti-dilution statute, if a plaintiff can show the 'likelihood of injury to business reputation or of dilution of the distinctive qualify of a mark' that plaintiff is entitled to injunctive relief").

In *H-D Michigan v. Bikers Dream*, defendants affixed plaintiff's model name trademarks onto non-Harley Davidson products. 48 U.S.P.Q.2d 1108, 1112, 1998 U.S. Dist. Lexis 17259 at *13 (C.D. Cal. 1998) (decided under a likelihood of dilution standard). The court found that such use of plaintiff's mark by defendant was likely to dilute the distinctive quality of those marks. Here, Defendants' use of the NBI marks on Infringing Safes dilutes the distinctiveness of NBI's famous marks. *See Andy's Sportswear*, 40 U.S.P.Q.2d 1542, 1996 U.S. Dist. Lexis 15583 (N.D. Cal. 1996) (granting TRO).

The relief Plaintiffs seek in this motion is supported by the injunctions entered against other marketers of bottle safes and can safes in this judicial district and others. *See [STRING CITE]*. Moreover, Defendants' use of the NBI marks exacerbates the potential for dilution by suggesting that more than one company can use these marks. *See Nike*, 2007 U.S. Dist. Lexis 66686 at *26 (defendant's use of NIKEPAL likely to dilute famous NIKE mark because escalating erosion of the famous NIKE mark would diminish its ability to serve as a source identifier).

The pervasive use of concealment devices like the Infringing Safes to hide illicit narcotics further supports NBI's tarnishment claims. *See Sahni*, 2007 U.S. Dist. Lexis 53768 at *12; *Coca-Cola v. Gemini Rising, Inc.*, 346 F. Supp. 1183 (E.D.N.Y 1972) (enjoining defendants' use of "Enjoy Cocaine" in famous Coca-Cola script).

2. Defendants are Causing Irreparable Injury to Plaintiffs and the Public

Consumers encountering Defendants' Infringing Safes are likely to become alarmed and angry with Plaintiffs. This irreparable harm to Plaintiffs, as well as the public, supports the grant of a preliminary injunction.

"Once the plaintiff has demonstrated a likelihood of confusion, it is ordinarily presumed that the plaintiff will suffer irreparable harm if injunctive relief is not granted." *Metro Pub. v. San Jose Mercury News*, 987 F.2d 637,

640 (9th Cir. 1993); *see also Sony Computer Entm't Am. Inc. v. GameMasters*, 87 F. Supp. 2d 976, 988 (N.D. Cal. 1999) (irreparable injury presumed where likelihood of success on the merits established). "The fact that plaintiff has had the symbol of its reputation placed in the hands of another is irreparable injury." *Sony*, 87 F. Supp. 2d at 984.

3. The Balance of Hardships Favors Plaintiffs

The sale of the Infringing Safes causes Plaintiffs to suffer more hardship than any harm Defendants would incur from the issuance of the preliminary injunction. Plaintiffs' loss of goodwill would be difficult to compensate in monetary terms. *JayAIR Corp. v. Muka Indus., Inc.*, 33 U.S.P.Q.2d 1304, 1308 (C.D. Cal. 1994) ("any losses caused by a failure to issue an injun–ction at this time would be difficult to fully compensate").

In *Reebok Int'l, Ltd. v. Marnatech Enters. Inc.*, 737 F. Supp. 1515 (C.D. Cal. 1989), the court granted a preliminary injunction in a trademark counterfeiting case and found that "[t]he harm to plaintiffs of denying the requested preliminary injunction outweighs the harm to the legitimate interests of Defendants . . . The equities weigh heavily in favor of plaintiff whose valuable trademarks and reputation are at risk through the counterfeiting activities of the Defendants." 737 F. Supp. at 1516; *see Dr. Seuss*, 109 F.3d at 1406. The balance of hardships here also weighs heavily in Plaintiffs' favor, especially given Defendants' intent to trade off of Plaintiffs' goodwill. Moreover, the only harm to Defendants, who sell many other products, including bottle safes and can safes bearing other trademarks, is the prohibition of their sale of Infringing Safes.

4. The Public Interest Supports Immediate Injunctive Relief

There is a strong public interest in preventing consumer confusion through the issuance of the requested injunctive relief in circumstances like this case. *See, e.g., Ferrellgas Ptnrs., L.P. v. Barrow*, 143 Fed. App'x. 180, 191 (11th Cir. 2005) (the public interest is served by injunctions against trademark infringement because they help to avoid confusion in the marketplace). Consumers and law enforcement are being duped by the Infringing Safes. The Drug Enforcement Agency and other law enforcement recognize these products as illegal drug paraphernalia. Plaintiffs' customers will be alarmed and angry at Plaintiffs' when they encounter Defendants' products. These factors strongly support the granting of the relief requested herein.

III. Conclusion

Plaintiffs are substantially likely to prevail on their claims against Defendants' unlawful conduct, are suffering irreparable injury, and have shown that the balance of harms and the public interest favor the grant of a temporary and preliminary injunction. Accordingly, Plaintiffs respectfully request that this Court enter the temporary restraining order, order for expedited discovery and recall, and the preliminary injunction requested herein.

Proposed Temporary Restraining Order

United States District Court
Central District of California
Western Division

NBI, INC., a North Carolina corporation, SUI CORPORATION, a Delaware corporation, Plaintiffs, vs. STASH SAFE WORLD, a California corporation, and DAVID KONG, an individual, Defendants.	Case No. [PROPOSED] ORDER FOR TEMPORARY RESTRAINING ORDER, ORDER FOR EXPEDITED DISCOVERY, INCLUDING A REQUEST FOR ENTRY ONTO DEFENDANTS' PREMISES FOR INSPECTION, AND A RECALL

This case having been presented to this Court on the ___ day of _____, 2008, upon the motion of Plaintiffs, NBI, Inc. ("NBI") SUI Corporation("SUI"), for a temporary restraining order, order of expedited discovery, including an inspection, and a recall, as well as a request for hearing on a motion for an order to show cause for preliminary injunction, and it appearing from the allegations of the Complaint, the Declarations of Trademark Counsel, Consumer Experience Director, Product Analyst, and Investigator and the accompanying Memorandum of Law that Plaintiffs are entitled to such relief; further appearing that Plaintiffs, their NBI and SUI marks and the public will be irreparably injured by the manufacture, advertising and sale of products by defendants Stash Safe World, Inc., and David Kong (hereinafter, collectively, "Defendants"), consisting of:

a) converted bottles bearing infringing NBI and SUI trademarks but filled with liquids that are not Plaintiffs' products; and

b) converted cans bearing infringing NBI trademarks.

This Court having granted Plaintiffs' motion for a temporary restraining order, order of expedited discovery, including an inspection, and a recall, as well as a request for hearing on a motion for an order to show cause for preliminary injunction with respect to Defendants, and it being further determined from the specific facts recited in the moving papers, memorandum of law, declarations and exhibits that Plaintiffs submitted that Plaintiffs are likely to succeed on the merits in showing that:

a) Defendants infringed the NBI and SUI marks in connection with the manufacture, advertising and sale of bottle safes that contain simulated soft drinks and drinking water; and

b) Defendants infringed the NBI marks in connection with the manufacture, advertising and sale of can safes.

Plaintiffs also are able to show that:

a) immediate and irreparable injury will occur if Defendants are not restrained;
b) the harm to Plaintiffs of denying the Order outweighs the harm to the Defendants' legitimate interests; and
c) harm to the public interest will occur if Defendants are not restrained; it is hereby ORDERED:

Temporary Restraining Order

1. That pending the hearing on _____, 2008, commencing at _____ a.m., unless the date of the hearing is extended by agreement of the parties and/or the Court, Defendants and their agents, servants, employees, officers, attorneys, successors and assigns, and all persons in active concert or participation with them who receive actual notice of such Order, are enjoined and restrained from:
   a) Manufacturing, distributing, selling, offering for sale, advertising or promoting, hiding or destroying, Infringing Safes consisting of bottles, hideaway bottles, stash bottles or bottle safes bearing any of Plaintiffs' trademarks, including the NBI and SUI trademarks or any materials bearing a colorable imitation of these trademarks (hereinafter "Bottle Safes");
   b) Manufacturing, distributing, selling, offering for sale, advertising or promoting, hiding or destroying, Infringing Safes consisting of cans, can safes or stash cans bearing any of Plaintiffs' trademarks, or any materials bearing a colorable imitation of these trademarks (hereinafter "Can Safes");
   c) Doing any other act or thing likely to confuse, mislead or deceive members of the public into believing that Defendants' Bottle Safes or Can Safes (collectively, "Infringing Safes") emanate from, or are connected with, licensed, sponsored or approved by Plaintiffs;
   d) Destroying, moving, hiding, distributing or otherwise disposing of any documents, equipment, machinery or things relating to the manufacturing, sale, distribution, advertising or promotion of the Infringing Safes, including documents and equipment relating to Defendants' manufacture of Infringing Safes, the identity of other sources or manufacturers of Infringing Safes, Defendants' distribution, sale, advertising and promotion of the Infringing Safes and documents relating to Defendants' purchase or receipt of bottles or labels bearing the NBI or SUI marks, or Defendants' purchase and

receipt of cans bearing the NBI marks. It being recognized that such documents shall consist of any writings, correspondence, notes, books, e-mail messages, memoranda, invoices, purchase orders, receipts, pamphlets, reports, account books, rolodex information, calendars, photographs, slides, videotapes, films, drawings, sketches, illustrative materials, magnetic recording tapes, computer records or data, websites, microfilm and other storage means by which information is retained in retrievable form, and all other materials whether printed, typewritten, handwritten, recorded, or reproduced by any process and whether in final or draft form; and it being recognized that such machinery consist of any article of production by which the Infringing Safes are made, altered, fashioned or put into final form;

e) Contacting, or having someone else contact, any other sources or manufacturers of Infringing Safes bearing Plaintiffs' trademarks, or any source of Defendants' bottles, cans or labels or other components of Defendants' Infringing Safes bearing these trademarks until further order of this Court; and

f) Assisting, aiding or abetting any other person or business entity in engaging in any of the activities prohibited in subparagraphs (a) through (e) above;

Bond

9. That a bond in the sum of $_____ be posted to secure the actions taken under this Order;

Service

10. That, sufficient cause having been shown, service of this Order shall be made by overnight mail;

Expedited Discovery

11. That Defendants shall respond to Plaintiffs' discovery requests by:
    a) Permitting Plaintiffs' counsel, persons acting under their supervision and a computer expert, in accordance with Plaintiffs' Request For Entry Onto Defendant's Premises For Inspection Pursuant To FRCP 34 and Order For Expedited Discovery that have been served upon Defendants, entry onto Defendants' premises where the manufacture and sale of the Infringing Safes have taken place, which are located at:
    1. Old Physical Address;
    2. New Physical Address;

       3. Corporate Address; and

       4. any other place that Defendants have manufactured, stored, sold or destroyed the Infringing Safes;

  b) Beginning on a date seven (7) days after the date Defendants have been served with a copy of this Order, or a date mutually agreed upon by the parties, for the purpose of inspecting and photographing the areas of Defendants' premises where they manufacture, sell or store the Infringing Safes for the purpose of inventorying the Infringing Safes, and Defendants shall provide access to and passwords for Defendants' computers, computer databases, files and hard drives used to store information pertaining to their business for the purpose of allowing the inspection and copying of any electronically stored information relating to the Infringing Safes;

  c) Producing documents and things responsive to Plaintiffs' First Requests For Production Of Documents And Things Pursuant To Order For Expedited Discovery that have been served upon Defendants and producing said documents and materials within ten (10) days after the date Defendants have been ordered to comply and have received Plaintiffs' documents requests at the offices of Local Counsel;

  d) Producing David Kong and a 30(b)(6) witness, as directed in Plaintiffs' deposition notices that have been served upon Defendants, beginning on a date fourteen (14) days after the date of this Order, at the offices of Local Counsel; and

  e) Thereafter responding to any supplemental interrogatories, document requests or deposition notices from Plaintiffs within ten (10) days of their service;

12. That Plaintiffs are also hereby permitted to serve expedited discovery requests upon the same terms described above upon any persons that Plaintiffs discover are acting in concert with Defendants, including, but not limited to, any manufacturers or sources of Defendants' Infringing Safes;

Recall

13. That, within seven (7) after the date Defendants have been ordered to comply, Defendants shall send a letter by United States mail, in a form and on a date approved by Plaintiffs, to each of Defendants' customers to whom they have sold Infringing Safes instructing them not to sell these products, indicating that Defendants shall refund to them the cost of these products, and requiring them to return these products to Defendants' location at Defendants' expense;

Preliminary Injunction

14. In accordance with Rule 65(b), that hearing on Plaintiffs' motion for a preliminary injunction shall be held on _____, 2008, at ____ _A.M., at the United States Court House for the Central District of California, Western Division, 312 N. Spring St., Los Angeles, California.

Dated: _____, 2008 ____ _____

United States District Judge

Motion for Temporary Restraining Order Against Unknown Defendants Planning to Sell Infringing Goods at a Musical Performance

In many situations of potential trademark counterfeiting or infringement, such as at flea markets, concerts, or athletic events, a trademark owner will not know the identity of a potential defendant, but the potential to stop them only arises during the event. For these situations, a "John Doe" suit that identifies the type of activity and the products to be sold at the event usually suffices for a court to issue a temporary restraining and seizure order that can be used on the counterfeiters when and where they are encountered, at least for the duration of the event. The next form is an example used in connection with a rock concert put on by the SMASHING PUMPKINS.

In the United States District Court for the Northern District of Illinois Eastern Division

WILLIAM CORGAN,	)	
	)	
Plaintiff,	)	
v.	)	Civil Action No. 00 C 2291
VARIOUS JOHN DOES, JANE	)	Honorable Charles P. Kocoras
DOES and XYZ COMPANIES,	)	
	)	
	)	Defendants.

Memorandum of Law in Support of Plaintiff's Motion for Temporary Restraining Order, Order of Seizure, and Preliminary Injunction
Introduction

The pleadings filed by Plaintiff William Corgan establish that Defendant bootleggers, and those acting in concert with them, have sold, and will continue to sell, or attempt to sell, bootleg t-shirts and other infringing bootleg merchandise. The pleadings further establish that Defendants are present, or almost certainly will sell, or attempt to sell, infringing merchandise in connection with the Smashing Pumpkins concert at the Aragon Entertainment Center in Chicago, Illinois on April 15 and 16, 2000, and at subsequent concerts on the Smashing Pumpkins' concert tour. The bootleg merchandise will bear the Smashing Pumpkins' name and trademarks without legal authority. Indeed, William Corgan has the exclusive right to sell and license the sale of merchandise bearing the name and mark Smashing Pumpkins both alone and in connection with various logos and designs ("SMASHING PUMPKINS Marks").

Plaintiff is entitled to a temporary restraining order, an order permitting seizure of the bootleg merchandise, and ultimately a preliminary injunction prohibiting these illegal acts. By using the SMASHING PUMPKINS Marks without authorization, Defendants and their cohorts are committing trademark counterfeiting, trademark infringement, and using a false designation of origin in violation of 15 U.S.C. §§ 1114, 1125(a), and violating state and common law.

Defendants can assert no defense to Plaintiff's claims. Moreover, not only is each bootleg sale irretrievably lost to Plaintiff, but the damage to Plaintiff's goodwill through the distribution of inferior merchandise cannot be calculated or remedied. The only way that these bootleggers can be stopped is through issuance of a temporary restraining order and order of seizure followed by a preliminary injunction.

The public interest would be served by issuance of the relief requested since the public interest favors the protection of legitimate property and contractual rights. In addition, the relief requested is the *only* method of protecting the public from inferior merchandise, including the infringing merchandise, which bear a counterfeit or infringing mark. Such merchandise is created and sold by individuals accountable to no one, whether for payment of royalties, income or sales taxes, or for quality control. There is no potential harm to any legitimate interest of Defendants or any other persons if the requested relief is granted.

Argument
I. The Sale of "Bootleg" Merchandise

Violates Plaintiff's Exclusive Rights

Plaintiff has the exclusive right to sell and license the sale of merchandise bearing the SMASHING PUMPKINS Marks. The sale of unauthorized bootleg merchandise by Defendants violates these rights and must be enjoined.

A. Defendants Are Infringing Plaintiff's Registered Service Mark In Violation of Section 32 of the Lanham Act

The owner of a federally registered service mark has a cause of action for service mark infringement against another who uses that owner's mark, or a colorable imitation thereof, in a manner likely to cause confusion, mistake or deception as to the source of the goods or services. 15 U.S.C. § 1114. In a trademark infringement case where the plaintiff seeks injunctive relief, the plaintiff shows a likelihood of success on the merits by establishing that

1) he has a protectable mark, and 2) that a "likelihood of confusion" exists
between the marks or products of the parties. *Meridian Mut. Ins. Co. v.
Meridian Ins. Grp.*, 128 F.3d 1111, 1115 (7th Cir. 1997).

Plaintiff owns a federal registration for the trademark and service mark
SMASHING PUMPKINS, U.S. Reg. No.1,900,492, for prerecorded audio
and audiovisual records in the field of music in a variety of media, posters,
bumper stickers and decals, wearing apparel and entertainment services. This
registration is prima facie evidence that the "validity of the registered mark and
of the registration of the mark, of the registrant's ownership of the mark, and of
the registrant's exclusive right to use the registered mark on or in connection
with the goods or services specified in the registration" 15 U.S.C. § 1115. The
mark has been continuously used since January 1989. Accordingly, the first
part of the infringement test is satisfied.

For part two of the test, likelihood of confusion is measured by the standard
enunciated by the Seventh Circuit in *Meridian*, 128 F.3d at 1115. Under this
standard, the Court should consider the following factors in determining the
likelihood of confusion:

> 1) the similarity between the marks in appearance and suggestion; 2) the
> similarity of the products; 3) the area and manner of concurrent use; 4) the degree
> of care likely to be exercised by consumers; 5) the strength of complaintant's
> mark; 6) actual confusion; and 7) intent of defendant to "palm off his product as
> that of another."
>
> *Id.* at 1115 (citations omitted).

None of these factors is dispositive. *Id.* However, the relevant factors
applied here favor Plaintiff.

The Seventh Circuit has noted that "[a] mark that is strong because of its
fame or its uniqueness, is more likely to be remembered and more likely to
be associated in the public mind with a greater breadth of products and
services, than is a mark that is weak because [it is] relatively unknown . . . ."
James Burrough Ltd. v. Sign of the Beefeater, 540 F.2d 266, 276 (7th Cir.
1976) (consumers are likely to understand the BEEFEATER mark to apply to
products other than alcohol and would believe that defendant's restaurant
was associated with the makers of BEEFEATER gin). Plaintiff's SMASHING
PUMPKINS Mark is a strong and famous mark, which heavily weighs against
bootleggers who sell spurious merchandise featuring any use of SMASHING
PUMPKINS. Due to the strength of Plaintiff's mark, consumers likely will
associate bootleggers' infringing and inferior goods with Plaintiff or as being
approved by Plaintiff.

Although Plaintiff need not show defendant bootleggers' wrongful intent
to establish infringement, the fact that it can show such intent is certainly "an
important factor bearing on the likelihood of confusion." *Computer Care v.
Service Systems Enter.*, 982 F.2d 1063, 1070 (7th Cir. 1992). Bootleggers' lack

of good faith exists in the fact that as unauthorized and unlicensed vendors, bootleggers are intentionally trading on the goodwill of Plaintiff's registered mark and name.

The fact that the "[infringer's] products are the kind that the public might very well attribute to [the plaintiff] . . . provides additional evidence of a likelihood of confusion." *Int'l Kennel Club of Chicago Inc. v. Mighty Star Inc.*, 846 F.2d 1079, 1089 (7th Cir. 1988). Consumers at Plaintiff's concerts are likely to believe that the counterfeit and spurious merchandise sold by bootleggers at or near the concert has been authorized by the Plaintiff, who will be selling similar merchandise at the concert.

There is a strong likelihood of confusion as to the source of any counterfeit or spurious goods sold by bootleggers if bootleggers are allowed to offer for sale any merchandise featuring the SMASHING PUMPKINS Marks. Without restraining bootleggers' activities and seizing their infringing merchandise, Plaintiff will suffer irreparable harm to its goodwill and diminished profits from direct sales and license royalties.

B. Defendants Are Violating Section 43(a) of the Lanham Act

The courts repeatedly have held that the use of registered and unregistered names, and logos of musical artists or musical events by bootleggers also violate section 43(a) of the Lanham Act, 15 U.S.C. § 1125(a). See orders identified in and attached to the accompanying Declaration of Victor K. Sapphire. *See also Moon Records et al. v. Various John Does*, 217 U.S.P.Q. 46 (N.D. Ill. 1981); *Brockum Co. v. Blaylock*, 729 F. Supp. 438 (E.D. Pa. 1990) (sale of bootleg t-shirts bearing names of rock groups violates section 43(a)); *Winterland Concessions Co. v. Creative Screen Design Ltd.*, 214 U.S.P.Q. 188 (N.D. Ill. 1981) (sales of bootleg t-shirts bearing the names of various rock artists violate § 43(a)); *Joel v. Various John Does*, 499 F. Supp. 791, 792 (E.D. Wis. 1980) (sale of t-shirts bearing the name of the artist Billy Joel violates section 43(a) of the Lanham Act).

Section 43(a) is designed to prevent a wide range of conduct involving both registered and unregistered names and logos. Section 43(a) provides in pertinent part:

> Any person who, on or in connection with any goods or services . . . . uses in commerce any word, term, name, symbol or device, or any combination thereof, or any false designation of origin, false or misleading description of fact, or false or misleading representation of fact which:
>
> (1) is likely to cause confusion, or to cause mistake, or to deceive as to the affiliation, connection, or association of such person with another person, or as to the origin, sponsorship or approval of his or her goods, services or commercial activities by another person, . . . shall be liable in a civil action by any person who believes that he or she is likely to be damaged by such act.

This broad prohibition against "unfair competition" covers not only confusion as to source or sponsorship between Defendants' goods and Plaintiff's goods, but it also prohibits the misappropriation of the efforts of others. McKenney and Long, *Federal Unfair Competition: The Lanham Act*, Section 2:04 (1989). Section 43(a) codifies the principle enunciated by the Supreme Court in *Int'l News Service v. Associated Press*, 248 U.S. 215 (1918) that "a party cannot reap where it has not sown." *See also R.R. Donnelley Corp. v. Illinois Bell Tel. Co.*, 595 F. Supp. 1202, 1206 (N.D. Ill. 1984) ("those who invest time, money and energy into the development of a product and its accompanying goodwill should be allowed to reap the advantages of their investment").

The elements of the claim for violation of Section 43(a) are (1) that the mark is valid and protectable, and (2) that the defendant's use of the mark is likely to cause confusion among the consuming public. *See Two Pesos, Inc. v. Taco Cabana*, 112 S. Ct. 2753, 2758 (1992). These two elements are met in this case. First, because the SMASHING PUMPKINS Marks are arbitrary rather than generic or merely descriptive when used in connection with merchandise, they are valid and protectable.

Second, Defendants' use is likely to cause confusion. SMASHING PUMPKINS Marks have become well known through widespread promotion of the band's concerts and music as well as extensive media publicity nationwide. Where, as here, Defendants are aware of Plaintiff's use of its marks, Defendants' intent is presumed to be in bad faith. *See AMF, Inc. v. Sleekcraft Boats*, 599 F.2d 341, 354 (9th Cir. 1979).

Defendants intend to cause confusion, and trade upon it. "[W]here intention to exploit its good will has been shown, the inference of likelihood of confusion is readily drawn because the alleged infringer has indicated by its actions that such confusion will indeed be created." *First Nationwide Bank v. Nationwide Savings and Loan*, 682 F. Supp 965, 976 (E.D. Ark. 1988). Defendants have manufactured bootleg merchandise for the sole purpose of selling it at Plaintiff's concerts. It is beyond dispute that Defendants have utilized, and will continue to knowingly utilize, the SMASHING PUMPKINS Marks to deceive the public and create the appearance that defendants' illegal merchandise is sponsored by or originated with Plaintiff. This is precisely the type of conduct Section 43(a) was designed to stop.

C. Unfair Competition

Such unfair competition is also prohibited by the common law. *See Int'l News Service v. Associated Press*, 248 U.S. 215 (1918) ("a party cannot reap where it has not sown"). Unfair competition is demonstrated where the defendant, without permission, uses the names or trademarks of plaintiff. *See Boston Prof'l Hockey Ass'n v. Del's Cap and Emblem Mfg.*, 510 F.2d 1004, 1010 (5th Cir. 1974) (use of another's name or trademark is unfair competition).

As established above, that test is met here: Any use by Defendants of Plaintiff's marks is without Plaintiff's permission.

D. Illinois Deceptive Trade Practices Act

Moreover, Illinois statutory law prohibits deceptive trade practices. 815 I.L.C.S. § 510/1-7 (Illinois Deceptive Trade Practices Act). Under the Illinois Deceptive Trade Practices Act, a "person engages in a deceptive trade practice when, in the course of his business . . . he . . . causes likelihood of confusion or of misunderstanding as to the source, sponsorship, approval or certification or goods or services . . . [or] as to the affiliation, connection or association with . . . another." As a consequence of Defendants' use of Plaintiff's marks, consumers are likely to be deceived into buying Defendants' merchandise, believing that it is sponsored by Plaintiff and that the proceeds of sales will go to charity. Plaintiff will suffer the loss of profits of these diverted sales.

Under the Act, a court may grant injunctive relief to a person likely to be damaged by deceptive trade practices. 815 I.L.C.S. § 510/3. As discussed below, it is likely that Plaintiff will be damaged by Defendants' sales of counterfeit and bootleg merchandise.

II. Plaintiff is Entitled to a Temporary Restraining Order

Order of Seizure, and a Preliminary Injunction

This action is aimed at bootleggers—groups of individuals who manufacture unauthorized merchandise and will attempt to sell it at the Smashing Pumpkins concerts. The only available remedy that can protect Plaintiff is injunctive relief, including an order of seizure.

A. An Injunction and Order of Seizure Are Appropriate

The courts repeatedly have issued ex parte temporary restraining orders and orders of seizure, in advance of concerts, to stop the sale of bootleg merchandise. *See, e.g.,* Exhibits to Victor K. Sapphire's Declaration. This procedure is specifically authorized by statute. Section 44 of the Lanham Act (15 U.S.C. § 1116(d)) specifically provides for ex parte injunctions and seizures to restrain the sale of counterfeit products. Moreover, 15 U.S.C. § 1116(a) broadly provides for injunctions "upon such terms as the court may deem reasonable" to prevent the infringement of registered trademarks and violations of section 43(a). 15 U.S.C. § 1116(a); *see also* 15 U.S.C. § 1118 (a court has the authority to order delivery, seizure and destruction of merchandise which violates registered trademark or section 43 (a) of the Lanham Act); 15 U.S.C. § 1126 (remedies for violation of registered trademarks available for acts of unfair competition); 28 U.S.C. § 1651(a) (court can enter all appropriate orders in aid of its jurisdiction); Fed. R. Civ. P. 64.

Moreover, under the traditional standard of Rule 65 of the Federal Rules of Civil Procedure, seizure orders should be granted. As described above, Plaintiff has demonstrated a likelihood of success on the merits. Moreover, in cases of trademark infringement and unfair competition such as this, the fact that there is a likelihood of confusion constitutes irreparable injury as a matter of law sufficient to satisfy the requirements of Rule 65(b)(1). *See In re Vuitton et Fils, S.A.*, 606 F.2d 1, 4–5 (2d Cir. 1979). Absent injunctive relief, in advance of the bootleg sales, the bootleg sales will occur and the defendants will disappear, making it impossible to remedy this ongoing violation of Plaintiff's rights.

B. A Temporary Restraining Order, Without Notice, Is Available to Enjoin Activities of Persons Whose Identities Are Unknown

Plaintiff is attempting to stop the bootleg activities of defendants whose identities are presently unknown, at the concert at the Aragon Entertainment Center in Chicago, Illinois, on April 15 and 16, 2000, and the subsequent concert venues on the tour. Indeed, the identities of the individual bootleggers will not be known until they are stopped and the goods seized. Even then, the bootleggers' identities may not be known, because bootleggers often refuse to give their true identities.

Federal courts throughout the country have enjoined "John Doe" bootleggers in this fashion. See orders identified to Victor K. Sapphire's Declaration. In each of these cases, the plaintiff brought an action against John and Jane Doe defendants, and the court issued a temporary restraining order and seizure order. *See also Moon Records v. Various John Does*, 217 U.S.P.Q. 46, 47 (N.D. Ill. 1981):

> The problem regarding identity of defendants will be met by requiring copies of the complaint and this restraining order to be served on all persons from whom the infringing merchandise is seized on February 26, 27, 28 and March 1, 1981. These persons will be asked to reveal their names so that they can be added as parties to the lawsuit and appear in court to contest the seizures at the hearing on March 2, 1981.

The temporary restraining order and order of seizure must not only issue against John and Jane Does but must be issued without Notice. As a practical matter, it is impossible to give notice to defendants whose identity is not yet known.

Here, the only effective remedy is an ex parte temporary restraining order and seizure order. Unless an injunction issues without notice, no injunction is possible; the identities of the defendants will not be determined until the goods are seized. Moreover, even if notice were given, the defendants would simply move their operations to avoid the injunction and the jurisdiction of this Court.

C. Plaintiff is Entitled to a Nationwide Preliminary Injunction

Absent such a nationwide injunction, complete relief here would be impossible to achieve. Plaintiffs would have to seek separate temporary restraining orders at every location on the tour. Such a series of lawsuits is impractical and cost prohibitive, and would, in any event, result in a terrible waste of the resources of both the parties and of the federal courts.

The bootlegging operation to be enjoined here appears to be a concerted action of many individuals acting together with the Defendants to be named in the preliminary injunction. Identical shirts have been found at several locations on previous tours, indicating that the bootleggers go from one location on the tour to another to sell their merchandise. Clearly, a nationwide injunction against Defendants and those acting in concert with them is appropriate and required if is to realize meaningful relief from Defendant's bootlegging activity.

A party that commits a tort, like the violations of Plaintiff's trademark rights alleged here, against an Illinois resident so that the injury is felt in Illinois submits itself to the jurisdiction of the Illinois courts. *Janmark v. Reidy*, 132 F.3d 1200, 1202 (7th Cir. 1997). Defendants are committing such torts against Plaintiff, an Illinois resident, and, thus, are subject to this Court's personal jurisdiction regardless of whether Defendants physically enter Illinois:

> [T]his court considers *Janmark* authoritative and finds the situation at hand factually indistinguishable from the one in *Janmark*. Both the plaintiff here and in *Janmark* are Illinois residents that suffered injury in Illinois in the form of bad financial consequences as a result of an alleged business tort that occurred outside the state. Thus, under *Janmark*, the court need not make findings about whether defendants "entered" Illinois.

Clearclad Coatings, Inc. v. Xontal Ltd., No. 98 C. 7199, 199 WL 652030 (N.D. Ill. Aug. 20, 1999) at *21. Since Plaintiff will personally serve each Defendant with process, each Defendant will properly be subject to this Court's jurisdiction.

Conclusion

For all of the foregoing reasons, Plaintiff respectfully requests that the Court grant its application for a temporary restraining order, order of seizure, and preliminary injunction order.

Respectfully submitted,

Motion for Temporary Restraining Order
Preventing Unfair Competition

In the United States District Court
for the Northern District of Illinois
Eastern Division

ASPEN MARKETING, INC., a California corporation,	)))
Plaintiff,	)
v.	)
CAROLYN STACK,	))
Defendant.	)

Memorandum in Support of Plaintiff's
Motion for Temporary Restraining Order and
Preliminary Injunction
I. Introduction

Plaintiff ("Aspen") moves for a temporary restraining order and a preliminary injunction (1) to enforce the terms of a written agreement whereby defendant ("Stack") agreed not to solicit or induce Aspen's employees to quit their employment, and (2) to enjoin Stack from interfering with Aspen's prospective contracts with its customers. Two Aspen employees are known to have been contacted by Stack, and an Aspen employee has intercepted a telephone call from Stack to a third employee. Four of Aspen's employees recently have submitted their resignations from Aspen; two of those are now employed by Stack's new employer.

II. Facts

Aspen, through its division Aspen Direct, is engaged in the business of, inter alia, providing direct mail marketing programs to businesses for those businesses to use in advertising and promoting their respective products and services. (Verified Complaint, ¶ 4). Through its Aspen Direct division, Aspen provides direct mail marketing programs particularly to automobile dealerships. (Verified Complaint, ¶ 5).

Aspen regularly has its key employees sign an Employee Confidentiality Agreement upon being hired. (Verified Complaint, ¶ 6). The Agreement, among other requirements, prohibits the employee from soliciting any other employee of Aspen to quit his or her employment, unless authorized to do so. (O'Rahilly Dec., ¶ 7, Exh. A).

Aspen extended an offer of employment to Stack to be Director of Marketing Support, a position responsible for supervising Aspen's support personnel. (O'Rahilly Dec., ¶ 3). Stack accepted the offer and signed the Employee Confidentiality Agreement on December 20, 1999. (O'Rahilly Dec., ¶ 7, Exh. A). Stack expressly agreed in the Employee Confidentiality Agreement not to "solicit or induce any employee or consultant of the Company to quit their employment or cease doing business with the Company," unless she was specifically authorized to do so by Aspen. Stack began her employment with Aspen on January 3, 2000. (O'Rahilly Dec., Exh. A, ¶ 13). By the terms of the contract, the Employee Confidentiality Agreement with Stack is governed by California law. (O'Rahilly Dec., Exh. A, ¶ 16).

Shortly after beginning her employment with Aspen, Stack requested a transfer to the position of Director of Special Events. (O'Rahilly Dec., ¶ 5). Aspen agreed to Stack's request and transferred her to the position of Director of Special Events. (O'Rahilly Dec., ¶ 5).

Around the same time, Stack made another request of Aspen, to be transferred from Aspen's Chicago office to its Detroit, Michigan office. Once again, Aspen agreed to Stack's request, and transferred her to Aspen's Detroit Office. (O'Rahilly Dec., ¶ 6). Aspen also agreed to pay Stack's costs to move from Chicago to Detroit. (O'Rahilly Dec., ¶ 6). Effective April 20, 2000, Stack resigned from Aspen. (O'Rahilly Dec., ¶ 2).

On or about May 5, 2000, Stack attempted to contact Aspen Account Executive Juan Bravo. (Pearce Dec., ¶¶ 2-4). The office operator of Aspen's Chicago office intercepted a telephone call defendant placed to Mr. Bravo while he was still employed by Aspen. (*Id.*) On June 2, 2000, Mr. Bravo terminated his employment with Aspen. (O'Rahilly Dec., ¶ 9). Stack also initiated a conversation with Aspen's Executive Creative Director Monte Wehrkamp. (Wehrkamp Dec., ¶ 2). In that conversation, which took place between the time she tendered her resignation and the time she left Aspen, Stack inquired whether Mr. Wehrkamp had any thoughts about what he would be doing in the future and if he left Aspen would he call her. (Wehrkamp Dec., ¶ 3). After leaving Aspen, Stack also initiated conversation with Aspen Senior Account Executive Julie Welsh. (Welsh Dec., ¶ 3). In that conversation Stack indicated to Ms. Welsh that given both their employment histories, it might be nice to work together someday and how appropriate it would be for them to do so. (Welsh Dec., ¶ 4).

On May 3, 2000, Diane Rosa, the Assistant to the Executive Vice President at Aspen Direct, terminated her employment with Aspen Marketing. (O'Rahilly Dec., ¶ 9). Ms. Rosa has begun employment with Stack's current employer, the advertising firm of Scanlon & Turner Advertising. (O'Rahilly Dec., ¶ 9).

On May 17, 2000, Pat Caraos, an Art Director at Aspen Direct, terminated her employment with Aspen Marketing. (O'Rahilly Dec., ¶ 9). Ms. Caraos has begun employment with Stack's current employer, Scanlon & Turner Advertising. (O'Rahilly Dec., ¶ 9).

For the last ten years, Aspen has had a business relationship with the Chicagoland NW Indiana Cadillac Dealers association ("CNWICD"). (O'Rahilly Dec., ¶ 12). Over that time period, Aspen's business with the CNWICD has generated gross revenues for Aspen of approximately $2,500,000. (O'Rahilly Dec., ¶ 12). The marketing programs Aspen sells to CNWICD are created by Aspen especially for the CNWICD. (O'Rahilly Dec., ¶ 13, 15; Verified Complaint ¶ 20, 22).

In 2000, Aspen prepared a program (the "Summer Clearance Campaign") comprised of two mail pieces for the CNWICD which was presented to the CNWICD at a May 1, 2000, meeting held in Park Ridge, Illinois. (O'Rahilly Dec., ¶ 13, Exhs. B and C). Stack was present at that meeting, and took part in Aspen's presentation of the program to CNWICD. (O'Rahilly Dec., ¶ 13). The Summer Clearance Campaign is comprised of two mail pieces prepared especially for CNWICD, which are proprietary to Aspen, and are the result of substantial labor and cost. (O' Rahilly Dec., ¶ 15). At the May 1, 2000, meeting, the CNWICD stated that one of the two mail pieces was the direction that CNWICD wanted to go and requested that Aspen make some modifications to the piece. (O'Rahilly Dec., ¶ 14). On or about May 24, 2000, a member of the CNWICD informed Aspen that the Summer Clearance Campaign contract probably would be awarded to Scanlon & Turner Advertising. (O'Rahilly Dec., ¶ 17).

Aspen estimates that it would have received profits from a contract with CNWICD in excess of $29,000 had it been awarded the CNWICD project. (O'Rahilly Dec., ¶ 18).

III. Argument

A. Aspen Is Entitled to a Temporary Restraining *Order* and a *Preliminary Injunction*

A court will grant a preliminary injunction if the movant demonstrates: (1) a reasonable likelihood of success on the merits, (2) that there exists no adequate remedy at law and that the movant will be irreparably harmed if the injunction is not issued, (3) that the threatened injury to the movant outweighs the threatened harm the injunction may inflict on the non-movant, and (4) that the granting of the preliminary injunction will not disserve the public interest. *Brunswick Corp. v. Jones*, 784 F.2d 271, 273–74 (7th Cir. 1986) (affirming a preliminary injunction barring a former employee from breaching a covenant not to compete with his former employer).

1. Likelihood of Success on the Merits

a. Breach of Contract

Under California law, courts recognize contractual provisions preventing a former employee from raiding her former employer to solicit other employees to leave. *Loral Corp., et al. V. Moyes*, 174 Cal. App. 3d 268 (Cal. Ct. App. 1985). The court noted that "The restriction presumably was sought by plaintiffs in order to maintain a stable work force and enable the employer to remain in business." *Id.* at 280.

Before commencing her employment with Aspen, Stack signed an Employee Confidentiality Agreement, "in consideration of the compensation and benefits from my employment." (O'Rahilly Dec., Exh. A). In that document, Stack agreed (*id.* ¶ 13):

> During and after my employment, I will not solicit or induce any employee or consultant of the Company to quit their employment or cease doing business with the Company, unless I am specifically authorized to do so by the Company.

Stack is known now to have contacted or attempted to contact at least three employees of Aspen. On or about May 24, 2000, she attempted to contact by telephone Aspen Account Executive Juan Bravo. (Pearce Dec., ¶ ¶ 2–4). On June 2, 2000, Mr. Bravo terminated his employment with Aspen. (O'Rahilly Dec., ¶ 9). Stack also initiated a conversation, between the time of her notice of resignation but before leaving Aspen, with Aspen's Executive Creative Director Monte Wehrkamp. In that conversation Stack inquired whether Mr. Wehrkamp had any thoughts about what he would be doing in the future and if he left Aspen would he call her. (Wehrkamp Dec., ¶ 3). After leaving Aspen, Stack also initiated a conversation with Aspen Senior Account Executive Julie Welsh. In that conversation Stack indicated to Ms. Welsh that given both their employment histories it might be nice to work together someday and how appropriate it would be for them to do so. (Welsh Dec., ¶ 4).

Two other employees of Aspen have left Aspen's employment to begin employment with Stack. (O'Rahilly Dec., ¶ 9). On May 3, 2000, Diana Rosa, the Assistant to the Executive Vice President of Aspen Direct, terminated her employment with Aspen and has begun working for Ms. Stack's current employer, Scanlon & Turner Advertising.[1] (Id.). And on May 17, 2000,

---

1. Ms. Rosa stated at the time she tendered her resignation that she was going to join a firm in Tampa, Florida. In fact, she is now employed by Scanlon & Turner Advertising in Oak Brook Terrace, Illinois.

Pat Caraos, an Art Director at Aspen, terminated his employment. Likewise, Mr. Caraos has begun employment with Scanlon & Turner Advertising.[2] (Id.)

These three confirmed contacts and two other apparent contacts with employees of Aspen are in violation of the Employee Confidentiality Agreement. Under California law, which by agreement of the parties governs the contract, Aspen is entitled to an injunction to prohibit further breach of the Agreement.[3] *Loral Corp., et al. V. Moyes*, 174 Cal. App. 3d 268 (Cal. Ct. App. 1985). Moreover, Stack already has agreed to injunctive relief in the Employee Confidentiality Agreement (*id.* ¶ 14):

> I agree that a violation of this Agreement may cause harm to the Company's reputation, customer relationships, and other aspects of its business for which an award of money damages would not be adequate. I, therefore, agree that the Company shall be entitled to a court order as appropriate to prevent me from violating this Agreement in addition to any claims for money damages or other relief.

b. Interference with Prospective

Economic Advantage

Illinois law prohibits a party from conducting tortious interference with the prospective economic advantage of another. *Dames & Moore v. Baxter & Woodman, Inc.*, 21 F. Supp. 817 (N.D. Ill. 1998). The elements of this tort are:

(1) A reasonable expectation by the plaintiff of entering into a valid business relationship
(2) The defendant's knowledge of the plaintiff's expectancy
(3) Purposeful interference by the defendant that prevents the plaintiff's legitimate interest from ripening into a valid business relationship
(4) Damages to the plaintiff resulting from such interference.

Id. at 825, *citing Fellhauer v. City of Geneva*, 142 Ill. 2d 495. Purposeful interference is found where, for example, the defendant employs wrongful means. *Id.* at 825.

Under these standards, Stack tortiously interfered with Aspen's prospective economic advantage with the Chicagoland NW Indiana Cadillac Dealers association ("CNWICD"). Aspen had a reasonable expectation of receiving

---

2. Mr. Caraos stated at the time he tendered his resignation that he was going to work for a firm in downtown Chicago. In fact, he is now employed by Scanlon & Turner Advertising in Oak Brook Terrace, Illinois.
3. It is worth noting that Illinois law would enforce a similar contract provision. *Arpac Corp. v. Murray*, 226 Ill. App. 3d 65 (Ill. App. Ct. 1992).

the contract from CNWICD for the Summer Clearance Campaign because of Aspen's past relationship with CNWICD, which had generated gross revenues for Aspen of approximately $2,500,000. (O'Rahilly Dec., ¶ 12). Stack had knowledge of Aspen's expectation of receiving a contract from CNWICD for the Summer Clearance Campaign because of her participation at the May 1, 2000, meeting.

Stack's unfair competition, which establishes the third element of the tort, is established through her solicitation of key Aspen personnel, in violation of her Employee Confidentiality Agreement. Furthermore, through her involvement in the presentation of the proposed Summer Clearance Campaign to CNWICD, as part of Aspen's inside team for that business proposal, she gained substantial knowledge of the type of program the CNWICD wanted. (*See* O'Rahilly Dec., ¶ 13–14). Therefore her conduct is not mere competition, but unfair competition resulting in interference with Aspen's prospective economic advantage from the CNWICD.

Lastly, Stack's interference has resulted in damages to Aspen in an amount over $29,000. (O'Rahilly Dec., ¶ 18).

Thus, Stack's conduct meets all of the elements of the tortious interference with contractual relations, and should be enjoined by this Court.

2. There is no Adequate Remedy at Law and Aspen will be Irreparably Harmed Without Entry of Preliminary Relief

Stack is known to have contacted at least three Aspen employees in violation of her contract; two other Aspen employees have left Aspen since Stack left and now are employed by Stack's current employer. The impact of Stack's breach of her contract is being felt by Aspen in many ways, including other employees' feeling that Aspen is becoming unstable. (O'Rahilly Dec., ¶ 11).

With respect to the interference with prospective economic advantage, Aspen risks permanently losing customers with whom it has had long-standing relations if Stack is not enjoined from unfairly competing through the use of Aspen employees she has hired away and Aspen's proprietary materials.

3. The Balance of Harm Favors Aspen

The balance of harm favors Aspen because Stack cannot be harmed through an order requiring her to abide by the terms of a confidentiality agreement she entered into, the relevant term of which is recognized by both California and Illinois law. *Loral Corp.*, et al. *V. Moyes*, 174 Cal. App. 3d 268 (Cal. Ct. App. 1985); *Arpac Corp. v. Murray*, 226 Ill .App. 3d 65 (Ill. App. Ct. 1992).

With respect to the interference claim, there is no harm to Stack in enjoining her from unfairly competing against Aspen with Aspen's employees she lured away, and with trade materials proprietary to Aspen.

4. Preliminary Relief will not Disserve the Public Interest

There is no disservice to the public interest in enforcing the terms of an employment contract between two parties. And there is no harm to competition in enjoining Stack from using Aspen employees she lured away and proprietary Aspen materials in an effort to prevent Aspen from concluding prospective contracts with Aspen's customers.

IV. Conclusion

Aspen therefore requests that the Court temporarily restrain Stack from further soliciting or inducing Aspen employees to quit their employment with Aspen and from interfering with Aspen's prospective contractual relations. Aspen further requests that the Court set a hearing on Aspen's motion for a preliminary injunction.

FORM 5.5

Motion for Temporary Restraining Order to Stop Marketing Campaign

In the United States District Court for the Northern District of Illinois Eastern Division

NORTHERN TRUST CORPORATION, a Delaware Corporation, Plaintiff, v. JPMORGAN CHASE & CO., a Delaware Corporation, Defendant.	Case No. 08-CV-0297 Judge William T. Hart Magistrate Judge Keys

Plaintiff's Memorandum in Support of its APPLICATION FOR TEMPORARY RESTRAINING ORDER and Motion for Preliminary Injunction
V. Introduction

Northern Trust, a private bank headquartered in Chicago, has for two years been running an advertising campaign—the biggest in its history—for its banking and personal financial services under the registered mark WHAT REALLY MATTERS.

On January 13, 2008, JPMorgan Chase, the New York megabank, launched a national advertising blitz for its banking services under the mark CHASE WHAT MATTERS. This mark is nearly identical to Northern Trust's WHAT REALLY MATTERS mark, and it contains Chase's famous housemark, CHASE. Chase will spend $70 million in the first two and a half months of the campaign, which will include Super Bowl ads, ads on Oprah Winfrey's pre-Academy Awards interview special, on ABC, CBS, NBC, and Fox, on yahoo. com and msn.com, on billboards and more. CHASE WHAT MATTERS will be as ubiquitous as the Golden Arches.

Chase's nationwide saturation advertising with a near-identical mark, especially one that also includes the famous CHASE housemark, will simply obliterate Northern Trust's mark. Consumers, including Northern Trust's clients and potential clients, will—incorrectly—associate Northern Trust's advertisements with Chase or will assume that they are somehow approved by Chase or that there is some association between Northern Trust and Chase. Put another way, Northern Trust will effectively end up running advertisements for Chase, the value and consumer goodwill of Northern Trust's mark will be wiped out, and Northern Trust's efforts to expand into new markets with the mark will be completely undermined. As a result, Northern Trust loses control over its corporate identity, goodwill, and reputation.

This constitutes serious and irreparable trademark harm to Northern Trust, known as "reverse confusion," which is expressly recognized in the Seventh Circuit. To prevent this irreparable harm, Chase must be restrained from any use of the CHASE WHAT MATTERS mark. The equities are strongly in Northern Trust's favor: Chase was fully aware of Northern Trust's mark before it launched its campaign. Chase could and should have chosen a noninfringing mark, such as "Chase What's Important" or "Chase The Dream." Instead, Chase decided to imitate Northern Trust's mark, thereby destroying it. This conduct must be stopped.

VI. Statement of Facts

A. Northern Trust and its Business

Northern Trust Corporation is a leading provider of banking, investment management, asset servicing, and fiduciary services, primarily for affluent individuals and families, as well as institutions. Affidavit of Ashly A. Iacullo, ¶ 2. Since 1889, Northern Trust has distinguished itself by its commitment to exceptional client service and the importance of building strong, long-lasting relationships. *Id.*

Excellence in client service is a core component of Northern Trust's cultural heritage. *Id.* Northern Trust places a premium on understanding clients and their specific needs. *Id.* Its success in earning the confidence of clients, as evidenced by its growth in assets under custody and managed assets, demonstrates how Northern Trust's unique array of products and services is receiving increased market acceptance. *Id.* Backed by its comprehensive understanding of clients' needs, Northern Trust is dedicated to delivering solutions-based products in the most user friendly and time-efficient ways possible. *Id.* Northern Trust's 85 U.S. offices are located within a 45-minute drive of approximately half of the nation's millionaire households. *Id.* Its close proximity to its personal clients is one of the characteristics that makes it unique. *Id.*

B. The What Really Matters Mark

In applications filed with the Trademark Office in July 2005, Northern Trust registered both its WHAT REALLY MATTERS mark and its THE FREEDOM TO FOCUS ON WHAT REALLY MATTERS mark. *Id.* ¶¶ 3–4. Both marks are registered in connection with banking services and related financial services.

Id. When Northern Trust applied to register these marks, the Trademark Office determined that there was "no similar registered or pending mark which would bar registration under Trademark Act Section 2(d)." *Id.* ¶¶ 5–6.

Indeed, prior to Chase's actions described below, no live federal trademark registration or application existed for marks containing the words "what" and "matters" in connection with banking services other than Northern Trust's marks. A search performed on the Trademark Office's website on January 13, 2008, shows only three entries for such marks. *Id.* ¶ 7. The first two are Northern Trust's registrations, the third is Chase's current application. *Id.*

| Start | List At: | | OR | Jump | to record: | | 3 **Records(s) found (This page: 1 ~ 3)** |

Refine Search what[bi] and matters[bi] and banking[gs] and | Submit |

Current Search: **S1: what[bi] and matters[bi] and banking[gs] and live[ld]** docs: 3 occ: 12

	Serial Number	Reg. Number	Word Mark	Check Status	Live/Dead
1	78673655	3363286	THE FREEDOM TO FOCUS ON WHAT REALLY MATTERS	TARR	LIVE
2	78673661	3360523	WHAT REALLY MATTERS	TARR	LIVE
3	77308911		CHASE WHAT MATTERS	TARR	LIVE

Had Chase performed this simple search at any time since July 2005 and prior to adopting the CHASE WHAT MATTERS mark (and, since it is a routine action to take when selecting a new mark, Chase likely did), it would have immediately found out about Northern Trust and its WHAT REALLY MATTERS Marks.

C. JPMorgan Chase & Co. and its Business

Chase is the third-largest banking institution in the U.S. *Id.* ¶ 8. It serves millions of U.S. customers, operates in more than 50 countries, and has more than 170,000 employees. *Id.* ¶ 9. Chase has issued more than 154 million credit cards and serves the public and small businesses through nearly 3100 bank branches, 9100 ATMs, and 280 mortgage offices. *Id.* ¶ 10. Chase also has loan-originating relationships with 15,000 automobile dealerships. *Id.* Chase is a component of the Dow Jones Industrial Average. *Id.* ¶ 9.

Chase's 2006 Annual Report states that Chase "increased checking accounts 14% to 10 million" and "added 438 net new branches . . . and 1,194 ATMs, including . . . 500 placed in Walgreens stores." *Id.* ¶ 11. As of 2006, Chase was the "#1 commercial bank in market penetration in Chase's retail footprint, almost double that of the next leading competitor." *Id.* ¶ 12.

The last several years have seen a surge in merger and acquisition activity within the banking industry. Recent examples include Wachovia's acquisitions of SouthTrust, Golden West Financial, and World Savings Bank, Fifth Third Bancorp's acquisition of Old Kent Financial Corp., as well as Bank of America's acquisitions of FleetBoston Financial Corp., MBNA Corporation, and LaSalle

Bank. *Id.* ¶ 13. Chase has been an active participant in this trend: in 2004, Chase acquired Bank One Corporation, which had been the sixth-largest bank in the United States. *Id.* Chase now occupies Bank One's former headquarters, two blocks from Northern Trust's main offices. *Id.* ¶ 20. In 2006, Chase acquired The Bank of New York's consumer, small business, and middle-market banking business. *Id.* ¶ 14. Most recently, at the same time as its launch of its CHASE WHAT MATTERS advertising campaign, the media reported Chase's acquisition of part of a mortgage portfolio belonging to British lender Northern Rock. *Id.* ¶ 15.

D. The CHASE WHAT MATTERS Mark and Campaign

On October 19, 2007, Chase filed a federal trademark application to register the mark CHASE WHAT MATTERS for banking and related financial services (App. Ser. No. 77/308,911). *Id.* ¶ 16. On December 28, 2007, the Trademark Office refused registration of the CHASE WHAT MATTERS mark based on a likelihood of confusion with Northern Trust's WHAT REALLY MATTERS registration. *Id.* ¶ 17. The Trademark Office found that the parties' marks and services were confusingly similar, reasoning as follows:

> [Chase]'s mark, CHASE WHAT MATTERS, is similar to the registered mark, WHAT REALLY MATTERS. The marks both contain the words "WHAT" and "MATTERS," which have the same sound, spelling, and meaning in the marks . . .
>
> [Chase]'s services, namely "Banking and related financial services," are similar to registrants' services, namely "banking services, personal and corporate trust services, funds investment, investment advice, and investment consultation services." . . .

Accordingly, registration is refused under § 2(d) of the Trademark Act based upon a likelihood of confusion.

(Emphasis added, citations omitted.) *Id.*

Despite being put expressly on notice by the Trademark Office about Northern Trust's mark and likelihood of confusion, Chase announced on January 9, 2008, that it planned to debut the CHASE WHAT MATTERS mark as the centerpiece of a national rebranding campaign designed for highest visibility among the entire U.S. public. *Id.* ¶ 18. This announcement was widely reported, including in *The New York Times. Id.* The CHASE WHAT MATTERS campaign is "the first overhaul of Chase's brand advertising since its 2004 merger with Bank One. The ads . . . will be used throughout the bank's wide range of consumer business, including credit cards, student loans and retail banking." *Id.* The CHASE WHAT MATTERS advertising campaign began with print ads in major newspapers on January 13, 2008, and in television commercials and other media starting on January 14, 2008. *Id.* ¶ 10.

A representative CHASE WHAT MATTERS print advertisement is attached to the Iacullo Affidavit as Exhibit S.

The first new CHASE WHAT MATTERS television advertisements aired yesterday during the "Today Show" on NBC and on "Good Morning America" on ABC, both starting at 7:00 a.m. EST. *Id.* Chase's plans include additional advertisements on ABC, CBS, and NBC nationally, as well as on various cable networks, including the Food Network, HGTV, and The History Channel. *Id.* Chase also plans to show advertisements featuring the CHASE WHAT MATTERS mark during such television programming as the Super Bowl pre-game show, Oprah Winfrey's pre-Academy Awards interview special, and popular prime-time shows such as "Grey's Anatomy," "American Idol," "Prison Break," and "Boston Legal." *Id.*

Online, CHASE WHAT MATTERS advertising will appear on high-impact websites such as <yahoo.com> and <msn.com>. *Id.* In addition to newspapers and magazines, Chase plans to showcase the CHASE WHAT MATTERS campaign in the March issue of *O*, Oprah Winfrey's magazine. *Id.* Chase also plans to make extensive use of outdoor and out-of-home advertising media, including subways, public transit stations, billboards, and movie theater trailers. *Id.* Finally, Chase has a website at chasewhatmatters.com that prominently displays the mark.

Chase executives say that they will spend more than $70 million on the CHASE WHAT MATTERS advertising campaign during the first two and one half months of 2008 alone. *Id.* ¶ 21.

VII. Argument

Temporary restraining orders are emergency remedies issued to maintain the status quo until a hearing can be held on an application for a preliminary injunction. *Coca-Cola Co. v. Alma-Leo U.S.A., Inc.*, 719 F. Supp. 725, 726 (N.D. Ill. 1989). "The standards for a temporary restraining order and a preliminary injunction are identical." *Bernina of Am. Inc. v. Fashion Fabrics Int'l, Inc.*, 2001 U.S. Dist. LEXIS 1211, 2001 WL 128164, at *1 (N.D. Ill. Feb. 9, 2001).

Northern Trust is entitled to a TRO and preliminary injunction because (1) it is likely to succeed on the merits, (2) it is suffering irreparable injury for which it has no adequate remedy at law, (3) the balance of harms favors Northern Trust, and (4) the public interest favors enjoining Chase. *See Eli Lilly & Co. v. Natural Answers, Inc.*, 233 F.3d 456, 461 (7th Cir. 2000).

A. Northern Trust Is Likely To Succeed on the Merits of its Claims

In the Seventh Circuit, a plaintiff needs only show a "better than negligible" likelihood of success on the merits to be entitled to a preliminary injunction. *Ty, Inc. v. Jones Grp. Inc.*, 237 F.3d 891, 897 (7th Cir. 2001). Northern Trust's likelihood of success far exceeds this minimal threshold. To prevail on its Lanham Act and state law claims, Northern Trust must show that (a) it has protectable trademark rights in the WHAT REALLY MATTERS marks and, (b) Chase's use of the CHASE WHAT MATTERS mark is likely to cause confusion. 15 U.S.C. § 1125(a); 15 U.S.C. § 1114; *Ty, Inc.*, 237 F.3d at 897.

1. Northern Trust Owns Protectable Trademark Rights in the WHAT REALLY MATTERS Marks

Northern Trust's ownership and use in commerce of the WHAT REALLY MATTERS marks is not in question. Through applications filed with the Trademark Office in July 2005, Northern Trust registered both its WHAT REALLY MATTERS mark and its THE FREEDOM TO FOCUS ON WHAT REALLY MATTERS mark. These marks have been used widely by Northern Trust in connection with its banking and financial services continuously since January 2006, and they appear prominently on Northern Trust's marketing materials.

2. Chase's Use of the CHASE REALLY MATTERS Mark is Likely to Cause Confusion

Chase's ad campaign is likely to cause confusion across the board. Northern Trust is especially concerned about reverse confusion. "Reverse confusion occurs when a large junior saturates the market with a trademark similar or identical to that of a smaller, senior user. In such a case, the junior user may not seek to profit from the goodwill associated with the senior user's mark. Nonetheless, the senior user is injured because the public comes to assume that the senior user's products are really the junior user's, or that the former has become somehow connected to the latter. The result is that the senior user loses the value of the trademark—its product identity, corporate identity, control over its goodwill and reputation, and ability to move into new markets." *Sands, Taylor & Wood Co. v. Quaker Oats Co.*, 978 F.2d 947, 957 (7th Cir. 1992) (emphasis added, citations and quotation marks omitted). *See also Peacable Planet, Inc., v. Ty, Inc.*, 362 F.3d 986, 992–93 (7th Cir. 2004) (same); *Custom Vehicles, Inc., v. Forest River, Inc.*, 476 F.3d 481, 484 (7th Cir. 2007) (same). *See generally Big O Tire Dealers, Inc., v. Goodyear Tire & Rubber Co.*, 561 F.2d 1365 (10th Cir. 1977). The present situation cannot be described better.

In determining whether confusion is likely, courts in this Circuit analyze the following factors: (1) the similarity between the marks in appearance and suggestion, (2) the similarity of the products or services, (3) the area and manner of concurrent use, (4) the degree of care likely to be exercised by consumers, (5) the strength of the complainant's mark, (6) actual confusion, and (7) the intent of the defendant to "palm off his products as those of another." *Sands*, 978 F.2d at 959. The weight accorded to these factors may vary depending on the facts of a case. *Meridian Mut. Ins. Co. v. Meridian Ins. Grp.*, 128 F.3d 1111, 1115 (7th Cir. 1997). Here, they overwhelmingly favor a finding of likelihood of confusion. *See, e.g., TV Land, L.P., v. Viacom Int'l, Inc.*, 908 F. Supp. 543, 550–55 (N.D. Ill. 1995) (granting preliminary injunction based on reverse confusion).

a) Similarity

The first factor, the similarity of the marks, favors Northern Trust. As the Trademark Office correctly noted in connection with the CHASE WHAT MATTERS application, Chase's and Northern Trust's marks "both contain the words 'WHAT' and 'MATTERS,' which have the same sound, spelling, and meaning." *See* Iacullo Aff. at ¶ 17. As a junior user, Chase has a duty to avoid confusion with Northern Trust's WHAT REALLY MATTERS marks. *See, e.g., Forum Corp. of North Am. v. Forum, Ltd.*, 903 F.2d 434, 440–41 (7th Cir. 1990).

Importantly, Chase uses its CHASE brand name in connection with WHAT MATTERS. This greatly exacerbates the likelihood of confusion. In reverse confusion cases, "the linking of the plaintiff's mark with the defendant's brand name is an aggravation, not a justification. *Sands*, 978 F.2d at 960. *See also id.* at 954 ('[I]t is precisely the strong association between Gatorade and "Thirst Aid' created by Quaker's ads that is likely to create confusion in this case").

b) Services

Both Northern Trust and Chase offer a full array of banking and related financial services under the marks in question. Their services are thus virtually the same.

c) Concurrent Use

Chase's advertising blitz is designed to reach the entire U.S. population. National TV ads will run on the Super Bowl pre-game show and on Oprah Winfrey's pre-Academy Awards interview special, as well as on ABC, CBS, NBC and Fox, including on the "Today Show," "Good Morning America," "Grey's Anatomy," "American Idol," "Prison Break," and "Boston Legal," in addition to channels such as Food Network, HGTV, and The History Channel. *See* Iacullo Aff. at ¶ 10. Online ads will appear on <yahoo.com> and <msn. com>. *Id.* Subways, public transit stations, billboards, and movie theater trailers will feature Chase's ads. *Id.* The Nation will be blanketed with CHASE WHAT MATTERS ads. There will be no escaping them.

Northern Trust's U.S. customers and potential customers will, of course, be exposed to Chase's ads as well. This consumer group has also been exposed to Northern Trust's own ad campaign involving the WHAT REALLY MATTERS

Marks. Thus, the marks will be used concurrently, and the viability of Northern Trust's marks in both Northern Trust's existing and new markets will be severely compromised.

d) Consumer Care

Consumer sophistication will be of no help in preventing the serious, indeed irreparable, harm that Northern Trust will suffer from Chase's saturation use of CHASE WHAT MATTERS. This lies in the very nature of Chase's ad campaign, which appears on all popular media (print, radio, TV, Internet), is designed to reach the entire U.S. population, and is fueled by expenditures in excess of $72 million through March of this year.

Northern Trust has a reputation, among its clients and potential clients, for "high-touch" service, and it uses the WHAT REALLY MATTERS mark to promote that service. Chase's ad campaign will be everywhere, and Northern Trust's clients and potential clients will inevitably see it. Chase's use of a near-identical mark, and especially in combination with the CHASE house mark, will confuse Northern Trust's clients and potential clients. Northern Trust's campaign, instead of strengthening Northern Trust's goodwill, will instead promote Chase's services, and will confuse Northern Trust's clients and potential clients about the distinctive nature of Northern Trust's services. This is exactly the kind of devastating trademark injury the Seventh Circuit described in *Sands, Taylor*.

The likelihood of consumers' false belief that Northern Trust has become connected with Chase in some form is aggravated by Chase's own history of merger and of acquiring other financial institutions. Chase has been an active acquirer of its banking competitors, purchasing Bank One Corporation in 2004, and The Bank of New York's consumer, small business, and middle-market banking business in 2006. *See* Iacullo Aff. at ¶¶ 13–14. Most recently, at the same time as the launch of its CHASE WHAT MATTERS campaign, Chase completed a widely reported acquisition of part of a mortgage portfolio belonging to British lender Northern Rock, a financial services company sharing the first element of its name with Northern Trust. *Id.* ¶ 15. Indeed, Chase itself is the result of a merger of the Chase Manhattan Corporation with J.P. Morgan & Co. *Id.* ¶ 13.

Consumer sophistication and care therefore do not mitigate the insidious harm that Northern Trust will suffer from the reverse confusion caused by Chase's acts.

e) Strength of Mark

The strength of a trademark "refers to the distinctiveness of the mark, or more precisely, its tendency to identify the goods sold under the mark as emanating from a particular . . . source." *Sands*, 947 F.2d at 959. In this situation, where reverse confusion is likely, the focus is on the commercial strength of Chase's mark, rather than on the strength of Northern Trust's mark. *Id*. 959–60. Moreover, "the conjunction of defendant's trademark and the allegedly infringing term may actually increase the misappropriation by linking defendant's name to plaintiff's goodwill." *Sands*, 947 F.2d at 954. This is particularly true in reverse confusion cases, where "the linking of the plaintiff's mark with the defendant's brand name is an aggravation, not a justification." *Id*. 960.

Both factors—strength of the junior mark and connection of the junior mark with an extremely famous housemark—are present here to the highest degree. The CHASE mark by itself is one of the most powerful and famous marks in the entire banking industry. The CHASE WHAT MATTERS advertising campaign, with expenditures of upward of $70 million in the first quarter of 2008 alone, will inevitably have an extremely powerful impact on consumers.

f) Actual Confusion

Chase is now launching its CHASE WHAT MATTERS campaign. Proof of actual confusion is not necessary to establish likelihood of confusion. *Sands*, 978 F.2d at 960; *Intn'l Kennel Club, Inc. v. Mighty Star, Inc.*, 846 F.2d 1079, 1090 (7th Cir. 1988).

g) Intent

Chase's launch of its advertisements with knowledge of Northern Trust's prior rights and of the Trademark Office's finding of likelihood of confusion, constitutes wrongful intent. *See, e.g.*, *Sands*, 978 F.2d at 961 (holding that "[i]n a reverse confusion case . . . the defendant by definition is not palming off or otherwise attempting to create confusion as to the source of his product [and t]hus the 'intent' factor of the likelihood of confusion analysis is essentially irrelevant in a reverse confusion case").

B. Northern Trust has no Adequate Remedy at Law and Will Suffer Irreparable Harm if this Court does not Restrain and Enjoin Chase's Use of the CHASE WHAT MATTERS Mark

Irreparable harm is presumed when a trademark plaintiff has shown a likelihood of success on the merits of its infringement claim. *Promatek Indus., Ltd. v. Equitrac Corp.*, 300 F.3d 808, 813 (Fed. Cir. 2002) (holding that "it is well settled that injuries arising from Lanham Act violations are presumed to be irreparable") (citation omitted); *Eli Lilly*, 233 F.3d at 469.

Northern Trust is certain to suffer irreparable harm if Chase is permitted to continue infringing its WHAT REALLY MATTERS mark. Northern Trust has spent millions of dollars and the past two years building client recognition of its WHAT REALLY MATTERS mark. Moreover, Northern Trust has spent many decades cultivating a certain image and reputation, which has now become closely linked with the WHAT REALLY MATTERS mark. Permitting Chase to use its ubiquitous presence to bulldoze Northern Trust's WHAT REALLY MATTERS Campaign with Chase's CHASE WHAT MATTERS campaign would destroy Northern Trust's investment in its own ad campaign and devastate its reputation as an independent private bank providing "high-touch" services to its clients.

This timing of Chase's launch of its CHASE WHAT MATTERS campaign makes injunctive relief particularly important. Chase launched the CHASE WHAT MATTERS campaign with print advertisements on January 13, 2008, and with television advertisements the next day. Chase plans to saturate the market with the CHASE WHAT MATTERS campaign, with advertisements during the Super Bowl and other prominent events. The longer Chase runs its infringing campaign, the greater the harm to Northern Trust. By enjoining Chase from continuing its infringing CHASE WHAT MATTERS campaign, this Court can mitigate consumer confusion, and hence harm to Northern Trust.

C. The Harm to Northern Trust Far Outweighs any Harm to Chase

The harm to Northern Trust associated with Chase's infringement of the WHAT REALLY MATTERS mark vastly outweighs any legitimate harm that Chase might claim. At present, Chase enjoys powerful brand recognition among the U.S. public for its banking services. Chase is now launching its CHASE WHAT MATTERS campaign. Northern Trust does not seek to interfere in any way with Chase's banking services, nor do those services depend on the CHASE WHAT MATTERS campaign. Chase's current brand image and recognition will suffer no harm whatsoever if the infringing campaign is enjoined. In short, a temporary restraining order and injunction will cause no cognizable harm to Chase.

Chase would lose the money it spent in ramping up for the infringing campaign. But that is entirely the result of Chase's own willful and reckless conduct. Northern Trust's WHAT REALLY MATTERS is a registered trademark. Northern Trust applied to register its mark in July 2005. Chase thus knew, or should have known, about Northern Trust's mark prior to applying to register the CHASE WHAT MATTERS mark in October 2007. In addition, the Trademark Office cited Northern Trust's WHAT REALLY MATTERS registration in its office action refusing registration to the CHASE WHAT MATTERS mark, giving Chase undeniable actual knowledge of Northern Trust's mark prior to the launch of Chase's campaign.

Moreover, Northern Trust advised Chase of its concern that the CHASE WHAT MATTERS mark infringes the WHAT REALLY MATTERS mark on January 9, 2008, the date that reports announcing Chase's new campaign first were published. Chase still decided to proceed with the CHASE WHAT MATTERS campaign. Any harm that flows to Chase from such behavior is not the sort that a court should consider when weighing the equities of a case. *See, e.g., Ty, Inc.*, 237 F.3d at 903; *Pride Commc'ns Ltd. P'ship v. WCKG, Inc.*, 30 U.S.P.Q.2d 1185, 1192 (N.D. Ill. 1994) (when defendants began using their mark they should have known of plaintiff's competing use; "they therefore acted at their peril that their own use would be enjoined").

D. The Public Interest Supports a Restraining Order and Immediate Injunctive Relief

The public interest supports an injunction to prevent consumer confusion. *See, e.g., Eli Lilly & Co*, 233 F.3d at 469. Until it is enjoined, Chase's CHASE WHAT MATTERS advertising campaign will continue to cause confusion, injuring the public. Immediate injunctive relief thus is necessary to prevent the public, including Northern Trust's clients and potential clients, from believing that Northern Trust has become associated with or acquired by Chase.

VIII. Conclusion

Northern Trust is likely to prevail on its claims against Chase and is suffering irreparable harm. The balance of harms and public interest favor the grant of a temporary restraining order and preliminary injunction. Accordingly, Northern Trust respectfully requests that this Court enter the requested order.

   Dated: January 16, 2008, Respectfully submitted,

Motion for Preliminary Injunction re Trademark, Copyright and Dilution Claims

In the United States District Court for the Northern District of Illinois Eastern Division

SAGE PRODUCTS, INC.,	)	
	)	
Plaintiff,	)	
	)	Civil Action No.
v.	)	
	)	
KIMBERLY-CLARK CORPORATION,	)	
Defendant.	)	

MEMORANDUM OF LAW IN SUPPORT OF
PLAINTIFF'S MOTION FOR PRELIMINARY INJUNCTION

Plaintiff, Sage Products, Inc. ("Sage"), submits this memorandum of law in support of its motion for preliminary injunction.

Background Facts

Sage is a leading manufacturer of health=care products. One of Sage's most successful products is its Comfort disposable washcloths ("Sage's washcloths"), which are premoistened washcloths for people who find conventional bathing difficult, such as the elderly and disabled. (Affinito Decl. ¶ 3). The cloths are designed to be warmed in a microwave prior to use so that they are more comfortable for the person being cleaned. Sage's Comfort product, first introduced in 1996, created and demonstrated a market for disposable washcloths. It is presently by far the leading disposable washcloth sold to hospitals and other healthcare providers. (Affinito ¶ ¶ 4, 8). Sage's washcloths now compete with several other companies' products in that market, including products made by Medline, Kendall, and Joey Bath. (Affinito ¶ 4). Sage has been the only significant disposable washcloth product sold directly to consumers at retail. (Affinito ¶ 15).

Since November 2000, Sage's standard Comfort washcloths have been packaged in a distinctive denim blue package design (the "Sage's Package"), attached as Exhibit 1 to this memorandum. The package is insulated so that the cloths, once heated for one minute, will stay warm for 45 minutes. The cloths have a light, pleasant fragrance and contain a high amount of moisture in part due to a special ingredient, Tencel, which increases absorbency. (Affinito ¶ 6).

Sage has registered its copyright in Sage's Package with the United States Copyright Office, Registration No. VA-106-380. In 2001, Sage sold over $25 million worth of Comfort washcloths in that package. The vast share of Sage's annual sales of that product comes from sales to healthcare providers, such as hospitals, healthcare facilities, and distributors for such facilities. Sage began selling the product at retail two and a half years ago, and has a substantial and growing presence in that market. The many national chains carrying Sage's product include Walgreen's, Osco, and CVS. (Affinito ¶ 7, 12).

Sage spent over $5.5 million dollars in 2001 to advertise and promote Sage's washcloths in the denim blue package through a variety of media, including direct marketing to physicians and other healthcare providers, attendance and exhibition at healthcare industry trade shows, and over the Internet via its websites at www.sageproducts.com and www.comfortbath. com. (Affinito ¶ 9, 10, and 14). Sage has engaged in extensive print advertising of the product in national publications such as *Good Housekeeping, Saturday Evening Post, Reader's Digest, Woman's Day, Working Mother, Quest, New Mobility, Exceptional Parent, Healthy Caregiver*, and *OT Practice*. Sage also has featured its denim blue package in advertising on national television. (Affinito ¶ 10). Although Sage's Comfort product competes with several others for sales to hospitals and other healthcare providers, none of those competitors uses packaging similar to Sage's package. (Affinito ¶ 11).

On or about November, 2001, Sage became aware that defendant Kimberly-Clark Corporation ("Kimberly-Clark"), a large manufacturer of tissue, personal care, and healthcare products, and a competitor of Sage, was beginning to sell a disposable washcloth product through retail outlets such as Walgreen's, Osco, and CVS. (Affinito ¶ 15). The package bears the Kimberly-Clark name but no other brand name appears on it. Like Sage's washcloths, Kimberly-Clark's washcloth packaging indicates the washcloths are intended for use by individuals who have difficulty with conventional bathing and are intended to be microwaved prior to application. However, Kimberly-Clark has been promoting the washcloths as part of its incontinence product line. (Affinito ¶ 17).

Kimberly-Clark's disposable washcloths are sold in the denim blue package ("Kimberly-Clark's Package") shown in Exhibit 2 attached to this memorandum. Unlike Sage's product, Kimberly-Clark's package is only partially insulated, so the cloths need to be repeatedly reheated rather than staying warm for 45 minutes. Kimberly-Clark's cloths are less thick, lack the ingredient Tencel, and contain less moisture than Sage's, with the result that they clean less well. They also have a strong fragrance unlikely to appeal to consumers. (Affinito ¶ 20). Because of the compositional differences, Kimberly-Clark's washcloths are designed to be heated in the microwave for only 30 seconds, rather than the one minute of heating used for Sage's product. This difference in heating time raises a serious risk that confusion caused by Kimberly-Clark's similar packaging will result in the overheating of Kimberly-Clark's cloths and potential injury or discomfort for users. Consumers familiar with Sage's package who purchase or use Kimberly-Clark's product may well attempt to warm defendant's product the same way they do Sage's, resulting in such overheating. This risk is particularly acute in the many hospitals that have pre-programmed a button on their microwaves to warm Sage's product for one minute. (Affinito ¶ 21, 22).

Sage has filed a complaint against Kimberly-Clark alleging copyright infringement, trade dress infringement, and trade dress dilution, and now moves for a preliminary injunction against Kimberly-Clark's use of the package shown above for its disposable washcloth product, and use of any other package or design that is substantially similar to, likely to be confused with, or likely to dilute the distinctiveness of Sage's Package.

Argument

A party is entitled to a preliminary injunction i: (1) it has some likelihood of prevailing on the merits of its claim, (2) it is without an adequate remedy at law, (3) the threatened injury outweighs any damage that the injunction would cause the nonmovant, and (4) the injunction will serve the public interest. *Ty, Inc. v. Jones Grp. Inc.*, 237 F.3d 891, 895 (7th Cir. 2001); *Meridian Mut. Ins. Co. v. Meridian Ins.* Grp., 28 F.3d 1111, 1114 (7th Cir. 1997). All of these factors confirm that the requested relief should be granted.

IX. Sage is Likely to Succeed on the Merits of its Claims

In this circuit, in order to demonstrate a likelihood of success, a party must demonstrate that its chances of prevailing are "better than negligible." *Ty,* 237 F.3d at 897. Sage's likelihood of success on the merits is far greater than negligible, as discussed below.

A. Sage is Likely to Succeed on its Claims of Copyright Infringement

Sage will succeed on the merits of its copyright infringement claims if it can show (1) ownership of a valid copyright, (2) substantial similarity between the copyrighted work and the allegedly infringing work, and (3) the defendant's access to the copyrighted work. *Atari, Inc. v. N. Am. Phillips Consumer Elec. Corp.*, 672 F.2d 607, 614 (7th Cir. 1982), *cert. denied,* 459 U.S. 880 (1982).

1. Sage Owns A Valid Copyright

Sage owns U.S. Copyright Registration VA-106-380 for its package. This certificate of registration constitutes "prima facie evidence of the validity of the copyright and of the facts stated in the certificate." 17 USC § 410(c). Sage has therefore established prima facie ownership of a valid copyright.

2. Kimberly-Clark's Packaging is Substantially Similar to Sage's Copyrighted Package

Kimberly-Clark's packaging for its disposable washcloths is substantially similar to Sage's copyrighted package. The packages are virtually identical in size, shape, and denim blue color. While Sage's package also has graphic water drops on its denim blue background, Kimberly-Clark's package incorporates a wash/fade effect on its denim blue so that, from even a short distance away, the visual effect is virtually identical to that of Sage's package. Kimberly-Clark's package also mimics the other color shades used on Sage's package, including the white label, navy blue, dark turquoise, and yellow shading. Both packages use stylized white silhouettes of the human form centered at the top of the label in a rectangular logo, and in the bottom half of the label both feature pictures of a person using the washcloth to clean the back right shoulder area. Although the packages are not identical in every aspect, the Kimberly-Clark package thoroughly mimics the "total concept and feel" of Sage's package, and is substantially similar to it. *Atari*, 672 F.2d at 619–20.

3. Kimberly-Clark Had Access to Sage's Package

In copyright cases, access may be either proven directly or inferred. *Selle v. Gibb*, 741 F.2d 896, 901 (7th Cir. 1984) (plaintiff can establish reasonable possibility of access when its work has been widely disseminated to the public). Access may be inferred from widespread public display of the copyrighted work. *Ty, Inc. v. GMA Accessories, Inc.*, 959 F. Supp. 936, 940 (N.D. Ill. 1997). The close similarity of the works also raises an inference of access. *Id.*

In this case, there is no question that Kimberly-Clark had access to Sage's denim blue package. Aside from Kimberly-Clark's imitation of Sage's design, Sage's product is far and away the market leader for disposable washcloths sold to hospitals and other healthcare providers. Until Kimberly-Clark entered the retail market with its disposable washcloth product, Sage's also was the only significant product in that market. (Affinito ¶ 15). Among its many promotional activities, Sage has advertised its product on national television, and extensively both in general interest magazines and in magazines focused on healthcare issues involving the elderly and disabled. (Affinito ¶ 9, 10, and 14). In preparing to enter the disposable washcloth market, consideration of Sage's product by Kimberly-Clark was unavoidable.

Like Sage, Kimberly-Clark actively markets and sells products to hospitals and other healthcare providers, and to retail consumers. According to its website, last year it earned approximately $1.3 billion from its healthcare products business, $5.4 billion from its personal care business, and $7.3

billion from its tissue products. It is selling its product in the same retail outlets as Sage and, unlike Sage's other competitors, is using a package that studiously mimics Sage's design. (Affinito ¶ 11,15). Kimberly-Clark unquestionably had access to Sage's Comfort product, and was aware of Sage's package when it designed and launched its disposable washcloth product. Because Kimberly-Clark's package is substantially similar to Sage's copyrighted package, and Kimberly-Clark, when designing its package, had access to Sage's copyrighted package, Sage is likely to succeed on its claim of copyright infringement.

B. Sage Is Likely to Succeed on its Claims of Trade Dress Infringement

Sage is likely to succeed in demonstrating that Sage's package is entitled to trade dress protection, and that there is a likelihood of confusion between Sage's package and Kimberly-Clark's package.

1. Sage's Product Is Entitled to Trade Dress Protection

Sage's Package is inherently distinctive and entitled to protection under the trademark laws. Courts have recognized that a product's trade dress is eligible for such protection when it is not functional and is either inherently distinctive or has acquired distinctiveness through use.

a) The Sage Design is Not Functional

The Supreme Court in *Inwood Labs. v. Ives Laboratories*, 454 U.S. 844 n. 10 (1982) defined a functional feature as one that Ais essential to the use of purpose of the article or [that] affects the cost or quality of the article. The Second Circuit has explained that the concern is that courts will hinder competition by granting a monopoly on a useful design, rather than protecting an indicator of source as intended by the trademark laws:

> The functionality defense . . . was developed to protect advances in functional design from being monopolized. It is designed to encourage competition and the broadest dissemination of useful design features. The question posed is whether by protecting the [plaintiff's] symbols we are creating a monopoly on the shape or form of some useful object, thereby limiting the sharing of utilitarian refinements in useful objects.

Warner Bros., Inc. v. Gay Toys, Inc., 724 F.2d 327, 331 (2d Cir. 1983). The elements of Sage's package cannot be said to be "essential to the use or purpose" of the product, nor do they "affect the cost or quality" of the product in this utilitarian fashion. *See Traffix Devices, Inc. v. Mktg. Displays, Inc.*, 532 U.S. 23 (2001) (endorsing the use of the *Inwood*

Laboratories functionality test). In package design and similar cases, the question is whether the protection of the *combination* [of elements] would hinder competition or impinge on the rights of others to compete effectively. *Hartford House Ltd. v. Hallmark Cards, Inc.*, 846 F.2d 1268, 1273 (10th Cir. 1988) (greeting card design held infringed). *See also Click Billiards, Inc. v. Sixshooters, Inc.*, 251 F.3d 1252 (9th Cir. 2001) (finding fact issues as to whether the overall image of plaintiff's pool hall was nonfunctional, distinctive, and infringed). Some courts have focused on whether there are viable alternative designs in the marketplace. *See, e.g., Click Billiards, supra* (availability of alternative designs is relevant to functionality inquiry); *Tools USA & Equip. Co. v. Champ Frame Straightening Equip. Inc.*, 87 F.3d 654 (4th Cir. 1996) (upholding jury verdict for plaintiff; combination of elements in mail-order catalog nonfunctional where, though information conveyed in the catalog was useful, competitors did not need to imitate plaintiff's presentation). Here, protection of the combination of the various design elements for Sage's product clearly would not hinder competition, and many alternatives are possible, as shown by the existing third-party products on the market.

b) The Sage Design Is Distinctive

In *Wal-Mart Stores, Inc. v. Samara Bros, Inc.*, 120 S.Ct. 1339, 1344 (2000), Justice Scalia, for a unanimous court, commented that in contrast to product designs, consumers are predisposed to regard [words and packaging] as [an] indication of the producer." *See also Qualitex v. Jacobson Prods. Co.*, 514 U.S. 159 (1995) (color alone may be protectable as a trademark; plaintiffs green-gold color for dry cleaning pads held infringed). Sage's package, with its multiple and arbitrarily selected design features, is inherently distinctive. *Compare Chevron Chem. Co. v. Voluntary Purchasing Grps. Inc.*, 659 F.2d 695, 702 (5th Cir. 1981), *cert. denied*, 457 U.S. 1126 (1982), in which, in holding an insect spray bottle's overall appearance inherently distinctive, the court stated:

> If the features of the trade dress sought to be protected are arbitrary and serve no function either to describe the product or assist in its effective packaging, there is no reason to require a plaintiff to show consumer connotations associated with such arbitrarily selected features.

That is the situation here. Some elements of Sage's package, of course, have an informational purpose. However, the overall combination of the graphic features of package, including the predominant denim blue color, have been arbitrarily chosen for an appealing presence on the shelf and in use by the consumer. The package therefore is inherently distinctive. *Cf. Computer Care v. Service Systems Enters. Inc.*, 982 F.2d 1063, 1069 (7th Cir. 1992) (trade dress of brochures, letters, and reports held inherently distinctive).

If Sage were required to show secondary meaning in the package, its sales success and extensive advertising would provide ample basis for doing so. Factors typically considered in determining whether a trade dress has secondary meaning include (1) exclusivity, length and manner of use; (2) nature and extent of advertising and promotion; (3) volume of sales and number of customers; (4) established place in the market; and (5) the extent to which purchasers actually identify the design with the product. *Echo Travel, Inc. v. Travel Assoc., Inc.*, 870 F.2d 1264, 1267 (7th Cir. 1989).

Here, Sage has been the exclusive user of this denim blue package for more than a year and is far and away the market leader in disposable washcloths. *Compare L.A. Gear v. Thom McAn Shoe*, 12 U.S.P.Q.2d 1001, 1010 (S.D.N.Y. 1989), *aff'd in part and rev'd in part*, 988 F.2d 1117, 1130 (Fed. Cir. 1993) (five months of marketing of plaintiff's new sport shoe design sufficient to establish secondary meaning). In addition to its many other promotional activities, Sage has had advertising featuring its denim blue packaging run in at least ten national publications, including *Reader's Digest, Good Housekeeping, Saturday Evening Post, Woman's Day,* and *Working Mother*. Advertising featuring the package also has been broadcast on national television.

A final secondary meaning factor, which can be critical, is intentional copying by the second user. If the second user has intentionally copied another's nonfunctional packaging design, it is strong evidence that the plaintiff's design indicates source, or else the second user would not have sought to benefit by copying it. *See Schwinn Bicycle Co. v. Ross Bicycle, Inc.*, 870 F.2d 1176, 1182 (7th Cir. 1989) (intentional copying of the plaintiff's design is probative evidence of secondary meaning); *Click Billiards, Inc. v. Sixshooters, Inc.*, 251 F.3d 1252 (9th Cir. 2001)("In appropriate circumstances, deliberate copying may suffice to support an inference of secondary meaning"); *M. Kramer Mfg. Co. v. Andrews*, 783 F.2d 421, 448 (4th Cir. 1986) (Evidence of intentional, direct copying establishes a prima facie case of secondary meaning).

Here, Kimberly-Clark has demonstrated its intention to copy by mimicking everything from package size, label shape,and colors, to the white silhouette in a rectangular logo and the three-tiered layout of the label, including a picture showing someone using the washcloth on the back of her right shoulder. The last is particularly noteworthy because Kimberly-Clark is promoting this product with its Depend and Poise incontinence products. The simulation of Sage's shoulder-scrubbing photograph makes little sense for an incontinence product. Kimberly-Clark also has chosen not to use either the packaging design or well-known brand names of its Depend and Poise product lines. (Affinito ¶ 17).

Given the sales success of the Sage product under this package, its extensive advertising and promotion of the product, and Kimberly-Clark's intentional copying, Sage's package has acquired further distinctiveness in addition to the package's inherent distinctiveness.

c) Kimberly-Clark's Package for Its Washcloths Is Likely to be Confused with Sage's Package

In *Meridian Mut. Ins. Co. v. Meridian Ins.* Grp., 28 F.3d 1111, 1115 (7th Cir. 1997), the Seventh Circuit set forth the following factors to consider in determining whether confusion is likely:

1. The similarity between the marks in appearance and suggestion
2. The similarity of the products
3. Area and manner of concurrent use
4. Degree of care likely to be exercised by consumers
5. Strength of the complainant's mark
6. Actual confusion
7. Intent of the defendant to "palm off his product as that of another".

See also Ty, Inc. v. Jones Grp. Inc., 237 F.3d 891, 897 (7th Cir. 2001).

As discussed above, Kimberly-Clark's washcloth package is highly similar to Sage's washcloth package. It has copied the overall commercial impression of the package, using the same size and shape, the same colors, and similar pictures and designs on its label. This factor favors finding a likelihood of confusion.

This close similarity in appearance is not excused by the placement of the Kimberly-Clark name on defendant's package. It has long been recognized that the presence of such a "housemark" may only aggravate the confusion problem, leading consumers to believe there is a license, approval, or other authorization relationship between the parties. *Int'l Kennel Club of Chicago v. Mighty Star, Inc.*, 846 F.2d 1079, 1088 (7th Cir. 1988) (defendant's housemark argument was "a smoke screen and a poor excuse"; consumers "would necessarily believe that [plaintiff] had licensed, approved, or otherwise authorized the defendant's use"); *Am. Trading, Inc. v. Russ Berrie & Co.*, 966 F.2d 1284, 1288 (9th Cir. 1992) ("the prominence of [defendant's] housemark may serve to create reverse confusion"), citing *Menendez v. Holt*, 128 U.S. 514, 521 (1888) (use by defendant of its house mark along with plaintiff's LA FAVORITA mark was "an aggravation and not a justification, for it is openly trading in the name of another upon the reputation acquired by the device of the true proprietor").

The products involved in this case are identical and directly competitive. Both are microwaveable, disposable washcloths that can be used in healthcare facilities and homes to clean people who have difficulty with conventional bathing. (Affinito ¶ 3). *McGraw Edison Co. v. Walt Disney Prods., Inc.*, 787 F.2d 1163, 1169 (7th Cir. 1986) (products are similar if they are the kind the public attributes to a particular source). Although Kimberly-Clark is promoting its product with its incontinence line, it also is presenting it as a "bathing cloth" product in competition with Sage's product.

Assessing the area and manner of concurrent use requires determining whether there is a relationship in use, promotion, distribution or sales between the parties' products. *Ty, Inc. v. Jones Grp. Inc.*, 237 F.3d 891, 900 (7th Cir. 2001). Kimberly-Clark only recently introduced its washcloth product, but it is targeting the exact same retail and healthcare markets as Sage has.

The parties' washcloths are relatively inexpensive, the suggested retail price for both being under four dollars. Because of their nature, the products are purchased frequently and without a high degree of care. *AHP Subsidiary Holding Co. v. Stuart Hale Co.*, 1 F.3d 611, 616 (7th Cir. 1993) ("consumers take less time purchasing low-cost items, and haste increases the possibility of confusion"). Furthermore, the washcloths are of particular interest to elderly consumers, who may have diminished eyesight and rely more on visual similarities in packaging.

Sage's package design is extensively advertised, and the product is the market leader. Sage's advertising and sales, along with Kimberly-Clark's intentional copying, confirm that Sage's package is a strong trade dress symbolizing source and goodwill for Sage. Sage's package, in fact, has been unique in the market until Kimberly-Clark's product appeared. The absence of *any* third-party product with a similar design also demonstrates the strength of Sage's trade dress. (Affinito ¶ 11). *Cf. Frehling Enters. Inc. v. Int'l Select Grp. Inc.*, 192 F.3d 1330, 1336 (11th Cir. 1999) ("Where there is a lack of third-party use, the mark's strength is enhanced, as it is more distinctive and therefore more easily recognized by consumers").

Proof of actual confusion is not required in an infringement case. While Sage believes actual confusion is occurring, such confusion is unlikely to be reported given the cost of these products. *Beer Nuts, Inc. v. Clover Club Foods Co.*, 805 F.2d 920, 928 (10th Cir. 1986) ("Purchasers are unlikely to bother to inform the trademark owner when they are confused about an inexpensive product"). Nonetheless, there already has been at least one instance where Kimberly-Clark's package was displayed in Sage's display unit. (Affinito ¶ 18).

Finally, it is clear that Kimberly-Clark adopted its imitative packaging with the intent of trading upon the goodwill Sage has developed in its package. As the second entrant into the market for microwaveable, disposable washcloths, it was Kimberly-Clark's obligation to choose a packaging design that avoided conflict with Sage's rights. *Forum Corp. of North Am. v. Forum, Ltd.*, 903 F.2d 434, 440 (7th Cir. 1990). Unlike Sage's other competitors, Kimberly-Clark instead adopted a highly similar package. In light of its actions, its billion dollar presence in the healthcare market, and Sage's status as market leader and only significant seller of this type of product, Kimberly-Clark obviously knew of Sage's package and made the conscious decision to imitate it.

Sage therefore has a substantial likelihood of success on the merits of its trade dress infringement claim.

d) Sage Is Likely to Succeed on Its Claims of Trade Dress Dilution

Sage also is likely to succeed on its claim of trade dress dilution. Its denim blue package has become famous in its market, and Kimberly-Clark's packaging for its washcloth product is likely to blur the distinctiveness of that trade dress and tarnish the reputation of Sage's product.

Courts look to several factors to determine whether a trademark is "famous" for purposes of dilution. These factors include the degree of inherent or acquired distinctiveness of the mark, the duration and extent of use of the mark, the duration and extent of advertising of the mark, the geographical extent of the trading area in which the mark is used, the channels of trade in which the mark is used, the degree of recognition in those trade channels, the nature and extent of use of similar marks by third parties, and whether the mark is registered. 15 USC § 1125(c); *Eli Lilly & Co. v. Natural Answers, Inc.*, 233 F.3d 456, 466 (7th Cir. 2000).

The Seventh Circuit has recognized that a mark or trade dress may be famous in a niche market and may be diluted by uses of similar marks or similar trade dresses in that niche. *Syndicate Sales, Inc. v. Hampshire Paper Corp.*, 192 F.3d 633, 641 (7th Cir. 1999). In this case, Sage's washcloth product is famous in the market for disposable washcloths sold to hospitals and at retail. As discussed above, Sage's denim blue package is inherently distinctive, and it has acquired further distinctiveness through widespread use and promotion. The product has been successfully sold nationwide, and it has been advertised extensively in general circulation magazines, health and nursing care trade journals, as well as on national television. Sage's washcloth product is the top-selling disposable washcloth sold to healthcare providers, and was, until Kimberly-Clark's introduction of its product, the only significant disposable washcloth sold to consumers at retail. (Affinito ¶ ¶ 4, 9, 10, 15).

Before Kimberly-Clark's entry into the market, Sage's package was unique and without imitators. There are *no* third parties, other than Kimberly-Clark, using similar packaging. As shown in the Declaration of Kym Affinito, Sage's competitors for sales to healthcare providers, such as Medline, Kendall, and Joey Bath all use substantially different packaging from Sage's. (Affinito ¶ 11).

Given its leadership position, Sage's package enjoys a high degree of recognition in the trade channels in which it is sold. Many hospitals have even specifically preprogrammed microwave buttons for warming Sage's product. (Affinito ¶ 22). Sage's package therefore constitutes a famous trade dress under the federal dilution statute.

Kimberly-Clark's use of its imitative packaging for washcloths is likely to dilute the distinctiveness of Sage's trade dress by blurring its commercial impression in the eyes of consumers. *Eli Lilly*, 233 F.3d at 468 (plaintiff need only prove a likelihood of dilution to prevail). Dilution by blurring occurs when "consumers see the plaintiff's mark used on a plethora of different goods and services, raising the possibility that the mark will lose its ability to serve as a unique identifier of plaintiff's product." *Id.* Cf. *Nabisco, Inc. v. PF Brands, Inc.,* 191 F.3d 208, 219 (2d Cir. 1999) ("A second major seller of goldfish-shaped, orange-colored, cheddar-flavored, bite-sized crackers, can hardly fail, in our view, to dilute the distinctiveness in the eyes of consumers of the senior mark in a goldfish-shaped, orange-colored, cheddar-flavored, bite-sized cracker"). Here, Sage's use of its denim blue package has been unique. A second major seller of a closely similar package can hardly fail to dilute the distinctiveness of Sage's package in the eyes of consumers.

Dilution by tarnishment also is likely because Kimberly-Clark's product is of lower quality, and its difference in heat retention raises injury and discomfort concerns. (Affinito ¶ 20–22); *Eli Lilly,* 233 F.3d at 468 (dilution by tarnishment occurs when similarity causes consumers to associate plaintiff's mark with defendant's inferior or offensive product). Sage's package is insulated to allow the cloths to stay warm for up to 45 minutes after heating. Kimberly-Clark's package is insulated only at the bottom, so that it does not stay warm as long as Sage's product. (Affinito ¶ 20). Kimberly-Clark's washcloths also are not as thick, have a less pleasant fragrance, and do not hold as much moisture as Sage's product, with the result that they cleanse less well (Affinito ¶ 20). The reputation of Sage's product therefore is likely to be tarnished by association with Kimberly-Clark's lesser quality product.

In addition to this quality issue, Kimberly-Clark's similar packaging creates a risk of injury to product users. Sage's washcloths are designed to be microwaved for one minute prior to use, whereas Kimberly-Clark's cloths are designed to only be microwaved for thirty seconds, or one-half as long. (Affinito ¶ 21). Consumers familiar with Sage's product who purchase Kimberly-Clark's similar-looking product may attempt to warm Kimberly-Clark's product the same way they warm Sage's washcloths, creating an overheated cloth that could injure the user. (Affinito ¶ 22). This risk is of particular concern in healthcare facilities, many of which currently have preprogrammed buttons on their microwave ovens to heat the Sage product. (Affinito ¶ 22). Mistaken use of the microwave to overheat Kimberly-Clark product for one minute rather than thirty seconds, because of confusion due to preprogramming or confusion based on prior usage of Sage's product, creates a risk of physical harm, or causing other discomfort. (Affinito ¶ 21–22).

Sage therefore has a substantially greater likelihood of success on its dilution claim than the "better than negligible" chance required by the Seventh Circuit for entitlement to a preliminary injunction. *Ty,* 237 F.3d at 897.

X. Sage is Likely to Suffer Irreparable Harm if an Injunction is Not Entered

In trademark and copyright cases, there is a presumption that the harm caused is irreparable and not susceptible to an adequate remedy at law. *Ty,* 237 F.3d at 902; *Atari, Inc. v. North Am. Philips Consumer Elec. Corp.*, 672 F.2d 607, 614 (7th Cir. 1982), *cert. denied*, 459 U.S. 880 (1982). That presumption is fully justified in this case. As in *Ideal Indus. Inc v. Gardner Bender, Inc.*, 612 F.2d 1018, 1025 (7th Cir. 1979), "the existence of irreparable injury is positively supported by the fact that the alleged trademark and the infringing use are identical, that the products are the same and that the markets are the same."

Here, Sage's and Kimberly-Clark's packages for their washcloth products are closely similar, are used on directly competitive products, and are sold and promoted in the same markets, namely, to retail consumers and healthcare providers. Consumers who mistakenly purchase Kimberly-Clark's product instead of Sage's product are likely to associate any dissatisfaction with Sage's product. This risk is particularly acute here because of the differences in quality and the risk of physical injury or discomfort that could arise if the Kimberly-Clark product is used in the same manner that consumers are used to using Sage's product, as discussed above. Kimberly-Clark's continued use of the packaging at issue here therefore exposes Sage to irreparable injury to its goodwill and reputation, and purchasers of Kimberly-Clark's product to risk of physical harm. The potential for irreparable injury clearly favors entry of a preliminary injunction.

XI. The Balance of Hardships Favors Sage

The balance of hardships favors issuance of a preliminary injunction. As discussed above, Sage faces potentially irreparable injury to its reputation and goodwill if a preliminary injunction is denied. By contrast, issuing a preliminary injunction will impose only a slight burden on Kimberly-Clark. Kimberly-Clark is just starting out as a new entrant in the market. Its package is not established or well known among consumers. An injunction would only require Kimberly-Clark to change its packaging design. It would not require Kimberly-Clark to cease selling products in competition with Sage's product, or even to change the name of its competitive product.

Given Kimberly-Clark's recent entry, any potential loss from an injunction is relatively slight, particularly for a company of Kimberly-Clark's size and market presence. *Storck USA, L.P. v. Farley Candy Co., Inc.*, 797 F. Supp. 1399, 1413 (N.D. Ill. 1992) (balance of harms weighed in favor of plaintiff with smaller product line and against defendant with a broader product line); *Soft Sheen Products, Inc. v. Revlon, Inc.*, 675 F. Supp. 408, 417 (N.D. Ill. 1987) (same); *Littlefuse, Inc. v. Parker-Hannifin Corp.*, 230 U.S.P.Q. 654, 661 (N.D. Ill. 1986) (same). Kimberly-Clark also assumed the risk of being enjoined when it chose such a similar package design. *Atari, Inc. v. North Am. Consumer Elec. Corp.*, 672 F.2d 607, 620 (7th Cir.), *cert. denied*, 459 U.S. 880 (1982) ("Advantages built upon a deliberately plagiarized make-up do not seem to us to give the borrower any standing to complain that his vested interests will be disturbed," quoting from *My-T-Fine Corp. v. Samuels*, 69 F.2d 76, 78 (2d Cir. 1934)); *Helene Curtis Indus., Inc. v. Church & Dwight Co.*, 560 F.2d 1325, 1333–34 (7th Cir. 1977), *cert. denied*, 434 U.S. 1070 (1978) (same); *Pride Commc'ns v. WCKG, Inc.*, 30 U.S.P.Q.2d 1185, 1192 (N.D. Ill. 1994) (when defendants began using their mark they should have known of plaintiff's competing use; "they therefore acted at their peril that their own use would be enjoined").

XII. The Public Interest Favors Entry of an Injunction

Injunctions in trademark and copyright cases are presumed to serve the public interest. *Atari*, 672 F.2d at 620 (preliminary injunctions in copyright cases "preserve the integrity of the copyright laws which seek to encourage individual effort and creativity by granting valuable, enforceable rights"); *Health O Meter, Inc. v. Terraillon Corp.*, 873 F. Supp. 1160, 1176 (N.D. Ill. 1995) ("The public's interest is best served by the employment of non-confusing trade dresses on similar products put out by competing companies"). In this case, there is not only a substantial likelihood of confusion, but such confusion could cause physical harm. There is a serious risk to the public that mistaken heating of Kimberly-Clark's product for one minute, rather than the 30 seconds it is designed for, will cause injury or discomfort. (Affinito ¶ 21–22). The public interest therefore will be fully served by entry of a preliminary injunction.

Conclusion

For the foregoing reasons, Sage requests entry of a preliminary injunction prohibiting Kimberly-Clark from using the packaging at issue here or any other product packaging that is confusingly similar to or dilutive of Sage's package.

   Respectfully submitted,

Response to Motion for Preliminary Injunction

United States District Court for
the District of Vermont

MOUNT SOFTWARE,	)		
Plaintiff,	)		
v.	)	Case No.:	
MIM CORPORATION,	)	Oral Argument Requested	
Defendants.	)		

I. Introduction

Plaintiff Mount–which markets a personal finance program called "PocketCash"–seeks to preliminarily enjoin MIM's use of the name, "MIM Cash for Pocket PC." Mount would hold MIM responsible for alleged reverse confusion because either "PocketCash" and "MIM® Cash for Pocket PC" are confusingly similar, or in the alternative, MIM is responsible for several erroneous references by the public to MIM's product as "Pocket Cash."

Mount's motion should be denied on the grounds that: (1) Mount first learned of this matter in February 1999 and has delayed in seeking preliminary relief, demonstrating it is not being irreparably harmed; (2) MIM has marketed its personal finance software under the trademarks CASH and MIM CASH for many years prior to Mount's release of its "PocketCash" program; (3) the term "pocket PC" is generic or merely descriptive in the industry for a handheld computer; (4) therefore, MIM is entitled under the Lanham Act to use its long-standing trademark coupled with this generic name to describe to consumers what the product is; (5) MIM is not liable for references by third parties to its software as "Pocket Cash"; (6) Mount does not have protectable rights in the name "PocketCash"; (7) there is no likelihood of confusion between "MIM® Cash for Pocket PC" and "PocketCash"; and (8) the balance of hardships tips decidedly in favor of MIM.

MIM continuously has used its marks MIM CASH and CASH in connection with financial management software since prior to Mount's use of PocketCash. Pocket PC is a generic or merely descriptive term in the computer industry, signifying a class of hand-held computers small enough to fit in one's pocket. MIM developed a version of its MIM CASH software exclusively for use on Pocket PCs, and called it MIM® Cash for Pocket PC. Under the Trademark Law, MIM is permitted to use the descriptive phrase Pocket PC to identify to consumers the specific application of the software.

Equity also favors denying the motion for a preliminary injunction. MIM advised Mount in February 1999 of its initial intent to call its software for Pocket PCs "MIM Pocket Cash." Mount responded, remarkably claiming rights to any mark including "pocket" and "cash" together. In order to avoid a dispute with Mount, MIM decided not to use "MIM Pocket Cash." MIM informed Mount by letter in February 2000 that the product would be called MIM® Cash for Pocket PC, and that the Pocket PCs would ship sometime in the first half of the year 2000. The manufacturers of the Pocket PCs with MIM® Cash for Pocket PC installed indeed began shipping in April 2000. Mount then complained that members of the public were calling the MIM software "Pocket Cash," and demanded that MIM change the name. MIM declined. Mount then waited three months until August 2000, to file its complaint, and waited yet another three months to file the pending motion.

II. Facts

A. MIM's CASH Product and Use of MIM® Cash for Pocket PC

Since 1991, MIM has used the term CASH in connection with personal finance software for desktop computers. (Ortiz Dec. ¶ 2; O'Callahan Dec., Exh. A). MIM has sold millions of copies of the software, and it has won numerous industry awards. (Ortiz Dec. ¶¶ 2–3). MIM has also advertised and promoted its CASH product extensively. (Jensen Dec., ¶ 2, Exhibit). In response to the phenomenal popularity of the CASH software and the advent of small-sized handheld computers, commonly called Pocket PCs, MIM developed CASH software suitable for use with Pocket PCs. (Sheldon Dec. ¶ 3 Yarble Dec. ¶ 4).

MIM uses the phrase "MIM® Cash for Pocket PC" to market its version of Cash for Pocket PCs. CASH and the famous MIM mark are accompanied by the generic or descriptive phrase "for Pocket PC" to describe the devices for which the software was written. (Yarble Dec. ¶ 4; O'Callahan Dec. ¶ 4, Exh. C). MIM's standard CASH program will not run on a Pocket PC. (Sheldon Dec. ¶ 5). MIM® Cash for Pocket PC, however, functions exclusively on the Windows CE operating system, within the more constrained technological parameters of a pocket PC. (*Id.* ¶¶ 4–5). Although smaller in size, MIM® Cash for Pocket PC is more than just a downsized version of the CASH application. (*Id.* ¶ 5). MIM® Cash for Pocket PC can be used as a stand-alone product or synchronized with the CASH software designed for desktop computers. (*Id.* ¶ 5).

In April 2000, MIM® Cash for Pocket PC was first sold to the public by original equipment manufacturers ("OEMs"), including Compaq, Casio and Hewlett-Packard, who include the application as an integral part of their Pocket PC units sold to consumers. (Sheldon Dec. ¶ 3).

B. Mount And Its PocketCash Product

Mount claims to have begun sales of personal financial management software under the alleged mark PocketCash in 1994, three years after MIM released its CASH product. (Prelim. Inj. Br. at 2). Mount sells its product primarily, if not exclusively, over the Internet. (*see* O'Callahan Dec. ¶ 11, Exh. H). Over the past six years, Mount alleges sales of over 6,000 copies of its Pocket Cash product, not all in the United States, and has expended a total of $20,000 in advertising. (Prelim. Inj. Br. at 2; Macia Dec., ¶ 6). Mount has not obtained a federal trademark registration of PocketCash. Nevertheless, Mount displays a federal trademark registration symbol in connection with the mark on its website, the software application itself, and related documentation. (O'Callahan Dec. ¶ 9, Exh. G).

C. Communications Between the Parties

On February 15, 1999, MIM wrote to Mount expressing concern about any use Mount might make of "PocketCash" in connection with financial planning software on a Windows CE Platform, also informing Mount of its original intention to use the name "MIM Pocket Cash" for the Pocket PC version of MIM CASH. (O'Callahan Dec., Exh. I). In response, by letter of February 26, 1999, Mount objected to MIM's use of "pocket" in conjunction with "cash" for personal finance software. (*Id.* Exh. J) Correspondence between MIM and Mount regarding their respective uses of "MIM Pocket Cash" and "PocketCash" continued over the next three months.

Throughout this period, Mount maintained its objection to MIM's use of "pocket" in conjunction with "cash." On April 22, 1999, Mount wrote to MIM that it had received numerous communications from customers and friends alerting it to MIM's proposed use of "Pocket Cash." (*Id.* Exh. K). Mount included a draft complaint and preliminary injunction motion seeking to prevent MIM from using "pocket" and "cash" in connection with any financial management software. On May 10, 1999, MIM informed Mount that it did not intend to use the name "MIM Pocket Cash." (*Id.* Exh. L).

On February 19, 2000, MIM informed Mount that it was naming its software product MIM® Cash for Pocket PC and that the software was in production and would be released to consumers in the first half of 2000. (*Id.* Exh. M). In April 2000, the various OEM's began sales of Pocket PC units which included MIM Cash for Pocket PC as part of the Pocket PC's built-in software. (Sheldon Dec., ¶ 3). During April and May 2000, Mount alleged three times in letters to MIM that it was aware of instances of erroneous use of "Pocket Cash" to describe MIM's software. (O'Callahan Dec., Exh. N). Although Mount became aware of what it characterizes as the public's alleged misuse of "Pocket Cash" to describe MIM's product at that time, Mount elected not to file its Complaint until August 30, 2000. It then waited until November 26, 2000, to file for injunctive relief - *three months* after Mount filed the underlying action, *seven months* after the Pocket PCs containing MIM CASH appeared on the market, *nine months* after it learned of MIM's intended use of the phrase "MIM® Cash for Pocket PC," *21 months* after it first objected to MIM's use of a name including the words "pocket" and "cash."

III. Argument

A. Mount Fails to Meet the Requirements for Obtaining a Preliminary Injunction

It is well settled that a preliminary injunction is a drastic and extraordinary remedy. *Med. Soc. of State of N.Y. v. Toia*, 560 F.2d 535, 538 (2d Cir. 1977). To qualify for a preliminary injunction, Mount must demonstrate (a) that it is likely to suffer irreparable injury absent the injunction, and (b) either (1) that it is likely to succeed on the merits of its claim or (2) that there exist sufficiently serious questions going to the merits to make them a fair ground for litigation and the balance of hardships tips decidedly toward the movant. *Jackson Dairy, Inc. v. H.P. Hood & Sons, Inc.*, 596 F.2d 70, 71 (2d Cir. 1979) (per curium).

The Second Circuit has characterized a showing of likely irreparable harm as perhaps the single most important prerequisite for the issuance of a preliminary injunction. *Bell & Howell: Mayima Co. v. Masel Supply Co.*, 719 F.2d 42, 45 (2d Cir. 1983) (*quoting* 11C. Wright & A. Miller, *Federal Practice and Procedure* § 2948 at 431 (1973)). When the applicant is unable to show a probability of success on the merits, it must make an even stronger showing of irreparable injury. *Triebwasser & Katz v. Am. Tel. & Tel. Co.*, 535 F.2d 1356, 1359 (2d Cir. 1976); *Jackson Dairy*, 596 F.2d at 74 (concurrence) ("the weaker the case on the merits, the stronger must be the showing of threat of irreparable injury").

1. Mount's Lengthy Delay in Seeking an Injunction Proves a Lack of Irreparable Harm

It is well settled that significant delay in bringing suit or applying for preliminary injunctive relief renders any presumption of irreparable harm inoperative. *Tough Traveler v. Outbound* Prods. 60 F.3d 964, 968 (2d Cir. 1995). Such a delay "tends to neutralize any presumption that infringement alone will cause irreparable harm pending trial and, such delay may alone justify the denial of a preliminary injunction." *Citibank, N.A. v. Citytrust*, 756 F.2d 273, 276 (2d Cir. 1985). The courts have rejected claims of irreparable harm for similar or lesser delays of time. *Id.* (delay of nine months after receiving notice in the press and ten weeks after receiving actual notice); *Tough Traveler*, 60 F.3d at 968 (delay of nine months after discovery of harm and four months after filing complaint); *Greenpoint Fin. Corp. v. The*

Sperry & Hutchinson Co. Inc., 116 F. Supp. 2d 405, 409 (S.D.N.Y. 2000) (delay of four months); *ImOn, Inc. v. Imagin On, Inc.*, 90 F. Supp. 2d 345, 350 (S.D.N.Y. 2000) (delay of 18 weeks; held the presumption of harm inoperative, but case decided no likelihood of confusion); *Eugene Biro Corp. v. Empire Diamond Corp.*, 40 U.S.P.Q.2d 1527, 1529–30 (S.D.N.Y. 1996) (delay of 10 months after defendant's refusal to cease and one year after plaintiff's alleged first notice of defendant's mark).

Mount's substantial delay in seeking preliminary relief, knowing MIM was proceeding with the name, precludes any finding of irreparable harm, and justifies the denial of Mount's motion. Mount delayed nine months after MIM informed Mount it would be using the name "MIM Cash for Pocket PC," in connection with MIM's CASH software for Pocket PCs. At the same time, MIM indicated to Mount that the product would be released in the first half of 2000. (O'Callahan Dec. Exh. M). It was almost 19 months from the time Mount served a draft preliminary injunction motion and brief before Mount actually sought preliminary relief. (*Id.* Exh. K). And it was 21 months between the parties' first discussion of this matter and the filing of this motion. (*Id.* Exh. I). Mount's delay in seeking enforcement of those rights undercuts the sense of urgency and indicates a reduced need for the drastic, speedy action of a preliminary injunction. *Citibank*, 756 F.2d at 276. This unreasonable delay indicates that any harm suffered by the applicant is not so severe as to be irreparable, particularly in light of Mount's failure to offer a reasonable explanation. *Tough Traveler*, 60 F.3d at 968 (unless the delay is attributable to plaintiff's ignorance or good faith efforts to investigate, delay alone may justify denial of preliminary injunction).

Mount offers no explanation for its delay. Mount was aware of MIM's intention to release a Pocket PC version of the CASH software almost two years before it applied for injunctive relief. On the basis of Mount's delay in seeking preliminary relief, especially when MIM explicitly stated to Mount that it had changed its name and was proceeding to market with the phrase MIM® Cash for Pocket PC, the Court should conclude Mount is suffering no irreparable harm and deny the motion for preliminary injunction.

2. Mount Has Not Established a Substantial Likelihood of Success

In order for Mount to establish a likelihood of success on the merits in a reverse confusion case, it must demonstrate (1) prior rights in a protectable trademark and (2) that consumers are likely to believe that MIM is the source of Mount's product. *Lang v. Retirement Living Publ'g Co., Inc.* 949 F.2d 576, 582 (2d Cir. 1991)[4]. Mount's case fails because (1) MIM has prior rights in

---

4. Mount alleges it has a claim of reverse confusion under 15 U.S.C. §§ 1114 and 1125 (Pl. Br. At 11). However, Mount does not have a claim of infringement under 15 U.S.C. §§ 1114 because it does not have a federal registration for PocketCash. Mount's

the mark CASH for financial planning software, and it has the right to use the descriptive phrase "for Pocket PC," and (2) Mount has presented *no evidence* that anyone believes MIM is the source of Mount's product.[5]

a) Mount Does Not Have Prior Protectable Rights

(1) MIM Has Senior Rights in the term CASH and "Pocket" is Generic or Merely Descriptive

MIM's continuous use of CASH in connection with financial management software pre-dates Mount's use of PocketCash by at least three years. (Ortiz Dec., ¶ 2). Over the past several years, MIM has sold over 50 million copies of its MIM® CASH software. (*Id.* ¶ 3).[6]

Mount's statement that MIM uses a mark comprised of "pocket" and "cash" is false both factually and legally. Rather, CASH and the famous MIM mark are accompanied by the generic or descriptive phrase "for Pocket PC" to inform consumers of the computer application for which the software was written. Furthermore, MIM's website shows that the software is sometimes referred to as "MIM Money for *the* Pocket PC" (emphasis added), further demonstrating that "Pocket PC" merely describes the specific platform for which this version of the MIM CASH program is written. (O'Callahan Dec. ¶ 4, Exh. C). This variation in usage further demonstrates MIM is not using Pocket PC as a trademark.

MIM has the right under the Trademark Law to use a generic or descriptive term for pocket-sized personal computers in connection with software designed to run on those computers. *Bristol-Myers Squibb Co. v. McNeil – P.P.C., Inc.*, 973 F.2d 1033, 1039–41 (2d Cir. 1992). A descriptive term immediately conveys to the public some information about the nature, characteristics or benefits of a product or service. *Id.* at 1040; *King-Size v. Frank's King Size Clothes, Inc.*, 547 F. Supp. 1138, 1156 (N.D. Ill. 1982) (KING-SIZE held to be descriptive of large men's clothing). The term "pocket" conveys to the public the size of the goods - a computer that is pocket sized in

---

only colorable claim is under 15 U.S.C. § 1125. Mount also alleges a claim of infringement under Vermont common law, but fails to cite any authority under Vermont law. (Pl. Br. at 1).

5. Concerning Mount's improper use of the federal trademark registration symbol, courts have found that such fraudulent use of the federal registration symbol constitutes unclean hands and estops a party from seeking relief for trademark infringement. *See e.g., L.F. Gaubert & Co. v. Inst. of Elec. & Elec. Eng'r, Inc.*, 563 F. Supp. 122, 128 (E.D. La. 1983) (preliminary injunction denied where plaintiff misused symbol "intentionally" or through careless disregard); *Urecal v. Masters*, 413 F. Supp. 873 (N.D. Ill. 1976) (misuse of symbol constitutes unclean hands and bars relief).

6. The issue of Mount's use of PocketCash in light of MIM's prior use of CASH and MIM CASH may be before the Court at another time.

order that it may be conveniently carried on one's person. (O'Callahan Dec. Exhs. D-F). Furthermore, the term Pocket PC is widely used throughout the computer industry to refer to small-sized computers of different manufacturers. Hundreds of articles on the Nexis database use the term Pocket PC to refer to computers of that size. (O'Callahan Dec. ¶ 8, Exh. F). These articles date back to at least 1987, more than six years before Mount alleges it first used PocketCash. (*Id.* ¶ 8, Exh. F; Prelim. Inj. Br. at 2). The term "PC" is commonly defined and used throughout the industry to identify a "personal computer." (O'Callahan Dec. ¶ ¶ 5 and 8, Exh. D, E and F).

A term may be shown to be generic or merely descriptive by public usage. *Ale House Mgmt. Inc. v. Raleigh Ale House, Inc.*, 205 F.3d 137 (4th Cir. 2000). Mount's claim to trademark rights notwithstanding, the terms "pocket" and "Pocket PC" were widely used by many parties long prior to Mount's use of PocketCash. (O'Callahan Dec. Exhs. E-F). The term is used in the stories from the Nexis database in connection with the products of at least 26 companies. (*Id.* Exh. E). These stories show that Pocket PC cannot function as a trademark. MIM is, therefore, entitled to use "Pocket PC" in the phrase MIM® Cash for Pocket PC to describe the computer device for which the MIM CASH software was developed. *Ale House Mgmt. Inc.*, 205 F.3d at 141. (internet search revealing over 100 uses of "ale house" sufficient to prove the term is generic).

Mount cannot assert a claim of trademark infringement against MIM based on alleged rights in a mark comprised of MIM's prior CASH trademark and the descriptive term "pocket." [7] The addition of the descriptive term "pocket" to CASH does not provide Mount protectable rights in "PocketCash." Even the United States Patent and Trademark Office has required disclaimer of the word "pocket" in a trademark registration because the word is merely descriptive. *In re EBS Data Processing, Inc.*, 212 U.S.P.Q. 964, 966 (TTAB 1981), the Board required the applicant to disclaim "Pocket Profile" in the registration of PHACTS POCKET PROFILE, for use in connection with a personal medical history summary. The Board took judicial notice of the definition of "pocket" as an adjective meaning reduced in size or condensed. "[T]he term 'Pocket Profile' merely describes applicant's condensed record of patient's medical information. This profile is condensed to pocket size in order that it may be conveniently carried on one's person. As such the term is merely descriptive of the goods." (*Id.*); *see Cunningham v. Laser Golf Corp.*, 222 F.3d 943, 947 (Fed. Cir. 2000) (LASERSWING likely to cause confusion with LASER for golf clubs; "swing" is a common term when referring to golf clubs).

---

7. Mount's State of Vermont registration affords no presumption regarding the validity or strength of its alleged mark. 9 V.S.A. §§ 2529 and 2530. The registration merely provides Mount the right to sue under Vermont law, yet Mount fails to cite *any* authority for suit under Vermont law.

The evidence, therefore, shows that MIM has prior rights in its marks CASH and MIM CASH in connection with software for financial management. Furthermore, there is much common usage of the phrase Pocket PC to describe the category of pocket-sized computers, since well prior to Mount's first sale of its PocketCash software. Given its prior rights in CASH, and the genericness or descriptiveness of Pocket PC, MIM cannot be enjoined from using the phrase MIM® Cash for Pocket PC.

(2) Third Party Use of "Pocket Cash"

Mount asks this Court to impose unprecedented liability on MIM for the public's descriptive use of "Pocket Cash" to refer to MIM's CASH software for Pocket PCs, even though MIM has neither sanctioned nor encouraged such use. Plaintiff offers no evidence that MIM ever has used or encouraged anyone to use the phrase "Pocket Cash" in connection with its CASH software for the Pocket PC application. To the contrary, MIM has instructed its OEMs that the product properly is called MIM® Cash for Pocket PC. (Yarble Dec. ¶ ¶ 6–7, Exh. A). Each OEM receives a copy of MIM's "Product Name Usage Guidelines," which states the product should be called "MIM® Cash for Pocket PC." (*Id.*). Mount's evidence is only unsworn statements in which some members of the public, not MIM, have used the term "Pocket Cash" to refer to the MIM® Cash for Pocket PC application. Furthermore, *none of the unsworn statements reflect confusion between the parties' products.*

Trademark law does not impose liability under the above circumstances. In *Illinois High School Ass'n v. GTE Vantage Inc.*, 99 F.3d 244 (7th Cir. 1996) *cert. denied*, 519 U.S. 1150 (1997), the Seventh Circuit affirmed, in effect, the principle that the media's appropriation of one party's alleged mark to describe a second party's service cannot be grounds for an infringement action against the second party. The Illinois High School Association ("IHSA") brought a trademark infringement action against GTE Vantage, a licensee of the mark "March Madness." IHSA asserted rights in the mark based on more than 50 years of use to designate the annual Illinois high school basketball tournament. A basketball tournament sponsored by the National Collegiate Athletic Association ("NCAA") was first called "March Madness" by sportscaster Brent Musberger in 1982. The media subsequently began to use the term for the NCAA tournament also held in March and also referred to by the public as "March Madness." GTE Vantage later licensed the mark from the NCAA for merchandise associated with the NCAA tournament.

IHSA filed an unsuccessful motion for preliminary injunction against GTE Vantage's use of "March Madness," alleging reverse confusion. The Seventh Circuit affirmed, analogizing to cases in which marks were made generic through public use of the marks to describe a general category of goods rather than one specific brand, and holding that "March Madness" had become a "dual-use term." "Whatever you call it, it's a name that the public has affixed to something other than, as well as, the Illinois high school basketball tournament." *Id.* at 247. The court commented that IHSA might have a remedy against the NCAA, "were [the] NCAA responsible for blotting out the exclusive association of "March Madness" with the Illinois high school basketball tournament." *Id.* at 246.

Similarly, in this case, Mount has no remedy against MIM because MIM is not responsible for any public use of "Pocket Cash" to refer to MIM® Cash for Pocket PC. In fact, unlike the defendants in two cases cited by Mount, *Big O Tire Dealer, Inc. v. Goodyear Tire & Rubber Corp.*, 408 F. Supp. 1219 (D. Colo. 1976) *aff'd as modified*, 561 F.2d 1365 (10th Cir. 1977); and *Banff, Ltd. V. Federated Dept. Stores, Inc.*, 841 F.2d 486 (2d Cir. 1988); MIM took specific measures to distinguish its CASH software for Pocket PCs from Mount's PocketCash product.[8] Defendant Goodyear asked Big O for a consent to use "Bigfoot" on its tires, Big O refused, and Goodyear proceeded with the launch of its "Bigfoot" campaign. Here, MIM informed Mount of its intent to launch "Pocket Cash," Mount protested, and MIM revised the name and launched MIM Cash for Pocket PC. Moreover, MIM has correctly referred to its product and has further provided its OEMs with "Product Name Usage Guidelines" that expressly instruct the OEMs to use the phrase MIM® Cash for Pocket PC. (Yarble Dec. Exh. A).

b) There is No Likelihood of Confusion

Plaintiff alleges MIM has caused reverse confusion. The Second Circuit has held that the only relevant confusion in a reverse confusion case is a belief by the senior user's purchasers or prospective purchasers that the senior user's product was produced by or affiliated with the junior user. *Lang*, 949 F.2d at 583 (2d Cir. 1991). The relevant confusion to be avoided is that which affects purchasing decisions, not confusion generally. *Id.* at 582–83; see also *W.W.W. Pharm. Co., Inc. v. Gillette Co.*, 984 F.2d 567, 574 (2d Cir. 1993).

Mount cites *Banff*, 841 F.2d 486, quoting the rule that "reverse confusion is the misimpression that the junior user is the source of the senior user's goods." Mount claims to satisfy the element of likelihood of confusion with proof that consumers have been mistakenly using Mount's trademark to identify MIM's

---

8. The reverse confusion cases cited by Mount also are inapposite in that they involved the adoption by the defendants of marks phonetically identical to the plaintiff's marks. (*See* Prelim. Inj. Br. at 4). In *Banff, Ltd.* the owner of the "Bee Wear" trademark for women's clothing sued Federated over its use of the mark "B Wear," also for women's clothing. In *Big O Tire Dealer, Inc.*, the owner of the mark "Big Foot" for tires sued Goodyear over its use of "Bigfoot," also for tires. MIMCash for Pocket PC is not phonetically identical to PocketCash.

product *and* have been confused as to the *source* of the parties' products. (Prelim. Inj. Br. at 8). Not one piece of evidence, however, shows that anyone believes that MIM is the source of Mount's product.

(1) Polaroid Factors

Mount has failed to show that there is a likelihood of confusion caused by MIM's use of MIM® Money for the Pocket PC and Mount's use of PocketCash. Likelihood of confusion is evaluated in light of the test established in *Polaroid Corp. v. Polrad Elec. Corp.*, 287 F.2d 492 (2d Cir.), *cert. denied*, 368 U.S. 820 (1961) (the strength of plaintiff's mark; the degree of similarity between the two marks; the proximity of the products; the likelihood the prior owner will bridge the gap; actual confusion; defendant's good faith in adopting its own mark; the quality of defendant's product; sophistication of the buyers)[9]. Each factor must be weighed "in the context of the others to determine if, on balance, a likelihood of confusion exists." *W.W.W. Pharm.*, 984 F.2d at 572. Moreover, a probability of confusion must exist, not merely a possibility. *Streetwise Maps, Inc. v. Vandam, Inc.*, 159 F.3d 739, 743 (2d Cir. 1998). Mount must show that an appreciable number of purchasers will be confused as to the source of the goods. *Id.*

The Strength of Plaintiff's Mark - The strength of PocketCash turns on whether the alleged mark has acquired secondary meaning so that it tends to identify Mount's business in the public eye. *Lang*, 949 F.2d at 580. Mount has not presented evidence that its alleged mark is distinctive in the marketplace. *Thompson Med. Co. v. Pfizer Inc.*, 753 F.2d 208 (2d Cir. 1985). As discussed above, "pocket" is a commonly used word for small-sized computers and related software. Mount describes its total sales over its six-year history as over 6,000 units in 70 countries, only an unknown portion of them in the United States. Mount has made an average expenditure of $3300 per year in advertising. These low sales and advertising figures negate any inference that PocketCash is associated in the public's mind with Mount. *Lang*, 949 F.2d at 580 (total of $85,000 in domestic and foreign sales in six years and extensive third party use of "choices" supports finding that "New Choices" is weak).

Even if the Court were to find Mount's alleged mark deserving of some protection, the combination of *Polaroid* factors weighs strongly against a finding of likelihood of confusion. *Streetwise*, 159 F.3d at 744.

The Degree of Similarity Between The Marks - The dissimilarities of marks in their entireties and differences in their commercial presentation are sufficient for a court to find the marks are not confusingly similar without further analysis of any other *Polaroid* factors. *Nabisco v. Warner-Lambert, Co.*, 220 F.3d 43, 46 (2d Cir. 2000); *Bristol-Myers Squibb Co. v. McNeil-PPC*,

---

9. Mount misstates the *Polaroid* factors in its brief. (Pl/ Br. at 12).

973 F.2d 1033, 1045–46 (packages for EXEDRIN PM and TYLENOL PM for analgesics not confusingly similar: "the prominence of the trade names on the two packages weighs heavily against a finding of consumer confusion."); *see also Streetwise Maps, Inc. v. Vandam, Inc.*, 159 F.3d 739 (2d Cir. 1998) (affirming dismissal of trademark infringement claim by owner of STREETWISE mark for tourist maps against user of STREET SMART for competing maps, finding that although trademarks sound similar, they are not confusingly similar in commercial context because of differences in folds, logos, colors and typefaces). In *Nabisco,* the Court held that "cumulative differences between the parties' products and in the commercial presentation of their mark creates distinct marketplace impressions" and, therefore, make confusion unlikely. *Id.* at 47. In that case, the plaintiff appealed from an order granting summary judgment to defendant on plaintiff's trademark infringement and unfair competition claims. Plaintiff owned the mark ICE BREAKERS for breath-freshening chewing gum and sued defendant for use of DENTYNE ICE for competing goods. The Court held that defendant's use of the famous housemark DENTYNE virtually eliminated any chance of confusion. *Id.* at 46. Moreover, whatever confusion existed, notwithstanding the use of the housemark, was dispelled by the other aspects of the parties' commercial presentations of their respective marks. *Id.* Specifically, the Court found that the parties presented their marks in different styles and typefaces, the product packaging differed in terms of dimension and shape, and the products were sold in different forms – plaintiff's product came as a traditional stick and defendant's was sold as a candy-coated pellet. *Id.* at 47.

Here, MIM® Cash for Pocket PC and Mount's alleged PocketCash mark are not similar. Moreover, MIM prominently uses its famous housemark to identify MIM® Cash for Pocket PC as part of its family of software products. MIM's housemark appears on its website in connection with the product and in the software itself. (O'Callahan Dec. ¶ 4 and 18, Exh. C; Sheldon Dec. ¶ 8). Use of MIM's famous house mark eliminates any likelihood of confusion. *Nabisco,* 220 F.3d at 47.

Even where two marks are similar, differences in logos may make confusion unlikely. When users access the MIM® Cash for Pocket PC software, they click on an icon showing the MIM® CASH mark. (O'Callahan Dec. ¶ 18). In addition, the multi-colored MIM® icon and MIM® CASH appears on every page as the application runs. (*Id.*) Mount's website, on the other hand, displays Mount's "mountain" logo. (O'Callahan Dec. ¶ 9, Exh. G). When users access the Mount software, they click on a Mount icon. (O'Callahan Dec. ¶ 19). Information on how to contact Mount also appears in the "About" section of the program. (*Id.*).

The Proximity of the Products - The fact that the parties' products are related is not dispositive, particularly where as here, the parties marks' are different and create distinct commercial impressions. *Nabisco,* 220 F.3d at 47. Moreover, the parties' products are sold through different channels in different forms, which diminishes any likelihood of confusion. *Computer Assoc. Int'l v. AJV Computerized Data Mgmt.*, 889 F. Supp. 630, 637 (S.D.N.Y. 1995). MIM licenses MIM® Cash for Pocket PC to OEMs, such as Casio, Hewlett-Packard and Compaq, who include it in their Pocket PCs sold to the public. (Sheldon Dec. ¶ 6) Mount, on the other hand, sells its software directly to consumers who download it onto their computers. (O'Callahan Dec. ¶ 11). The differences between the parties' product forms and the different commercial presentations of MIM® Cash for Pocket PC and PocketCash make it unlikely that confusion will result from their simultaneous use. *Nabisco*, 220 F.3d at 47.

Actual Confusion - Mount presents no evidence of actual confusion - that consumers believe that the PocketCash product emanates from MIM. Nor did Mount present evidence that purchasing decisions were affected by confusion. *Lang*, 949 F.2d at 583. Instead, the web-postings cited by Mount merely show that some consumers have used the phrase "Pocket Cash" to refer to MIM's product. This does not show confusion as to source; rather, consumers are at most attaching the descriptive word "pocket" to MIM's CASH mark to refer to MIM® Cash for Pocket PC. The lack of confusion as to source is underscored by the fact that the majority of the newsgroup postings referred to by Mount are taken from a MIM CASH newsgroup and websites dedicated to MIM products.

Defendant's Good Faith – Contrary to Mount's assertions of intentional wrongdoing, MIM adopted the phrase MIM® Cash for Pocket PC in good faith. The test for establishing bad faith is "whether the defendant adopted its mark with the intention of capitalizing on plaintiff's reputation and goodwill and any confusion between his and the senior user's product." *Lang*, 949 F.2d at 583 (quoting *Edison Bros. Stores, Inc. v. Cosmark, Inc.*, 651 F. Supp. 1547, 1560 (S.D.N.Y. 1987)). Prior knowledge of Mount's alleged mark does not necessarily give rise to an inference of bad faith. *Id.* at 583-84. Mount has put forth no evidence that MIM intended to promote confusion between the products or capitalize on Mount's alleged goodwill. Here, as in *W.W.W. Pharmaceutical*, the relative size and market strengths of the parties indicate that MIM had no intent to trade on Mount's reputation and therefore did not act in bad faith. "Given [MIM's] name recognition and goodwill, and [Mount's] obscurity, any confusion would have redounded to [Mount's], rather than [MIM's], benefit." *W.W.W. Pharm.*, 984 F.2d at 575.

Moreover, MIM's combination of its mark CASH with the generic or descriptive phrase "for Pocket PC" to describe its product evidences its good faith. *Streetwise*, 159 F.3d at 745. In *Streetwise*, the defendant had prior use of the term "smart" for maps and combined it with the descriptive term "street" to form the mark STREETSMART for maps. Plaintiff sued for trademark infringement based on its registered mark STREETWISE for maps. The Court held that defendant's mark was not identical to plaintiff's. Instead, defendant created a different name by combining a descriptive term with a mark it had previously used. *Id.* at 745–46. The mark STREETSMART merely reflected the product's characteristics. Although defendant knew of plaintiff's mark, it did not believe its mark was infringing. *Id.* at 746. Similarly, MIM selected a phrase that merely describes the Pocket PC version of its CASH product. MIM had no intention of capitalizing on Mount's alleged goodwill.

In fact, it is Mount that incorporated MIM's CASH mark in Mount's alleged mark PocketCash. Mount asks this court to take the unprecedented stance that MIM is responsible for the public's incorrect use of its name, in spite of MIM's explicit decision to use a phrase distinct from PocketCash, and regardless of the fact that MIM has instructed its licensees regarding its proper use. (Yarble Dec. ¶ ¶ 5–8).[10]

The Quality of Defendant's Product - Mount has offered no evidence that MIM® Cash for Pocket PC is of poor quality. A small collection of postings to web newsgroups or chat rooms is anecdotal evidence at best and does not demonstrate anything other than the minor problems encountered by a handful of customers. As in *Computer Assoc. Int'l.*, 889 F. Supp. at 638, there is no evidence that MIM's product has suffered from anything more than the normal glitches that often accompany a new product into the market.

Sophistication of the Buyers - Confusion is less likely where the consumers are sophisticated. *Computer Assocs. Int'l.*, 889 F. Supp. at 638. Here the parties' products are financial management software. Courts have routinely held that consumers exercise care in choosing and using financial management instruments and tools. *See, e.g., Nat'l Inf. Corp. v. Kiplinger Wash. Editors*, 771 F. Supp. 460, 465 (D. Col. 1991) (consumers of financial publications are likely to exercise care in their purchasing decisions); *Am. Express Co. v. CFK, Inc.*, 947 F. Supp. 310, 318 (E.D. Mich.1996) (finding confusion unlikely: "(t)he fact that consumers must apply for, and receive, an American Express Credit Card, or deliberately solicit financial services from a company suggests a certain level of sophistication"); *Computer Assoc. Int'l.*, 889 F. Supp. at 638 (buyers unlikely to confuse the parties' tax preparation software). In addition, MIM's CASH software for pocket PCs is installed in handheld computers that cost several hundred dollars, while Mount's software sells for about $30.00. (O'Callahan Dec. ¶ 11, Exh. H). The fact that the Pocket PCs that include MIM's CASH software cost several times

---

10. Mount's inclusion of MIM's counsel's letter in which he told Mount that he felt the public would expect MIM's product to be called "Pocket Cash" because of its naming convention is not evidence that MIM intended the public to refer to its product as such. The letter merely states that consumers would expect to call a product by a particular name, not that they would call it that in any event. Mr. Behm's letter was written before the introduction of the product and its name to the market. Therefore, the letter does not express an opinion as to what the public will in fact call MIM's product, as it ultimately was named.

the price of Mount's software, makes confusion unlikely. (O'Callahan Dec. ¶ 20, Exh. O); *see Computer Assoc. Int'l.*, 889 F. Supp. at 638.[11]

3. There are not Sufficiently Serious Questions Going To the Merits and the Balance of Hardships Favors MIM

As set forth above, Mount has failed to raise sufficiently serious questions going to the merits. Moreover, forcing MIM to cease use of "MIM® Cash for Pocket PC" would cause substantial hardship to MIM, its third party OEMs, and to the public. (Manley Dec. ¶ 6; Sheldon Dec. ¶ ¶ 10–12). The resulting disruption of sales and distribution of Pocket PCs, and the resulting delay in MIM's providing another version of MIM® Cash for Pocket PC software to its OEM customers would furthermore damage the goodwill MIM has built up with OEMs, consumers and the marketplace in general. (Manley Dec. ¶ 7; Sheldon Dec. ¶ 9–11).

Although the phrase "MIM® Cash for Pocket PC" appears only in the "Help" file of the software, in a small number of messages that appear only during initial user setup and in a small number of messages that appear in generally rare conditions, the injunction Mount requests would stop shipment of the OEM's Pocket PCs thereby causing substantial hardship to MIM, its OEMs and its customers. (Manley Dec. ¶ ¶ 6–8; Sheldon Dec. ¶ 9–12). In order to remove the phrase from its software, MIM would have to develop new software to provide the OEMs, a process that can take up to four to six weeks. (Sheldon Dec. ¶ 9; Manley Dec. ¶ 6). The OEMs, who specially design and manufacture the ROM chips for their Pocket PCs, would have to cease production of all units and open existing inventory to replace or reflash the ROM chip to remove the name. (Manley Dec. ¶ ¶ 6–7; Sheldon Dec.

---

11. Mount's citation of authority on the issuance of injunctions is also inapposite. Ten of the eleven "Second Circuit Trademark Injunction Cases" cited by Mount are factually distinguishable. In five of the cases, the marks used by the plaintiffs and defendants were phonetically or visually identical. *Banff, Ltd. v. Federated Dept. Stores, Inc.*, 841 F.2d 486 (2d Cir. 1988); *Nature's Bounty, Inc. v. SuperX Drugs Corp.* 490 F. Supp. 50 (E.D.N.Y. 1980); *Selchow & Righter Co. v. McGraw-Hill Book Co.*, 580 F.2d 25 (2d Cir. 1978); *Warner-Lambert Co. v. Northside Dev. Corp.*, 86 F.3d (2d Cir. 1996); *Sterling Drug, Inc. v. Bayer AG*, 14 F.3d 733 (2d Cir. 1994). In four of the cases, the court found bad faith on the part of the defendant. *Maternally Yours, Inc. v. Yours Maternity Shop, Inc.*, 234 F.2d 538, 110 U.S.P.Q. 462 (2d Cir. 1956); *Les Ballets Trockadero de Monte Carlo, Inc. v. Trevino*, 945 F. Supp. 563 (S.D.N.Y. 1996); *Kookai, S.A. v. Shabo*, 950 F. Supp. 605 (S.D.N.Y. 1997); *Russian Kurier, Inc. v. Russian Am. Kurier, Inc.*, 899 F. Supp. 1204 (S.D.N.Y. 1995). In *Plus Products v. Plus Discount Foods, Inc.*, 722 F.2d 999 (2d Cir. 1983), plaintiff had used its mark for approximately 40 years. In the eleventh case, *Lobo Enter. v. Tunnel, Inc.*, 822 F.2d 331 (2d Cir. 1987), the trial court denied the preliminary injunction, and the appellate court vacated the denial because the trial court relied too heavily on an improper characterization of defendant's target audience.

¶ ¶ 7, 9 and 10). The OEMs cannot simply replace a single program on the ROM chip. (Sheldon Dec. ¶ 10). This process would take the OEMs four to twelve weeks, and is one of the most expensive parts of the manufacturing process (Manley Dec. ¶ 6; Sheldon Dec. ¶ 10). Such delay would cause a significant disruption of the OEMs business, especially harmful since the Pocket PC market is still developing and extremely competitive. (Manley Dec. ¶ 8; Sheldon Dec. ¶ 11). MIM's OEMs would have great difficulty in recovering market share and recouping business losses caused by such delay. (Manley Dec. ¶ 8; Sheldon Dec. ¶ 12).

On the other hand, Mount's dilatory conduct and the absence of any actual confusion indicate that Mount is not suffering any irreparable harm during the pendency of this action. Mount will suffer no hardship if the Court denies the preliminary injunction, as Mount has shown no consumer confusion between the parties. Given Mount's considerable delay in moving for preliminary relief, there will be no hardship to Mount in waiting until trial for a decision on the merits. Under all these circumstances, the hardship of an injunction would be far greater for MIM and its OEMs than the denial of the injunction would be for Mount.[12]

B. The Public Interest Will Be Disserved by the Injunction

The public interest would also be disserved by entry of the requested injunction. OEMs would be unable to sell their pocket PCs that include the MIM CASH software. (Sheldon Dec. ¶ 12). The demand for product is outstripping supply, as the market for pocket PCs is growing at an energetic pace. (Manley Dec. ¶ 4; Sheldon Dec. ¶ 12). Distributors are experiencing delays in receiving the product. (Manley Dec. ¶ 4). If an injunction were entered, consumers would have even greater difficulty finding and purchasing handheld devices. (Manley Dec. ¶ 4 and 8; Sheldon Dec. ¶ 12).

Moreover, consumers should be able to identify software by appropriate descriptive terms, commonly used in the industry. As set forth above, Pocket PC is a generic or merely descriptive term in the computing industry for pocket-sized computers. (O'Callahan Dec., Exhs. E and F). The requested injunction would complicate communication with computer users, not only by MIM, but by OEMs as well. For these reasons, the public will not be served by entry of an injunction.

---

12. Mount's cases in support of its balance of hardship arguments are not on point. Mount cites *Fisian Horticulture, Inc. v. Vigoro Indus. Inc.*, 30 F.3d 466 (3d Cir. 1994). The Third Circuit, however, adopts a different standard of reverse confusion and like-lihood of confusion than the Second Circuit. Mount also cites *Corning Glass Works v. Jeannette Glass Co.*, 308 F. Supp. 1321 (S.D.N.Y. 1970), *aff'd*, 432 F.2d 784 (2d Cir. 1970). This was a case of contributory infringement where, unlike here, defendant's actions were severe and fraudulent.

V. Conclusion

Mount sat and watched as MIM brought its MIM® Cash for Pocket PC software to market. Then it sought preliminary relief. Mount's extraordinary delay provides sufficient grounds to deny Mount's motion. Mount would have this Court enjoin MIM from using "MIM CASH" with the generic or descriptive term Pocket PC, which merely identifies the application for which the software was designed. MIM's prior rights in CASH, by more than three years, make Mount's request all the more remarkable. Lastly, the balance of harms weighs considerably in favor of denying the motion, on account of the considerable harm that would befall both MIM and the manufacturers of the computers which carry MIM's software, were the injunction to be entered.

Should the Court decide to enter an injunction, MIM respectfully requests leave to address the issue of an appropriate injunction bond. For all the reasons set forth above, however, MIM respectfully requests that the Court deny Mount's motion for a preliminary injunction.

Respectfully submitted,

Additional Response to Motion for Preliminary Injunction

In the United States District Court
Northern District of Illinois
Eastern Division

CENTIV, INC., a Delaware Corporation,	)
Plaintiff,	)
	) Case No. 02-CV-7316
v.	)
	) Honorable Rebecca R. Pallmeyer
INCENTIVE SYSTEMS, INC., a	) Magistrate Judge Schenkier
Massachusetts Corporation d/b/a CENTIV,	)
Defendant.	)

Defendant's Memorandum in Opposition to Plaintiff's Motion For Preliminary Injunction Introduction

Defendant Incentive Systems, Inc. d/b/a Centiv ("ISI") hereby submits this Memorandum in Opposition to Plaintiff Centiv, Inc.'s Motion for Preliminary Injunction to enjoin ISI from using the mark CENTIV in its business.

Plaintiff comes before the Court raising a hue and cry about actual confusion, and asking for a drastic remedy—to force ISI, a fairly large and well-established company, to change its name and identity.

It is true that there has been some confusion (mostly in terms of incorrectly addressed emails) among individuals who are neither customers nor prospective customers of either party, such as job applicants, a vendor and at least one individual at Yahoo. This evidence, however, while indicative of some level of corporate nuisance, does not entitle the Plaintiff to the drastic relief it seeks. This is for several key reasons:

The authorities are clear that "confusion" which has not occurred in the relevant purchasing marketplace does not generally present cognizable harm under the Lanham Act. See, infra, pp. 13–15.

In this case, no customer or potential customer has ever been confused, and the services offered by the Plaintiff and the defendant are so vastly different— far more different than is implied in Plaintiff's misleading portrayal—that no confusion will ever occur in either Plaintiff's marketplace or ISI's.

The confusion that does exist (which, interestingly, is so far all in one direction) can be remedied by far less drastic measures than the Plaintiff seeks here.

As described below, ISI's product is a multimillion dollar software system bought by sophisticated corporate customers after months of discussions and meetings. The individuals who buy ISI's product will not be confused about the source of the product and will likely never have heard of the Plaintiff since the Plaintiff and ISI operate in entirely different channels of trade. ISI adopted its CENTIV name and mark as a shortening or abbreviation of its already-existing INCENTIVE® trademark, which is federally registered and has been used in commerce continuously since 1997. To force ISI to change its name now would wreak incalculable harm on its goodwill and its customer relationships; in contrast, the Plaintiff is currently suffering no burden other than the administrative hassles caused by forwarding a handful of e-mails and correcting a one-paragraph news story. The balance of harms is against the Plaintiff.

Finally, to the extent the Plaintiff might ever have been entitled to the relief it seeks, it has waived that right by recently emailing an accusatory press release concerning this suit to industry analysts who cover ISI but who, prior to the email, had never even heard of the Plaintiff—thereby creating confusion where none existed, interfering in ISI's business relationships, and precluding any entitlement to equitable relief.

Facts

The Parties Sell Non-Competing Products

ISI is a software vendor with its corporate headquarters located in Bedford, Massachusetts. ISI has approximately 134 employees and annual sales projected in the amount of $29,000,000. *See Affidavit of Nancy McIntyre* ("McIntyre Aff."), ¶ 2.

Since 1997, ISI has sold Enterprise Incentive Management ("EIM") software and services. That is, ISI sells computer software and services to large companies for the design and management of sophisticated employee compensation programs. McIntyre Aff., ¶ 3. For example, a typical large company will have employees who calculate the commission and/or bonus of each employee, according to each individual's incentive compensation plan. In the absence of an EIM software product, they would do so by using internally developed software or commercially available spreadsheets and calculators. ISI's software products (the current release of which is called Centiv/EIM™) automates that process, integrates with an existing software platform to collect all the necessary data, performs complex calculations, provides advanced reporting functions, and allows a much greater degree of flexibility to change the incentive plans and other benefits. *See Affidavit of John Desmond* ("Desmond Aff."), ¶ 3.

ISI's products are not purchased online, off the shelf, or on an impulse basis by its customers. The products and services are expensive, costing a minimum of $500,000. The average price paid by ISI's customers this year is over $2 million. When considered together with the hardware that must be purchased from another vendor to implement ISI's product, the typical customer is looking at a $4 to $6 million expenditure. The purchasing process lasts an average of four to eight months, and involves repeated conferences, demonstrations, and prolonged contract negotiations, containing a minimum of five face-to-face meetings and more than a dozen in larger deals. The selection of the software vendor is usually made by a committee comprised of the head of compensation, Human Resources, sales operations (for a commission system), the Finance organization, and the Information Technology group. After the product is licensed, ISI then provides implementation services, technical support, and extensive training to the customer personnel in how to use the software. The user of the software is typically the compensation manager or the commissions manager in the central corporate headquarters. McIntyre Aff., ¶ 4; Desmond Aff., ¶ 6.

In contrast, the Plaintiff is not a software company (except to the extent that its services, like most companies' services, utilize software to some degree). Instead, the Plaintiff offers customized "point-of-purchase" (or "POP") marketing services to manufacturers and mass retailers through the internet. The Plaintiff has approximately 31 employees and annual sales in the amount of $12 million. McIntyre Aff., ¶¶ 5–6.

According to its website, the Plaintiff offers three different services. The first is called "Instant Impact," a system which allows users to order customized in-store point-of-purchase materials remotely using Internet-based templates. In a website demonstration, the Plaintiff illustrates its service by showing that from remote locations, sellers of retail products such as Smirnoff Vodka can create signage such as pop-up table tents, indoor banners, and posters that say "Summer Time Special $15.95." The Plaintiff then delivers the materials within 48 hours. The Plaintiff advertises that the service is "so simple no training is required," "even first time users can make a great looking sign" and "[n]o special equipment or technical experience is required." McIntyre Aff., ¶ 6.

The Plaintiff also offers "Design" services. If the customer is unable to create a design template on its own, the Plaintiff's "skilled and experienced design department will create highly effective templates" that "reflect a corporate brand identity through colors, fonts, logos, etc." Lastly, the Plaintiff offers "Print Production" services. This includes digital printing and finishing capabilities (including mounting, laminating, and trimming). McIntyre Aff., ¶¶ 7–8.

In its 2001 Annual Report, the Plaintiff summarizes its services as follows:

> For many years, retailers and manufacturers who sell their products through retail channels have utilized POP signage to promote products and services to consumers. Typically, that signage has been produced using manual methods (chalkboards, markers, etc.) by in-store personnel, or printed at a central corporate location using standard lithography printing methods and distributed to retail stores. Recent advances in software and hardware have created a new market for customer POP signage using display graphic printers, software and media. This technology allows retailers and wholesalers to quickly and easily create, print and display retail signs that are more responsive to their needs in full color with photo-realistic quality. McIntyre Aff., ¶ 9.

The Products are Marketed and Sold to Different Customers through Different Channels

The parties market and sell their products to entirely different customers. The overwhelming majority of ISI's existing and prospective customers are located in the following industries: financial services, telecommunications, technology, manufacturing and medical/pharmaceutical. Consumer goods companies are not a focus of ISI's sales effort. ISI has 65 customers (out of which 16 are through an independent distributor). Out of these customers, only four engage in the retail sale of consumer goods in any fashion, and only one of the four focuses the majority of its business on retail consumer sales.[13] The remaining customers sell their goods and services exclusively to businesses. McIntyre Aff., ¶ 10. In addition, none of the companies in the "pipeline" of potential sales and customer-specific presentations currently in process sell retail consumer goods. McIntyre Aff., ¶ 11.

The Plaintiff, on the other hand, "markets its products to companies that sell packaged consumer goods . . ." *See Affidavit of William M. Rychel* ("Rychel Aff."), ¶ 24. Unlike ISI's customers, the Plaintiff's customers focus primarily on the retail sale of consumer products, such as alcohol, soda beverages and household products. *See* Rychel Aff., ¶ 24.

ISI markets its products to managers in charge of employee compensation, typically located within human resources and information technology departments of large corporations. For example, ISI markets its products to potential customers at a series of trade shows across the country for human resources and compensation executives. These tradeshows concern compensation issues, but do not concern marketing or advertising issues.

---

13.   While Kinkos is one of the four customers of ISI who sells consumer goods, there is very little likelihood of confusion on the part of Kinkos as it is a competitor of the Plaintiff that markets point-of-purchase advertising services.

To the best of ISI's knowledge, the Plaintiff has never attended any of these trade shows. McIntyre Aff., ¶ 12.

As opposed to compensation and human resources personnel, the Plaintiff's product is designed to be used by marketing, brand, and retail managers. ISI does not promote its products to marketing, advertising, or retail personnel because the software does not pertain, in any way, to promotional or signage activities. McIntyre Aff., ¶ 13.

Neither the Plaintiff nor ISI identifies the other as a competitor in any of its materials or filings. McIntyre Aff., ¶ 14.

Both parties engage in partnerships with companies to enhance the effectiveness of their products. The Plaintiff engages in partnerships "to solve print communication problems" with advertising agencies, graphic design firms, event marketing firms, promotional marketing firms, print brokers, commercial printers, print industry suppliers, and B2B exchanges. In contrast, ISI engages in partnerships with systems integrators, compensation design firms, software firms, and human resource strategy firms. McIntyre Aff., ¶ 15.

ISI Shortens its Name from Incentive Systems to Centiv

By virtue of consistent use in commerce since 1997, ISI owns rights in the trademarks INCENTIVE® and INCENTIVE SYSTEMS(with design)® in the field of EIM software and services. ISI owns U.S. Registrations Numbers 2,404,594 and 2,503,423 for these trademarks. McIntyre Aff., ¶ 16.

On July 29, 2002, ISI announced that it was shortening its name to "Centiv" as its corporate identity and brand. ISI decided to shorten its product and company brand name when it became apparent that its competitors were claiming to offer "incentive management" products, and ISI needed to differentiate from such terms. ISI did not choose the name "Centiv" for the purpose of confusing customers, stealing customers from the Plaintiff, or misappropriating the Plaintiff's goodwill. The name and mark CENTIV was chosen because it is a logical and easily recognizable derivative of the mark INCENTIVE®, on which ISI had already spent millions of dollars to establish as a recognized brand. (ISI's advertising expenses for fiscal year 2002 totaled $1.65 million.) It is a shorter form of ISI's current brand that is more distinctive and differentiated in the incentive compensation market. At the time of the change, ISI created a flash video for its customers and partners that visually shows how "Centiv" was created from "Incentive" by dropping the "In" and "e." McIntyre Aff., ¶ 17.

The logo used by ISI contains a carrot design (which is intended to be the graphic equivalent of an incentive), the mark CENTIV with the letter "C" capitalized, and the name "INCENTIVE SYSTEMS" clearly printed underneath the carrot and "Centiv." At no time does the logo ever display the name "Centiv" without the carrot and the name "INCENTIVE SYSTEMS" printed underneath. The logo appears on ISI 's letterhead, throughout ISI's website, and on most if not all of ISI's marketing materials. ISI does not have any immediate plan to remove the name "INCENTIVE SYSTEMS" from the logo. McIntyre Aff., ¶ 18. ISI has also named its product line "Centiv/EIM™." Like the logo, the term "Centiv" never appears by itself when ISI refers to its product line. McIntyre Aff., ¶ 19.

To promote the change from "Incentive" to "Centiv," ISI engaged in an expansive and wide-ranging marketing campaign that included the following: letters and e-mail notices to approximately 7000 partners, existing customers, and prospective customers; redesign of its website; press releases; print advertisements; and printing the logo on its letterhead and company paraphernalia (i.e., mugs, mouse pads, etc.). McIntyre Aff., ¶ 20.

There is No Confusion Among Customers or Investors

The types of customers who use ISI's incentive compensation services are completely different from those customers who engage the Plaintiff for its point-of-purchase advertising services. To the best of Defendant's knowledge, (i) there is not a single customer who has purchased products from both ISI and the Plaintiff, (ii) no existing or prospective customer has ever confused ISI with the Plaintiff, and (iii) ISI has never received a single e-mail that was intended for the Plaintiff. McIntyre Aff., ¶¶ 21–23. In addition, ISI is not aware of any person in the venture capital or investment community ever being confused between the parties or their products. McIntyre Aff., ¶ 24.

ISI Will be Irreparably Harmed if the Injunction Issues

The software industry relating to incentive compensation services is highly competitive. Establishing a brand identity that is recognized and trusted in the marketplace is a crucial component for succeeding in the industry. Thus far, ISI has invested substantial resources and capital to shift its brand identity in the marketplace from "Incentive" to "Centiv." ISI would be severely and irreparably harmed if it were enjoined from marketing its products under the mark CENTIV. McIntyre Aff., ¶ 31.

The immediate out-of-pocket costs of announcing a name change and removing the CENTIV mark would be extremely high. Even more damaging, however, is the immeasurable loss of confidence and brand recognition in ISI from its partners, existing customers, industry analysts, and prospective customers. A name change, coming on the heels of the recent change from "Incentive" to "Centiv" (i.e., two name/identity changes in less than three months), would hopelessly confuse ISI's identity among its existing and potential customers. In addition, the change would be viewed within the industry as arbitrary, indecisive, and signaling a change in the direction of ISI, even though this is not the case. This would result in loss of goodwill and sales which could not be quantified. McIntyre Aff., ¶ 32.

The Plaintiff Is Intentionally Causing Confusion

The Plaintiff has issued a press release stating that it has filed this action against ISI and that "[i]t's difficult to believe that Incentive Systems has chosen to knowingly violate our rights as owners of this mark." On October 15, 2002, the Plaintiff's Chief Marketing Officer, John Bauer, forwarded a copy of the press release by e-mail to an industry analyst named Steven Bonadio with the following message: "Your name and email address were provided to me as an industry analyst who might be interested in the attached press release, which is effective today." *See Affidavit of Steven Bonadio* ("Bonadio Aff."), ¶ 2. Mr. Bonadio forwarded the e-mail and press release to his contact at ISI, stating: " . . . how they got my e-mail is beyond me. What's this all about?" *See Affidavit of Robert Conlin* ("Conlin Aff."), ¶ ¶ 2–4.

Mr. Bonadio is an analyst for META Group, Inc., a large firm which performs consulting and analysis in the information technology field. While Mr. Bonadio covers and analyzes a number of companies selling enterprise software, including ISI, he does not cover the point-of-purchase marketing products sold by the Plaintiff. Prior to receiving the email and press release from the Plaintiff, Mr. Bonadio had never heard of the Plaintiff or its services. Bonadio Aff., ¶ 2.

ISI has also been contacted by two other IT industry analysts who received similar e-mails from the Plaintiff with the press release attached. Like Mr. Bonadio, neither of these analysts had ever heard of the Plaintiff or its product prior to receiving the e-mails and press release from the Plaintiff. Conlin Aff., ¶ 7.

Argument

"A preliminary injunction is a very serious remedy, 'never to be indulged in except in a case clearly demanding it.'" *Barbecue Marx, Inc. v. 551 Ogden, Inc.*, 235 F.3d 1041, 1044 (7th Cir. 2000) (*quoting Schwinn Bicycle Co. v. Ross Bicycles, Inc.*, 870 F.2d 1176, 1184 (7th Cir. 1989)). In order to obtain a preliminary injunction, the Plaintiff must first show (1) a likelihood of success on the merits of its claim, (2) an inadequate remedy at law and irreparable harm if the injunction does not issue, (3) the balance of harm to each party of granting or denying the injunction and (4) the public interest. *See, e.g., RWT Corp. v. Wonderware Corp.*, 931 F. Supp. 583, 586 (N.D. Ill. 1996). The Court must then balance all four factors using a "sliding scale" approach. *Id.*[14]

---

14. The Plaintiff argues that it "need only prove that it has a 'better than negligible' likelihood of success on the merits at this preliminary injunction stage." This is not the necessarily the case, however, under the "sliding scale" approach. Instead, the Plaintiff need only *initially* prove that it has a better than negligible likelihood of success on the merits for the Court to *then* balance the likelihood of success with the

I. Plaintiff is Unlikely to Succeed on the Merits

In the trademark context, likelihood of success on the merits requires a showing by the Plaintiff that (1) it has a protectable mark, and (2) a "likelihood of confusion" exists between the marks or products of the parties. *E.g., Meridian Mut. Ins. Co. v. Meridian Ins. Grp. Inc.*, 128 F.3d 1111, 1115 (7th Cir. 1997).

A. The Plaintiff's Protectable Rights are Limited by ISI's Prior Rights

The Plaintiff has a protectable mark in the sense that the Plaintiff is using it in commerce and the U.S. Patent Trademark Office has approved it for issuance. However, there is a serious question as to whether the Plaintiff has protectable rights to the CENTIV mark that trump those of ISI. Instead, the Plaintiff's rights to the CENTIV mark may be subservient to ISI's rights to the mark based on ISI's continuous use of its existing (and registered) mark INCENTIVE since 1997. Indeed, "Centiv" is a common shorthand version or abbreviation of "Incentive." *See Archer Daniels Midland Co. v. Narula*, 2001 WL 804025, at *9 (N.D. Ill. July 12, 2001) (unregistered abbreviations with secondary meaning entitled to protection under trademark law).[15] "Centiv" also sounds very much like "Incentive," and there is a strong likelihood that someone hearing one name may confuse it for the other. *See G.D. Searle & Co. v. Chas, Pfizer & Co.*, 265 F.2d 385, 387 (7th Cir. 1959). Therefore, if there were any meaningful likelihood of confusion between the marks (which ISI maintains is not the case), such confusion would exist regardless of whether ISI calls itself " Incentive" or "Centiv"—thus, it would be the Plaintiff infringing on ISI's rights, rather than vice versa.

For example, in Paragraph 15 of the Rychel Affidavit, the Plaintiff complains that job applicants reviewing electronic postings have mistakenly sent applications to the Plaintiff that were meant for ISI. Exhibit 8 to the Affidavit shows, however, that the job postings by ISI were for "Incentive Systems," not "Centiv." Nevertheless, the applicants apparently confused "Centiv" for "Incentive Systems." This may give rise to ISI's priority use of the mark CENTIV. For example, in *Forum Corp. of North Am. v. Forum, Ltd.*, 903 F.2d 434, 440–41 (7th Cir. 1990), the Plaintiff shortened its mark from

---

hardships to the parties. *See Int'l Kennel Club of Chicago v. Mighty Star, Inc.*, 846 F.2d 1079, 1084 n.5 (7th Cir. 1988). In *Maxim's Ltd. v. Badonsky*, 772 F.2d 388, 391 (7th Cir. 1985), the court explained that the degree of likelihood of success that Plaintiff must demonstrate varies inversely with the extent of irreparable harm on the Plaintiff's side.

15. *See also Tamko Roofing Prod. Inc. v. Ideal Roofing Co., Ltd.*, 2002 WL 338112, at *16 (1st Cir. Mar. 7, 2002) ("There are circumstances in which abbreviations of trademarks may be protectable as independent marks.").

"The Forum Corporation of North America" (which it had been using since 1971) to "The Forum" in the early 1980s. The defendant began using the mark "The Forum Ltd." in 1980. *Id.* at 436–37. The court held that even though plaintiff shortened its registered mark to resemble defendant's mark after defendant started using its mark, plaintiff's use of "The Forum" did not infringe defendant's "The Forum Ltd." mark. *Id.* at 440–41.

B. There is No Likelihood of Confusion Among Customers

In any case, there is no likelihood of confusion. There has never been a single instance of confusion by existing or prospective customers of either party. The products do not compete with each other in any way and are sold to different customers through different channels.

In the Seventh Circuit, Courts look at the following seven factors to determine whether a likelihood of success on the merits exists: (1) the similarity between the marks in appearance and suggestion, (2) the similarity of the products, (3) the area and manner of concurrent use, (4) the degree of care likely to be exercised by consumers, (5) strength of complainant's mark, (6) actual confusion, and (7) the intent of the defendant to "palm off his product as that of another." *E.g., Rust Env't & Infrastructure, Inc. v. Teunissen*, 131 F.3d 1210, 1216 (7th Cir. 1987). "'[N]one of the seven factors alone are dispositive, and the weight accorded to each factor will vary from case to case.'" *Id.* at 1217 (*quoting Smith Fiberglass Prods., Inc. v. Ameron, Inc.*, 7 F.3d 1327, 1329 (7th Cir. 1993)). These factors weigh in favor of ISI, and the Plaintiff is unable to establish a likelihood of success on the merits of its claims.

Due to the emphasis the Plaintiff has placed on the alleged incidents of confusion in its brief, ISI will first address the "actual confusion" factor and then the remaining six.

1. There is No Actual Confusion of Trademark Significance

The instances of confusion alleged by the Plaintiff do not involve any customers or prospective ones. Rather, they involve misdirected inquiries and messages from current and prospective employees, a potential supplier, and a news reporter.[16] Such inquiries, however, do not amount to actionable confusion and are insufficient to establish trademark infringement. In *Liquid*

---

16. As noted above, the fact that the electronic job posting listed positions for "Incentive Systems" and "Centiv" shows that the confusion by the applicants was not between "Centiv" the Defendant and "Centiv" the Plaintiff, but between "Incentive Systems" (in which ISI has clearly superior rights) and "Centiv."

Controls Corp. v. Liquid Control Corp., 802 F.2d 934, 940 (7th Cir. 1986), the Seventh Circuit Court of Appeals held:

> In the case before us **the only evidence of confusion is occasional misdirected mail**. This confusion would seem to arise merely because of the similarity of names. **Section 43(a) [of the Lanham Act] does not protect the plaintiff from this sort of confusion.**

(emphasis and brackets added). Similarly, in *Therma-Scan, Inc. v. Thermoscan, Inc.*, 295 F.3d 623, 635–36 (6th Cir. 2002), the Court held that 18 misdirected e-mail messages (6 of which were from consumers) did not support finding a likelihood of confusion. Similar holdings from this Circuit and others abound.[17] Indeed, the cases also hold that the confusion must involve a "significant" number of consumers, which is certainly not the case here. *See, e.g., Rust. Env't & Infrastructure, Inc.*, 131 F.3d at 1218 (evidence of "rare and trivial" confusion from customers did not support likelihood of confusion); *Knaack Mfg. Co. v. Rally Accessories, Inc.*, 955 F. Supp. 991, 1005 (N.D. Ill. 1997) ("[L]ikelihood of confusion must occur to a significant number of consumers and not merely in an isolated situation.").[18]

Nor does the fact that the two companies use similar Internet URLs change the outcome. Instead, the confusion alleged by the Plaintiff amounts to little more than "initial interest confusion" resulting from the parties having similar internet and e-mail addresses. The courts have found that this type of confusion, even among customers, is nonactionable. In *Chatam Int'l. v. Bodum, Inc.*, 157 F. Supp. 2d 549, 559 (E.D. Pa. 2001), the court held that initial interest confusion did not support a trademark action between Chambord liqueur (with the URLs "chambordonline.com," "chambord.net," and "chambordliqeur.com") and Chambord coffee makers (with the URL "chambord.com"): "Internet surfers are inured to the false starts and excursions awaiting them in this evolving medium." *Id.* Similarly, in *Hasbro, Inc. v. Clue*

---

17. *See, e.g., Ziebart Int'l Corp. v. After Market Assoc., Inc.*, 802 F.2d 220, 228 (7th Cir. 1986) (finding no actual confusion based on misdirected communication); *Lang v. Retirement Living Publ'g Co.*, 949 F.2d 576, 584 (2d Cir. 1991) (upholding summary judgment for infringement defendant despite 400 misdirected phone calls since there was no evidence linking these calls to any effect on consumers' purchasing decisions); *Nutri Systems, Inc. v. Con-Stan Indus., Inc.*, 809 F.2d 601, 606–07 (9th Cir. 1987) (finding evidence of several misdirected letters and checks deemed "thin" and "trivial": "The court acted properly in finding that any actual confusion was de minimis ").

18. *See also Door Sys., Inc. v. Pro-Line Door Sys., Inc.*, 83 F.3d 169, 173 (7th Cir. 1996) ("[W]e think it wholly unlikely that any significant number of consumers would be misled. And that is the test."); *Homeowners Grp. Inc. v. Home Mktg. Specialists, Inc.*, 931 F.2d 1100, 1110 (6th Cir. 1991) (finding even where parties were in direct competition, "isolated instances of actual confusion are not conclusive or entitled to great weight").

Computing, Inc., 66 F. Supp. 2d 117, 119 (D. Mass. 1999), the court held that a computer consulting business with the Internet domain name "clue.com" did not infringe on the trademark of the CLUE board game. The court explained that though consumers may initially go to the wrong Internet website, they will realize they are at the wrong site and go to an Internet search engine to find the right one. *Id.* at 125. The court held that "'initial confusion on the part of web browsers . . . is not cognizable under the trademark laws.'" *Id.* (ellipses in original) (*quoting Teletech Customer Care Mgmt. Inc. v. Tele-Tech Co.*, 977 F. Supp. 1407, 1414 (C.D. Cal. 1997)).

In sum, the relevant question is not whether two companies' similar names are causing communications to be misdirected or a news reporter to be confused. The question is whether the companies' use of the same trademark is likely to cause confusion among prospective purchasers of their respective goods and services. "Only confusion among the consuming public, or 'in the market place,' is relevant where trademark infringement or unfair competition is at issue." *See Heico Inc. v. Heico Corp.*, 1991 WL 335366, at *9 (Ill. Cir. Sept. 19, 1991), 21 U.S.P.Q.2d 1334, 1341 (noting that business associates, media, auditors, would-be-investors, banks, and insurance companies are not "customers" or "consumers" for purposes of establishing likelihood of confusion). "[T]he issue in trademark litigation is what a mark means to consumers, not to the industry." *Id.*[19]

2. The Marks are Not Identical

"A court must look not just at the words contained in the mark, but the effect of the combination of the words, the typeface used and any accompanying logos ('the perceptual gestalt')." *See Hyatt Corp. v. Club Regency Int'l, S.A.*, 1986 WL 8029, at *5 (N.D. Ill. July 14, 1986). "The marks must be compared in light of what occurs in the marketplace, not sitting side by side on a podium in the courtroom." *Knaack Mfg. Co.*, 955 F. Supp. at 1000.

Here, ISI's use of "Centiv" is different from the Plaintiff's, whether compared side by side or in the marketplace. ISI's mark is rectangular in shape, has a capital "C" with black writing, has an orange carrot symbolizing the incentive concept, and has the name "INCENTIVE SYSTEMS" written below it (a clearly differentiating reference to ISI's corporate name and former marketplace identity). The Plaintiff's mark, however, is square in shape, is in all lower

---

19. *See also Dorr-Oliver, Inc. v. Fluid-Quip, Inc.*, 94 F.3d 376, 380–82 (7th Cir. 1996) ("The requirement of consumer confusion is vital to protecting the basic policies behind federal trademark law . . . . the Lanham Act is concerned with 'consumer confusion when choosing to purchase, or not purchase, the items, not public confusion at viewing them from afar.'"); *Astra Pharm. Prods. v. Bechman Instruments, Inc.*, 718 F.2d 1201, 1206 (1st Cir. 1983) ("If likelihood of confusion exists, it must be based on the confusion of some relevant person; i.e., a customer or purchaser.").

case letters, is blue, and contains an arrow pointing into the opening of a large "C." The different symbols, colors, fonts and shapes, coupled with the symbolism of the carrot and the use of "INCENTIVE SYSTEMS" on ISI's mark, alerts consumers that these are different companies and precludes confusion between the two. *See Knaack Mfg. Co.*, 955 F. Supp. at 1000 (finding WeatherGUARD and WEATHER GUARD marks not identical due to different capitalization, type face, graphics, and coloring). In the marketplace, ISI relies heavily on its website and written materials to advertise its product, as is likely the case for the Plaintiff. As a result, potential customers in the marketplace will see the different logos when considering whether to purchase the point-of-purchase advertising services of the Plaintiff or the incentive compensation software of ISI. Taken as a whole and considered in the context of the marketplace, the two marks are not identical and are unlikely to cause confusion among customers.

3. The Products are Not Similar and do Not Compete With Each Other

The products sold by ISI do not overlap, in any way whatsoever, with the products sold by the Plaintiff. The Plaintiff's characterization of both products as "business enterprise solution services" is quite misleading. Although both companies use the Internet to provide part of their services, the similarity goes no further. The Plaintiff's product creates customized point-of-purchase advertising materials, such as banners, posters, signs and pop-up tents for companies that sell packaged retail products. ISI's product automates sophisticated employee incentive compensation plans for large corporations. ISI's product has nothing to do with advertising or marketing. The products are completely different from each other and are not likely to cause customer confusion.

Cases in this jurisdiction and elsewhere are clear that even identical marks do not create confusion where they operate in different markets. In *Knaack Mfg. Co.*, 955 F. Supp. at 1000, the court held that there was no likelihood of confusion between plaintiff's "WEATHER GUARD" tool boxes and storage equipment and defendant's "WeatherGUARD" car covers. The court reasoned that, despite their similarity, consumers were unlikely to confuse the marks because the products did not compete with each other. *Id.* at 1001. The court also explained that because the parties carried entirely different product lines, it was "even less likely that customers would believe that the two product types come from the same source." *Id.* There are numerous similar holdings from this jurisdiction and others.[20]

---

20. *See Somat Corp. v. Somat Corp.*, 1992 WL 315198, at *6–7 (N.D. Ill. Oct. 26, 1992) (no likelihood of confusion between Somat of Pennsylvania waste disposal company and

4. The Products Are Sold to Different Customers through Different Channels

This factor "relates to the parties' targeted market: to whom and how are the parties' services and products offered." *Hyatt Corp.*, 1986 WL 8029 at *6. In *Knaack Mfg. Co.*, 955 F. Supp. at 1001, the court also held that there was no likelihood of confusion between the marks "WEATHER GUARD" and "WeatherGUARD" because plaintiff did 95 percent of its business through mass retailers while defendant did no business through this channel at all:

> The evidence was clear that these companies, based on market realities, are not in the same industry. They exhibit at different trade shows, they use different channels of distribution and they have not come into contact with one another in the business world, except in court.[21]

Like the products in *Knaack Mfg. Co.*, the products in this case are sold to different customers through different channels. All of the Plaintiff's customers sell retail consumer goods, which makes sense, as the Plaintiff's entire service is geared toward increasing its customers' point-of-purchase sales to consumers. In stark contrast, only one of ISI's 65 customers is primarily in the business of selling retail goods to consumers. Further, 61 of ISI remaining 64 customers sell their products and services exclusively to other businesses, none of whom have any need for point-of-purchase marketing materials. There is also no overlap between the industries in which the parties' customers sell their products. The Plaintiff's customers focus on the alcohol, beverage, hardware store and health club industries, while ISI's customers are located in the financial services, telecommunications, technology, manufacturing and medical/pharmaceutical industries.

Somat of Illinois portable computer company); *Heico Inc.*, 1991 WL 335366, at *12, 21 U.S.P.Q.2d at 1341 (no likelihood of confusion between Heico jet engines and Heico flues for wood-burning furnaces); *Elec. Data Sys. Corp. v. EDSA Micro Corp.*, 23 U.S.P.Q.2d 1460 (TTAB 1992) (no likelihood of confusion between similar software marks since the software products performed different, unrelated functions); *Elec. Design & Sales, Inc. v. Elec. Data Sys. Corp.*, 954 F.2d 713, 717, 21 U.S.P.Q.2d 1388 (CAFC 1992) (no likelihood of confusion between opposer's and applicant's use of the identical term "EDS" in the electronics field since the goods and services were different in nature); *Borg-Warner Chem., Inc. v. Helena Chem. Co.*, 225 U.S.P.Q. 222 (TTAB 1983) (no likelihood of confusion between uses of the identical term BLENDEX on chemical compositions where one product was used in the industrial arts while the other was used in pesticides and fertilizers).

21. *See also Heico Inc.*, 1991 WL 335366, at *9, 21 U.S.P.Q.2d at 1341 (noting that neither party sold its products through unsolicited catalogs or the public at large, but instead through in-house sales department, the court held that there was no reason to think that jet engines were sold to the same customers or through the same channels as industrial sewer cleaning equipment).

The parties also market their products to different groups within their customers. In *Somat Corp. v. Somat Corp.*, 1992 WL 315198, at *5 (N.D. Ill. Oct. 26, 1992), the court held that there was no likelihood of confusion between noncompeting products, even though they were purchased by the same customers, because "the devices were purchased by different people and are used in different capacities in each of these organizations." ISI markets its products to human resources and compensation executives, while the Plaintiff markets its products to marketing and advertising executives.[22] The parties market to none of the same customers; attend none of the same trade shows; advertise through none of the same channels; and partner with none of the same distributors and vendors. There is no overlap.

5. Corporate Customers Exercise a High Degree of Care when Purchasing the Products Sold by Both Parties

Corporations that purchase expensive, sophisticated products are less likely to be confused by similarities between the sellers' names than consumers who purchase less expensive products off the shelf. *See Somat*, 1992 WL 315198, at *4 (finding a high degree of care is likely to be exercised by purchasers of advanced portable computer system costing hundreds of thousands of dollars). In *Rust Env't & Infrastructure, Inc.*, 131 F.3d at 1217, the court held that there was no likelihood of confusion between the environmental consulting firm formerly known as "Donahue & Associates" and a competitor with the same name, "Donahue & Associates." The court emphasized that "the relevant market of consumers is composed of sophisticated buyers of services in a highly specialized technical field," and such consumers "are likely to look beyond a firm's name before making any contractual commitments." *Id.*

In this case, the customers of both the Plaintiff and ISI are the quintessential discriminating customers who are unlikely to be confused between the parties or their products. Both products are very expensive, ranging from the hundreds of thousands to millions of dollars (The total outlay for ISI's product, including the necessary hardware to run the software, is approximately $4 to $6 million.) Both products are purchased by discriminating, high-level corporate executives, and ISI's product is a sophisticated software system requiring extensive training in its use. In addition, the purchasing process

---

22. Attached as Exhibit 7 to the Rychel Aff. is an email to the Plaintiff from a trade show planner asking if the Plaintiff was interested in participating in a Human Resources Technology conference. In response, John Bauer, the Plaintiff's Chief Marketing Officer, stated that he does "not see a fit with our product offering and HR Technology." The fact that the Plaintiff does not attend any of the trade shows for human resources and compensation executives at which ISI markets its products to potential customers is telling, as it shows that ISI sells a different product, to different customers, through different channels.

for ISI's products averages 4 to 8 months and involves repeated conferences, demonstrations, and prolonged contract negotiations, containing five to twelve meetings. Under these circumstances, it is utterly inconceivable that a company, after spending months reviewing and negotiating the purchase of a highly sophisticated and multimillion dollar incentive compensation software system, would confuse ISI with the Plaintiff.

6. The Plaintiff's Mark is Weak

The Plaintiff's use of the CENTIV mark is weak because it is used as an element of numerous other registered marks, and it is not particularly well known to the public. "If the mark is weak, its protection may have an 'extremely narrow scope'; and may indeed by limited to similar goods similarly marketed." *Knaack Mfg. Co.*, 955 F. Supp. at 1003 (*quoting Telemed Corp. v. Tel-Med, Inc.*, 588 F.2d 213 (7th Cir. 1978)). "[A] measure of a mark's strength or weakness is whether a significant number of third-parties use the same or a similar mark." *Id.* On the Federal Register alone one can find such registered and published marks as: E-CENTIVES, Reg. No. 2,373,242; ICENTIVES, Serial No. 75/609,028; PIN-CENTIVES, Reg. No. 1,968,685; SMARTCENTIVE, Serial No. 78/052936; GAMECENTIVE, Serial No. 78/052,934; CLICKCENTIVE.COM, Serial No. 75/867229; NETCENTIVES, Reg. No. 2,442,912; DREAMCENTIVES, Reg. No. 2,552,038; BETCENTIVES, Serial No. 76/132740; PARKCENTIVES, Serial No. 78/022,427; and others. Some of these marks cover goods and services that are closely related to the Plaintiff's field,[23][11] and all of them have priority over the Plaintiff's mark.

It is not enough to show that a mark is coined or invented to establish that it is strong for purposes of a likelihood of confusion analysis. *See Heico Inc.*, 1991 WL 335366, at *10, 21 U.S.P.Q.2d at 1341. "[A] trade-mark has the advantage of strength where its owner has invested a considerable amount in advertising or can point to a long period of time during which his mark was used on a great quantity of articles, as symbolic of his business." *Telemed*, 588 F.2d at 219 (*quoting* 3 R. Callahan, *Unfair Competition and Trade-Marks* § 82.1 (2d ed.)). Here, the Plaintiff's use of the CENTIV mark is weak, particularly when compared to ISI's use of the INCENTIVE mark. The Plaintiff has not invested a considerable amount of advertising in the mark (hundreds of thousands of dollars total, compared to millions of dollars spent yearly by ISI) or used the mark for a long period of time (since April 2001, compared to ISI's continuous use since 1997).

---

23. *See* www.e-centiv.com, which advertises the following on the front page of its web-site: "Industry Spotlight: Consumer Packaged Goods. New technologies are changing the way CPG manufacturers market their brands."

7. There is No Intent by ISI to Palm Off its Product

"[I]n the trademark infringement context, 'intent' refers to the intent to confuse customers, not merely the intent to use a mark that is already in use somewhere else." *Meridian Mut. Ins. Co.*, 128 F.3d at 1120. Here, there is no intent by ISI to confuse customers about the identity of the parties or products. ISI has nothing to gain by doing so, as the parties market completely different products to entirely different customers. Instead, the purpose of choosing the name "Centiv" is that it is an abbreviation for ISI's full name, "Incentive Systems," on which ISI has already spent millions of dollars establishing in the incentive compensation industry.

II. The Balance of Hardships Favors ISI

A. The Balance of Harms Tip in Favor of ISI

Although there is a presumption of irreparable harm in the trademark context, "the significance of that fact is rather minimal; for what is necessary is that whatever irreparable injury there is to the plaintiff *outweigh* the injury to the defendant . . ." *See Maxim's Ltd.*, 772 F.2d at 392 (emphasis in original). The balance of harms in this case decidedly favors ISI, thereby precluding the Plaintiff's motion for injunctive relief regardless of the Court's findings as to the Plaintiff's likelihood of success on the merits. *See id.* at 391–92.

If the injunction issues, ISI will suffer extreme and irreparable harm to its entire business. The incentive compensation software industry is highly competitive, and establishing a recognized and trusted brand identity in the marketplace is a crucial component for success. If forced to change its name, ISI would lose an immeasurable amount of confidence from its customers and partners. In addition, a second name change in a three-month span would hopelessly confuse ISI's identity among its existing and potential customers and be viewed within the industry as arbitrary, indecisive, and signaling a change in the direction of ISI (even though this is not the case). ISI would also lose the substantial capital and resources it has already invested in its shift from doing business as "Incentive" to "Centiv."

The Plaintiff, on other hand, has not alleged, must less shown, that a single customer has ever confused the parties or their products. Nor has the Plaintiff demonstrated that ISI's use of the CENTI V mark has caused it to sustain any serious damages whatsoever. Instead, the Plaintiff complains of misdirected communications. Curiously, the confusion appears to be all in one direction—people trying to reach ISI are apparently reaching the Plaintiff by mistake (but the converse is not true). This suggests that the only burden the Plaintiff is suffering is the minor administrative hassle associated with correcting or forwarding the communications.

Moreover, instead of taking steps to minimize future misdirected communication or other confusion, the Plaintiff is actively creating confusion where none existed by sending notices of the lawsuit to industry analysts who have never even heard of the Plaintiff or its products. As argued below, this amounts to unclean hands and bars the Plaintiff from any equitable relief whatsoever. As for balancing of the harms, it is a factor weighing against the Plaintiff.

B. Relief Other Than Enjoining the Use of the Centiv Mark Could Protect the Plaintiff

If the Court is inclined to grant injunctive relief, measures other than enjoining ISI's use of the CENTIV mark will protect the Plaintiff against the possibility of confusion among customers and others. This is not a case in which customers of the Plaintiff are mistakenly using the services of ISI, or one in which ISI is misappropriating the good will generated by the Plaintiff. Instead, the problems encountered in this case concern misdirected communications, primarily in the form of e-mails. The Court could prevent the occurrence of future misdirected communications (and potential confusion generally) by ordering the following measures:

Both companies take steps to automatically route any misdirected e-mails to the proper recipient.

ISI prominently places a message on the front page of its website stating that if the user is looking for the Plaintiff, the user can, with one click of the mouse, link directly to the Plaintiff's website.

ISI prominently displays its logo on all materials viewed by the public.

ISI could potentially change the URL of its website and e-mail address from www.centivinc.com.

ISI has offered in writing to discuss the above measures with the Plaintiff and has been rebuffed. Similarly, the Plaintiff has not asked for injunctive relief along these lines, but insists on a total name change. ISI respectfully suggests that, given the Plaintiff's difficulties with the balance of harms and the merits, the Court (exercising its discretion in equity) could consider the above measures *sua sponte*, or could simply respond to the Plaintiff's "all or nothing" approach by ruling that it is entitled to nothing.

III. Granting the Injunction Will Negatively Affect the Public Interest

The public interest is served by freedom of trade and business competition. *See Platinum Home Mortgage Corp. v. Platinum Fin. Grp. Inc.*, 149 F.3d 722, 726 (7th Cir. 1998); *Hyatt Corp.*, 1986 WL 8029 at *4. Because the parties' products, customers, and channels of trade are completely different from each other, an injunction will not enhance in any way the freedom of trade or business competition in the point-of-purchase marketplace. However, if ISI is enjoined from using the CENTIV mark, the harm flowing to ISI will weaken its position in the incentive compensation marketplace and render it less competitive.

IV. The Plaintiff is Barred from Equitable Relief by Its Unclean Hands

In addition to failing to satisfy the elements of the four-part test for preliminary injunctions, the Plaintiff is barred from the equitable relief it seeks because it comes before the Court with unclean hands. Under the unclean hands doctrine, "'one seeking equitable relief cannot take advantage of his own wrong.'" *Polk Bros, Inc. v. Forest City Enter., Inc.*, 776 F.2d 185, 193 (7th Cir. 1985) (*quoting Fair Auto. Repair, Inc. v. Car Serv. Sys., Inc.*, 128 Ill. App. 3d 763, 471 N.E.2d 554, 558 (1984)). "'If the plaintiff creates or contributes to the situation on which it relies, the court denies equitable relief in order to deter the wrongful conduct.'" *Id.*

Here, the Plaintiff has sent copies of its press release saying that ISI has intentionally infringed the Plaintiff's mark to analysts who cover ISI's industry but not the Plaintiff's. Before receiving the press releases, none of the analysts had ever heard of the Plaintiff. The analysts are now asking ISI who the Plaintiff is and whether ISI has infringed the Plaintiff 's mark. Thus, the Plaintiff has taken active steps to increase the likelihood of confusion.

Furthermore, there is no valid reason for the Plaintiff's actions. Because the analysts cover a different industry, there was no danger that they might confuse the Plaintiff for ISI. Instead, the Plaintiff sent the press release to the industry analysts for the sole purpose of harassing and exerting pressure upon ISI to acquiesce to the Plaintiff's demands for a name change. The Plaintiff's actions constitute intentional interference with existing and prospective business relations and unfair and deceptive trade practices. The Plaintiff cannot now with unclean hands come before this Court sitting in equity and expect to obtain the extraordinary relief which it seeks.

V. Bond Securing ISI's Damages

As explained more fully above, ISI will be severely harmed if it is enjoined from using the CENTIV mark. If (despite all the above arguments) the Court issues the relief requested by the Plaintiff, ISI requests that the Plaintiff be required to post a bond in the amount of one million dollars ($1,000,000) to protect ISI's interests in the event that ISI prevails after a full trial on the merits. *See* Fed. R. Civ. P. 65(c).[24]

---

24. *See Schawbel Corp. v. Conair Corp.*, 122 F. Supp. 2d 71, 85–86 (D. Mass. 2000) (issued bond of $1,000,000 to protect defendant after preliminary injunction was granted against it in suit for patent infringement).

Conclusion

For all the foregoing reasons, Defendant Incentive Systems, Inc. d/b/a Centiv respectfully requests that this Court deny Plaintiff's Motion for Preliminary Injunction.

Date: October _____, 2002, Respectfully submitted,

CHAPTER
6

Motion to Dismiss

One of the first considerations for any litigator after receiving a complaint is whether any of the plaintiff's claims may be dismissed on procedural grounds or for failure to state a claim. *See* Fed. R. Civ. P. 12(b). Since both trademark and copyright claims present questions under federal law, generally, the only Rule 12(b) motions available are for lack of personal jurisdiction or for failure to state a claim.

Recent Supreme Court decisions have made clear that a pleading must do more than merely allege the elements of a claim but must state facts from which a claim can adduced. *See Bell Atl. Corp. v. Twombly*, 550 U.S. 544, 555 (2007); *Ashcroft v. Iqbal*, 129 S. Ct. 1937, 1949 (2009), In short, a federal complaint that is nothing more than an "unadorned, the-defendant-unlawfully-harmed-me accusation" is fair game for a 12(b)(6) motion.

At least one empirical study found a slight increase in federal complaint dismissal rates in the short amount of time since the *Twombly* and *Iqbal* decisions. *See* Hatamyar, Patricia W., *The Tao of Pleading: Do* Twombly *and* Iqbal *Matter Empirically?*, 59 AM. U. L. REV. 553, 556 (2010) (compiling data that suggests the following dismissal rates: 46 percent pre-*Twombly*; 48 percent *Twombly* to *Iqbal*; 56 percent post-*Iqbal*).

The authors assume some level of familiarity with the standards for asserting a motion to dismiss. The examples below focus on motions specific to trademark and copyright litigation.

Motion to Dismiss for Failure to Properly Plead a Trademark

One of the basic elements of a federal trademark infringement claim is the ownership of a mark. If the plaintiff does not own a protectable mark, then it has no right to complain, and its complaint must be dismissed.

Since trademark rights in the United States are acquired through use, a federal registration is not required to pursue a lawsuit. A claim for trademark infringement based upon an unregistered mark or trade dress may be brought under Section 43(a) of the Lanham Act. Without a registration, however, a plaintiff does not receive the statutory presumptions of validity and right to exclusive use.

Thus, the most common type of motion to dismiss a common-law trademark infringement claim rests upon lack of a trademark, usually because the alleged mark is not a mark at all, but a generic term, a descriptive term for which plaintiff has failed to sufficiently plead secondary meaning or functional trade dress. Other examples may come to mind, but the essential character of such a motion is the failure by the plaintiff to assert a protectable mark.

Motion to Dismiss for Failure to Properly Plead a Trademark

Plaintiff's Motion to Dismiss Defendant's Counterclaim

Plaintiff, by its attorneys, hereby moves this Court for an order dismissing the Counterclaim filed by Defendant with prejudice pursuant to Fed. R. Civ. P. 12(b)(6), stating as follows:

Introduction

1. Defendant filed four bare-bones counterclaims against Plaintiff that avoid specific allegations of fact and instead simply recite legal conclusions. Counts I, II, and III are based upon Defendant's conclusory assertion that it owns common-law trademarks to the phrase and to an unspecified logo. Under any pleading standard, that bare conclusion is inadequate to establish Defendant's ownership of a protectable trademark, and these counts must be dismissed.
2. Moreover, this pleading deficiency cannot be cured because Defendant simply cannot establish a protectable trademark. In fact, the U.S. Trademark Trial and Appeal Board has squarely rejected Defendant's attempt to register a trademark on the phrase "_____," and expressly ruled in a detailed written opinion that the phrase is generic and therefore cannot be a valid trademark.
3. Count IV of Defendant's counterclaim fails for a separate reason: It is a mirror image of the request for a declaratory judgment in Plaintiff's Complaint. Under established law, such mirror-image claims should be dismissed.
4. For all these reasons, Defendant's Counterclaim should be dismissed with prejudice pursuant to Fed. R. Civ. P. 12(b)(6).

Legal Standard

5. Rule 12(b)(6) authorizes the Court to dismiss a pleading for "failure to state a claim upon which relief can be granted." *See* Fed. R. Civ. P. 12(b)(6). In deciding a Rule 12(b)(6) motion to dismiss, the Court should treat the non-movant's well-pleaded allegations as true and should construe the allegations in the light most favorable to the non-movant; in order to survive dismissal, however, a pleading must contain more than unsupported legal conclusions. *See Advocacy Org. for Patients & Providers v. Auto Club Ins. Ass'n*, 176 F.3d 315, 319 (6th Cir. 1999); *see also id.* at 325 ("The 'reasonableness' of these charges is a legal conclusion, wholly unsupported by allegation of fact, and therefore it need not be accepted as true for purposes of 12(b)(6) review"). In *Bell Atl. Corp. v. Twombly*, 550 U.S. 544, 555 (2007), the U.S. Supreme Court explained that "a formulaic recitation of the elements of a cause of action will not do," and that "[f]actual allegations must be enough to raise a right to relief above the speculative level . . . ." The Supreme Court reiterated in *Ashcroft v. Iqbal*, 129 S. Ct. 1937, 1949 (2009), that the federal pleading standard "demands more than an unadorned, the-defendant-unlawfully-harmed-me accusation." The Supreme Court emphasized that legal conclusions in a pleading "must be supported by factual allegations," and that conclusory allegations are "not entitled to be assumed true." *Id.*, 129 S. Ct. at 1950–51.

Argument

6. For the reasons discussed below, Plaintiff respectfully submits that Counts I–III of the Counterclaim should be dismissed with prejudice because Defendant does not and cannot plead that it owns a legally protectable trademark, and that Count IV of the Counterclaim should be dismissed with prejudice because it is a mirror image of Plaintiff's declaratory judgment claim.[1]

---

1. While it is not necessarily germane to this Rule 12(b)(6) motion, Defendant's counterclaim fails to disclose that, under the first-sale and fair-use doctrines, a repackager is legally entitled to use the original publisher's name to identify the original source of the product, *even if that name were deemed to be a valid trademark. See Prestonettes, Inc. v. Coty*, 264 U.S. 359, 368–69 (1924) (first-sale doctrine); *ETW Corp. v. Jireh Pub., Inc.*, 332 F.3d 915, 920–21 (6th Cir. 2003) (fair-use doctrine). Moreover, contrary to Defendant's allegations, Plaintiff's product contains a clear repackaging notice, prominently stating that: "This audiobook has been repackaged by Plaintiff, a wholly separate and distinct company from the publisher. Plaintiff, _____."

A. Counts I–III Should be Dismissed with Prejudice Because Defendant Fails to Adequately Plead that it owns a Protectable Trademark

7. Defendant's entire effort to plead that it owns a legally protectable trademark consists of the following: "'Defendant' and Defendant's logo are Defendant's common law trademarks." (Counterclaim, ¶ 18.) Defendant does not attempt to allege how or when it acquired any common-law trademark. It never identifies or describes its "logo." It does not claim that it ever registered a supposed trademark, and as explained more fully below, the U.S. Trademark Trial and Appeal Board expressly ruled that Defendant could not register a trademark on the phrase "Defendant" because that term is generic. Defendant does not even bother to allege how, when, or even whether the phrase "Defendant" or the unspecified "logo" has been used in the course of trade or commerce.

8. Under any pleading standard, Defendant's bare assertion that it owns a trademark is inadequate. *See Seybert v. Nat'l Ctr. for Missing & Exploited Children*, No. 09-169, 2009 U.S. Dist. LEXIS 103427, at ** 6–7 (E.D. Tex. Aug. 10, 2009) (holding that the "legal conclusion that [the plaintiff] owns a common law trademark" is "not entitled to the assumption of truth" on a motion to dismiss), *adopted*, 2009 U.S. Dist. LEXIS 103427 (E.D. Tex. Nov. 5, 2009). To prove the existence of a "valid and legally protectable trademark," Defendant must show that its purported trademark is either "inherently distinctive" or that it has "acquire[d] distinctiveness through secondary meaning." *DeGidio v. West Grp. Corp.*, 355 F.3d 506, 509–10 (6th Cir. 2004). Secondary meaning is acquired "in the marketplace." *Id.* at 513. Defendant utterly failed to plead when, how, for what period of time, or whether it used the purported trademarks in the course of trade or commerce. It offers no allegations establishing that any consumers associate the phrase "_____" or any logo with Defendant's products. It also fails to allege that the phrase "_____" or the "logo" is inherently distinctive, or that either purported trademark has acquired secondary meaning in the marketplace.

9. In sum, under *Seybert* and the other authorities discussed herein, Defendant's bald allegation that it owns common-law trademarks is not supported by any factual allegations and therefore fails the pleading

standard established by *Twombly* and *Iqbal*. Indeed, this bare legal conclusion would fail under any standard, and it is not entitled to a presumption of truth under Rule 12(b)(6). Counts I through III of Defendant' Counterclaim fail on this basis alone and should be dismissed with prejudice.

B. Counts I–III Should Be Dismissed with Prejudice Because Defendant Cannot Cure its Failure to Plead that it Owns a Protectable Trademark to the Phrase "_____"

10. Furthermore, to the extent that Defendant's Counterclaim is based upon its allegations of a common-law trademark to the phrase "_____," its failure to adequately plead its ownership of that trademark is not curable. The phrase "_____" cannot be a legally protectable trademark because it is a purely generic term. "Generic terms can never be trademarks . . . ." *DeGidio v. West Grp. Corp.*, 355 F.3d 506, 510 (6th Cir. 2004) (*quoting* 2 McCarthy on Trademarks and Unfair Competition § 11:2 (4th ed. 2003)); *see also Le Book Pub., Inc. v. Black Book Photography, Inc.*, 418 F. Supp. 2d 305, 311 (S.D.N.Y. 2005) ("The word '_____' is a generic term and cannot be registered as a trademark").[2]

11. Defendant failed to notify the Court that the U.S. Trademark Trial and Appeal Board ("TTAB") already has ruled that Defendant is not entitled to trademark protection for the phrase "_____" because it is generic. *See In re Defendant* (Trademark Trial & Appeal Board) (attached as Exhibit A). Defendant submitted an application to the U.S. Patent and Trademark Office to register a trademark for the phrase "_____." The Trademark Examining Attorney refused registration "on the ground that _____, when used in connection with [such goods] is generic and, thus, incapable of functioning as a source identifying mark." *Id.* at * 1.

12. In a thorough and detailed written opinion, the TTAB reviewed the factual record, considered the arguments of Defendant's counsel, and squarely rejected Defendant's appeal, finding that the Office had met its "burden of proving genericness by 'clear evidence.'" *Id.* at *2. Thus, the TTAB expressly found "the designation '_____' to be generic." *Id.* at ** 19–20."

13. This Court may take judicial notice of the Trademark Trial and Appeal Board's decision and may consider it in deciding this Rule 12(b)(6)

---

2. Defendant's purported claims under state law "follow the same analysis" as its claims under federal law. *See Rock & Roll Hall of Fame & Museum, Inc. v. Gentile Prods.*, 134 F.3d 749, 754 (6th Cir. 1998).

motion. *See, e.g., Kaempe v. Myers*, 367 F.3d 958, 965 (D.C. Cir. 2004) (taking judicial notice of "documents recorded by the PTO" because, among other things, "the cited documents are public records subject to judicial notice on a motion to dismiss"); *HTC Corp. v. IPCom Gmbh & Co., KG*, 671 F. Supp. 2d 146, 151 n.3 (D.D.C. 2009) (taking judicial notice of PTO pleadings on a motion to dismiss counterclaims and to strike affirmative defenses; "A court may take judicial notice of court documents and other public records"). The TTAB decision is particularly important because it contains a detailed review of a well-developed factual record, an analysis of relevant legal authorities, and a well-reasoned explanation of the findings reached by the TTAB after a proceeding in which Defendant was represented by counsel. Moreover, a "decision of the PTO, and certainly the TTAB, is to be accorded great weight." *Murphy Door Bed Co., Inc. v. Interior Sleep Sys., Inc.*, 874 F.2d 95, 101 (2d Cir. 1989).

14. Therefore, Defendant cannot allege that is owns a legally protectable trademark consisting of the phrase "_____." Because this defect is not curable, Counts I–III of the Counterclaim should be dismissed with prejudice.

C. Defendant's Mirror-Image Declaratory Judgment Claim Should be dismissed with Prejudice

15. Count IV of the Counterclaim simply asks for a declaratory judgment that Defendant's "use of the label '_____' or other similar label on its retail versions is lawful and may continue." (Counterclaim, ¶ 39.) Plaintiff's Complaint seeks a declaratory judgment that precisely the same conduct is unlawful and may not continue. Count IV of the Counterclaim is therefore nothing more than a mirror image of a claim in the Complaint.

16. "[C]ourts should dismiss or strike a redundant counterclaim when 'it is clear that there is a complete identity of factual and legal issues between the complaint and the counterclaim.'" *Pettrey v. Enter. Title Agency, Inc.*, No. 05-1504, 2006 U.S. Dist. LEXIS 83957, at * 9 (N.D. Ohio Nov. 17, 2006) (quoting *Aldens, Inc. v. Packel*, 524 F.2d 38, 51–52 (3d Cir. 1975)). In *Pettrey*, the court dismissed counterclaims and explained its decision as follows:

Here, there is a complete identity of factual and legal issues and the Court harbors no doubt whatsoever that Defendants' declaratory judgment counter-claims will be rendered moot by the adjudication of Plaintiffs['] claims. Defendants seek nothing more than a proclamation that the acts alleged by Plaintiffs are not in fact unlawful.

Id. at * 10. Thus, "no useful purpose would be served by retaining Defendants' declaratory judgment counterclaims." *Id. See also Erickson v. Brock & Scott, PLLC*, No. 09-02461, 2009 U.S. Dist. LEXIS 114331, at ** 13–14 (W.D. Tenn. Dec. 8, 2009) (where the complaint alleged that the defendant violated a statute, and the counterclaim sought a declaration that the defendant did not violate the statute, the court dismissed the counterclaim "as redundant" because it was "factually and legally identical" to the complaint and "will be rendered moot by the disposition of [plaintiff's] Complaint").

As in *Pettrey* and *Erickson*, Count IV of the Counterclaim is nothing more than a mirror image of the Complaint. It simply seeks a declaration that the conduct alleged in the complaint is, in fact, legal. Because Count IV raises only issues that are factually and legally identical to those raised in the Complaint, Count IV should be dismissed with prejudice.

Conclusion

For all the reasons stated above, Plaintiff respectfully requests that this Court dismiss Defendant's Counterclaim with prejudice pursuant to Fed. R. Civ. P. 12(b)(6) and award Plaintiff all further and additional relief that this Court deems proper under the circumstances.

Motion to Dismiss for Lack of Personal Jurisdiction and Simultaneously for Venue Transfer where Defendants Have Insufficient Contacts to Support Jurisdiction

While motions to dismiss for lack of personal jurisdiction are common throughout all types of disputes in federal and state court, one unique aspect of such motions in the context of trademark litigation is allegations based upon the use of a trademark on a website. Courts generally have adopted a sliding scale test based upon the interactivity of a website to determine whether a court has jurisdiction over the defendant because of the potential for people living in the forum to interact with that website. *See Zippo Mfg. Co. v. Zippo Dot Com, Inc.*, 952 F. Supp. 1119, 1124 (W.D. Pa. 1997).

Another consideration in trademark claims is the common tactic of asserting claims against the individuals involved in the business of a company accused of infringement. Trademark and copyright cases follow traditional principles for piercing the corporate veil and officer liability for corporate conduct.

FORM 6.2

Motion to Dismiss for Lack of Personal Jurisdiction and Simultaneously for Venue Transfer where Defendants Have Insufficient Contacts to Support Jurisdiction

In the United States District Court
for the Northern District of Illinois
Eastern Division

MORE CUPCAKES, LLC,	)	
	)	Case No. 09 CV 3555
Plaintiff,	)	
v.	)	Judge Kocoras
	)	Magistrate Judge Valdez
LOVEMORE LLC, ANGELA B.	)	
CROSSMAN,		
and ANDREA R. CROSSMAN,	)	
Defendants.	)	

Defendants' Memorandum in Support of Motion to Dismiss for Lack of Personal Jurisdiction, 12(B)(6) Motion to Dismiss Individual Defendants, and in the Alternative, Motion to Transfer

Defendants Lovemore LLC and Angela B. and Andrea R. Crossman (collectively referred to hereinafter as "Defendants") submit this memorandum in support of their motion to dismiss for lack of personal jurisdiction, to dismiss the Complaint against Angela B. and Andrea R. Crossman (collectively, the "Crossman Defendants") for failure to state a claim upon which relief may be granted, and in the alternative, to transfer venue to the Eastern District of New York.

Based on the allegations that Plaintiff, More Cupcakes, LLC ("Cupcakes"), set forth in its Complaint, the facts set forth in the Declaration of Angela B. Crossman (the "Crossman Decl."), the Declaration of Paul W. Leicht (the "Leicht Decl."), and the authorities cited herein, the Court should dismiss the Complaint for lack of personal jurisdiction over the Defendants because they lack the minimum contacts with Illinois to support personal jurisdiction. In addition, the Complaint states no cognizable claim against the Crossman Defendants and should be dismissed. Finally, and in the alternative, even if the Court finds personal jurisdiction over the Defendants, the Court should transfer this case to the United States District Court for the Eastern District of New York because the material events in dispute occurred there, numerous, important non-party witnesses reside there and litigating this case in Chicago presents a significant burden upon the Defendants.

A. Background

Cupcakes brings this suit under the Lanham Act claiming that Lovemore's T-Shirts infringe on Cupcakes' alleged LOVE MORE trademark for T-shirts. Complaint, ¶ 3. Lovemore LLC ("Lovemore") is a New York limited liability company formed and owned by the Crossman Defendants, who live and work in Brooklyn, New York. Complaint, ¶¶ 3–4. All of Lovemore's operations, assets, and personnel are located in New York. Crossman Decl., ¶ 7. As a new business, Lovemore's operations are small, and its total sales to date are about $8200. Crossman Decl., ¶ 13. Cupcakes alleges that Lovemore does business throughout the United States by offering its LOVEMORE apparel for sale through its website (www.chooselovemore.com). Complaint, ¶ 3. Although Lovemore's shirts are available through its website, the majority of its sales to date (57 percent) have been to consumers in New York. Crossman Decl., ¶ 16 By contrast, as of the filing of the Complaint, Lovemore's relevant sales in Illinois amount to two shipments for only $140.00—about 1 percent of its $8225.07 total sales.[3]

III. The Court Does Not Have Personal Jurisdiction Over the Defendants

A. Defendants are not Subject to General or Specific Jurisdiction in Illinois

In this case, the Court may exercise personal jurisdiction over Defendants only upon a showing that they have "purposefully established minimum contacts within" Illinois such that Defendants may "reasonably anticipate being haled into court" in Illinois because Lovemore has purposefully availed itself of the privilege of conducting business there. *Hyatt Int'l Corp. v. Coco,* 302 F.3d 707,

---

3. Cupcakes also contends that "at least one shipment has been ordered from and has arrived in Illinois, in this district" since Cupcakes LOVE MORE registration issued on June 2, 2009. Complaint, ¶ 3. That shipment of $108.00 in products was purchased on June 4, 2008, by Adriana Sosa, a legal assistant working from the same office address as counsel for Cupcakes. Crossman Decl., ¶ 14; Leicht Decl. Lovemore submits that Cupcakes itself, through its counsel, orchestrated this purchase in preparation for this litigation. Thus, other than one sale initiated by Cupcakes, Lovemore's sales to Illinois amount to $140.00—only 1% percentof its $8,225.07 in total sales. Crossman Decl., ¶ 15.

716 (7th Cir. 2002); *RAR, Inc. v. Turner Diesel, Ltd.*, 107 F.3d 1272, 1276 (7th Cir. 1997) (citing *Burger King Corp. v. Rudzewicz*, 471 U.S. 462, 476 (1985).[4]

Personal jurisdiction may be either general or specific. General jurisdiction exists over a defendant who has had "continuous and systematic" contacts with the forum. *Purdue Research Found. v. Sanofi-Synthelabo, S.A.*, 338 F.3d 773, 787 (7th Cir. 2003) (citing *Helicopteros Nacionales de Colombia, S.A. Hall*, 466 U.S. 408, 416 (1984); *Hyatt*, 302 F.3d at 713; *RAR*, 107 F.3d at 1277). Specific jurisdiction requires "sufficient minimum contacts between [Defendants], this litigation, and [Illinois] to permit us to say that it would be fundamentally fair to require [Defendants] to participate in this litigation and to be bound by the judgment of a court sitting in [Illinois]." *Purdue*, 338 F.3d at 780.

Here, Cupcakes alleges that the Court has jurisdiction over Defendants because Lovemore has offered to ship infringing products to all states, including Illinois, and Lovemore has made at least one shipment to the Northern District of Illinois. Complaint, ¶ 3. These allegations do not establish general or specific jurisdiction over Defendants.

1. Defendants are Not Subject to General Jurisdiction in Illinois

General jurisdiction exists over a defendant who has such "continuous and systematic" contacts with the forum that it is "tantamount to the [defendant] being constructively present in the state to such a degree that it would be fundamentally fair to require it to answer in [that state's] court in **any** litigation arising out of **any** transaction or occurrence taking place **anywhere** in the world." *Purdue*, 338 F.3d at 787 (emphasis added).

The Complaint does not remotely allege that Defendants have "continuous and systematic" contacts with Illinois, nor could it. Lovemore does not own property or assets in Illinois. Crossman Decl., ¶ 8. Lovemore is not licensed to do business in Illinois; Lovemore does not maintain employees, offices, agents, or bank accounts in Illinois; the Crossman Defendants do not reside in Illinois; Lovemore does not maintain phone or fax listings in Illinois;

---

4. Personal jurisdiction must comport with Fifth Amendment Due Process, and the defendant must be amenable to service from the court. The defendant is amenable to service (1) when a court in the state in which the district court is located would have jurisdiction in accordance with the provisions of the state's long-arm statute, or (2) when it is authorized by a statute of the United States. Fed. R. Civ. P. 4(k). Illinois permits courts to exercise jurisdiction on any basis permitted by the Illinois and United States Constitutions. 735 ILCS § 5/2-209(c). "There is no operative difference between the limits imposed by the Illinois Constitution and the federal limitations on personal jurisdiction." *Hyatt*, 302 F.3d at 715 (citing *RAR*, 107 F.3d at 1276). Thus, a single inquiry of whether the Constitution permits the exercise of personal jurisdiction over *Lovemore* is sufficient. *Id.*

Lovemore does not advertise in Illinois; Lovemore's employees do not travel to Illinois for work; Lovemore does not pay taxes in Illinois; and Lovemore does not recruit employees in Illinois. Crossman Decl., ¶¶ 8–12; *see Richter v. Instar Enter. Int'l, Inc.,* 594 F. Supp. 2d 1000, 1006 (N.D. Ill. 2009) (defendant who lacked offices, employees, and agents in Illinois did not reside in Illinois and did not advertise in Illinois in any way other than allowing Illinois residents access to its website was not subject to general jurisdiction).

Instead, Cupcakes contends that Lovemore has sold products in Illinois, relying on a single purchase that Cupcakes (or its counsel) made in preparation for this litigation. Complaint, ¶ 3 and Exs. 6, 7, and 8. The Court should disregard this manufactured transaction and exclude it from the jurisdiction analysis. *E.g., Watchworks Inc. v. Total Time Inc.,* 2002 WL 424631, at *15 (N.D. Ill. Mar. 19, 2002) (personal jurisdiction was not established where plaintiff had only provided evidence of a sale and shipment to plaintiff's investigator in Illinois); *ISI Brands Inc. v. KCC Int'l Inc.,* 458 F. Supp. 2d 81, 88 (E.D.N.Y. 2006) (no personal jurisdiction where two orders shipped to forum state were placed online by plaintiff's counsel during pendency of litigation).

Apart from this artificial "contact," Lovemore has sold $140.00 of goods to Illinois, and these sales account for 1 percent of Lovemore's $8225.07 total sales. Including the $108.00 purchase that Cupcakes made—only 3 percent of Lovemore's sales were to Illinois. Courts routinely hold that a small percentage of sales in the forum state will not support general jurisdiction. *See Richter,* 594 F. Supp. 2d at 1007 (holding that contact with the forum state is not substantial where a defendant's sales in a state represents both a small percentage of defendant's total sales and a small volume of sales overall); *McGill v. Gigantex Techs. Co.,* 2005 WL 3436403, at *8 (N.D. Ill. Dec. 12, 2005) (no general jurisdiction over defendant where sales to Illinois were only 3.5 percent of its total sales); *Berndorf Belt Sys., Inc. v. Harwood Rubber Prods., Inc.,* 2001 WL 800090, at *4 (N.D. Ill. July 16, 2001) (no general jurisdiction where defendant generated only 1 percent of its annual receipts from Illinois). Lovemore's de minimis sales to Illinois cannot support general personal jurisdiction over Lovemore.

2. The Court Does Not Have Specific Jurisdiction Over Lovemore

The Court may exercise specific jurisdiction where the suit arises out of or relates to the defendant's minimum contacts with the forum state. *Hyatt Int'l Corp.* at 716. Here, Cupcakes alleges that Lovemore does business by offering its products throughout the United States (including in Illinois) via its website at www.chooselovemore.com. Complaint, ¶ 3. Cupcakes further alleges that it was damaged in Illinois by Lovemore's supposed infringement of Cupcakes' registered mark during the nine days between the issuance of that registration and the filing of the Complaint. Complaint, ¶ 21. Cupcakes alleges no other contacts by Lovemore to justify specific jurisdiction.

a). Lovemore's Web Site Does Not Support Specific Jurisdiction

Cupcakes alleges that Lovemore does business by infringing T-shirts throughout the United States via its website at www.chooselovemore.com. Complaint, ¶ 3. Whether a defendant's website supplies sufficient contact with the forum to establish specific jurisdiction is evaluated under the sliding scale test first articulated in *Zippo Mfg. Co. v. Zippo Dot Com, Inc.*, 952 F. Supp. 1119, 1124 (W.D. Pa. 1997). *See Richter*, 594 F. Supp. 2d at 1007. Under this test, "the more interactive the website is the greater the likelihood that the defendant had established contacts that comport with the requirements of personal jurisdiction." *Id.* at 1012 (citing *Zippo Mfg. Co.*, 952 F. Supp. at 1124). Personal jurisdiction requires "deliberate and repeated" contacts, and the test presses on the "nature and quality of the contacts with the forum and not the quantity of those contacts." *Id.* Moreover, such contacts must be extensive and intended to be ongoing and directed to the jurisdiction. *See Lindgren v. GDT, LLC,* 312 F. Supp. 2d 1125, 1131 (S.D. Iowa 2004) (holding that website offering point-of-sale transactions, in contrast to continuous user accounts or long-term contracts, are not sufficient contacts for personal jurisdiction). Here, Lovemore does not have extensive contacts with Illinois and has no ongoing directed contacts to support specific personal jurisdiction.

Although its website is accessible to any Internet user, Lovemore has not intentionally directed its website to Illinois and has derived only very few sales, consisting of two shipments, from Illinois. Such minimal sales to Illinois do not support jurisdiction. *See Graduate Mgmt. Admission Council v. Raju,* 241 F. Supp. 2d 589, 595 (E.D. Va. 2003) (two shipments to the forum's residents and a testimonial from a customer from the forum state on its website did not establish specific jurisdiction). That Lovemore's website, like any other, is accessible in Illinois does not render Lovemore's actions purposely directed at Illinois. *See Lindgren,* 312 F. Supp. 2d at 1131 (no personal jurisdiction where the "[defendant's] Website is both commercial and highly interactive, [and] the site is arguably no more directed at [the forum state] than at Uzbekistan. The fact that someone who accesses defendant's Website can purchase [defendant's product] does not render defendant's actions 'purposely directed' at this forum"). In short, Lovemore's de minimis sales to Illinois and putative contact with Illinois through its website do not support specific jurisdiction.

b). The "Effects Test" Does Not Support Specific Jurisdiction over Defendants

Specific jurisdiction may also be established under the effects test established in *Calder v. Jones,* 465 U.S. 783 (1984). *See Euromarket Designs, Inc. v. Crate & Barrel, Ltd.,* 96 F. Supp. 2d 824, 835 (N.D. Ill. 2000). Although not entirely clear, the Complaint states that Lovemore infringed Cupcakes' "statutory rights" for nine days after its registration issued on June 2, 2009. Complaint, ¶ 17. Even if Cupcakes asserts jurisdiction over Lovemore based on this "effect," that theory offers no basis for jurisdiction.

Under the effects test, personal jurisdiction is proper when the defendant's "intentional tortuous actions expressly aimed at the forum state cause harm to the plaintiff in the forum state, and the defendant knows such harm is likely to be suffered", *Richter*, 594 F. Supp. 2d at 1010 (citations omitted). The effects test distinguishes intentional tortuous actions from untargeted negligence. *Id.* at 1011. *See Calder*, 465 U.S. at 789–90 (defendants who had written a disparaging article about the plaintiff knew that their actions could potentially injure the plaintiff in the state where she lived and where the publication they worked for had its largest circulation). Absent evidence of deliberate and knowing infringement, the Court cannot find that Lovemore could have anticipated being haled into court in Illinois. *See Richter*, 594 F. Supp. 2d at 1012; Crossman Decl., ¶ 17. As in *Richter,* Lovemore has not knowingly or deliberately infringed the rights asserted by Cupcakes. *Id.* at 1011; Crossman Decl., ¶ 17. Thus, under Rule 12(b)(2), Lovemore lacks the necessary minimum contacts necessary to establish personal jurisdiction in Illinois.

B. The Fiduciary Shield Doctrine Precludes Personal Jurisdiction over the Crossman Defendants in Illinois

Cupcakes alleges that the Court has jurisdiction over the Crossman Defendants because they are the founders and principals of Lovemore and are personally responsible for directing the business activities of Lovemore, including its infringement of the alleged LOVE MORE mark for T-shirts. Complaint, ¶ 4. Even should the Court find jurisdiction over Lovemore, the Court should nevertheless dismiss the Crossman Defendants because Cupcakes has not (and cannot) establish any separate grounds for personal jurisdiction over them.

Other than their roles as principals of Lovemore, the Crossman Defendants have no contact with Illinois whatsoever. Indeed, the Crossman Defendants have not travelled to Illinois at any time relevant to this dispute. Crossman Decl., ¶ 5. Their conduct as members and principals of Lovemore cannot, as a matter of law, support jurisdiction over their person, and the Crossman Defendants cannot be haled into court here.

The Crossman Defendants' only "contacts" with Illinois result from their employment with Lovemore. Under the "fiduciary shield doctrine" recognized by the Illinois Supreme Court in *Rollins v. Ellwood*, 141 Ill.2d 244 (1990), these business contacts with Illinois do not support the exercise of personal jurisdiction over the Crossman Defendants. In *Rollins*, the court held that:

> [it would be] unfair and unreasonable, under Illinois' due process clause and the tenets of our concept of the jurisdictional power of the Illinois courts, to assert

personal jurisdiction over an individual who seeks . . . to serve [the interests] of his employer . . .

141 Ill.2d at 280. *See also Clipp Designs, Inc. v. Tag Bags*, 996 F. Supp. 766, 768 (N.D. Ill. 1998) (personal jurisdiction does not exist over an individual whose presence and activity in the forum state were "solely on behalf of his employer or other principal").

The doctrine applies where the plaintiff cannot provide equitable reasons for the court to disregard the corporate entity. *Id.* at 769. Courts have recognized that the corporation and its founders' interests may be compatible but hold that this does not necessitate finding that the corporation is a sham corporation or that application of the fiduciary shield is precluded. *See Modern Aids, Inc. v. Lil' Drug Store Prods. Inc.*, 1993 WL 239054, at *3 (N.D. Ill. June 24, 1993). Here, Cupcakes alleges no facts to challenge the legitimacy of Lovemore as a "sham corporation" and gives no reason for the Court to disregard that business entity such that the Crossman Defendants should be haled into Illinois court individually.

IV. The Court Should Dismiss Complaint Against the Crossman Defendants Under Rule 12(b)(6)

Cupcakes also fails to allege a cognizable claim against the Crossman Defendants. To withstand a motion to dismiss under Rule 12(b)(6), Cupcakes must allege "sufficient facts to outline a cause of action, proof of which is essential to recovery." *The Drink Grp. v. Gulfstream Commc'ns, Inc.*, 7 F. Supp. 2d 1009, 1010 (N.D. Ill. 1998). While the Complaint does not need detailed factual allegations, Cupcakes' obligation to provide the grounds of its entitlement to relief requires "more than labels and conclusions, and a formulaic recitation of the elements of a cause of action will not do." *Bell Atl. Corp. v. Twombly*, 127 S. Ct. 1955, 1964–65 (2007); *accord Jennings v. Auto Meter Prods. Inc.*, 495 F.3d 466, 472 (7th Cir. 2007). Here, the Complaint's factual allegations do not raise a right to relief above the speculative level, even should the Court assume that all of Cupcakes' allegations are true. *Id.*

"Personal liability for the wrongdoing of a corporation cannot be imposed upon an individual merely because that individual is an officer of the corporation." *Dev. Indus., Inc. v. Rockwell Graphic Sys., Inc.*, 1992 WL 100908, at *3 (N. D. Ill. 1992). Cupcakes has not asserted any facts to establish a separate cause of action against the Crossman Defendants. Cupcakes alleges only that the Crossman Defendants are independently liable for Lovemore's alleged infringement because they are responsible for directing the business activities of Lovemore as the founders and principals of the company. Complaint, ¶ 4. These allegations do not establish a cognizable claim. Fed. R. Civ. P. 12(b)(6).

The law has long recognized that absent "some special showing, the managing officers of a corporation are not liable for the infringements of such corporation, though committed under their general direction." *Dangler et al. v. Imperial Mach. Co.*, 11 F.2d 945, 947 (7th Cir. 1926). Courts have interpreted the "special showing" requirement as a heightened pleading requirement. *See Jones Day v. Blockshopper LLC*, 2008 WL 4925644 at *5(N.D. Ill. Nov. 13, 2008) (allegations that individual defendants cofounded, registered, and owned defendant corporation did not satisfy the special showing required to hold an individual officer liable). "The mere fact that officers incorporated the defendant [corporation is] innocuous in the absence of allegations that, at the time of incorporation, they were motivated by some improper purpose or acting outside the scope of their corporate duties." *The Drink Grp.*, 7 F. Supp. 2d at 104. Here, there are no allegations that the Crossman Defendants organized Lovemore for any improper purpose or acted outside of their duties to Lovemore. Thus, Cupcakes' allegations against the Crossman Defendants "fall woefully short of the special showing requirement in *Dangler*." *Id.* (allegations that individual defendants incorporated the defendant corporation failed to meet special showing requirement).

Furthermore, Cupcakes' allegations against the Crossman Defendants regarding their direction of the alleged infringement are conclusory statements that standing alone fall short of Cupcakes' obligation to present a claim with some supporting facts. *See id.* This Court has not hesitated to dismiss actions against individual corporate officers absent some alleged wrongdoing on the part of the individual officers. *See id.* (allegations that individual defendants were the principal and driving force behind the infringement stated no claim for personal liability); *Dev. Indus.*, 1992 WL 100908 at *3 (allegations that individual defendants were "the moving, conscious, and dominant force behind [the defendant corporation's] offending conduct" failed to state a claim). Thus, Cupcakes alleges no facts that meet the minimum threshold of notice pleading under Rule 12(b)(6),and the Complaint should be dismissed against the Crossman Defendants. *Id.*

V. In the Alternative, the Court Should Transfer this Action to the Eastern District of New York

The Court enjoys broad discretion to transfer this case from its present inconvenient forum to the Eastern District of New York, where Defendants are located. 28 U.S.C. § 1404(a) provides:

> For the convenience of the parties and witnesses, in the interest of justice, a district court may transfer any civil action to any other district or division where it might have been brought.

See also Sassy, Inc. v. Berry, 406 F. Supp. 2d 874, 875 (N.D. Ill. 2005) ("The decision to transfer is left to the sound discretion of the trial court.").

Transfer of venue is appropriate when the following three requirements are met: (1) venue is proper in both the transferor and transferee districts, (2) the transfer is for the convenience of the parties and witnesses, and (3) the transfer serves the interests of justice. *Sassy, Inc.*, 406 F. Supp. 2d at 875; *Chukwu v. Air France*, 218 F. Supp. 2d 979, 988 (N.D. Ill. 2002). Here, should the Court find personal jurisdiction: all three requirements are met.

A. Venue is Proper in this District and in the Eastern District of New York

1. Venue is Proper in the Northern District of Illinois

If the Court finds personal jurisdiction, venue is technically proper in this District because this action, which is not founded solely on diversity of citizenship, may be brought in a judicial district that may exercise personal jurisdiction over a corporate defendant. 28 U.S.C. § 1391(c). Thus, upon the Court's finding personal jurisdiction, venue would be proper here.

2. Venue is Proper in the Eastern District of New York

Venue is proper in the Eastern District of New York because Lovemore is a New York limited liability company with its principal place of business in Brooklyn, New York, and the Crossman Defendants also reside in that juridical district. Crossman Decl., ¶ 4; 28 U.S.C. § 1391(b)(1).

Further, a substantial part of the events giving rise to the claims occurred in New York. 28 U.S.C. § 1391(b)(2). Lovemore tested and promoted its T-shirt products in New York. Crossman Decl., ¶ 18. Lovemore hired and oversaw a design team that developed the mark in New York. Crossman Decl., ¶ 20. Lovemore also hired photographers, printing centers, makeup artists, and models to promote the mark in New York. Crossman Decl., ¶ 21. The decisions concerning the branding and marketing of Lovemore's goods were made in New York. Crossman Decl., ¶ 18.

Moreover, all events relating to Lovemore's allegedly infringing conduct occurred in the Eastern District of New York. Lovemore developed and produces its allegedly infringing products in New York. Crossman Decl., ¶ 23. Lovemore created and designed the website that Cupcakes alleges Lovemore uses to sell its products in New York. Crossman Decl., ¶ 24. Thus, because Lovemore allegedly committed acts in New York that lead to the claimed infringement, venue is appropriate in the Eastern District of New York under 28 U.S.C. § 1391(b)(2).

B. Transfer is Convenient for the Parties and Witnesses

Having determined that an action could properly be brought in either the transferor or transferee district, the Court then should consider the convenience of the parties and witnesses. *See Chukwu,* 218 F. Supp. 2d at 988. Factors in weighing the parties and witnesses' convenience are (a) the plaintiff's choice of forum, (b) the situs of the material events, (c) ease of access to sources of proof, (d) the individual residences and the respective abilities of the parties to bear the expense of trial in a particular forum, (e) availability and cost of obtaining attendance of witnesses, and (f) the convenience of the parties. *Id.* Here, the convenience factors overwhelmingly favor transfer to the Eastern District of New York.

1. Cupcakes' Choice of Forum has Minimal Value Because the Central Activities Giving Rise to This Action Did Not Occur in Illinois

The plaintiff's choice of forum "is not absolute and will not defeat a well-founded motion to transfer." *Wen Prods. Inc. v. Master Leater, Inc.,* 899 F. Supp. 384, 385–86 (N.D. Ill. 1995). "The weight given to plaintiff's choice of forum is lessened if the chosen forum has [a] relatively weak connection with the operative facts giving rise to the claim." *Int'l Truck and Engine Corp. v. Dow-Hammond Trucks Co.,* 221 F. Supp. 2d 898, 904 (N.D. Ill. 2002). This is true even in cases where the chosen forum is plaintiff's home forum. *Id.* This Court has not hesitated to transfer trademark infringement actions for the convenience of the parties and witnesses. *Id.* at 905–06; *SRAM Corp. v. Sunrace Roots Ent. Co., LTD.,* 953 F. Supp. 257, 259–60 (N.D. Ill. 1997) (plaintiff's choice of home forum insufficient to defeat motion to transfer venue in trademark infringement action); *Wen Prods.,* 899 F. Supp. at 385–86 (same).

The central activities giving rise to the causes of action occurred in New York, not Illinois. Therefore, Cupcakes' filing of its Complaint in this judicial district is entitled to minimal weight.

2. New York is the Situs of the Material Events

"Lanham Act cases generally focus on the activities of the alleged infringer, its employees, and its documents; therefore, the location of the infringer's place of business is often **the critical and controlling consideration**." *See Interlochen Ctr. for the Arts v. Interlocken Int'l Camp, Inc.,* 2002 WL 31040346, at *5 (N.D. Ill. Sept. 12, 2002) (quotations omitted) (emphasis added); *SRAM Corp.,* 953 F. Supp. at 259; *Habitat Wallpaper and Blinds, Inc. v. K.T. Scott Ltd. P'ship,* 807 F. Supp. 470, 475 (N.D. Ill. 1992).

Here, the central activities for the alleged trademark infringement occurred in New York. As noted, Lovemore's creation and development of its products took place in New York, its sales and marketing of its products are directed from New York, and Lovemore's relevant documents and employees are in New York. Crossman Decl., ¶¶ 18–25.

Because Lovemore's alleged infringement occurred in New York, this forum's connection to this dispute is tenuous at best. In such circumstances, cases are routinely transferred to the relevant forum. *See, e.g., Int'l Truck and Engine Corp.,* 221 F. Supp. 2d at 904 (venue transferred to California in trademark infringement suit where California was situs of the infringing activity).

3. New York Provides Relative Ease of Access to Sources of Proof

All documents related to Lovemore's testing and initial promotion of its T-Shirt products are located in New York. Crossman Decl., ¶ 19. Lovemore's design team, as well as photographers, printing centers, makeup artists, and models who are familiar with Lovemore's use and development of its mark are located in New York. Crossman Decl., ¶¶ 20–25. Cupcakes alleges that Lovemore does business in its infringing products via its website. Complaint, ¶ 3. Lovemore's website activities were designed, planned, and implemented in New York, not Illinois. *See Ty Inc., v. Beanie World,* 1999 WL 782092, at *3 (N.D. Ill. Sept. 27, 1999) (transferring case where defendant's "internet activities were designed, planned, and implemented in Florida, not Illinois"). Furthermore, the mere fact that Lovemore sold $140 worth of goods in Illinois does not make it the situs of material events. *See id.* at *2 (sales of only $300 in Illinois through defendants website did not make it the situs of material events). Hence, this factor strongly favors transfer. *Int'l Truck and Engine Corp.,* 221 F. Supp. 2d at 904–05 (finding ease of access to proof favored venue transfer where defendant's activities in requested venue were what led to the dispute).

4. The Convenience of Witnesses Strongly Favors Transfer

In deciding whether a case should be transferred pursuant to Section 1404(a),"the convenience of the witnesses is one of the most important factors to be considered." *Moore v. A&T Latin Am. Corp.,* 177 F. Supp. 2d 785, 790 (N.D. Ill. 2001). Congruently, Courts address two other important related factors—the availability of the compulsory process to require the presence of unwilling witnesses and the cost of obtaining attendance of the willing witnesses. *Ful Inc. v. Unified School Dist. Number 204,* 839 F. Supp. 1307, 1312 (N.D. Ill. 1993). These factors are important because obtaining live testimony of witnesses at trial is preferred over other means of presenting evidence. *Ful Inc.,* 839 F. Supp. at 1312 ("the presence of potential non-party witnesses outside the subpoena power of the court, weighs heavily in a transfer decision"); *Bally Mfg. Corp. v. Kane,* 698 F. Supp. 734, 738 (N.D. Ill. 1988) (same).

Here, the convenience to the witnesses strongly warrants transfer of this case to the Eastern District of New York. First, it is Lovemore's understanding that no third-party witnesses residing in this district have personal knowledge of events relating to Lovemore's allegedly infringing conduct. Crossman Decl., ¶ 26. Second, the great majority of material non-party witnesses are in New York. Crossman Decl., ¶ 25. Lovemore hired a design team of three individuals to continue development of the LOVEMORE mark in New York. Crossman Decl., ¶ 20. Lovemore hired a printing service, three photographers, and 22 models in New York to develop its business under the LOVEMORE mark. Crossman Decl., ¶ 21. Such witnesses include:

- David–individual who tested and promoted Lovemore T-shirts in December 2007
- Christopher–individual who tested and promoted Lovemore T-shirts in December 2007
- Anya–individual who photographed Andrea Crossman in Lovemore T-shirt at New York comedy club and posted photos on Flickr website in April 2008
- Sarah–individual who wore and promoted Lovemore T-shirt on CBS's televised *Amazing Race,* filmed worldwide, in April–May 2008
- Terence–individual who wore and promoted Lovemore T-shirt on CBS's televised *Amazing Race,* filmed worldwide, in April–May 2008
- Alvaro–individual who worked on designing and developing Lovemore brand identity materials and website in May 19–July 2008
- Jessica–individual who worked on designing and developing Lovemore logo and website in August 2008
- Nicolas–individual who worked on designing and developing Lovemore logo and website in August 2008
- Jocelyn–individual who worked on designing and developing Lovemore logo and website in August 2008
- Michael–individual who worked on printing postcards and business cards in October–November 2008
- Meg–individual who photographed Lovemore web catalogue in November 2008
- Bowen–individual who assisted photographer of Lovemore web catalogue in November 2008
- Lisa–individual who created makeup artistry for Lovemore web catalogue shoot in November 2008

Testimony from these witnesses is highly probative of the fact that Lovemore has prior commercial use of the LOVE MORE mark. Crossman Decl., ¶ 25. Thus, even at this early stage of the litigation, there are at least 12 material New York area non-party witnesses, and as many as 32 New York area non-party witnesses, that would be subject to the subpoena power of the Eastern District of New York, but not this Court.

Since these witnesses are not under Defendants' control, it is unlikely that Defendants would be able to secure their voluntary appearance at trial. *See Ramsey v. Fox News Network, LLC*, 323 F. Supp. 2d 1352, 1356 (N.D. Ga. 2004) (noting that no presumption exists that non-party witnesses will agree to testify at trial voluntarily). Significantly, Defendants would also be unable to compel these witnesses to testify at trial because they are outside of this Court's subpoena power. Therefore, Defendants would be forced to present their testimony by deposition.

The prospect of using lengthy deposition testimony from these key witnesses unfairly prejudices Defendants by impeding their ability to present an effective case at trial. *See, e.g., In re Eastern Dist. Repetitive Stress Injury Litigation*, 850 F. Supp 188, 194 (E.D.N.Y. 1994) (stating that "depositions, however, even when videotaped, are no substitute for live testimony."); *Haworth, Inc. v. Herman Miller, Inc.*, 821 F. Supp. 1476, 1479 (N.D. Ga. 1992) (transferring case where other forum provided compulsory process over key witnesses).

Even videotaped depositions would not cure the prejudice to Defendants' ability to present an effective case at trial. *Household Fin. Servs., Inc. v. Prestige Fin. Servs. Corp.*, 1999 WL 608705, at *2 n.8 (N.D. Ill. Aug. 6, 1999) ("The possibility of taking videotaped depositions does not save plaintiffs from transfer. Live witness testimony is superior to either printed or taped depositions").

Because the Court should not be forced to rely on deposition testimony when another suitable forum could obtain live testimony can be obtained, Defendants' ability to compel material non-party witnesses to testify at trial presents a paramount reason to transfer this case to the Eastern District of New York. *See Waites v. First Energy Leasing Corp.*, 605 F. Supp. 219, 222–23 (N.D. Ill. 1985) (granting defendants' request to transfer venue, despite the fact that plaintiff identified material witnesses located in Illinois, because virtually all of defendants' material witnesses resided in New York).

Second, assuming that the New York-based witnesses were willing to testify at trial, the cost of obtaining their attendance in Illinois would be much greater than in New York. Even at this early stage of the litigation, it is apparent that the vast majority of the non-party witnesses for this case reside in or near New York, not Illinois. Crossman Decl., ¶¶ 25–26. If the Court transfers the case to New York, Defendants would incur minimal travel costs for the aforementioned witnesses: for example, the cost of gas mileage, instead of thousands of dollars per witness for airfare from New York to Illinois, hotel accommodations, and food. Thus, the convenience of the witnesses strongly favors transfer of this case to New York.

5. The Convenience of the Parties Favors Transfer to New York

In assessing the convenience to the parties in transferring venue, courts have considered the parties' respective residences and their ability to bear the expense of the litigation in a particular forum. *SRAM Corp.*, 953 F. Supp. at 259–60; *Wen Products*, 899 F. Supp. at 385–86. Here, because Lovemore and Cupcakes are both small companies with small workforces, Crossman Decl., ¶ 13, their respective abilities to bear the cost of traveling witnesses within their control (e.g., employees and experts) are the same. *SRAM Corp.*, 953 F. Supp. at 259–60; *Wen Prods.*, 899 F. Supp. at 386. Thus, the cost of attendance of witnesses within either Lovemore or Cupcakes' control is neutral. *See Household Fin.*, 1999 WL 608705, at *2 (recognizing that the "cost of attendance of witnesses within either party's control is neutral, as one of the parties will have to incur the time and expense of securing the attendance of such witnesses regardless of whether this case is litigated here or in Florida").

The cost of attendance for material non-party witnesses, however, the majority of whom are located in New York, would be considerably lower were this case litigated in New York. Moreover, to the extent any of these witnesses are unwilling to testify, only the Eastern District of New York would have the ability to compel their attendance, as these witnesses would be outside the subpoena power of this Court. *E.g., Sky Valley Ltd. P'ship v. ATX Sky Valley*, 776 F. Supp. 1271, 1277 (N.D. Ill. 1991) (granting motion to transfer, holding that "[t]he factor weighing most heavily in favor of transfer is the location of the third party witnesses in California," and further explaining that "[t]he interest of justice is better served by ensuring the presence of live witness testimony . . . Thus the presence of third party witnesses outside the subpoena power of this court is a factor which weighs heavily in favor of transferring this case").

For the reasons discussed above, Defendants will be greatly inconvenienced if it is required to try this action in Illinois. The party and non-party witnesses Defendants plans to call at trial are located in New York. Even if they could gain their cooperation in the absence of a subpoena, Defendants would incur the significantly greater cost of flying numerous non-party witnesses from New York to Illinois and back and providing them with hotel accommodations, if the case proceeds in Illinois. *Sky Valley*, 776 F. Supp. at 1277; *Int'l Truck*, 221 F. Supp. 2d at 905. Accordingly, this factor favors a transfer of venue to New York.

C. Public Interest Favors Transfer

After considering the convenience of the parties and witnesses, courts evaluate the public interest in having the case litigated in the transferee or transferor forum. *Chukwu*, 218 F. Supp. 2d at 989. Public interest factors include (a) the relationship of the community to the issues in the litigation and the desirability of resolving controversies in their locale, (b) the Court's familiarity with applicable law, and (c) congestion of the respective dockets. *Id.* Here, two of these factors favor transfer to New York, and the other is neutral.

1. New York has a Relationship to the Litigation and an Interest in its Resolution

Lovemore has made 57 percent of its total sales in New York, while it has made about 1 percent of its total sales in Illinois. Crossman Decl., ¶ ¶ 13–16. Because all events relating to Lovemore's allegedly infringing conduct occurred in New York, and the majority of Lovemore's total sales occurred in New York, that state has a strong interest in this action. *See SRAM Corp.*, 953 F. Supp. at 259–60 (finding factor favored defendant's request to transfer venue where the vast majority of the alleged infringing sales occurred in the district where venue was sought); *Wen Prods.*, 899 F. Supp. at 386 (finding district to which transfer was granted had an interest in the case because the defendant resided in and conducted its alleged trademark infringement within the state); *Habitat Wallpaper*, 807 F. Supp. at 475 (finding district to which transfer was granted had an interest because virtually all acts that would constitute alleged infringement took place within the state). The central activities and situs of the material events for Lovemore's alleged trademark infringement are in New York. Thus, New York has a special interest in the resolution of this matter that Illinois does not have.

Lastly, Cupcakes is seeking permanent injunctive relief to prevent Lovemore from using the LOVEMORE and LOVE MORE marks on shirts. Complaint, Prayer ¶ a. The nature and extent of any such injunctive relief will necessarily have a distinct local effect in New York. *See Int'l Truck,* 221 F. Supp. 2d at 905; *Habitat Wallpaper,* 807 F. Supp. at 475 (plaintiff's assertion of claim for injunctive relief militated in favor of transfer because, if granted, the injunction would require enforcement in Massachusetts). Based upon the foregoing, New York has a relationship to the litigation and a strong interest in its resolution that exceeds any interest of Illinois.

2. New York Courts are Familiar with Trademark Cases

The trademark claims underlying the Complaint are based on federal law, 15 U.S.C. § 1125(a) ("the Lanham Act"), for which there is general nationwide uniformity. Thus, the Eastern District of New York will be familiar with the applicable law.

3. Resolution of the Matter Will Be Expeditious in New York

Federal Court Management Statistics for the period ending September 30, 2008, indicate that there are 7162 cases pending in the Eastern District of New York, while there are 7398 cases pending in the Northern District of Illinois. Furthermore, resolution of this matter will be expeditious in the Eastern District of New York, given that there "the action [will be] litigated in

the forum that is closer to the action." *See Ty Inc.*, 1999 WL 782092, at
* 4. Accordingly, this factor favors transfer.

VI. Conclusion

For the reasons set forth above and the authorities cited herein, Defendants
urge the Court to dismiss the Complaint for lack of personal jurisdiction
because they lack the minimum contacts with Illinois to support personal
jurisdiction. Defendants further request that the Court dismiss all claims against
the Crossman Defendants for failure to state a cause of action. Finally, and
in the alternative, even if the Court finds personal jurisdiction over Defendants,
the Court should transfer this case to the United States District Court for the
Eastern District of New York where the material events in dispute occurred and
where numerous non-party witnesses reside.

Respectfully submitted,

Motion to Dismiss Dilution Claim

A claim for dilution under the Lanham Act has become much more
difficult to plead since recent amendments to the Lanham Act made clear
that a trademark must be famous among the general consuming public of
the United States to qualify for protection under the Act. For example,
courts have found the following marks to be famous: NISSAN, NIKE, PEPSI,
STARBUCKS, VICTORIA'S SECRET, and VISA. Marks found not to be famous
for purposes of Lanham Act dilution protection include MENSA, the Texas
Longhorn Logo, BLUE MAN GROUP, CLUE, and TREK. Obviously, the
threshold of fame is very high. Niche fame or limited geographic fame is
insufficient. Thus, dilution claims are ripe for motions to dismiss based upon
the insufficient fame of the alleged mark.

Motion to Dismiss Dilution Claim

In the United States District Court
for the Northern District of Llinois
Eastern Division

K-C INC.,	)	
K-C LLC,	)	
Plaintiffs,	)	
	)	Case No.
vs.	)	
	)	The Hon. John W. Darrah
MDI, INC.,	)	
	)	Magistrate Judge Arlander Keys
Defendant.	)	

II. Defendant's Memorandum of Law in
Support of its Motion to Dismiss Plaintiffs'
Dilution Claim Under 43(C) of the Lanham Act
III. Introduction

Plaintiffs K-C Inc. and K-C LLC (collectively, "K-C") allege that defendant, MDI, Inc. ("MDI"), diluted K-C's Red Mark (as defined in the Complaint) " after the Red Mark was distinctive and **famous in the relevant industry**." (Comp., ¶ 13) (emphasis added). A mark must be **widely recognized by the general consuming public of the United States** to qualify for protection under Section 43(c) of the Lanham Act, as amended by the Trademark Dilution Revision Act of 2006 ("TDRA"). 15 U.S.C. § 1125(c)(2) (emphasis added). Thus, K-C has failed to plead that its Red Mark has the requisite level of fame necessary to support a claim for dilution. MDI therefore moves to dismiss K-C's claim for federal trademark dilution (Count IV of the Complaint) under Fed. R. Civ. P. 12(b)(6) for failure to state a claim upon which relief can be granted.

IV. Background

K-C markets and sells disposable, -colored face masks for use in the medical industry. MDI markets and sells disposable, purple-colored face masks for use in the medical industry.

The parties litigated in 2005 over, among other things, lavender-colored face masks marketed by MDI to which K-C objected. The parties settled the 2005 litigation through a confidential settlement agreement.

K-C now complains that MDI's purple-colored face masks, which MDI developed to comply with the settlement and which MDI has sold since 2005, dilute K-C's Red Mark. K-C has not, however, properly pled a dilution claim under the Lanham Act—and cannot—because the parties market their face masks only to the medical industry.

V. Argument

A. MDI Has Met the Standard on its Motion to Dismiss

Accepting the allegations in the Complaint as true, K-C nevertheless has failed to allege facts that plausibly suggest that relief is warranted for its dilution claim. *Jang v. A.M. Miller & Assocs.*, 122 F.3d 480, 483 (7th Cir. 1997); *see also DiChristofano v. Neiman Marcus Grp. Inc.*, 2007 U.S. Dist. LEXIS 50001, *2–3 (N.D. Ill. July 11, 2007); *Allstate Ins. Co. v. Mathison*, 2002 U.S. Dist. LEXIS 11541, *3 (N.D. Ill. June 26, 2002) (J. Darrah) (Dismissal proper when it appears beyond doubt that Plaintiff can prove no set of facts to support the allegations in his or her claim).

Furthermore, K-C's own allegations prevent its dilution claim from proceeding because the Complaint states that K-C's Red Mark is only famous in the relevant industry. *See Ill. Tool Works, Inc. v. Chester Bros. Machined Prods.*, 2006 U.S. Dist. LEXIS 57316, *14–15 (N.D. Ill. July 27, 2006) (dismissing false advertising claim under the Lanham Act where plaintiff failed to allege facts found to be prerequisite to asserting a false advertising claim); *Thermal Zone Prods. Corp. v. Echo Eng., Ltd.*, 1993 U.S. Dist. LEXIS 12708, *12–13 (N.D. Ill. Sept. 14, 1993) (dismissing claim under Illinois Anti-Dilution Act where plaintiff's allegations of competition between parties placed claim squarely outside of precedent excluding claims by competitors). MDI therefore requests that the Court dismiss this claim.

B. K-C Fails to Allege That its Red Mark is Famous Among the General Consuming Public of the United States

K-C alleges that its "Red Mark" is famous only **"in the relevant industry."** (Complaint, ¶ 13) (emphasis added). To obtain relief under Section 43(c) of the Lanham Act, the mark at issue must be famous among the **general public**. In particular, the TDRA states: "a mark is famous if it is widely recognized by the general consuming public of the United States as a designation of source of the goods or services of the mark's owner." 15 U.S.C. § 1125(c)(2).

The enactment of the TDRA added this definition of fame to prevent claims, such as K-C's, based solely on a mark with niche market fame. "[The TDRA] strengthens the requirement of fame by making it clear that the mark must be 'widely recognized by the general consuming public of the United States,' **the bill rejects the application of the law to so-called 'niche' fame among a few people or in a small part of the United States.**" *Trademark Dilution Revision Act of 2005: Hearing on H.R. 683 Before the Subcomm. on Courts, the Internet, and Intellectual Property of the H. Comm. on the Judiciary,* 109th Cong. 46 (2005) (statement of Mark A. Lemley, William H. Neukom Professor of Law, Stanford Law School) (emphasis added).

To date, no court in the Seventh Circuit has considered niche market fame under the TDRA.[5] Courts that have considered claims of dilution under the TDRA have explicitly found that niche market fame is insufficient. *See, e.g., Jarritos, Inc. v. Los Jarritos,* 2007 U.S. Dist. LEXIS 32245, at *53 (N.D. Cal. May 2, 2007) (". . . the TDRA revised the Federal Trademark Dilution Act to deny protection to marks that are famous only in 'niche' markets.") *citing Century 21 Real Estate LLC v. Century Ins. Group,* 2007 U.S. Dist. LEXIS 9720, at *43 (D. Ariz. Feb. 9, 2007) (same); *Dan-Foam A/S & Tempur-Pedic, Inc. v. Brand Named Beds, LLC,* 2007 U.S. Dist. LEXIS 33301, at *30 (S.D.N.Y. May 4, 2007) (Inclusion of "widely recognized by the general consuming public of the United States" in definition of "famous" under the TDRA intended to reject dilution claims based on niche fame, but denying defendant's motion for summary judgment on dilution because plaintiff submitted evidence that its mark was in use on a national level and widely known among consumers.).

Courts that have applied the TDRA have specifically denied relief under the TDRA to trademark owners whose marks had acquired only niche market fame, including, for example, in limited geographic areas. *See Cosi, Inc. v. WK Holdings,* 2007 U.S. Dist. LEXIS 31990 (D. Minn. May 1, 2007); *see also The Christopher B. Smithers Foundation, Inc. v. St. Luke's-Roosevelt Hospital Center,* 2003 U.S. Dist. LEXIS 373, at *15 (S.D.N.Y. Jan. 13, 2003) (A mark has only niche market fame if its "fame [is] limited to a particular channel of trade, segment of industry or service or geographic region."). In *Cosi,* the court dismissed plaintiff's dilution claim because the COSI mark was not sufficiently famous to warrant dilution protection. *Id.* at *5–6. Despite plaintiff's operation of over 110 restaurants in 16 states and sale of franchises in 47 states and select foreign countries, the court refused to accept plaintiff's assertion that the public viewed COSI as a national chain. *Id.* Measuring fame against marks like VICTORIA'S SECRET and LOUIS VUITTON, the court found that plaintiff's use of the COSI mark in "a small number of states" did not qualify it as famous under the new standard. *Id.* at *6. K-C's allegation that its Red Mark is famous

---

5. Prior to the enactment of the TDRA, the Seventh Circuit suggested that it would accept claims of dilution based on niche market fame among competitors within the same market. *See Syndicate Sales, Inc. v. Hampshire Paper Corp.,* 192 F.3d 633, 640–41 (7th Cir. 1999). To the extent that precedent in this Circuit previously found niche market fame sufficient to state a dilution claim, MDI submits that the TDRA has overruled such precedent.

in the relevant industry likewise does not qualify it for dilution protection. *See also Hamzik v. Zale Corp.*, 2007 U.S. Dist. LEXIS 28981, at *15 (N.D.N.Y. Apr. 19, 2007) (Plaintiff's failure to allege facts suggesting that his mark was famous under the meaning of the TDRA required dismissal of dilution claim).

VI. Conclusion

For the foregoing reasons, MDI requests that this Court grant its motion to dismiss Plaintiffs' dilution claim.

Respectfully submitted,

MDIMDI

Motion to Dismiss Claims for Trademark Infringement and Related Torts

In many cases, a plaintiff asserts federal and state law claims related to its trademark and unfair competition claims. While this "kitchen sink" approach may be warranted in some circumstances, often, one or more of these claims will not be supported by the facts at hand. Generally, it is the better practice to assert only claims that have a good probability of overcoming a motion to dismiss, both because it shows the court that the claims are serious and because losing a substantive motion early in a case often disheartens the client.

Below is an example from one of the many class actions filed against Google in recent years over its business model. This example focuses on a codefendant that sought to extract itself from the lawsuit entirely by requesting the dismissal of all claims against it.

FORM 6.4

Motion to Dismiss Claims for Trademark Infringement and Related Torts

United States District Court
Northern District of Illinois

VULCAN GOLF, LLC,	)	
Individually And On Behalf of All Others	)	
Similarly Situated,	)	
Lead Plaintiff,	)	
	)	
v.	)	No. 07 CV 3371
	)	
GOOGLE, INC., OVERSEE.NET,	)	Judge Charles P. Kocoras
SEDO LLC, DOTSTER, INC., AKA	)	Magistrate Judge Geraldine
		Soat Brown
REVENUEDIRECT.COM,	)	
INTERNET REIT, INC. d/b/a IREIT, INC.	)	
and JOHN DOES I–X.,	)	
Defendants.	)	

Eastern Division

Memorandum of Defendant Internet Reit, Inc in Support of its Motion to Dismiss
I. Introduction

Plaintiff Vulcan Golf, LLC ("Plaintiff" or "Vulcan") sued Defendant Internet REIT ("Ireit") and the other defendants based on an isolated dispute involving two domain names registered by a single defendant other than Ireit. Despite the lack of any quarrel with Ireit, Plaintiff asserts claims against Ireit for purported RICO, consumer fraud, cybersquatting, and trademark violations on behalf of the potentially millions of entities that have their own trademarks. Even if the Court were to accept as true the allegations of Vulcan's Complaint, those allegations fail to state a claim against Ireit for any of the 12 counts of the Complaint. Accordingly, as discussed more fully below, the Complaint should be dismissed as to Ireit.

II. Statement of Facts

A. Defendant Ireit

Ireit acquires, develops, and monetizes domain names and web properties. Complaint ("Comp.") ¶ 49; *see also* http://www.Ireit.com/index.php. Ireit is a Delaware corporation having its principal place of business in Houston, Texas. Comp. ¶ 49. Ireit owns and manages a portfolio of domain names. *Id.*

Ireit has enrolled in the AdSense program run by Google Inc. ("Google"), which is an Internet advertising program for domain names. *Id.* ¶ ¶ 56(x)–(y), 79, 97.

B. Plaintiff

Vulcan is the lead plaintiff in this purported class action against Ireit and the other named and unnamed defendants. Comp. ¶ ¶ 6. Plaintiff is an Illinois corporation with its principal place of business in St. Charles, Illinois. *Id.* ¶ 16. Plaintiff reportedly was founded "to design and manufacture high performance innovative game improvement golf clubs." *Id.* ¶ 17. Plaintiff allegedly owns the trademark VULCAN and the trade name Vulcan Golf. *Id.* ¶ ¶ 18, 23.

C. Allegations Against Ireit

Plaintiff asserts 12 counts on its own behalf and on behalf of a purported class of "similarly situated entities and individuals" ("Class") against Ireit and the other named defendants (Google; Oversee.net; Sedo LLC; Dotster, Inc., a/k/a Revenuedirect.com) and unnamed defendants (John Does I–X) (collectively, "Defendants"). Comp. ¶ 6. The purported Class consists of owners of marks that "one or more of the Defendants" have allegedly infringed. *Id.* ¶ 24.

Plaintiff asserts against all Defendants claims pursuant or relating to the Lanham Act, 15 U.S.C. § 1051 *et seq.*, including trademark infringement, under 15 U.S.C. § 1114(1), false designation of origin under 15 U.S.C. § 1125(a), dilution under 15 U.S.C. § 1125(c), and cybersquatting under 15 U.S.C. § 1125(a); Racketeering Influenced Corrupt Organizations Act ("RICO") under 18 U.S.C. § 1962(c) and (d); the Illinois Consumer Fraud and Deceptive Business Practices Act under 815 ILCS § 505/2; the Illinois Uniform Deceptive Trade Practices Act under ILCS § 510/2, and "the identical or substantially similar consumer fraud and fair trade practices acts of the various states, and various states' common law." *Id.* ¶ 6.

Plaintiff fails to identify even a single mark or domain name that Ireit allegedly registered, licensed, or utilized that infringes, dilutes, or somehow violates any rights of Plaintiff. Instead, Plaintiff merely contends that Ireit owns the domain name <mantbank.com>, for which Ireit uses Google's AdSense program. *Id.* ¶¶ 386–94. Importantly, Plaintiff fails to allege that it owns or has any rights to <mantbank.com> or any related trademark. Plaintiff fails to identify the owner of a mark supposedly infringed by the domain <mantbank.com> and fails to allege that any such person is a member of the purported Class.

III. Analysis

A. Plaintiff Lacks Standing to Sue Ireit

1. There Is No Allegation That Ireit Harmed Plaintiff

Because Plaintiff lacks standing, the Court should dismiss all claims pursuant to Rule 12(b)(1). Plaintiff must "assert [its] own legal rights and interests, and cannot rest [its] claim to relief on the legal rights or interests of third parties." *Warth v. Seldin*, 422 U.S. 490, 499–500 (1975); *Lujon v. Defenders of Wildlife*, 504 U.S. 555, 560–61 (1992); *see also Am. Fed'n of Gov't Emp., Local 2119 v. Cohen*, 171 F.3d 460, 465 (7th Cir. 1999) ("Obviously, if a plaintiff cannot establish standing to sue, relief from this court is not possible, and dismissal under 12(b)(1) is the appropriate disposition").

While courts may look beyond the pleadings in a Rule 12(b)(1) motion, *Roman v. United States Postal Service*, 821 F.2d 382, 385 (7th Cir. 1987), the Complaint itself shows that Plaintiff lacks standing to sue Ireit. Plaintiff does not allege that Ireit committed any acts that harmed Plaintiff itself. Instead, the Complaint makes clear that the only domain names that allegedly harmed the Plaintiff were "wwwvulcangolf.com" and "volcangolf.com." Comp. ¶ 200. The Complaint alleges that both of these offending domain names were registered by defendant Dotster. Comp. ¶ 200. The Complaint does not allege that Ireit had anything to do with "wwwvulcangolf.com" or "volcangolf.com."

Plaintiff relies entirely on hypothetical claims that might be asserted by non-parties to establish standing for its claims against Ireit. This is improper. Unless and until a class is certified in this case, the claims of alleged class members are simply not relevant. *See Warth*, 422 U.S. at 502 (named plaintiffs "must allege and show that they personally have been injured, not that injury has been suffered by other, unidentified members of the class to which they belong and which they purport to represent").[6] Plaintiff may not bring claims against Ireit "through the back door of a class action." *Allee v. Medrano*, 416

---

6. Moreover, a plaintiff's claim must present more than "abstract questions of wide public significance which amount to generalized grievances . . . ." *Valley Forge Christian College v. Am. United for Separation of Church & State, Inc.*, 454 U.S. 464, 474–75 (1982). This principle is closely related to the constitutional requirement of personal "injury in fact." *Id.*, 454 U.S. at 475.

U.S. 802, 828–29 (1974) (Burger, C.J., concurring in part and dissenting in part). It is black letter law that "if none of the named plaintiffs purporting to represent a class establishes the requisite of a case or controversy with the defendants, none may seek relief on behalf of himself or any other member of the class." *O'Shea v. Littleton*, 414 U.S. 488, 494 (1974); *see also Robinson v. City of Chicago*, 868 F.2d 959, 968 (7th Cir. 1989) (class action may not be certified unless the named plaintiff has standing).

Where, as here, Plaintiff cannot trace an injury it has suffered to Ireit, Plaintiff lacks standing to sue Ireit. *See, e.g., Angel Music, Inc. v. ABC Sports, Inc.*, 112 F.R.D. 70, 75 (S.D.N.Y. 1986) (copyright owner injured by one infringer did not have standing to bring a class action against all alleged infringers under theory of alleged "industry-wide policy"); *Matte v. Sunshine Mobile Homes, Inc.*, 270 F. Supp. 2d 805, 826 (W.D. La. 2003) (rejecting attempt by 16 mobile home owners to bring class action against 282 defendants comprising all mobile home manufacturers, because they could trace no injury to the conduct of defendants from whom they did not purchase a mobile home); *Easter v. Am. West Fin.*, 381 F.3d 948, 962 (9th Cir. 2004) (named plaintiffs lacked standing to bring class action against lenders who did not hold and had never held a named plaintiff's loan).

2. There Is No Allegation That Ireit Injured Plaintiff Through a RICO Violation

Nor do Plaintiff's RICO allegations provide standing to sue Ireit. To have standing under RICO, a plaintiff must allege that he has been "injured in his business or property by reason of a [RICO] violation." 18 U.S.C. § 1964(c); *Evans v. City of Chicago*, 434 F.3d 916, 924 (7th Cir. 2006). This provision requires a plaintiff to show that an actionable RICO violation was the proximate cause of the *plaintiff's* injury for standing to sue under RICO. *Holmes v. Securities Investor Prot. Corp.*, 503 U.S. 258, 268 (1992); *Gas Tech. Inst. v. Rehmat*, No. 05 C 2712, 2006 WL 3422190, at *13 (N.D. Ill. 2006).

The Complaint basically alleges that defendant Dotster had an agreement with defendant Google to share profits from "wwwvulcangolf.com" and "volcangolf.com," and that this agreement somehow creates an actionable RICO claim. The Complaint fails to allege any agreement by Ireit with any party that relates in any way to these two domain names or to Plaintiff Vulcan Golf. Plaintiff fails to allege that Ireit did anything whatsoever to assist Dotster or Google to profit from "wwwvulcangolf.com" or "volcangolf.com." Nor does Plaintiff allege that Ireit committed any other RICO predicate act that damaged Plaintiff Vulcan Golf. The Complaint's RICO allegations against Ireit instead rely on an alleged conspiracy between Ireit and Google to harm other, hypothetical, unnamed future class members. Comp. ¶ ¶ 169–79. These allegations fail to state that Ireit committed any RICO predicate acts that were a proximate cause of Vulcan Golf's own injuries. Hence, Plaintiff lacks standing to sue Ireit under RICO. Because Plaintiff fails to plead *any* facts or claims against Ireit that establish standing, all 12 counts asserted against Ireit in Plaintiff's Complaint should be dismissed pursuant to Rule 12(b)(1) .

B. Plaintiff's RICO Allegations Are Not Pleaded with Particularity as Required by Federal Rule of Civil Procedure Rule 9(b)

A plaintiff must plead RICO fraud claims with particularity pursuant to Rule 9(b). *EQ Fin. Inc. v. Personal Fin. Co.*, 421 F. Supp. 2d 1138, 1146 (N.D. Ill. 2006); *Builders Bank v. First Bank & Trust Co. of Illinois*, No. 03 C 4959, 2004 WL 1497766, at *2 (N.D. Ill. 2004). Here, Plaintiff bases its RICO claims on alleged mail and wire fraud. To plead mail and wire fraud with particularity, Plaintiff must, at a minimum, state "who initiated the communication, when the communication took place, the contents of the communication, and how that communication furthered the scheme to defraud." *Builders Bank*, 2004 WL 1497766, at *2. The extreme length of Plaintiff's Complaint should not be mistaken for particularity: "A complaint can be long-winded, even prolix, without pleading with particularity. Indeed, such a garrulous style is not an uncommon mask for absence of detail." *Williams v. WMX Tech. Inc.*, 112 F.3d 175, 178 (5th Cir. 1997).

Plaintiff's RICO counts are fatally deficient in many areas:

- **Time**—Plaintiff's conclusory allegations that "Defendants" placed "matter and things" in "post offices" and transmitted "matter and things" by wire are insufficient. There is not a single date tied to a single communication to which Ireit was a party in the entire 127-page Complaint. Plaintiff must allege the *exact date* of *each* communication Plaintiff claims constituted a predicate act. *Builders Bank*, 2004 WL 1497766, at *3.
- **Place**—Plaintiff fails to identify where any alleged predicate act took place other than to state that they all took place at unspecified "post offices."
- **Content**—Plaintiff's reference to "matter and things" fails to identify the content of the communications. Plaintiff's further clarification of "including but not limited to contracts, invoices, correspondence, and payments," would encompass everything that an ordinary business would mail or transfer over the wire. In order to satisfy Rule 9(b), Plaintiff must allege exactly *what was said or done* in *each* communication at issue that constituted actionable mail or wire fraud. *EQ Fin.*, 421 F. Supp. 2d at 1147.
- **Method**—Plaintiff broadly alleges that all defendants committed predicate acts by the use of mail or wire. But Plaintiff must allege for *each* communication whether it was made through mail, Internet, telephone, or some other means. *EQ Fin.*, 421 F. Supp. 2d at 1147.

- ***Identities of the Parties***—Plaintiff fails to allege who made any of the communications. The Seventh Circuit has specifically held that it is not sufficient to "lump" a group of defendants together and allege that the group sent communications or the group members communicated with each other. *Viacom, Inc. v. Harbridge Merchant Servs., Inc.*, 20 F.3d 771, 778 (7th Cir. 1994). The complaint must specifically identify which party sent each communication that forms the basis for a predicate act, and to whom the communication was sent. *Id.*

Plaintiff's RICO allegations do not satisfy a single requirement of Rule 9(b) and should, therefore, be dismissed.

C. Plaintiff's Consumer Protection Claims Are Not Pleaded with Particularity as Required by Rule 9(b)

Consumer protection claims that sound in intentional misrepresentation and fraud, as opposed to negligent misrepresentation, must be pleaded with particularity pursuant to Rule 9(b). *Veal v. First Am. Sav. Bank*, 914 F.2d 909, 912–13 (7th Cir. 1990); *Siegal v. Shell Oil Co.*, 480 F. Supp. 2d 1034, 1039–40 (N.D. Ill. 2007). Here, Plaintiff alleges intentional misrepresentation and fraud. *See* Comp. ¶ ¶ 591, 595 (alleging that all defendants committed "fraud, false promise, misrepresentation, and concealment," and "Defendants have knowingly, intentionally, and deliberately engaged in conduct that creates a likelihood of confusion.") Because Plaintiff alleges intentional fraud, Plaintiff must plead:

> (1) "the identity of the person making the misrepresentation" (the "who"), (2) the "content of the misrepresentation" (the "what"), (3) "the time" the misrepresentation occurred (the "when"), (4) "the place" of the misrepresentation (the "where"), and (5) the "method by which the misrepresentation was communicated to the plaintiff" (the "how").

Siegal v. Shell Oil Co., 480 F. Supp. 2d 1034, 1039–40 (N.D. Ill. 2007).
Just like Plaintiff's RICO claims, Plaintiff fails to allege any of these requisite facts. Instead, Plaintiff merely recites the legal elements of a consumer protection claim and alleges facts related only to "wwwvulcangolf.com" and "vulcangolf.com"—domains that have *nothing* to do with Ireit. Moreover, the Complaint fails to identify the party supposedly making the misrepresentations. The Complaint instead lumps all the defendants together and makes conclusory statements that they all engaged in deceptive practices. *See Sears v. Likens*, 912 F.2d 889, 893 (7th Cir. 1990) (rejecting complaint that "lumped together" multiple defendants because the complaint was "bereft of any detail concerning who was involved in each allegedly fraudulent activity"). The Complaint also fails to allege the time or place of any of the representations.

Although the Complaint alleges that Ireit owns "many deceptive domain names," it fails to identify a single one, let alone allege the specific facts required for the consumer protection claim.

D. Plaintiff's Complaint Fails to State Any Claim for Relief and Should Be Dismissed Pursuant to Rule 12(b)(6)

Plaintiff's Complaint fails to state a claim against Ireit in any of its 12 counts. The Court should thus dismiss Plaintiff's claims pursuant to Rule 12(b)(6). The Supreme Court recently clarified the standard for dismissal under Rule 12(b)(6):

> While a complaint attacked by a Rule 12(b)(6) motion to dismiss does not need detailed factual allegations, . . . a plaintiff's obligation to provide the "grounds" of his "entitle[ment] to relief" requires more than labels and conclusions, and a formulaic recitation of the elements of a cause of action will not do . . . Factual allegations must be enough to raise a right to relief above the speculative level, . . . on the assumption that all the allegations in the complaint are true (even if doubtful in fact).

Bell Atl. Corp. v. Twombly, 127 S. Ct. 1955, 1964–65 (2007) (internal citations omitted).

Although Plaintiff asserts 12 causes of action, the basis for each boils down to two domain names, "wwwvulcangolf.com" and "volcangolf.com." As noted above, Ireit has nothing to do with these two domain names. The Complaint's allegations against Ireit are nothing more than a "formulaic recitation of the elements" of each of Plaintiff's causes of action. The Complaint fails to allege any facts whatsoever to support a claim that Ireit has harmed Plaintiff Vulcan Golf.[7]

1. Counts I and II Must Be Dismissed Because Plaintiff Fails to Plead a Cognizable RICO Claim

Count I asserts a claim under Section (c) of RICO, 18 U.S.C. § 1962(c); and Count II asserts a claim under Section (d) of RICO, 18 U.S.C. § 1962(c). These sections provide:

> (c) It shall be unlawful for any person employed by or associated with any enterprise engaged in, or the activities of which affect, interstate or foreign

---

7. For brevity, Ireit adopts by reference the additional Rule 12(b)(6) grounds set forth in the other defendants' motions to dismiss, rather than restating those grounds in Ireit's brief.

commerce, to conduct or participate, directly or indirectly, in the conduct of such enterprise's affairs through a pattern of racketeering activity or collection of unlawful debt.

(d) It shall be unlawful for any person to conspire to violate any of the provisions of subsection (a), (b), or (c) of this section.

RICO does not cover all instances of wrongdoing. *Gamboa v. Velez*, 457 F.3d 703, 705 (7th Cir. 2006). To state a civil RICO claim based upon mail and wire fraud, Plaintiff must show that Ireit (1) controls or operates an enterprise, (2) engaged in a pattern of racketeering activity, (3) which constituted a scheme to defraud Plaintiff about a material fact, (4) involving use of the mails and wire in furtherance of the scheme, and (5) the scheme proximately caused injury to Plaintiff. *See McDonald v. Schencker*, 18 F.3d 491, 494 (7th Cir. 1994); *see also Holmes*, 503 U.S. at 268 (requiring proximate cause with respect to injury).[8]

Plaintiff fails to adequately plead injury sufficient to have standing, as well as at least the following three essential elements of a RICO claim: (1) a cognizable RICO enterprise, (2) predicate racketeering activity, or (3) conspiracy.

a. Plaintiff Lacks Standing Because it has Failed to Plead Direct Injury

Plaintiff utterly fails to allege that Ireit is the proximate cause of Plaintiff's own alleged injury. In order to have RICO standing, Plaintiff must allege that a fraudulent statement by Ireit caused a direct injury to Plaintiff. *See Phoenix*

---

8. Although RICO provides civil remedies for private parties under certain exacting conditions, the statute was expressly enacted for the purpose of "seek[ing] the eradication of organized crime in the United States." *Katzman v. Victoria's Secret Catalogue*, 167 F.R.D. 649, 654 (S.D.N.Y. 1996) (quoting Pub. I., No. 91-452). It is fundamentally a criminal statute aimed at preventing the infiltration of business enterprises by organized crime. *See United States v. Turkette*, 452 U.S. 576 (1981); *Russello v. United States*, 464 U.S. 16 (1983). As such, RICO should not lightly be applied against civil defendants unless the plaintiff plainly satisfies its burden as to each and all of the requisite elements. Courts have long recognized that "[c]ivil RICO is an unusually potent weapon—the litigation equivalent of a thermonuclear device." *Miranda v. Ponce Fed. Bank*, 948 F.2d 41, 44 (1st Cir. 1991). Because the "mere assertion of a RICO claim . . . has an almost inevitable stigmatizing effect on those named as defendants, . . . courts should strive to flush out frivolous RICO allegations at an early stage of the litigation." *Figuero Ruiz v. Alegria*, 896 F.2d 645, 650 (1st Cir. 1990). *See also Philatelic Found. v. Kaplan*, 647 F. Supp. 1344, 1347 (S.D.N.Y. 1986) (finding that criminal law origins of civil RICO present "difficulties," if not an outright "dilemma," requiring courts to "struggle[] . . . [for] principled conclusions" lest "garden variety" misconduct impermissibly be transformed into the proverbial federal case).

Bond & Indemnity Co. v. Bridge, 477 F.3d 928, 932 (7th Cir. 2007), *rehearing en banc denied* (Apr. 17, 2007) (holding "that the direct victim may recover through RICO whether or not it is the direct recipient of the false statements") (*citing Israel Travel Advisory Serv., Inc. v. Israel Identity Tours, Inc.*, 61 F.3d 1250, 1257 (7th Cir. 1997)). However, the "injury must be direct rather than derivative," and "business rivals may not use RICO to complain about injuries derivatively caused by mail frauds perpetrated against customers." *Id.* at 933 (*quoting Israel Travel*, 61 F.3d at 1258). Plaintiff fails to allege any direct injury resulting from Ireit or any other defendant's conduct.

In *Anza v. Ideal Steel Supply Corp.*, 126 S. Ct. 1991 (2006), the Court applied a proximate cause requirement to a § 1962(c) RICO claim alleging mail fraud as a predicate act. The *Anza* Court relied on the standard in *Holmes*, that provides that a plaintiff's right to sue "require[s] a showing that the defendant's violation not only was a 'but for' cause of his injury, but was the proximate cause as well." *Anza*, 126 S. Ct. at 1996 (*quoting Holmes*, 503 U.S. at 268). Further, the Court stated that a compensable injury flowing from a § 1962(c) injury "necessarily is the harm caused by the predicate acts . . . for the essence of the violation is the commission of those acts in connection with the conduct of an enterprise." *Id.* (*quoting Sedima S.P.R.L. v. Imrex Co.*, 473 U.S. 479, 497 (1985)).

Plaintiff fails to allege how Ireit, or any other defendant, is the "proximate cause" of any trademark owner's alleged RICO injury. "When a court evaluates a RICO claim for proximate causation, the central question it must ask is whether the alleged violation led directly to the plaintiff's injuries." *Anza*, 126 S. Ct. at 1998. Here, Plaintiff brings a RICO mail fraud claim based on its alleged loss of sales resulting from Plaintiff's customer's mistyping of a web address that results in the customer seeing paid advertisements which might result in the customer failing to purchase what it would have otherwise purchased from Plaintiff. In this case, as in *Anza*, the "cause of [Plaintiff's] asserted harm" is a "set of actions . . . entirely distinct from the alleged RICO violation." *Anza*, 126 S. Ct. at 1997. As the Seventh Circuit noted in similar circumstances, the mail fraud statute "does not protect vendors to persons who may be deceived, and firms suffering derivative injury from business torts therefore must continue to rely on the common law and the Lanham Act rather than resorting to RICO." *Israel Travel Advisory Service, Inc.*, 61 F.3d at 1258. Thus, Plaintiff fails to allege that Ireit caused Plaintiff's alleged injuries or the injuries of any putative class member.

b. Plaintiff Fails to Plead the Existence of a RICO "Enterprise" Over Which Ireit "Exercised Control"

Plaintiff's RICO claims should be dismissed for the additional reason that Plaintiff has failed to plead the existence of a RICO enterprise or that Ireit exercised control over the alleged enterprise.

(i) No "Enterprise"

In order to satisfy Section 1962(c)'s pleading requirements, a plaintiff must plead each defendants' participation in the operation or management of an "enterprise," as that term is defined for purposes of the statute. *See Richmond v. Nationwide Cassel L.P.*, 52 F.3d 640, 645 (7th Cir. 1995); *Reeves v. Ernst & Young*, 507 U.S. 170, 183 (1993)). For purposes of the RICO statute, "enterprise" "includes any individual, partnership, corporation, association, or other legal entity, and any union or group of individuals associated in fact although not a legal entity." 18 U.S.C. § 1961(4). Plaintiff fails to identify an enterprise because the Complaint does not allege any identifiable structure, any common purpose, or any independent existence separate from the alleged racketeering activity.

While a RICO enterprise can be formal or informal, some type of identifiable organizational structure is required. *See U.S. v. Korando*, 29 F.3d 1114, 1117 (7th Cir. 1994) ("The hallmark of an enterprise is a 'structure.'"); *see also Bachman v. Bear, Stearns & Co.*, 178 F.3d 930, 931 (7th Cir. 1999) (finding a loose-knit association of entities cannot constitute a RICO "enterprise" where it involves no organization beyond an alleged conspiracy to commit fraud). Thus, a RICO "enterprise" must be an "ongoing 'structure' of persons associated through time, joined in purpose, and organized in a manner amenable to hierarchical or consensual decision-making." *Richmond*, 52 F.3d at 644. To properly allege a RICO enterprise, a Plaintiff is required to identify "a 'command structure' separate and distinct from" the individual defendants which allegedly comprise the enterprise." *Stachon v. United Consumers Club, Inc.*, 229 F.3d 673, 676 (7th Cir. 2000).

Plaintiff's sole attempt to allege the existence of an "enterprise" is to allege the following open-ended and amorphous "Enterprise":

> The following group of individuals and entities, associated in fact, constitute an interstate "Enterprise" under RICO: (1) Defendant Google, (2) the Parking Company Defendants, (3) all AdWords Participants/Advertisers, (4) all AdSense Participants/Publishers, (5) all other individuals and entities participating in Defendant Google's AdSense and AdWordsNetworks and/or the Google Advertising Network, (6) Defendant Google Search Partners, and (7) other unnamed Co-conspirator Defendants that agreed to and engaged in the unlawful actions described herein.

Comp. ¶ 429. The group as defined by Plaintiff lacks the requisite separate command structure. Plaintiff's alleged enterprise is nothing more than a group of wholly independent entities, known and unknown, who as a group lack any distinct existence and structure. *See Richmond*, 52 F.3d at 645 (dismissing a RICO action naming a string of entities, known and unknown, as a RICO enterprise because "a nebulous, open-ended description of the enterprise does not sufficiently identify this essential element of the RICO offense").[9]

While Plaintiff does allege that the members of the alleged enterprise share a common purpose, the purpose alleged is so vague that it would make the parties to every business transaction members of an enterprise. An adequately alleged enterprise must have "a common purpose of engaging in a course of conduct." *Richmond*, 52 F.3d at 645. Plaintiff alleges that the "members of the Enterprise . . . share the common purpose of maximizing their profits and market share through cooperation, participation, fraternization, and utilization of the extensive international network" of online commerce. Comp. ¶ 441. Such a generic purpose is insufficient to allege an enterprise, according to the Seventh Circuit:

> [D]iverse parties, such as these [alleged members of the enterprise], customarily act for their own gain or benefit in commercial relationships. Given the commercial nature of the various parties' relationships . . . and the independent interests necessarily governing those relationships, the amended complaint fails to dispel the notion that the different parties entered into agreements . . . for their own gain or benefit.

Stachon, 229 F.3d at 677 n.4. Given that the alleged members of the enterprise in this case are all for-profit entities, Plaintiff has done nothing to allege an enterprise with a common purpose that goes beyond normal business relations.

The alleged pattern of racketeering activity is also insufficient to allege an enterprise. "The enterprise needs to be something more than just the pattern of racketeering activity. 'Otherwise two statutory elements—enterprise and pattern—would be collapsed into one.'" *Korando*, 29 F.3d at 1117 (citation omitted). Even if Plaintiff adequately alleged in an amended complaint a conspiracy to defraud, Plaintiff would be no closer to alleging an enterprise. A conspiracy to defraud "is not an enterprise unless every conspiracy is also an enterprise for RICO purposes, which the case law denies." *Bachman*, 178

---

9. The Complaint also does not satisfy the "separateness" requirement: "[S]ection 1962(c) requires separate entities as the liable person and the enterprise which has its affairs conducted through a pattern of racketeering activity." *Haraco, Inc. v. Am. Nat'l Bank and Trust Co.*, 747 F.2d 384, 400 (7th Cir. 1984). Plaintiff apparently tries to circumvent the "separateness" requirement for the enterprise by randomly adding entities wholly disconnected to the alleged fraud. The Seventh Circuit rejected a similarly misconceived attempt by the *Richmond* Plaintiff to allege an enterprise because "[n]ot one of the non-defendant entities, supposedly constituent parts of the 'enterprise,' [was] described as playing a role in the [alleged fraud]." *Richmond*, 52 F.3d at 645. To the extent that Plaintiff has identified defendants and the entities making up the enterprise, not one of the additional entities in the alleged enterprise "play[s] a role" in the alleged fraud. Plaintiff thus fails to allege an enterprise with any identifiable structure.

F.3d at 932 (affirming a dismissal for failure to allege an enterprise even though plaintiff alleged a conspiracy to defraud that lasted for years). Thus, Plaintiff fails to identify an enterprise because it alleges no structure, no common purpose and no identity separate from the alleged racketeering.

(ii) No "Exercise of Control" By Ireit

In order to allege a 1962(c) violation, Plaintiff must also allege that Ireit "conduct[ed] or participate[d], directly or indirectly, in the conduct of such enterprise's affairs." 18 U.S.C. § 1962(c). The Supreme Court has held that "to conduct" "indicates some degree of direction" and that "to participate," "one must have some part in directing th[e] affairs" of the enterprise. *Reeves*, 507 U.S. at 178–79; *see also U.S. v. Cummings*, 395 F.3d 392, 397 (7th Cir. 2005) ("Supreme Court precedent teaches that this language 'indicates some degree of direction . . .'). Indeed, "one is not liable under [§ 1962(c)] unless one has participated in the operation or management of the enterprise itself." *Reeves*, 507 U.S. at 183. Further, the Plaintiff must allege "that the defendants conducted or participated in the conduct of the *"enterprise's* affairs," not just their *own* affairs." *Id.* at 185 (emphasis in original). "[M]ere participation in the activities of the enterprise is insufficient." *Goren v. New Vision Int'l, Inc.*, 156 F.3d 721, 727 (7th Cir. 1998). An allegation of "the existence of a business relationship between the[] defendants and the enterprise" does not satisfy the operation or management test. *Id.* at 728. Even performing services for an enterprise "with knowledge of the enterprise's illicit nature, is not enough to subject an individual to RICO liability under § 1962(c)." *Id.*

Plaintiff fails to allege that Ireit managed or operated the alleged enterprise. Plaintiff contends that every Defendant in this case is a "person" within the meaning of 18 U.S.C. § 1961(3)," and thus by inference managed or operated the affairs of the alleged enterprise. Comp. ¶ 428. While Plaintiff provides the "formulaic recitation of the elements," *see* Comp. ¶¶ 439, 440, 459, 508, 510, 521, nowhere does the Plaintiff provide a factual basis for its blanket allegation that Ireit "conduct[ed]" or had "some part in directing" the affairs of the enterprise. *See* Comp. ¶ 442. Nothing in the alleged facts would raise "above the speculative level" the possibility that Ireit operated or managed the affairs of the enterprise. *See Twombly*, 127 S. Ct. at 1965.[10] Thus, Plaintiff has failed to plead the necessary conduct or participation under § 1962(c).

---

10. Nor is it even plausible that Ireit somehow manages the affairs of Google, let alone all of the other defendants.

c. Plaintiff Has Failed to Adequately Plead Predicate "Racketeering Activity"

In order to plead a RICO violation, Plaintiff must plead that a defendant committed a pattern of predicate acts (or racketeering activity) enumerated in Section 1961(c) of the RICO statute. Cybersquatting and trademark infringement are not enumerated RICO predicate acts. Plaintiff bases its RICO allegations upon alleged mail and wire fraud in violation of 18 U.S.C. §§ 1341 and 1343. *See* Comp. ¶ 446–56. The elements of mail fraud require "(1) a scheme or artifice to defraud with the intent to defraud; (2) through a deception about a material fact; and (3) the use of the mails (or interstate telecommunication) to further the fraud." *Corley v. Rosewood Care Ctr. Inc.*, 152 F. Supp. 2d 1099, 1108 (C.D. Ill. 2001).

(i) No Scheme To Defraud

"A necessary element of a scheme to defraud is the making of a false statement or material misrepresentation, or the concealment of a material fact." *Williams v. Aztar Ind. Gaming Corp.*, 351 F.3d 294, 299 (7th Cir. 2003) (dismissing a mail fraud claim for failing to allege a misrepresentation). Stated simply, a scheme to defraud requires allegations of fraud, which Plaintiff simply has not made. While Plaintiff alleges fraud in mailed invoices and contracts, that allegation completely fails the particularity requirement of Rule 9(b) as discussed above. Thus, the only allegation that might possibly pass muster is the alleged "Illegal Infringement Scheme" relating to the alleged acts of cybersquatting. As detailed below, however, the Complaint's cybersquatting allegations do not amount to fraud or deceit.

Plaintiff vaguely alleges that Ireit and the other Defendants committed mail and wire fraud to effectuate an "Illegal Infringement Scheme" that supposedly injured Plaintiff. Comp. ¶ ¶ 446–456. In the attempt to create a false impression of mail and wire fraud, Plaintiff lists a multitude of mail and wire transactions inherently implicated in the Internet advertising industry. *Id.* at ¶ ¶ 450(a)–(t), 451. Plaintiff, however, fails to offer any allegations to establish how Ireit lied to, or concealed material facts from, Plaintiff, any putative plaintiff, or any of Plaintiff's potential customers in any alleged attempt to defraud any of them. Nor does Plaintiff identify any fraudulent or false statement by Ireit, or for that matter, any other defendant.

(ii) No Deception About a Material Fact

Even if Plaintiff could allege that Ireit acted with intent to defraud, Plaintiff must further allege that the fraud was material. Additionally, a false statement is material where it has "'a natural tendency to influence . . . the decision of the decisionmaking body to which it was addressed.'" *U.S. v. Gee*, 226 F.3d 885, 891 (7th Cir. 2000). The Complaint fails to allege any fraudulent statement, much less any *materially* fraudulent statement by Ireit. Vulcan's alleged potential customers who mistype a domain name address are the only alleged persons possibly making a decision. It is difficult to imagine a statement by Ireit that would influence the decision of potential Vulcan customers with respect to domain names and websites with which Ireit has absolutely no connection. Plaintiff completely fails to demonstrate the materiality of any statement by Ireit as it regards any decision made by Vulcan's potential customers.

(3) Not Mailed for the Purpose of Executing a Fraudulent Scheme

Even if Plaintiff had properly alleged trademark infringement or cybersquatting, allegations of mailings will not convert either of these acts into a predicate act under § 1961(1). Other than the fraud alleged in ¶ 450 (a)–(b) of the Complaint, Plaintiff has failed to allege any act subject to RICO because cybersquatting and trademark infringement are not included in the § 1961(1) list of predicate acts. *See Miranda*, 948 F.2d at 48 ("Congress painstakingly enumerated a complete list of predicate acts in 18 U.S.C. § 1961(1)."). Further, the nonfraudulent use of the mail or wires will not convert an act excluded from the predicate acts of § 1961(1) into a predicate act. *See Evercrete Corp. v. H-Cap Ltd.*, 429 F. Supp. 2d 612, 631 (S.D.N.Y. 2006) (dismissing RICO claims because willful trademark infringement does not become racketeering simply through the use of interstate mail or wires); *see also Smith v. Jackson*, 84 F.3d 1213, 1217 (9th Cir. 1996) (rejecting RICO claims that do no more than allege copyright infringement—prior to the addition of criminal copyright as a predicate act).

d. Plaintiff Fails to Plead a "Conspiracy" Under Section 1962(d)

Because Plaintiff fails to allege an act of racketeering under § 1962(a)–(c), it cannot allege conspiracy under § 1962(d). The Supreme Court has held "that a person may not bring suit under § 1964(c) predicated on a violation of § 1962(d) for injuries caused by an overt act that is not an act of racketeering or otherwise unlawful under the statute." *Beck v. Prupis*, 529 U.S. 494, 507 (2000). Since Plaintiff has failed to allege adequately a § 1962(c) violation, and has not even attempted to allege a § 1962(a) or (b) violation, Plaintiff may not allege conspiracy under § 1962(d) based simply on the plain language of that statute.

While a violation of § 1962(c) is not essential to plead a § 1962(d) violation, Plaintiff has not alleged the necessary elements of a § 1962(d) conspiracy. "[T]he touchstone of liability under § 1962(d) is an agreement to participate in an endeavor which, if completed, would constitute a violation of the substantive statute." *Slaney v. Int'l Amateur Athletic Fed.*, 244 F.3d 580, 600

(7th Cir. 2001) (*quoting Goren*, 156 F.3d at 732). The *Goren* court explained that a RICO conspiracy requires both an agreement to participate in the enterprise and an agreement to commit two predicate acts:

> From a conceptual standpoint a conspiracy to violate RICO can be analyzed as composed of two agreements . . . an agreement to conduct or participate in the affairs of an enterprise and an agreement to the commission of at least two predicate acts . . . If either aspect of the agreement is lacking then there is insufficient evidence that the defendant embraced the objective of the alleged conspiracy.

Goren, 156 F.3d at 732 Thus, allegations of mere "affiliation" with an enterprise or mere agreement to commit criminal acts does not satisfy the pleading requirements of § 1962 *(id)*. *See Goren*, 156 F.3d at 732.

While Plaintiff recites the formula "in furtherance of a conspiracy" multiple times (*see* Comp. ¶ ¶ 8, 13, 465–69, 501(t), 513, 517–23), Plaintiff fails to allege that Ireit "conspired knowingly to facilitate the activities of anyone to whom § 1962(c) would apply—namely, an operator or manager of the . . . RICO enterprise." *See U.S. v. Cummings*, 395 F.3d at 398. Plaintiff does not allege that Ireit agreed to conduct or participate in the affairs of the alleged enterprise, nor does Plaintiff allege that Ireit agreed to commit mail or wire fraud. "It is well established that a complaint may be dismissed if it contains only conclusory, vague and general allegations of a conspiracy." *Goren*, 156 F.3d at 733 (citing the Third Circuit for the proposition that "a conspiracy claim must contain supportive factual allegations describing the general composition of the conspiracy, some or all of its broad objectives, and the defendant's general role in the conspiracy."). Plaintiff's vague and conclusory allegations of association with an enterprise are simply insufficient to state a claim under § 1962(d). For the foregoing reasons, Plaintiff's RICO claims against Ireit should be dismissed.

2. Count III Must Be Dismissed Because Plaintiff Fails to Assert a Cybersquatting Claim Against Ireit

Plaintiff also fails to establish a claim against Ireit under the Anticybersquatting Consumer Protection Act ("ACPA"), 15 U.S.C. § 1125(d).[11] To state an ACPA claim, Plaintiff must allege that (1) it owns a distinctive or famous mark entitled

---

11. (1)(A) A person shall be liable in a civil action by the owner of a mark, including a personal name which is protected as a mark under this section, if, without regard to the goods or services of the parties, that person
    (i) has a bad-faith intent to profit from that mark, including a personal name which is protected as a mark under this section; and

to protection, (2) Ireit owns a domain name that is "identical or confusingly similar to" Plaintiff's mark, and (3) Ireit registered that domain name with the bad-faith intent to profit from it. *Id.* Plaintiff has not alleged and cannot prove these requisite elements because Ireit does not own any domain name that infringes Plaintiff's rights.

Plaintiff loosely hinges its cybersquatting claim against Ireit on the allegation that Ireit owns the domain name <mantbank.com>. Comp. ¶ 386. However, Plaintiff alleges no rights to <mantbank.com> and thus has no standing to bring a claim regarding that domain name under the ACPA. Moreover, Plaintiff fails to allege that "mantbank.com" is a distinctive or famous mark or otherwise entitled to protection, or that the domain name was registered with the bad-faith intent to profit from it. 15 U.S.C. § 1125(d)(1)(A) . Accordingly, Count III against Ireit must be dismissed.

3. Counts IV, V, and VI Must Be Dismissed Because Plaintiff Fails to Allege That Ireit Infringed, Falsely Designated, or Diluted Plaintiff's Registered Trademark

Because Plaintiff fails to allege that Ireit used, infringed, falsely designated, or diluted any of Plaintiff's marks, Counts IV, V, and VI alleged against Ireit fail to state a claim and should be dismissed.

a. There Has Been No Trademark Infringement by Ireit Under 15 U.S.C. § 1141(1)

Count IV of the Complaint alleges trademark infringement under 15 U.S.C. § 1114(1). To assert a claim under that provision, Plaintiff must show that (1) its marks are registered, (2) Ireit used the marks in commerce without Plaintiff's consent, and (3) Ireit's unauthorized use is likely to confuse consumers or deceive the public. *Id.; see also S Indus. Inc. v. Stone Age Equip., Inc.*, 12 F. Supp. 2d 796, 803 (N.D. Ill. 1998). Plaintiff cannot meet this burden because Ireit has not, and Plaintiff has not alleged that Ireit has, used any mark owned by Plaintiff in commerce.

As noted above, Plaintiff lacks standing to enforce rights in trademarks to which Plaintiff has no legal interest. The clear language of the statute accords

---

(ii) registers, traffics in, or uses a domain name that
   (I)   in the case of a mark that is distinctive at the time of registration of the domain name, is identical or confusingly similar to that mark;
   (II)   in the case of a famous mark that is famous at the time of registration of the domain name, is identical or confusingly similar to or dilutive of that mark; or
   (III) is a trademark, word, or name protected by reason of section 706 of Title 18 or section 220506 of Title 36.

a cause of action to only the owner of a mark. 15 U.S.C. § 1114(1). The only domain name that Plaintiff identifies in its Complaint that is linked to Ireit is <mantbank.com>. Comp. ¶ 386–87. Once again, however, Plaintiff has no rights to <mantbank> and thus has no standing to bring trademark claims against Ireit. Since Ireit is not alleged to have owned or used a domain name confusingly similar to a trademark owned by Plaintiff, Count IV against Ireit should be dismissed.

b. There Has Been No False Designation of Origin by Ireit Under 15 U.S.C. § 1125(a)

Plaintiff's "false designation of origin" claim fails for essentially the same reasons as its trademark infringement claim. Section 43(a) of the Lanham Act protects unregistered trademarks in the much the same way; 15 U.S.C. § 1141 protects marks registered with the United States Patent and Trademark Office. [12]

As with its claim for trademark infringement, Plaintiff fails to allege that Ireit used any false designation of origin or made any false or misleading description or misrepresentation of fact as to Plaintiff's marks. Nor has Plaintiff identified any such false designation or misleading description. Vague and unsupported allegations under 15 U.S.C. § 1125(a) are not sufficient to withstand dismissal. *See, e.g., Sweet v. City of Chicago*, 953 F. Supp 225, 231 (N.D. Ill. 1996) (finding plaintiff's § 1125(a) claim warranted dismissal because it "merely makes the conclusory assertion that confusion is likely and sets forth no facts that would permit a conclusion that patrons of the Art Fair are likely to be confused as to the origin or sponsorship of the Art Fair").

c. There Has Been No Trademark Dilution by Ireit

Plaintiff has alleged no basis for its trademark dilution claim against Ireit in Count VI of the Complaint. To state a claim for dilution under federal law, Plaintiff must allege (1) it owns a famous mark, (2) Ireit used the mark after

---

12. This section provides:

> (1) Any person who, on or in connection with any goods or services, or any container for goods, uses in commerce any word, term, name, symbol, or device, or any combination thereof, or any false designation of origin, false or misleading description of fact, or false or misleading representation of fact, which
>
> > (A) is likely to cause confusion, or to cause mistake, or to deceive as to the affiliation, connection, or association of such person with another person, or as to the origin, sponsorship, or approval of his or her goods, services, or commercial activities by another person,
> >
> > . . .
>
> shall be liable in a civil action by any person who believes that he or she is or is likely to be damaged by such act. 15 U.S.C. § 1125(a).

it became famous, (3) Ireit's use of the mark caused it to be diluted, and (4) Ireit's use of the marks was "in commerce."[13] 15 U.S.C. § 1125(c)(1). Plaintiff fails to allege facts that satisfy any of these four requirements. Specifically, Plaintiff has not contended it owns a famous mark, that Ireit has used Plaintiff's famous mark, that Ireit has diluted Plaintiff's famous mark, or that Ireit's use of Plaintiff's famous mark was commercial or in commerce. 15 U.S.C. § 1125(c)(1). Plaintiff's sole basis for asserting a dilution claim against Ireit appears to be that Ireit allegedly registered the domain name <mantbank. com>, but Plaintiff fails to allege it has any rights in any trademark similar to "mantbank," let alone that any such mark is famous and diluted by Ireit. Count VI thus fails to state a claim against Ireit under the federal dilution statute and should be dismissed.

4. Count VII Must Be Dismissed Because Plaintiff Has No Claim for Consumer Fraud or Deceptive Trade Practices

In Count VII, Plaintiff asserts a defective claim under §2 of the Illinois Consumer Fraud and Deceptive Business Practices Act ("ICFA") and §2 of the Illinois Deceptive Trade Practices Act ("DTPA"), 815 ILCS 505/2 and 815 ILCS 510/2. To state a claim under the ICFA, a private plaintiff must plead: (1) a deceptive act or practice by the defendant, (2) the defendant's intent that the plaintiff rely on the deception, (3) the occurrence of the deception in the course of conduct involving trade or commerce, and (4) actual damage to the plaintiff (5) proximately caused by the deception. *Avery v. State Farm Mut. Auto. Ins. Co.*, 216 Ill.2d 100, 180, 835 N.E.2d 801, 850 (2005). Although an ICFA plaintiff need not necessarily be an Illinois resident, ICFA does not apply to "fraudulent transactions which take place outside Illinois." *Avery*, 835 N.E.2d at 853.

In the present case, the only assertion of any connection to Illinois is the fact that Plaintiff's principal place of business is located in St. Charles, Illinois. Compl. ¶ 16. Neither Ireit, nor any of the other defendants, is based in Illinois, nor is there any allegation that any relevant transaction occurred in Illinois. Compl. ¶ ¶ 25–55. Plaintiff attempts to sidestep this obvious pleading deficiency by alleging, in conclusory fashion, that Ireit "has engaged in acts or omissions within this judicial district causing injury . . . ." Compl. ¶ 50. It is well established, however, that this allegation is insufficient to establish

---

13. 15 U.S.C. § 1125(c)(1) provides in relevant part as follows:

> Subject to the principles of equity, the owner of a famous mark that is distinctive, inherently or through acquired distinctiveness, shall be entitled to an injunction against another person who, at any time after the owner's mark has become famous, commences use of a mark or trade name in commerce that is likely to cause dilution by blurring or dilution by tarnishment of the famous mark, regardless of the presence or absence or actual or likely confusion, of competition, or of actual economic injury.

the "requisite nexus" with Illinois to warrant application of the ICFA. *See, e.g., Avery*, 835 N.E.2d at 854; *Rohlfing v. Manor Care, Inc.*, 172 F.R.D. 330, 340, n.10 (N.D. Ill. 1997) (where the only connection with Illinois is the headquarters of the defendant or the fact that a scheme "emanated" from Illinois, the Consumer Fraud Act "does not apply to the claims of the non-Illinois plaintiffs"). Plaintiff has not alleged that Ireit committed, or that Plaintiff was injured as a result of, any deceptive act committed by Ireit in Illinois. Moreover, Plaintiff cannot manufacture a nexus to Illinois by prophesizing that an unnamed, putative plaintiff in a class yet to be certified may ultimately establish such a nexus.

The lack of an Illinois nexus applies equally to Plaintiff's DTPA claim, just as with Plaintiff's ICFA claim. *See Rohlfing*, 172 F.R.D. at 340 n.9, citing *Phillips Petroleum Co. v. Shutts*, 472 U.S. 797, 821 (1985) (recognizing that Due Process Clause forbids a forum state from applying its own law to every member of a class unless the state has a significant contact or significant aggregation of contacts to the claims asserted by each member of the plaintiff class).

Count VII also fails against Ireit because misrepresentation is a necessary element for such claims. *Web Commc'n Grp. Inc. v. Gateway 2000, Inc.*, 889 F. Supp. 316, 323 (N.D. Ill. 1995) (dismissing consumer fraud claims where plaintiff failed to identify any misrepresentation by movants affecting consumers); *Indus. Specialty Chems. v. Cummins Engine Co., Inc.*, 902 F. Supp. 805, 812–13 (N.D. Ill. 1995) (granting motion to dismiss claims under the Act due to lack of actionable misrepresentations by defendant). Significantly, Plaintiff does not, and cannot, identify *any* misrepresentation by Ireit that has injured Plaintiff. For this additional reason, Plaintiff's ICFA and DTPA claims should be dismissed.

5. Plaintiff is Not Entitled to Declaratory Relief Under Count VIII

Plaintiff is not entitled to the requested declaratory relief because Plaintiff fails to adequately plead any claims against Ireit under Counts I through VII of the Complaint. In the absence of any cognizable claim against Ireit, there is no "actual controversy." Moreover, the declaratory relief sought merely tracks Plaintiff's other claims, all of which are deficient for the reasons detailed above. Accordingly, this Court should dismiss Count VIII of Plaintiff's Complaint as directed against Ireit.

6. Count IX Should Be Dismissed Because Plaintiff Does Not Have a Valid Common Law Claim for Trademark Infringement Against Ireit

The principles of trademark law and the tests for infringement under the Illinois common law are essentially the same as under the federal Lanham

Act. *See Berghoff Rest. Co. v. Lewis W. Berghoff, Inc.*, 357 F. Supp. 127, 130 n.3 (N.D. Ill. 1973), *aff'd*, 499 F.2d 1183 (7th Cir. 1974). Therefore, Plaintiff's claim for trademark infringement under Illinois common law is deficient for the reasons set forth above in the discussion of Counts IV and V. Accordingly, Count IX as alleged should be dismissed.

7. Count X Should Be Dismissed Because Plaintiff Fails to Allege That Ireit Has Contributorily Infringed Plaintiff's Trademark Rights

Plaintiff fails to allege (nor does Plaintiff have standing to allege) a justiciable trademark infringement claim against Ireit, because Ireit has not used any mark, name or term confusingly similar to a mark owned by Plaintiff. Consequently, Plaintiff's attempt to assert a *contributory* infringement claim against Ireit also fails. To properly plead a claim for contributory trademark infringement, Plaintiff must allege that Ireit (1) intentionally induced a third party to infringe Plaintiff's mark, or (2) supplied a product to a third party with actual or constructive knowledge that the product was being used to directly infringe Plaintiff's mark. *See Inwood Labs., Inc. v. Ives Labs., Inc.*, 456 U.S. 844, 854 (1982); *Hard Rock Cafe Licensing Corp. v. Concession Servs., Inc.*, 955 F.2d 1143, 1148 (7th Cir. 1992); *SB Designs v. Reebok Int'l, Ltd.*, 338 F. Supp. 2d 904, 911–12 (N.D. Ill. 2004). Contributory infringement requires proof of direct infringement of Plaintiff's mark by a third party, as well as the defendant's intent and knowledge of the wrongful activities of the infringer. *David Berg & Co. v. Gatto Int'l Trading Co.*, 884 F.2d 306, 311 (7th Cir. 1989).

Plaintiff fails to allege these essential elements of a claim for contributory infringement: ownership of a valid trademark confusingly similar to a domain name with knowledge by Ireit that other parties were allegedly infringed Plaintiff's marks, and Ireit's contribution to or inducement of that infringement. *See Monotype Imaging, Inc. v. Bitstream Inc.*, 376 F. Supp. 2d 877, 892 (N.D. Ill. 2005) (finding that contributory infringement requires proof of direct infringement by third party, as well as defendant's intent and knowledge of wrongful activities of third party). Accordingly, Count X as asserted against Ireit fails to state a claim for contributory infringement and should be dismissed.

8. Count XI Should Be Dismissed Because Plaintiff Fails to Adequately Plead an Intentional Interference with any Current or Prospective Economic Advantage

Plaintiff fails to plead an intentional interference claim against Ireit. In order to state a claim for tortious interference with prospective economic advantage, Plaintiff must allege that (1) it had a reasonable expectancy of a valid business relationship, (2) Ireit knew about the expectancy, (3) Ireit intentionally interfered with the expectancy and prevented it from ripening into a valid business relationship, and (4) the intentional interference injured Plaintiff.

Ali v. Shaw, 481 F.3d 942, 946 (7th Cir. 2007). Illinois courts have made it clear that "A plaintiff states a cause of action only if it alleges a business expectancy with a specific third party as well as action by the defendant directed towards that third party." *Assoc. Underwriters of Am. Agency, Inc. v. McCarthy*, 356 Ill. App. 3d 1010, 826 N.E.2d 1160, 1169 (1st Dist. 2005). *See also Ali*, 481 F.3d at 946.

In this case, Plaintiff vaguely refers to "third party Internet consumers" as third parties with whom it had a business expectancy with which Defendants allegedly interfered. Compl. ¶ ¶ 628–32. But Plaintiff fails to identify any specific third party with whom it had a business expectancy *or* any specific action Ireit took toward that party to Plaintiff's detriment. *Schuler v. Abbott Labs.*, 265 Ill. App. 3d 991, 994–95, 639 N.E. 2d 144, 147 (1st Dist. 1993). Accordingly, Count XI as alleged against Ireit is subject to dismissal.

9. Count XII Should Be Dismissed Because Plaintiff Fails to Plead a Cognizable Unjust Enrichment Claim Against Ireit

Plaintiff's unjust enrichment count also fails to state a claim on which relief can be granted. To state a claim for unjust enrichment in Illinois, Plaintiff must allege that (1)Ireit unjustly retained a benefit to Plaintiff's detriment; and (2) Ireit's retention of that benefit would violate the fundamental principles of justice, equity, and good conscience. *See Scott v. GlaxoSmithKline Consumer Healthcare, L.P.*, 2006 U.S. Dist. LEXIS 18630 at *12–13 (N.D. Ill. Apr. 12, 2006); see *also Sudicky v. Allied Tube & Conduit*, 1999 U.S. Dist. LEXIS 16794 (N.D. Ill. Oct. 22, 1999) (dismissing an unjust enrichment claim because [u]nder Illinois law, no person is unjustly enriched unless the retention of the benefit would be unjust) (internal quotation marks omitted).

Plaintiff fails to recite any benefit retained by Ireit to the detriment of Plaintiff. In fact, Plaintiff has not pled *any* factual allegation linking Ireit to any alleged injury to Plaintiff or the absence of a remedy provided by law. Accordingly, Count XII as alleged against Ireit must be dismissed.

E. In the Alternative, Plaintiff Should Be Required to Provide a More Definite Statement of its Claims

At the very least, Ireit cannot defend this lawsuit without a more definite statement from Plaintiff. "When a complaint is so vague or ambiguous that a party cannot reasonably be required to frame a responsive pleading, courts can order a more definite statement under Fed. R. Civ. P. 12(e)." *Kutzle v. Thor Indus. Inc.*, No. 03 C 2389, 2003 WL 21654260, at *4 (N.D. Ill July 14, 2003); *Bowers v. Crystal Valley, R. V.*, No. 95 C 7527, 1996 WL 169415, at *1 (N.D. Ill. Apr. 9, 1996).

Plaintiff's allegations against Ireit are simply too vague to allow Ireit to answer. In order to frame an answer, even a simple good-faith denial, Ireit must know at least the following:

- Which domain names Ireit owns that Plaintiff claims infringe upon Plaintiff's trademark rights or amount to cybersquatting
- What Ireit did in violation of Illinois' consumer protection laws that harmed Plaintiff
- What Ireit possesses that rightfully belongs to Plaintiff and forms the basis of Plaintiff's unjust enrichment claim
- Who Ireit induced to infringe upon Plaintiff's trademark and how Ireit did so
- How Ireit intentionally interfered with Plaintiff's prospective economic advantage
- What RICO predicate acts Ireit committed that harmed Plaintiff
- Who Ireit conspired with to harm Plaintiff.

The Complaint's ambiguity stems not from its lack of words but from its failure to justify any reason for including Ireit in this lawsuit and explain what Ireit supposedly has done to harm Plaintiff. Without knowing these things, Ireit will not be able to make a good-faith answer to Plaintiff's lawsuit. Unless the Complaint is dismissed, the Court should thus order a more definite statement pursuant to Rule 12(e).

IV. Conclusion

For the foregoing reasons, Internet Ireit, Inc. respectfully requests that the Court dismiss Counts I through XII of Plaintiff's Complaint as alleged against Internet Reit, Inc. with prejudice.

Respectfully Submitted,

Motion to Dismiss Claims Preempted by Copyright Claim

Claims under state law for misappropriation, breach of contract, tortious interference, unjust enrichment, and the like often accompany copyright claims, but when they assert nothing more than the copying of material subject to copyright, they are preempted. Below is a typical motion asking for dismissal of a claim that merely seeks redress for the same conduct alleged to infringe the plaintiff's copyright.

United States District Court
Southern District of New York

ENERGY INTELLIGENCE GROUP, INC., a corporation,	))	05-CV-8314 (MGC-FM)
Plaintiff,	)	DEFENDANT'S MEMORANDUM OF
v.	)	LAW IN SUPPORT OF ITS MOTION
BP AMERICA, INC., a corporation,	)	TO DISMISS PLAINTIFF'S BREACH
Defendant.	)	OF CONTRACT CLAIM

Defendant BP America, Inc. ("BP") moves to dismiss Plaintiff Energy Intelligence Group, Inc.'s ("EIG's") claim for breach of contract (Count Two of the Complaint) under Fed. R. Civ. P. 12(b)(6) for failure to state a claim upon which relief can be granted. The alleged breach of contract claim is preempted under Section 301 of the Copyright Act, 17 U.S.C. § 301.

The complaint alleges that BP violated EIG's rights in the *Oil Daily* publication (the "OD"), a newsletter published by EIG and distributed to subscribers via e-mail in Portable Document Format ("PDF"), by forwarding the e-mail containing the PDF copy of the OD to non-subscribers within BP in violation of the Copyright Act. Count Two alleges that the same acts constitute breach of the contract between EIG and BP for the subscriptions. EIG does not allege that BP has engaged in any activity distinct from the alleged violations of EIG's rights under the Copyright Act.

I. Complaint
The complaint, filed September 27, 2005, states EIG's breach of contract claim under Count II in paragraphs 17, 18, 31 and 32 as follows:

17. Upon information and belief, Defendant copied, exhibited, transmitted,displayed and distributed the Work to numerous individuals, without implied or express authority, nor with Energy Intelligence's express and/or implied permission.
18. Energy Intelligence did not grant Defendant any right to copy, exhibit, transmit, and/or display the Work or any issue of OD in its entirety and beyond the limited license granted under the subscription.

EIG's copyright infringement allegations excerpted from paragraphs 22 and 23 of the complaint below state the same activities:

31. The transaction between Defendant and Energy Intelligence involves a legally enforceable contract in which Engery Intelligence licensed Defendant's use of OD. The contract provided for a single user e-mail subscription to OD. The contract does not allow for Defendant to copy,

exhibit, transmit, display and distribute any of the publications as a whole or in their entirety and only granted such rights to portions of the publications.

32. Upon information and belief, Defendant has breached its contract with Energy Intelligence by unlawfully copying, exhibiting, transmitting, displaying and distributing OD beyond the scope provided for in contract,including but not limited to, unauthorized use of the volume in Exhibit C.

Thus, EIG's breach of contract claim is identical in substance to EIG's copyright infringement claim.

II. Argument

A. Preemption Doctrine

State laws are subject to preemption under Section 301 of the Copyright Act if they create "legal or equitable rights that are equivalent to any of the exclusive rights within the general scope of copyright as specified by Section 106 in works of authorship that are fixed in a tangible medium of expression and come within the subject matter of copyright as specified by sections 102 and 103." 17 U.S.C. § 301(a); *see also eScholar LLC v. Otis Educ. Sys. Inc.*, 387 F. Supp. 2d 329, 331–32 (S.D.N.Y. 2005) (Robinson, J.). Claims brought pursuant to state law are preempted when "(1) the particular work to which the claim is being applied falls within the type of works protected by the Copyright Act under 17 U.S.C. §§ 102 and 103, and (2) the claim seeks to vindicate legal or equitable rights that are equivalent to one of the bundle of exclusive rights already protected by copyright law under 17 U.S.C. § 106." *Briarpatch Ltd., L.P. v. Phoenix Pictures, Inc.*, 373 F.3d 296, 305 (2d Cir. 2004); *see also NBA v. Motorola, Inc.*, 105 F.3d 841, 848 (2d Cir. 1997).

A state law cause of action is preempted if it is employed in such a manner as to create an equivalent right to a right granted under copyright, even though other applications of the same cause of action may be valid. *See eScholar LLC*, 387 F. Supp. 2d at 332. That is, if the state law claim is predicated upon the same conduct as that underlying the copyright claim, e.g., an act of reproduction, performance, distribution or display, then such a claim is nothing more than a reincarnation of the copyright claim and is preempted.

If an extra element is required instead of or in addition to such acts, then there is no preemption. *Id.*

B. EIG's Contract Claim is Redundant Under Preemption Doctrine

To determine whether a state law claim is qualitatively different from a copyright claim, courts examine what the plaintiff seeks to protect and the manner in which the work is protected. *Id.* Courts generally take a restrictive view of what extra elements transform an otherwise equivalent claim into one that is qualitatively different from a copyright infringement claim. *Id.* citing *Briarpatch*, 373 F.3d at 306; *see also NBA*, 105 F.3d at 851 (citation omitted).

A breach of contract claim is preempted if it is based merely upon "allegations that the defendant did something that the copyright laws reserve exclusively to the plaintiff (such as unauthorized reproduction, performance, distribution, or display)." *American Movie Classic v. Turner Entm't Co.*, 922 F. Supp. 926, 931 (S.D.N.Y. 1996) (Schwartz, J.) (finding breach of contract claim preempted where the basis of the claim was defendant's violation of plaintiff's exclusive exhibition rights in violation of the parties' agreement); *see Cooper v. Sony Records Int'l*, 60 U.S.P.Q.2d 2008, 2012 (Berman, J.) (finding claim that defendant "wrongfully commercially exploited the Masters" in violation of a contract between the parties was the essence of plaintiff's copyright infringement claim, and therefore, was preempted).

EIG's breach of contract claim is based solely upon allegations that BP unlawfully copied and distributed the OD, which are the identical allegations in EIG's copyright infringement claim. *Compare* Compl. ¶¶ 31–32 *with* Compl. ¶¶ 22–23, *supra*. Thus, EIG's breach of contract claim: (1) seeks to protect the same material—the OD; (2) in the same manner—by prohibiting the copying, exhibition, transmission, display, and distribution of the OD; and (3) by enforcing the same rights—EIG's exclusive right to copy and distribute the OD, as EIG's claim under the Copyright Act. This is precisely the type of claim to which the preemption doctrine is intended to apply. *See AMC*, 922 F. Supp. at 931.

Courts do not permit breach of contract claims pled in the same manner as EIG has pled its breach of contract claim here to survive preemption. For example, in *eScholar*, the district court granted defendant's motion to dismiss plaintiff's breach of contract claim where the plaintiff alleged that the defendant breached the parties' agreement by "copying materials belonging to eScholar and distributing the copied materials without eScholar's written consent." *eScholar*, 387 F. Supp. 2d at 331, 333 (affirming magistrate's report and recommendation). In *AMC*, the plaintiff claimed that the defendant violated the plaintiff's right to exhibit classic films during an exclusive time window in breach of the license defendant granted to plaintiff. *AMC*, 922 F. Supp. at 929. The plaintiff asserted that the defendant had violated plaintiff's rights by airing these films on defendant's movie channels during times that, under the license, plaintiff had the exclusive right to exhibit them on cable television. *AMC*, 922 F. Supp. at 928. The plaintiff asserted no allegations that the defendant breached any provisions of the agreement other than those providing the plaintiff with the exclusive right to exhibit the films at agreed upon times. The court found these breach of contract allegations preempted under the Copyright Act. *AMC*, 922 F. Supp. at 932. In *Cooper*, the plaintiffs asserted breach of contract claims arising out of defendant's allegedly wrongful exploitation of plaintiffs' copyrighted recordings after the agreement granting defendant's such right had terminated. *Cooper*, 60 U.S.P.Q.2d at 2012. The court found that plaintiffs had not asserted any allegation that defendant breached any provisions of the parties' agreement other than those providing defendant with the right to commercially exploit the recordings, and therefore, the breach of contract claim was preempted. *Id.* at 2014.

The cases in this District where a breach of contract claim has not been preempted by the Copyright Act are distinguishable from the case at bar. In those cases, something more than a mere allegation that a right granted under the Copyright Act has been violated in breach of an agreement between the parties was present. *See, e.g., Sharp v. Patterson*, 73 U.S.P.Q.2d 1481 (S.D.N.Y. 2004) (Lynch, J.) (contract claim based on plaintiff's agreement to work on romantic sections of novel in exchange for payment); *Torah Soft Ltd. v. Drosnin*, 224 F. Supp. 2d 704 (S.D.N.Y. 2002) (Francis IV, Mag. J.) (promise to market software in conjunction with book); *Lennon v. Seaman*, 63 F. Supp. 2d 428 (S.D.N.Y. 1999) (Sand, J.) (contract required defendant employee to hold information learned during the course of his employment in confidence); *Katz Dochrermann & Epstein, Inc. v. Home Box Office*, 50 U.S.P.Q. 2d 1957 (S.D.N.Y. 1999) (Griesa, J.) (finding that plaintiff's contract claim sought to "enforce a promise to pay for the use of [an] idea alone," regardless of any rights plaintiff could have acquired under the Copyright Act to the expression of the idea). In *Architectronics, Inc. v. Control Systems, Inc.*, the court denied defendant's request for summary judgment on plaintiff's breach of contract claim because "breach of contract claims are qualitatively different from claims for copyright infringement and therefore are not preempted." 935 F. Supp. 425 at 441 (S.D.N.Y. 1996) (Mukasey, J.).

Architectronic's breach of contract claim rested upon the defendants' purported agreements to keep the plaintiff's product, which included copyrightable software code, confidential. There was also an agreement concerning the defendant's potential development of a derivative work based on the plaintiff's product and code. The defendant allegedly developed a derivative product, although the existence of a license to do so was in question. Thus, plaintiff's claim, although partially based on the defendant's alleged creation of a derivative work based on plaintiff's computer code, was not a mere allegation of copyright infringement in violation of an agreement.

C. This Circuit Has Not Adopted a Per Se Rule That Breach of Contract Claims Are Never Preempted by Copyright Infringement Claims

Although some courts have adopted a per se rule that the promise inherent in a contract provides the extra element necessary to avoid preemption of breach of contract claims by copyright infringement claims, regardless of the right sought to be protected under the contract, the Second Circuit has not followed this rule. *See eScholar*, 387 F. Supp. 2d at 332. Moreover, application of such a per se rule has been criticized. *See Selby v. New Line Cinema Corp.*, 96 F. Supp. 2d 1053, 1060–61 (C.D. Cal. 2000) (adopting a case-by-case analysis depending on the specific terms of the contract and rights sought to be vindicated and rejecting a per se rule that breach of contract claims are never preempted by the Copyright Act); *see also* 1 Melville B. Nimmer & David Nimmer, Nimmer on Copyright § 1.01[B][1][a] (2005) (advocating case-by-case analysis and criticizing blanket approach of non-preemption of breach of contract claims).

III. Conclusion

Because it is preempted by the Copyright Act, BP requests this Court to dismiss EIG's claim for breach of contract (Count Two of the Complaint) under Fed. R. Civ. P. 12(b)(6) for failure to state a claim upon which relief can be granted.

Motion to Dismiss Fraud Claim Before the TTAB

Recently, claims for fraud on the patent and trademark office have become common in TTAB proceedings because of the decision in *Medinol v. Neuro Vasx, Inc.*, 67 U.S.P.Q. 2d 1205 (T.T.A.B. 2003). *Medinol* and its progeny essentially held that filing a trademark application or renewal of a registration that claimed use of a mark on goods with which the mark actually was not used, but the recent decision in *In re Bose Corp.*, 580 F.3d 1240, 91 U.S.P.Q. 2d 1938 (Fed. Cir. 2009), has changed the standard for pleading fraud on the PTO. Or, as many commentators have pointed out, returned the standard to its original state. Nevertheless, the trademark litigator should be prepared to defend against such claims for the foreseeable future.

In the United States Patent and Trademark Office Trademark Trial and Appeal Board

In The Matter of Registration No. 2,757,300,	)	
JELLIFISH		
JELLI FISH KIDS, INC.	)	
Petitioner,	)	
v.	)	Cancellation No.: 92052358
JELLIFISH INT'L CORP. USA,	)	
	)	Registrant.

Registrant's Partial Motion to Dismiss

Pursuant to Rule 12(b)(6) and Rule 9(b) of the Federal Rules of Civil Procedure and Section 503 of the *Trademark Trial and Appeal Board Manual of Procedure* (TBMP), Registrant, Jellifish Int'l Corp. USA, moves the Trademark Trial and Appeal Board for an order dismissing Petitioner's, Jelli Fish Kids, Inc.'s, fraud claim with prejudice. In support of this motion, Registrant states as follows:

I. Petitioner's Fraud Claim

Petitioner alleges that Registrant uses its JELLIFISH mark only in connection with guitar picks and has ceased use on all other goods listed in the registration. Petition for Cancellation ("Pet.") ¶ 4. Based on this allegation, Petitioner claims that Registrant's Sec. 8 and 15 Affidavit, which lists all the goods set forth in the registration, is fraudulent and the registration should be cancelled pursuant to 15 U.S.C. §1064. Pet. ¶¶ 6–7.

This is the sum total of Petitioner's fraud claim.

II. Bose and the New Fraud Standard

On August 31, 2009, the Court of Appeals for the Federal Circuit issued its decision in *In re Bose Corp.*, 580 F.3d 1240, 91 U.S.P.Q. 2d 1938 (Fed. Cir. 2009). In *Bose*, the Court of Appeals overruled the Board's existing fraud standard as set forth in *Medinol v. Neuro Vasx, Inc.*, 67 U.S.P.Q. 2d 1205 (T.T.A.B. 2003). The Court found that in *Medinol* and its progeny, the Board had "erroneously lowered the fraud standard to a simple negligence standard." *Bose*, 91 U.S.P.Q. 2d at 1940. The Court instituted far more stringent pleading and proof requirements for fraud claims, which are binding in all subsequent Board proceedings. *Id* at 1940–42.

In *Asian and Western Classics B.V. v. Selkow*, 92 U.S.P.Q. 2d 1478 (T.T.A.B. 2009), the Board explained in detail the *Bose* pleading requirements for fraud claims, as follows:

- The elements of the fraud claim must be alleged with particularity under F. R. Civ. P. 9(b). *Id.* at 1478.
- "The pleadings must contain explicit rather than implied expression of the circumstances constituting fraud." *Id.* (internal citation and quotation marks omitted).
- "Pleadings of fraud made on information and belief, when there is no allegation of specific facts upon which the belief is reasonably based are insufficient." *Id.* at 1479 (internal citation and quotation marks omitted).
- The pleader must "know of facts that support the pleading or that evidence showing the factual basis is likely to be obtained after reasonable opportunity for discovery or investigation." *Id.* (internal citation and quotation marks omitted).

- The pleading must contain an allegation of intent. *Id.*
- While intent may be alleged generally, "the pleadings must allege sufficient underlying facts from which a court may reasonably infer that a party acted with the requisite state of mind." *Id.*
- Allegations that the registrant "knew or should have known" its representations were false or misleading are insufficient to plead fraud. *Id.*

III. Argument

Bose totally invalidates Petitioner's fraud claim. The claim meets not a single one of the *Bose* requirements. This shows a complete lack of any supporting facts whatsoever. The fraud claim should be dismissed with prejudice on that basis alone.

Moreover, *Bose* observed that "[b]ecause practically all of the user's substantive trademark rights derive from continuing use, when a trademark is still in use, nothing is to be gained from and no public purpose is served by cancelling the registration of the trademark." *Id.* at 1942 (internal citation and quotation marks omitted). Petitioner has admitted that Registrant's mark is in use. *See* Pet. at ¶ ¶ 4, 6–7. Therefore, Registrant's registration will not be cancelled, and Petitioner's fraud claim cannot possibly succeed. The fraud claim should be dismissed with prejudice.

IV. Conclusion

For all the reasons set forth above, Petitioner's fraud claim should be dismissed with prejudice.

Respectfully submitted,

Opposition to Motion to Dismiss for Lack of Personal Jurisdiction Based Upon Insufficient Contacts with the Forum State

Just as motions to dismiss for lack of personal jurisdiction based on website interactivity and contacts are common against complaints, litigators should be prepared to argue why contacts are sufficient to justify keeping a complaint in their chosen forum. Frequently, such arguments entail detailing all of a defendant's contacts with the forum, as shown below.

Additionally, trademark plaintiffs have the distinct advantage of relying upon the effects test of *Calder v. Jones*, 465 U.S. 783 (1984), which stated simply, permits the owner of a trademark to assert jurisdiction over an accused infringer because the effect of the infringement will be felt predominantly where the trademark owner is located. While this doctrine is not always followed, it provides trademark owners with an often effective means of keeping suits in their home court.

Plaintiff's Memorandum in Opposition to Defendant's Motion to Dismiss for Lack of Personal Jurisdiction Introduction

Plaintiff, based in California, brings this action to stop Defendant's cybersquatting and infringement of Plaintiff's trademark. Defendant is a serial cybersquatter who has registered 75 domain names that combine Plaintiff's trademark with a city or other geographic area, e.g., <Plaintiff's Marksanfrancisco.com>. By his own admission, Defendant registered these infringing domain names in an attempt to profit from the use of Plaintiff's trademark in a nationwide marketing scheme. *See* Affidavit of Defendant's Principal, attached to Defendant's Motion to Dismiss ("Defendant's Principal Aff."), ¶ ¶ 3–8, 14.

Defendant has specifically targeted California by engaging in the following conduct: (1) registering and attempting to use domain names that infringe the trademark of a California-based business in a deliberate attempt to trade on the goodwill of that trademark; (2) registering 15 infringing domain names that target and refer to geographic locations in California, more than twice the number of infringing domain names targeting any other state; and (3) implementing a business plan that involves soliciting contracts with California service professionals offering services in California.

Defendant now seeks to avoid personal jurisdiction in this forum with his present Motion to Dismiss (Doc. 11). As discussed below, the Court may properly exercise personal jurisdiction over Defendant in this case. To the extent the Court has any doubt on this issue, Plaintiff requests limited discovery to address more fully the issues raised in Defendant's motion. Accordingly, Plaintiff respectfully requests that the Court deny Defendant's Motion to Dismiss or, alternatively, grant Plaintiff limited discovery to establish further Defendant's contacts with California.

I. Statement of the Case

Plaintiff advertises and sells Plaintiff's products ("Plaintiff's Systems"), and it owns a federal trademark registration for PLAINTIFF'S MARK for "Plaintiff's Goods" (the "Plaintiff's Mark"). (Doc. 1, Complaint ("Compl.") ¶ ¶ 8, 12). Plaintiff sells its Plaintiff's Systems through a direct sales force and third-party distributors, and it promotes its goods on the Internet through its primary website located at <www.Plaintiff'sMark.com>. (Declaration of Plaintiff's Chief Marketing Officer ("CMO Decl.") ¶ 6; Compl. ¶ 15). Plaintiff, which is located in California, employs approximately 999 people, approximately 666 of whom are located in California. (CMO Decl. ¶ 3).

The State of California constitutes one of the most significant markets for Plaintiff's Systems, if not the most significant market. (CMO Decl. ¶ 7).

For example, approximately 25 percent of sales of Plaintiff's Systems in the United States are made to service professionals and others in the State of California. *Id.* Among other reasons, Southern California's concentration of service professionals renders it a primary market for Plaintiff's Systems. *Id.*

Defendant is an individual residing in Texas. (Compl. ¶ 6). Defendant registered 75 domain names that incorporate Plaintiff's Mark combined with a city or other geographic area (the "PLAINTIFF'S MARK Domain Names"). (Compl. ¶ 17). The PLAINTIFF'S MARK Domain Names include 25 domain names that incorporate a total of 15 geographic locations in California, including Beverly Hills, Oakland, County, Riverside, Sacramento, San Bernardino, San Diego, San Francisco, and San Jose. *Id.* The PLAINTIFF'S MARK Domain Names that incorporate California locations account for more than 25 percent of all the PLAINTIFF'S MARK Domain Names and constitute more than twice as many locations as any other state. *See id.* The PLAINTIFF'S MARK Domain Names include only four locations within Defendant's home state of Texas, and the only other states with more than one are Florida and Ohio (with three and two, respectively). *See id.*

In his affidavit, Defendant admits that he intends to contract with service professionals in the cities for which he has registered PLAINTIFF'S MARK domains. (Defendant's Principal Aff. ¶ 14). He admits that "I intended to use the Plaintiff's Mark domain names as soon as I made an agreement with a service professional in the city whose name is contained in the domain names I purchased." *Id.* According to his "business method," Defendant claims that he intends to develop websites at each of the PLAINTIFF'S MARK Domain Names for service professionals located in the corresponding geographic location. *Id.* at ¶¶ 4, 14. These service professionals would pay Defendant each time a consumer contacted the service professional for treatment through the PLAINTIFF'S MARK Domain Name. *Id.* at ¶ 6. Currently, the websites located at the PLAINTIFF'S MARK Domain Names contain links to websites offering products and services for related to Plaintiff's Systems, including the products and services of Plaintiff's competitors. *See, e.g.,* Declaration of Paralegal ("Paralegal Decl.") ¶ 8, and Exhibits F and G to Paralegal Decl. For example, the website located at <www.sanfranciscoPlaintiff'sMark.com> displays a link to Competitor's services offered in San Francisco. (Exhibit F to Paralegal Decl.).

Defendant portrays himself only as an individual who has registered these PLAINTIFF'S MARK Domain Names, but in actuality he operates a company called Defendant's Company that engages in advertising nationwide, including in California. For example, Defendant's personal e-mail address is "Defendant's Principal@Defendant'sCompany.com," and he signs his e-mails with "Defendant's Principal, Defendant'sCompany.com." (Paralegal Decl. ¶ 4, Ex. A). On his website at <www.Defendant'sCompany.com>, Defendant, through Defendant's Company, admits that it "operates |nationally" and claims to represent Fortune 500 clients. *See* Exhibit B to Paralegal Decl. Defendant's Company website also allows users to

"Schedule a Complimentary Consultation" by providing their name, e-mail address, telephone number, how they prefer to be contacted, and the best time to call. *Id.* In addition, Defendant's Company website also allows users to submit online customer payments. *Id.* California residents can access and utilize the services offered on Defendant's Company website.

Despite Defendant's sworn statement in his affidavit and statements in his Motion to Dismiss that he has "never sold products in or to California," (Defendant's Principal Aff. ¶ 18), or "contracted with any California resident whereby the contract would be performed in whole or in part in California," (Mot. to Dismiss 2), he appears to have done those very things. A recently inactive website indicates that Defendant, through Defendant's Company, contracted with a specific service professional, with a location in Los Angeles, California, to provide website advertising services.[14] (Exhibit C to Paralegal Decl.).

Applying the law to the above record demonstrates that Defendant is subject to personal jurisdiction in this forum.

II. Analysis

A. Defendant Is Subject to Specific Personal Jurisdiction in This Forum

1. Standard

Before a trial or hearing, a plaintiff is required only to make a prima facie showing of jurisdiction. *Rio Properties, Inc. v. Rio Int'l Interlink*, 284 F.3d 1007, 1019 (9th Cir. 2002); *Data Disc, Inc. v. Sys. Tech. Assocs., Inc.*, 557 F.2d 1280, 1285 (9th Cir. 1977). Allegations in the complaint that are uncontroverted must be taken as true, and all factual disputes construed in a light most favorable to the plaintiff. *Rio Properties,* 284 F.3d at 1019.

In the Ninth Circuit, courts engage in a two-step process for determining whether or not exercise of personal jurisdiction over a defendant is proper. *Taubler v. Giraud,* 655 F.2d 991, 993 (9th Cir. 1981). In the first step, the court determines if the state's long-arm statute applies. If it does, the court then analyzes whether or not application of the long-arm statute complies with constitutional Due Process requirements. *Id.*

---

14. Defendant also makes various statements in his Motion to Dismiss that are outside the scope of the present Motion. Plaintiff does not address these statements, which are inappropriate in this procedural context.

2. Personal Jurisdiction Under California's Long-Arm Statute

Under California law, "[a] court of this state may exercise jurisdiction on any basis not inconsistent with the Constitution of this state or of the United States." Cal. Civ. Proc. Code § 410.10 (West Year). Because California grants personal jurisdiction to the fullest extent allowed under the Constitution, this Court need only analyze whether or not the exercise of personal jurisdiction in this case comports with Due Process. *Taubler,* 655 F.2d at 993.

3. This Court has Specific Jurisdiction over Defendant

Personal jurisdiction may be founded on either general jurisdiction or specific jurisdiction. *Panavision Int'l, L.P. v. Toeppen,* 141 F.3d 1316, 1320 (9th Cir. 1998). In this case, Defendant is subject to specific jurisdiction based on the current record of the case, including the facts alleged in the Complaint and Defendant's own affidavit, which contains facts that all but admit specific jurisdiction. *See* Defendant's Principal Aff. ¶ ¶ 8, 14.

The Ninth Circuit applies a three-part test to determine if a district court may exercise specific personal jurisdiction:

(1) The nonresident defendant must . . . perform some act by which he purposefully avails himself of the privilege of conducting activities in the forum, thereby invoking the benefits and protections of its laws

(2) The claim must be one which arises out of or results from the defendant's forum-related activities

(3) Exercise of jurisdiction must be reasonable.

Panavision, 141 F.3d at 1320.

Contrary to Defendant's contention that "Plaintiff must satisfy each element of the Ninth Circuit's three-prong test in order to defeat this Motion to Dismiss," (Mot. to Dismiss 10), the Ninth Circuit has abandoned the rule that Defendant cites and now applies a more "flexible approach" that emphasizes reasonableness over strict satisfaction of all three prongs. *See Ochoa v. J.B. Martin & Sons Farms, Inc.,* 287 F.3d 1182, 1189 n.2 9th Cir. 2002 (citations omitted).

Where, as here, the plaintiff's claims sound in tort, the Court should analyze the first prong under the "purposeful direction" test.[15] Under this test, also

---

15. *See Panavision,* 141 F.3d at 1321 (describing trademark infringement as "akin to a tort case"); *Polar Bear Prods. Inc. v. Timex Corp.,* 384 F.3d 700, 720 (9th Cir. 2004) (explaining that, for purposes of statute of limitations, "trademark infringement generally sounds in tort"). Courts often use the phrase "purposeful availment," in shorthand fashion, to include both purposeful availment and purposeful direction. *See, e.g., Harris Rutsky & Co. Ins. Servs. v. Bell & Clements Ltd,* 328 F.3d 1122, 1129 (9th Cir.

called the *Calder* "effects test" after the Supreme Court's decision in *Calder v. Jones*, 465 U.S. 783 (1984), purposeful direction has three requirements: "the defendant allegedly [must] have (1) committed an intentional act, (2) expressly aimed at the forum state, (3) causing harm that the defendant knows is likely to be suffered in the forum state." *Yahoo! Inc. v. La Ligue Contre Le Racisme et L'Antisemitisme*, 433 F.3d 1199, 1206 (9th Cir. 2006) (internal citation omitted). Notably, the *Yahoo!* court clarified that the "brunt" of the harm need not be felt in the forum state as long a jurisdictionally sufficient amount is suffered there, even if more harm might have been suffered in another state. *Id.* at 1207.

a) Defendant Purposefully Directed His Actions at the Forum State

Defendant's actions in this case satisfy all three requirements of the "purposeful direction" or *Calder* test, thus satisfying the first prong of the specific personal jurisdiction analysis. Alternatively, Defendant meets the first prong of the specific jurisdiction test because of the nature of the websites located at each of the PLAINTIFF'S MARK Domain Names.

As for the "purposeful direction" test: *First*, Defendant intentionally registered 75 domain names that incorporate the well-known Plaintiff's Mark in its entirety. Indeed, Defendant admits that he intentionally chose to incorporate PLAINTIFF'S MARK in his PLAINTIFF'S MARK Domain Names "with plans to explore existing and new relationships with service professionals . . .," (Defendant's Principal Aff. ¶ 8), a substantial number of whom are in California.

Second, Defendant expressly aimed his conduct at California when he used a mark owned by Plaintiff, a California-based company. In *Panavision Int'l v. Toeppen*, the court found that the defendant cybersquatter, who registered the plaintiff's trademarks as his domain names and subsequently sought to sell them to the plaintiff, a California corporation, had expressly aimed his actions at California. For, "[defendant's] conduct, as he knew it likely would, had the effect of injuring [plaintiff] in California where [plaintiff] ha[d] its principal place of business." *Id.* at 1322.

In addition, Defendant in this case used California locations in more than 25 percent of the PLAINTIFF'S MARK Domain Names, more than twice the number of PLAINTIFF'S MARK Domain Names that include locations from any other state. To that end, Defendant admits his intention to enter into contracts

---

2003) (internal citation omitted). Availment and direction are, in fact, two distinct concepts, and a purposeful direction analysis is most often used in suits sounding in tort. *See, e.g., Dole Food Co., Inc. v. Watts*, 303 F.3d 1104, 1111 (9th Cir. 2002); *Ziegler v. Indian River County*, 64 F.3d 470, 473 (9th Cir. 1995) (noting that the Ninth Circuit applies different purposeful availment tests to contract and tort cases).

with service professionals in the cities and geographic areas included in the PLAINTIFF'S MARK Domain Names, which include nine areas in California. (Defendant's Principal Aff. ¶ 14). In turn, prospective consumers from the area can then contact the service professionals through Defendant's website and using Defendant's telephone number. *Id.* at ¶ 6 ("The phone number is owned by me but forwards any calls directly to the service professional"). Thus, if Defendant's "business method" is successful, the largest concentration of consumers likely to be deceived by Defendant's use of Plaintiff's Mark will be located in California, which has the most locations of all PLAINTIFF'S MARK Domain Names. This is especially true here because the State of California is one of the most significant markets for Plaintiff's Systems, constituting approximately 25 percent of Plaintiff's Systems sales in the United States. (CMO Decl. at ¶ 7). Accordingly, this factor supports a finding of personal jurisdiction. *See Indianapolis Colts, Inc. v. Metro. Baltimore Football Club Ltd. P'ship*, 34 F.3d 410, 411–12 (7th Cir. 1994) (in trademark infringement action, finding personal jurisdiction in Indiana over Maryland defendant's use of "Baltimore CFL Colts," where largest concentration of consumers likely to be confused were Indianapolis Colts fans in Indiana, even though the defendant had not yet licensed "Baltimore CFL Colts" merchandise in Indiana).

Third, Defendant is causing harm it knows is likely to be suffered in the forum state. When a company's trademarks are infringed, the company suffers harm in its primary place of business. *Panavision,* 141 F.3d at 1321; *see also Mattel Inc. v. MCA Records, Inc.,* 296 F.3d 894, 899 (9th Cir. 2002) (personal jurisdiction over foreign defendants upheld where defendants allegedly infringed plaintiff's trademarks and distributed infringing materials in the forum state). As Plaintiff is headquartered in California, a jurisdictionally sufficient amount of harm will be felt in California. *See Panavision,* 141 F.3d at 1321 (finding that the defendant knew the plaintiff would suffer harm in California because, although a Delaware corporation, the plaintiff's principal place of business was in California); *Rio Properties,* 284 F.3d at 1020 (finding injury to Nevada headquartered corporation in Nevada where defendant registered the plaintiff's RIO trademark as part of the defendant's domain name and advertised services to Nevada residents); *Mad Dogg Athletics, Inc. v. NYC Holding,* 565 F. Supp. 2d 1127 1130 (C.D. Cal. 2008) ("by trafficking in domain names bearing infringements of the trademarks of a California business, Defendant both purposefully availed itself of the benefits of the forum state and committed a tort directed at, and likely to cause harm in, the forum state of California").

Based on the foregoing, Defendant has purposefully directed his conduct at California, and his arguments to the contrary are unavailing. Defendant relies primarily on *Cybersell, Inc. v. Cybersell, Inc.,* 130 F.3d 414 (9th Cir. 1997), a case whose "narrow scope . . . became apparent" after the *Panavision* decision. *See Meade Instruments Corp. v. Reddwarf Starware LLC,* 47 U.S.P.Q.2d

1157, 1159 (C.D. Cal. 1998). In *Cybersell*, the defendant did nothing more than post an essentially passive website using the name "Cybersell," and this occurred before the plaintiff even had a federal service mark registration for CYBERSELL. *Cybersell*, 130 F.3d at 419 ("All that [the defendant] did was post an essentially passive home page on the web, using the name 'Cybersell,' which [the plaintiff] was in the process of registering as a federal service mark."). Otherwise, the defendant had "no contacts with Arizona [the forum state]," "did nothing to encourage people in Arizona to access its site," and "there is no evidence that any part of its business . . . was sought or achieved in Arizona." *Id.* at 415, 419.

In contrast, Defendant in this case registered the PLAINTIFF'S MARK Domain Names *after* Plaintiff obtained a federal trademark registration for Plaintiff's Mark, contemplated that people of California would access his sites by using geographic locations in California in the PLAINTIFF'S MARK Domain Names, and has admitted that he seeks to contract with service professionals in California, which will be a substantial portion of his business. Unlike in *Cybersell*, the Defendant here has done "something more" than just register the PLAINTIFF'S MARK Domain Names. *See Panavision*, 141 F.3d at 1322 (explaining that "something more" is required to show purposeful direction than just posting a passive website). There is no state in the nation that has a higher concentration of geographic areas in the PLAINTIFF'S MARK Domain Names than California, evidencing Defendant's intent to direct his activities "in a substantial way" to California. Defendant's actions, therefore, provide the "something more" that satisfies this element of the purposeful direction test.

In addition to satisfying the "purposeful direction" test, Defendant independently satisfies the purposeful availment prong of the specific jurisdiction test because of his websites located at the PLAINTIFF'S MARK Domain Names (another fact that distinguishes *Cybersell*). In determining whether a defendant's activity on the Internet subjects a defendant to personal jurisdiction, the Ninth Circuit applies a "sliding scale" approach, under which "jurisdiction is directly proportionate to the nature and quality of defendant's commercial activity conducted on the Internet." *Quokka Sports, Inc. v. Cup Int'l Ltd.*, 99 F. Supp. 2d 1105, 1111 (N.D. Cal. 1999) (citing *Cybersell*, 130 F.3d at 418). Under this approach, "at one end of the spectrum is a situation where defendant clearly does business over the Internet and so personal jurisdiction is proper, and at the other end of spectrum is a situation where defendant simply posts information on a website accessible to users in foreign jurisdictions and so personal jurisdiction is not proper." *See Coremetrics, Inc. v. Atomic Park.com, LLC*, 370 F. Supp. 2d 1013, 1019 (N.D. Cal. 2005) (explaining test in parenthetical).

The websites located at the PLAINTIFF'S MARK Domain Names are not merely passive websites. They display active webpages that include links to websites offering, among other things, various services that directly compete with Plaintiff's products and services. *See* Exhibits F and G to Paralegal Decl.

For example, the website located at <www.sanfranciscoPlaintiff'sMark.com> displays a link to Competitor's services offered in San Francisco. [16] *See* Exhibit F to Paralegal Decl. The harm in this case, therefore, results directly from the interactive links, because users looking for service professionals offering Plaintiff's Systems treatment in the San Francisco area instead will be directed to competing services.

In summary, Defendant's contacts with California in this case are not, as Defendant suggests, "random," "fortuitous," or "attenuated." *Burger King Corp. v. Rudzewicz*, 471 U.S. 462, 475 (1985). *See* Mot. to Dismiss 10. Rather, Defendant deliberately targeted California by using the trademark of a California-based company in his PLAINTIFF'S MARK Domain Names, including nine California locales in the PLAINTIFF'S MARK Domain Names, and implementing a plan to contract with service professionals all over the State of California. Defendant cannot be willing to conduct business all over the State of California but be unwilling to litigate here when that business injures a company headquartered in California.

b). Plaintiff's Claims Arise Out of and Relate to Defendant's Actions Directed at the Forum State

The second requirement of the test for specific personal jurisdiction is whether or not the plaintiff's claims arise out of and relate to defendant's activities in the forum state. The Ninth Circuit requires a showing that "the plaintiff . . . would not have been injured "but for" the defendant['s] . . . conduct directed toward' plaintiff in the forum state. *Panavision*, 141 F.3d at 1322."

Here, Plaintiff would not have been injured "but for" Defendant's registration of the PLAINTIFF'S MARK Domain Names and deliberate infringement of the trademark rights of Plaintiff, a company headquartered in this forum. In *Panavision*, the court found that "[the plaintiff's] registration of Panavision's trademarks as his own domain names on the Internet had the effect of injuring Panavision in California." *Id.* Based on this, the court

---

16. Defendant claims that GoDaddy, the registrar through which he registered the PLAINTIFF'S MARK Domain Names, is responsible for this content. (Defendant's Principal Aff., ¶ ¶ 10–13). Defendant, however, chose to use GoDaddy as his registrar and was required to agree to GoDaddy's Parked Page Service Agreement, the terms of which authorize GoDaddy to post the very pages from which Defendant tries to distance himself. (*See* Paralegal Decl. Ex. D, E.). In similar circumstances, World Intellectual Property Organization (WIPO) panels deciding domain name disputes have found that a defendant cannot claim ignorance of GoDaddy's practices. *See, e.g., Owens Corning v. NA*, WIPO Case No. D2007-1143, *available at* http://www.wipo.int/amc/en/domains/decisions/html/2007/d2007-1143.html. (October 1, 2007) (finding that Respondent must have known that Internet users seeking information about Complainant's products would then find themselves at a website placed by GoDaddy advertising other goods and services).

concluded that, "[b]ut for [the defendant's] conduct, this injury would not have occurred." *Id.* For identical reasons, Plaintiff's injury would not have occurred "but for" Defendant's conduct, and this prong is satisfied.

c). Exercise of Personal Jurisdiction over Defendant is Reasonable

Once the court finds that the first two specific jurisdiction factors are satisfied, there is a presumption that the exercise of jurisdiction is reasonable. *Ballard v. Savage*, 65 F.3d 1495, 1501 (9th Cir. 1995) (citing *Sher v. Johnson*, 911 F.2d 1357, 1364 (9th Cir. 1990)). The defendant then bears the "heavy burden of rebutting the strong presumption in favor of jurisdiction." *Id.* Here, Defendant cannot carry that heavy burden.

In determining whether or not specific jurisdiction over a defendant is reasonable, courts weigh the following seven factors:

> (1)The extent of the defendant's purposeful interjection; (2) the burden on the defendant of defending in the forum; (3) the extent of conflict with the sovereignty of the defendant's state; (4) the forum state's interest in adjudicating the dispute; (5) the most efficient judicial resolution of the controversy; (6) the importance of the forum to the plaintiff's interest in convenient and effective relief; and (7) the existence of an alternative forum.

Panavision, 141 F.3d at 1323 (citing *Burger King*, 471 U.S. at 476–77).

(i). Defendant Purposefully Interjected Himself into California's Affairs

This factor measures the degree of the defendant's interjection into the forum state, even where, as here, that interjection is sufficient to satisfy the purposeful availment or direction prong. *Panavision*, 141 F.3d at 1323. In *Panavision*, the Ninth Circuit found that the defendant's degree of interjection was "substantial" where it registered a California company's trademarks as his domain names and sent a letter to the plaintiff demanding money to release the domain names. *Id.*; *see also Quokka Sports, Inc.*, 99 F. Supp. 2d at 1113 (finding that New Zealand defendants purposefully interjected their website into the California and United States markets where they registered a ".com" address and had content directed at U.S. consumers). Likewise, in this case, Defendant has registered the trademarks of a California-based corporation as his domain names, has registered the highest proportion of those PLAINTIFF'S MARK Domain Names using geographic locations in California, admittedly plans to contract with California service professionals, and uses the PLAINTIFF'S MARK Domain Names for websites directed to California consumers. This factor favors Plaintiff.

(ii) Burden on Defendant of Litigating in this Court

Plaintiff has chosen to file this suit in California, where it is located. Although Defendant is located in Texas, this factor does not weigh against finding California to be a reasonable choice of forum. The mere fact that Defendant is an individual does not tilt this factor in his favor. In *Panavision*, the Ninth Circuit held that an individual residing in Illinois was not so inconvenienced at having to litigate in California as to deprive him of Due Process. *Panavision*, 141 F.3d at 1323.

In addition, although Defendant portrays himself as only an individual without resources to litigate in California, he operates a company that touts itself as a "national" business serving Fortune 500 companies. *See* Exhibit B to Paralegal Decl. Defendant also admits he registered the PLAINTIFF'S MARK Domain Names for the purpose of contracting with service professionals in at least nine California locations. Again, Defendant cannot be willing to conduct business all over the State of California but be unwilling to litigate here when that business injures a company headquartered in California.

Accordingly, this factor also supports the exercise of jurisdiction.

(iii) Extent of Conflict Between the Sovereignty of California and Texas

Trademark infringement and cybersquatting are both issues governed by federal law, and Plaintiff's state law claims for unfair competition under the common law and the California Unfair Practices Act mirror the federal standard for trademark infringement under the Lanham Act. *See Cleary v. News Corp.*, 30 F.3d 1255, 1262–63 (9th Cir. 1994) ("This Circuit has consistently held that state common law claims of unfair competition and actions pursuant to California Business and Professions Code § 17200 are 'substantially congruent' to claims made under the Lanham Act." (internal citations omitted)). Therefore, there is no sovereignty conflict between California and Texas.

(iv) The Forum State's Interest in Adjudicating the Dispute

"California maintains a strong interest in providing an effective means of redress for its residents tortiously injured." *Panavision*, 141 F.3d at 1323 (quoting *Gordy v. Daily News, L.P.*, 95 F.3d 829, 836 (9th Cir. 1996)). Plaintiff's principal place of business is in California, which is sufficient for this factor to favor Plaintiff. *Id.*

(v) The Most Efficient Judicial Resolution of the Controversy

This factor mainly concerns the location of witnesses and evidence. Given modern advances in travel and communication, however, this factor no longer weighs heavily in the reasonableness analysis. *Id.; see also Quokka*

Sports, Inc., 99 F. Supp. 2d at 1113–14. Because Plaintiff is headquartered in California, the vast majority of Plaintiff's witnesses and documents regarding its use of the Plaintiff's Mark are located in California. Moreover, as Defendant is a sole proprietor, it would clearly appear that more witnesses will be located in California than in Texas.

(vi) The Relation of the Forum to Plaintiff's Interest in Convenient and Effective Relief

Plaintiff chose California as the forum in which to seek relief because Plaintiff is located in California, it suffers harm caused by Defendant's trademark infringement at its principal place of business in California, and its marketing and sales of products bearing the trademarks at issue are administered from this location as well. As such, this forum is most convenient and effective for Plaintiff.

(vii) The Existence of an Alternative Forum

Courts accord great weight to the plaintiff's choice of forum. *Piper Aircraft Co. v. Reyno,* 454 U.S. 235, 241 (1981). While Texas could be a potential alternative forum, Plaintiff has chosen to bring suit in this Court, which is also an appropriate forum.

In summary, each of the factors discussed above weighs in favor of finding that this Court's exercise of personal jurisdiction over Defendant is reasonable. As indicated above, satisfaction of the first two prongs of the specific jurisdiction analysis creates a presumption that jurisdiction is reasonable, and the defendant bears a heavy burden to rebut that presumption. *Ballard,* 65 F.3d at 1501 (9th Cir. 1995) (citation omitted). Defendant has failed to meet his burden in this case.

B. Plaintiff Requests Discovery if There Is Any Doubt as to Jurisdiction

The record establishes this Court's personal jurisdiction over Defendant. If there is any doubt on this point, however, Plaintiff requests limited discovery to determine, among other things, the full extent of Defendant's contacts with California, how he chose the nine California cities or geographic areas he used in the PLAINTIFF'S MARK Domain Names, his marketing efforts directed at service professionals in those areas, and similar information. Discovery may be especially necessary in this case because Plaintiff has learned facts that are inconsistent with statements in Defendant's sworn affidavit and Motion to Dismiss. *See infra,* Section II.

"A court may permit discovery to aid in determining whether it has in personam jurisdiction." *Data Disc,* 557 F.2d at 1285 n.1 (citing *Wells Fargo & Co. v. Wells Fargo Express Co.,* 556 F.2d 406, 430 n.24 (9th Cir. 1977)).

Discovery in this situation can be granted "where pertinent facts bearing on the question of jurisdiction are controverted or where a more satisfactory showing of the facts is necessary." *Id.*

In addition, Plaintiff does not have sufficient facts to determine whether Defendant is subject to general jurisdiction in California. A defendant whose activities in a forum state are "substantial" or "continuous and systematic" may be subject to general jurisdiction in that state. *Panavision*, 141 F.3d at 1320. Although Defendant admits that "[i]n some of the cities I have existing contracts with service professionals who may provide Plaintiff's Systems," he does not indicate which cities, how many service professionals, or for how long these contracts have existed. (Defendant's Principal Aff., ¶ 14). These facts are relevant in determining whether Defendant is subject to general jurisdiction in California. Moreover, as stated above, Defendant's affidavit minimizing his contacts with California may not be credible.

Accordingly, if the Court finds that the current record does not establish personal jurisdiction over Defendant, Plaintiff respectfully requests an opportunity to take limited discovery for a sixty (60) day period to respond fully to Defendant's Motion to Dismiss.

III. Conclusion

For the reasons stated above, the current record sufficiently demonstrates that Defendant is subject to personal jurisdiction in this forum. Defendant has targeted California specifically by (1) infringing trademarks owned by a corporation whose principal place of business is in California; (2) registering fifteen PLAINTIFF'S MARK Domain Names (more than 25 percent of the total number of PLAINTIFF'S MARK Domain Names) that include geographic locations in California and are directed to California consumers; and (3) using these domain names as part of an admitted scheme to obtain business from California service professionals who offer services in California. Accordingly, Plaintiff requests that the Court deny Defendant's Motion to Dismiss for Lack of Personal Jurisdiction or, alternatively, allow Plaintiff to engage in limited discovery to establish that Defendant is subject to personal jurisdiction in this forum.

Motion to Dismiss Counterclaim for Partial
Cancellation Before the TTAB

A familiar tactic in the TTAB is for an applicant to counterclaim for partial cancellation of a trademark registration in an effort to avoid a finding of likelihood of confusion. The TTAB is supposed to conduct its likelihood of confusion analysis strictly upon the bases of (1) the marks as registered/ applied for, and (2) the goods/services covered by the applicable registration/ application. Use of the marks, nevertheless, often comes into play.

Applicants seeking to limit an opposer's challenge may assert counter-claims for partial cancellation of a registration, as was the case in the proceeding below.

In the United States Patent and Trademark Office
Before the Trademark Trial and Appeal Board

FORD MOTOR COMPANY,	)	
Opposer,	)	
	)	Opposition No. 111,804
v	)	
	)	
EQUIPMENT TECHNOLOGY, INC.,	)	
Applicant.	)	

Opposer's Motion to Dismiss Counterclaim

Opposer hereby moves pursuant to Rule 503 of the Trademark Trial and Appeal Board Manual of Procedure and Rule 12(b)(6) of the Federal Rules of Civil Procedure to dismiss Applicant's counterclaim for failure to state a claim upon which relief can be granted, or, in the alternative, for entry of judgment in Opposer's favor on Applicant's counterclaim pursuant to Rule 504 of the Trademark Trial and Appeal Board Manual of Procedure and Rule 12(c) of the Federal Rules of Civil Procedure. In support of this motion, Opposer states as follows:

I. Factual Background

Opposer owns and has for many years continuously used the mark Cougar Head design for "automobiles and their structural parts, wheels and wheel covers," and is the owner of United States Trademark Registration No. 1,359,117 (hereinafter "Opposer's Registration"). Applicant seeks to register the trademark ETI & Design for "structural truck parts, namely, truck mounted personnel lifts with articulating and telescopic booms, hydraulic and electrically operated utility truck beds and outriggers." Applicant has filed United States Trademark Application No. 75/271,306 to register the ETI & Design mark (hereinafter the "Opposed Application"). Opposer timely filed a Notice of Opposition to the Opposed Application on September 16, 1998. After numerous consented extensions of time, Applicant answered the Notice of Opposition on December 7, 2000. Applicant filed a counterclaim with its answer that states as follows:

> On information and belief, the Registrant only uses its COUGAR & Design trademark in connection with goods that are sold through authorized dealers, therefore, Applicant requests that the identification of goods in Registration

No. 1,359,117 be restricted based on Section 18 of the Lanham Act as follows: automobiles and their structural parts, wheels, and wheel covers *sold through authorized dealers*. (Emphasis added).

Opposer now moves to dismiss Applicant's counterclaim.

II. Argument

A party seeking to restrict or limit the description of goods in a trademark registration must plead and prove that (1) the entry of the proposed restriction will avoid a finding of likelihood of confusion, and (2) the opponent is not using its mark on those goods or services that will be effectively excluded from the registration if the proposed restriction is entered. *Eurostar, Inc. v. "Euro-Star" Reitmoden GmbH & Co., KG*, 34 U.S.P.Q. 2d 1266, 1269 (T.T.A.B. 1994). Applicant has not only failed to satisfy the pleading require-ments that the Board established in *Eurostar*, but also will be unable to prove that entering the proposed restriction will avoid a finding of likelihood of confusion. Applicant's counterclaim must therefore be dismissed.

A. Applicant Has Failed to Plead a Claim for Partial Cancellation

Applicant's counterclaim consists of a bare bones allegation that Opposer has not used the mark described in the Opposed Registration on goods other than those sold through "authorized dealerships." Applicant has failed to allege that restricting the Opposed Registration would eliminate a likelihood of confusion, and has therefore failed to satisfy the threshold pleading requirements that the Board established in *Eurostar*. Applicant's counterclaim therefore fails to state a claim for relief and must be dismissed.

B. Applicant Cannot Prove That the Restriction That It Seeks Would Eliminate the Likelihood of Confusion

Furthermore, even if Applicant were to amend its counterclaim to allege that the restriction it seeks would eliminate any likelihood of confusion, it is clear that it would not be able to prove that the proposed restriction would have this effect. Opposer is therefore entitled to judgment as a matter of law on Applicant's counterclaim.

1. Applicant's Proposed Restriction To Opposer's Registration Would Not Eliminate Any Overlap In The Trade Channels

It is settled law that the goods and services described in a trademark application or registration are presumed to move in all channels of trade that would be normal for such goods, and that they would be purchased by all potential buyers thereof. *See e.g., Canadian Imperial Bank of Commerce v. Wells Fargo Bank Nat'l Assoc.*, 811 F.2d 1490, 1492 (Fed. Cir. 1987) ("where likelihood of confusion is asserted by an opposer, the issue of likelihood of confusion must be resolved . . . in the absence of any specific limitations in the application and registration, on consideration of the normal and usual channels of trade and methods of distribution"); *In Re Cross Country Paper Prods. Inc.*, 2001 TTAB LEXIS 84 at *1 (T.T.A.B. Jan. 31, 2001) ("where the goods in the cited registration are broadly described as to their nature and type, it is presumed that . . . the identified goods move in all channels of trade which would be normal for such goods and that they would be purchased by all potential buyers thereof"); *In Re Smith and Mehaffey*, 1994 TTAB LEXIS 19 at *3 (T.T.A.B. June 15, 1994) ("Applicant's argument that its goods . . . do not travel in the channels of trade normally associated with clothing is unavailing because, since the identification is unrestricted as to channels of distribution, we must consider the goods to travel in all channels appropriate for goods of this type"); *Am. Hygienic Labs. Inc. v. Tiffany & Co.*, 12 U.S.P.Q. 2d 1979, 1983 (T.T.A.B. 1989) ("because there is no restriction in the application with respect to channels of trade, we must presume that applicant's goods are sold in all channels of trade for those products, including the channels of trade . . . in which opposer sells its products).

The Opposed Application does not set forth any restrictions as to trade channels or methods of distribution. It must therefore be presumed that Applicant's goods are, or will be, sold in all channels of trade for those products, including through "authorized dealers." *Am. Hygienic Labs.* 12 U.S.P.Q. 2d at 1983. Even if Opposer's Registration were restricted in the manner proposed by the Applicant, therefore, the trade channels would still overlap. Because Applicant's proposed restriction to Opposer's Registration would not eliminate the overlap in trade channels, the restriction would not eliminate a likelihood of confusion.

2. Even If Applicant's Proposed Restriction Eliminates the Overlap in Trade Channels, It Nevertheless Fails to Eliminate the Likelihood of Confusion

Applicant's counterclaim is further flawed because the restriction that it seeks to impose on Opposer's Registration, even if it eliminates an overlap in trade channels, nevertheless does not eliminate the likelihood of confusion. Likelihood of confusion generally turns on the confusion of actual or potential purchasers. *Elec. Design & Sales, Inc. v. Elec. Data Sys. Corp.*, 954 F.2d 713, 716 (Fed. Cir. 1992). In the case of automobiles and automobile parts and accessories, the Board has recognized that the issue is not whether the products are sold in the same dealerships, but rather whether customers would have reason to believe that the goods originate from a common source if sold under the same or a similar mark. *Saab-Skania AB v. Sparkomatic Corp.*, 1993 TTAB LEXIS 11 at *8 (T.T.A.B. Mar. 17, 1993) (owner of a car who encounters car speakers with same or substantially similar to the mark on their car is likely to assume a common source, sponsorship, or endorsement).

Applicant seeks to restrict Opposer's Registration to cover only "automobiles and their structural parts, wheels, and wheel covers sold through authorized dealers." Even if Applicant's counterclaim were read to state that Opposer only sells its automobiles and automobile parts through authorized car dealerships through which new vehicles are customarily sold, Applicant would still not be able to prove that restricting Opposer's Registration to these trade channels would eliminate the likelihood of confusion. In *Saab-Skania AB*, the manufacturer of the Saab 9000 series of automobiles opposed an application to register the mark 9000 SERIES for "automotive stereo speakers." *Saab-Skania*, 1993 TTAB LEXIS 11 at *1. TTAB 1993. The applicant argued that there were differences in the trade channels because opposer's new cars were sold through dealerships whereas applicant's goods were sold in auto parts stores and through mass marketers. *Id*. at *5. Acknowledging that there was no evidence that the applicant's goods were sold through opposer's dealerships, the Board nevertheless found an overlap in the trade channels and purchasers because:

> A car owner who is looking for replacement speakers at a mass merchandiser or an auto accessory or parts store, upon encountering speakers bearing a mark which is the same as or substantially similar to the trademark on his or her car, is likely to assume a common source or sponsorship, or at least endorsement of the accessory by the automaker.

Id. at **9–10.

Similarly, even if Applicant were to establish that its products are not sold in Opposer's dealerships and that Opposer does not sell its goods outside of its dealerships, this would not be sufficient to demonstrate that restricting Opposer's Registration would eliminate the likelihood of confusion. A consumer familiar with Opposer's Cougar Head mark and the products sold under that mark may reasonably believe that Applicant's truck beds, outriggers, and truck lifts sold under the same or a highly similar mark originate from or are endorsed by the Opposer, even if Applicant's goods are not sold in Opposer's dealerships. Applicant also disregards the possibility that Opposer's dealerships may also sell goods manufactured by other companies and the existence of the used car and used auto part markets for Applicant's and Opposer's goods. Therefore, even if Applicant is able to demonstrate that Opposer itself only sells its goods through its own dealerships, Applicant will nevertheless be unable to demonstrate that the likelihood of confusion will be eliminated by restricting Opposer's registration.

Opposer is therefore entitled to judgment as a matter of law on Applicant's counterclaim.

III. Conclusion

WHEREFORE, Opposer requests that Applicant's counterclaim be dismissed.

Respectfully submitted,

Motion to Dismiss Copyright Infringement Claim for Lack of Subject Matter Jurisdiction

Another effective attack at the pleading stage against a copyright claim is to assert that the plaintiff does not own a valid copyright. There are many different bases for such an assertion. Below is an example based upon a licensing arrangement. Because ownership of a copyright registration is a jurisdictional requirement, such motions are aimed at the court's subject matter jurisdiction.

United States District Court Northern District of Illinois Eastern Division

MEDICAL BILLING CONSULTANTS, INC.)	
d/b/a Medbillz.com,)	
Plaintiff,)	
v.)	Case No. 01C 9148
)	Judge Moran
INTELLIGENT MEDICAL OBJECTS, INC.)	Magistrate Judge Nolan
Defendant)	.

Memorandum in Support of Defendants' Motion to Dismiss for Lack of Subject Matter Jurisdiction and Failure to State a Claim

I. Introduction

This dispute arises from the development and licensing of computer software from defendant, Intelligent Medical Objects, Inc. ("IMO"), to plaintiff, Medical Billing Consultants Inc. ("MedBillz"). After IMO sent MedBillz a notice of termination of the license agreement for failure to make royalty payments, MedBillz filed this suit. As more fully discussed below, the Complaint should be dismissed for two independent reasons.

First, the complaint should be dismissed under Rule 12(b)(1) for lack of subject matter jurisdiction. Diversity jurisdiction is not available, and federal question does not exist because the copyright claim is derivative of a dispute over ownership, as explained in the recent Seventh Circuit decision, *Int'l Armor & Limousine Co. v. Moloney Coachbuilders, Inc.*, 2001 U.S. App. LEXIS 25131 (7th Cir. Nov. 26, 2001).

The complaint should also be dismissed under Rule 12(b)(6) for failure to state a claim upon which relief can be granted. MedBillz claims copyright in a work called "IMO CPT Enhanced." However, the exhibits to the complaint specifically state that IMO is the owner of that work and that MedBillz is merely a licensee.[17] As a result, MedBillz lacks ownership of the copyright on which its claim is based. Supplemental jurisdiction over the remaining state law claims falls with the collapse of Plaintiff's copyright claim.

II. Background

On January 17, 2000, the parties entered into a Consulting Agreement in which IMO agreed to provide consulting services for the development of website relating to medical bills. The website was designed to work with various preexisting coding systems and enhancements that are not owned by Medbillz, but may be licensed from IMO or third parties, including a coding system known as "CPT," owned by the American Medical Association, and an enhancement to that system called "IMO CPT Enhanced," owned by IMO.

The website was delivered to MedBillz on September 15, 2000, and is now operated by a third party through a separate agreement with MedBillz. The parties entered into a License Agreement dated September 15, 2000, ("License Agreement'), which grants MedBillz the right to use IMO CPT Enhanced on the MedBillz website.

On September 15, 2001, MedBillz failed to make a minimum royalty payment due to IMO on the anniversary of the license agreement. IMO sent a Notice of Default, but MedBillz did not respond or cure the default. IMO next sent a Notice of Termination. MedBillz followed with this lawsuit.

III. Discussion

A. Motion to Dismiss For Lack of Subject Matter Jurisdiction

The Complaint alleges that the jurisdiction of this court arises from a federal question involving copyright infringement. However, the complaint shows that the copyright claim is entirely derivative of and dependent on contract issues involving ownership of the copyright. Therefore, it appears that this court lacks subject matter jurisdiction for the reasons recently explained by Judge Posner in *Int'l Armor & Limousine Co. v. Moloney Coachbuilders, Inc.*, 2001 U.S. App. LEXIS 25131 (7th Cir. Nov. 26, 2001) *Change text to (Moloney)*.

As explained in *Moloney*, the mere fact that a federal right is involved does not create federal question jurisdiction: "a dispute about ownership of a copyright does not arise under federal law, even though the dispute could not exist but for the property right created by copyright" (citing *T.B. Harms Co. v.*

---

17. The relevant Exhibits to the Complaint (Exhibits A, C, and D) are attached to this Memorandum for convenient reference.

Eliscu, 339 F.2d 823 (2d. Cir. 1964)). This principle has been adopted by the Seventh Circuit. *See Saturday Evening Post Co. v. Rumbleseat Press, Inc.*, 816 F.2d 1191 (7th Cir. 1987).

In *Moloney*, the Court of Appeals applied this principle to dismiss a trademark dispute after three years of federal court litigation, stating:

> Because in this case the only serious dispute is how the contracts of 1986 and 1990 allocate ownership rights in the *Moloney* name and business history (as applied to stretch limousines), the same principle leads to the conclusion that there is no federal jurisdiction. The dispute arises under the law of contracts; any trademark claims are entirely derivative of the contract issue.

Similarly here, the rights of the parties in the copyrighted work at issue are controlled by the agreements attached to the Complaint as Exhibits, and the copyright claim is thus derivative of the rights conferred by those agreements. As a result, *Moloney* compels the conclusion that there is no federal question jurisdiction.

Since there is no federal question or diversity jurisdiction, the court also lacks supplemental jurisdiction over the remaining state law claims.

B. Motion to Dismiss For Failure to State a Claim

Plaintiff's claim for copyright infringement also must be dismissed because the Complaint, including the Exhibits, demonstrates that Plaintiff is not the owner of "IMO CPT Enhanced," the work at issue. Instead, Plaintiff is the licensee of IMO CPT Enhanced and has specifically acknowledged IMO's ownership of that work at issue in the agreements attached as Exhibits to the Complaint.

A Motion to Dismiss under Rule 12(b)(6) should be granted when the Complaint demonstrates that the Plaintiff cannot prevail on its claim. Rule 10(c) provides that the Exhibits attached to the Complaint shall be considered part of the Complaint for the purpose of a motion to dismiss. To state a valid claim for copyright infringement, the plaintiff must properly allege ownership of the copyrighted work. Here, the Exhibits attached to the Complaint show that plaintiff is not the owner of the work at issue. Therefore, Count I of the Complain fails to state a claim for copyright infringement and should be dismissed. Moreover, since subject matter jurisdiction relies on the copyright claim, and not on diversity, the remaining state law claims must also be dismissed for lack of supplemental jurisdiction.

Plaintiff's claim of copyright infringement is based on the allegation that IMO "created a competing identical internet website product called 'IMO CPT Enhanced,' on IMO's website, which recreates the database of CPT codes, provides a search engine for access to coding information, and in all respects functions identically to the MedBillz.com site." Compl. ¶ 57. As relief, Plaintiff demands that IMO remove "IMO CPT Enhanced" from IMO's website and turn over all contracts and other records concerning access to IMO CPT Enhanced. Compl. 22.

Paragraph 27 of the Complaint alleges the basis of Plaintiff's copyright ownership claim:

> 27. The Consulting Agreement further stated '[e]xcept as set forth below in this Section 6, all right, title, and interest, including copyright interests and any other intellectual property rights, in the Software and other materials provided by Consultant per this Agreement as specified in Exhibit A, shall be the property of the Customer [MedBillz]

MedBillz totally ignores the specific reservation of rights stated in Section 6 of the Consulting Agreement. Following the language quoted by Plaintiff in Paragraph 27 of the Complaint, the Consulting Agreement states:

> 6.2 Reservation of Consultant's [i.e., IMO's] Rights. Notwithstanding Section 6.1 . . . . Consultant also reserves and retains ownership of the works identified in Attachment D, which Consultant created before entering into this Agreement or enhancements to those works required by the Customer.

Attachment D of the Consulting Agreement (included in the Complaint as page 12 of Exhibit A) lists the reserved works and specifically includes "IMO CPT Enhanced," among others.

The Copyright Assignment dated August 11, 2000, referenced in Paragraphs 48 and 54 of the Complaint and attached to the Complaint as Exhibit C, assigns the works acquired by MedBillz under the Consulting Agreement, namely "unpublished web page designs, computer screen displays and computer programs and related documentation." The Assignment does not indicate any transfer of ownership from IMO to plaintiff of "IMO CPT Enhanced."

Further confirming IMO's ownership of IMO CPT Enhanced is the License Agreement referenced in Paragraph 104 of the Complaint and attached to the Complaint as Exhibit D. This agreement entered on September 17, 2000, grants Plaintiff a nonexclusive license to embed IMO's databases, including IMO CPT Enhanced, in MedBillz's system. Paragraph 6 of the License provides that IMO "has and shall have exclusive title to and ownership of all Service and Integrated Service products . . . ." The "Integrated Service" owned by IMO is defined in the preamble of the License to include the products listed on Exhibit A of the License Agreement and specifically includes IMO CPT Enhanced. (That exhibit is attached to the Complaint as page 11 of Exhibit D.)

In summary, it is clear from the Exhibits to the Complaint that IMO is the owner of all right, title, and interest in IMO CPT Enhanced. As a result, plaintiff's claim that IMO has infringed plaintiff's copyright in IMO CPT

Enhanced is false, cannot be proved, and must be dismissed. Further, the court lacks supplemental jurisdiction over the remaining state law claims.

IV. Conclusion

For these reasons, we ask this Court to grant Defendant's Motion to Dismiss for Lack of Subject Matter Jurisdiction and Failure to State a Claim.

Respectfully submitted,

Opposition to Motion to Dismiss by Foreign Corporation Claiming Lack of Sufficient Contacts and Failure to State a Claim

Trademark and copyright cases often cross international boundaries and when they do, defendants frequently assert that they are not subject to jurisdiction in the United States. The Federal Rules, however, under FRCP 4(k)(2) provide for jurisdiction over defendants that have sufficient contacts with the United States as a whole but not a particular forum. Below is an example of a motion using this argument to bring a defendant into U.S. federal court.

Opposition to Motion to Dismiss by Foreign Corporation Claiming Lack of Sufficient Contacts and Failure to State a Claim

In The United States District Court for the Northern District of Illinois Eastern Division

MDI, INC.	Case No.
an Illinois Corporation,	Judge Castillo
Plaintiff,	Magistrate Judge Mason
v.	
SAINTLY COMMUNICATIONS STRATEGIES, INC.,	
et al.,	
Defendants.	

MDI's Response To Saintly Communications Strategies' Motion To Dismiss

SCS was the linchpin of a fraudulent telemarketing operation. It listened to each recorded call, offered"customer service," arranged to charge customer accounts, and arranged to ship infringing products. In short, it did everything but make the telemarketing calls.

SCS and its associates cloaked their operation in a myriad of corporations and funds transfer mechanisms, either to avoid liability or detection. Even SCS's U.S. address for "customer service" was phony, and complaints ended up in a dead letter file in a mail drop in New York.

Under the "MDI Savings" telemarketing scheme, Defendants Abu and Wang, identifying themselves as MDI Savings, called elderly people offering to sell them worthless "pharmaceutical discount packages" for $398 each. SCS communicated with Wang, and probably Abu, every day. It heard recordings from every call, supposedly to "verify" that customers consented to have their bank accounts charged. It also received numerous calls from "MDI Savings" consumers complaining about Wang and Abu. Through these recordings and customer complaints, SCS knew that Wang and Abu berated or tricked elderly customers into consenting, yet there is no evidence that SCS ever rejected a single one of the verifications. Indeed, SCS, under the guise of offering "customer service," either lied to consumers seeking refunds or outright refused to refund the money, getting paid every time that it approved a charge to a customer's account.

Later, SCS lied to MDI as well, claiming in its sworn discovery responses that it had "no direct involvement" in the operation, that it "had no knowledge of the information requested concerning any persons placing such telemarketing calls," and that "there is no relationship between SCS and the individuals or entities placing the 'MDI Savings' telemarketing calls."

After approving the $398 charge, SCS, using the name MDI Savings, caused payment processors to withdraw the money, including from accounts in Illinois, and caused fulfillment companies to ship infringing packages, again for an entity called "MDI Savings."

Consumers and state Attorneys General began calling the plaintiff, MDI, Inc., to lodge complaints. MDI is a large well-regarded seller of medical supplies. The injury to MDI' reputation is obvious.

Argument

I. Standard

For the purposes of SCS's 12(b)(6) motion, the court should accept the allegations in the Second Amended Complaint as true and should draw all reasonable inferences in MDI's favor. *Christensen v. County of Boone, Illinois,* 483 F.3d 454, 457 (7th Cir. 2007). For the purposes of SCS's 12(b)(2) motion, the court should accept MDI's allegations as true unless controverted by defendant's affidavits, with any disputes in the evidence resolved in favor of jurisdiction. *Purdue Research Foundation v. Sanofi-Synthelabo, S.A.,* 338 F.3d 773, 782 (7th Cir. 2003).

SCS has submitted an affidavit in support of its motion, but that affidavit never disputes the jurisdictional allegations in MDI's complaint, namely, that SCS directed payment processors to deduct funds from Illinois banks in connection with "MDI Savings," and that in connection with various non-"MDI Savings" operations, SCS has directed the deduction of funds from Illinois banks, directed the shipment of fulfillment products to Illinois consumers, and communicated on a regular basis with Illinois consumers.

II. The Court has Personal Jurisdiction over SCS

A. General Jurisdiction

This Court has personal jurisdiction over SCS because SCS has continuous and systematic general business contacts with Illinois. *Helicopteros Nacionales de Colombia, S.A. v. Hall,* 466 U.S. 408, 416 (1984). Under the concept of general jurisdiction, "a firm that does business in Illinois on a regular basis may be sued in an Illinois court even if the plaintiff's cause of action does not grow out of that business," provided that "the business done by the defendant in Illinois be intentional, substantial, and continuous rather than inadvertent, trivial, or sporadic, that it continue up to the time of suit, and that it evidence a purpose on the part of the defendant to avail himself of the protection of the laws of

Illinois." *Asset Allocation and Mgmt. Co. v. Western Employers Ins.*, 892 F.2d 566, 570 (7th Cir. 1989).

SCS's general contacts are systematic and intentional and are undertaken on a regular basis and with knowledge that Illinois residents and banks were involved. It has provided customer service to Illinois residents in connection with various telemarketing schemes and has directed the deduction of funds from banks throughout Illinois. Second Amended Complaint (hereinafter "Compl."), ¶ 40. MDI conclusively identified four such telemarketing operations, but its investigations indicate that there were many more—by their very nature, these investigations were bound to uncover only a fraction of SCS's activities, yet they still indicated that a high percentage of SCS's telemarketing operations involved Illinois consumers. *See* Exhibit 1. The verification recordings and other customer data make clear from the outset with whom SCS is dealing, and SCS has the final say as to which customers are charged and which are not. Compl. ¶ 35. Thus, every time that SCS directs the removal of funds from an Illinois bank, directs the shipment of fulfillment packages to Illinois consumers, communicates with Illinois consumers, or provides refunds to Illinois consumers, it does so of its own volition and with knowledge of the consumers' status as Illinois residents.[18] SCS has thus purposefully availed itself of the protection of the laws of the State of Illinois, and personal jurisdiction is proper here.

SCS does not deny that it has provided customer service to Illinois residents in connection with the other telemarketing operations. Nor does it deny that it has directed, and continues to direct, payment processors to deduct funds from Illinois banks. Instead, it makes the conclusory argument that MDI has failed to present sufficient general contacts with Illinois.

As shown above, MDI has established general personal jurisdiction over SCS. However, to the extent that SCS argues to the contrary, it is SCS's own wrongdoing which has deprived MDI of additional jurisdictional facts. See MDI's pending Motion To Compel Jurisdictional Discovery and Reply in support.[19] It is unjust for SCS to deprive MDI of jurisdictional facts and then try to use that lack of knowledge to form the basis of a motion to dismiss. Thus, to the extent the Court believes that general jurisdiction is lacking, MDI

---

18. SCS's knowledge is further confirmed by the paperwork SCS and its payment processors submit to banks, which prominently displays the address of the customer and the banks with whom SCS is dealing. *See* Affidavits attached as Exhibit 2 and Exhibit 3.

19. How many Illinois consumers has SCS serviced? How long do these calls last? What sort of business is transacted during these calls? Does SCS ever send e-mails or letters to these Illinois consumers? Does it ever call them? How often does SCS give refunds to Illinois consumers? From how many Illinois banks has SCS ordered funds deducted, and what were the total amounts? These are all questions that have a direct bearing on general jurisdiction, but SCS simply won't answer them. By providing false discovery responses and then refusing to supplement them as required by Rule 26(e), SCS has denied MDI and the Court the full picture regarding its general contacts with Illinois.

asks the Court to order SCS to produce the withheld jurisdictional discovery and to allow MDI to file an additional brief before ruling. Alternatively, as a penalty for SCS's ongoing refusal to provide jurisdictional discovery, MDI asks the Court to rule that personal jurisdiction has been established over SCS, or at the very least to shift the burden of proof on jurisdiction from MDI to SCS. *See, e.g., Ins. Corp. of Ir. v. Compagnie Des Bauxites*, 456 U.S. 694, 707–09 (1982) (finding that the district court did not abuse its discretion in deeming personal jurisdiction established as a sanction for defendant's failure to comply with jurisdictional discovery); *Koehler v. Bank of Berm. Ltd.*, 2003 WL 289640, *12–13 (S.D.N.Y. Feb. 11, 2003) (ordering the jurisdictional burden of proof shifted as a sanction against defendant who contested personal jurisdiction but did not cooperate in jurisdictional discovery).

B. Specific Jurisdiction Under the Effects Doctrine

As a defendant who harmed an Illinois trademark owner and reached into the state in connection with its trademark infringement, SCS is subject to personal jurisdiction under the effects doctrine.

The Seventh Circuit adopted the effects doctrine, first recognized by the Supreme Court in *Calder v. Jones*, 465 U.S. 783 (1984), in *Indianapolis Colts, Inc. v. Metropolitan Baltimore Football Club*, 34 F.3d 410 (7th Cir. 1994). In that case, the Court held that jurisdiction over an out-of-state trademark infringer was proper in Indiana, even when the defendant had no contacts with Indiana, because the plaintiff was based there and was therefore injured there. *Id.* at 411–12. Thus, under the effects doctrine, "specific jurisdiction can be proper when the injury occurs in Illinois, even if all of the other relevant conduct took place elsewhere." *Int'l Molding Mach. Co. v. St. Louis Conveyor Co.*, 2002 WL 1838130, *4 (N.D. Ill. Aug. 12, 2002).

The court in *Indianapolis Colts* noted that some sort of entry into the state is required. *Indianapolis Colts*, 34 F.3d at 412. In *Calder*, the defendant's "entry" was the subsequent sale by third parties of magazines containing a defamatory article, while in *Indianapolis Colts*, the defendant's "entry" was the subsequent broadcast by third parties of infringing football games. Other courts have similarly held that the threshold for entry under the effects doctrine is very low. *See, e.g., Ridell, Inc. v. Monica*, 2003 WL 21799935, *3 (N.D. Ill. July 25, 2003) (finding personal jurisdiction in trade secrets case where defendant mailed a single advertisement to an Illinois consumer); *Sys. Designs, Inc. v. New Customware Co., Inc.*, 248 F. Supp. 2d 1093, 1099–1102 (D. Utah 2003) (finding personal jurisdiction in trademark infringement case where plaintiff was based in Utah, and defendant listed companies "with a large Utah presence" as clients on its website, even though defendant "did not have deliberate or repeated contacts with Utah"); *U.S. Tsubaki, Inc. v. Indus. Research Team*, 2001 WL 99696, *3 (N.D.Ill. Feb. 1, 2001) (finding personal jurisdiction in Lanham Act case where plaintiff was based in Illinois, and Canadian defendant distributed 4 copies of infringing report to Illinois consumers, out of a total of 2275 copies distributed nationally); *Nida Corp. v. Nida*, 118 F. Supp. 2d 1223, 1231 (M.D. Fla. 2000) (finding personal jurisdiction in trademark infringement case where California defendant derived $27,428 in revenue from Florida between 1995 and 2000, against the backdrop of $1,000,000 in nationwide revenue in 1999 alone); *Brown v. CitiCorp*, 1998 WL 341610, *5 (N.D. Ill. June 22, 1998) (finding personal jurisdiction in patent and copyright case where defendant did no business in Illinois but advertised its infringing services in Illinois); *Heroes, Inc. v. Heroes Found.*, 958 F. Supp. 1, 3–5 (D.D.C. 1996) (finding personal jurisdiction in trademark infringement case where defendant placed a single infringing advertisement in a forum newspaper and operated a passive website accessible to forum residents).

SCS has sufficient minimum contacts with Illinois to satisfy due process requirements under the effects doctrine. SCS selected consumers with Illinois bank accounts as proper "MDI Savings" customers, then directed payment processors to make deductions from these Illinois banks, with SCS deriving a financial benefit from each transaction.[20] Compl. ¶¶ 35–36. SCS knew that these were Illinois banks, as it reviewed the verification recordings containing this information and then instructed its payment processors accordingly. Compl. ¶¶ 35–36. This knowledge is confirmed by the paperwork submitted by SCS's payment processors, which prominently list the Illinois addresses of the banks. *See* Exhibit 2, ¶ 3; Exhibit 3, ¶ 3. Later, SCS fielded customer service calls from some of these Illinois banks regarding the "MDI Savings" charges. *See* Exhibit 1, ¶ 7. Even if these Illinois bank transactions were a small fraction of the total number of transactions ordered by SCS, personal jurisdiction is still proper under the effects doctrine, as these transactions were performed using the MDI trademark, with knowledge of MDI's ownership of the MDI trademark and the harm that would be felt to MDI in Illinois. Compl. ¶¶ 36, 46. These activities have indeed caused MDI and its reputation irreparable harm, with numerous consumers being confused into believing that the "MDI Savings" telemarketing operation was affiliated with or endorsed by

---

20. Only SCS knows how many Illinois banks it targeted. MDI confirmed two and found a likely third, but those were merely the banks that happened to call SCS. *See* Exhibit 1, ¶ 7; Exhibit 2, ¶ 2; Exhibit 3, ¶ 2. The paperwork sent to the banks did not include SCS's phone number, but rather the payment processor's, so there was no doubt many more Illinois banks affected. *See* Exhibit 1, ¶ 8. Indeed, by sifting through just a sample of the 250 hours of "MDI Savings" verification recordings, MDI found a fourth Illinois bank targeted by the scheme, one that had never called SCS, indicating that there are likely dozens more. *See* Exhibit 1, ¶ 9. As part of the jurisdictional discovery authorized by this Court, MDI sought documents from SCS that would reveal every Illinois bank from which SCS ordered the withdrawal of "MDI Savings" funds, but SCS refused to comply. *See* Exhibit 1, ¶ 10.

MDI and some consumers and law enforcement officials contacting MDI to express such a belief. Compl. ¶ 49.

SCS does not dispute that it instructed payment processors to deduct "MDI Savings" funds from Illinois banks. Instead, it suggests that it cannot be subject to personal jurisdiction because a third party carried out these activities. The Supreme Court expressly rejected this argument in *Calder*. In *Calder*, authors of a defamatory article argued that they could not control where their employer distributed a magazine, yet the court still held them subject to jurisdiction. *Calder*, 465 U.S. at 789. *Calder* attributed the subsequent foreseeable actions of their employer to the defendants, a far broader ruling than the situation faced here, where SCS exercised independent discretion and directed the payment processors to deduct funds.

Numerous other courts have also ruled that a defendant cannot escape the reach of the courts by using an intermediary to carry out its wrongdoing. *See, e.g., Finley v. River North Records, Inc.,* 148 F.3d 913, 916 (10th Cir. 1998) (finding personal jurisdiction over out-of-state defendant in fraudulent inducement case, even though defendant retained a booking agent to carry out the fraudulent activity); *Indianapolis Colts, Inc. v. Metro. Baltimore Football Club Ltd. P'ship*, 34 F.3d 410, 412 (7th Cir. 1994) (finding personal jurisdiction over out-of-state trademark infringer, even though third-party cable companies physically broadcast the football games that reached the forum state); *Brown v. SBC Commc'ns, Inc.,* 2007 WL 684133, *3 (S.D. Ill. Mar. 1, 2007) (finding personal jurisdiction over out-of-state telecommunications service provider, even though it used intermediary "billing clearinghouses" to levy fraudulent telephone charges, and it was "three steps removed from the customer"); *Morris v. Khadr*, 415 F. Supp. 2d 1323, 1336 (D. Utah 2006) (finding personal jurisdiction over foreign terrorist, even though defendant used a third party to carry out the attack that harmed the plaintiffs); *Worldtronics Int'l. Inc. v. Ever Splendor Enterprise Co., Inc.,* 969 F. Supp. 1136, 1141 (N.D. Ill. 1997) (finding personal jurisdiction over foreign patent infringer, even though the infringer "ships the accused product f.o.b. outside of Illinois to a customer who ships the product to Illinois, albeit sometimes through yet another customer"); *Heroes, Inc. v. Heroes Found.,* 958 F. Supp. 1, 3 (D.D.C. 1996) (finding personal jurisdiction over trademark infringer even though a third party placed the infringing advertisement in a forum newspaper); *Ragold, Inc. v. Ferrero, U.S. A., Inc.,* 506 F. Supp. 117, 120 (N.D. Ill. 1980) (finding personal jurisdiction over out-of-state defendant even though it used an independent advertising agency to distribute the false advertisements at issue in the case).

Under these circumstances, it was foreseeable that SCS would be required to answer for its actions in Illinois. Exercising personal jurisdiction over SCS will not offend traditional notions of fair play and substantial justice. Illinois has an interest in adjudicating this case because MDI is an Illinois company, and SCS's activities caused injury in Illinois and because SCS directed the fraudulent withdrawal of funds from Illinois banks. Moreover, SCS has not claimed that it would be unduly burdensome to litigate in Illinois, and it would not. *Board of Trustees v. Elite Erectors, Inc.*, 212 F.3d 1031, 1037 (7th Cir. 2000) ("easy air transportation, the rapid transmission of documents, and the abundance of law firms with nationwide practices, make it easy these days for cases to be litigated with little extra burden in any of the major metropolitan areas.").

C. Specific Jurisdiction by Transaction of Business and Commission of a Tort

SCS is also subject to personal jurisdiction in Illinois because, by virtue of the "MDI Savings" bank transactions, it transacted business and committed tortious acts in this state.[21] Under the Illinois Long-Arm Statute, a court sitting in Illinois may exercise specific jurisdiction over a defendant who engages in "the transaction of any business within this State" or "the commission of a tortious act within this State." 735 ILCS 5/2–209(a).

Fraud is a tort, as is trademark infringement. *See, e.g., Habitat Wallpaper and Blinds, Inc. v. K.T. Scott Ltd. P'ship,* 807 F. Supp. 470, 473 (N.D. Ill. 1992). "Illinois courts have held that the commission of a single tortious act in Illinois brings a defendant within the scope of § 2-209(a)(2), even if the defendant has no other contact with Illinois." *Id.* at 473, n.2. *See also Magnum Feeders, Inc. v. Bloedorn,* 1995 WL 743747 (N.D. Ill. Dec. 12, 1995) (finding personal jurisdiction over out-of-state trademark infringer whose only contacts with Illinois were the sale of $865 in infringing bird cages, or 0.0074 percent of defendant's total infringing sales). Moreover, submitting a request into Illinois to obtain payment for a fraudulent transaction is a tortious act under the Long-Arm Statute. *See, e.g., Czarnowski Display Servs. Inc. v. Bell,* 2004 WL 1613553, *3 (N.D. Ill. July 19, 2004). SCS facilitated telemarketing fraud and infringed the MDI trademark by directing "MDI Savings" deductions from Illinois banks. Comp. ¶ ¶ 35–36. As such, even if these Illinois bank transactions were few in number, they nonetheless give rise to personal jurisdiction as tortious acts committed in Illinois.

A single transaction or solicitation in Illinois may be sufficient to confer personal jurisdiction, even if the defendant never physically entered Illinois, provided that the lawsuit arises out of that transaction. *See, e.g., Burger King Corp. v. Rudzewicz,* 471 U.S. 462, 476 (1985); *R.E. Davis Chemical Corp. v. Int'l Crystal Lab., Inc.,* 2004 WL 2191328, *4 (N.D. Ill. Sep. 27, 2004);

---

21. As discussed above, neither the "transacts business" nor "tortious act" analysis is altered by the fact that SCS directed payment processors to carry out these activities, as the courts have held that a defendant cannot evade personal jurisdiction by using an intermediary to carry out its wrongdoing.

Westnofa USA Inc. v. British Design (U.S.A.) Corp., 1983 WL 420, *2 (N.D. Ill. Nov. 8, 1983). By directing its payment processors to deduct funds from Illinois banks, SCS transacted business within Illinois, and MDI's complaint arises out of that business. This provides a separate basis for this Court to assert personal jurisdiction over SCS.

D. Jurisdiction Pursuant to Fed.R.Civ.P. 4(k)(2)

Should the Court conclude that if Illinois lacks personal jurisdiction over SCS, jurisdiction would still be proper under Fed.R.Civ.P. 4(k)(2), which covers defendants "who do not reside in the United States, and have ample contacts with the nation as a whole, but whose contacts are so scattered among states that none of them would have jurisdiction." *ISI Int'l, Inc. v. Borden Ladner Gervais*, 256 F.3d 548, 551 (7th Cir. 2001).

Given the public policy concerns behind Rule 4(k)(2), the threshold for minimum contacts with the United States is low. *See, e.g., Adams v. Unione Mediterranea Di Sicurta*, 364 F.3d 646, 651 (5th Cir. 2004) (finding sufficient contacts with the United States as a whole where defendant insurance company paid claims to 155 U.S. companies from 1991 to 1994 and insured 260 shipments to the United States between 1989 and 1995); *Graduate Mgmt. Admission Council v. Raju*, 241 F. Supp. 2d 589, 599–600 (E.D. Va. 2003) (finding jurisdiction proper under Rule 4(k)(2) based on foreign defendant's electronic contacts with the United States, even though defendant did not physically enter the country, noting that "to find otherwise would not only frustrate [plaintiff's] attempts in this case to vindicate its rights under United States law, by requiring [plaintiff] to turn to foreign courts to vindicate those rights against a likely elusive defendant, it would also provide a blueprint whereby other individuals bent on violating United States trademark and copyright laws could do so without risking suit in a United States court.").

SCS has had sufficient contacts with the United States, both from a specific jurisdiction and general jurisdiction standpoint, to permit the application Rule 4(k)(2) in this case. SCS has provided customer service, directed the withdrawal of funds, and directed the shipment of fulfillment products to tens of thousands of U.S. banks and citizens, with MDI's claims arising out of many of those activities.[22]

SCS purposefully availed itself of the protection of the laws of the United States, and it could therefore reasonably anticipate being haled into a U.S.

---

22. Based on the Identacall verification recordings described in MDI's complaint, there were at least 5000 "MDI Savings" customers, spread throughout the United States. SCS claims that the "MDI Savings" operation lasted for less than a year, and that SCS has provided customer support for dozens of other telemarketing operations over the past several years. Thus, it is a conservative estimate that SCS has had business contacts with tens of thousands of U.S. customers and their banks.

court. First, SCS derives a substantial economic benefit from its dealings with U.S. consumers and banks.[23] The more U.S. consumers that SCS approved, the more SCS was paid, with the funds being deducted from U.S. bank accounts and then wired directly to SCS from a U.S. bank. Compl. ¶¶ 35, 37. Second, by providing such extensive assistance to telemarketing schemes that it knew or should have known to be fraudulent—and in some cases engaging in fraudulent activity itself—it was entirely foreseeable that SCS would harm citizens of the United States. *See, e.g., Mwani v. bin Laden,* 417 F.3d 1, 14 (D.C. Cir. 2005) (jurisdiction proper under Rule 4(k)(2) where defendants did not have sufficient minimum contacts with any one state, but could reasonably anticipate being haled into U.S. court by virtue of the harms they caused to U.S. citizens).

To avoid the daunting situation where a plaintiff has to "traipse through the 50 states, asking whether each could entertain the suit," the Seventh Circuit provides the following solution:

> A defendant who wants to preclude use of Rule 4(k)(2) has only to name some other state in which the suit could proceed. Naming a more appropriate state would amount to a consent to personal jurisdiction there (personal jurisdiction, unlike federal subject-matter jurisdiction, is waivable). If, however, the defendant contends that he cannot be sued in the forum state and refuses to identify any other where suit is possible, then the federal court is entitled to use Rule 4(k)(2).

ISI Int'l, 256 F.3d at 552. Thus, in accordance with Rule 4(k)(2) and the decision in *ISI Int'l,* MDI calls upon SCS to state in its reply brief the states in which it believes this lawsuit can proceed. Should SCS fail to do so, then in accordance with Seventh Circuit precedent, MDI asks this Court to maintain jurisdiction over SCS pursuant to Rule 4(k)(2).

III. MDI Has Stated Valid Claims for Trademark Infringement and Telemarketing and Consumer Fraud

A. Telemarketing and Consumer Fraud Claims

The "MDI Savings" telemarketers misrepresented the actual cost of the "MDI Savings" package, fraudulently claimed to be calling from consumers' banks in order to obtain their bank account information, caused consumers' bank accounts to be debited without their actual authorization, and failed

---

23. SCS was paid over $80,000 for the "MDI Savings" operation alone. *See* Exhibit 1, ¶ 11. Again, taking at face value SCS's claims that "MDI Savings" was a small part of its dozens of overall telemarketing operations, that means SCS has derived substantial revenue, likely millions of dollars, from its dealings with U.S. consumers and banks.

to establish proper mechanisms by which consumers could obtain a refund. (Compl. ¶ ¶ 28, 31–33, 51). These acts constituted deceptive and abusive telemarketing practices. *See* 15 U.S.C. § 6102(a)(1); 16 C.F.R. §§ 310.3–310.4.

SCS assisted and facilitated the "MDI Savings" telemarketing fraud. (Compl. ¶ ¶ 34–44, 52). As a result, SCS is liable under the Telemarketing Fraud Act as well. *See* 15 U.S.C. § 6102(a)(2) ("The Commission shall include in such rules respecting deceptive telemarketing acts or practices a definition of deceptive telemarketing acts or practices . . . which may include acts or practices of entities or individuals that assist or facilitate deceptive telemarketing"); 16 C.F.R. § 310.3(b) ("It is a deceptive telemarketing act or practice and a violation of this Rule for a person to provide substantial assistance or support to any seller or telemarketer when that person knows or consciously avoids knowing that the seller or telemarketer is engaged in" deceptive or abusive telemarketing); *F.T.C. v. Leisure Time Marketing, Inc.*, 2001 WL 34133935, *2 (M.D. Fla. June 18, 2001) (defining "substantial assistance and support" as including "performing customer service functions for an entity engaged in telemarketing including, but not limited to, receiving or responding to consumer complaints").[24]

These deceptive and abusive telemarketing practices irreparably harmed MDI because consumers and law enforcement officials believed MDI was the entity responsible for them, and MDI therefore suffered damages to its business and reputation well in excess of $50,000. (Compl. ¶ ¶ 49, 54). Thus, MDI has been "adversely affected by" a "pattern or practice" of deceptive and abusive telemarketing, and therefore has standing to bring suit under the Telemarketing Fraud Act. 15 U.S.C. § 6104(a).

SCS argues that this harm is not enough to give MDI standing, because MDI is seeking "statutory damages under the Lanham Act" rather than actual damages. However, MDI is not seeking statutory damages under the Lanham Act, as that statute does not provide for statutory damages for the claims MDI is asserting. Rather, as shown in its prayer for relief, MDI is seeking "an award for damages due to the injury to its business reputation and the loss of its goodwill by reason of Defendants' engagement in or substantial assistance to deceptive and abusive telemarketing practices, and by Defendants' offer to sell and sales of goods and services not emanating from MDI but identified with

---

24. SCS argues, without citation to any authority, that SCS cannot be liable for assisting the telemarketing fraud because it did not monitor the instrumentality of the fraud. There is no basis for such a requirement in the statute or case law, but regardless, MDI has pleaded facts showing that SCS *did* monitor the instrumentality of the telemarketing fraud. (Second Am. Compl. ¶ ¶ 34–44, 61).

MDI's MDI trademark." (Compl. 20). *See also* 15 U.S.C. § 1117(a) (trademark infringer subject to an award of "any damages sustained by the plaintiff").[25]

SCS notes that the Senate originally limited the "adversely affected" language to purchasers, financial institutions, and credit card companies. But SCS fails to mention that the House had no such limitation. *See* H. Rep. No. 103-20, 1993 WL 54276, *10 ("Subsection (a) permits injured persons, including individuals, partnerships, and corporations, to bring civil actions to enforce the rules promulgated under the bill."). The Senate and the House each passed their own respective versions of the bill, but on July 25, 1994, the House asked the Senate to accept the broader language, and on August 2, 1994, the Senate did so. *See* Exhibit 4. Thus, while the Senate originally contemplated the narrow standing language noted by SCS, it accepted the House's broader version, which means that an aggrieved trademark holder such as MDI does have standing to file suit under the Telemarketing Fraud Act. *See, e.g., 800-JR Cigar, Inc. v. GoTo.Com,* 437 F.Supp.2d 273, 296 (D.N.J. 2006) ("[T]he Act states that those persons who are 'adversely affected' are authorized to bring a civil action against a deceptive telemarketer. First, GoTo argues that it is the public, not JR Cigar itself, that has been allegedly deceived by GoTo's actions and that JR Cigar therefore lacks standing to bring a claim. This argument is without merit. JR Cigar is most certainly aggrieved by practices (if proven) that take unfair advantage of its marks and divert customers away from its website.").

---

25. SCS cites cases supporting dismissal where a plaintiff made speculative claims for damages, but none of those decisions is on point. In *Ryan v. Mary Immaculate Queen Center,* 188 F.3d 857, 860 (7th Cir. 1999), plaintiff accused defendant of conspiring in an unlawful search, but failed to plead any facts regarding when the conspiracy was formed or what its terms were. Similarly, in *Fries v. Helsper,* 146 F.3d 452, 457 (7th Cir. 1988), plaintiff accused defendant judge of conspiring with litigants to deny his earlier claim, but failed to plead any facts regarding the nature of the conspiracy. In *Piscotta v. Old Nat'l Bancorp,* 499 F.3d 629, 632 (7th Cir. 2007), plaintiffs accused defendant bank of failing to protect their personal data, but never alleged that defendant's failure led to any identity theft or loss of money from their accounts. In *Dunkin Donuts Inc. v. N.A.S.T., Inc.,* 428 F. Supp. 2d 761 (N.D. Ill. 2005), the court found that defendant failed to submit enough evidence to support its counterclaim for damages, but that decision was on *summary judgment,* not a motion to dismiss, and the defendant had failed to produce any evidence of damages in discovery. Finally, as summarized by Justice Stevens, *Bell Atlantic Corp. v. Twombly,* 127 S. Ct. 1955 (2007) had nothing to do with damages but rather with a failure to plead liability in the first place: "The Court does not suggest that an agreement to do what the plaintiffs allege would be permissible under the antitrust laws. *Nor does the Court hold that these plaintiffs have failed to allege an injury entitling them to sue for damages under those laws.* Rather, the theory on which the Court permits dismissal is that, so far as the Federal Rules are concerned, no agreement has been alleged at all." *Id.* at 1984 (emphasis added).

B. Trademark Claims

MDI has stated a valid claim for SCS's direct trademark infringement. Section 32 of the Lanham Act makes actionable a defendant's "use in commerce" of the plaintiff's mark "in connection with the sale, offering for sale, distribution or advertising of any goods or services."[26] 15 U.S.C. § 1114(1). Courts have construed "use in commerce" broadly in the context of infringement and unfair competition claims. *See, e.g., United We Stand America, Inc. v. United We Stand, America*, 128 F.3d 86, 90–93 (2nd Cir. 1997) (defendant's use of mark as a source identifier while soliciting funds qualified as "use in commerce," even though defendant never sold any goods or services in connection with the mark); *Council of Better Business Bureaus, Inc. v. Bailey & Assoc., Inc.*, 197 F. Supp. 2d 1197, 1212 (E.D. Mo. 2002) (defendant's distribution of documents bearing the BBB mark constituted "use in commerce," even though defendant did not use the mark with its own goods or services and often used the mark "after a sale, presumably to make the customer comfortable with the purchase."); *Jews For Jesus v. Brodsky*, 993 F. Supp. 282, 309 (D.N.J. 1998) ("The requirement that the activities of an infringer be done 'in connection with any goods or services,' does not require the infringer to actually cause goods or services to be placed into the stream of commerce. Rather, all that is needed is that the trademark violation be 'in connection' with any goods or services.").

SCS's actions fall well within the language of 15 U.S.C. § 1114(1). After deciding which customers to include in the "MDI Savings" program, SCS directed payment processors to deduct funds from consumers' bank accounts under the "MDI Savings" name and directed fulfillment companies to ship "MDI Savings" packages to consumers. (Compl. ¶¶ 34–36, 38, 42–43). The deduction of funds and the shipment of goods all prominently featured the MDI trademark.[27] (Compl. ¶¶ 36, 38, 41). As a result of SCS's actions, consumers are likely to be confused as to the source of origin of the "MDI Savings" goods and services; in fact, consumers have already been confused. (Compl. ¶¶ 49, 56).

---

26. This is broader than the definition cited by SCS, which actually applies to registrability and not infringement. *See McCarthy on Trademark and Unfair Competition*, J. Thomas McCarthy, § 23:11.50 (4th Ed. 2008) ("If one were to substitute the Lanham Act § 45 definition of 'use in commerce' into the § 32(1) infringement requirement, the result would be awkward and inept. It would be a robotic statutory reading divorced from the meaning and history of what trademark "use" signifies for acquiring rights as opposed to infringing someone else's trademark rights.").

27. The Lanham Act broadly defines "commerce" as "all commerce which may lawfully be regulated by Congress." 15 U.S.C. § 1117. Wire transfers and shipments of goods qualify under this definition, as Congress has passed laws regulating both.

SCS argues that MDI failed to explicitly allege that these activities constituted use in commerce. This argument is without merit. MDI's allegations refer to SCS's "use" of the trademarks, and deducting funds and shipping products are "in commerce." SCS offers no case law to support the notion that under the liberal notice pleading provisions of Rule 8(a), a plaintiff must explicitly recite the words "use in commerce" in order to state a valid claim. See Council of Better Business Bureaus, 197 F. Supp. 2d at 1213 (rejecting the same argument as "merely a matter of semantics"). The one case cited by SCS, Rescuecom Corp. v. Google, Inc., 456 F. Supp. 2d 393 (N.D.N.Y. 2006), merely held that Google's sale of keywords in connection with its search engine results did not constitute use of the mark in commerce, because this was an internal use within Google's software and not visible to the public. In sharp contrast, consumers in the instant case did encounter the MDI trademark in connection with Defendants' goods and services, which explains why many were actually confused.

MDI has also stated a valid claim for SCS's contributory trademark infringement. Contributory trademark infringement occurs where "a manufacturer or distributor intentionally induces another to infringe a trademark, or if it continues to supply its product to one whom it knows or has reason to know is engaging in trademark infringement." Inwood Labs. Inc. v. Ives Labs. Inc., 456 U.S. 844, 854 (1982). The courts have recognized that contributory trademark infringement is a valid claim in the context of both goods and services. See, e.g., Hard Rock Cafe Licensing Corp. v. Concession Servs. Inc., 955 F.2d 1143, 1149 (7th Cir. 1992) (holding that contributory trademark infringement applies to services as well as goods, and noting that a flea market operator would be liable for contributory trademark infringement if it knew of or was willfully blind to a vendor's direct infringement). In the context of services, some courts have gone so far as to require a plaintiff to plead that a defendant directly controlled and monitored the instrumentality of infringement used by the direct infringer. See, e.g., Lockheed Martin Corp. v. Network Solutions, Inc., 194 F.3d 980, 984 (9th Cir. 1999). The Seventh Circuit has not adopted the Lockheed Martin "control and monitoring" standard.

Courts have consistently permitted contributory trademark infringement claims to go forward in the context of services. See, e.g., Adidas Am. Inc. v. Kmart Corp., 2007 WL 2915594, *9 (D. Or. Oct. 3, 2007) (denying the defendant's motion for summary judgment on contributory trademark infringement where the defendant "provides the space for the allegedly infringing activities, processes the sales of the allegedly infringing products, and receives a portion of the gross revenue from those sales"); Habeeba's Dance of the Arts, Ltd. v. Knoblauch, 430 F. Supp. 2d 709, 715 (S.D .Ohio 2006) (holding that the plaintiff stated a valid claim for contributory trademark infringement against the YWCA for hosting a dance symposium, which the YWCA knew or should have known was being presented using an infringing trademark, and noting that liability would ultimately turn on "how substantially involved" the YWCA was in the business operations of the direct infringer); *Gucci Am. Inc. v. Hall & Assoc.* 135 F. Supp. 2d 409 (S.D.N.Y. 2001) (holding that the plaintiff stated a valid claim for contributory trademark infringement against an ISP that provided web-related services to a customer which the ISP knew or should have known was posting infringing content); *Century 21 Real Estate Corp. v. R.M. Post, Inc.*, 8 U.S.P.Q. 2d 1614 (N.D. Ill. 1988) (holding that the plaintiff stated a valid claim for contributory trademark infringement against a phone book publisher who knew or should have known that it had printed an infringing advertisement).

SCS's actions satisfy these requirements for contributory trademark infringement. SCS directed the payment processors to deduct "MDI Savings" funds from bank accounts and directed the fulfillment companies to ship out "MDI Savings" packages. (Compl. ¶ ¶ 35–36, 38). Moreover, SCS supplied numerous services to the "MDI Savings" infringers. (Compl. ¶ ¶ 34–43). SCS continued these actions even though it knew or should have known of the "MDI Savings" infringements. (Compl. ¶ ¶ 44, 61). SCS directly controlled and monitored the instrumentality of these infringements. (Compl. ¶ ¶ 44, 61). Specifically, SCS listened to sales recordings and decided which consumers to approve and which consumers to reject, directed the deduction of funds from consumers' bank accounts, directed the shipment of infringing packages, and worked to block consumers from cancelling the transactions. (Compl. ¶ 35–36, 38, 42–43). In that the MDI trademark was used in connection with these activities, MDI has supported its allegation that SCS directly controlled and monitored the infringers' instrumentality of infringement. Thus, MDI has stated a valid claim that SCS committed contributory trademark infringement by (1) inducing the payment processors and fulfillment company to infringe the MDI trademark, and (2) continuing to supply its services to the "MDI Savings" telemarketers even though it knew or should have known of their infringements.[28]

Conclusion

For the foregoing reasons, MDI respectfully requests that the Court deny SCS's motion to dismiss.

Respectfully submitted,

---

28. To the extent that it is inconsistent for MDI to allege that SCS's directions to the payment processors and fulfillment companies constituted both contributory and direct infringement, such inconsistent allegations are permissible at the pleadings stage. *See* Fed. R. Civ. P. 8(d)(2); *Limousine Werks, Inc. v. Flaherty Mfg., Inc.*, 1989 WL 8553, *4 (N.D. Ill. Jan. 31, 1989) ("a pleader may set forth inconsistent legal theories in his pleading and will not be forced to select a single theory on which to seek recovery.").

*MDIMDI*Opposition to Motion to Dismiss
Copyright Claim and Related Torts

Trademark and copyright cases often involve novel issues of technology and infringement, which often result in motions to dismiss. Below is an example of a response to a motion to dismiss aimed at facts that did not, at the time, easily fall into a particular trademark or copyright claim.

Opposition to Motion to Dismiss Copyright Claim and Related Torts

In the United States District Court for the Central District of California

TICKETMASTER CORPORATION, a corporation, and TICKETMASTER ONLINE-CITYSEARCH, INC., a corporation	))))	CV 99-7654 HLH (BQRx)
	)	Hon. Henry L. Hupp
Plaintiffs,	)	
		MEMORANDUM OF LAW IN
v.	)	RESPONSE TO DEFENDANT'S
	)	MOTION TO DISMISS
TICKETS.COM, INC., a corporation, Defendant.	)))	

In response to the Defendant's Motion to Dismiss Plaintiffs' Complaint, plaintiffs submit this memorandum in opposition.

I. Nature of the Case

Plaintiffs filed this lawsuit to stop defendants from misappropriating content from the plaintiffs' Internet website (the "Ticketmaster Web Site"), from unlawfully hyperlinking to the Ticketmaster website's internal pages, and from disseminating false and misleading information to the consuming public and disrupting plaintiffs' relationships with their customers. In "free-riding" off of plaintiffs' efforts, defendant has made unauthorized reproductions of the Ticketmaster website, has siphoned advertising revenue away from the Ticketmaster website, and has misled consumers about the source of online tickets, miscellaneous event information, and ticket availability on the Ticketmaster website.

II. Factual Background

Plaintiff, Ticketmaster Corporation, is a nationwide retailer of tickets for concerts, sporting events, and theater shows. Ticketmaster sells tickets though ticket outlets, over the phone, and via the Internet at its website <www.ticketmaster.com>. (Compl. ¶ 14.) Ticketmaster's exclusive licensee, Ticketmaster Online-City Search, Inc., operates the Ticketmaster website.[29] *Id.* ¶ 8. Visitors to the site can obtain, in addition to tickets, general information on events, artists, and venues as well as souvenir merchandise. *Id.*

Ticketmaster designs and constructs its site primarily for the convenience of its consumers but also to optimize its sales. *Id.* ¶ 10. The entry point for the website is the Ticketmaster Home Page, which usually provides a feature story regarding an upcoming or ongoing event and also instructs the visitor on how to navigate through the site. *Id.* ¶ 16. Built into the Ticketmaster Home Page is a site counter, which records the number of visitors to the site. Tickermaster calculates advertising fees based in part on this site counter's figures. *Id.* ¶ 17. The Ticketmaster Home Page also displays a link to the Terms and Conditions page, which sets out the terms governing use of the site by visitors. *Id.* ¶ 18. Another feature of the site are the Event Pages—separate webpages dedicated to each event, which furnish information about the particular event, venue, artist, seating and other items. *Id.* ¶ 22.

Defendant, Tickets.com, sells tickets to concerts, shows, and sporting events at its website www.tickets.com. *Id.* ¶ 25. Unlike Ticketmaster however, Tickets.com does not have ticket retailing rights for many of the events that it promotes on its site. Instead, it relies primarily on its network of ticket "brokers" or "scalpers," who charge steep premiums over and above the face value of a ticket. *Id.* ¶ 26. Hence, on its event pages, Tickets.com will typically supply a link to, or other contact information for, its affiliated ticket broker. For certain events, Tickets.com also provides a link to the Ticketmaster website that bypasses the Ticketmaster Home Page and goes directly to the corresponding internal Ticketmaster Event Page where consumers can purchase tickets (the "Unauthorized Deep Link"). *Id.* ¶¶ 27, 41. Ticketmaster has not authorized these links and has repeatedly objected to their placement.

Soon after construction of the Tickets.com website, Ticketmaster learned that Tickets.com was using the Ticketmaster website as its source for event information, scavenging Ticketmaster's site using a "spider" or "webcrawler" program, which extracts information from the Ticketmaster website and downloads it to the Tickets.com website. *Id.* ¶¶ 31, 32, 44, 45, 56–60. Ticketmaster also discovered that defendant was frequently supplying false or misleading information about Ticketmaster. On some occasions, Tickets.com would provide the wrong phone number for Ticketmaster's local service. *Id.* ¶¶ 36, 38. On other occasions, it would fail to list the Ticketmaster website as a source for tickets or would claim falsely that no tickets were available on the Ticketmaster website. *Id.* ¶¶ 39–40, 79–86.

---

29. For convenience, plaintiffs are collectively referred to as Ticketmaster.

After cease and desist requests proved unavailing, Ticketmaster filed an eight-count Complaint charging Tickets.com with unlawful conduct in the operation of its website. The Complaint alleges causes of action for (1) copyright infringement, (2) breach of contract, (3) false advertising, (4) misappropriation, (5) unfair competition, (6) trespass, (7) unjust enrichment, and (8) tortious interference with prospective economic advantage. Ticketmaster's lawsuit seeks injunctive and monetary relief.

III. Analysis

A. Ticketmaster's first Claim for Relief States a Valid Cause of Action for Copyright Infringement

Tickets.com's motion to dismiss Ticketmaster's claim for copyright infringement reflects a fundamental misreading and misunderstanding of the Complaint. Ticketmaster is not claiming copyright protection over the raw event data. Rather, it is Tickets.com's repeated unauthorized reproduction of most, if not all of, Ticketmaster's copyrighted website for purposes of obtaining the raw event data and of fixing its deep link that is the subject of Ticketmaster's copyright claim. Tickets.com's preoccupation with establishing that "facts are not protectible" completely misses the point.

1. Ticketmaster's Copyright Infringement Claim

Ticketmaster's First Claim for Relief charges Tickets.com with infringing Ticketmaster's copyrights by "accessing the Ticketmaster Web Site, thereby downloading copies of pages of the website, and reproducing and displaying all or portions of these pages, without Ticketmaster's approval or authorization." (Compl. ¶ 90.) The Complaint alleges that

Tickets.com makes these downloaded copies as part of its effort to (1) plunder the site for event data, and (2) construct deep links to Ticketmaster's Event Pages. (*See, e.g.,* Compl. ¶ ¶ 45, 77.)

Nowhere in the Complaint does Ticketmaster assert that they own a copyright in the facts and data regarding events. The gravamen of Ticketmaster's claim is that Tickets.com unlawfully copies Ticketmaster's copyrighted webpages when it downloads those pages for programming its webcrawlers and constructing deep links. It is this conduct that violates Ticketmaster's "exclusive rights of reproduction and display under 17 U.S.C. § 106." (Compl. ¶ 90.), and on this central allegation, Tickets.com is silent.

Put simply, Tickets.com's motion with respect to this claim presents this Court with two issues: (1) whether Ticketmaster has a valid copyright registration for its website; and (2) whether by downloading copies of

Ticketmaster's website, Tickets.com has created an unauthorized copy in violation of federal copyright law. This Court should not be misled by Tickets.com's efforts to portray this case as something it is not. As set forth below, the allegations of Ticketmaster's complaint, which are accepted as true for purposes of this motion, properly state a claim for relief, and therefore, Tickets.com motion to dismiss the copyright infringement claim *should* be denied.

2. Ticketmaster's Copyright Infringement Claim is Valid

Copyright protection affords its owner the exclusive right to reproduce a copyrighted work, to prepare derivative works based on the copyrighted work, to distribute, and to display a copyrighted work. 17 U.S.C. § 106. To prove copyright infringement, a plaintiff must demonstrate (1) ownership of a valid copyright, and (2) copying of expression protected by the copyright beyond the scope of any license. *Triad Sys. Corp. v. Southeastern Express Co.*, 64 F.3d 1330, 1335 (9th Cir. 1995). Ticketmaster has alleged facts sufficient to meet each of these requirements.

Ticketmaster has attached to their Complaint certificates of registration for the Ticketmaster Web Page. (Compl. Ex. E.) These certificates constitute prima facie evidence of the validity of Ticketmaster's copyright. 17 U.S.C. § 410(c); *Triad*, 64 F.3d at 1335. While Tickets.com devotes much time to arguing that the copyright registrations do not extend to the event data—a proposition with which Ticketmaster does not take issue—Tickets.com does not dispute the validity of the registrations for the website itself. Indeed, it acknowledges, as it must, that for purposes of this motion, the registrations must be assumed to be valid. (Def. Mem. at 11.)

Moreover, in downloading virtually all of Ticketmaster's website pages, Tickets.com has undoubtedly copied the protected portions of Ticketmaster's copyrighted work. Courts in this circuit have consistently held that the transfer of computer software into a computer's Random Access Memory or RAM is sufficient to create a copy under the Copyright Act. *MAI Sys. Corp. v. Peak Computer, Inc.*, 991 F.2d 511, 519 (9th Cir. 1993), *cert. denied*, 114 S. Ct. 671 (1994); *Triad*, 64 F.3d at 1335 (holding that when an entire software program is copied, protected elements of the software are necessarily copied for copyright infringement purposes); *Sony Computer Entm't, Inc. v. Connectix Corp.*, 48 F. Supp.2d 1212, 1218 (N.D. Cal. 1999) (finding that source code downloaded from the Internet created a copy); *Sega Enters. Ltd. v. MAPHIA*, 948 F. Supp. 923 (N.D. Cal. 1996) (finding copying was established when game files were uploaded to or downloaded from defendant's online bulletin board); see also *Playboy Enters. Inc. v. Frena*, 839 F. Supp. 1552, 1559 (M.D. Fla. 1993) (ruling that the "display right precludes unauthorized transmission of the display from one place to another, for example, by a computer system").

Unless this copying is authorized, it constitutes copyright infringement. *MAI Sys.,* 991 F.2d at 518.

MAI Systems provides strong support for Ticketmaster's copyright claim. The plaintiff, a computer manufacturer sued an independent computer service provider for copyright infringement. The plaintiff claimed that when servicing its computers, the defendant made an unauthorized copy of the plaintiff's copyrighted operating system by turning on the machine and booting it up. *Id.* at 518. The district court ruled that the loading of the copyrighted work into the computer was a sufficiently fixed version of the work to constitute a copy. *Id.* Because the service provider did not have a license for the operating system, the court granted the plaintiff's motion for summary judgment. *Id.* The defendant challenged this ruling on appeal, but the Ninth Circuit rejected the challenge and affirmed. *Id.* at 519; *see also Triad,* 64 F.3d at 1335 (affirming grant of preliminary injunction on copyright infringement claim); *Sony,* 48 F. Supp. 2d at 1221 (granting preliminary injunction on copyright infringement claim); *Sega,* 948 F. Supp. at 931–32 (granting summary judgment and preliminary injunction on copyright claim); *Playboy,* 839 F. Supp. at 1557 (granting summary judgment on copyright claim).

Tickets.com's actions in this case are indistinguishable from those of the defendants in the cases cited above. The Complaint describes occasions on which Tickets.com has downloaded Ticketmaster's webpages thousands of times. (Compl. ¶¶ 57–60.) Every time it downloads one of Ticketmaster's pages, Tickets.com is reproducing on its own computer Ticketmaster's copyrighted material. Hence, each download represents a copy for purposes of the Copyright Act.

Moreover, the Complaint is replete with facts showing that Tickets.com makes these copies without Ticketmaster's authorization. For example, the Complaint recounts Ticketmaster's correspondence with Tickets.com requesting to no avail that Tickets.com cease its webcrawling and deep linking. (Compl. ¶¶ 47, 49.) When Tickets.com refused, Ticketmaster attempted to block Tickets.com's actions using technical means, but Tickets.com circumvented those blocks. (Compl. ¶¶ 42, 43.)

Tickets.com does not dispute that it lacks Ticketmaster's authorization; far from it, Tickets.com's motion is premised on its belief that it can, with impunity, repeatedly and systematically copy Ticketmaster's copyrighted website for its own commercial purposes, without Ticketmaster's permission. That Ticketmaster permits the general public to use its website to view event information and buy tickets does not grant Tickets.com a license to copy the website for purposes of commercial competition. *Microstar v. Formgen, Inc.,* 942 F. Supp. 1312, 1318 (S.D. Cal. 1996), *aff'd* in relevant part, *rev'd* in other part, 154 F.3d 1107 (9th Cir. 1998). In *Microstar,* Formgen made and distributed a copyrighted computer game and encouraged players to use its software to create new "levels" for the game and share them with others.

942 F. Supp. at 1314–15. Microstar downloaded hundreds of these player-created "levels" from the Internet, packaged them, and sold them. Formgen claimed that Microstar committed copyright infringement. Microstar defended that it had an implied license to use Formgen's copyrighted material because Formgen permitted its players to use them in creating new levels. In rejecting Microstar's claim and finding copyright infringement, the court noted that Formgen's encouraging of its players to use its copyrighted software for noncommercial purposes did not permit Microstar to copy that software for commercial competition. *Id.* at 1318. Similarly, Ticketmaster's public display of event information does not give rise to an automatic license allowing its competitors to indiscriminately copy and plunder its website for their own commercial purposes.

Nor does the fact that Tickets.com does not commercially display the copied we pages absolve it of liability. It is sufficient that it reproduces the copyrighted webpages as a means of achieving its commercial ends. In *Sony*, the plaintiff had obtained copyright protection for the source code used in its video game consoles. *Sony*, 48 F. Supp. 2d at 1215. The defendant manufactured video game emulators—software programs that allow personal computers to run games manufactured for the plaintiff's system without having to purchase the console. *Id.* To construct its emulator, the defendant obtained two copies of the plaintiff's source code. First, it downloaded a version of the source code from the Internet. When that version proved to be unworkable, the defendant removed the microchip containing the source code from one of the plaintiff's products and downloaded the microchip's contents onto a disk. *Id.* at 1216. It then used that code to build the emulator. As the final step in the emulator's construction, the defendant replaced the plaintiff's code with its own code, so the emulator was never sold with the plaintiff's code inside. *Id.* The plaintiff sued for copyright and trademark infringement and moved for a preliminary injunction.

After first finding that the plaintiff had showed valid copyright ownership by submitting the copyright registration for its source code, the court ruled that in downloading the plaintiff's code from the Internet and from the microchip, plaintiff had copied plaintiff's protected work in violation of the Copyright Act. *Id.* at 1218. In so doing, the court rejected the defendant's argument that because it did not sell a product containing the plaintiff's code, its use of the code was simply developmental and therefore fair use. *Id.* Noting that the defendant had used the code to build the emulator and its new code, the court dismissed this argument as "insufficient." *Id.*

Likewise, any contention here that Tickets.com is not infringing upon Ticketmaster's copyright because it is only appropriating the event data for its own commercial use must fail because it rests on too narrow of a construction of the Copyright Act. As *Sony* makes clear, the unauthorized reproduction of a copyrighted work remains unlawful even if no effort is made by the defendant to commercially market the copyright-protected aspects of the work. It is sufficient that the copyrighted work was reproduced as a means to developing the commercial ends.

As such, Ticketmaster's First Claim for Relief properly establishes a viable claim for copyright infringement.

B. Tickets.com's Unauthorized Deep Linking is Actionable

Ticketmaster does not dispute the useful role that hypertext links play in the making the World Wide Web easier to navigate. To the contrary, in typical situations, links are placed in good faith and do not present any problems. But when the use of those links is designed to interfere with and undermine the linked website's ability to transact business, that conduct should not be condoned simply because it occurs on the Internet.

Ticketmaster alleges that Tickets.com's unauthorized deep linking is designed to interfere with and undermine Ticketmaster's ability to take full advantage of the Ticketmaster Web Site. Tickets.com accomplishes this in several ways:

- The deep link siphons advertising revenue away from Ticketmaster's site to Tickets.com's site
- By appropriating selected Ticketmaster's webpages onto its own site, Tickets.com interferes with Ticketmaster's ability to distribute its products in the manner it chooses
- By selectively omitting the link for certain events, Tickets.com misleads consumers into believing wrongly that Ticketmaster has no tickets available

Each of these theories is described in more detail below.

First, by installing a deep link instead of a link to the Ticketmaster Home Page, Tickets.com sends consumers to Ticketmaster's site without their visits being detected by Ticketmaster's site counter. (Compl. ¶ 71.) Because advertising revenue is ultimately based on the number of visits to the Ticketmaster Home Page, the Unauthorized Deep Link succeeds in lowering the Ticketmaster Web Site's advertising revenue. Meanwhile Tickets.com, a competitor of Ticketmaster, uses the deep links to attract more traffic to its site and ultimately to increase its revenue. As a result, the deep link uses Ticketmaster's own we pages to unfairly shift advertising revenue from Ticketmaster to one of its self-proclaimed competitors. Second, the Unauthorized Deep Link undermines Ticketmaster's investment in, and its ability to transact business on, its own website. Ticketmaster has invested much effort and expense in constructing the Ticketmaster Web Site. A great deal of thought and creativity has gone into designing and ordering the pages. The site does more than simply sell tickets; for example, it provides its own information about various artists and events, and it sells merchandise.

(Compl. ¶ 8.) Like a traditional bricks-and-mortar business, the Ticketmaster Web Site is designed in a manner that promotes and markets all the various products and services available on the site in the hope that visitors will purchase them. (*See* Compl. ¶ 10.)

By hijacking particular pages from the Ticketmaster Web Site for its own commercial use, the Unauthorized Deep Link undermines Ticketmaster's ability to sell its products in the manner it chooses because it circumvents Ticketmaster's site design. Tickets.com free rides on Ticketmaster's investment, gaining visitors in the process, while Ticketmaster's efforts in designing the site are wasted. Tickets.com's parasitical business model discourages those like Ticketmaster because there is less incentive for them to be creative in their own site design, if they are unable to protect that creativity against a freeloading competitor.

Finally, the deep link is deceptive. By repeatedly posting incorrect event and ticket information, Tickets.com's deep link to the Ticketmaster Web Site ultimately misleads consumers. For instance, when Tickets.com's website—the self-proclaimed "ultimate resource for event information and tickets"—omits a deep link to the Ticketmaster Web Site and states that tickets are only available from one of its affiliated ticket scalpers, when in fact, tickets are available from the Ticketmaster Web Site at face value, Ticketmaster loses potential sales as well as goodwill among their customers. Consumers, who are confronted with either paying exorbitant premiums—a portion of which, upon information and belief, go directly to Tickets.com—or foregoing the event completely, also lose. (Compl. ¶¶ 39–40, 82–86.) Likewise, Ticketmaster is obviously harmed when Tickets.com provides phone listings purportedly for Ticketmaster's ticket-by-phone service but which turn out to be phone numbers for competitors or for pornographic chat lines. *Id.* ¶ 36, Exs. I, J, K.

In addition to breaching Ticketmaster's terms and conditions (*see supra* Sec. III.D), the Unauthorized Deep Link is actionable because it tortiously interferes with Ticketmaster's relationships with its consumers and advertisers. Moreover, in misleading ticket buyers about ticket availability on the Ticketmaster Web Site and luring them into buying tickets from Tickets.com ticket scalpers, the Unauthorized Deep Link also constitutes an unfair business practice.

1. Ticketmaster's Allegations Regarding the Unauthorized Deep Link State a Claim for Tortious Interference with Prospective Economic Advantage

To state a claim for tortious interference, a plaintiff must allege facts showing the following: (1) the existence of an economic relationship between the plaintiff and a third party, (2) awareness of the relationship on the part of the defendant, (3) intentional conduct by the defendant designed to disrupt that relationship, (4) actual disruption of the relationship, and (5) damage to the plaintiff. *Los Angeles Land Co. v. Brunswick Corp.*, 6 F.3d 1422, 1429 (9th Cir. 1993).

Ticketmaster's complaint sets forth facts supporting each of these elements. First, the facts alleged demonstrate that Ticketmaster has established a lucrative and successful relationship with consumers. During 1998, consumers purchased approximately 3 million tickets through the website, and an additional 1.6 million through the first five months of 1999. (Compl. ¶ 14.) Plainly, Ticketmaster has a valuable economic relationship with the ticket-buying public, which it should reasonably expect to continue.

Additionally, Ticketmaster has a relationship with its advertisers. As set forth in the Complaint, the Ticketmaster Web Site earns revenues through the placement of advertisements, and advertisers pay for space on the site based on the number of visitors counted on its home page. (Compl. ¶ 17.) Ticketmaster's continued relationship with its advertisers is also valuable.

Tickets.com's awareness of these relationships cannot be disputed, particularly here, where all the allegations of the complaint must be treated as true. In its motion, Tickets.com acknowledges that its role is to provide ticketing information collected from many different sources. Since Ticketmaster is by far one of the world's leading ticket retailers—in Tickets.com's words, "the dominant player in the market"—Tickets.com would be hard-pressed to claim that it was ignorant of Ticketmaster's status with consumers or with advertisers. (Compl. ¶ 7.)

Ticketmaster's complaint alleges that the Unauthorized Deep Link is unlawfully designed to disrupt Ticketmaster's relationship with its customers and advertisers. (Compl. ¶¶ 128–30.) The means by which the deep link does this have been described in detail above and need only be summarized here. The Unauthorized Deep Link (1) siphons advertising revenues from Ticketmaster to Tickets.com, (2) interferes with Ticketmaster's ability to sell their products in the manner they choose by hijacking select pages and engrafting them onto Tickets.com's site, and (3) misleads consumers about event information and the availability of tickets on the Ticketmaster Web Site.

Ticketmaster has alleged disruption and damages as a result of the Unauthorized Deep Link. (Compl. ¶¶ 129–30.) The fact that precise damages cannot be estimated at this time is not fatal to Ticketmaster's claim at this stage in the proceedings. *See, e.g., Lowell v. Mother's Cake & Cookie Co.*, 79 Cal. App. 3d 13, 144 Cal. Rptr. 664 (Cal. Ct. App. 1978).

Tickets.com's only substantive argument for its motion to dismiss this claim is that there is nothing wrongful about providing a deep link. (Def. Mot. 24). That linking may, as a general proposition, be a beneficial feature does not affect Ticketmaster's allegations, which for purposes of this motion must be assumed as true. "[A]n action for interference with prospective business advantage will lie where the right to pursue a lawful business is intentionally interfered with either by unlawful means or by means otherwise lawful when there is a lack of sufficient justification." *Id.* at 668 (reversing grant of demurrer on interference with prospective business advantage claim). Hence, the wrongful conduct need not necessarily be unlawful, merely that which does not fall within the confines of fair competition. *Id.* Moreover, wrongfulness may be gleaned from the defendant's motives. *Id.* In this case, Tickets.com's motives are clearly not innocent. Despite repeated requests to cease its deep linking, Tickets.com continues to include the link (or remove it when misrepresenting ticket availability). And, when Ticketmaster erects technical barriers, Tickets.com deliberately circumvents them. Put simply, Tickets.com's business requires that it be able to appropriate the Ticketmaster Event Pages for its own use, regardless of the effect that appropriation has on Ticketmaster's consumers and advertisers.

2. Ticketmaster's Allegations Regarding the Unauthorized Deep Link State a Claim for Unfair Business Practices

The Unfair Business Practices Act proscribes "any unlawful, unfair, or fraudulent business practice and unfair, deceptive, untrue or misleading advertising." Cal. Bus. & Prof. Code §§ 17200 et. seq. (West Year) To be actionable, a practice need not be unlawful, merely unfair or fraudulent. *In re Morpheus Lights, Inc.,* 228 B.R. 449, 455 (N.D. Cal. 1998). To determine whether a business practice is unfair, the trier-of-fact must assess the harm inflicted by the practice on the victim and balance that against the motives and justifications of the alleged wrongdoer. *Id.* Tickets.com's persistent placement of the Unauthorized Deep Link is an unabashed attempt to divert revenue from Ticketmaster's site to its own. As such, it constitutes a plainly unfair practice with no lawful jurisdiction.

The statute also contains a separate provision prohibiting false advertising. Cal. Bus. & Prof. Code §§ 17500 (West Year). That provision forbids any statement that "is untrue or misleading, and which is known, or which by the exercise of reasonable care should be known to be untrue or misleading." *Cairns v. Franklin Mint Co.,* 24 F. Supp. 2d 1013, 1036 (C.D. Cal. 1998). To be actionable, a statement need not be wrong only "likely to deceive." *Id.* at 1037. Hence, a "perfectly true statement couched in such a manner that it is likely to mislead or deceive the consumer" is sufficient. *Day v. AT&T Corp.,* 63 Cal. App. 4th 325, 332, 74 Cal. Rptr. 2d 55, 59 (Cal. Ct. App. 1998). A statement that is actionable under the false advertising provisions of the Lanham Act will necessarily be actionable under the Unfair Business Practices Act. *Freeman v. Time, Inc.,* 68 F.3d 285, 289 (9th Cir. 1995); *Cairns,* 24 F. Supp. 2d at 1037.

As discussed above, the allegations of Tickets.com's false statements and omissions regarding ticket availability on the Ticketmaster Web Site are sufficient to state a claim for relief. Visitors to Tickets.com's site could reasonably conclude that the links and references to Ticketmaster's site are authorized or that Ticketmaster's and Tickets.com's sites are somehow affiliated.

(Compl. ¶ 70.) In cases where Tickets.com has removed from its event pages links to the Ticketmaster's site, even though Ticketmaster indeed has tickets, visitors could reasonably conclude that the absence of a link means that Ticketmaster has no tickets available. (Compl. ¶¶ 39–40, 82–86.) The visitors then would either have to pay the premium fee charged by Tickets.com's scalper affiliate or miss the event. The Unfair Business Practices Act plainly encompasses this type of consumer deception. *See, e.g., Cairns*, 24 F. Supp. 2d at 1037 (finding allegations that defendants' advertisements misleadingly implied that defendant was affiliated with plaintiff stated a valid claim under § 17500 of the Unfair Business Practices Act).

C. There is No First Amendment Right to Deep Link

Tickets.com claims that its placement of the Unauthorized Deep Link is protected by the First Amendment. (Tickets.com's Br. 22.) Putting aside the fact that Tickets.com offers no support for its claim, it is an argument that is specious for several reasons.

Tickets.com's reliance on the Pentagon Papers case and others cited in its memorandum is misguided. (Tickets.com's Br. 22.) Those cases each dealt with political or communicative speech. To the extent that Tickets.com's placement of a link on its site constitutes protected speech, it would be commercial speech at best. *See Central Hudson Gas & Elec. Corp. v. Public Serv. Comm'n of New York*, 447 U.S. 557, 561 (1980) (defining commercial speech as "expression related solely to the economic interests of the speaker and its audience").

Because commercial speech tends to be more durable than other forms of expression, the First Amendment provides less protection to commercial speech. *Id.* Restraint on speech that is deceptive or relates to illegal activity, for example, is not protected by the First Amendment. And, even if the speech is protected, it may be restrained if the government interest is substantial, the restraint advances that interest, and the restraint is not more extensive than necessary to serve that interest. *Id.* at 566.

In this instance, Tickets.com's right to place or not place an Unauthorized Deep Link is not protected by the First Amendment. As set forth above, Tickets.com trumpets its site as providing comprehensive information regarding ticket availability from all sources. In providing or omitting a link to Ticketmaster's site, Tickets.com explicitly informs consumers about Ticketmaster's ability to supply tickets to a given event. Ticketmaster has alleged facts that show that Tickets.com's information is not always correct. As a result, consumers are likely to be misled into not buying tickets or into buying tickets at scalper prices, a portion of which goes to Tickets.com. The First Amendment offers no protection for such commercially deceptive speech.

IV. Conclusion

For the foregoing reasons, Ticketmaster respectfully requests that Defendant's Motion to Dismiss be denied.

Respectfully submitted,

Response to Motion to Dismiss False Advertising Claim for Failure to Plead with Particularity Under Fed. R. Civ. P. 9(b)

The Lanham Act also provides redress against false and misleading statements of fact. In some circumstances, defendants will attempt to defend against such claims by arguing that they are subject to the heightened pleading standard of Fed. R. Civ. P. 9(b). Generally, this is not the case, as illustrated below.

Response to Motion to Dismiss False Advertising Claim for Failure to Plead with Particularity Under Fed. R. Civ. P. 9(b)

United States District Court Southern District of Ohio Western Division

CELSIS, INCORPORATED,	:	Case No. C-1-02-900
Plaintiff,	:	Judge Weber
vs.	:	Magistrate Judge Sherman
BIOTRACE, INCORPORATED,	:	RESPONSE TO MOTION TO DISMISS
a corporation d/b/a COGENT	:	FOR FAILURE TO PLEAD LANHAM
TECHNOLOGIES,	:	ACT CLAIM WITH PARTICULARITY
Defendant.		

I. Introduction

Plaintiff, Celsis, Incorporated ("Plaintiff") brought this action for false advertising, deceptive trade practices, unfair competition, and related claims based on Defendant's dissemination of promotional materials containing false and misleading comparative statements. Defendant has moved to dismiss Plaintiff's false advertising claim under the Lanham Act, 15 U.S.C. § 1125(a) (1)(B), for failing to plead that claim with particularity under Rule 9(b) of the Federal Rules of Civil Procedure ("Rule 9(b)"). As discussed below, this Court must deny Defendant's Motion because Rule 9(b) does not apply to Lanham Act claims. Moreover, even if Rule 9(b) did apply, Plaintiff's complaint satisfies the standard.

II. Analysis

A. Lanham Act Claims Are Not Subject To Fed. R. Civ. P. 9(b)

Defendant's Motion to Dismiss is premised on the proposition that Lanham Act claims must be pleaded with particularity under Rule 9(b). *See* Defendant's Memorandum in Support of Motion to Dismiss For Failure to Plead Lanham Act Claim With Particularity ("Defendant's Memorandum") at p. 5. The plain language of Rule 9(b) has no such requirement, and Defendant's argument for extending Rule 9(b)'s application is not supported.

1. Logical Application of Supreme Court Precedent Precludes Application of Rule 9(b)

The Supreme Court has held that Rule 9(b) is limited to the two very specific instances expressly named in the Rule: claims of fraud and mistake. *See Leatherman v. Tarrant County Narcotics and Coord. Unit*, 507 U.S. 165, 168 (1993). While *Leatherman* concerned municipal liability under 42 U.S.C § 1983, the Court's rule is logically applicable to Lanham Act claims. The Court's rule was that those claims which that are not expressly included in the rule are excluded.

As the Supreme Court explained:

> Rule 9(b) does impose a particularity requirement in two specific instances. It provides that "[i]n all averments of fraud or mistake, the circumstances constituting fraud or mistake shall be stated with particularity." Thus, the Federal Rules do address in Rule 9(b) the question of the need for greater particularity in pleading certain actions, but do not include among the enumerated actions any reference to complaints alleging municipal liability under § 1983. *Expressio uniusest exclusio alterius*. [the expression of one thing is the exclusion of another]

The Court then explained that bringing claims other than fraud and mistake within Rule 9(b) is not within the purview of judicial decisions.

> Perhaps if Rules 8 and 9 were rewritten today, claims against municipalities under § 1983 might be subjected to the added specificity requirement of Rule 9(b). But that is a result which must be obtained by the process of amending the Federal Rules, and not by judicial interpretation.

Thus, since Plaintiff alleges a Lanham Act violation, not fraud, its pleading is not subject to Rule 9(b).

Significantly, in all of the Lanham Act decisions in which Leatherman has been applied, the courts have held that Rule 9(b) does not control.

For example, in *Stubbs Collections, Inc. v. Davis*, 2000 WL 381947 (N.D. Tex. Apr. 14, 2000), a Lanham Act case Defendant cites with approval, the court cited *Leatherman* as controlling. The court held that Lanham Act claims fall outside Rule 9(b) in that "Rule 9(b) requires particularity in pleading **only** for those actions specifically enumerated by the rule—fraud or mistake." *Id.* citing *Leatherman, supra* (emphasis in original). The *Stubbs* court explained that Lanham Act claims are not fraud claims:

> A claim of fraud requires not only the making of a false statement but also the intent to defraud the victim . . . Again the [Lanham Act] does not require intent to deceive as a necessary element of a Section 1125(a) violation. Therefore,

> Plaintiff's federal Lanham Act claims do not allege claims of fraud and are not
> subject to Rule 9(b)'s particularity in pleading requirements.

Stubbs, 2000 WL 381947, *5.

The court in *John P. Villano Inc. v. CBS, Inc.*, 176 F.R.D. 130 (S.D.N.Y. 1997),
another Lanham Act case that followed *Leatherman* and refused to apply Rule
9(b), echoed the same logic. There the court stated:

> . . . the particularity requirement of Rule 9(b) is limited to averments of "fraud or
> mistake.". . . No matter how parsed, a claim of false advertising under the
> Lanham Act—one of a panoply of trademark torts created by the Act—is not
> identical to a claim of fraud. Fraud requires, not just the making of a statement
> known to be false, but also, inter alia, a specific intent to harm the victim and
> defraud him of his money or property (citations omitted) . . . Consequently, a
> claim of false advertising under § 1125 . . . falls outside the ambit of Rule 9(b) and
> may not be the subject of any heightened pleading requirement. *Leatherman v.
> Tarrant County Narcotics and Coord. Unit*, 507 U.S. 165, 168 (1993).

In addition, while the Sixth Circuit has not addressed Rule 9(b) in the
Lanham Act context, no court in the Sixth Circuit has ever held that rule 9(b)
applies to Lanham Act claims. *See Riser v. WSYX-TV ABC-6*, 2002 U.S. Dist.
LEXIS 23654 (S.D. Ohio July 17, 2002) (attached as Exhibit A) (applying Rule
8 standard); *see also Sara Lee Corp. v. ConAgra, Inc.*, 1993 U.S. Dist. LEXIS
18881 (W.D. Mich. Nov. 18, 1992) (attached hereto as Exhibit B*); Syncor
Intern. Corp. vs. Newbaker*, 12 F. Supp. 2d 781, 783–84 (W.D. Tenn. 1998)
(applying Rule 8(a) to test sufficiency of pleading for Lanham Act claim);
Finnsugar Bioproducts, Inc. v. Monitor Sugar Co., 2002 U.S. Dist. LEXIS 25014
at *37–38 (E.D. Mich. June 11, 2002) (attached hereto as Exhibit C) adopted by
Finnsugar Bioproducts, Inc. v. Monitor Sugar Co., 2002 U.S. Dist. LEXIS 23565
(E.D. Mich. Sep. 30, 2002) (applying Rule 8 pleading standard to Lanham
Act claim); *WHS Entm't Ventures v. United Paperworkers Int'l Union*, 997 F.
Supp. 946 (M.D. Tenn. 1998*); Hobart Mfg. Co. v. Mullins Mfg. Corp.*, 8 F.R.D.
329 (N.D. Ohio 1947) (finding that plaintiff's Lanham Act claim satisfied Rule
8 and denying defendant's motion for more definite statement*); IA, Inc. vs.
Thermacell Tech. Inc.* 983 F. Supp. 697 (E.D. Mich. 1997).

2. The Cases Defendant Cites All Held That Rule 9(b) Does Not Apply, Avoided the Issue or Missed Leatherman

Defendant cites many cases on this issue but all of the cases (a) held that
Rule 9(b) does not apply to Lanham Act cases, b) avoided deciding the issue,
or c) missed the Supreme Court's decision in *Leatherman*.

Three of Defendant's cases directly support Plaintiff's position. As noted above,
Stubbs Collections, Inc. v. Davis, 2000 WL 381947 (N.D. Tex. Apr. 14, 2000)

held that Rule 9(b) does not apply to Lanham Act cases. The court in *Century 21 Real Estate Corp. v. Re/Max South County*, 882 F. Supp. 915 (C.D. Cal. 1994) expressly declined to apply Rule 9(b), stating that "a Lanham Act claim is not subject to the strict pleading requirement of Rule 9 fraud claims . . ." *Id.* at 927.[30] Finally, the court in *Max Daetwyler Corp. v. Input Graphics, Inc.*, 608 F. Supp. 1549, 1556 (E.D. Pa. 1985), noted that the Lanham Act claim before it, as opposed to a pure fraud claim, did not need to satisfy Rule 9's pleading requirements.

In two other cases Defendant cites the court expressly avoided deciding the issue, merely finding that the plaintiffs' complaints were sufficient even if Rule 9(b) applied.[31] In one of these cases, *Nutrition & Fitness, Inc. v. Mark Nutritionals, Inc.*, 202 F. Supp. 2d 431, 434 (M.D.N.C. 2002), the court correctly noted that no appellate court has ever ruled that Lanham Act claims are subject to the heightened pleading requirements under Rule 9(b) or otherwise. *Id.*

Yet another case on which Defendant relies, *Ellis v. Provident Life & Accident Insurance Co.*, 3 F. Supp. 2d 399 (S.D.N.Y. 1998), is inapposite because it involved a New York state negligent misrepresentation claim, not a federal Lanham Act claim. *Ellis*, 3 F. Supp. 2d at 411.

Textile Deliveries, Inc. v. Stagno, 1990 WL 155709 (S.D.N.Y. Oct. 9, 1990), in which the court applied Rule 9(b) to a Lanham Act case, was decided before the Supreme Court's decision in *Leatherman*. Moreover, the two subsequent decisions on this point in the Southern District of New York declined to apply Rule 9(b). As noted above, the court in *John P. Villano Inc. v. CBS, Inc.*, 176 F.R.D. 130 (S.D.N.Y. 1997), expressly applied *Leatherman* in doing so. *See also Bio-Technology Gen. Corp. v. Genentech, Inc.*, 886 F. Supp. 377, 383 (S.D. N.Y. 1995) ("Defendant . . . urges that this court apply the strictures of Rule 9(b) to Lanham Act claims, however, the Second Circuit has not held that this court need do so . . .").

The court in *Sanderson v. Brugman*, 2001 WL 699876 (S.D. Ind. May 29, 2001), the only other case which applied Rule 9(b) to a Lanham Act claim, did not mention the Supreme Court's *Leatherman* decision. In fact, it did not cite to one other case in which a court has held that Rule 9(b) applies to Lanham Act claims.

---

30. Defendant's quotation from *Century 21* in footnote 3 of its Memorandum is misleading because it suggests that the court there required something more than placing the defendant on notice of claims against it. In fact, the court in *Century 21* dismissed the plaintiff's particular Lanham Act claim because the claim was not raised in its amended complaint at all and, therefore, the defendant had not been put on notice of it. *Century 21*, 882 F. Supp. at 927. Defendant has made no such claim here.

31. These cases are *Federal Express Corp. v. U.S. Postal Service*, 40 F. Supp. 2d 943, 950 (W.D. Tenn. 1999), and *Nutrition & Fitness, Inc. v. Mark Nutritionals, Inc.*, 202 F. Supp. 2d 431, 434 (M.D.N.C. 2002).

Clearly, application of Rule 9(b) to Plaintiff's Lanham Act claim would, by judicial interpretation, extend Rule 9(b) to a claim not enumerated in the Rule and directly contradict *Leatherman*. It would also violate the logic of the Lanham Act cases interpreting Rule 9(b), and it would alter Sixth Circuit practice. Defendant can cite to no persuasive precedent for taking such an unprecedented step. Accordingly, this Court should follow the directive and logic of *Leatherman* and the post-*Leatherman* decisions that expressly apply it to Lanham Act cases, and Defendant's Motion should be denied.

B. Plaintiff's Complaint Satisfies Rule 9(b)

Plaintiff's complaint provides Defendant with fair notice of Plaintiff's claims by (1) attaching tables from Defendant's false promotional materials; (2) specifying false statements in the tables; and (3) pleading, on information and belief, additional facts, such as the falsity of the statements and dissemination of the materials. Thus, Plaintiff's Lanham Act claim passes muster, even if Rule 9(b) is applied.

1. Under Rule 9(b) Plaintiff Need Only Provide Defendant With Fair Notice of the Substance of Plaintiff's Claims

The Sixth Circuit has stated that the purpose of Rule 9(b)'s particularity requirement is "to provide a defendant fair notice of the substance of plaintiff's claim in order that the defendant may prepare a responsive pleading." *Michaels Bldg. Co. v. Ameritrust Co., N.A.*, 848 F.2d 674, 679 (6th Cir. 1988). The appellate court has further held that, in ruling on Rule 9(b) motions to dismiss, courts must factor in Fed. R. Civ. P. 8's requirement of a short and plain statement of the claim and simple, concise, and direct allegations. *Michaels*, 848 F.2d at 679. Finally, the court has held that Rule 9 (b) must be construed liberally. *Id*.

2. Plaintiff Has Provided Defendant With Fair Notice

Defendant complains that Plaintiff has not alleged the "who, when, where and to whom" parameters of Defendant's false promotional materials and that Defendant has improperly plead facts on information and belief. Def. Mem. 6–10. However, under the relevant case law Defendant approves, Plaintiff has properly alleged these parameters and its pleading on information and belief is appropriate. *Federal Express Corp. v. U.S. Postal Serv.* 40 F. Supp. 2d 943, 950 (W.D. Tenn. 1999); *In Re Sirrom Capital Corp.*, 84 F. Supp. 2d 933, 939 (M.D. Tenn. 1999).

Defendant cites *Federal Express Corp. v. U.S. Postal Service*, 40 F. Supp. 2d 943, 950 (W.D. Tenn. 1999), with approval. In *Federal Express*, a Lanham Act case in which the plaintiff's pleading was closely analogous to Plaintiff's pleading here, the court held that the complaint was sufficient, even if Rule 9(b) were applied.[32] There, as here, the plaintiff alleged false advertising or promotion. There, as here, the plaintiff supported its allegation by pointing to defendant's materials and enumerating the statements in the materials that were false. Specifically here, Plaintiff has attached the relevant tables from Defendant's false promotional materials to its Complaint and, over ten paragraphs, has specified the false statements and implications in those tables. Compl. ¶¶ 14–22.

The *Federal Express* court held that such pleading satisfied Rule 9(b) because they provide the defendant sufficient notice to prepare responsive pleadings. *Federal Express*, 40 F. Supp. 2d at 951. By pointing to the false materials in the complaint and enumerating the false statements in those materials, the plaintiff in *Federal Express* and Plaintiff here identified the misleading statements and how they were misleading. Moreover, the attachment of a portion of Defendant's false promotional materials provides Defendant with adequate notice of the who, where, and when of the false statements. As the *Federal Express* court held, these allegations are sufficient to identify (a) the defendant as the source of the statements—the *"who"* communicated the misleading [materials] component; b) identify the place of the statements as the advertisement at issue—the *"where"* component; and c) provide the dates of the false statements—the *"when"* component. *See id.* at 951–52. Here, plaintiff has also pleaded the "to whom" component (Compl. ¶ 14).

None of the other cases Defendant cites for Plaintiff's alleged Rule 9 pleading obligations was a Lanham Act case; they are all fraud cases. Accordingly, none of the other cases Defendant cites is relevant.

Defendant's other complaint, that Plaintiff has pled some of the above facts on information and belief, merely seeks to profit from the fact that much of the evidence is in Def's. Mem. For example, Defendant faults Plaintiff for pleading the inaccuracy of the promotional materials on information and belief. Def's. Mem. 7. However, Defendant fails to mention that Plaintiff does not have a complete copy of the promotional materials; it only has the tables from the materials.[33] Since the tables provide evidence of falsity but do not constitute the complete materials, Plaintiff responsibly pled falsity on information and belief. Defendant's complaint that plaintiff alleged the recipients of the materials on information and belief is similarly a simply opportunistic argument. Def's. Mem. 8. Defendant, not Plaintiff, has all the

---

32. As noted above, the court did not decide whether Rule 9(b) applies to Lanham Act claims. Rather, it held that even if it did the plaintiff's pleading was adequate.
33. Defendant provided Plaintiff with a copy of the materials in prelitigation settlement discussions but only on the grounds that they were not used for any purpose other than such discussions.

facts relating to whom Defendant distributed its promotional materials. Since Plaintiff has clearly pled the materials, Defendant can easily inform itself of these facts. And, clearly Defendant has done this, since it admits at least one customer to whom it distributed the promotional materials. (Def's. Mem. n.1).[34]

Moreover, as Defendant acknowledges, where, as here, the information pled is exclusively in the possession of the defendant, pleading on information and belief satisfies Rule 9(b). *See Michaels*, 848 F.2d at 680; *Picard Chemical Inc. v. Perrigo Co.*, 940 F. Supp. 1101, 1114 (W.D. Mich. 1996); *In Re Sirrom Capital Corp.*, 84 F. Supp. 2d 933, 939 (M.D. Tenn. 1999) (internal citation omitted) ("[A]n exception to this rule exists for matters that are peculiarly within the knowledge of the opposing party.").

Defendant essentially asks this Court to dismiss Plaintiff's Complaint because Plaintiff has been unable to obtain the complete promotional materials and information regarding their distribution—materials and information that only Defendant has in its possession. Defendant has not, however, complained that the allegations do not give it adequate notice of Plaintiff's claims. Therefore, Defendant's Motion must be denied.

III. Conclusion

For the foregoing reasons, Defendant's motion should be denied. In the alternative, if this Court finds that Plaintiff has failed to satisfy Rule 9(b), Plaintiff requests that it be allowed to amend its Complaint.[35]

---

34. Defendant's footnote No. 1 reveals its true motivation for its motion, i.e., that it cannot get discovery through Plaintiff's Complaint. Defendant admits that Plaintiff's failure to plead all of the "customers" who may have received the promotional materials "is at the heart of this motion."

35. Defendant has yet to file a responsive pleading in this matter and, therefore, Plaintiff has a right to amend its Complaint as a matter of course. Fed. R. Civ. P. 15(a).

Response to Motion to Dismiss Copyright Infringement Claim

Defendants in copyright infringement claims may attempt to dismiss a claim by arguing at the pleading stage that two works are so different that the claims should not even be heard by the court. Such motions often fail because of the fact-intensive nature of the substantial similarity requirement, and below is an example of a simple response to such a motion.

Response to Motion to Dismiss Copyright Infringement Claim

In the United States District Court
for the Northern District of Illinois
Eastern Division

FRANZ COLLECTION INC. a California Corporation; and Seagull Décor Co., Ltd. a Taiwan Corporation Plaintiffs, v. DALE TIFFANY, INC. a California Corporation Defendant.	))))))))))))))	Civil Action No. 04C 6342 Judge Castillo Magistrate Judge Keys

Response to Defendant's Motion to Dismiss

XXIII. Introduction

Defendant claims that Plaintiffs failed to state a cause of action. Plaintiffs alleged valid copyrights and that Defendant is infringing those copyrights. That is all that is required. Defendant's motion should therefore be denied.

I. Legal Standard

The purpose of a motion to dismiss is to test the sufficiency of the complaint, not to decide its merits. *See Gibson v. City of Chicago*, 910 F.2d 1510, 1520 (7th Cir. 1990). When considering a motion to dismiss, well-pleaded allegations in the complaint are accepted as true. *See Turner/Ozanne v. Hyman/Power*, 111 F.3d 1312, 1319 (7th Cir. 1997). Any ambiguities in the complaint are construed in favor of the plaintiff. *See Kelly v. Crosfield Catalysts*, 135 F.3d 1202, 1205 (7th Cir. 1998). A court should dismiss a claim only if "it is clear that no relief could be granted under any set of facts that could be proved consistent with the allegations of the complaint." *Cook v. Winfrey*, 141 F.3d 322, 327 (7th Cir. 1998). Only notice pleading is required: "Rule 8(a) . . . requires that a claim for relief need contain, in addition to a statement concerning jurisdiction and a demand for judgment, only a short and plain statement of the claim showing that the pleader is entitled to relief." *Id*. Thus, "[a] Rule 12(b)(6) motion cannot be used to dismiss a complaint on the ground that it does not include information that Rule 8 does not require it to contain." *Id*. at 328. Plaintiffs are free, in defending against Defendant's motion, "to allege without evidentiary support any fact [they] please[] that are consistent with the complaint in order to show that there is a state of facts within the scope of the complaint that if proved . . . would entitle [them] to judgment." *Wallace Computer Servs. Inc. v. Adams Bus. Forms, Inc.*, 837 F. Supp. 1413, 1416 (N.D. Ill. 1993) (internal citation omitted).

II. Argument

A. Plaintiffs' Complaint Meets the Notice Pleading Requirements of the Federal Rules

Plaintiffs complaint states a cause of action for copyright infringement. Plaintiffs allege valid copyright registrations. *See* Compl. ¶ ¶ 7–9. Plaintiffs allege that Defendant is infringing three of Plaintiffs' copyrighted designs. *See* Compl. ¶ ¶ 17–20; 27. This is all that is required. *See* Fed. R. Civ. Pro. 8(a). *See also* Fed. R. Civ. P. Form 17. Nevertheless, Plaintiffs plead additional facts, not required by the Federal Rules, including access and similarity (Compl. ¶ ¶ 18–20; 22–24). Thus, Plaintiffs state a claim for copyright infringement, and Defendant's motion should be denied. *See generally Store Décor Divison of Jas Int'l, Inc. v. Stylex Worldwide Indus. Ltd.*, 767 F. Supp. 181 (N.D. Ill. 1991) (denying defendant's motion to dismiss plaintiff's copyright infringement claim and denying defendant's motion to transfer venue).

B. Defendant Does Not Establish That, as a Matter of Law, it Must Prevail

To prevail on its motion to dismiss, Defendant must establish that no reasonable jury could find substantial similarity. *See, e.g., S.C. Johnson & Son, Inc. v. Turtle Wax, Inc.*, No. 89 C 5792, 1989 WL 134802 (N.D. Ill. Oct. 17, 1989). Defendant does not meet this high burden. Defendant's Designs are substantially similar to Plaintiffs' Copyrighted Designs. Defendant's primary argument is that a side-by-side comparison of the Infringing Designs and Plaintiffs' Copyrighted Designs requires this Court to conclude that no jury could find substantial similarity. *See* Defendant's Memorandum of Law In Support Of Its Motion To Dismiss Or, Alternatively, To Transfer Venue ("Defendant's Memo"), at 7–12.

Defendant argues, at great length, that these designs are not substantially similar. *See* Def's Mem. at 8–12. Specifically, Defendant points to several alleged minor differences. *See id.* at 10–12. As noted in Plaintiffs' September 30 Memorandum of Law, such minor differences are inapposite. *See Wildlife Express Corp. v. Carol Wright Sales, Inc., Inc.*, 18 F.3d 502, 510–11 (7th Cir. 1994) (holding that slight differences were of minor importance in such an evaluation and did not preclude a finding of infringement). *See also Novelty Textile Mills, Inc. v. Joan Fabrics Corp.*, 558 F.2d 1090, 1094 n.6 (2d Cir. 1977) (noting that mere changes in color scheme of a copied design does not usually protect a defendant from the charge of infringement).

Here, the similarities are clear. The sculpted designs, the positioning and appearances of the frogs and lotus leaves, the positioning and layout of the lilies, and the color scheme and arrangement of the wisteria are all examples of such similarities. Quite simply, when evaluating their overall look and feel, Defendant's Infringing Designs capture the total concept and feel of Plaintiffs' Copyrighted Designs.

Moreover, while the side-by-side comparisons are helpful, Defendant is asking the Court to decide the designs are not substantially similar as a matter of law without having seen the works in question. Defendant claims that the deposit copy differs from the picture in the complaint (reproduced above). *See* Def's Mem. at 11–12. This is false. The two pictures are of the same design, merely from different angles. Defendant's confusion establishes that relying solely on pictures of three-dimensional sculpted works is problematic. *Cf. Stillman v. Leo Burnett Co., Inc.*, 720 F. Supp. 1353, 1355 n.1 (N.D. Ill. 1989) (holding that a court cannot reject a copyright infringement claim at the pleading stage unless the parties have provided the court with the works in question).

1. Plaintiffs' Additional Allegations Support a Finding of Copyright Infringement

Plaintiffs allege that Defendant had access to the Plaintiffs' Copyrighted Designs. *See* Compl. ¶¶ 22–23. Defendant concedes this. *See* Defendant's Response to Plaintiffs' Motion for Preliminary Injunction, at 2. In addition, Plaintiffs allege that Defendant's conduct was intentional and willful. *See* Compl. ¶ 28. In cases of intentional infringement, courts routinely view the types of differences described by Defendant (Def's Mem. 10–12) as an attempt to disguise misconduct. *See Atari, Inc. v. North Am. Philips Consumer Elec. Corp.*, 672 F.2d 607, 620–21 (7th Cir. 1982), *superseded by statute on other grounds.* Moreover, customers at a recent tradeshow thought Dale Tiffany's designs were from the Plaintiffs. *See* Compl. ¶ 24. This confusion is strong evidence of copyright infringement. *See Atari*, 672 F.2d at 619 (holding that evidence of consumer confusion suggested plaintiffs were likely to prevail on the copyright infringement claim). All of these facts, when taken as true, lead to the inescapable conclusion that a reasonable finder of fact *could* find for Plaintiffs. Defendant's motion should therefore be denied.

2. Defendant's Remaining Arguments are Inapposite at this Stage

Defendant makes several additional arguments as to why Plaintiff cannot ultimately prevail. Defendant argues that Plaintiffs' claims must fail because the only similarity is the subject matter (Def's Mem. 8), Plaintiffs' expressions can only be expressed in a limited number of ways (Def's Mem. 9), and the only similarities involve nonprotectable elements of Plaintiffs' Designs (Def's Mem. 10). This is not the place to address such arguments. As the Seventh Circuit has held, the purpose of a 12(b)(6) motion is not to decide the merits of a case. *See Gibson v. City of Chicago*, 910 F.2d 1510, 1520 (7th Cir. 1990).

Moreover, all of these arguments were considered and rejected in *Wallace Computer Services, Inc. v. Adams Business Forms, Inc.*, 837 F. Supp. 1413 (N.D. Ill. 1993). In *Wallace*, the plaintiff brought suit alleging that defendant had copied the cover of its telephone message book by using the pose of a hand with a pen positioned over the message book. Defendant's filed a motion to dismiss, arguing that plaintiff's claim must fail because the only similarity was the subject matter plaintiff's expression could only be expressed in a limited number of ways and the only similarities involve nonprotectable elements (*Id.* at 1417–19). The court rejected all three arguments in denying the motion to dismiss, concluding that "the plaintiff has a plausible claim that it owns a protectible expression in the overall layout [] and that the defendant copied some of plaintiff's protectible expression." *Id.* at 1419. Here, as in *Wallace*, Defendant's arguments should be rejected. *See also S.C. Johnson & Son, Inc. v. Turtle Wax, Inc.*, No. 89 C 5792, 1989 WL 134802 (N.D. Ill. Oct. 17, 1989) (rejecting defendant's argument that the plaintiff's copyright infringement claim failed as a matter of law).

IV. Conclusion

Plaintiffs own valid copyrights in their Franz Collection. Defendant had access to this collection and copied it. A reasonable jury could conclude that Defendant's Infringing Designs are substantially similar to Plaintiffs' Copyrighted Designs. Thus, Defendant's Motion to Dismiss should be denied.

Respectfully submitted,

CHAPTER

7

Written Discovery

Much civil litigation over trademark and copyright infringement involves written discovery. The principal tools—interrogatories, requests for document production, and requests for admissions—are addressed in this chapter, and discovery by deposition, covered in Chapter 8. Each type of written discovery request serves a different purpose and counsel should be familiar with the rules governing each.

Interrogatories, governed by Federal Rule 33, can serve to elicit responses to specific questions, but because the other side's lawyers often are involved in preparing the responses, unlike asking a question at a deposition, they are best used for identifying potential deponents or obtaining short admissible answers to general questions. The Southern District of New York, for example, allows interrogatories only as to certain topics until near the close of discovery. The Federal Rules limit a party to propounding 25 interrogatories, including sub-parts.

Requests for production, governed by Federal Rule 34, are the bread and butter of written discovery in litigation because documents serve as the basis for most proof in a case. Such requests also can seek examples of a product or prior versions of a work. They also can include inspection of a physical location, though this often is not necessary in trademark and copyright matters.

Requests for admission, governed by Federal Rule 36, have the same flaw as interrogatories – the other side's counsel will review and craft the answers. Nevertheless, using requests to admit to authenticate documents or establish relatively uncontroversial facts can reduce the overall cost of trial. It often is useful to include documents as attachments if they are to be authenticated. Additionally, failure to properly responds to requests to admit can lead to sanctions or the requests being admitted.

Plaintiff's Interrogatories
(TRADEMARK INFRINGEMENT and DILUTION)

The following interrogatories represent the basic questions asked to support a typical trademark infringement and dilution claim. They can be used in federal litigation or in a proceeding before the TTAB.

Plaintiff's First Set of Interrogatories

Pursuant to Fed. R. Civ. P. 33, Plaintiff requests that Defendant answer the interrogatories below, subject to the following definitions and instructions.

Definitions and Instructions

A. "Plaintiff" means ABC Corporation, its predecessors, successors and related entities, and their officers, directors, employees, agents and representatives.

B. "Defendant" means XYZ, Inc., its predecessors, successors and related entities, and their officers, directors, employees, agents and representatives.

C. As used herein, the phrase "Contested Mark" means Defendant's _____ trademark, including any variations thereof.

D. As used herein, the phrase "Plaintiff's Mark" means Plaintiff's _____ trademark identified in paragraph ____ of the Complaint.

E. As used herein, the term "document" includes but is not limited to all electronically stored information, writings, correspondence, books, memoranda, e-mails, computer print-outs, Internet web pages, invoices, contracts, purchase orders, receipts, pamphlets, publications, catalogs, labels, packaging, displays, advertisements, promotional materials, photographs, slides, videotapes, films, artwork, drawing, sketches, illustrative materials, circulars, price lists, layouts, tear sheets, magnetic recording tapes, microfilms, and other storage means by which information is retained in retrievable form, and other material, whether printed, typewritten, handwritten, recorded or reproduced by any mechanical or electronic process, including but not limited to information stored on a computer hard drive.

F. Whenever an interrogatory inquires about documents, please furnish either a copy of, or the following information about, each document:

1. the date of the document;
2. a general description of the document;
3. a general description of the subject matter to which it pertains;

    4. the names and addresses of all persons receiving or shown the documents or copies thereof;

    5. the names and addresses of the persons in whose custody, possession or control the documents are presently maintained; and

    6. if a privilege is claimed as to a document, identify each such document and state the nature of the privilege claimed.

G. If a privilege is relied upon in declining to provide any information or document in response to an interrogatory or a part thereof, identify the nature of the privilege and

    1. For documents, provide the following: (a) the basis for the privilege; (b) the date of the document; (c) the originator of the document, to whom it is addressed, and all persons who were sent or shown copies; and (d) a general description of the type of document and the subject matter to which it pertains; and

    2. For oral communications, provide the following: (a) the basis of the privilege; (b) the date and place of communication; (c) the name of the person making the communication and the names of persons present while the communication was made and, where not apparent, the relationship of the persons present to the person making the communication; and (d) the general subject matter of the communication.

H. As used herein, the term "person" includes any corporation, division, agency or other entity, as well as an individual.

I. Whenever an interrogatory inquires about the identity of a person and that person is an individual, the information requested includes:

    1. The person's full name;

    2. The person's employer;

    3. The person's position or title; and

    4. In the case of persons not employed by Defendant, the person's last known address and telephone number.

J. Whenever an interrogatory inquires about the name or identity of a person and the person is a corporation, division, agency, association or other entity, the information requested includes its full name and current address.

K. As used herein "and" as well as "or" shall be construed disjunctively or conjunctively as necessary to bring within the scope of the interrogatory all responses which might otherwise be construed to be outside its scope.

L. As used herein, "relate to," "related to" and "relating to" shall mean comprising, directly or indirectly mentioning or describing, pertaining or referring to, being connected with, reflecting upon or resulting from the stated subject matter.

M. The singular shall include the plural and the present tense shall include the past tense and vice versa in order to bring within the scope of the interrogatory all responses which might otherwise be construed to be outside its scope.

Interrogatories

1. Identify each good and/or service with which Defendant has used, uses, or plans to use the Contested Mark, and state the date on which each such good and/or service was first offered for sale or is planned to be offered for sale.

2. Identify the person(s) most knowledgeable about Defendant's conception, consideration, design, development, creation, selection, adoption, use, or plans to use the Contested Mark, and state each such person's role and responsibility and the period of time during which each such person had such involvement.

3. Identify the persons most knowledgeable concerning Defendant's promotion and advertising or planned promotion and advertising of goods and/or services in connection with the Contested Mark.

4. Identify the persons most knowledgeable concerning Defendant's use or plans to use the Contested Mark.

5. Identify the persons primarily responsible for the preparation or approval of advertisements or promotions for goods and/or services marketed or that Defendant plans to market in connection with the Contested Mark.

6. State Defendant's annual dollar and unit volume of sales and/or anticipated annual dollar and unit volume of sales in the United States for each good and/or service sold in connection with the Contested Mark.

7. Describe the channels of trade through which each good and/or service marketed in connection with Contested Mark has been, is or will be sold.

8. Identify the types of outlets and representative specific outlets in the United States through which each good and/or service marketed in connection with the Contested Mark has been, is or will be offered or sold.

9. Identify all media in which each good and/or service marketed in connection with the Contested Mark has been, is or will be advertised or promoted, including specific publications, websites, materials and means of communication, and state the period of time each medium has been or will be used.

10. State Defendant's annual marketing expenses or anticipated marketing expenses for each type of advertising or promotion Defendant has used or plans to use for goods and/or services marketed in connection with the Contested Mark.

11. Identify each use, former use, planned use or claim of use by Defendant or any third party of any name or mark consisting in whole or in part of [overlapping portions of marks], and the persons who have knowledge of such use, former use, planned use or claim of use.

12. Identify each formal or informal investigation, research endeavor, search, survey, test, poll, or study of any kind, including but not limited to trademark searches, trademark surveys, focus groups and name selection research, that Defendant has conducted, caused to be conducted, or has knowledge of, relating to any name or mark consisting in whole or in part of [overlapping portions of marks] or Plaintiff's, Defendant's or any third party's use of such a name or mark, and each person having knowledge relating thereto.

13. Identify any rights that Defendant has granted (e.g., through a license, assignment, security interest, or any other means of transfer) to any third party or acquired from any third party in any name or mark comprised in whole or in part of [overlapping portions of marks] and the persons most knowledgeable concerning each such grant or acquisition.

14. Describe separately each of Defendant's federal, state, or domain name registrations of, applications to register, or any attempt to register any mark comprised in whole or in part of [overlapping portions of marks] and identify the persons most knowledgeable about each such registration, application, or attempted registration.

15. Describe separately any formal or informal objections made by or directed against Defendant that relate to Defendant's use or planned use of, or claimed rights in, any name or mark consisting in whole or in part of [overlapping portions of marks] and identify the persons most knowledgeable about each objection.

16. Identify each instance of confusion, mistake or association of any kind between Plaintiff or its use of Plaintiff's Mark, and Defendant or its use of the Contested Mark, and identify each person with knowledge of each such instance.

17. Describe how Defendant first became aware of Plaintiff's use of Plaintiff's Marks and identify each person with knowledge relating thereto.

18. If Defendant intends to rely upon the opinion of an expert in connection with the defense of this proceeding, provide the information set forth in Rules 26(a)(2)(A) and (B) of the Federal Rules of Civil Procedure for each expert.

19. Identify each person who provided information or documents for, or otherwise assisted in the preparation of, the answers to the above interrogatories or the responses to Plaintiff's First Request For Production Of Documents.

Plaintiff's Interrogatories
(FALSE ADVERTISING)

The following interrogatories are taken from a lawsuit involving allegedly misleading claims made in an advertisement comparing competitive products. They seek substantiation for the claims, which were based upon scientific studies.

PLAINTIFF, INCORPORATED,	:	PLAINTIFF'S FIRST
Plaintiff,	:	SET OF
vs.	:	INTERROGATORIES
DEFENDANT, INCORPORATED,	:	
Defendant.	:	

In accordance with Rule 33 of the Federal Rules of Civil Procedure, plaintiff, Plaintiff, Incorporated ("Plaintiff"), requests that defendant, Defendant, Incorporated ("Defendant"), answer under oath the interrogatories set forth below, subject to the following definitions and instructions:

Definitions and Instructions

A. As used herein, the term "Plaintiff" includes Plaintiff, Incorporated, its predecessors in interest, affiliates, subsidiaries and related organizations, and the officers, directors, employees, agents and representatives thereof.

B. As used herein, the term "Defendant" includes Defendant, Incorporated, its predecessors in interest, affiliates, subsidiaries and related organizations, and the officers, directors, employees, agents and representatives thereof, and without limitation Cogent Technologies.

C. As used herein, the term "Reagent" means any biochemical reagent that is used in the detection of microbial contamination in food or beverage products.

D. As used herein, the term "Comparative Advertisement" means Defendant's February 2001 promotional piece comparing Defendant and Plaintiff Reagents, including but not limited to exhibits, addenda, protocols, methodology and documents that comprise, in whole or in part, such materials.

E. As used herein, the terms "Market" and "Marketing" shall include any and all activities that may be undertaken to foster sales of a product or service, including but not limited to, advertising, promotion and sales activities.

F. As used herein, the term "Test" means any and all reviews, studies, experiments or other forms of analysis.

G. As used herein, the term "document" is synonymous in meaning and equal in scope to the usage of this term in Fed. R. Civ. P. 34(a), including but not limited to all writings, correspondence, books, memoranda, e-mails, invoices, contracts, purchase orders, receipts, pamphlets, publications, studies, catalogues, labels, packaging, displays, photographs, slides, videotapes, films, artwork, drawings, sketches, illustrative materials, circulars, price lists, advertisements, layouts, tear sheets, magnetic recording tapes, microfilm, computer records or data, electronically stored information, web pages, and other storage means by which information is retained in retrievable form, and other material, whether printed, typewritten, handwritten, recorded, transmitted or reproduced by any mechanical or electronic process, including but not limited to information stored on a computer hard drive or server.

H. Whenever an interrogatory inquires about documents, please furnish the following information as to each:
1. The date of the document;
2. A general description of the document;
3. A general description of the subject matter to which it pertains;
4. The names and addresses of the addressor, addressee, and all persons receiving or shown the document or copies thereof;
5. The names and addresses of the persons in whose custody, possession or control the document is presently maintained;
6. If a privilege is claimed as to a document, identify each such document and state the nature of the privilege claimed, the nature of the document, its date and, if it is a communication, the name of the sender and all recipients.

I. As used herein, the term "person" includes any corporation, division, agency, or other entity, as well as an individual.

J. Whenever an interrogatory inquires about the name or identity of a person and that person is an individual, the information requested includes:
1. The person's full name;
2. The person's employer;
3. The person's position or title;
4. The person's last known address.

K. Whenever an interrogatory inquires about the name or identity of a person and the person is a corporation, division, agency, or other entity, the information requested includes the full name and current address of said corporation, division, agency, or other entity.

L. As used herein, "and" as well as "or" shall be construed disjunctively or conjunctively as necessary in order to bring within the scope of the interrogatory all responses which might otherwise be construed to be outside its scope.

M. As used herein, the singular shall always include the plural, and the present tense shall always include the past tense, and vice versa.

N. Whenever an interrogatory herein calls for information or materials over the course of time, it shall be construed to ask for information and materials only from January 1, 1999, to the present.

O. Whenever an interrogatory herein calls for information or materials, it shall be construed to ask for information and materials related to activities in the United States.

Interrogatories

II.   Identify each person who has information relating to Defendant's creation, use and distribution of the Comparative Advertisement, and describe the general areas of responsibility of each such person.

III.   Identify each person who is responsible for and knowledgeable about Defendant's Marketing of its Reagents and Reagent based products or services in the United States, and describe the general areas of responsibility of each such person.

IV.   Identify each person who has information relating to each Test described or mentioned in the Comparative Advertisement, including each person who participated in decisions concerning, or preparations or acquisitions for, or who conducted, analyzed, or reported the results of, such Tests.

V.   Identify each method and medium, including but not limited to advertising, publication of studies in journals, marketing pieces, presentations, reports, and sales calls, that Defendant has used to Market the Reagent identified or described in the Comparative Advertisement.

VI.   Identify each method and medium, including but not limited to advertising, publication of studies in journals, marketing pieces, presentations, reports, and sales calls, that Defendant has used to Market its Reagents and Reagent based products or services in the United States.

VII.   Identify each person who has information relating to any Tests that have been identified, described, or in any manner referred to, in any medium or used as part of any method, other than the Comparative Advertisement, to Market Defendant's Reagents and Reagent based products or services in the United States, including each person who participated in decisions concerning, or preparations or acquisitions for, or who conducted, analyzed, or reported the results of, such Tests.

VIII. Identify the date of, each person involved in, and each person who has knowledge of, any meeting or communication among any employees of Defendant, between any such person and a third party or between any third parties that related or referred to the Comparative Advertisement, the Tests described or mentioned in the Comparative Advertisement or the distribution of the Comparative Advertisement and/or such Tests.

IX. State Defendant's monthly dollar and unit volumes of sales of, and monthly unit distribution volume for, the Reagent identified or described in the Comparative Advertisement in the United States.

X. Describe the protocols and methodology for, the Reagents and volumes of Reagent used in, the timing sequences of, and the date and location of the acts that comprised, the Tests described or mentioned in the Comparative Advertisement, including but not limited to "control" and "duplicate" Tests.

XI. Identify the equipment and materials used or otherwise involved in the Tests described or mentioned in the Comparative Advertisement, including but not limited to: a) the reagent kit, including part number, serial/lot number, catalog number, kit number, expiration date of Reagents and source; and b) the instruments, including serial number and calibration factors, and the protocols.

XII. Identify each entity and individual to whom the Comparative Advertisement has been distributed, shown, or made available, and each entity and individual who has knowledge of the Comparative Advertisement or the results and conclusions detailed in the Comparative Advertisement, and identify the dates on which the Comparative Advertisement or its results or conclusions were distributed, shown or made available to each entity and individual.

XIII. Identify each entity and individual to whom any materials used to Market Defendant's Reagents and Reagent based products or services in the United States have been distributed, shown, or made available.

XIV. If Defendant intends to rely upon the opinion of an expert in this action, provide the information that would be set forth under Fed. R. Civ. P. 26(a)(2)(A) and (B) for each expert.

Plaintiff's Interrogatories
(COPYRIGHT INFRINGEMENT)

Plaintiffs' First Set of Interrogatories to Defendant

In accordance with Rule 33 of the Federal Rules of Civil Procedure, plaintiffs request that defendant, within the time period prescribed by the Court, answer each of the interrogatories set forth below, subject to the following definitions:

Definitions

A. As used herein, the term "Plaintiffs" include plaintiffs, plaintiffs' affiliates, their predecessors in interest, their subsidiaries and related organizations, and the officers, directors, employees, agents and representatives thereof.

B. As used herein, the term "Defendant" includes defendant, its affiliates, its successors and/or predecessors in interest, subsidiaries and related organizations, and officers, directors, employees, agents and repre-sentatives.

C. As used herein, the term "Document" means the broadest definition of the term "Document" permissible under Fed.R.Civ.P. 34(a) and case law interpreting it, and includes but is not limited to all writings, correspondence, e-mails, books, memoranda, invoices, contracts, purchase orders, receipts, pamphlets, publications, catalogs, labels, packaging, displays, photographs, slides, videotapes, films, artwork, drawings, sketches, illustrative materials, circulars, price lists, layouts, tear sheets, magnetic recording tapes, microfilms, and other storage means by which information is retained in retrievable form, and other material, whether printed, typewritten, handwritten, recorded or reproduced by any mechanical or electronic process, including but not limited to information stored on a computer hard drive.

D. Whenever an interrogatory inquires about Documents, please furnish either a copy of, or the following information about, each Document:
   (1). the date of the Document;
   (2). a general description of the Document;
   (3). a general description of the subject matter to which it pertains;
   (4). the names and addresses of the address or, addressee, and all persons receiving or shown the Documents or copies thereof;
   (5). the names and addresses of the persons in whose custody, possession or control the Documents are presently maintained; and

(6). if a privilege is claimed as to a document, identify each such Document and state the nature of the privilege claimed.

E. As used herein, the term "Person" includes any corporation, division, agency or other entity, as well as any individual.

F. As used herein, "Plaintiffs' Designs" means the artworks described in Paragraphs 18 through 21 of the Complaint.

G. As used herein, "Plaintiffs' Collection" means the copyrighted collection described in Paragraphs 5 through 10 and 18 through 21 of the Complaint.

H. As used herein, "Defendant's Designs" refer to those allegedly infringing works described in Paragraphs 23 though 25 of the Complaint.

I. Whenever an interrogatory inquires about the name of a Person and the Person is an individual, the information requested includes:

(1). the Person's full name;

(2). the Person's employer;

(3). the Person's position or title; and

(4). the Person's last known address and telephone number.

J. Whenever an interrogatory inquires about the name or identity of a Person and the Person is a corporation, division, agency or other entity, the information requested includes the full name and current address of said corporation, division, agency or other entity.

K. As used herein, "and" as well as "or" shall be construed disjunctively or conjunctively as necessary in order to bring within the scope of the interrogatory all responses which might otherwise be construed to be outside its scope.

L. As used herein, "relate to, " "related to" and "relating to" shall mean comprising, directly or indirectly mentioning or describing, pertaining or referring to, being connected with, reflecting upon or resulting from the stated subject matter.

M. As used herein, the singular shall always include the plural and the present tense shall always include the past tense, and vice versa.

Interrogatories

1. Identify the person most knowledgeable about the design, manufacture, production, marketing or sale of Defendant's Designs, including the information each individual possesses.

2. Describe with specificity the design process for Defendant's Designs, including the timeline for the design and production of each piece, all sources of inspiration for each piece, the place of design and name of designer(s).

3. Identify with specificity the place of production or manufacture of Defendant's Designs and name of those responsible for production or manufacture.

4. Identify the number of orders and sales for each of Defendant's Designs, including how many of those orders have been filled, and if not yet filled, when Defendant intends to ship those pieces or fill those orders.
5. Identify the number of pieces of Defendant's Designs that have been manufactured and where those pieces, not already shipped, are being stored, and how many of each piece are being stored in each location.
6. Identify the name and location of each wholesaler, retailer, catalog company, direct mail account, or any other entity that currently has or at any time in the past had offered Defendant's Designs for sale.
7. Identify and briefly describe each account that has ordered Defendant's Designs and the volume of Defendant's Designs ordered.
8. Identify every instance of actual confusion, mistake or association, which has or may have occurred between Plaintiffs, Plaintiffs' Designs, or Plaintiffs' Collection and Defendant or Defendant's Designs, and identify each Person with knowledge of each such instance.
9. Identify all of Defendant's means of promoting, advertising, or marketing Defendant's Designs, including, but not limited to, sales representative showrooms, gift shows, catalogs, brochures, trade journals, trade shows, and trade publications, and the beginning and end date of each type of promotion.
10. From the date of Defendant's first sale of any of Defendant's Designs to the present, set forth the annual dollar and unit volumes of Defendant's sales of each piece and the state in which the sales took place.
11. Set forth separately for each year Defendant's annual gross revenue and net profits, from Defendant's Designs, including each specific category of expense deducted from gross revenue to arrive at net profits.
12. If Defendant intends to argue that Defendant's Designs are not infringing because they were independently developed, state the complete factual basis for this defense.
13. Identify each person who has furnished information or otherwise assisted in the preparation of an answer to one or more of these interrogatories and the answer or answers for which each such person provided such information or other assistance.

Defendant's Interrogatories
(TRADEMARK INFRINGEMENT)

Defendant's First Set of Interrogatories

[Definitions and Instructions Omitted]

Interrogatories

1. Identify each person having information regarding plaintiff's use and registration of the Mark.
2. Identify each person who has had primary responsibility for the promotion, advertising and sale of products plaintiff offers for sale under the Mark since 1985.
3. Describe the channels of trade through which the products plaintiff offers for sale under the Mark are sold or distributed to consumers.
4. Identify all products in connection with which plaintiff uses or plans to use the Mark.
5. State plaintiff's yearly dollar volume of sales for the last five years for each product plaintiff offers for sale under the Mark.
6. Identify each person or agency who has participated in the creation or distribution of advertisements or promotions for the products plaintiff offers for sale under the Mark and state the period of time during which each such person or agency has participated.
7. State plaintiff's yearly expenditures for the last five years with respect to the advertising and promotion of products plaintiff offers for sale under the Mark.
8. Identify each publication in which products plaintiff offers for sale under the Mark have been advertised.
9. Identify all assignments, licenses or other transfers of rights in the Mark granted by or to plaintiff.
10. Identify each person having information relating to any formal or informal trademark searches or investigations which relate to the Mark.
11. Identify each person having information relating to any market studies, surveys, focus groups or other studies which relate to the Mark or products plaintiff offers for sale under the Mark.
12. Identify each expert which plaintiff expects to call as a witness in this proceeding and state the subject matter on which each expert is expected to testify.
13. Identify and detail each instance of actual confusion between plaintiff or the products plaintiff offers for sale under the Mark and Defendant or the products defendant offers for sale under Defendant's Mark.

14. Identify and detail any formal or informal objections to plaintiff's use of the Mark.
15. Identify and detail any formal or informal objections by plaintiff to use by others of the Mark or any other name, mark or term which plaintiff believed to be confusingly similar to its Mark.
16. For each present or former third party use or registration of a name, mark or term comprised in whole or in part of the Mark or any variation thereof of which plaintiff is aware, identify (a) the third party, (b) the name, mark or term, (c) the products for which it was used and/or registered, and (d) the period of time during which it was or has been used and/or registered.
17. Identify each person who provided information or documents for responses to the above interrogatories or Defendant's First Request For Production of Documents.

FORM 7.5
Plaintiff's Request for Production of Documents
(TRADEMARK INFRINGEMENT and DILUTION)

Requests for documents generally are similar across trademark and unfair competition cases. Below is a typical example.

Plaintiff's First Set of Document Requests

Pursuant to Fed. R. Civ. P. 34 and 37 C.F.R. § 2.120, Plaintiff requests that Defendant make available for inspection and copying at a mutually convenient place, the documents described herein, subject to the following definitions and instructions:

Definitions and Instructions

N. "Plaintiff" means Plaintiff, its predecessors, successors and related entities, and their officers, directors, employees, agents and representatives.

O. "Defendant" means Defendant, its predecessors, successors and related entities, and their officers, directors, employees, agents and representatives.

P. As used herein, the phrase "Defendant's Mark" means defendant's trademark described in paragraph 20 of the Complaint.

Q. As used herein, the phrase "Plaintiff's Marks" means the trademarks identified in paragraph 7 of the Complaint.

[ADDITIONAL DEFINITIONS AND INSTRUCTIONS OMITTED]

Requests for Production

1. All documents identified in response to Plaintiff's First Set of Interrogatories.
2. All documents that relate or refer to Defendant's conception, consideration, design, development, creation, selection, adoption, or first use of the Defendant's Mark.
3. Specimens of or documents that show each good and/or service with which Defendant has used, uses or plans to use the Defendant's Mark.
4. Documents sufficient to reveal the date of Defendant's first sale or anticipated first sale of each of the goods and/or services offered in connection with the Defendant's Mark.
5. Specimens of each product, label, sign, display, trade dress, wrapper, packaging, promotion, advertisement, point-of-sale material and any

marketing material Defendant has used, uses or plans to use in connection with the Defendant's Mark.

6. Documents sufficient to identify Defendant's annual dollar and unit volumes of sales for each good and/or service sold in connection with the Defendant's Mark since Defendant's introduction of each such good and/or service.

7. Documents that reveal the territorial areas in the United States in which Defendant has marketed, markets or plans to market each good and/or service offered in connection with the Defendant's Mark.

8. Documents that reveal the channels of trade through which Defendant promotes, advertises or markets, or plans to promote, advertise or market each good and/or service offered in connection with the Defendant's Mark.

9. Documents that disclose the types of outlets and representative specific outlets through which products and/or services offered in connection with the Defendant's Mark are, have been, or will be offered or sold.

10. All documents that relate or refer to the marketing of, or plans to market, goods and/or services in connection with the Defendant's Mark, including, but not limited to:
    a) all advertising and promotional materials that contain, relate or refer to the Defendant's Mark including, but not limited to documents that relate or refer to the creation, development, approval, preparation of, proposals for, and distribution or planned distribution of said materials; and
    b) representative specimens of all advertisements, promotional materials, website pages, or other documents Defendant uses or plans to use in the advertising or promotion or planned advertising or promotion of goods and/or services in connection with the Defendant's Mark.

11. Documents that reveal Defendant's annual marketing expenses or planned expenses for goods and/or services marketed in connection with the Defendant's Mark, including but not limited to, expenses for advertising and promotion.

12. All documents that constitute, relate or refer to any grant or acquisition through assignment, license, or other transfer of any rights to or from Defendant in any name or mark comprised in whole or in part of Defendant's Mark

13. All documents that relate or refer to Plaintiff and Plaintiff's use of Plaintiff's Marks, including all documents that relate or refer to the circumstances under which Defendant first became aware of Plaintiff's use of Plaintiff's Marks.

14. All documents that relate or refer to any instances of confusion, mistake, or deception that has or may have occurred between Plaintiff

or Plaintiff's use of Plaintiff's Marks, and Defendant or Defendant's use of the Defendant's Mark.

15. All documents that constitute, relate, or refer to any formal or informal investigation, research endeavor, search, survey, test, poll, or study of any kind, including but not limited to trademark searches, trademark surveys, focus groups and name selection research, that Defendant has conducted, caused to be conducted, or has knowledge of pertaining to the Plaintiff's Marks, the Defendant's Mark, or pertaining to the markets for the goods or services offered in connection with any of the aforesaid names or marks.

16. All documents that relate or refer to Defendant's decision to register the Defendant's Mark in the United States Patent and Trademark Office.

17. All documents that constitute, relate, or refer to any federal, state, or domain name registration of, application to register, or any attempt made by Defendant to register any mark comprised in whole or in part of Defendant's Mark.

18. All documents that relate or refer to each use, former use, planned use or claim of use by Defendant or any other party of any name or mark consisting in whole or in part of Defendant's Mark.

19. All documents that constitute, relate, or refer to any formal or informal objections made by or directed against Defendant relating to or referring to Defendant's use or planned use of, or claimed rights in, any name or mark consisting in whole or in part of Defendant's Mark.

20. All documents that constitute, relate, or refer to any contacts Defendant has had with experts in connection with this proceeding.

Requests for Production of Documents
(FALSE ADVERTISING)

[DEFINITIONS AND INSTRUCTIONS OMITTED]

Requests

1. Any and all documents referred to in Defendant's responses to Plaintiff's First Set of Interrogatories.

2. All documents that constitute, or relate or refer to Defendant's Advertisement, including but not limited to documents that constitute, or relate or refer to Defendant's creation of the Advertisement.

3. A specimen of each document or material, including but not limited to ads, promotional pieces, articles, press releases, sales sheets and correspondence, that Defendant has used to market its products or services in the United States and that has included, identified, described, or in any manner referred to the claims identified in paragraph 20 of the Complaint.

4. All documents that constitute, or relate or refer to each claim described or mentioned in the Advertisement, including but not limited to all documents that constitute, or relate or refer to the acts that comprised, the protocols and methodology for, the claims identified in paragraph 20 of the Complaint, and the identity of each person who made decisions about, or participated in any manner in conducting or reporting on such claims.

5. All documents that constitute, or relate or refer to each claim included, identified, described, or in any manner referred to in any materials used to market Defendant's products or services in the United States, and the identity of each person who made decisions about, or participated in any manner in conducting or reporting on, such claims.

6. All documents that identify or relate or refer to the instruments and other equipment used or otherwise involved in conducting the tests described or mentioned in the Advertisement, including but not limited to protocols for use of the instruments and other equipment used in such tests.

7. Access for inspection to the equipment described in Request No. 6.

8. Access to the actual products used in the tests described or mentioned in the Advertisement.

9. All documents that relate or refer to Plaintiff's products that are the subject of the Advertisement, including but not limited to all documents that relate or refer to Defendant's procurement of such products.

10. All documents that relate or refer to Defendant's decision to create and use the Advertisement, and to run the tests described or mentioned in the Advertisement.

11. All documents that relate or refer to Defendant's distribution and other uses of the Advertisement and the tests described or mentioned in the Advertisement.

12. All documents that relate or refer to Defendant's distribution and other uses of any materials used to market Defendant's products or services that included, identified, described, or in any manner referred to, a test.

13. All documents that relate or refer to the dissemination or distribution of the Advertisement or any aspect of the Advertisement by third parties.

14. All documents that relate or refer to the dissemination or distribution of any materials used to market Defendant's products or services by third parties.

15. Representative specimens of each type of material that Defendant has used to market its products or services in the United States.

16. Documents that reveal Defendant's monthly dollar and unit volumes of sales of, and monthly unit distribution volume for, the product identified or described in the Advertisement in the United States.

17. Documents that reveal Defendant's expenses for the Advertisement and for the tests described or mentioned in the Advertisement.

18. All documents that reveal, or relate or refer to the manner in which Defendant recognized or recorded its costs related to the Advertisement and the tests described or mentioned in the Advertisement.

19. All documents that reveal, or relate or refer to the manner in which Defendant has recognized or recorded its costs related to the marketing materials produced in response to Request No. 3 and any tests included, identified, described, or in any manner referred to in such marketing materials.

20. All documents that constitute, or relate or refer to any meeting or communications among employees of Defendant, between any such person and a third party or between any third parties that in any manner related or referred to the Advertisement, the tests

described or mentioned in the Advertisement or the distribution of
the Advertisement and/or such tests.

21.   All documents that constitute, or relate or refer to tests performed
by or for any third party that in any manner related to the
Advertisement.

22.   All documents that constitute, or relate or refer to the reactions or
actions of third parties that have related, or referred to, or arisen
from, any aspect of the Advertisement or its distribution.

23.   Alwl documents that constitute, or relate or refer to any contacts or
the results of contacts Defendant has had with experts in
connection with this proceeding.

FORM 7.7

Defendant's Requests for Admission

SUNAMERICA CORPORATION)
(formerly SUN LIFE GROUP OF)
AMERICA, INC.), a Delaware)
corporation, and SUN LIFE)
INSURANCE COMPANY OF AMERICA,)
INC., a Maryland corporation)
Plaintiffs and)
Counterdefendants,)
v.)

SUNLIFE ASSURANCE COMPANY OF)
CANADA, a Canadian corporation,)
and SUN LIFE ASSURANCE COMPANY)
OF CANADA (U.S.), a Delaware)
corporation,)
Defendants and)
Counterclaimants.)

Defendants' Request for Admissions (Set I)

In accordance with Rule 36 of the Federal Rules of Civil Procedure and subject to the sanctions of rule 37(c) of the Federal Rules of Civil Procedure, defendants, Sun Life Assurance Company of Canada and Sun Life Assurance Company of Canada (U.S.) request that plaintiffs, SunAmerica Corporation and Sun Life Insurance Company of America, Inc. (hereinafter "SunAmerica"), admit or deny the following:

1. As to Exhibit 1 attached hereto:
   (a) It is a true and correct copy of a federal registration certificate for the mark SUN & Design, Registration No. 1,245,580, filed on the Principal Register in the United States Patent and Trademark Office;
   (b) It is a genuine and authentic copy of the registration certificate for Registration No. 1,245,580;
   (c) Registration No. 1,245,580 is valid and subsisting and owned by Sun Refining and Marketing Company, Philadelphia, Pennsylvania;
   (d) The mark SUN & Design depicted in Registration No. 1,245,580 has been used by Sun Refining and Marketing Company in connection with extending credit to others for the purchases of gasoline and other automotive related goods and services by means of a credit card;

(e) The mark SUN & Design depicted in Registration No. 1,245,580 is currently being used by Sun Refining and Marketing Company in connection with extending credit to others for the purchases of gasoline and other automotive related goods and services by means of a credit card.

2. As to Exhibit 2 attached hereto:

   (a) It is a true and correct copy of a federal registration certificate for the mark SUN BANKS OF FLORIDA, INC. & Design, Registration No. 1,013,709, filed on the Principal Register in the United States Patent and Trademark Office;

   (b) It is a genuine and authentic copy of the registration certificate for Registration No. 1,013,709;

   (c) Registration No. 1,013,709 is valid and subsisting and owned by Sun Banks, Inc., Orlando, Florida;

   (d) The mark SUN BANKS OF FLORIDA, INC & Design has been used by Sun Banks Inc. in connection with banking and bank-related services;

   (e) The mark SUN BANKS OF FLORIDA, INC. & Design is currently being used by Sun Banks, Inc. in connection with banking and bank-related services.

3. As to Exhibit 3 attached hereto:

   (a) It is a true and correct copy of a federal registration certificate for the mark SUN BANK 24, Registration No. 1,111,061, filed on the Principal Register in the United States Patent and Trademark Office;

   (b) It is a genuine and authentic copy of the registration certificate for Registration No. 1,111,061;

   (c) Registration No. 1,111,061 is valid and subsisting and owned by Sun Banks, Inc., Orlando, Florida;

   (d) The mark SUN BANK 24 has been used by Sun Banks, Inc. in connection with banking services; namely, automatic teller services.

   (e) The mark SUN BANK 24 is currently being used by Sun Banks, Inc. in connection with banking services, namely automatic teller services.

4. As to Exhibit 4 attached hereto:

   (a) It is a true and correct copy of a federal registration certificate for the mark SUNSET, Registration No. 803,602, filed on the Principal Register in the United States Patent and Trademark Office;

   (b) It is a genuine and authentic copy of the registration certificate for Registration No. 803,602;

   (c) Registration No. 803,602 is valid and subsisting and owned by Sunset Life Insurance Company of America, Olympia, Washington;

   (d) The mark SUNSET has been used by Sunset Life Insurance Company of America in connection with underwriting life, health and accident insurances;

(e) The mark SUNSET is currently being used by Sunset Life Insurance Company of America in connection with underwriting life, health and accident insurances.

5. As to Exhibit 5 attached hereto:
   (a) It is a true and correct copy of a federal registration certificate for the mark SUN BANK, Registration No. 1,144,487, filed on the Principal Register in the United States Patent and Trademark Office;
   (b) It is a genuine and authentic copy of the registration certificate for Registration No. 1,144,487;
   (c) Registration No. 1,144,487 is valid and subsisting and owned by Sun Banks of Florida, Inc., Orlando, Florida;
   (d) The mark SUN BANK has been used by Sun Banks of Florida, Inc. in connection with banking and bank-related services;
   (e) The mark SUN BANK is currently being used by Sun Banks of Florida, Inc. in connection with banking and bank- related services.

6. As to Exhibit 6 attached hereto:
   (a) It is a true and correct copy of a federal registration certificate for the mark SUNSOURCE & Design, Registration No. 1,307,415, filed on the Principal Register in the United States Patent and Trademark Office;
   (b) It is a genuine and authentic copy of the registration certificate for Registration No. 1,307,415;
   (c) Registration No. 1,307,415 is valid and subsisting and owned by Sunwest Bank of Albuquerque, N.A., Albuquerque, New Mexico;
   (d) The mark SUNSOURCE & Design depicted in Registration No. 1,307,415 has been used by Sunwest Bank of Albuquerque, N.A. in connection with insurance and financial services—namely, underwriting travel insurance, insurance, life insurance and accident and health insurance services, banking services, credit card services and stock broker services;
   (e) The mark SUNSOURCE & Design depicted in Registration No. 1,307,415 is currently being used by Sunwest Bank of Albuquerque, N.A. in connection with insurance and financial services - namely, underwriting travel insurance, insurance, life insurance and accident and health insurance services, banking services, credit card services and stock broker services.

7. As to Exhibit 7 attached hereto:
   (a) It is a true and correct copy of a federal registration certificate for the mark SUNVEST, Registration No. 1,315,001, filed on the Principal Register in the United States Patent and Trademark Office;
   (b) It is a genuine and authentic copy of the registration certificate for Registration No. 1,315,001;
   (c) Registration No. 1,315,001 is valid and subsisting and owned by Southern Investment Management, Inc. d.b.a. Sunvest Asset Management, Atlanta, Georgia;

(d) The mark SUNVEST has been used by Southern Investment Management, Inc. d.b.a. Sunvest Asset Management in connection with investment counseling and management services;

(e) The mark SUNVEST is currently being used by Southern Investment Management, Inc. d.b.a. Sunvest Asset Management in connection with investment counseling and management services.

8. As to Exhibit 8 attached hereto:

(a) It is a true and correct copy of a federal registration certificate for the mark SUN POINT & Design, Registration No. 1,430,522, filed on the Principal Register in the United States Patent and Trademark Office;

(b) It is a genuine and authentic copy of the registration certificate for Registration No. 1,430,552;

(c) Registration No. 1,430,522 is valid and subsisting and owned by Sun Point Savings Bank, Lake Worth, Florida;

(d) The mark SUN POINT & Design depicted in Registration No. 1,430,522 has been used by Sun Point Savings Bank in connection with banking services;

(e) The mark SUN POINT & Design depicted in Registration No. 1,430,522 is currently being used by Sun Point Savings Bank in connection with banking services.

9. As to Exhibit 9 attached hereto:

(a) It is a true and correct copy of a federal registration certificate for the mark SUNTRUST, Registration No. 1,513,027, filed on the Principal Register in the United States Patent and Trademark Office;

(b) It is a genuine and authentic copy of the registration certificate for Registration No. 1,513,027;

(c) Registration No. 1,513,027 is valid and subsisting and owned by SunTrust Banks, Inc., Atlanta, Georgia;

(d) The mark SUNTRUST has been used by SunTrust Banks, Inc. in connection with financial and insurance services;

(e) The mark SUNTRUST is currently being used by SunTrust Banks, Inc. in connection with financial and insurance services.

10. As to Exhibit 10 attached hereto:

(a) It is a true and correct copy of a federal registration certificate for the mark SUNWEST BANK & Design, Registration No. 1,226,889, filed on the Principal Register in the United States Patent and Trademark Office;

(b) It is a genuine and authentic copy of the registration certificate for Registration No. 1,226,889;

(c) Registration No. 1,226,889 is valid and subsisting and owned by Sunwest Bank, Tustin, California;

(d) The mark SUNWEST BANK & Design depicted in Registration No. 1,226,889 has been used by Sunwest Bank in connection with banking services;

(e) The mark SUNWEST BANK & Design depicted in Registration No. 1,226,889 is currently being used by Sunwest Bank in connection with banking services.

[11 through 34 intentionally omitted]

35. As to Exhibit 35 attached hereto:
    (a) It is a true and correct copy of a federal registration certificate for the mark SUNRISE PROFESSIONAL DATA SERVICES, Registration No. 1,370,478, filed on the Principal Register in the United States Patent and Trademark Office;
    (b) It is a genuine and authentic copy of the registration certificate for Registration No. 1,370,478;
    (c) Registration No. 1,370,478 is valid and subsisting and owned by Sunrise Datacorp, Citrus Heights, California;
    (d) The mark SUNRISE PROFESSIONAL DATA SERVICES has been used by Sunrise Datacorp in connection with data processing services in the field of billing and accounting services for business professionals and small business;
    (e) The mark SUNRISE PROFESSIONAL DATA SERVICES is currently being used by Sunrise Datacorp in connection with data processing services in the field of billing and accounting services for business professionals and small business.
36. As to Exhibit 36 attached hereto:
    (a) It is a true and correct copy of a federal registration certificate for the mark ON THE SUNNY SIDE OF THE STREET, Registration No. 562,062, filed on the Principal Register in the United States Patent and Trademark Office;
    (b) It is a genuine and authentic copy of the registration certificate for Registration No. 562,062;
    (c) Registration No. 562,062 is valid and subsisting and owned by North Adams Hoosac Savings Bank, North Adams, Massachusetts;
    (d) The mark ON THE SUNNY SIDE OF THE STREET has been used by North Adams Hoosac Savings Bank in connection with processing and handling of deposits and withdrawals in checking and savings accounts, and mortgage and loan financing;
    (e) The mark ON THE SUNNY SIDE OF THE STREET is currently being used by North Adams Hoosac Savings Bank in connection with processing and handling of deposits and withdrawals in checking and savings accounts, and mortgage and loan financing.

7.3 Response to Requests for Admissions

In the United States District court For the Northern District Of Georgia
Atlanta Division

v.

Sunlife assurance canada, and sun life assurance company) of Canada (U.S.),
delaware Defendants' Response To Plaintiffs' Request For Admissions

General Objections

Defendants object to each request in which plaintiffs seek to have defendants admit or deny characterizations given by plaintiffs to copies of documents which speak for themselves. Defendants also object to plaintiffs' use of the word "documents" or "document" in each request on the ground that the use is vague and ambiguous, as it is unclear whether plaintiffs are referring to original documents or photocopies.

Subject to their general objections, defendants answer and object to plaintiffs' request for admissions as follows:

Request no. 1

As to the documents made available to Defendants for inspection and copying numbered SA 00829 through SA 00838:

- (a). they are genuine and authentic documents from the corporate files of Plaintiffs;
- (b). document SA 00829 is a copy of an envelope postmarked August 7, 1989 addressed to "Sun Life of Canada" at the then-current mailing address of Sun Life of America;
- (c). document SA 00831, which incudes a reference to "Sun Life of Canada Insurance Company," is a copy of a paper included among the contents of the envelope referenced in part (b);
- (d). the envelope and paper referenced in parts (b) and (c) were received by Sun Life of America;
- (e). the paper referenced in part (c) was intended to be received by an entity affiliated with Defendants;
- (f). they evidence an instance of confusion between Sun Life of America and an entity affiliated with Defendants.

Response

- a. Defendants admit that the cited documents are genuine and authentic, but neither admit nor deny that they are from plaintiffs' corporate files, as the information necessary to respond to that portion of this request is in the possession of plaintiffs, and is not available to defendants by means of reasonable inquiry.

b.   Admitted, except that defendants neither admit nor deny that the address is for "a then-current mailing address of Sun Life of America," as that is a matter neither within the knowledge of defendants nor readily obtainable by means of reasonable inquiry.

c.   Defendants neither admit nor deny this request. This is a matter not within the knowledge of defendants nor readily obtainable by means of reasonable inquiry.

d.   Defendants neither admit nor deny this request. The information necessary to respond is in the possession of plaintiffs and not available to defendants by means of reasonable inquiry.

e.   Defendants neither admit nor deny this request. This is a matter not within the knowledge of defendants nor readily obtainable by means of reasonable inquiry.

f.   Defendants neither admit nor deny this request. This is a matter not within the knowledge of defendants nor readily obtainable by means of reasonable inquiry.

Request no. 2

As to the document made available to Defendants for inspection and copying numbered SA 00839:

(a).   it is a genuine and authentic document from the corporate files of Plaintiffs;

(b).   it evidences an instance in which a stockbroker obtained his client's approval to purchase $100,000 of Sun Life of America products, requested a "Sun Life" application from his home office, and received an application for products provided by an entity affiliated with Defendants; and

(c).   it evidences an instance of confusion between Sun Life of America and an entity affiliated with Defendants.

Response

a.   Defendants admit that the cited documents are genuine and authentic, but neither admit nor deny that they are from plaintiffs' corporate files, as the information necessary to respond to that portion of this request is in the possession of plaintiffs, and is not available to defendants by means of reasonable inquiry.

b.   Defendants neither admit nor deny this request. This is a matter not within the knowledge of defendants nor readily obtainable by means of reasonable inquiry.

c. Defendants neither admit nor deny this request. This is a matter not within the knowledge of defendants nor readily obtainable by means of reasonable inquiry.

Request no. 3

As to the documents made available to Defendants for inspection and copying numbered SA 00840 through SA 00844:

(a). they are genuine and authentic documents from the corporate files of Plaintiffs;

(b). document SA 00841 is a copy of an envelope bearing a postmark of February 27, 1989 addressed to "Sun Life Insurance Company of America" at an address of an entity affiliated with Defendants;

(c). document SA 00844, which includes a reference to "Sun Life Insurance Company of America," is a copy of a paper included among the contents of the envelope referenced in part (b);

(d). the envelope and paper references in parts (b) and (c) were received by an entity affiliated with Defendants;

(e). the paper referenced in part (c) was intended to be received by Sun Life of America;

(f). the envelope referenced in part (b) includes a communication from an employee of an entity affiliated with Defendants indicating that the paper referenced in part (c) was misdirected;

(g). document SA 00840 is a copy of an envelope postmarked March 6, 1989 transmitting the envelope and paper referenced in parts (b) and (c) from an entity affiliated with Defendants to Sun Life of America; and

(h). they evidence an instance of confusion between Sun Life of America and an entity affiliated with Defendants.

Response

a. Defendants admit that the cited documents are genuine and authentic, but neither admit nor deny that they are from plaintiffs' corporate files, as the information necessary to respond to that portion of this request is in the possession of plaintiffs, and is not available to defendants by means of reasonable inquiry.

b. Admitted.

c. Admitted.

d. Admitted.

   e.   Defendants neither admit nor deny this request. This is a matter not within the knowledge of defendants nor readily obtainable by means of reasonable inquiry.
   f.   Admitted.
   g.   Defendants neither admit nor deny this request. This is a matter not within the knowledge of defendants nor available by means of reasonable inquiry. Defendants further state that there is no message or other indication on the cited documents which might permit defendants to otherwise respond.
   h.   Defendants neither admit nor deny this request. This is a matter not within the knowledge of defendants nor readily obtainable by means of reasonable inquiry.

Request no. 4

As to the documents made available to Defendants for inspection and copying numbered SA 00845 through SA 00847:

   (a).   they are genuine and authentic documents from the corporate files of Plaintiffs;
   (b).   document SA 00845 is a copy of an envelope postmarked January 4, 1989, addressed to "Sun Life Insurance Company of America" at a then-current post office box used by Sun Life of America;
   (c).   document SA 00846, which includes a reference to "MFS/SUN LIFE (U.S.)," is a copy of a paper included among the contents of the envelope referenced in part (b);
   (d).   the envelope and paper referred to in parts (b) and (c) were received by Sun Life of America;
   (e).   the paper referred to in part (c) was intended to be received by an entity affiliated with Defendants; and
   (f).   they evidence an instance of confusion between Sun Life of America and an entity affiliated with Defendants.

Response

   a.   Defendants admit that the cited documents are genuine and authentic, but neither admit nor deny that they are from plaintiffs' corporate files, as the information necessary to respond to that portion of this request is in the possession of plaintiffs, and is not available to defendants by means of reasonable inquiry.
   b.   Admitted, except that defendants neither admit nor deny that the address is for "a then-current post office box used by Sun Life of America," as that is a matter neither within the knowledge of defendants nor readily obtainable by means of reasonable inquiry.

c.   Defendants neither admit nor deny this request. This is a matter not within the knowledge of defendants nor readily obtainable by means of reasonable inquiry.

d.   Defendants neither admit nor deny this request. The information necessary to respond is in the possession of plaintiffs and not available to defendants by means of reasonable inquiry.

e.   Defendants neither admit nor deny this request. This is a matter not within the knowledge of defendants nor readily obtainable by means of reasonable inquiry.

f.   Defendants neither admit nor deny this request. This is a matter not within the knowledge of defendants nor readily obtainable by means of reasonable inquiry.

Request no. 5

As to the documents made available to Defendants for inspection and copying numbered SA 00850 through SA 00851:

(a).   they are genuine and authentic documents from the corporate files of Plaintiffs;

(b).   document SA 00851 is a copy of an envelope postmarked January 10, 1989, addressed to the attention of Joan Bennett at "Sun Life Insurance Company of America" at its then current address;

(c).   document SA 00850, which includes a memo dated January 8, 1989, to Joan Bennett, is a copy of a paper included among the contents of the envelope referenced in part (b);

(d).   the envelope and paper referenced in parts (b) and (c) were received by Sun Life of America;

(e).   the paper referenced in part (c) was intended to be received by an entity affiliated with Defendants;

(f).   Joan Bennett was an employee of an entity affiliated with Defendants as of January 10, 1989; and

(g).   they evidence an instance of confusion between Sun Life of America and an entity affiliated with Defendants.

Response

a.   Defendants admit that the cited documents are genuine and authentic, but neither admit nor deny that they are from plaintiffs' corporate files, as the information necessary to respond to that portion of this request is in the possession of plaintiffs, and is not available to defendants by means of reasonable inquiry.

b. Admitted, except that defendants neither admit nor deny that the address is "its then current address," as that is a matter neither within the knowledge of defendants nor readily obtainable by means of reasonable injury.

c. Defendants neither admit nor deny this request. This is a matter not within the knowledge of defendants nor readily obtainable by means of reasonable inquiry.

d. Defendants neither admit nor deny this request. The information necessary to respond is in the possession of plaintiffs and not available to defendants by means of reasonable inquiry.

e. Defendants neither admit nor deny this request. This is a matter not within the knowledge of defendants nor readily obtainable by means of reasonable inquiry.

f. Admitted.

g. Defendants neither admit nor deny this request. This is a matter not within the knowledge of defendants nor readily obtainable by means of reasonable inquiry.

Request no. 6

As to the document made available to Defendants for inspection and copying numbered SA 00852:

(a). it is a genuine and authentic document from the corporate files of Plaintiffs;

(b). it is a copy of letter dated August 3, 1988, to a Vice President of Sun Life of America requesting information concerning an annuity provided by Defendants;

(c). the letter referenced in part (b) was received by Sun Life of America;

(d). the letter referenced in part (b) was intended to be received by an entity affiliated with Defendants; and

(e). it evidences an instance of confusion between Sun Life of America and an entity affiliated with Defendants.

Response

a. Defendants admit that the cited document is genuine and authentic, but neither admit nor deny that it is from plaintiffs' corporate files, as the information necessary to respond to that portion of this request is in the possession of plaintiffs, and is not available to defendants by means of reasonable inquiry.

b. Denied.

c. Defendants neither admit nor deny this request. The information necessary to respond is in the possession of plaintiffs, and is not available to defendants by means of reasonable inquiry.

d. Defendants neither admit nor deny this request. This is a matter not within the knowledge of defendants nor readily obtainable by means of reasonable inquiry.

e. Defendants neither admit nor deny this request. This is a matter not within the knowledge of defendants nor readily obtainable by means of reasonable inquiry.

Request no. 7

As to the documents made available to Defendants for inspection and copying numbered SA 00853 through SA 00856:

(a). they are genuine and authentic documents from the corporate files of Plaintiffs;

(b). document SA 00853 is a copy of an envelope addressed to Mr. Jacques Guilmette at "Sun Life Assurance Company of Canada" at the then-current address of Sun Life of America;

(c). document SA 00854 is a copy of a paper dated August 12, 1988, included among the contents of the envelope referenced in part (b);

(d). the envelope and paper referenced in parts (b) and (c) were received by Sun Life of America;

(e). the paper referenced in part (c) was intended to be received by an entity affiliated with Defendants;

(f). Jacques Guilmette was an employee of an entity affiliated with Defendants as of August 12, 1988; and

(g). they evidence an instance of confusion between Sun Life of America and an entity affiliated with Defendants.

Response

a. Defendants admit that the cited document is genuine and authentic, but neither admit nor deny that it is from plaintiffs' corporate files, as the information necessary to respond to that portion of this request is in the possession of plaintiffs, and is not available to defendants by means of reasonable inquiry.

b. Admitted, except that defendants neither admit nor deny that the address is "the then-current address of Sun Life of America," as that is a matter neither within the knowledge of defendants nor readily obtainable by means of reasonable inquiry.

c. Defendants neither admit nor deny this request. This is a matter not within the knowledge of defendants nor readily obtainable by means of reasonable inquiry.

d. Defendants neither admit nor deny this request. The information necessary to respond is in the possession of plaintiffs and not available to defendants by means of reasonable inquiry.

e. Defendants neither admit nor deny this request. This is a matter not within the knowledge of defendants nor readily obtainable by means of reasonable inquiry.
f. Admitted.
g. Defendants neither admit nor deny this request. This is a matter not within the knowledge of defendants nor readily obtainable by means of reasonable inquiry.

Request no. 8

As to the document made available to Defendants for inspection and copying numbered SA 00857:

(a). it is a genuine and authentic document from the corporate files of Plaintiffs;
(b). it is a copy of an envelope having a mailing label addressed to Mr. Roger Milton at "Sun Life Insurance Company of Canada" at an address used at one time by Sun Life of America;
(c). the envelope referenced in part (b) was received by Sun Life of America;
(d). the envelope referenced in part (b) was intended to be received by an entity affiliated with Defendants; and
(e). it evidences an instance of confusion between Sun Life of America and an entity affiliated with Defendants.

Response

a. Defendants admit that the cited documents are genuine and authentic, but neither admit nor deny that they are from plaintiffs' corporate files, as the information necessary to respond to that portion of this request is in the possession of plaintiffs, and is not available to defendants by means of reasonable inquiry.
b. Admitted.
c. Defendants neither admit nor deny this request. The information necessary to respond is in the possession of plaintiffs, and is not available to defendants by means of reasonable inquiry.
d. Defendants neither admit nor deny this request. This is a matter not within the knowledge of defendants nor readily obtainable by means of reasonable inquiry.
e. Defendants neither admit nor deny this request. This is a matter not within the knowledge of defendants nor readily obtainable by means of reasonable inquiry.

Request no. 9

As to the documents made available to Defendants for inspection and copying numbered SA 00873 through SA 00874:

(a). they are genuine and authentic documents from the corporate files of Plaintiffs;

(b). document SA 00873 is a copy of a letter dated July 5, 1989, addressed to "Sun Life Insurance Company of America" at its then-current address;

(c). document SA 00874, which includes a reference to "Sun Life of Canada," is a copy of a paper enclosed with the letter referenced in part (b);

(d). the letter and paper referenced in parts (b) and (c) were received by Sun Life of America;

(e). the paper referenced in part (c) was intended to be received by an entity affiliated with Defendants; and

(f). they evidence an instance of confusion between Sun Life of America and an entity affiliated with Defendants.

Response

a. Defendants admit that the cited documents are genuine and authentic, but neither admit nor deny that they are from plaintiffs' corporate files, as the information necessary to respond to that portion of this request is in the possession of plaintiffs, and is not available to defendants by means of reasonable inquiry.

b. Admitted, except that defendants neither admit nor deny that the address is "the then-current address of Sun Life of America," as that is a matter neither within the knowledge of defendants nor readily obtainable by means of reasonable inquiry.

c. Defendants neither admit nor deny this request. This is a matter not within the knowledge of defendants nor readily obtainable by means of reasonable inquiry.

d. Defendants neither admit nor deny this request. The information necessary to respond is in the possession of

e. plaintiffs and not available to defendants by means of reasonable inquiry.

f. Defendants neither admit nor deny this request. This is a matter not within the knowledge of defendants nor readily obtainable by means of reasonable inquiry.

g.   Defendants neither admit nor deny this request. This is a matter not within the knowledge of defendants nor readily obtainable by means of reasonable inquiry.

[Requests 11 through 116 intentionally omitted]

Request no. 117

Prior to adopting the name SUN FINANCIAL GROUP, either or both of Defendants was aware of Sun Life of America's use of the name *SUN* FINANCIAL to promote products or services to the public.

Response

Defendants admit that prior to adopting the name SUN FINANCIAL GROUP they were aware of plaintiffs' use of *SUN* FINANCIAL SERVICES, but deny that any protectable rights accrued to plaintiffs by virtue of that use and further state that defendants had been using "SUN FINANCIAL" to refer to their business since the late 1970's and long prior to plaintiffs' use of SUN FINANCIAL SERVICES as part of a mailing address.

Request no. 118

Prior to adopting the name SUN FINANCIAL GROUP, either or both of Defendants was aware of Sun Life of America's use of the name SUN FINANCIAL SERVICES to promote products or services to the public.

Response

See answer to Request 117.

Request no. 119

Prior to adopting the name SUN FINANCIAL GROUP, either or both of Defendants was aware of Sun Life of America's use in advertising materials of one or more terms containing both "SUN" and "FINANCIAL."

Response

See answer to Request 117.

CHAPTER

8

Depositions

I. Deposition Preparation

The deposition often plays a crucial role in discovery in civil litigation and this is no less true in trademark and copyright litigation. Both types of actions almost exclusively take place in federal court and, therefore, under the federal rules. Litigators must be familiar with the federal rules, especially rule 30, which covers depositions. In trademark litigation, the most important deposition often is the 30(b)(6) deposition of a corporate party.

Rule 30(b)(6) requires the party calling the deposition to "describe with reasonable particularity the matters for examination." Nevertheless, recent decisions have held that questions outside of the topics identified in the deposition notice are fair game and a deponent may not refuse to answer such questions. The topics identified in the deposition notice are used by the deposed party to identify people who can speak to each topic.

Taking an effective deposition comes down to knowing what you want out of a particular deposition and proper preparation.

The following are five "Deposition Gets" that work for any deposition.

Get the facts: what facts - good or bad - does this witness know.

Get the names: who else has information about the facts.

Get the admissions: if possible, obtain admissions from the witness on elements of the claims - this is by far the hardest thing to do at a deposition.

Get ready for trial: pin the witness down on his or her testimony so they have no wiggle room at trial to alter their testimony - or else look less than honest in front of the fact-finder.

Get to know the witness: learning how the witness will seem to a fact-finder is almost as important as what they say; an adverse witness who appears smug, dissembling, or combative may turn off a jury, or a judge, and help your case even if what they say does not.

Preparing for a deposition generally involves preparing a deposition outline – a document to guide your questioning. Not everyone's outline will look the same. Some attorneys prefer to have specific questions written out, others want nothing more than a few bullet points.

A. Deposition Outline

Below is an example of a typical deposition outline in a trademark infringement matter

1. Admissions Sought

    a. Acme Solutions was aware of the fact that GEAR EXCHANGE was a mark owned and used by Cadillac Machinery prior to registering the domain name <gearexchange.com>.

b. Acme Solutions was aware of the fact that GEAR EXCHANGE was a mark owned and used by Cadillac Machinery prior to using it in the content of its website located at <gearexchange.com>.

c. Acme Solutions had reason to believe that the GEAR EXCHANGE mark was owned and used by Cadillac Machinery prior to its registration of the domain name <gearsolutions.com>.

d. The purpose of the <gearexchange.com> website was to divert customers from Cadillac Machinery.

e. The purpose of the <gearexchange.com> website was to cause confusion with Cadillac Machinery.

f. Acme Solutions' activities created a likelihood of confusion or misunderstanding as to affiliation, connection, or association with or certification by another.

2. Information Sought

g. Whether or not Acme Solutions indicated to Spain that it was aware of Cadillac Machinery's ownership and use of the mark GEAR EXCHANGE.

h. Whether or not Acme Solutions instructed Spain to include the GEAR EXCHANGE mark in the content of its website with the intent of diverting or confusing consumers.

i. Any information regarding possible bad faith on the part of Acme Solutions in connection with registration of the domain name <gearexchange.com>.

j. Any indication of actual or likely consumer confusion.

3. Deposition Questions

a. *General Background of Witness*
   i. Age?
   ii. Formal Education?
   iii. Where are you currently employed?
   iv. For how long has the business been established?
   v. What is your current position?
      1. How long have you held this position?
      2. Please describe the nature of your job duties and responsibilities in this position.
   vi. Do you have any former employment or were you formerly engaged in any other business endeavors?

b. *Chronology of Deponent's Role in the Situation*
   i. When did you first become aware of Acme Solutions?
   ii. Had you done work for Acme Solutions prior to working on the <gearexchange.com> website?

1. What projects?
2. What are the dates on which you did work for Acme Solutions?

iii. When were you first contacted by Acme Solutions regarding the website <gearexchange.com>?
   1. Who were you contacted by?
   2. By what means were you contacted? (phone, e-mail?)

iv. What was the nature of your work on the website <gearexchange.com>?

v. Had the domain name <gearexchange.com> already been obtained by Acme Solutions prior to them contacting you regarding designing a new website?
   1. If not, when was the domain name purchased in relation to when you were hired to design Acme Solutions' new website?

vi. Were you ever asked by Acme Solutions to comment on, give an opinion regarding or help choose a domain name, including but not limited to the domain name <gearexchange.com>?

vii. Please describe the nature of Acme Solutions' use of the GEAR EXCHANGE mark on the <gearexchange.com>.

viii. As the designer of the site, what kind of liberty, if any, did you have regarding the content of the site and the way the information on the site was presented?
   1. Whose decision was it to include the GEAR EXCHANGE mark in the content of the website?
   2. Did you get any input as to whether or not the GEAR EXCHANGE mark was included in the content of the website?

c. *Authentication and Explanation of Documents*

   i. Please verify that you are the person named in each of the following documents.

   ii. Do you recall the circumstances surrounding creation or transmission of any of these documents?

   iii. Please explain, to the best of your ability, why you are named in these documents, and explain the s ignificance of the content of these documents.

II. Witness Preparation

What does the witness need to know about the deposition process?

The deposition process is new to most witnesses. It is useful to describe the logistics and setting. Most depositions take place in a conference room, not open court. The persons present will be the opposing counsel and other representatives of the party, the witness, his attorney, and the court reporter preparing a written record of the statements made. The judge is not present, but it may be necessary to contact the court by phone to resolve objections to questions. Some depositions are videotaped.

The role of counsel should be explained. The opposing counsel is seeking information, admissions and contradictions that she may exploit at trial. She will be asking questions and creating a record to determine and limit the scope of testimony the witness can provide at trial.

The counsel representing the witness is trying to ensure that testimony is accurate and to protect privileged communications. Thus, counsel may make objections as to the form of the questions, allowing the witness to answer, or objections regarding the disclosure of privileged information, instructing the witness to refrain from answering. Usually the counsel representing the witness will say little if the witness has been properly prepared and the opponent is an effective questioner. The witness may be surprised by the lack of involvement from defending counsel, so advanced warning is merited.

It is also useful for a witness to know how the deposition will be used. Excerpts may be used in court submissions to support motions. Excerpts may be read as testimony at trial. Live witnesses may be impeached by inconsistent statements at trial.

What is the difference between preparation and improper coaching?

Coaching crosses the line by telling a witness what to say. It is unethical to encourage a witness to lie. Preparation does not tell a witness what to say or encourage lying. Instead, preparation is the process of helping a witness understand the issues, review the relevant record, understand the deposition process.

It is important to ensure that the witness understands the deposition process and how to conduct themselves. It is also critical to ensure that the witness understands the legal issues involved and theory of the case. A truthful answer can be misleading or damaging if not placed in proper context. A prepared witness can be helped to avoid such problems. Consider, for example, the famous case of the lost ear. The witness is asked, "did you see my client bite off the ear?" The truthful answer is "no" and ends there if the witness follows all of the usual procedural admonitions. The truthful answer by the prepared witness, who understands the theory of the case, goes on to add, "but I saw him spit it out."

What rules apply to deposition preparation?

There is no specific rule of federal procedure relating to witness preparation.

The Rules of Evidence apply in that a witness may be asked to reveal any documents or material used to refresh recollection. Thus, outlines, memoranda and documents shown to a witness may be revealed.

The rules of privilege apply in that any advice given by a lawyer to her client during preparation is immune from disclosure as a privileged communication and materials prepared by the attorney in connection with litigation are protected as attorney work product.

Ethical rules apply with respect to dishonest testimony.

What should you do to help party witnesses prepare?

Some say you do not win a deposition, you only avoid losing. Therefore, witness preparation can be essential to preventing problems in your case that arise from inaccurate admissions or facts. It can also be the key to avoiding embarrassing surprises from inconsistent statements or impeaching documents.

It is important to allow sufficient time for preparation. Experienced counsel know that witness preparation is likely to take as much time or more than the actual deposition. The measure of successful preparation is whether all reasonable inquiries were anticipated and discussed in advance so that there were no surprises during the deposition.

The preparation sessions will usually cover several areas:

1) The background and relevant information known by the witness.
2) The nature of the issues and information likely to be pursued.
3) The nature of the claims made in the lawsuit.
4) Ground rules for witness conduct.
5) Review of key documents and prior testimony.
6) Practice questioning

What preparation should counsel do before meeting with witnesses?

Just as witness preparation is key, so to is advanced preparation by counsel. Counsel will want to understand the pleadings, the prior testimony, relevant documents and relevant statutes and case law. Counsel should also attempt to anticipate the questions and issues that opposing counsel is likely to pursue. It is useful to prepare as if counsel were taking the deposition. See the sample deposition outline for an example of the type of preparation that is useful for taking and defending depositions.

What are the guidelines for witnesses?

The seminal guidelines are: (1) answer the question, and (2) tell the truth. The rest of the general guidelines elaborate on these key principles. See attached witness guidelines.

What problems should you anticipate during preparation?

Most problems can be avoided by thorough preparation. Some key problem areas arise from the nature of particular types of witnesses.

1) **"the loquacious salesman"**—Some witnesses have careless grasp of the truth and will agree with most anything asked of them. These types aim to please. They will require a firm discussion about the need to stick to the facts no matter what.
2) **"the overzealous executive"**—Many witnesses have jobs where they are trained to have answers. They put 2 and 2 together to reach 4, even if they don't know the facts or answer with certainty. These

witnesses need to be warned to stick to their actual knowledge and avoid assumptions and conclusions about what probably happened.

3) **"the dishonest president"**—Some witnesses believe they can hide bad facts. These witnesses may have something to hide or may simply want to avoid disclosure of weaknesses. They need to be encouraged to tell the whole truth and not avoid bad facts or other weaknesses. Bad facts revealed while the case is being prepared can be managed by counsel. Bad facts revealed at trial without prior warning can destroy an otherwise meritorious case.

4) **"the too-busy CEO"**—Some witnesses think they are too important, busy or smart to spend time preparing for a deposition. They need to understand the importance and risks of the deposition process to their own interests and those of the company.

5) **"the lawyer wannabe"**—These witnesses want to be an advocate. They think they can outsmart the questioner. Remind them that the goal is to tell the truth, not "win" the deposition.

May you show the witness documents during preparation?

It is common for counsel to show documents to witnesses during preparation, but witnesses may be asked to reveal the documents they looked at during preparation. If documents were used to refresh witness recollection, opposing counsel may be entitled to have them produced.

Are there different rules for non-party witnesses?

The principal difference between preparation of party and non-party witnesses is that of privilege. Advice given to a party witness is immune from disclosure as a privileged communication. In contrast, statements made to witness you do not represent are not privileged and are fair subjects for questioning during the deposition. The witness, therefore, may be asked what counsel said to her during preparation. This can be embarrassing or damaging if counsel has made ill-advised requests, disclosures, or statements to the witness.

III. Deposition Defense

What rules apply to deposition defense?

The Federal Rule of Civil Procedure regarding conduct at depositions is Rule 30.

What are the "usual stipulations"?

It's an old joke. The veteran lawyer asks the novice counsel at the deposition if the "usual stipulations" apply. Not wishing to appear green, the novice agrees. The joke: there are no "usual stipulations." Rather, there are a series of common issues addressed by stipulation, often at the start of a deposition, but the exact stipulation needs to be stated or no one will no what is meant. The areas covered by stipulation often include:

1) What objections will be reserved for trial (all objections, none, only questions as to form).
2) Whether the witness will review, correct, and sign the deposition transcript.
3) Whether signature is waived, may be made without notary, may be made in front of any notary, or must be made in front of the reporter taking the deposition.

What objections can you make at depositions?

The parties may stipulate that all objections expect for form are reserved for trial. This is the norm in federal cases. As a result, counsel is not required to make objections regarding relevance, materiality, or hearsay during the deposition. These may be reserved until the testimony is presented to the court. Objection as to form however will be waived unless made on the record at the deposition. This rule generally applies to any improper questions that could be corrected at the time of the deposition. For example, objections relating to questions that are compound, ambiguous or misleading should be made on the record or they may be waived. In these situations, opposing counsel will have the opportunity to rephrase the question or press ahead with the witness responding despite the objection.

Objections regarding questions calling for privileged information should be made on the record to prevent a waiver of privilege through disclosure. In addition to stating the objection, the witness will be instructed not to answer.

The Relevant Rule of Civil Procedure controls the manner in which the objection is made:

Rule 30(d)(1) Any objection during a deposition must be stated concisely and in a non-argumentative and non-suggestive manner. A person may instruct a deponent not to answer only when necessary to preserve a privilege, to enforce a limitation directed by the court, or to present a motion under Rule 30(d)(4).

How do you deal with improper questions or behavior from opposing counsel?

Examples of improper behavior include bullying or badgering the witness, threats of retaliation, profanity, and similar tactics that impede fair testimony. Preventing improper tactics by opposing counsel can be difficult. Protests stated plainly on the record may help and may preserve a record that can be presented later to the court. The written record, however, does not always reveal the full scope of improper tactics. Sometimes even a short break can cool tempers and end improper tactics. Videotaping the deposition may deter improper behavior. If counsel persists and you are confident that opposing counsel's behavior is improper, you may terminated the deposition and seek a protective order. In extreme cases you may seek to conduct the deposition under court supervision. The Federal Rules provide the following procedure:

> Rule 30(d) (4)—At any time during a deposition, on motion of a party or of the deponent and upon a showing that the examination is being conducted in bad faith or in such manner as unreasonably to annoy, embarrass, or oppress the deponent or party, the court in which the action is pending or the court in the district where the deposition is being taken may order the officer conducting the examination to cease forthwith from taking the deposition, or may limit the scope and manner of the taking of the deposition as provided in Rule 26(c). If the order made terminates the examination, it may be resumed thereafter only upon the order of the court in which the action is pending. Upon demand of the objecting party or deponent, the taking of the deposition must be suspended for the time necessary to make a motion for an order. The provisions of Rule 37(a)(4) apply to the award of expenses incurred in relation to the motion.

May you talk to the witness during breaks?

It is generally considered improper to interrupt and discuss testimony with the witness while a question remains pending, except for the purpose of preserving privilege. During a break between questions, however, it is proper to speak to the witness unless an order has been entered to prevent such discussions.

When should you cross-examine at a deposition?

You are not required to conduct any examination at the deposition. If the witness will appear at trial, you may reserve questioning until that time. You may also call the same witness at a later date for a deposition.

If the witness will not appear at trial or will be unavailable for later questioning, cross-examination may be desirable, particularly if the witness is a party you do not represent.

If the witness has left an unclear or incorrect record on a key point, cross-examination may be needed.

What do you do after the deposition?

Both counsel and witness will want to read and correct the transcript. Counsel may point out mistakes to the witness and prepare errata sheets. Incorrect testimony correctly transcribed may be changed, but doing so may entitle opposing counsel to question the witness further about the changes. The applicable Rule states:

Rule 30(e)—Review by Witness; Changes; Signing. If requested by the deponent or a party before completion of the deposition, the deponent shall have 30 days after being notified by the officer that the transcript or recording is available in which to review the transcript or recording and, if there are changes in form or substance, to sign a statement reciting such changes and the reasons given by the deponent for making them. The officer shall indicate in the certificate prescribed by subdivision (f)(1) whether any review was requested and, if so, shall append any changes made by the deponent during the period allowed.

IV. Deposition Guidelines for Witnesses

1. Tell the truth (and nothing but the truth)

Obviously it is important for the witness to tell the truth. They should not deliberately hide harmful facts if responsive to a direct question. It is equally important to recognize that the witness should only testify to the truth. Not what they think might have happened, probably happened, or could have happened.

2. Don't speculate, volunteer, or agree

The witness should not guess about what may have happened, or volunteer that someone else might know the answer and that the answer might be contained in documents or notes. The witnesses should also be cautious about agreeing with summaries of the testimony provided by counsel. Hesitate to let counsel put words into your mouth.

3. Answer the question (and nothing else)

Don't provide answers to what you think counsel is trying to ask. Simply answer the questions asked as directly and simply as possible. Don't engage in added commentary or side talk. Although chitchat may seem innocent, it can be used to your disadvantage.

4. Take your time (understand the question, understand your answer)

You have the right to understand the question and should be sure you have heard it completely before responding. The deposition should not be an ordinary conversation. Pause and consider what you will say before committing your response to the record.

5. Don't help the lawyer (she is not your friend)

Remember that opposing counsel is trying to win a case by damaging you or your company. It is serious business. You are there to answer questions on the record, nothing more.

V. Sample Deposition Witness Preparation Outline

A. Witnesses
   1. Dr. Cassey Smith

    2. Ms. Judy Jones
B. Location
    1. Noon, September 4, 2001, Law Offices of Arnold I. Attorney, 77 West Washington Street.
C. Case Chronology
    1. December 1, 1997—Smith entered into Retainer Agreement with Johnson & Associates.
    2. October 1, 1999—Litigation Cost Agreement between Smith and North American.
    3. February 22, 2000—Motion for Summary Judgment granted
    4. March, 2000—Johnson and Anderson withdraw
    5. March 30, 2000—Judgment entered on Jury's verdict for $35,000
    6. December 21, 2000—Motions for attorneys' fees denied
D. Legal Position
    1. The amount of work done by Mr. Johnson was unreasonable and unauthorized.
       a) The amount in controversy was about $35,000.
       b) Counsel expanded scope of case unnecessarily and without client approval.
       c) The court found that counsel's actions were unreasonable and denied request for attorneys' fees.

"[D]espite the fact that early in the course of litigation it was objectively clear that the extent of the infringement was not great, and that the value of Plaintiff's claim was minuscule in comparison to the amount of attorneys fees plaintiff was incurring, plaintiff continued to purse and extraordinarily aggressive litigation strategy . . . . Plaintiff's strategy was objectively unreasonable in light of the potential value of his case."

    2. Defendant has fully paid an amount that is reasonable for the work authorized.
E. Admissions Sought
    1. Smith hired Johnson and Charlie to represent him in copyright dispute.
    2. Smith agreed in writing to pay hourly fees, expenses, interest on unpaid invoices and attorneys' fees in event of breach.
    3. North Central agreed to pay attorneys fees for Smith.
    4. Client instructed counsel to take vigorous action.
    5. Client authorized or approved all actions by counsel.
    6. Client never objected to actions by counsel
    7. Client never objected to bills
    8. The hourly rates charged are reasonable
    9. The case was complicated and unusual
    10. Client ultimately prevailed as a result of work down by counsel

F.   Outline
   1.   Background
        a)   Education
        b)   Medical experience
        c)   Current Business

   2.   Creation of Book—Self-Test Guide

   3.   Retention of Johnson & Associates
        a)   Why did Smith retain Johnson?
        b)   Identification of Retainer Agreement

   4.   Retention of Charlie & Loom
        a)   Why did Smith use Charlie as local counsel?

   5.   Agreement by North Central to Pay Fees

   6.   Copyright Infringement Action
        a)   Why was case filed?
        b)   What was the strategy?
        c)   What did client seek?

   7.   Communication with Counsel
        a)   How did parties communicate?
        b)   What instructions did client give counsel?
        c)   What information did counsel provide client?
        d)   Did client require prior approval?

   8.   Authorization of Work Performed
        a)   Did client authorize work performed?
        b)   Was client informed of work performed?
        c)   Did client object to any work perform?
        d)   Did counsel do any work over the objections of client?

   9.   Payments Made
        a)   What payments were made?
        b)   When?
        c)   How much?

   10.   Basis for Withholding Additional Payments
        a)   Why did Smith withhold payments?
        b)   When?
        c)   Any discussions with counsel about excessive charges?

   11.   Objections Made To Services
        a)   Did Smith object to counsel's conduct?
        b)   Why did Smith change counsel?

CHAPTER
9

Discovery Disputes

Many cases may be won at trial or in briefs, but most cases are won (or lost) during the discovery process. Effective and efficient discovery can give your client a distinct advantage, even if the facts or law appeared to be against it at the pleading stage. Most litigators, knowing the importance of discovery, will do what they can to thwart your efforts, inevitably leading to discovery disputes.

Although discovery disputes can be very contentious, they need not be—a good rapport with opposing counsel is the best way to overcome such disputes. Many litigators view "compromise" as a dirty word that shows weakness in a case or position, but clients don't see it that way; and more and more frequently, clients are coming to understand that failure to cooperate in discovery can result in exponential increases in litigations costs. Always bear in mind that both sides are advocating for their clients, and intelligent people can disagree about the appropriateness of certain discovery techniques and the amount of information that should be shared during litigation. It is incumbent upon each litigator to draw an appropriate line between cost of the discovery provided or obtained and the benefit of reduced litigation costs resulting from a compromise.

Discovery disputes should not be ignored while allegedly more important tasks are completed. Addressing a discovery dispute quickly and head-on will bring you and your client closer to resolving the case overall and will yield better results for the client's bottom line. Disputes that linger find their way into briefs and discussions before the court, which rarely wants to hear about them.

A telling example of a court fed up with parties' discovery disputes is Judge Presnell's Order that counsel for the parties play rock, paper, scissors to decide the location of a 30(b)(6) deposition. *See Avista Mgmt. Inc. v. Wausau Underwriters Ins. Co.*, 6:05-cv-1430 (M.D. Fla. June 6, 2006). The parties had brought numerous discovery disputes to the court's attention before this, and the offices for both parties' counsel were located in the same county. These are the types of disputes that should be resolved so that only differences on significant matters need be heard by the court.

Every communication with opposing counsel should be written with the understanding that it may come before the court, or other decision-maker, when the parties cannot agree. Unreasonable demands, vitriol, and obstinacy may seem like good ideas when a letter or e-mail is written with the goal of convincing the other side that your position is right, and they just won't listen, but it will make your client and you appear to be unreasonable when those same words are reviewed by a neutral.

Generally, the sequence of events in a discovery dispute follow this pattern: one party makes a request during discovery—an interrogatory, document request, request to admit, deposition question, etc.—and the other party believes the request is inappropriate so it objects, provides an inadequate response, or fails to respond at all. What do you do at that point? One thing you usually cannot do is immediately file a motion to compel. Nearly every federal court, and the TTAB, now has a meet and confer requirement before a discovery dispute may be brought before them for decision. *See, e.g.,* Southern District of New York Local Civil Rule 37.2 (requiring informal conference with the Court before a motion may be filed); Northern District of Illinois Local Civil Rule 37.2 (requiring consultation in good faith to resolve the parties' differences and a recitation of such efforts in the request); Central District of California Local Civil Rule 37-1 (requiring counsel for the parties to confer in good faith, in person in some circumstances); and Central District of California Local Civil Rule 37-2.1 (request to consider dispute must be filed as a stipulation of the issues in dispute). Although different courts have different rules about addressing discovery disputes, generally, sending a detailed deficiency letter and following up with a phone call to discuss the issues raised therein usually is sufficient to meet any court's requirement, and it also has the added benefit of potentially resolving the dispute. Of course, if that does not work, then it is time to file a motion to compel.

Counsel should be aware that different forums provide for different sanctions. Federal courts have the full powers of Fed. R. Civ. P. 37 and the power of civil contempt to require a noncompliant party to pay for the moving party's fees and costs incurred in bringing the motion. If the motion is brought pursuant to a subpoena, the party seeking an order to compel or for sanctions must move in the issuing court. The TTAB has no authority to issue monetary sanctions, but it can provide other sanctions, such as evidentiary presumptions and determinations on the merits of specific issues.

Objections to Written Discovery Requests

Written discovery often is the beginning of the discovery process in a case. Objections to written discovery often are the beginning of any discovery dispute. Below is a template for preparing common objections to discovery in trademark and copyright disputes. Despite common practice, general objections are ineffective, and specific objections should not be conclusory statements about a particular discovery request; otherwise, should they come before a court for resolution, the court will have no basis for determining the validity of an objection to a written request.

Template for Objections to Written Discovery

Plaintiff objects to Interrogatory No. __ on the ground that the term "__" is vague and ambiguous.

Plaintiff objects to Interrogatory No. __ on the ground that it is duplicative of Interrogatory No. __.

Plaintiff objects to Interrogatory No. __ on the grounds that it is overly broad and unduly burdensome to the extent that it asks for "all" documents that "__."

Plaintiff objects to Interrogatory No. __ on the grounds that it is not likely to lead to the discovery of relevant evidence because it seeks "__."

Plaintiff objects to Interrogatory No. __ to the extent it seeks information shielded from discovery by the attorney-client privilege or the work-product doctrine.

Plaintiff objects to Interrogatory No. __ to the extent it seeks confidential and proprietary business information in the absence of an appropriate protective order.

Objections to Deposition Questions

The deposition often is crucial to discovery in a civil case. This is equally true for trademark and copyright litigation where issues of intent and knowledge often play a crucial role in assessing a party's position before trial. As in every other federal case, objections during depositions serve to preserve them for trial, although most protective orders and stipulations explicitly preserve objections to deposition testimony, even if an objection is not stated on the record of a deposition.

A deponent may be instructed not to answer only when necessary to preserve a privilege, to enforce a limitation on evidence directed by the court, or to protect a witness from examination "being conducted in bad faith or in such a manner as to annoy, embarrass, or oppress the deponent or party." *Morales v. Zondo, Inc.*, 204 F.R.D. 50, 53 (S.D.N.Y. 2001). Counsel advising a deponent not to answer a question should know ahead of time that a successful motion to compel an answer may result in fee shifting for the follow-up deposition. *See* Fed. R. Civ. P. 30(d)(2). Additionally, counsel taking the deposition may adjourn it and submit the objection for resolution to the emergency judge sitting in the jurisdiction where the deposition is being held, though practically, such an adjournment is rarely used. Instead, the best practice is to advise the other side, on the record, that failure to answer a question may result in the deposition being retaken at a later date at the deponent's expense. While this may not result in an answer to the question posed, it will preserve counsel's admonition for the record.

The following objection checklist is not exhaustive, but it is a good starting point for the objections that a defending attorney may use during a deposition. These objections should be stated simply: "Objection, the question. . .

- assumes facts not in evidence."
- is speculative."
- is leading."
- is vague/ambiguous/unintelligible."
- has been asked and answered."
- is compound."
- is designed to harass the deponent."
- mischaracterizes the exhibit presented to the deponent."
- calls upon the witness to address an exhibit that lacks authentication."
- calls for privileged information. I am instructing the witness not to answer with respect to any information protected by the attorney/client privilege."

Deficiency Letters

The first step in addressing inadequate written discovery responses should be a deficiency letter that lays out each and every improper objection to a request, inadequate response to an interrogatory, and insufficient production of documents. Below are examples of such a letter. They are deliberately detailed and provide a flavor for the type of letter that should be sent not long after receiving inadequate responses.

It should also be noted that the TTAB has special rules for the extent to which a party can obtain discovery because of the necessarily limited relevance of certain information to the question of registrability, so deficiency letters in TTAB proceedings should reference the specific section of the Trademark Board Manual of Procedure to lend arguments more credibility. *See* TBMP § 414.

FORM 9.1
Deficiency Letters

Dear Guillermo:

Thank you for the objections and written responses to discovery of Defendant that you provided on August 27, 2008. As set forth in more detail below, we believe many of Defendant's objections are baseless attempts to circumvent its discovery obligations. To avoid forcing us to seek the Court's intervention, we ask that Defendant withdraw these objections and supplement its responses on or before September 20, 2008.

Defendant's Objections Regarding Plaintiff's Trademark Registrations

Defendant objects to: (a) Interrogatory Nos. 4, 5, 6, 7, 8, 9, 10, 12, 13, and 14 on the basis that it must "ascertain for itself what trademarks are registered in the name of Plaintiff because Plaintiff has never provided the Respondent with certificates of registration of trade marks. . ."; (b) Document Request Nos. 1, 2, 3, 4, 5, 6, 7, 8, 9, 10, 11, 12, 13, 14, and 29 on the basis that the requests are ". . . vague as to what constitutes the 'Mexican product' since Plaintiff has not provided the Respondent with any certificate of registration for any trademark it claims to possess. . ."; and (c) Admission Request Nos. 1, 2, 5, 6, 7, 8, 9, 10, 11, 12, 16, 19, and 21 on the basis that "Plaintiff has not shown to Defendant the certificates of registration of the 'Infringed marks' and Plaintiff cannot assume that the definition of 'Infringed marks' given by Plaintiff is correct."

These objections have no merit. Defendant's refusal to respond to these discovery requests violates its discovery obligations. Paragraph 8 of the Complaint specifically identifies Plaintiff's federal registrations, the marks registered, and the goods for which Plaintiff uses the marks. Thus, the Complaint provides more than sufficient information for Defendant to respond. Moreover, Plaintiff's federal registrations may be viewed through the United States Patent and Trademark Office ("USPTO") website, in the unlikely event that you or Defendant need additional detail. See www.uspto.gov. Indeed, as a matter of law, Defendant has constructive notice of the contents of Plaintiff's federal registrations. See 15 U.S.C. § 1072. Thus, your client is fully aware of the contents of Plaintiff's federal trademark registrations referenced in Plaintiff's discovery requests. Furthermore, Defendant must respond to these requests to the extent they are not objectionable, which it did not do. See FED. R. CIV. P. 33(b)(3), 34(b)(2)(C), 36(a)(4).

Objections to Interrogatories

- *Interrogatory No. 1*: This interrogatory seeks the identity of Defendant's affiliate entities and its owners, officers, employees, etc. You object to this interrogatory on the basis that it is overbroad and not reasonably calculated to lead to the discovery of admissible evidence, but you do not provide a specific reason for this objection. *See* Fed. R. Civ. P. 33(b) (4) (grounds for an objection must be stated with specificity). The information sought bears directly on this case, including the identity of witnesses and other persons with relevant information. Defendant, also without explanation, objects to this interrogatory as seeking "unnecessary and confidential and sensitive business information." Information regarding Defendant's affiliates, officers, and employees is not privileged or otherwise protected as confidential. Thus, this objection is meritless, and we ask that Defendant supplement its response with the information that we seek.
- *Interrogatory No. 3*: Defendant objects to this interrogatory as vague and overbroad but provides no specific reason for this objection. Moreover, your statement that Defendant and Latin have no "affiliation" is not responsive because you do not fully describe Defendant's relationship with Latin otherwise. Thus, this objection is baseless, and we ask that Defendant supplement its response with the information that we seek, specifically, that Defendant identify the companies' relationship, if any.
- *Interrogatory Nos. 4–10, 12–14*: Defendant objects to these interrogatories as unduly burdensome and overbroad but give no specific reason for any objection as it relates to each interrogatory. *See* Fed. R. Civ. P. 33(b)(4) (grounds for an objection must be stated with specificity). These interrogatories require Defendant to identify persons with knowledge of facts relevant to Plaintiff's claims, purchase and sale information regarding the products at issue, the locations from which Defendant has sold the products at issue and, instances of consumer confusion. The identity of individuals with relevant information and the purchase and sale information sought are within Defendant's knowledge and relate directly to Plaintiff's claims. Once again, these objections are unfounded, and we ask that Defendant supplement its response.
- *Interrogatory No. 11*: Defendant objects to this interrogatory as overbroad, unduly burdensome, vague, and not reasonably calculated to lead to the discovery of admissible evidence. Again, you provide no specific reason for these objections as the Federal Rules require. This interrogatory seeks information concerning the extent of Defendant's infringement of Plaintiff's marks, including marks other than the Infringed marks. Thus, it is directly relevant to Plaintiff's claims of trademark infringement. Defendant, also without explanation, further objects to this

interrogatory as seeking "sensitive and confidential business information." Information regarding Defendant's sales of foreign soft drinks in the United States, and the brands of those soft drinks is not privileged or otherwise protected as confidential. Defendant's objection has no merit, and we ask that Defendant supplement its response.

- *Interrogatory No. 14*: Without any explanation, Defendant objects to this interrogatory as vague as to consumer confusion and mistake. These terms are directly from the Federal Trademark Act and, therefore, have clear meanings. According to your unexplained objections of overbreadth and undue burden, Defendant admits that it has encountered so many instances of consumer confusion and mistake, that it cannot bear the burden of identifying those instances. Consumer confusion is central to Plaintiff's claims. Defendant must supplement its response.

- *Interrogatory No. 15*: Again without any explanation, Defendant objects to this interrogatory as overbroad, unduly burdensome, vague, and not reasonably calculated to lead to the discovery of admissible evidence. The identity of the persons responsible for the maintenance and preservation of Defendant's electronically stored information is directly relevant to your client's records concerning the purchase and sale of the products at issue in this dispute. Defendant must supplement its response with the information that we seek.

Objections to Document Requests

- *Document Request Nos. 2–5*: Defendant, without explanation, objects to these requests as seeking "sensitive and confidential business information that is not relevant." To the extent Defendant wishes to invoke the attorney-client privilege or work-product doctrine, it must identify and describe those materials under Rule 26(b)(5) and provide a privilege log. We reject, however, Defendant's attempt to withhold as "sensitive" all documents related to Defendant's sale of Mexican product, its decisions and timing of those sales, and Defendant's sources for the Mexican product that it sells and/or has sold. If particular documents truly are confidential, Defendant must identify them and produce them under an appropriate protective order that Defendant would need to obtain from the Court.

- *Document Request Nos. 7–8*: Again, Defendant, without explanation, objects to these requests as seeking "sensitive and confidential business information that is not relevant." Invoices related to Defendant's purchases and sales of Mexican product are not privileged and are not otherwise protected as confidential. This objection has no merit, and Defendant must provide documents responsive to this request.

- *Document Request No. 9*: Defendant objects to this document request as "vague as to consumer confusion or mistake." Again, these terms are directly from the Federal Trademark Act and, therefore, have clear meanings. Thus, please withdraw this objection and provide documents responsive to this request.
- *Document Request No. 10*: Defendant, without explanation, objects to this request as seeking "sensitive and confidential business information that is not relevant." Catalogs, brochures, and other marketing materials that suppliers and/or potential suppliers of Mexican product are directly related to Defendant's purchases and sales of Mexican product. These documents are not privileged and are not otherwise protected as confidential. This objection has no merit, and Defendant must provide documents responsive to this request.
- *Document Request No. 11*: Again without explanation, Defendant objects to this request as seeking "sensitive and confidential business information that is not relevant." Documents sufficient to identify the quantity of Mexican product sold by Defendant are not privileged and are not otherwise protected as confidential. This objection has no merit, and Defendant must provide documents responsive to this request.
- *Document Request No. 13–14*: Defendant, without explanation, objects to this request as seeking "sensitive and confidential business information that is not relevant." Documents that show Defendant's profits and the calculation of its profits derived from Defendant's sales of Mexican product relate to a central component of Plaintiff's claims. These documents are not privileged and are not otherwise protected as confidential. Defendant must provide documents responsive to these requests. If particular documents truly are confidential, Defendant must identify them and produce them under an appropriate protective order that Defendant would need to obtain from the Court.
- *Document Request No. 15*: Defendant, without explanation, objects to this request as vague, overbroad, and unduly burdensome. The discovery rules do not permit Defendant to withhold documents related to the defenses that Defendant has invoked in this litigation. Defendant must provide documents responsive to this request.
- *Document Request Nos. 18, 19, 20, and 21*: Defendant objects to these requests as "not relevant" but refuses to provide documents to the extent that they are not objectionable. Documents concerning the entities related to Defendant, the individuals involved in Defendant's infringing sales operations, Mr. Zabaleta-Valdez's participation in that business are relevant, if not central, to Plaintiff's claims and Defendant's defenses. Defendant must provide documents responsive to these requests.
- *Document Request Nos. 22 and 25*: Defendant objects to these requests as vague and overbroad, without any specified reason. Defendant's relationship with Latin Products bears directly on the litigation because

both entities participated in Defendant's improper sales of Mexican soft drinks under the INFRINGED marks. This objection has no merit, and Defendant must provide documents responsive to these requests.

- *Document Request No. 24*: Defendant objects to this request as vague and overbroad, without any specified reason. The law does not permit Defendant to withhold documents that would identify all locations where it does business. Defendant must provide documents responsive to this request.

- *Document Request No. 26*: Defendant objects to this request as seeking privileged work product and attorney-client communications. This request asks only for opinions of counsel upon which Defendant intends to rely to defend against claims of willful trademark infringement. Since we are only asking for documents that would be introduced in Court to support Defendant's contention on point, Defendant must produce such documents or waive any defense that it relied on the advice of counsel. Thus, please confirm that Defendant has no such documents or withdraw this objection and provide a response by the deadline we have provided.

- *Document Request No. 27*: Defendant objects to this request as "seeking privileged sensitive and confidential business information." To the extent Defendant wishes to invoke the attorney-client privilege or work-product doctrine, it must identify and describe those materials under Rule 26(b)(5) and provide a privilege log. If particular documents truly are confidential, Defendant must identify them and produce them under an appropriate protective order that Defendant would need to obtain from the Court. Otherwise, these documents are relevant to damages incurred by Plaintiff as the result of Defendant's infringing conduct. This objection is baseless, and Defendant must provide documents responsive to this request.

- *Document Request No. 29*: Again without explanation, Defendant objects to this request as seeking "sensitive and confidential business information that is not relevant." The Mexican product that Defendant sold is central to this litigation. Specimens of those products are not privileged and are not otherwise protected as confidential. Defendant must provide documents responsive to this request.

Despite Defendant's above-detailed failure to properly respond to our discovery requests, we will accept supplemental responses to these discovery requests if Defendant retracts these baseless objections and provides proper responses on or before September 20, 2008. To the extent you wish to discuss or clarify any specific request or objection, please contact us to set up a time before September 20, 2008, to meet and confer by telephone to address those specific concerns. Otherwise, should Defendant maintain its refusal to honor its discovery obligations, we will seek relief from the Court, including an award of Plaintiff's attorneys' fees and costs under Rule 37.

Cordially,

Dear Gary:

We write to address deficiencies in your responses to our discovery requests. We note initially that the protective order obviates your objections that certain discovery requests seek "proprietary, confidential or commercially sensitive documents." Please immediately produce all documents and information withheld on that basis. The same goes for the numerous documents and interrogatory responses that you expressly withheld until entry of a protective order.

Document Requests

For many document requests, you agree to make documents available for inspection at Defendant's facilities. Please let us know the dates and times when we may conduct an inspection. I suggest we shoot for early January.

You object to several requests on the grounds that they are "overly broad" or "unduly burdensome." For each such request, please state whether documents have been withheld on the basis of these objections, which we believe to be unfounded.

You claim several requests are "harassing." For each such request, please state whether documents have been withheld on the basis of that objection. Further, you do not identify any intrusion, annoyance, or other burden that would justify a refusal to respond. The requests seek relevant and discoverable information and documents. For instance, Document Request No. 5 seeks documents "sufficient to identify" dates and amounts of payments received and owed to Defendant since 2000. Document Request No. 6 requests documents or information "sufficient to identify" persons making or owing such payments as identified in Document Request No. 5. That's perfectly reasonable and not "harassing."

We hereby clarify Document Request No. 28 to seek documents sufficient to identify persons under Defendant's employ from 2004 to 2006. They are potential witnesses, and we are entitled to discover their identity.

You object to several requests on the grounds that they seek attorney-client privileged information and/or communications (e.g., Document Request Nos. 10, 11, and 21). But you have not given us a privilege log. Please do so right away. It must include the basis for privilege, date of document, originator, recipient, and all persons who were sent or shown copies, and a description of the type of document and the subject matter to which it pertains.

You claim several requests seek irrelevant documents (e.g., Document Request Nos. 5–7, 17, 22, 23, 27, and 28). For each such request, please state whether documents have been withheld on the basis of that objection, which we believe to be unfounded.

Document Requests Nos. 1, 2, and 3

You do not object to these requests, yet your production is plainly incomplete. This request seeks, among other things, all drafts of the claimed copyrighted works, all materials related to any claim of actual damages, as well as all documents relating or referring to the copyright registration, including but not limited to the copyright application, drawings, any correspondence between the Plaintiff and the Copyright Office, and all documents relating in any way to the timing of the copyright registration. These materials are at the heart of the case, and we are entitled to all of them. Please produce them.

Document Request No. 3

You claim that "any facts or circumstances that may limit or bar Plaintiff's recovery" is overly broad, vague, and ambiguous. The overbreadth objection in plainly meritless, and you cannot rely on it to hold back any documents. We also don't see vagueness and ambiguity in the request. Please explain what you do not understand, so we can clarify if appropriate.

Document Request No. 4

You claim this request is "vague and ambiguous." We hereby clarify that the request's reference to "First Set of Requests for Production of Documents" should be replaced by "First Request for Interrogatories."

Document Request Nos. 5–9

Please state whether any documents related to the Yorkville site have been withheld on the basis of your objections, or confirm that your discovery is complete. Also, please state whether there are any documents that you are planning not to make available for inspection.

Document Request No. 10

Please state whether any documents have been withheld on the basis of your objections, or state that your production is complete.

Document Request No. 11

While you have agreed to produce responsive, nonprivileged documents, no responsive documents have been produced. Please produce all responsive documents, or state that your production is complete.

Document Request Nos. 12 and 13

While you don't object to these requests, no responsive documents have been produced. Please produce all responsive documents, or state that your production is complete.

Document Request Nos. 14 and 19

You object to these requests on the ground that responsive documents "are publicly available." The objection is meritless. If you have legal support for your position, please provide it to us. Moreover, there must be many responsive documents that are not publicly available, so the premise of your objection is incorrect. Also, you have no basis to restrict production to the "Copyrighted Work" and the "Yorkville Site," as you do regarding request no. 14. Please produce all responsive documents, or state that your production is complete.

Document Request Nos. 15 and 17

You state that you will produce responsive documents, if any. You have no basis to restrict production to the "Copyrighted Work" and the "Yorkville Site," as you do regarding request no. 15. Please produce all responsive documents, or state that your production is complete.

Document Request Nos. 16 and 18

You claim that "oral contract or understanding" in request no. 16 is vague and ambiguous. But you don't object to the same language in request no. 18. In any event, Defendant defines "oral contract or understanding" as any verbal or spoken communication or agreement between the parties, not memorialized in writing. With that clarification, please produce all responsive documents, or state that your production is complete. You have, of course, no basis to restrict production to the "Copyrighted Work" and the "Yorkville Site," as you do regarding request no. 16.

Document Requests Nos. 20–27

It appears that no responsive documents have been produced. Please produce all responsive documents, or state that your production is complete. As I said before, you have no basis to restrict production to the "Copyrighted Work" and the "Yorkville Site," as you do regarding requests nos. 22, 26, and 27.

In sum, your document production to date appears notably paltry and incomplete. Please supplement it fully at your earliest convenience.

Interrogatories

Interrogatory Nos. 1, 3, 9, and 10

You claim the contents of Mr. Bonham's June 29, 2006 letter is governed by FRE 408. Defendant notes that documents and/or information that may be inadmissible at trial are nevertheless still discoverable. Facts or circumstances surrounding the letter may potentially lead to other discoverable information to which Defendant is entitled under the Federal Rules of Civil Procedure. At this point, it is premature to withhold information and documents on the basis that they are inadmissible as evidence at trial. Subject to this objection, Plaintiff agrees to produce Plaintiff's business records upon the entry of the protective order. Since the protective order has been entered, we expect Plaintiff's business records will be forthcoming.

Interrogatory Nos. 2 and 13

Plaintiff responds to these interrogatories, stating that no information is known. Plaintiff also fails to produce any documents responsive to these interrogatories. We remind Plaintiff of its continuing duty to investigate and supplement its discovery throughout the course of the pending litigation. Defendant expects Plaintiff to supplement these responses and provide any document and/or information responsive to these interrogatories.

Interrogatory Nos. 5 and 6

Plaintiff states that information responsive to these interrogatories can be ascertained from Plaintiff's business records and will be made available upon the entry of a protective order. Since the protective order has been entered, as we've stated before, we expect Plaintiff's business records will be forthcoming. Please also provide any other responsive information that cannot be deduced from these business records.

Interrogatory No. 7

Plaintiff objects to this interrogatory on the grounds of the attorney-client privilege and attorney work product doctrine. To the extent that your objections invoke the attorney-client privilege or attorney work product doctrine, please supply a privilege log including the following information: basis for privilege, date of document, originator, recipient, and all persons who were sent or shown copies.

We hope to resolve these discovery concerns without having to resort to a motion to compel. Please respond to these deficiencies no later two weeks from today.

Cordially,

Dear Paul:

We have reviewed Applicant's Answers to Opposer's First Set of Interrogatories. As an initial matter, we note that your client's responses are untimely and, therefore, all objections to our interrogatories are waived. *See* Fed. R. Civ. P. 33(b)(4). This is true, also, for responses to our document requests, both the two you sent last night and those we still have not received. Your client's interrogatory answers were served on February 8, 2010, despite your written commitment in the parties' Notice of Agreement on Expert Disclosure, signed by you and filed with the Board, to provide them by January 29, 2010. Aside from being untimely, Applicant's answers also suffer from the following specific deficiencies:

Confidentiality: You raise general and specific objections on the ground of confidentiality and refuse to provide information in response to Interrogatories 16, 19, and 28 on that ground. As we stated in our February 9, 2010, e-mail, the Board's standard protective order already is in place and, therefore, confidentiality is not a proper objection. *See* 37 C.F.R. 2.116(g). Accordingly, Applicant may not withhold any information based on this objection.

Interrogatory No. 1: In response to this interrogatory, you refuse to identify the dates on which each of Applicant's goods or services was first offered because you assert that the phrase "was first offered" is vague and ambiguous in that "offered" is unqualified. Your objection is disingenuous, as you yourself use the same term in response to Interrogatory No. 22 when you state that "the product was offered as a subscription-free service until 2007." Clearly, you understand the meaning of this term, which is commonly used in the trademark context, and your client's refusal to answer appears to us to be in bad faith. Please provide the requested information immediately.

Interrogatory No. 2: The answers provide only a telephone number for the individuals listed in response to this interrogatory. The definitions section of our interrogatories indicates that, when Applicant identifies an individual, she is also requested to provide additional contact information, including an employer, position, and address. At a minimum, we must have a current e-mail address for each of the individuals identified in response to this interrogatory.

Interrogatory No. 16: As stated above, the objection to this interrogatory on the ground of confidentiality is improper given that the Board's standard protective order automatically is in place in this proceeding. Moreover, even in the absence of a protective order, this objection would be misplaced given that the interrogatory seeks information related only to historical use of the Mark, which is central to any trademark dispute. Please provide all information requested in this interrogatory immediately.

Interrogatory No. 17: This interrogatory asks Applicant to identify with particularity any and all uses of the Mark by Applicant prior to February 19, 2007. You objected by claiming that the term "uses" is vague and ambiguous and refused to provide an answer. You know that your objection is disingenuous in this context, since the term "use" is defined in the Lanham Act. *See* 15 U.S.C. § 1127 ("'Use' of a mark means the bona fide use of such mark made in the ordinary course of trade, and not made merely to reserve a right in a mark"). Consistent with this definition, please provide a response to this question immediately.

Interrogatory No. 19: As stated above, your objection to this interrogatory on the ground of confidentiality is improper given that the Board's standard protective order automatically is in place in this proceeding. Moreover, your objection is also misplaced given that the interrogatory seeks information related only to historical use of the Mark. Please provide the information requested in this interrogatory immediately.

Interrogatory Nos. 21 and 26: Your objection that sales and marketing figures for goods or services offered in connection with the Mark are not relevant is without merit. These figures are relevant and discoverable. *See* TBMP § 414(18). Please provide the information requested in this interrogatory immediately.

Interrogatory No. 23: You object that identifying the number of consumers who have used or purchased Applicant's goods or services for each year since its inception is burdensome and oppressive, and that the information is irrelevant. We do not believe this request is burdensome. However, to move this matter forward, we will limit this request by asking Applicant only to identify the number of consumers who have used or purchased Applicant's goods or services in 2005, 2006, and 2007, by year. This information is undisputedly relevant to the issue of priority, which your client has asserted as a defense in this proceeding.

Interrogatory No. 28: As stated above, your objection to this interrogatory on the ground of confidentiality is improper given that the Board's standard protective order automatically is in place in this proceeding. Moreover, this information is both relevant and discoverable. *See* TBMP § 414(4), (6). Please provide the information requested in this interrogatory immediately.

This is clearly not an exhaustive list of all of the deficiencies in your interrogatory answers, but in the interest of time, we rest on this list and the initial observation in this letter that EVERY objection to our requests was waived when your client failed to serve objections by the agreed deadline. As I indicated in my voice mail last night, we are very disappointed that your client has apparently decided not to participate in good faith in discovery in this proceeding. We still hope we may be able to resolve these concerns without the need to take them to the Board. To avoid a request for sanctions, however, we must have a full, complete, and good-faith response to these deficiencies—and your client's verification of her completed interrogatory answers—no later than this Friday.

Response to Deficiency Letter

Responding to a deficiency letter is more difficult than writing one because it requires the lawyer to consider the arguments of his adversary and address them in a reasonable manner. Conceding discovery objections that address requests that do not go to the heart of a case often will invite compromise from your adversary and convey the impression that you want to be fair and reasonable. To do otherwise invites the arbiter of the dispute—whether the judge for the case, the magistrate, an interlocutory attorney, or another neutral—to view you as the unreasonable party. On the other hand, you likely asserted objections because you thought they were proper and legitimate. Standing your ground in the face of unconvincing arguments is essential to the lawyer's practice. Below is just one example of a response to a deficiency letter that gives where appropriate without giving too much.

FORM 9.2
Response to Deficiency Letter

Dear Mr. Davis:

We write in response to your correspondence dated February 22, 2005, regarding Opposer's Response to Applicant's First Set of Interrogatories.

You clarified the term "use" in Interrogatory Nos. 1, 4, 8, and 13, to be understood as Opposer used the term "use" in Paragraph 10 of the Notice of Opposition. Without waiver of its other objections, Opposer will produce responsive, nonprivileged documents related to the use of the configurations, as understood by Opposer, referenced in Interrogatory Nos. 1, 4, 8, and 13.

You clarified the phrase "each business" in Interrogatory No. 2 as "each commercial enterprise, whether for-profit or nonprofit." Opposer continues its objection as the phrase remains vague and unclear, but to the extent that it understands the phrase, Opposer will produce responsive, nonprivileged documents for Interrogatory No. 2.

With respect to Interrogatory Nos. 6, 7, 16, 22, 24, and 25, you state simply that you consider the word mark to be relevant. Could you please provide an explanation of why, as we fail to see the relevance.

You corrected a typographical error in Interrogatory No. 7 and therefore Opposer withdraws its objection on the ground that no "third party [is] mentioned in Interrogatory No. 7." Without waiver of its other objections, Opposer will produce responsive, nonprivileged documents for Interrogatory No. 7.

You clarified the phrase "Opposer race car shape" in Interrogatory No. 18 as the "outline or contour" of "the automobile Opposer purportedly developed in 1963, as claimed by Opposer in paragraph 3 of the Notice of Opposition." Without waiver of its other objections, Opposer will produce responsive, nonprivileged documents for Interrogatory No. 18.

You state that you fail to see the reasoning behind Opposer's objection to Interrogatory No. 23 that the word mark is irrelevant to this proceeding. We stand by this objection as the issue in this proceeding is whether Applicant is entitled to register the configuration in the opposed application. Royalties for the word mark are irrelevant.

We trust that the above analysis satisfies the issues raised in your February 22, 2005, letter. We continue to gather responsive documents from our client and will produce documents as they become available. You should expect more documents and information within the next couple of weeks.

If you have any questions, please feel free to contact us.

Best regards,

Chapter 9.3–Motions to Compel

After attempting to resolve a dispute through the exchange of deficiency letters and responses, as well as having a discussion on any remaining issues, if disputes remain there is nothing to do but file a motion to compel under Fed. R. Civ. P. 37. The first motion below is a straightforward motion to compel where one party failed to respond to discovery entirely. It also lays the groundwork for seeking sanctions along with the motion to compel under Fed. R. Civ. P. 37. Generally, the severity of the sanctions will be commensurate with the severity of the misconduct by one side or the other. Where both sides have tried to resolve their differences in good faith, the party seeking sanctions likely will not get them, or will only obtain the sanction of requiring the other side to respond without objection, but some courts are far more harsh, including granting fees and costs associated with the filing of a successful motion.

Motion to Compel Discovery

Plaintiff's Motion to Compel Discovery

Pursuant to Rules 37(a) and (d) of the Federal Rules of Civil Procedure, Plaintiff moves this Court to compel Defendants to respond to Plaintiff's discovery requests issued on October 23, 2008. In support of this Motion, Plaintiff states as follows:

1. On October 23, 2008, Plaintiff served its First Set of Document Requests and First Set of Interrogatories on Defendants by first class mail, with a courtesy copy sent via e-mail. True and correct copies of Plaintiff's first sets of document requests and interrogatories are attached hereto as **Exhibit A**.

2. Defendants did not serve responses to Plaintiff's discovery requests by the November 25, 2008 deadline. Decl. of Plaintiff's counsel ¶ 4.

3. While the parties continued to discuss settlement, counsel for Plaintiff informed counsel for Defendants that Plaintiff expected Defendants to respond to Plaintiff's outstanding interrogatories and document requests. On February 23, 2009, counsel for Plaintiff sent Defendant's counsel an e-mail stating that if Defendants did not accept the latest settlement proposal by March 2, 2009,[1] the settlement would be withdrawn, and Defendants would need to produce responsive documents by no later than March 9, 2009. Decl. of Plaintiff's counsel ¶ 5, Ex. 1. On February 24, 2009, Defendant's counsel responded: "I understand. I will inform my client accordingly." *Id.* ¶ 6, 8 Ex. 2.

4. After further discussions regarding the proposed settlement, on March 6, 2009, Plaintiff's counsel sent Defendant's counsel a further e-mail stating that Plaintiff must receive by March 13, 2009, either the settlement agreement signed by Defendants or responses to Plaintiff's discovery. *Id.* ¶ 7, Ex. 3. Defendants have yet to sign the settlement agreement or provide their responses to Plaintiff's discovery requests. *Id.* ¶ 8.

5. During the week of March 16, 2009, counsel for Plaintiff called Defendant's counsel, more than once, to meet and confer about Defendants' failure to respond to Plaintiff's outstanding discovery requests. Decl. of Plaintiff's counsel ¶ 3. Although Plaintiff's counsel did not reach Defendant's counsel, he left voice mail messages. *Id.* Based on these messages, Defendant's counsel was fully aware that a motion to compel would be filed if Defendants failed to live up to their discovery obligations. *Id.* Plaintiff's counsel has made several follow up telephone

---

1. The parties subsequently agreed to extend this date until March 13, 2009.

calls to Defendant's counsel, but Defendants' counsel has not returned Plaintiff's counsel's messages. *Id.* ¶ 4.

6. Defendants' complete failure to respond to Plaintiff's discovery constitutes sanctionable conduct pursuant to Fed. R. Civ. P. 37(d), and entitles Plaintiff to an order compelling Defendants to respond to the outstanding interrogatories and document requests pursuant to Fed. R. Civ. P. 37(a)(3)(B)(iii) and (iv) and awarding to Plaintiff its reasonable expenses, including attorneys' fees, caused by such failure. Moreover, by failing to provide timely objections to Plaintiff's discovery requests, Defendants have waived their ability to object to these requests. *See, e.g.,* Fed. R. Civ. P. 33(b)(4).

7. Pursuant to Fed. R. Civ. P. 37(d)(1)(B), Plaintiff certifies that it has attempted in good faith to confer with Defendants about their failure to respond to Plaintiff's discovery requests. Defendant's counsel has failed to return Plaintiff's counsel's numerous phone calls on this subject, thus necessitating the filing of this Motion and the involvement of this Court. *See* Decl. of Plaintiff's counsel ¶ ¶ 3–4.

WHEREFORE, Plaintiff respectfully requests that this Court enter an order:

A. Compelling Defendants to produce documents responsive to Plaintiff's First Set of Document Requests served on October 23, 2008 and to provide full and complete answers to Plaintiff's First Set of Interrogatories served on October 23, 2008;

B. Ruling that any objections to Plaintiff's First Set of Interrogatories and First Set of Document Requests are waived by Defendants' failure to serve a timely response;

C. Granting Plaintiff an award its reasonable expenses, including attorneys' fees, caused by Defendants' failure to produce documents and failure to answer Plaintiff's interrogatories, including Plaintiff's fees and expenses associated with the filing of this motion; and

D. Granting Plaintiff such other and further relief as this Court sees fit. Respectfully submitted

Motion to Compel and Extend Deadlines

Opposer's Motion to Compel Discovery
And Extend Remaining Deadlines

In accordance with Rule 2.120(e) of the Trademark Rules of Practice, Opposer moves to compel discovery from Applicant and to extend all remaining deadlines by sixty (60) days. Applicant has failed to supplement its incomplete discovery responses or otherwise address the deficiencies Opposer detailed in a six-page letter sent on August 28, 2009. Applicant also has not produced a single document in this proceeding, improperly relying on the fact that Opposer is still in the process of gathering its own documents for production. Opposer also requests a sixty (60)-day extension of discovery to allow sufficient time to complete discovery after receiving Applicant's documents. In further support of its motion, Opposer states the following:

I. Opposer has opposed Applicant's application to register the Mark for the Goods based on Opposer's family of trademarks for related goods. Opposer owns numerous registrations for its family of marks, as shown in Paragraph 3 of its Notice of Opposition.

II. On April 1, 2009, the parties each served interrogatories and requests for production of documents. Attached as Exhibits 1 and 2 to the Declaration of Phillip Barengolts are Opposer's First Set of Interrogatories and First Set of Requests for Production of Documents ("Opposer's Discovery Requests"). (See Declaration of Phillip Barengolts ("Barengolts Decl.") ¶ 4, attached hereto as Exhibit A; Exhibits 1 and 2). Opposer also served a notice of a Rule 30(b)(6) deposition. (Barengolts Decl. ¶ 5).

III. On June 22, 2009, Applicant responded to Opposer's Discovery Requests with insufficient written answers and no documents. (Barengolts Decl. ¶ 6; Exhibits 3 and 4). Opposer provided written responses to Applicant's discovery requests around that same date.

IV. On August 26, 2009, Opposer's counsel contacted Applicant's counsel suggesting that the parties agree to extend discovery by sixty (60) days, given that neither party had produced any documents and that the applicant's answer remained insufficient. (Barengolts Decl. ¶ 7). Applicant would only agree to a thirty (30)-day extension, on the condition that Opposer produce all documents within 30 days and not seek any additional extensions. (Barengolts Decl. ¶ 7). Opposer could not agree to this request, in large part because 30 days is not sufficient time for Opposer to complete discovery after receipt of Applicant's documents.

V.   On August 28, 2009, Opposer's counsel contacted Applicant's counsel by phone and sent Applicant a letter addressing the deficiencies in Applicant's discovery responses. (Barengolts Decl. ¶ ¶ 8, 9; Exhibit 5).

VI.   On September 4, 2009, Opposer's counsel followed up with Applicant's counsel by phone to determine if the deficiencies detailed in the August 28th letter would be addressed. (Barengolts Decl. ¶ 10).

VII.   To date, Applicant has not responded to Opposer's letter.

VIII. Fact discovery in this matter is set to close on September 21, 2009.

IX.   Opposer now moves to compel discovery based on Applicant's deficient responses and failure to produce documents.

Objections Based on Confidentiality

X.   In response to Interrogatories 6 and 10 and Document Requests 3, 7–11, 13, 14, and 21, Applicant objected that the requests seek confidential and proprietary business information. This objection is not applicable because the Board's standard protective order is in place pursuant to Rule 2.116(g) of the Trademark Rules of practice and the parties' explicit agreement to abide by it following a discussion during the initial discovery conference. *See* 37 C.F.R. § 2.116(g); (Barengolts Decl. ¶ 3). Accordingly, to the extent Applicant withheld or plans to withhold information or documents based upon this objection, Applicant must supplement its answers to include the withheld information.

Specific Deficiencies in Applicant's Interrogatory Responses

XI.   Opposer's Interrogatory No. 6 states:

State Applicant's annual dollar and unit volume of sales and/or anticipated annual dollar and unit volume of sales in the United States for each good and/or service sold in connection with the mark.

Applicant objected on the basis of confidentiality and that the interrogatory fails to specify the years for which information is requested, stating that it would provide a summary of information upon entry of a protective order. As noted above, confidentiality is not a proper basis for an objection. In addition, Opposer clarified in its August 28, 2009, letter that this interrogatory seeks Applicant's dollar and unit volume of sales since the first use date of the mark, which Applicant claims is June 1, 2006. Applicant has failed to supplement its response. There can be no doubt that Opposer is entitled to this information. *See Sunkist Growers, Inc. v. Benjamin Ansel Co.*, 229 U.S.P.Q. 147, 149 (T.T.A.B. 1985) ("gross annual sales figures are relevant to these proceedings and must be provided"); *Am. Optical Corp. v. Exomet, Inc.*, 181 U.S.P.Q. 120, 123 (T.T.A.B. 1974) (information concerning extent of sales is relevant and applicant must furnish round figures); TBMP § 414(18) (annual sales figures are proper matters for discovery).

XII. Opposer's Interrogatory No. 8 states:

Identify the types of outlets and representative specific outlets in the United States through which each good and/or service marketed in connection with the mark is or will be offered or sold.

Applicant responded that the term "outlets" is vague, ambiguous, and unintelligible in this context and failed to provide any response. In its August 28, 2009, letter, Opposer clarified that "outlets" means the places from which a prospective consumer could purchase or order a good or service sold under the mark. Applicant has failed to supplement its response, even though Opposer is entitled to this information. *See J.B. Williams Co. v. Pepsodent G.m.b.H.*, 188 U.S.P.Q. 577, 580 (T.T.A.B. 1975) ("[A] party must respond to an interrogatory concerning the classes of customers who purchase its products sold under the mark. . .").

XIII. Opposer's Interrogatory No. 9 states:

Identify all media in which each product and/or service sold under the mark has been or will be advertised or promoted, including specific publications, websites, materials and means of communication, and state the period of time each medium has been or will be used.

Applicant's answer that "Applicant's services are not advertised or promoted in the media" is insufficient and unresponsive. Opposer knows that Applicant promotes its services on its website at <www.Applicant.com>, one medium specifically identified in the interrogatory. Opposer also provided other examples of media in its August 28, 2009, letter, including any other websites, brochures or marketing materials, print advertisements, radio advertisements, television advertisements, direct marketing pieces, and face-to-face presentations. Applicant has failed to supplement its response, even though this information is relevant to this proceeding. *See In re E.I. du Pont de Nemours & Co.*, 177 U.S.P.Q. 563, 567 (C.C.P.A. 1973) (identifying the "similarity or dissimilarity of established, likely-to-continue trade channels" as a factor relevant to likelihood of confusion).

XIV. Opposer's Interrogatory No. 10 states:

State Applicant's annual marketing expenses or anticipated marketing expenses
for each type of advertising or promotion Applicant has used or plans to use
for goods and/or services marketed in connection with the mark.

Applicant objected to this interrogatory on the basis of confidentiality
and that the interrogatory fails to specify the years for which information is
requested, stating that it would provide a summary of information upon entry
of a protective order. As stated above, confidentiality is not the proper basis
for an objection. In addition, Opposer clarified in its August 28, 2009, letter
that this interrogatory seeks information since the first use date of the mark,
which Applicant claims is June 1, 2006. Applicant has failed to supplement its
response. There can be no doubt that Opposer is entitled to this information.
See Sunkist Growers, Inc. v. Benjamin Ansel Co., 229 U.S.P.Q. 147, 149
(T.T.A.B. 1985) ("The Board has held that annual sales and advertising figures
of recent years given in round numbers for specific goods bearing the involved
mark(s) are proper matters for discovery. . ."); TBMP § 414(18) (annual
advertising figures are proper matters for discovery).

XV. Interrogatory No. 11 states:

Identify each use, former use, planned use or claim of use by Applicant or any
third party of any term or mark consisting in whole or in part of and the persons
who have knowledge of such use, former use, planned use or claim of use.

Applicant responded, after raising several objections, that it used the mark
but does not use any other term that consists in whole or in part of Opposer's
mark and has no knowledge of such use or plans of such use. Opposer stated
in its August 28, 2009, letter that this response was insufficient because
Applicant has not included information regarding the use of the mark in
connection with other products, or in other variations (e.g., different designs
or displays), or on other materials (e.g., marketing materials or brochures).
Applicant has failed to supplement its answer, even though the information
Opposer seeks is relevant to this proceeding. *See In re E.I. du Pont de Nemours
& Co.*, 177 U.S.P.Q. at 567 (identifying the "variety of goods on which a mark
is or is not used (house mark, 'family' mark, product mark)" as a factor in
determining likelihood of confusion).

Applicant Has Not Produced Any Documents

XVI.   On June 22, 2009, Applicant indicated in written responses to
Opposer's documents requests that it would be producing documents.
It has failed to do so. Applicant has now taken the position that it will

not produce documents because Opposer had not yet produced documents.

Applicant's position is baseless. The law is clear that Applicant's discovery obligations are not excused, even if Opposer has not provided adequate responses. *See Miss America Pageant v. Petite Prods. Inc.*, 17 U.S.P.Q. 2d 1067, 1070 (T.T.A.B. 1990) ("The Board has taken the position that a party is not relieved of its discovery obligations in spite of the fact that its adverse party has wrongfully failed to fulfill its own obligations."); *see also* Fed. R. Civ. P. 26(d). Here, Applicant's position is especially unfounded given that Opposer has provided written discovery responses. In addition, Opposer's task of gathering responsive documents is necessarily time consuming, given its long history of using the many trademarks in its family of marks. By contrast, Applicant has only one mark at issue, which has been in use for less than four years.

Applicant, therefore, has no legitimate basis to withhold its documents and should be ordered to produce them.

Rule 2.120(e) Certification

XVIII. Opposer has made a good-faith effort to confer with Applicant to resolve the issue presented in this motion pursuant to TBMP § 523.02 and C.F.R. § 2.120(e). Counsel for Opposer spoke with counsel for Applicant by phone on August 28, 2009, and raised Applicant's failure to produce any documents. (Barengolts Decl. ¶ 8). Opposer also sent Applicant a letter informing Applicant that it still had an obligation to produce documents despite the fact that Opposer was still gathering its own documents for production. (Barengolts Decl. ¶ 9). That letter also identified each specific deficiency in Applicant's discovery responses. Opposer followed up by phone a week later but has not received a response. (Barengolts Decl. ¶ 10). Despite these efforts, the parties have failed to reach agreement.

Opposer, which continues to gather its own responsive nonprivileged documents, is committed to producing such documents to the extent they are reasonably available within 45 days of the filing of this motion.

WHEREFORE, Opposer respectfully requests that the Board issue an order:

A. compelling Applicant to produce all responsive documents;
B. compelling Applicant to provide full and complete discovery responses as individually outlined above;
C. suspending proceedings with respect to all matters not germane to this motion, including suspension with respect to all of the parties' upcoming

deadlines and the September 21, 2009, close of fact discovery, pursuant to 37 C.F.R. § 2.120(e)(2); and

D. extending all remaining deadlines by sixty (60) days from the date of ruling on this motion, to allow the parties adequate time to receive Applicant's amended or supplemental discovery responses and take depositions.

See the Appendix for the sequence of papers filed by the parties in the heated discovery disputes between SunAmerica and Sun Life.

Motions to Deem Admitted

Fed. R. Civ. P. 36 provides a powerful tool for limiting the scope of litigation, but it often is not used and frequently is misunderstood. Unlike pleadings, requests to admit can relate to almost any matter in controversy. Fed. R. Civ. P. 36(a)(1)(A). Moreover, they must be addressed substantively; otherwise, they may be deemed admitted. Fed. R. Civ. P. 36(a)(4), (6). "A matter admitted under this rule is conclusively established unless the court, on motion, permits the admission to be withdrawn or amended." Fed. R. Civ. P. 36(b).

To have matters presented in a request for admission deemed admitted, requesting counsel must file a motion of the type shown below.

Motion to Deem Admitted

United States District Court for the
District of Nebraska

PLAINTIFF,)	
)	Case No. 8:03 CV 493
Plaintiff,)	
v.)	
)	PLAINTIFF'S
MONEY MAKERS AUTOMOTIVE)	MOTION TO DEEM
	ADMITTED THE
SURPLUS, INC., MIDWEST MOTOR)	MATTERS SET FORTH IN
PARTS CO., and SAF AUTO PARTS,)	PLAINTIFF'S FIRST SET OF
)	REQUESTS FOR ADMISSION
Defendants.)	

Plaintiff's Motion to Deem Admitted
Plaintiff's First Set of Requests for Admission

Pursuant to Local Rule 7.1 and Rule 36(a) of the Federal Rules of Civil Procedure, Plaintiff ("Plaintiff"), asks this Court to deem admitted certain matters set forth in Plaintiff's First Set of Requests for Admission because Defendants' responses failed to either admit or deny those Requests, in contravention of the Federal Rules of Civil Procedure. Defendants have repeatedly ignored the federal and local rules of civil procedure throughout this proceeding, and have thereby impeded the discovery process. Accordingly, this Court should exercise its discretion to deem admitted requests for admission to which Defendants have not properly responded.

I. Facts
A. Statement of Compliance With NELR 7.1

Counsel for the parties conferred on October 21, 2004, concerning the substance of this motion but were unable to reach agreement regarding the relief Plaintiff requests from the Court. (Declaration of Matthew A. Griffin, attached as Ex. 1).

B. Defendants' Responses to Plaintiff's First Set of Requests for Admission

On August 9, 2004, Plaintiff served its First Set of Requests for Admission ("Requests," attached hereto as Ex. 2). On September 10, 2004, the Defendants served their Responses ("Responses," attached hereto as Ex. 3). Defendants responded to the majority of Plaintiff's Requests ("Subject Requests") by stating only that "Defendant neither admits nor denies [the corresponding] Request for Admission." (*See* Ex. 3 at Responses Nos.: 4, 13–64, 111, 114–18, 126–27, 132–33, 135–37 ("Infirm Responses")). These bald refusals to admit or deny are inadequate under Rule 36(a) of the Federal Rules of Civil Procedure.

II. Argument

A. The Federal Rules Provide for Insufficient Responses to Requests for Admission To Be Deemed Admitted

Upon finding that responses to requests for admission do not comply with the requirements of Fed. R. Civ. P. 36, courts may deem the matter admitted. Fed. R. Civ. P. 36; *Rhone Poulenc Rover, Inc. v. The Home Indem. Co.*, 1992 U.S. Dist. LEXIS 20249 (E.D. Pa. Dec. 29, 1992) (deeming admitted requests where party stated that it could neither admit nor deny the request).

1. Defendants' Responses to the Requests for Admission are Insufficient

There are only three acceptable responses to a request for admission. First, an answering party may "specifically deny the matter, or [second] set forth in detail the reasons why the answering party cannot truthfully admit or deny the matter." Fed. R. Civ. P. 36(a). Third, a party may state that it lacks information or knowledge sufficient to respond, but only if "the party states that the party has made reasonable inquiry and that the information known or readily obtainable by the party is insufficient to enable the party to admit or deny." Fed. R. Civ. P. 36(a).

A general statement that the answering party can neither admit nor deny, unaccompanied by reasons, is an insufficient response. Fed. R. Civ. P. 36(a); *United States v. Kenealy*, 646 F.2d 699, 703 (1st Cir. 1981) ("Rule 36 requires specificity, detailed explanation when a truthful answer cannot be framed, good faith, and fairness"; deeming admitted the requests for admission); *Donley v. Cole*, 1988 U.S. Dist. LEXIS 11130 (D. Kans. Sept. 22, 1988) (deeming admitted requests for admission where party was in possession of documents that were the subject of the requests for admission, yet stated that she could neither admit nor deny the authenticity of those documents); *Rhone Poulenc Rover, Inc. v. The Home Indem. Co.*, 1992 U.S. Dist. LEXIS 20249 (E.D. Pa. Dec. 29, 1992) (deeming admitted requests where party stated that it could neither admit nor deny the request).

Indeed, even refusals to admit or deny on the alleged basis of a lack of sufficient knowledge or information will be deemed admitted unless the answering party makes a showing that it had first conducted a reasonable inquiry in preparing its responses. *See In re Sweeten*, 56 B.R. 675, 678 (Bankr. E.D. Pa. 1986) (deeming inadequate party's responses that it had insufficient information and knowledge to admit or deny where answering party made no showing of reasonable inquiry).

Here, each Infirm Response consists of only a cursory, boilerplate response that "Defendants neither admit nor deny" the Request, without explaining the reasons for Defendants' inability to admit or deny. Moreover, Defendants do not describe any inquiry they undertook to obtain information that would have enabled a proper response.[2] Because Defendants' Infirm Responses neither admit nor deny the matter contained in the Requests, nor explain their inability to respond properly, nor describe their attempt to obtain necessary information, the Infirm Responses are insufficient under Rule 36(a) of the Federal Rules of Civil Procedure.

2. This Court Should Deem the Infirm Responses Admitted

This Court has the discretion to order the Referenced Admissions admitted. Fed. R. Civ. P. 36(a); *United States v. Kenealy*, 646 F.2d at 702–03 (trial court within its discretion in deeming matters admitted). Such a remedy is especially appropriate where the answering party fails to undertake reasonable inquiry. *Rhone Poulenc Rover, Inc. v. The Home Indem. Co.*, 1992 U.S. Dist. LEXIS 20249 (E.D. Pa. Dec. 29, 1992). Where the infirm responses are part of a pattern of disregard for a party's discovery obligations, it is yet more appropriate for the Court to enter such an Order. *Kenealy*, 646 F.2d at 703

---

2. Indeed, Defendants could easily have obtained the information necessary to admit many of Plaintiff's requests for admission. For example, Requests Nos. 13–63, seek admissions of facts related to Plaintiff's trademark registrations in the United States Patent and Trademark Office. Defendants could easily have accessed publicly-available information from the Trademark Office's Internet website found at "www.uspto.gov." Instead, the Defendants responded to these requests with the same nonresponsive answers neither admitting nor denying the matters referenced, without even provided detailed reasons—or any reasons whatsoever—for such answers, as required by Rule 36(a). By not making even reasonable strides to obtain such information or knowledge, the Defendants have demonstrated their utter disregard for the rules of discovery and the discovery process.

(upholding order deeming admissions where party's "cavalier conduct in [the] litigation").

Defendants' Infirm Responses refuse to admit or deny the matters set forth in Plaintiff's Requests for Admission. Defendants have not provided any reasons for failing to admit or deny the Requests. Nor have Defendants conducted any inquiry—let alone a reasonable inquiry—in preparation of their responses. Such omissions alone justify deeming the Subject Requests admitted.

III. Conclusion

Because Defendants' Infirm Responses do not comply with the requirements of Rule 36(a) of the Federal Rules of Civil Procedure and because Defendants have consistently disregarded the Federal Rules of Civil Procedure, Plaintiff respectfully moves this Court to deem the admitted the following Subject Requests: Request Nos. 4, 13–64, 114–18, 126–27, 132–33, and 135–37.

Protective Orders

When one side in a litigation asks for discovery that is not easily subject to objection, a motion for a protective order may be necessary. While it is more typical for the parties to agree on an order for protection (see below) for confidential and proprietary information, or even trade secrets, in some circumstances one party will want to protect itself from discovery that otherwise would be required of it.

The most common example of the type of order counsel may seek in trademark and copyright disputes is protection from the attempted deposition of a senior executive. A typical example of such a motion is below.

Standard Two-Tier Stipulated Protective Order in a Federal Case

Stipulated Protective Order

Pursuant to the stipulation of the parties and in accord with the provisions of Rule 26(c) of the Federal Rules of Civil Procedure,

IT IS HEREBY ORDERED THAT:

1. The content of any document or thing produced by any party or third party, any interrogatory answer made by any party, any photograph, note, sketch, or other recordation taken of a party's facility, equipment or method of operation, any deposition testimony taken and any exhibit marked by any party in this action, any information learned as a result of an inspection under Rule 34, Fed. R. Civ. P., and any other information, document or thing received from a party or third party in the course of this litigation (hereinafter collectively identified as "information"), except published information of any origin and nonpublished information which is publicly available, is subject to this Protective Order.

2. Any party to this action who reasonably believes that any such information is a trade secret or other confidential research, development, or commercial information within the meaning of Rule 26(c), Fed. R. Civ. P., shall have the right through its counsel to designate such information "CONFIDENTIAL" in accordance with Paragraphs 3 or 5 below. Such designated information shall thereafter be subject to the terms of this Protective Order, and use or disclosure of information so designated shall be restricted as set forth herein.

3. To designate information as confidential information and thereby subject it to this Protective Order, the party disclosing the information shall place upon the document, thing, paper, or other tangible embodiments of the information, a legend substantially as follows:

Confidential: Subject To Protective Order

Except as otherwise set forth herein, nontangible information shall be expressly designated as confidential information subject to this Protective Order at the time of its disclosure or such status shall be confirmed in writing by the disclosing party within a reasonable time after the disclosure.

4. The information designated "CONFIDENTIAL: SUBJECT TO PROTECTIVE ORDER" as discussed in paragraph 3 above, and all

tangible embodiments thereof, all copies thereof, the substance thereof and all information contained herein ("Confidential Material"):

(a) shall not be disclosed or distributed by counsel or any other person receiving, viewing or hearing the Confidential Material ("Receiving Person") to any person other than to (1) counsel (including their secretaries, paralegals, and other regular employees) for either party; (2) parties or partners, directors and officers of a party to the extent such disclosure is necessary for the trial or preparation for trial of the captioned action; (3) expert witnesses or consultants hired by counsel for either party, who are assisting counsel in preparation of this action for trial; and (4) the Court and its employees;

(b) shall not be used by any person for any other lawsuit or for any purpose other than the preparation for and trial of this case;

(c) shall be filed with the Court, should filing be desired or required, in a sealed wrapper, accompanied by a motion to place the document containing such information under seal. Upon approval by the Court, the document shall be placed under seal and shall not be disclosed by any person except upon further order of the Court. On the sealed envelope or container shall be affixed the caption of this action and a statement substantially in the following form:

CONFIDENTIAL: SUBJECT TO PROTECTIVE ORDER—This envelope contains documents which have been filed in this case by _____ [name of party] and are not to be opened nor the contents thereof to be displayed or revealed except by the Court or upon order of the Court;

(d) shall not be disclosed to any person within the categories of paragraphs 4(a)(2) and 4(a)(3), unless the provisions of paragraph 7 of this Protective Order are agreed to and followed.

5. To designate information as for attorneys' review only and thereby subject it to this Protective Order, the party disclosing the information shall place upon the document, thing, paper, or other tangible embodiments of the Information, a legend substantially as follows:

Confidential: Attorneys Only

Except as otherwise set forth herein, nontangible information shall be expressly designated as for attorneys' review only subject to this Protective Order at the time of its disclosure or such status shall be confirmed in writing by the disclosing party within a reasonable time after the disclosure. A party designating information for attorneys' review only shall do so only upon a good faith belief that disclosure other than subject to these terms may cause the party to suffer serious competitive or commercial damage.

6. The information designated "CONFIDENTIAL: ATTORNEYS ONLY" as discussed in paragraph 5 above, all tangible embodiments thereof, all copies thereof, the substance thereof and all information contained therein (collectively, "Attorneys Only Material"):
   (a) shall not be disclosed or distributed by counsel or any other person receiving, viewing or hearing the Attorneys Only Material ("receiving person") to any person other than to (1) outside counsel (including their secretaries, paralegals, and other regular employees) for either party; (2) inside counsel for Plaintiff and Defendant (including their secretaries and paralegals); (3) independent consulting or testifying experts hired by counsel for either party, not affiliated with or employed by either of the parties, who are assisting counsel in preparation of this action for trial; and (4) the Court and its employees;
   (b) shall not be used by any person for any other lawsuit or for any purpose other than the preparation for and trial of this case;
   (c) shall be filed with the Court, should filing be desired or required, in a sealed wrapper, and accompanied by a motion to place the document containing such information under seal. Upon approval by the Court, the document shall be placed under seal and shall not be disclosed by any person except upon further order of the Court. On the sealed envelope or container shall be affixed the caption of this action and a statement substantially in the following form:

CONFIDENTIAL: ATTORNEYS ONLY—This envelope contains documents which have been filed in this case by _____ [name of party] and are not to be opened nor the contents thereof to be displayed or revealed except by the Court or upon order of the Court;

and
   (d) shall not be disclosed to any person within the category of paragraph 6(a)(2) unless the provisions of paragraph 7 of this Protective Order are agreed to and followed.
7. Prior to disclosing any Confidential Material or Attorneys Only Material to any person described in paragraphs 4(a)(2), 4(a)(3), or 6(a)(2), counsel for the respective party(ies) shall explain the contents of this Protective Order to that person. The receiving person shall agree to be bound by the terms of this Protective Order and, for all persons in the categories identified in subparagraphs 4(a)(3) and 6(a)(2) of this Protective Order, shall execute a declaration identical to Exhibit "1"

attached hereto. Counsel for the respective party(ies) shall maintain the originals of all such declarations.

8. Documents need not be designated as Confidential Material or Attorneys Only Material at the time of a document inspection pursuant to Rules 33(c) or 34, Fed. R. Civ. P.; however, such documents shall be so designated at the time copies are delivered to the opposing party. An interrogatory answer shall be so designated at or prior to the time the answer is served on an opposing party by placing the appropriate notation prominently on each answer containing information deemed confidential. Failure to designate documents or tangible things as Confidential Material or Attorneys Only Material at the time of production shall not constitute a waiver of such claim if the designation is made within a reasonable time thereafter.

9. The parties may agree on any method of production of documents. The following procedure is to be followed in any inspections of the parties' original documents and things:
   (a) The inspections shall be limited to counsel for the parties, their partners and their employees;
   (b) All documents and things produced for inspection will temporarily be treated as if they had been stamped "CONFIDENTIAL: ATTORNEYS ONLY" pursuant to the Protective Order regarding confidential information. For the purposes of these documents and things, it will not be necessary for the producing party to have them stamped confidential, and the producing party will not be deemed to have waived any confidential designation by the lack of a confidential legend on the documents and things at the time of inspection; and
   (c) During the course of the inspection, the inspecting personnel will tag those documents that are to be copied and later provided. Upon obtaining photocopies of the tagged documents, the producing party will then stamp the "CONFIDENTIAL: SUBJECT TO PROTECTIVE ORDER" or "CONFIDENTIAL: ATTORNEYS ONLY" legend on those documents that the producing party believes should be so designated. Upon receipt of the photocopied documents, the inspecting personnel will no longer be required to treat as Confidential Material or Attorneys Only Material those documents and things that do not bear the appropriate legend. However, the inspecting personnel will continue to treat as Attorneys Only Material all other documents that were reviewed but were not tagged to be photocopied.

10. (a) During any deposition, hearing, or trial, Confidential Material may be disclosed to any deponent or witness (i) who is indicated on the face of the document to be its originator, author or recipient of a copy of said document; or (ii) who has been designated under

Fed. R. Civ. P. 30(b)(6) by the producing party; or (iii) other persons entitled hereunder to have access to Confidential Material, including court reporters hired by counsel of either party who are not and have never been affiliated with the parties; and to no other persons unless prior authorization is obtained from counsel respecting the producing party or from the Court. During any deposition, hearing, or trial, Attorneys Only Material may be disclosed to any deponent or witness (i) who is indicated on the face of the document to be its originator, author, or recipient of a copy of said document; or (ii) who has been designated under Fed. R. Civ. P. 30(b)(6) by the producing party; or (iii) other persons entitled hereunder to access to Attorneys Only Material; and to no other persons unless prior authorization is obtained from counsel representing the producing party or from the Court.

(b) Parties may, on the record during a deposition, hearing or trial or in writing within thirty (30) days after receipt of a deposition, hearing or trial transcript, designate to all parties any pages or lines thereof containing Confidential Material or Attorneys Only Material. Unless testimony is designated as Attorneys Only Material at or before the time of the deposition, all deposition testimony shall be treated as Confidential Material for a period of 30 days after the taking of the deposition. Thereafter, the deposition will only be covered by this Protective Order if specifically designated as either Confidential Material or Attorneys Only Material. The portion of any deposition, hearing, or trial transcript so designated shall be transcribed or marked by each party as a separate record, and access thereto shall be limited in accordance with the terms of this Protective Order.

11. The termination of proceedings in this action shall not relieve any person to whom confidential information was disclosed from the obligation of maintaining the confidentiality of such information in accordance with the provisions of this Protective Order.

12. Upon final termination of this action, each party shall assemble and, as agreed, shall either destroy or return within thirty (30) days all items designated as Confidential Material or Attorneys Only Material. Written verification of destruction shall be given immediately after such destruction, and receipt of material returned to the supplier shall be acknowledged in writing. Notwithstanding the foregoing, to the extent such items are incorporated into any attorney work product, a single copy of each such item may be retained in outside counsel's files.

13. Any document or testimony transcript designated as Confidential Material or Attorneys Only Material pursuant to this Protective Order will be treated pursuant hereto, unless confidentiality is waived in writing by the party asserting it or a Court order is obtained in accordance with Paragraph 16. To aid the Court in considering

requests pursuant to Paragraph 16, the parties agree that
Confidential Material or Attorneys Only Material shall not
include information that:

(a) was, is, or becomes public knowledge, not in violation of this
Protective Order, as shown by written documents;

(b) was previously known to the receiving party or was developed
independently by the receiving party, as shown by written
documents.

14. Allowance of an initial inspection of documents (including physical
objects) shall not constitute a waiver of the attorney/client privilege or
work product immunity with respect to any document so inspected.
Furnishing of copies to the opposing party also shall not constitute a
waiver of the attorney/client privilege or work-product immunity with
respect to any document or physical object so furnished, if within a
reasonable period of time after the opposing counsel's receipt of such
documents, the producing party designates any such document as
within either the attorney/client privilege or work product immunity
and requests return of any such documents to the producing party.
Upon request by the producing party for return of any such documents
designated as within either the attorney/client privilege or work-
product immunity, the receiving party immediately shall return to the
producing party all copies of such documents and shall destroy all
notes or summaries made regarding such documents. Nothing herein
shall prevent the receiving party from challenging the propriety of the
attorney/client privilege or work-product immunity designation by filing
an appropriate motion with the Court.

15. Nothing in this Protective Order shall foreclose or limit any party from
asserting that any information designated Confidential Material or
Attorneys Only Material pursuant to this Protective Order is, in fact, not
protectable as such within the meaning of Rule 26(c), Fed. R. Civ. P.,
and/or paragraph 14 above. The failure to designate information in
accordance with this Protective Order and the failure to object to a
designation at a given time shall not preclude the filing of a motion at a
later date seeking to impose such designation or challenging the
propriety thereof.

16. The parties may by written stipulation waive all or any part of their
rights under this Protective Order, and any party may seek an order of
the Court modifying this Protective Order. Any party shall also have the
right to apply to the Court for an order modifying or vacating the
structures on disclosure imposed by this Protective Order as applied to
any item or items designated pursuant hereto. In the event of a
challenge to an assertion of confidentiality, the party asserting
confidentiality shall have the burden of proving that the information is,
in fact, confidential.

17. To the extent that any discovery is taken of any person who is not a party to this action ("Third Party"), and in the event such Third Party or any party contends that the discovery sought involves confidential proprietary material, then such Third Party shall be asked to agree to execute and to join in and be bound by this Protective Order and then such Third Party's confidential information shall be protected by this Protective Order.

18. The Court shall retain jurisdiction over the parties for purposes of enforcement of this Protective Order.

Dated: SO ORDERED:

[CAPTION]

Declaration of <<_____>>
Re: Stipulated Protective Order
With Respect to Confidential
Information and Documents

I, _____, declare that:

1. My address is _____

2. My present employer is _____
   and the address of my present employment is
   _____

3. I have read and know the contents of the Stipulated Protective Order dated _____, 2010.

4. I am one of the persons described in the Protective Order, and I am executing this Declaration and agreeing to be bound by its terms in order to satisfy the conditions provided in the Protective Order prior to the disclosure to me of any confidential information under the Protective Order.

5. I have read and I shall be fully bound by the terms of the aforesaid Protective Order.

6. All such documents and information which are disclosed to me pursuant to the Protective Order shall be maintained by me in strict confidence and I shall not disclose or use the original or any copy of, or the subject of, such documents and/or information except in accordance with the aforesaid Protective Order.

7. I shall not use or refer to any of the aforesaid documents and/or information, or copies thereof, other than in connection with the above-entitled action and as provided in the Protective Order.

8. I shall, upon being notified of the termination of the above-entitled action, return all copies of such documents to counsel from whom I receive such documents, and I shall destroy any notes and/or

memoranda I have regarding the aforesaid documents and/or
information.

9. I do and shall subject myself to the continuing jurisdiction of the Court
over my person, wherever I shall be, for the enforcement of the
aforesaid Protective Order.

10. I declare under penalty of perjury under the laws of the United States of
America that the foregoing is true and correct.

Date: _____   _____

[SIGNATURE]

Motion for Protective Order to Stop the Deposition of a Senior Executive

A common discovery tactic is to seek the deposition of a senior executive who
may or may not have knowledge about a fact in question in the case. This
strategy frequently is designed to involve the senior executive in question to
help force the executive's company to the settlement table because that executive will not want to be deposed or to take any time out of his or her busy
schedule.

Depositions of senior executives frequently are unnecessary unless they
may potentially have specific knowledge about a party's claims or defenses
that another employee of the party does not have. Below is an example of a
motion for protective order seeking to stop such a deposition.

Traditionally called a "motion to quash," it is a creature of Fed. R. Civ. P.
45(c)(3), which permits a court to fashion an appropriate protective order,
including prohibiting the deposition of a person subject to the subpoena,
when that person would be subjected to "undue burden." This is the argument used to protect senior executives.

Motions to quash a subpoena must be filed in the court that issued the
subpoena, i.e., often not the court in which the case is pending.

Motion for Protective Order to Quash Subpeona

Plaintiff's Memorandum of Law In Support of Its Motion For Protective Order Quashing Subpoena of Senior Executive
Introduction

This lawsuit is pending before the United States District Court for the District of Massachusetts. Plaintiff ("Plaintiff") intervened as a third-party plaintiff to bring an action against Defendant for infringing Plaintiff's famous trademarks.

Counsel for Defendant issued a subpoena on March 12, 2002, for the deposition of Senior Executive. Copies of the subpoena and deposition notice are attached as Exhibit 1. Senior Executive is the President of Plaintiff's Financial Business, the arm of Plaintiff that offers financing, and a Vice President of Plaintiff. *See* Declaration of Senior Executive, attached hereto as Exhibit 2 (hereafter "Senior Executive Decl.") ¶ 3.

Plaintiff requests that this Court enter a protective order quashing the subpoena of Senior Executive, or, in the alternative, order that a less intrusive discovery method be used, for the following reasons:

1. Senior Executive, President of Plaintiff's Financial Business, is a high level officer, who has no unique knowledge of the matters at issue;
2. Senior Executive has never had any responsibility for or discussions about Plaintiff's trademarks;
3. Senior Executive has extensive responsibilities and an extremely busy schedule, making an oral deposition unduly burdensome;
4. Any knowledge Senior Executive may have about Defendant was obtained around the time this lawsuit commenced and is not relevant to Defendant's defense; and
5. Plaintiff does not know the purpose of Senior Executive's deposition and may be willing to stipulate to the facts Defendant wishes to establish.

Facts
I. Background of Senior Executive

Senior Executive is President and Chief Operating Officer of Plaintiff's Financial Business and Vice President of Plaintiff. (Senior Executive Decl. ¶ 2). He has been employed by Plaintiff in various capacities for over 28 years. (Senior Executive Decl. ¶ 4). During that time, Senior Executive has never had any responsibilities for or discussions about Plaintiff's trademarks or its efforts to police, protect or develop its trademarks. (Senior Executive Decl. ¶ ¶ 9–10).

In his current position, Senior Executive has responsibility over all of Plaintiff's Financial Business's worldwide operations, including all regional sales offices, dealer support, field operations, product development, marketing, and insurance products globally. (Senior Executive Decl. ¶ 3). In addition, Senior Executive is responsible for Plaintiff's Financial Business's North American Diversified operations, which include Commercial Lending Services as well as financing subsidiaries. (Senior Executive Decl. ¶ 3). Senior Executive's extensive responsibilities require a great deal of time and attention.

II. The Subpoena of Senior Executive

On March 12, 2002, prior to deposing any of Plaintiff's witnesses, Defendant attempted to serve Senior Executive with a subpoena to take his deposition. Counsel for Plaintiff notified counsel for Defendant that it represented Senior Executive. Even so, counsel for Defendant attempted again to serve Senior Executive, refused to allow Plaintiff's Financial Business's in-house counsel to accept service for Senior Executive, and twice sent a process server to Senior Executive's home.

Neither the subpoena nor the deposition notice stated why or on what topics Defendant planned to depose Senior Executive. Presumably, Defendant is seeking this deposition because Senior Executive purchased a product from Defendant in November 2000, around the same time that this action was originally brought. However, Senior Executive's deposition will not uncover any material facts because Senior Executive has no unique knowledge relevant to this case.

At the time he bought the product, Senior Executive would not have known that Defendant's use of the trademarks infringed Plaintiff's rights. *See* (Senior Executive Decl. ¶ 7). Senior Executive would not have known whether Plaintiff had licensed the marks to Defendant. (Senior Executive Decl. ¶ 8). He would have had no reason to inquire about it since Senior Executive has never had any direct responsibility for trademark matters. (Senior Executive Decl. ¶ ¶ 8, 9). Thus, Senior Executive's deposition can establish nothing other than that he bought a car, a fact that is not in dispute.

On April 23, 2002, counsel for Plaintiff sent Defendant's counsel a letter explaining that Senior Executive has no relevant knowledge and will not be made available for a deposition unless Defendant can explain why it needs to depose him. A copy of this letter is attached. On April 25, 2002, Defendant's counsel responded, again demanding the deposition but not explaining the reasons for it. Plaintiff's counsel called Defendant's counsel on April 26, 2002, offering to provide interrogatory responses or responses to written deposition questions. Defendant's counsel did not respond.

Argument

III. The Discovery Sought by Defendant Should Be Obtained from Plaintiff Employees with Knowledge of the Facts at Issue

Senior Executive is a high-level employee with responsibility for a multibillion dollar operation. Therefore, Defendant's request to depose him imposes undue burden both on Senior Executive and Plaintiff. *See Baine v. General Motors Corp.*, 141 F.R.D. 332, 334 (M.D. Ala. 1991) (prohibiting deposition of GM Vice President on grounds that it was burdensome and that information might be available from other sources). Defendant has not even tried to obtain discovery from another source or in a less burdensome manner. It is obliged to do so under the Federal Rules. Most importantly, Senior Executive has no knowledge of any facts underlying the suit. Deposing him is not only burdensome, it is wasteful.

Fed. R. Civ. P. 45(c)(3)(A)(iv) provides that: "On a timely motion, the court by which a subpoena was issued shall quash or modify the subpoena if it. . . subjects a person to undue burden." Fed. R. Civ. P. 26(b)(2) provides that:

> [T]he frequency or extent of use of the discovery methods. . . shall be limited by the court if it determines that: (i) the discovery sought. . . is obtainable from some other source that is more convenient, less burdensome, or less expensive. . . or (iii) the burden or expense of the proposed discovery outweighs its likely benefit, taking into account the needs of the case. . . the importance of the issues at stake in the litigation, and the importance of the proposed discovery in resolving the issues.

In accordance with these rules, the subpoena issued for the deposition of Senior Executive should be quashed.

IV. Senior Executive Has No Unique Knowledge Regarding The Facts at Issue In This Case

A party seeking to depose a senior company officer must generally demonstrate that the officer has "unique personal knowledge" of the matters at issue. *Baine*, 141 F.R.D. at 322, 335. The deposition should not be allowed if the information can be obtained through interrogatories or the deposition testimony of other persons. *Id.* (citing *Cmty. Fed. Sav. & Loan Assoc. v. Federal Home Loan Bank Bd.*, 96 F.R.D. 619, 621–22 (D.D.C. 1983) (when a party seeks to depose high-level decision-makers who are removed from the daily subjects of the litigation, the party must first demonstrate that the would-be deponent has unique personal knowledge of the matter in issue).

Other courts have similarly recognized the need to protect high-level corporate executives from potentially harassing discovery. In *Mulvey v. Chrysler Corp.*, 106 F.R.D. 364 (D.R.I. 1985), the Court noted that the chairman of

Chrysler, Lee Iacocca, was an individual who could easily be subjected to unwarranted harassment and abuse, and that courts had a duty to recognize his vulnerability. *Id.* at 366. The Court in *Mulvey* directed the plaintiff to serve interrogatories upon Lee Iacocca, and if the answers warranted, then the plaintiff could request an oral deposition. *Id.; see also Crown Cent. Petroleum Corp. v. Garcia*, 904 S.W.2d 125 (Tex. 1995) (when a party seeks to depose a high-level corporate official, the trial court should first determine whether the party seeking the deposition has arguably demonstrated that the official has unique or superior personal knowledge of discoverable information).

Here, Senior Executive is removed from the subject matter of this litigation, and he has no knowledge about Defendant's activities. Senior Executive has no responsibilities regarding the trademarks at issue, and he has not ever been involved in any discussion concerning those marks. *See* (Senior Executive Decl. ¶ 9). Senior Executive did not know that Defendant's actions were infringing until he was subpoenaed. (Senior Executive Decl. ¶ 2).

Furthermore, Senior Executive cannot provide any evidence to support Defendant's acquiescence and laches defenses. These defenses require that the defendant rely upon and be prejudiced by the plaintiff's actions, or that the plaintiff give the defendant affirmative consent to use a mark. *See Sara Lee Corp. v. Kayser-Roth Corp.*, 81 F.3d 455, 461, 462 (4th Cir. 1996), *cert. denied*, 519 U.S. 976 (1996). Senior Executive's purchase of Defendant's car can hardly have lulled Defendant into a false sense of security since Defendant was sued for infringement at the same time Senior Executive bought his car.

Because deposing one of Plaintiff's high-level executives who has no knowledge about the matters at issue in this suit would be unduly burdensome, Plaintiff requests that this Court quash Senior Executive's subpoena.

V. Defendant Has Not Attempted To Obtain The Sought After Discovery By Other Means Or From Other Sources

If Senior Executive had discoverable information (he does not), it would likely be available from other Plaintiff witnesses. Defendant has not yet taken the deposition of any Plaintiff witness, nor any 30(b)(6) deposition of Plaintiff. Defendant in fact does not know what information it will learn from its depositions of Plaintiff. Hence, there is no reason to take Senior Executive's deposition at least until Defendant discovers if Plaintiff's other witnesses will fulfill its needs.

Furthermore, if Defendant reveals its reasons for seeking this deposition, Plaintiff may be willing to stipulate to the facts that Defendant wishes to establish. Even if counsel for Plaintiff and Defendant cannot come to an agreement with regard to the sought after discovery, Defendant should exhaust less intrusive discovery methods before forcing a high level Plaintiff officer to expend valuable time answering Defendant's discovery requests.

Response to Motion to Quash Subpoena of Senior Executive

Response to Motion for Protective Order
And Order Quashing Subpoenas
I. Introduction

As Defendant correctly states, after the jury found Defendant liable for trademark infringement and imposed compensatory and punitive damages on Defendant, the trial court vacated the award for corrective advertising damages and ordered a new trial on corrective advertising damages only, allowing additional discovery on this issue. (Def's Mot. 3)

Pursuant to the trial court's scheduling order, the parties have since engaged in extensive written discovery and have freely redeposed each other's representatives without objections from the other side. For example, Defendant has redeposed Plaintiff's representatives and has noticed (for December, 11, 2001), the deposition of Plaintiff's President, who was also deposed prior to the first trial and testified there. Likewise, Plaintiff has redeposed Defendant's Chief Information Officer.

In short, Defendant's sudden resistance to the parties' well-established and ongoing *modus operandi* lacks all justification. Moreover, the contested depositions are central to Plaintiff's development of evidence for the corrective advertising trial.

II. Argument

A. The Testimony of Defendant's Former Chief Executive Officer and Vice President of Marketing is Crucial

In response to the trial court's posttrial ruling, for the new trial (unlike for the original trial) Plaintiff is basing its calculations of corrective advertising damages on the specific conduct Defendant has engaged in with regard to advertising and marketing. Ex. 1, Response to Rule to Show Cause 5–6. In order to properly assess these damages, Plaintiff has sought to discover evidence on the specifics of Defendant's advertising and marketing.

Defendant's Former Chief Executive Officer and Vice President of Marketing held those positions until the beginning of 2005. They were directly responsible for the oversight and direction of Defendant's most intense advertising and promotional efforts to date, a $25 million ad campaign that took place after the trial and caused awareness of the Defendant's brand to jump from 10 percent in November 2004 to 50 percent in December 2004.

In their positions, they were responsible for making decisions regarding the focus of Defendant's advertising, the demographic markets that would be targeted, and the media in which Defendant's advertising would be placed. As a result, they possess information that is critical to determining corrective advertising damages, which is based on the specific efforts undertaken to promote the Defendant's brand. These efforts, moreover, spectacularly increased after the trial under their tenure. Obviously, neither their successors nor other employees of Defendant can meaningfully testify to the decisions that they personally made on Defendant's advertising and marketing activities and strategy.

B. There is No Basis for a Protective Order

Under Rule 26, Defendant must demonstrate "good cause" to obtain a protective order limiting discovery. *See, e.g. Blankenship v. Hearst*, 519 F.2d 418, 429 (9th Cir. 1975) (party seeking a protective order must meet a "heavy burden"); *In re Gupta Sec. Litig.*, 1994 WL 675209, *3 (N.D. Cal. Sep. 24, 1994).

Plaintiff has not had "ample opportunity" to depose these witnesses on the issues relevant to the new corrective advertising trial. Fed. R. Civ. P. 26(b)(2)(ii). The previous depositions took place prior to the first trial and prior to Plaintiff's current court-ordered approach to calculating corrective advertising damages. Plaintiff plainly has the right to discover relevant evidence from these witnesses.

Defendant has not demonstrated that the "burden or expense of the proposed discovery outweighs its likely benefit." Fed. R. Civ. P. 26(b)(2)(iii). The benefit to Plaintiff in conducting these depositions is that they provide the only chance to obtain crucial evidence for Plaintiff's calculation of corrective advertising damages. In contrast, the only burden articulated by Defendant is that its trial counsel, based in Indiana, would have to defend the depositions in California.[3] This inconvenience is marginal and does not outweigh the benefits to be gained from these depositions.

III. Conclusion

For all of the above reasons, Plaintiff requests this court to deny Defendant's Motion for Protective Order and Order Quashing Subpoenas.

---

3. This is particularly unpersuasive given that numerous depositions of Defendant representatives have taken place in California, where Defendant's headquarters are located, without so much as a hint of protest from Defendant's counsel. Further, these depositions were initially scheduled in the days immediately following the deposition of the CIO. Defendant's counsel would not have been required to make a separate trip to California for either of these depositions had the instant motion not been filed.

This is particularly unpersuasive given that numerous depositions of Defendant representatives have taken place in California, where Defendant's headquarters are located, without so much as a hint of protest from Defendant's counsel. Further, these depositions were initially scheduled in the days immediately following the deposition of the CIO. Defendant's counsel would not have been required to make a separate trip to California for either of these depositions had the instant motion not been filed.

Standard Order of Protection of the
Trademark Trial and Appeal Board

Provisions for Protecting Confidentiality of Information
Revealed During Board Proceeding

Information disclosed by any party or non-party witness during this proceeding may be considered confidential, a trade secret, or commercially sensitive by a party or witness. To preserve the confidentiality of the information so disclosed, either the parties have agreed to be bound by the terms of this order, in its standard form or as modified by agreement, and by any additional provisions to which they may have agreed and attached to this order, **or** the Board has ordered that the parties be bound by the provisions within. As used in this order, the term "information" covers both oral testimony and documentary material.

Parties may use this standard form order as the entirety of their agreement or may use it as a template from which they may fashion a modified agreement. If the Board orders that the parties abide by the terms of this order, they may subsequently agree to modifications or additions, subject to Board approval.

Agreement of the parties is indicated by the signatures of the parties' attorneys and/or the parties themselves at the conclusion of the order. Imposition of the terms by the Board is indicated by signature of a Board attorney or Administrative Trademark Judge at the conclusion of the order. If the parties have signed the order, they may have created a contract. The terms are binding from the date that the parties or their attorneys sign the order, in standard form or as modified or supplemented, or from the date of imposition by a Board attorney or judge.

Terms of Order

1) Classes of Protected Information

The Rules of Practice in Trademark Cases provide that all inter partes proceeding files, as well as the involved registration and application files, are open to public inspection. The terms of this order are not to be used to undermine public access to files. When appropriate, however, a party or witness, on its own or through its attorney, may seek to protect the confidentiality of information by employing one of the following designations.

Confidential—Material to be shielded by the Board from public access.

Highly Confidential—Material to be shielded by the Board from public access *and* subject to agreed restrictions on access even as to the parties and/or their attorneys.

Trade Secret/Commercially Sensitive—Material to be shielded by the Board from public access, restricted from any access by the parties, and available for review by outside counsel for the parties and, subject to the provisions of paragraph 4 and 5, by independent experts or consultants for the parties.

2) Information Not to Be Designated as Protected

Information may not be designated as subject to any form of protection if it (a) is, or becomes, public knowledge, as shown by publicly available writings, other than through violation of the terms of this document; (b) is acquired by a nondesignating party or non-party witness from a third party lawfully possessing such information and having no obligation to the owner of the information; (c) was lawfully possessed by a nondesignating party or non-party witness prior to the opening of discovery in this proceeding, and for which there is written evidence of the lawful possession; (d) is disclosed by a nondesignating party or non-party witness legally compelled to disclose the information; or (e) is disclosed by a nondesignating party with the approval of the designating party.

3) Access to Protected Information

The provisions of this order regarding access to protected information are subject to modification by written agreement of the parties or their attorneys, or by motion filed with and approved by the Board.

Judges, attorneys, and other employees of the Board are bound to honor the parties' designations of information as protected but are not required to sign forms acknowledging the terms and existence of this order. Court reporters, stenographers, video technicians, or others who may be employed by the parties or their attorneys to perform services incidental to this proceeding will be bound only to the extent that the parties or their attorneys make it a condition of employment or obtain agreements from such individuals, in accordance with the provisions of paragraph 4.

- **Parties** are defined as including individuals, officers of corporations, partners of partnerships, and management employees of any type of business organization.
- **Attorneys** for parties are defined as including **in-house counsel** and **outside counsel**, including support staff operating under counsel's direction, such as paralegals or legal assistants, secretaries, and any other employees or independent contractors operating under counsel's instruction.
- **Independent experts or consultants** include individuals retained by a party for purposes related to prosecution or defense of the proceeding but who are not otherwise employees of either the party or its attorneys.

- **Non-party witnesses** include any individuals to be deposed during discovery or trial, whether willingly or under subpoena issued by a court of competent jurisdiction over the witness.

Parties *and* their attorneys shall have access to information designated as confidential *or* highly confidential, subject to any agreed exceptions.

Outside counsel, but not in-house counsel, shall have access to information designated as trade secret/commercially sensitive.

Independent experts or consultants, non-party witnesses, *and* any other individual not otherwise specifically covered by the terms of this order may be afforded access to confidential *or* highly confidential information in accordance with the terms that follow in paragraph 4. Further, independent experts or consultants may have access to trade secret/commercially sensitive information if such access is agreed to by the parties or ordered by the Board, in accordance with the terms that follow in paragraphs 4 and 5.

4) Disclosure to Any Individual

Prior to disclosure of protected information by any party or its attorney to any individual not already provided access to such information by the terms of this order, the individual shall be informed of the existence of this order and provided with a copy to read. The individual will then be required to certify in writing that the order has been read and understood and that the terms shall be binding on the individual. No individual shall receive any protected information until the party or attorney proposing to disclose the information has received the signed certification from the individual. A form for such certification is attached to this order. The party or attorney receiving the completed form shall retain the original.

5) Disclosure to Independent Experts or Consultants

In addition to meeting the requirements of paragraph 4, any party or attorney proposing to share disclosed information with an independent expert or consultant must also notify the party which designated the information as protected. Notification must be personally served or forwarded by certified mail, return receipt requested, and shall provide notice of the name, address, occupation and professional background of the expert or independent consultant.

The party or its attorney receiving the notice shall have ten (10) business days to object to disclosure to the expert or independent consultant. If objection is made, then the parties must negotiate the issue before raising the issue before the Board. If the parties are unable to settle their dispute, then it shall be the obligation of the party or attorney proposing disclosure to bring the matter before the Board with an explanation of the need for disclosure and a report on the efforts the parties have made to settle their dispute. The party objecting to disclosure will be expected to respond with its arguments against disclosure or its objections will be deemed waived.

6) Responses to Written Discovery

Responses to interrogatories under Federal Rule 33 and requests for admissions under Federal Rule 36, and which the responding party reasonably believes to contain protected information shall be prominently stamped or marked with the appropriate designation from paragraph 1. Any inadvertent disclosure without appropriate designation shall be remedied as soon as the disclosing party learns of its error, by informing all adverse parties, in writing, of the error. The parties should inform the Board only if necessary because of the filing of protected information not in accordance with the provisions of paragraph 12.

7) Production of Documents

If a party responds to requests for production under Federal Rule 34 by making copies and forwarding the copies to the inquiring party, then the copies shall be prominently stamped or marked, as necessary, with the appropriate designation from paragraph 1. If the responding party makes documents available for inspection and copying by the inquiring party, all documents shall be considered protected during the course of inspection. After the inquiring party informs the responding party what documents are to be copied, the responding party will be responsible for prominently stamping or marking the copies with the appropriate designation from paragraph 1. Any inadvertent disclosure without appropriate designation shall be remedied as soon as the disclosing party learns of its error, by informing all adverse parties, in writing, of the error. The parties should inform the Board only if necessary because of the filing of protected information not in accordance with the provisions of paragraph 12.

8) Depositions

Protected documents produced during a discovery deposition, or offered into evidence during a testimony deposition shall be orally noted as such by the producing or offering party at the outset of any discussion of the document or information contained in the document. In addition, the documents must be prominently stamped or marked with the appropriate designation.

During discussion of any nondocumentary protected information, the interested party shall make oral note of the protected nature of the information.

The transcript of any deposition and all exhibits or attachments shall be considered protected for 30 days following the date of service of the transcript by the party that took the deposition. During that 30-day period, either party may designate the portions of the transcript, and any specific exhibits or attachments that are to be treated as protected, by electing the appropriate designation from paragraph 1. Appropriate stampings or markings should be made during this time. If no such designations are made, then the entire transcript and exhibits will be considered unprotected.

9) Filing Notices of Reliance

When a party or its attorney files a notice of reliance during the party's testimony period, the party or attorney is bound to honor designations made by the adverse party or attorney, or non-party witness, who disclosed the information, so as to maintain the protected status of the information.

10) Briefs

When filing briefs, memoranda, or declarations in support of a motion, or briefs at final hearing, the portions of these filings that discuss protected information, whether information of the filing party, or any adverse party, or any non-party witness, should be redacted. The rule of reasonableness for redaction is discussed in paragraph 12 of this order.

11) Handling of Protected Information

Disclosure of information protected under the terms of this order is intended only to facilitate the prosecution or defense of this case. The recipient of any protected information disclosed in accordance with the terms of this order is obligated to maintain the confidentiality of the information and shall exercise reasonable care in handling, storing, using, or disseminating the information.

12) Redaction; Filing Material With the Board

When a party or attorney must file protected information with the Board, or a brief that discusses such information, the protected information or portion of the brief discussing the same should be redacted from the remainder. A rule of reasonableness should dictate how redaction is affected.

Redaction can entail merely covering a portion of a page of material when it is copied in anticipation of filing but can also entail the more extreme measure of simply filing the entire page under seal as one that contains primarily confidential material. If only a sentence or short paragraph of a page of material is confidential, covering that material when the page is copied would be appropriate. In contrast, if most of the material on the page is confidential, then filing the entire page under seal would be more reasonable, even if some small quantity of nonconfidential material is then withheld from the public record. Likewise, when a multipage document is in issue, reasonableness would dictate that redaction of the portions or pages containing confidential material be affected when only some small number of pages contain such material. In contrast, if almost every page of the document contains some confidential material, it may be more reasonable to simply submit the entire document under seal. Occasions when a whole document or brief must be submitted under seal should be very rare.

Protected information and pleadings, briefs, or memoranda that reproduce, discuss, or paraphrase such information, shall be filed with the Board under seal. The envelopes or containers shall be prominently stamped or marked with a legend in substantially the following form:

Confidential

This envelope contains documents or information that are subject to a protective order or agreement. The confidentiality of the material is to be maintained and the envelope is not to be opened, or the contents revealed to any individual, except by order of the Board.

13) Acceptance of Information; Inadvertent Disclosure

Acceptance by a party or its attorney of information disclosed under designation as protected shall not constitute an admission that the information is, in fact, entitled to protection. Inadvertent disclosure of information that the disclosing party intended to designate as protected shall not constitute waiver of any right to claim the information as protected upon discovery of the error.

14) Challenges to Designations of Information as Protected

If the parties or their attorneys disagree as to whether certain information should be protected, they are obligated to negotiate in good faith regarding the designation by the disclosing party. If the parties are unable to resolve their differences, the party challenging the designation may make a motion before the Board, seeking a determination of the status of the information.

A challenge to the designation of information as protected must be made substantially contemporaneous with the designation, or as soon as practicable after the basis for challenge is known. When a challenge is made long after a designation of information as protected, the challenging party will be expected to show why it could not have made the challenge at an earlier time.

The party designating information as protected will, when its designation is timely challenged, bear the ultimate burden of proving that the information should be protected.

15) Board's Jurisdiction; Handling of Materials After Termination

The Board's jurisdiction over the parties and their attorneys ends when this proceeding is terminated. A proceeding is terminated only after a final order is entered, and either all appellate proceedings have been resolved, or the time for filing an appeal has passed without filing of any appeal.

The parties may agree that archival copies of evidence and briefs may be retained, subject to compliance with agreed safeguards. Otherwise, within 30 days after the final termination of this proceeding, the parties and their attorneys shall return to each disclosing party the protected information disclosed during the proceeding, and shall include any briefs, memoranda, summaries, and the like, which discuss or in any way refer to such information. In the alternative, the disclosing party or its attorney may make a written request that such materials be destroyed rather than returned.

16) Other Rights of the Parties and Attorneys

This order shall not preclude the parties or their attorneys from making any applicable claims of privilege during discovery or at trial. Nor shall the order preclude the filing of any motion with the Board for relief from a particular provision of this order or for additional protections not provided by this order.

By Agreement of the Following, effective:

_____

[insert signature date]

_____

[print or type name and title of individual signing for defendant]

_____

[print or type name and law firm of attorney for defendant]

_____

[print or type name and title of individual signing for plaintiff]

_____

[print or type name and law firm of attorney for plaintiff]

By Order of the Board, effective _____.

_____

[print or type name and title of Board attorney or judge imposing order]

Motion for Sanctions

The Courts and the TTAB have the power to enforce their discovery orders and to impose sanctions upon a party that does not comply with discovery. Typical sanctions for failure to provide discovery include fee and costs shifting, instructions to the jury, evidentiary presumptions. In the most egregious circumstances, default judgment may even be granted as a sanction. A few examples of sanction motions follow.

Motion for Sanction of Default Judgment for Failure to Provide Discovery

IN THE UNITED STATES PATENT AND TRADEMARK OFFICE

Before the Trademark Trial And Appeal Board

PRAXAIR, INC.,) and PRAXAIR TECHNOLOGY, INC.,) Opposers,) v.) MILNER-FENWICK, INC.,) Applicant.)	Opposition No. 91177015

Opposers' Motion for Sanction of Default Judgment

Opposers, Praxair, Inc. and Praxair Technology, Inc. (collectively, "Praxair"), request the sanction of entry of default judgment against Applicant, Milner-Fenwick, Inc. ("Milner"), because of Milner's failure to comply with the Board's May 7, 2008, Order (the "Order") compelling discovery. *See* Trademark Board Manual of Procedure §§ 411.04 and 527.01(a); *see also* 37 CFR § 2.120(g)(1) and Fed. R. Civ. P. 37(b)(2). In support of its request, Praxair states as follows:

I. On April 27, 2007, Praxair filed its Notice of Opposition. Milner filed its answer on July 27, 2007.

II. On October 26, 2007, Praxair served Milner with its first sets of interrogatories and document requests ("Praxair's Discovery Requests"). Milner did not respond to Praxair's Discovery Requests.

III. As a result, on February 4, 2008, Praxair moved to compel Milner's responses to Praxair's Discovery Requests ("Motion to Compel") pursuant to 37 CFR § 2.120(e). Milner did not respond to the Motion to Compel.

IV. On May 7, 2008, the Board issued an order requiring Milner "to provide full and complete responses, without objection" to Praxair's Discovery Requests within thirty days. The Order required Milner to respond to Praxair's Discovery Requests by June 6, 2008, ". . .failing which, the Board may entertain a motion for sanctions, including the entry of judgment. . ."

V. As of the filing date of the instant motion, Milner has not complied with the Board's Order, has not contacted Praxair and has not responded to Praxair's Discovery Requests.

VI. Milner's failure to comply with the Order and respond to Praxair's Discovery Requests entitles Praxair to the sanction of default judgment. 37 CFR § 2.120(g)(1). The Board has granted default judgment as a sanction in similar circumstances in the past. See MHW Ltd. v. Simex, Aussenhandelsgesellschaft Savelsberg KG, 59 USPQ2d 1477, 1487 (TTAB 2000) (granting motion for sanction of default judgment due to respondent's failure to comply with Board order and disregard for discovery obligations); Philippe de Rothschild, S.A. v. Styl-Rite Optical Mfg. Co., 55 USPQ2d 1848, 1854 (TTAB 2000) (same); Unicut Corp. v. Unicut, Inc., 222 USPQ 341 (TTAB 1984) (same).

VII. Entry of default judgment against Milner is appropriate here because Milner has ignored the Board's Order and completely failed to participate in discovery. As a result, Praxair is precluded from preparing its case against Milner.

WHEREFORE, Praxair respectfully requests that the Board enter default judgment against Milner and sustain Praxair's opposition to Milner's pending application for the mark FROM HOSPITAL TO HOME, Application Ser. No. 78/729,094.

Respectfully submitted,

FORM 9.11
Motion to Compel and for Sanctions

Plaintiff's Motion to Compel And for Discovery Sanctions

Plaintiff moves this Court pursuant to Fed. R. Civ. P. 37(a)(2)(A) to compel the production of various documents requested by Plaintiff in discovery but not produced by defendant and for sanctions under Fed. R. Civ. P. 37(a)(4). As grounds for its motion, Plaintiff states as follows:

1. On April 24, 2002, Plaintiff served defendant with Plaintiff's First Request for Production of Documents. Among other documents, the Requests sought production of:
   a) any and all documents referred to in defendant's responses to Plaintiff's First Set of Interrogatories (Request No. 1);
   b) any and all documents defendant provides, or has provided, to potential investors in the planned theme park defendant has promoted under the Contested Mark (Request No. 14); and
   c) any and all documents discussing, relating to, or referring to potential investors in the planned theme park defendant has promoted under the Contested Mark (Request No. 15).
2. On May 7, 2002, Plaintiff served defendant with Plaintiff's Second Request for Production of Documents. Among other documents, those Requests sought production of:
   a) all documents used in connection with defendant's provision of each service marketed in connection with the Contested Mark (Request No. 43);
   b) all documents that constitute, relate, or refer to any research done by or for defendant in connection with his planned theme park, including but not limited to all documents that constitute, relate or refer to the "research in the areas of real estate, business structures, population trends, census data, consumer research, and competitor analysis" defendant identifies at its Internet URL (Request No. 55); and
   c) all documents that constitute, relate or refer to defendant's use or investment of any money received from investors in the planned theme park defendant has promoted under the Contested Mark (Request No. 58).
3. Defendant served his Responses to Plaintiff's First and Second Requests for Production on May 20, 2002. Defendant did not object to any of the aforementioned Requests, responding simply that documents responsive to each Request were "produced."
4. On August 1, 2002, counsel for Plaintiff wrote to defendant's counsel regarding certain deficiencies in defendant's production.

Specifically, Plaintiff noted the absence of a number of documents referred to in interrogatory answers and requested that, to the extent documents were available only in electronic form, defendant produce a copy of his hard drive. Plaintiff specifically noted defendant's failure to produce the partnership packet in response to Request No. 1 and that only one document was produced in response to Request No. 14 regarding documents provided to potential investors.

5. In response to the August 1, 2002 deficiency letter, defendant served Defendant's First Supplemental Answers to Plaintiff's First and Second Set of Interrogatories, but produced no further documents.

6. Plaintiff followed up on defendant's supplemental answers and requested that defendant confirm in writing that there were no further responsive documents, which defendant did by letter of counsel dated October 2, 2002.

7. Notwithstanding defendant's assurance that no further responsive documents existed, during his deposition on November 21, 2002, defendant referred to a number of documents that were called for by Plaintiff's requests but that were not produced. Defendant's own testimony clearly indicates that the documents do exist. In some cases, defendant even claimed to have provided the document at issue to his lawyer. Specifically, the following requested materials were referred to by defendant:

   a) the partnership agreement (referred to on p. 91 of the deposition transcript and called for by Request Nos. 1, 14 and 15);

   b) records of all investors in the partnership (referred to on p. 94 and called for by Request Nos. 15 and 58);

   c) records of Internet transactions regarding partnership units (referred to on p. 95 and called for by Request Nos. 15 and 58);

   d) documents reflecting the investment of funds received from the sale of partnership units (referred to on pp. 97-98 and called for by Request Nos. 15 and 58);

   e) the partnership packet provided to potential investors (referred to on p. 102 and called for by Request Nos. 1 and 14);

   f) records of recipients of partnership packets (referred to on p. 103 and called for by Request Nos. 1, 14, and 15); and

   g) articles regarding theme parks other than those owned by The Walt Disney Company (referred to on p. 108 and called for by Request Nos. 1 and 55).

8. In a final attempt to avoid Court intervention on this matter, on December 6, 2002, counsel for Plaintiff wrote to defendant's counsel, specifically referring to the documents defendant has failed to produce and requesting that defendant make himself available for further deposition questioning regarding those documents. Defendant has not responded to that letter.

9. Each of the documents referred to above was requested and repeatedly followed up on by Plaintiff. Plaintiff therefore respectfully submits that it has made a good faith effort to discover the documents without intervention by this Court.
10. As a result of defendant's failure to timely produce the requested documents, Plaintiff was unable to depose defendant regarding those documents during the time period allowed under Fed. R. Civ. P. 30(d).

WHEREFORE, Plaintiff respectfully requests that the Court order defendant to produce each of the documents referred to in Paragraph 7 above. Plaintiff also requests that the Court order defendant to appear for further deposition questioning regarding the documents he has withheld. Plaintiff further requests that the Court impose sanctions against defendant pursuant to Fed. R. Civ. P. 37(a)(4), awarding Plaintiff its attorneys' fees and costs relating to Plaintiff's efforts to obtain the requested discovery without Court intervention, the filing of this motion, and continuing defendant's deposition regarding the withheld documents.

FORM 9.12

Motion for Sanctions

In the United States District Court
For the Northern District of Illinois
Eastern Division

MEDICAL BILLING CONSULTANTS, INC.,)	
d/b/a Medbillz.com)	
Plaintiff,)	
)	Case No.:
v.)	
)	Hon. James B. Moran
INTELLIGENT MEDICAL OBJECTS, INC.)	
)	Magistrate Judge Nan R. Nolan
Defendant.)	

Motion to Compel and for Sanctions

Pursuant to Rule 37 of the Federal Rules of Civil Procedure, defendant moves for an order compelling plaintiff to provide answers to defendants' Interrogatories. In support of this motion, defendants state as follows:

1. On June 4, 2002, at a status conference held in chambers, this Court instructed plaintiff's counsel to respond to contention interrogatories concerning its copyright claim. Plaintiff's counsel stated plaintiff would respond in ten (10) days.
2. On June 4, 2002, defendants served their contention interrogatories in accordance with the Court's instructions at the status conference. (Exhibit A).
3. Defendants did not receive any response to the interrogatories within ten days as specified at the June 4, 2002, status conference.
4. On June 20, 2002, defendants sent a letter to plaintiff's counsel inquiring about the response. (Exhibit B).
5. On June 24, 2002, defendants' counsel discussed this issue with plaintiff's counsel, who stated he would discuss the issue further with his co-counsel, On June 25, 2002, the parties appeared before Magistrate Judge Nolan to schedule a settlement conference.
6. Despite counsel's representation, defendants did not receive any response on June 25, 2002. Instead, plaintiff's served detailed notices of taking depositions. (Exhibit C).

483

7. On July 3, 2002, defendants again wrote regarding plaintiff's failure to answer the interrogatories. (Exhibit D).
8. Defendants certify that they have made a good faith effort to resolve this discovery dispute, including discussions in person and by phone, as outlined above. However, as of the filing of this motion, defendants have not received any answer to the interrogatories or any commitment to provide answers. As a result, defendants have been forced to incur substantial legal expense that would have been unnecessary if plaintiff had complied with the obligations established at the June 4, 2002, status conference.

WHEREFORE, defendants request this Court to order plaintiff to:

(1) provide answers responsive to defendants' interrogatories and
(2) reimburse defendants' for their attorneys' fees and costs incurred in bringing this motion.

Respectfully submitted,

CHAPTER

10

Electronic Discovery

Although electronic records always have been discoverable,[1] on December 1, 2006, the Federal Rules of Civil Procedure were amended to address the problems created by the explosion of electronically stored information (ESI) in litigation.

Rule 26(b)(2) now requires a search for all ESI that is "in the possession, custody, or control of the party." Rule 34(a) has added "electronically stored information" to "documents" and tangible "things" as a third category of items that may be requested in discovery. The rules divide ESI into two categories: "reasonably accessible" and "not reasonably accessible." The search for responsive documents, including ESI, must be done at the time that litigation is reasonably anticipated and certainly no later than the first pretrial discovery-related meeting, which is required to be within 99 days of the filing of the complaint. Fed. R. Civ. P. 16(b). *See Pension Comm. of the Univ. of Montreal Pension Plan v. Banc of Am. Sec., LLC,* No. 05 Civ. 9016, 2010 U.S. Dist. LEXIS 4546, 2010 WL 184312 (S.D.N.Y. Jan. 15, 2010).

ESI includes e-mail, word processing documents, databases, voicemail messages, instant messages, text messages, websites, and any other information stored in an electronic format. ESI can be found on corporate servers, corporate or home computers, cell phones, flash drives, voicemail servers, backup tapes, and various other devices. Reasonably accessible ESI would be a subset of all ESI and includes any information a party routinely accesses or uses, but may not include disaster data stored on backup tapes or discs, deleted data, or other data that requires significant cost, effort, or burden to produce.

A party seeking discovery of ESI that is not "reasonably accessible" may need a court order to obtain it based on a showing of good cause. The good cause analysis weighs the requesting party's need for the information and availability of the information from another source against the burden on the responding party of obtaining it from sources that are difficult to access.

Discovery of ESI is expensive and can be contentious. Courts have dealt with the issues surrounding discovery of ESI in various manners. Of particular note is the Seventh Circuit's Electronic Discovery Pilot Program. *See* http://www.ilcd.uscourts.gov/Statement%20%20Phase%20One.pdf. The court clearly expresses a preference for a collaborative effort by the parties, although it remains to be seen how many litigants accept the proposed standing order promulgated by the court.

Discovery of ESI often requires hiring a computer forensics vendor to search a company's systems for relevant information. The vendor compiles documents responsive to search queries based upon terms provided to the vendor.

---

1. *See, e.g., Playboy Enter. Inc. v. Welles,* 60 F. Supp. 2d 1050, 1052–53 (S.D. Cal. 1999) (court allowed the plaintiff to obtain a mirror image of the defendant's computer hard drive in order to recover deleted e-mail messages).

The parties should agree on these terms but can seek relief from the court, which will impose terms upon the parties. Obviously, it is preferable for search terms to come from the parties who know the issues in their case far better than the court.

Some examples of the types of search terms usually used in trademark litigation include:

- The parties' trademarks and variations on the spellings of the marks (note that most vendors will search for variations on search terms, but it helps in trademark cases to be specific about variations on spellings because some may be more important than others, especially if confusion over two similarly spelled marks is at issue)
- The names of individuals employed by the parties involved with the products at issue
- Potential targets for the marketing of products, e.g., specific customer names or target demographics, especially if market overlap is at issue
- Geographic areas where the products are sold
- Terms associated with consumer inquiries about products
- The names of third parties involved with the creation, selection, and adoption of the marks, as well as licensees and marketing companies for the products

Rule 37(f) protects companies from sanctions for deleting e-mails as part of the "routine, good-faith operation of an electronic information system." An entity usually is protected if it took "reasonable steps to preserve the information after it knew or should have known the information was discoverable." This amendment has not been interpreted as a broad-based immunity, however, especially if a party made no effort to preserve electronic evidence when such evidence potentially could be discoverable. *See Pension Comm., supra.* Thus, once a party is on notice of a potential lawsuit, even routine document destruction policies could have negative consequences if the party does not preserve potentially relevant information.

Lawyers often, rightfully, have a concern about preserving privilege in discovery, but discovery of ESI often results in the advertent exchange of privileged documents. While commentators have spent much time on analyzing how to deal with such occurrences, the reality is that counsel should agree that any such inadvertently produced documents will be returned to the other side as soon as they are discovered by the receiving party and destroyed.

Document retention policies should be regularly enforced and should provide for the review, retention, and destruction of documents, including ESI, received or created in the ordinary course of business. The policy should identify documents that the company and its employees must maintain, how long they should be retained, and when they should and will be destroyed.

Businesses should train their employees, follow the document retention policy, and regularly audit the efficacy of the policy. The document retention policy must also contain a procedure for preserving all relevant documents as soon as a company learns that litigation is filed or anticipated. In intellectual property matters, this would be when the conflict is first recognized or cease and desist letters are sent or received. Waiting to retain documents until after a lawsuit is actually filed is too late. Extra caution must be taken with any information that could be used as evidence. For example, it is a best practice to place a "litigation hold" on documents, especially employee e-mail, that may be relevant to a case.

I. Recommended Steps to Reduce Risk and Ensure Compliance

A. Maintain a Document Retention Policy for Paper and Electronic Data

A document retention policy instructs employees on the types of documents and data that must be retained and for how long. Such a policy will promote efficiency, reduce storage and administration costs, help ensure compliance with federal and state laws and regulations, and help protect a party in litigation.

Such policies should be prepared by in-house counsel in conjunction with IT staff familiar with the company's information management systems.

B. Know Where Data Resides

A "data" map that documents where each type of data is stored (servers, laptops, home PC's, mobile devices, etc.) is an effective way to track potential sources of evidence. Also, such a map may reveal risk management issues that had not previously been considered. The contents of backup tapes in the ordinary course of business should be catalogued, which should save time and costs.

C. Have a Litigation Response Plan

As previously discussed, extra caution must be taken with any information that could be used as evidence. A business may want to select key personnel in the IT department who can assist with issues that may arise in future litigation.

This team will be responsible for keeping counsel apprised of recently acquired technologies that affect data storage or relate to the business's document retention program. This team also can serve as potential Rule 30(b)(6) witnesses who have knowledge of and can later articulate their expertise with all aspects of the company's computer processing and storage capabilities.

Top Ten Tips for E-Discovery from the Honorable John J. Hughes, Magistrate (Ret.), District of New Jersey, U.S. District Court, Trenton, New Jersey

1. Talk with your client about establishing a retention/preservation policy to avoid potential sanctions during litigation.
2. Talk with your adversary to establish "rules of the game" before you start playing to avoid later disagreements.
3. Identify your "electronic information representative" and establish a working relationship with your client's IT personnel to get on the same wavelength about the client's information systems and how they can help you with your case.
4. Educate the judge about the e-discovery issues in the case—don't assume that a particular judge understands your issues; we all come from different backgrounds and experiences.
5. Continuing disclosure is required under the Rules; someone will forget the PDA, and you have an obligation to remember.
6. Be specific in discovery requests if you truly want to obtain the information—the days of "any and all"—"in any form" are over.
7. Articulate "Good Cause" for production when requesting documents that go above and beyond the ordinary and specify the factual basis for the judge that shows the production is necessary to prepare your case.
8. Explain "Undue Hardship" in opposing a request for production and offer certification as to the precise cost in time/money/loss of productivity.
9. Connecting "e-discovery" with "e-trial" because the purpose of discovery is to prepare for trial or settlement—at least that's what the Rules say.
10. Be professional because your reputation is your most effective litigation skill but the one most easily lost.

1. Cost-Shifting for Electronic Discovery

Electronic discovery has added significant expense to an already expensive discovery process in U.S. litigation. Cooperating with your adversary is the best course for limiting the cost and burden of this discovery. While cost-shifting analysis will not generate much case law, it is of practical importance to clients because of the potential shifting of the expense. Exacerbating that expense by failing to cooperate in discovery does not serve clients well, as exemplified in a seminal series of cases decided by Judge Scheindlin of the U.S. District Court for the Southern District of New York, *Zubulake v. UBS Warburg LLC*, 217 F.R.D. 309 (S.D.N.Y. 2003) ("Zubulake I"). There, Zubulake, the plaintiff in a sexual discrimination lawsuit, requested that UBS, the plaintiff's former employer, produce all e-mails related to her. UBS produced approximately 100 pages of e-mails, but the plaintiff requested that e-mails be culled from any available source, including backup tapes, because she was aware that certain relevant e-mails were missing from the production. UBS objected that such discovery was too costly ($175,000 exclusive of attorney review time).

The parties reached an initial agreement that plaintiff would name a few individuals whose e-mail accounts should be reviewed for relevant information and then discuss with the defendant how the relevant e-mails would be retrieved. *Id.* at 313. After plaintiff named certain individuals, UBS did not produce any further documents and claimed to have produced all of the e-mails in those individuals' accounts but admitted that it had not retrieved e-mails stored on backup tapes. The Court first required UBS to produce for deposition someone knowledgeable about UBS's retention policies to explain the issues surrounding obtaining e-mails from storage tapes and the burden of producing it. Thereafter, plaintiff moved to compel UBS to produce the e-mails in storage.

The Court found that such discovery was relevant, and plaintiff was entitled to it. *Id.* at 317. The Court noted that there is a presumption that the producing party bears the burden of responding to discovery requests. "Thus, cost-shifting should be considered only when electronic discovery imposes an 'undue burden or expense' on the responding party." *Id.* at 318, quoting Fed. R. Civ. P. 26(c).

The Court divided data into accessible and inaccessible, with the producing party completely responsible for the burden and cost of producing data that was accessible, while cost-shifting was available for inaccessible data. In particular, accessible data consists of (1) active, online data, such as that stored on hard drives; (2) near-line data, such as optical disks that can be automatically retrieved; and (3) offline storage/archives, such as removable optical disks or magnetic tape media, which are labeled and stored in a shelf or rack, usually stored for disaster recovery or for archival purposes. *Id.* at 318–19. Inaccessible data consists of (4) backup tapes; and (5) erased, fragmented, or damaged data. *Id.* at 319.

The Court then created a seven-factor test to assess the necessity of cost shifting for the production of inaccessible data:

(1) The extent to which the request is specifically tailored to discover relevant information
(2) The availability of such information from other sources

(3) The total cost of production, compared to the amount in controversy
(4) The total cost of production, compared to the resources available to each party
(5) The relative ability of each party to control costs and its incentive to do so
(6) The importance of the issues at stake in the litigation
(7) The relative benefits to the parties of obtaining the information

Id. at 322.

The Court indicated that these factors should be weighed in descending order, except that factor (6) can sometimes predominate. In order to conduct this analysis, the Court requested that the defendant produce a sample from five backup tapes to better conduct the cost-shifting analysis. The cost-shifting analysis based on this sample was done in *Zubulake v. UBS Warburg LLC,* 216 F.R.D. 280 (S.D.N.Y. 2003) ("Zubulake II").

In Zubulake II, the plaintiff requested that UBS produce any relevant documents on the remaining backup tapes, and UBS requested that the entire cost be shifted to plaintiff. The Court ruled that the plaintiff must share 25 percent of the cost of restoring backup tapes on which these documents may be contained.

UBS had produced detailed evidence of the costs involved in restoring and reviewing the five backup tapes: $19,003.43. The remaining estimated cost was $273,649.39, including attorney-review cost. The Court engaged in a detailed analysis of each factor under the previously announced test. Of particular importance was the review of e-mails culled from the tapes that related to the matter, i.e., to the first factor. Plaintiff claimed that 68 of 600 produced e-mails were relevant, including 6 in particular.

The Court found that the marginal utility of these e-mails was potentially very high, and the e-mails were available from no other source, however, because none of the e-mails contained evidence of sexual discrimination against the plaintiff, the Court found the first two factors only slightly favored against cost shifting.

The Court then assessed factors 3, 4, and 5 by extrapolating from UBS's costs in restoring the first 5 tapes, namely $2,304.93 per tape, to $165,954.67 for the remaining 72 tapes. The Court compared this figure to the potential amount in controversy, which was millions, and found that the cost of discovery was not disproportionate. The Court did find that although UBS had exponentially more resources than plaintiff, plaintiff or her attorneys could contribute to discovery costs, especially given that they claimed over $19 million were at stake. Thus, this factor weighed against cost shifting but did not rule it out. The ability of the parties to control costs was neutral because the plaintiff could not further tailor her discovery requests while UBS could not do anything but choose a vendor to restore the tapes, and it had already chosen one. Factor (6) was found to be irrelevant. The benefit of the parties obtaining the information weighed strongly in favor of cost shifting because the defendant would not restore the tapes otherwise.

Ultimately, the Court put 25 percent of the cost of restoring the backup tapes on the plaintiff. It is noteworthy that the Court only shifted the cost of restoring the backup tapes and found explicitly that the cost of reviewing the data revealed on those backup tapes was not shiftable because once the data was restored, it would be accessible, and therefore, not subject to cost shifting.

FORM 10.1
Litigation Hold Letter

Dear Client:

The Federal Rules of Civil Procedure recently have been revised to require the retention of documents, including electronically stored information ("ESI"), relevant to contemplated litigation. Because you have been sued by XYZ Corp. ("Plaintiff"), we are writing to advise you that you should establish, if you have not done so already, a litigation hold concerning documents and ESI relevant to matters involving this dispute.

In particular, you should take steps to preserve all documents and ESI, including e-mail, word processing files, spreadsheets, databases, website iterations, electronically stored graphics, calendars, text messages, files stored on PDAs, and other electronic communication and information, pertinent to these potential proceedings so they are not deleted or destroyed pursuant to routine document retention procedures. Documents and ESI may be stored in various locations, such as individual work stations, laptops, PDAs, cell phones, the voice mail system, home computers, company servers, backup tapes and services, and removable media. You also should suspend any routine document/electronic file destruction policies so that relevant evidence is not inadvertently destroyed.

The scope of the litigation hold extends to all documents and ESI that might possibly be relevant to issues in the proceeding or that reasonably could lead to the discovery of relevant evidence. The particular materials of relevance include without limitation:

- The selection, clearance, and adoption of the Trademark for the various goods and services with which it is used and registered
- The use, advertising, promotion, and marketing of the Trademark
- The licensing of the Trademark
- The applications and registrations for the Trademark
- The value of the Trademark, the goodwill the Trademark symbolizes, and the public perception of the Trademark
- The manufacture, distribution, and sale of products bearing the Trademark
- Internal communications concerning any actual or potential proceedings involving the Trademark, including any actual or potential proceedings involving the Trademark
- Investigations concerning any actual or potential proceedings involving the Trademark, including any actual or potential proceedings involving the Trademark
- Instances of confusion between Trademark and any of Plaintiff's or any third-party marks

- Negotiations with Plaintiff or any third parties involving the Trademark
- Other business relationships or communications involving the Trademark

The above list is not exhaustive, and you may not have documents relevant to each category listed above, but these are the general categories of materials that should be preserved. Any doubts about the relevance of a document or ESI should be resolved in favor of preservation.

We recommend that you (or others at your instruction) send a written litigation hold memorandum, as soon as is practical, to all personnel who potentially have custody or control of pertinent documents and ESI, including information technology (IT) personnel and any third parties responsible for maintaining your networks, servers, and computer systems that contain the pertinent documents and those individuals responsible for implementing any document retention policies. The memo should refer questions to you or another appropriate contact within your company, or you can have them directed to us. Thereafter, you should send periodic written reminders to help ensure that the hold remains in effect during the pendency of the litigation.

Should discovery be taken in any proceeding, it is essential that you be able to represent (e.g., in a declaration or deposition of the relevant personnel) that you promptly instituted a litigation hold and that no pertinent documents have been lost or destroyed. Courts have imposed severe sanctions on parties that have not strictly observed these document retention requirements in the context of litigation.

We are available to discuss the above information with you in more detail and answer any questions you may have. It also would be helpful to identify and speak with any key IT personnel to help ensure your company complies with these requirements. Please do not hesitate to contact us.

Document Preservation Notice to be Used Internally by Clients

Frequently, clients will want to distribute a litigation hold themselves. Below is an example of a letter meant to be distributed by in-house counsel.

Document Preservation Notice to be Used
Internally by Clients

Important Legal Notice Regarding Document Preservation

Dear Colleagues:

The Company is engaged in trademark litigation in the United States, in which it is asserting that its trademarks have been infringed.

U.S. law prohibits the destruction of records, files, and documents, including electronically stored information ("ESI"), that may be relevant to the case. Accordingly, until further written notice, we must take the necessary steps to preserve such documents and ESI, and to suspend any routine document retention or destruction policies that might otherwise operate to destroy documents of a certain age. Our duty to retain documents extends to trademark licensees and related companies that may have relevant documents.

Therefore, we must immediately take steps to preserve all documents and ESI, including e-mails, word processing files, spreadsheets, databases, website iterations, electronically stored graphics, calendars, text messages, files stored on PDAs, and other electronic communication and information, pertinent to these potential proceedings so they are not deleted or destroyed pursuant to our routine document retention procedures. Documents and ESI may be stored in various locations, such as individual work stations, laptops, PDAs, cell phones, the voice mail system, home computers, company servers, backup tapes and services, and removable media. Because of our obligations, all routine document/electronic file destruction policies related to the relevant trademarks, and marketing and sale of products bearing those marks, as well as online advertising, are suspended, so that relevant evidence is not inadvertently destroyed.

This extends to all documents and ESI that might possibly be relevant to issues in the litigation or that reasonably could lead to the discovery of relevant evidence. The particular materials of relevance include (without limitation):

- Documents concerning the use, advertising, promotion and marketing of products under the marks in the United States
- Documents concerning the manufacture, distribution, and sale of products bearing the marks in the United States
- Documents concerning enforcement of rights in the marks in the United States
- Documents concerning the registration, clearance, and adoption of the marks in the United States
- Documents concerning any damage suffered or anticipated by the Company as the result of the infringement
- Documents concerning the defendant or its trademark, if any

The above list is not exhaustive, but it provides general guidelines on the types of documents that must be preserved. Any doubts about the relevance of a document or ESI should be resolved in favor of preservation.

Because severe sanctions may be imposed on parties that have not strictly observed these document retention requirements in the context of litigation, we appreciate your cooperation.

Please let us know if you have any questions or comments.

Best regards,

Associate General Counsel

FORM 10.3
Protocol for Computer Inspection

Stipulated Terms and Conditions Governing the Inspection and Imaging of Defendant's Computer

The parties have arrived at a mutually acceptable protocol for the inspection and mirror imaging of Defendant's computer. They jointly submit these proposed terms and conditions ("Inspection Order") for approval by the Court. The parties agree that this Inspection Order shall not be effective unless and until approved by the Court.

1. Plaintiff shall select a neutral, independent computer forensics expert having specific and demonstrated expertise in the field of electronic discovery ("Expert") to obtain a Mirror Image of the hard drive of the desktop computer used by Defendant to conduct its business and by Defendant's managing member for personal matters including the recordation of family, medical and financial affairs ("Computer"). As used herein, "Mirror Image" shall mean a forensic duplicate, which replicates bit for bit, sector by sector, all allocated and unallocated space, including slack space, on the computer's hard drive. The services of the Expert shall be paid by Plaintiff.

2. After the Expert has been selected, all communications between the expert and Plaintiff or its counsel shall take place either in the presence of Defendant's counsel or through written or electronic communication with a copy to Defendant's counsel. Other than the acts and services provided for herein, the Expert shall not perform any other services for Plaintiff related to this case without Defendant's express consent.

3. The Expert and any of its personnel engaged in obtaining the Mirror Image shall execute agree in writing to abide and be bound by the Protective Order already in place in this action and the Inspection Order.

4. To the extent the Expert has direct or indirect access to information protected by or on grounds of privilege, confidentiality, and/or personal privacy, such "disclosure" will not result in a waiver of such privilege, confidentiality, or privacy. Plaintiff shall not assert in this litigation that any such disclosure to the Expert constitutes any waiver by Defendant of such privilege, confidentiality, or privacy.

5. Defendant shall make the Computer available to the Expert at the office of its Counsel, at a mutually agreeable time within ten (10) days of entry of this Inspection Order. The Expert shall promptly make two (2) Mirror Images of the Computer's hard drive, a process which is expected to be completed in not more than eight (8) hours. He or she

may not remove the Computer from Counsel's office. No one other than the Expert, Defendant's managing member, and Defendant's counsel may be present during the process.

6. Once the Expert obtains the Mirror Image (and transfers such images to disks), Expert shall provide Defendant's Counsel with one set of the disk(s) in a format that readily allows the images to be printed. To the extent possible, the Expert shall also provide to Defendant's Counsel (a) the available information showing when any recovered "deleted" file was deleted, and (b) the available information about the deletion and contents of any deleted file that cannot be recovered.

7. Within thirty (30) days of the receipt of the recovered documents and data, Defendant's counsel shall review the records for privilege and responsiveness, appropriately supplement Defendant's responses to discovery requests, and send to Plaintiff's counsel all responsive and nonprivileged documents and information. Counsel shall also furnish a privilege log, which claims each privilege expressly and describes the nature of the documents, communications, or things not produced or disclosed in a manner that, without revealing information itself privileged or protected, will enable other parties to assess the applicability of the privilege or protection.

8. If Plaintiff disagrees with Defendant's privilege designation, then the parties shall present the issues to the undersigned for resolution, but only after a meeting to resolve the issues where each document is discussed. If the parties are unable to agree, then the matter may be presented by motion to the Court for resolution, and Defendant shall provide to the Court copies of the disputed documents *in camera*.

9. In addition to a privilege log, Defendant's counsel shall also furnish a log of any documents and data recovered from the Computer that refer or relate to any product bearing the mark, whether it is Defendant's or Plaintiff's trademarked brand product. This "relevance log" shall describe the nature of the documents, communications or things not produced or disclosed in a manner that, without revealing the information itself that is claimed to be irrelevant or nonresponsive, will enable Plaintiff to assess the applicability of the relevance or nonresponsiveness claim. For purposes of clarification, information relating to personal matters separate and apart from the subjects described above, including the recordation of family, medical, and financial affairs, shall not be included in the "relevance log."

10. Only the Expert and its personnel assigned to this project are authorized to inspect or otherwise handle the Computer or the Mirror Images generated. No employee of Plaintiff or its counsel will inspect or otherwise handle the Computer or the Mirror Images. The Expert will be the sole custodian of and shall retain the second set of the "Mirror Image" disk(s) in strict confidence until this proceeding and all

appeals are concluded. At the end of this litigation, the Expert shall then destroy the records and confirm such destruction to the satisfaction of Defendant of all documents retrieved from the disk(s) throughout the course of this litigation.

Dated: _____, 2010 SO ORDERED:

Response to Motion to Compel Production of Computer Records

In the United States District Court
For the Northern District of Illinois
Eastern Division

MEDICAL BILLING CONSULTANTS, INC	)	
d/b/a Medbillz.com)	)	
Plaintiff,)	)	
	)	Case No.:
v.		
	)	Hon. James B. Moran
INTELLIGENT MEDICAL OBJECTS, INC.)	)	Magistrate Judge Nan R. Nolan
Defendants	)	

Defendants' Opposition to Plaintiff MBC's Motion to Compel Inspection of Computer Records

Defendant, Intelligent Medical Objects, Inc. ("IMO"), opposes MBC's motion to compel inspection of computer records on the following grounds and request a briefing schedule to more fully address its objection to MBC's motion. In short, IMO opposes the motion because IMO has already produced the e-mail communications demanded by MBC, and MBC's demand to permit inspection of IMO's physical computer records is unreasonably broad and intrusive in requiring disclosure of irrelevant but proprietary information of IMO and its customers unrelated to this action and communications protected by the attorney-client privilege.

1. IMO has no objection to producing e-mail correspondence relating to IMO's dealings with MBC and has already searched for, collected, and produced all e-mail records reasonably available to it that appeared to be relevant and responsive to MBC's discovery demands for communications relating to MBC. Over 1500 pages of e-mail correspondence have been produced since January 2002.
2. On December 31, 2002, MBC sent a letter to IMO's counsel demanding that IMO also produce e-mail and other electronic correspondence between IMO and Dr. Smith, a former employee of IMO and current president of a non-party. The demand was not limited to communications relating to MBC. MBC demanded that the

e-mails be provided within two weeks. *See* Declaration of Sam Davis. In Support of Plaintiff MBC's Motion to Compel Inspection of Computer Records ("Davis Decl.") Ex. A.

3. On January 7, 2003, during a discovery conference, IMO's counsel told MBC that it appeared the demand for e-mail communications with Dr. Smith after his employment involved a new demand that would take additional time. IMO's counsel agreed to search for such e-mail communications and expected to produce them in 30 days as permitted by the Federal Rules.

4. IMO and its counsel needed adequate time to search for the requested e-mail, due in part to the other demands of this case, including its response to the Rule 56(f) motion on January 3, 2003; preparation for and attendance at a settlement conference held on January 15, 2003; reaction to the subpoenas served by MBC on over 50 of IMO's customers and business relations on January 20 and 21, 2003; as well as other matters.

5. IMO's agreement to produce the e-mail communications is noted in MBC's letter of January 17, 2003, insisting on a substantive response to the demand no later than January 22, 2003. (Davis Decl. Ex. B.).

6. On January 20, 2003, IMO wrote MBC again stating that it intended to respond to the request for the Almeida e-mail communications by January 30, 2003. (Davis Decl. Ex. C.).

7. On January 27, 2003, during a discovery conference, IMO's counsel again informed MBC's attorneys that it would produce the Smith e-mails later that week.

8. On January 28, 2003, IMO's counsel wrote MBC stating that:

The requested e-mail communications have now been gathered and are available for your inspection and copying. It appears these e-mail communications primarily involve Dr. Smith's terms of severance and matters relating to work for other clients. We therefore object to your demand on the grounds that the documents are not relevant to the Medbillz project or responsive to any properly framed production demand. We also object to the demand to the extent it seeks disclosure of confidential business information or trade secrets of IMO or third parties. Nevertheless, without waiving those objection or any previously stated objections, these documents will be made available to you for inspection at our offices beginning Wednesday, January 29, 2003, at a mutually convenient time, once we have received written agreement from you that documents identified as Attorney's Eyes Only will be disclosed only to counsel of record in this case and will not be used for any purpose other than this lawsuit (emphasis added).

(Davis Decl. Ex. E.).

9. On January 30, 2003, IMO counsel wrote MBC's counsel identifying by Bates number the Smith e-mail communications available for inspection. *See* Exhibit A attached hereto.

10. Notwithstanding IMO's offer to produce the Smith e-mail documents on January 29, 2003, MBC did not contact IMO to make any arrangements to review or copy the documents. Instead, IMO received MBC's motion on January 31, 2003, incorrectly claiming that IMO has refused to produce e-mail communications relating to MBC. In fact, IMO has already produced such e-mail communications. Regrettably, if MBC had reviewed the production of e-mail communications prior to filing this motion it would have learned that the production included the e-mail communication (IMO 06195), which MBC incorrectly claims has never been produced. *See* (Davis Decl. Ex. H.).

11. IMO has made a good faith effort to respond to MBC's numerous and quite burdensome demands for the production of documents. After conducting several searches of its records, IMO believes all relevant and discoverable e-mail communications relating to MBC have been produced. It also is willing to conduct further searches to address specific concerns of MBC.

12. IMO does object to MBC's demand to permit inspection of physical computer records by an MBC forensic expert. As a computer software consultant, developer and licensor, IMO's business involves the use of many computers containing trade secrets and confidential business information for many clients and others. MBC has not previously presented any formal discovery request to permit such inspection. The demand as framed by MBC in its motion to compel, seeking inspection of "any servers, hard drives and any other data storage media used by defendants from their first meeting with MBC until this litigation was initiated," is objected to for many reasons:

   (a) The demand seeks disclosure of information that is irrelevant to the lawsuit in that it would require disclosure of information regarding work of clients unrelated to this dispute, seeks disclosure of trade secrets or other confidential business information that is unrelated to this dispute, and also would require disclosure of communications protected by the attorney-client privilege.

   (b) The demand is too broad in seeking inspection of all computers and data storage devices used from later 1999 when IMO first met with MBC to later 2001 when MBC filed this suit.

   (c) The demand is unduly burdensome on IMO's business operations given that IMO has already conducted searches for requested electronic documents on its computers and has produced thousands of pages of such documents, including the documents maintained in its computer records for the work on the MBC project. Given that extensive production, it is unlikely that any material information would be uncovered by the burdensome interference caused by the direct inspection of IMO's computer records by MBC's forensic expert.

WHEREFORE, MBC's motion to compel should be denied. IMO received MBC's motion to compel on January 31, 2003, and requests additional briefing time to respond more fully with legal memoranda and affidavits to support its opposition to MBC's motion to compel inspection of computer records.

Respectfully submitted,

Deposition of a Corporate IT Representative

Below is a list of deposition topics for a 30(b)(6) deposition notice to assess a party's efforts to preserve and produce ESI.

1. The hardware and software used to create ESI
2. The storage, retention and gathering of ESI
3. Any policies and procedures related to the maintenance and management of ESI.
4. Employees responsible for the maintenance and management of ESI
5. Efforts taken to respond to any litigation hold letter issued in this lawsuit

These topics represent general areas for exploring the other side's compliance with its electronic discovery obligations.

Deposition Questions for Custodian of ESI

Deposing a party's ESI custodian is the best method to assess a party's compliance with its discovery obligations concerning ESI. In preparing to depose a party's 30(b)(6) representative for maintaining ESI, an outline of topics and questions is essential. Below are specific topics to address and questions to ask during such a deposition that can be incorporated into a 30(b)(6) deposition outline.

FORM 10.5
ESI Deposition Outline

I. Explore deponent's background, role and responsibilities
    A. If deponent is not responsible for managing the company's ESI, ask why he/she has been produced in response to the 30(b)(6) notice on topics related to ESI.
    B. Ask which topics the deponent is addressing from the 30(b)(6) notice.
II. Information Technology (IT) Department General Information
    A. Describe your IT department.
        1. What is the structure of the IT department?
        2. Who is the head of the IT department (CIO)?
        3. Are there any outside vendors that provide IT services to your company? If yes,
            a) what are their responsibilities?
            b) who is your primary contact at [vendor]?
            c) how are they involved in managing your company's electronic information?
        4. What is the relationship of the IT department to the legal department?
III. Handling of ESI
    A. How is electronic information typically stored and saved by the company?
        1. Is there a document management system?
            a) Describe it.
        2. Where is information stored?
            a) Centralized on servers?
            b) Decentralized on individual work stations?
    (1) It is theoretically possible that people could store documents on their local computers.
            c) How are general business records stored?
                (1) Paper?
                (2) Electronic?
    B. Does the company have a policy for managing ESI?
        1. [If written policy already produced, explore this topic through the document and ask the below questions in reference to the written policy].
        2. Describe the policy.
            a) How was it implemented in this case?
            b) Who was responsible for implementing it [ask about any e-mails or letters, e.g., litigation holds, sent to employees to preserve and maintain ESI]?

        c) Is there a document destruction policy?
          (1) Are e-mails ever automatically deleted?
            (a) What is the schedule?
            (b) How was this determined?

3. What does the company typically do to preserve and maintain its ESI when it reasonably anticipates litigation?
    a) What did the company do to preserve and maintain its ESI in this case?
    b) Who was involved?
    c) What were their roles?
    d) What was your role?

4. How are employees contacted when it is necessary to preserve and maintain ESI?
    a) How did you learn about the need to preserve and maintain ESI in this case?
    b) Who contacted you?
      (1) Explore.
    c) Who did you contact?
      (1) Identify each person contacted and their titles.
    d) How did you contact these people?

5. When the legal department needs to gather ESI, what steps are taken to involve the IT department?
    a) What steps were taken in this case?
    b) Who was involved?

IV. Location of ESI
  A. Describe your company's computer systems.
    1. What kind of hardware does your company use?
      a) Work computers.
      b) Networking/servers.
        (1) Co-location site?
        (2) Cloud-based storage or Software as a Service (SaaS) implementations?
      c) Removable storage.
      d) Home computers—are employees permitted to use them for work?
        (1) How are files transferred from a home computer to a work computer?
        (2) Is access from home tracked?
          (a) Produce logs.
          e) PDAs/Smartphones.
          f) Voice mail.
          g) Backup disks/tapes.
          h) Anything else?

2. What kind of software does your company use?
   a) Operating system.
   b) Office productivity suite.
   c) Document management, including restoration software.
   d) E-mail.
   e) Instant Messaging.
   f) Financial/Accounting.
   g) Databases.
   h) Collaboration applications.
   i) Employee monitoring, e.g., keystroke monitoring, web tracking, time tracking.
   j) Customer relations management software [especially useful in trademark cases].
   k) Desktop publishing.
   l) Graphics.
   m) Anything else?
3. Describe your company's Internet access policy for employees.
   a) Are logs maintained?
4. Any industry specific hardware or software systems?
   a) Explore their functionality with an eye toward identifying systems that could be mined for information.
5. Backup systems
   a) Describe your company's backup systems.
      (1) What is backed up?
   (a) Anything else?
      (2) How?
      (3) When?
      (4) Who is responsible or is it automated?
      (5) Where is backed up information stored?
   b) How are backed up files restored?
      (1) How much does it cost?
      (2) How long does it take?
V. Company website
   A. When did your company website first go live?
   B. Who designed it?
   C. Who provided the content?
   D. Who oversees website content?
   E. Are past iterations of the website preserved?
      1. How?
      2. Where?
      3. By whom?
   F. Does the content need to be approved by anyone?
      1. Who?
   G. Describe the functionality of the website.

H. What information can be obtained from the website?
I. Does the company post content to websites other than its own [e.g., Facebook, YouTube, blogs]?
   1. To what other websites does it post content?
   2. What type of content?
   3. Why does it post this content to these websites?
   4. Who is responsible for this content?
J. Does the company have a blog separate from its website?
K. Does the company host or participate in chats online?
   1. Where?
   2. When?
   3. Who participates?
   4. Are logs kept?
L. Does the company have an Intranet?
   1. What is on the Intranet?
   2. Who is responsible for it?
   3. Who has access to it?

APPENDIX A

Sun Life - A Case Study in Discovery Disputes

In the United States District Court for the Northern District of Georgia Atlanta Division

SUNAMERICA CORPORATION (formerly SUN LIFE GROUP OF AMERICA, INC., a Delaware corporation, and SUN LIFE INSURANCE COMPANY OF AMERICA, INC., a Maryland corporation, Plaintiffs,	)
v.	) CIVIL ACTION) FILE NO.
SUN LIFE ASSURANCE COMPANY OF CANADA, a Canadian corporation, and SUN LIFE ASSURANCE COMPANY OF CANADA (U.S.), a Delaware corporation, Defendants.	) 1:89-CV-1315-JTC)))))

Defendants' Motion to Compel Discovery

Defendants-counterclaimants, Sun Life Assurance Company of Canada and Sun Life Assurance Company of Canada (U.S.), hereby move this Court, pursuant to Rule 37 of the Federal Rules of Civil Procedure and Rule 225-4 of the Local Rules of this Court, for an Order compelling plaintiffs to provide answers and produce documents in response to the Interrogatories and Document Requests set forth in the Memorandum In Support Of Defendants' Motion To Compel Discovery filed concurrently herewith. Defendants-counterclaimants further request that they be allowed a reasonable period of time in which to take any necessary discovery relating to plaintiffs' belated interrogatory answers and production of documents.

In support of this motion, defendants submit the aforesaid Memorandum and the attached Certification Of Counsel Pursuant To Local Rule 225-4(b).

Certification of Counsel Pursuant to Local Rule 225-4(b)

My name is David C. Hilliard. I am a member of the bar of the State of Illinois and am a partner in the law firm Pattishall, McAuliffe, Newbury, Hilliard & Geraldson. I am lead counsel in this action and submit this Certification pursuant to Local Rule 225-4(b) and in support of Defendants' Motion To Compel Discovery.

I hereby certify that I have conferred with opposing counsel in a good-faith attempt to resolve by agreement the controversies reflected in Defendants' Motion To Compel Discovery but was unable to do so. Defendants' counsel has on numerous occasions stated that some or all of the documents and information sought in the Motion To Compel will be provided, but to date none of it has been. Since November 5 marks the close of discovery, defendants cannot wait any longer for the requested documents and interrogatory answers and must file the Motion To Compel in order to protect their position. However, in the event that further documents and answers are subsequently provided by plaintiffs that render moot any or all of the issues raised in the Motion To Compel, defendants will promptly withdraw the Motion as to any and all such issues that are rendered moot.

Memorandum in Support of Defendants' Motion To Compel Discovery

***

The disputes that have given rise to this motion to compel, however, are not, as far as we are aware, based on any of the objections filed by plaintiffs. Rather, this motion to compel seeks an Order requiring plaintiffs to provide interrogatory answers and documents that they have specifically undertaken to provide but so far have not provided.

***

Argument

The purpose of modern pretrial discovery is the disclosure of facts "to the fullest practicable extent." *United States v. Proctor & Gamble Co.,* 356 U.S. 677, 682, (1988); *Dollar v. Long. Mfg.,* 561 F.2d 613, 616 (5th Cir. 1977). Discovery procedures under the Federal Rules of Civil Procedure constitute "a liberal and integrated scheme for the full disclosure of relevant information." *Osterneck v. Barwick Industries, Inc.,* 82 F.R.D. 81, 84 (N.D. Ga. 1979).

Under Rule 37(a)(3) of the Federal Rules, an evasive or incomplete answer is to be treated as a failure to answer. It is well established, moreover, that the courts have wide latitude in requiring further answers to discovery requests. *Roberson v. Great American Insurance Companies of New York,* 48 F.R.D. 404, 410 (N.D. Ga. 1969).

Set forth below is the full text of each of the Interrogatories and Document Requests as to which defendants seek an Order compelling discovery. In each instance, the text of the Interrogatory or Request is followed by a brief statement of the reasons that defendants believe they are entitled to an Order compelling production of the answers or documents called for. For the sake of brevity, some of the Interrogatories and Document Requests are set forth in groups, followed by a statement of grounds supporting the motion that are applicable to all of the Interrogatories or Requests in the group.

Interrogatory Nos. 9 and 17

The text of Interrogatory Nos. 9 and 17 is set forth below:

Interrogatory No. 9. "With reference to the allegation in paragraph 48 of your Complaint that 'Plaintiffs have been and will be required to expend significant time, effort, and money on corrective efforts and advertising in order to maintain the good will of Plaintiffs' marks":

Describe in detail the corrective advertising in which you have engaged and in which you plan to engage;

Provide the exact amount of money you have expended and plan to expend on corrective advertising and describe the method by which you calculated such amount;

Identify the marks referred to;

Identify all representative samples, written communications, records of oral communications, and other documents upon which you rely in support of this allegation; and

Identify the persons who are most knowledgeable concerning the subject matter of this interrogatory."

Interrogatory No. 17. "Describe in detail the damages which you contend you are entitled to in this action, describe the manner of calculation, and identify all documents, including, but not limited to, any damages studies, which support your allegation that you are entitled to damages or which analyze the extent of your alleged damages."

Plaintiffs originally refused to answer Interrogatory Nos. 9 and 17 at all, on the ground that defendants' Interrogatories, including subparts, allegedly exceeded the limit of 40 specified in Local Rule 225-2. Plaintiffs took the position that they were free to refuse to answer any interrogatories they wished, as long as they were equal in number to the alleged excess over 40. Defendants disputed plaintiffs' claim that the Interrogatories exceeded the limit, as well as their claimed right thus to select Interrogatories that they would not answer.

As a result of a discovery conference held by counsel for the parties in November 1989 with respect to deficiencies claimed by defendants concerning plaintiffs' discovery responses as of that time, plaintiffs agreed to answer Interrogatories 9 and 17. That agreement was memorialized in an exchange of letters between counsel. . .

Defendants are entitled to answers to these important Interrogatories, both of which go to the issue of damages claimed by plaintiffs in this case. Indeed, plaintiffs have included an entire separate count in their Complaint (Count V), entitled "Damages For Corrective Advertising And Remedial Actions," asserting claims for damages that are addressed specifically by Interrogatory 9 and more generally by Interrogatory 17. In addition, plaintiffs make the extraordinary claim that they are entitled to recover from defendants the purchase price, in excess of $1,000,000, which plaintiffs recently paid to acquire from a third party, rights in the SUNAMERICA name. This claim, as well as all other claims for damages, are addressed by Interrogatory 17. Plaintiffs cannot, we submit, make such unusual damages claims and at the same time expect to avoid all discovery concerning them.

Second Document Request No. 4

The text of defendants' Second Document Request No. 4 is set forth below:

Second Document Request No. 4. "All documents which refer or relate to any discontinuance of the sale or provision, or to any consideration given to discontinuing the sale or provision of any product or service in connection with which plaintiffs have used any name or mark consisting in whole or in part of the word 'sun.'"

Subject to their General Objections, plaintiffs agreed to produce documents responsive to this Request. However, other than annual reports in which reference is made to the fact that plaintiffs have sold off their traditional life insurance businesses, plaintiffs have produced no documents in response to Second Request No. 4. It hardly seems possible, however, that no such documents exist, given the established fact that plaintiffs have sold off their prior life insurance business to Durham Life, Savers' Life and other life insurance companies. There must be, inter alia, correspondence with the purchasers and potential purchasers, agreements with the purchasers, and internal memoranda relating to these sales of SUNAMERICA's life insurance business. Yet no such documents have been produced to defendants.

Second Document Request No. 10

The text of defendants' Second Document Request No. 4 is set forth below:

Second Document Request No. 10. "All documents which refer or relate to any decision to discontinue sales or to any consideration of discontinuing sales of life insurance or any life insurance product."

Subject to their General Objections, plaintiffs agreed to produce documents responsive to this Request. However, other than annual reports in which reference is made to the fact that plaintiffs have ceased selling life insurance products, plaintiffs have produced no documents in response to Second Request No. 10. Plaintiffs have admitted, however, that within the past few years, they made decisions to discontinue sales of all life insurance products, including single-premium life insurance products. It is simply not credible that plaintiffs would have no documents relating to such important decisions.

***

****

SUNAMERICA CORPORATION (formerly) SUN LIFE   )
GROUP OF AMERICA, INC.),) a Delaware corporation,
and SUN) LIFE INSURANCE COMPANY OF
AMERICA,) INC., a Maryland corporation,)

)

Plaintiffs,   )

)

v.   ) CIVIL ACTION FILE
) NO. 1:89-CV-1315-JTC

SUN LIFE ASSURANCE COMPANY OF   )
CANADA, a Canadian corporation,   )
and SUN LIFE ASSURANCE COMPANY OF)   )
CANADA (U.S.), a Delaware   )
corporation,   )

)

Defendants.   )

)

Plaintiffs' Response to Defendants' Motion to Compel Discovery

***

Procedural History of the Case

. . . on November 5, 1990, the last day of discovery, [Defendants] filed the
present motion. . . The Motion to Compel. . . states Defendants' objections to
the sufficiency of Plaintiffs' production in only the vaguest of terms. Therefore,
it is virtually impossible for Plaintiffs to determine exactly what deficiencies
Defendants believe exist in the documents produced. To a large degree,
it appears that Defendants are unhappy with the fact that the documents
produced do not support Defendants' theories rather than with any failure to
produce relevant documents.

    . . . Plaintiffs assert that to the extent Defendants move to compel additional
discovery regarding Defendants' first interrogatories and first document
requests, such a motion should be denied as untimely inasmuch as
Defendants, by their tardiness, have waived any objections to Plaintiffs'
responses.

    With respect to Defendants' second document requests, Plaintiffs assert that
many of Defendants' second document requests are unnecessarily duplicative
of Defendants' first document requests or are so broad as to encompass
virtually every document in the possession of Plaintiffs. Further, to the extent
such documents exist, Plaintiffs believe they have produced all the documents

responsive to Defendants' second document requests that are in Plaintiffs' possession, custody, or control other than those which were subject to earlier agreements narrowing the scope of such requests.

***

Argument and Citation of Authorities

A. Applicable Legal Standards

Local Rule 225-4(a) requires opposing counsel to "make a good faith effort to resolve by agreement among themselves any disputes which arise in the course of discovery." As stated by Judge Pollack of the United States District Court for the Eastern District of Pennsylvania, a rule requiring the parties to confer prior to filing a motion to compel and to so certify in such a motion

> is not merely a formalistic requirement developed by [the courts] to increase the volume of each discovery motion filed. It was intended to reduce the unnecessary burden on the court and added expense to the parties caused by the expectation that the court would interject itself in minor pretrial skirmishes.
>
> * * *
>
> Discovery disputes should not be referred to the court unless such serious differences exist between counsel that further efforts at negotiations are pointless or unless court intervention is necessary to resolve a disputed issue of law.

Crown Cork & Seal Company, Inc. v. Chemed Corp., 101 F.R.D. 105, 106–07 (E.D. Pa. 1984). In *Crown Cork,* the defendant's motion to compel was denied where the only evidence that counsel for the parties had conferred was a letter from defendant's counsel inquiring as to the availability of nine witnesses for depositions followed by a series of telephone calls between counsels' secretaries.

Similarly, in *Madden v. Cleland,* 105 F.R.D. 520, 526 (N.D. Ga. 1985), Judge Vining denied the defendants' motion to compel where the defendants' counsel failed to consult with the plaintiff's counsel prior to filing the motion and the defendants' counsel failed to include a Certification of Counsel as required by Local Rule 225-4(b).

B. Defendants Have Waived Their Right to Additional Discovery With Respect to Their Interrogatories and First Requests for Production of Documents and Things

With respect to Defendants' First Interrogatories and Requests for Production of Documents and Things, the parties held a discovery conference (which lasted the entire afternoon) on November 21, 1989, at Defendants' request to discuss Plaintiffs' objections and responses. At that conference, counsel for the parties reviewed each and every interrogatory and document request served by Defendants and Plaintiffs' objections and responses thereto in excruciating detail. . . Plaintiffs' counsel believed fully fulfilled their part of the agreement reached at the discovery conference. . .Defendants now assert that these responses were incomplete.

C. Defendants' Second Document Are Overbroad and Duplicative and Defendants Motion to Compel Is Unjustified

Despite Plaintiffs' production of an enormous number of documents pursuant to Defendants' first document requests, Defendants served a second set of document requests. Many of these second document requests were repetitive and merely duplicated previous requests. In fact, Defendants concede in their memorandum in support of their Motion to Compel that second document request 38 merely duplicates first document request 18. Furthermore, many of Defendants' second document requests were vaguely drafted and excessively broad in scope. However, subject to these objections, Plaintiffs have produced a large volume of documents responsive to Defendants' second document requests.

Plaintiffs believe they have produced all documents in the possession, custody, or control that are responsive to Defendants' second document requests. To the extent Defendants contend otherwise, Plaintiffs show that the parties might be able to settle their dispute without the intervention of the Court if the Defendants would participate in a discovery conference in good faith and would specifically identify any documents they believe have not been produced which were not the subject of the prior agreement between the parties regarding the scope of such requests. Accordingly, Defendants' motion to compel with respect to Plaintiffs' responses to Defendants' second document requests should be denied. Plaintiffs respectfully suggest that Defendants' counsel should participate in a discovery conference in good faith with respect to Defendants' second document requests if they believe there are specifically identifiable documents that are appropriately subject to discovery and have not been produced.

In the United States District Court for the Northern District of Georgia Atlanta Division

SUNAMERICA CORPORATION (formerly SUN LIFE GROUP OF AMERICA, INC.), a Delaware corporation, and SUN LIFE INSURANCE COMPANY OF AMERICA, INC., a Maryland corporation, Plaintiffs, v. SUN LIFE ASSURANCE COMPANY OF CANADA, a Canadian corporation, and SUN LIFE ASSURANCE COMPANY OF CANADA (U.S.), a Delaware corporation, Defendants.	))))))))) CIVIL ACTION FILE NO.) 1:89-CV-1315-JTC))))))))

Order of Court

. . . Defendants' Motion to Compel is GRANTED. . .

Defendants have also moved to compel discovery. Defendants seek to compel responses to Interrogatories and a First Set of Document Requests served by defendants on August 15, 1989, and a Second Set of Document Requests served by defendants on June 13, 1990. Defendants notified plaintiffs on October 27, 1990, of the interrogatories and requests that had not yet been answered. Defendants correspondingly filed this Motion to Compel on November 5, 1990.

In response, plaintiffs claim that defendants' requests under the Interrogatories and First Set of Document Requests have already been addressed and are now untimely. Plaintiffs claim the defendants' Second Set of Document Requests are overly broad and duplicative of the earlier request. Plaintiffs claim that defendants should participate in a discovery conference to resolve these issues.

The Court finds that plaintiffs have an obligation to comply fully with defendants' discovery requests. Conclusory objections of untimeliness, overbreadth, or the need for a discovery conference do not limit plaintiffs' discovery obligations. The Court hereby ORDERS the plaintiffs to fully respond to defendants' discovery requests. Defendants' Motion to Compel is GRANTED.

In the United States District Court for the Northern District of Georgia Atlanta Division

SUNAMERICA CORPORATION	)
(formerly SUN LIFE GROUP OF	)
AMERICA, INC.), a Delaware	)
corporation, and SUN LIFE	)
INSURANCE COMPANY OF AMERICA,	)
INC., a Maryland corporation	)
Plaintiffs and	)
Counterdefendants,	)
v.	)
SUNLIFE ASSURANCE COMPANY OF	)
CANADA, a Canadian corporation,	)
and SUN LIFE ASSURANCE COMPANY	)
OF CANADA (U.S.), a Delaware	)
corporation,	)
	)
Defendants and	)
Counterclaimants.	)

Defendants' Motion for Order Admitting Requests for Admissions

Defendants-counterclaimants, Sun Life Assurance Company of Canada and Sun Life Assurance Company of Canada (U.S.), hereby move this Court, pursuant to Rule 36 of the Federal Rules of Civil Procedure and Rule 225-4 of the Local Rules of this Court to determine the sufficiency of Plaintiffs' Response To Defendants Requests For Admissions (Set II), as set forth in the Memorandum In Support Of Defendants' Motion For Order Admitting Requests For Admission filed concurrently herewith, and to order that the identified requests are admitted or, in the alternative, that plaintiffs be required to serve amended responses.

***

Memorandum in Support of Defendants' Motion for Order Admitting Requests for Admissions

As is more fully set forth below, in responding to numerous requests set forth in Defendants' Requests for Admissions (Set II), plaintiffs have failed to make the reasonable inquiry required by Rule 36 of the Federal Rules of Civil Procedure and, if admissions are not made, defendants will be required to incur the expense of taking many third-party depositions to establish what should not be contested facts. Defendants have advised plaintiffs in writing that defendants' investigation establishes the facts as to which admissions are sought, and have provided them in writing with the necessary information to enable them easily to confirm those facts. Defendants therefore have moved for an order admitting those requests or, in the alternative, that plaintiffs be ordered to amend their responses. The grounds for defendants' motion are as follows:

1. In this action, plaintiffs contend that defendants' use of names and marks containing the word "Sun" for insurance and annuity products and services infringes plaintiffs' use of marks containing the word "Sun" for similar products and services.

2. Attached as Exhibit A is a copy of defendants' second set of request for admissions concerning various third party names and marks containing the word "Sun" for insurance and annuity-related products and services.[1] The requests deal with current use of such names and marks, acquiescence by plaintiffs to such use, and related matters.

3. The existence of third-party uses and registrations of similar marks is commonly part of the likelihood of confusion analysis in trademark infringement cases, and the relevance of defendants' requests therefore is indisputable. *See, e.g.* McCarthy, *Trademarks* and *Sun Banks of Florida, Inc. v. Sun Federal Savings and Loan Association,* 651 F.2d 313, 316 (5th Cir. 1981) ("we find the extensive third party use of the word 'Sun' impressive evidence that there would be no likelihood of confusion between Sun Banks and Sun Federal").

4. Defendants have conducted investigations to verify current use and addresses for the third party uses listed in Defendants' Requests and to obtain some of the specimens attached to Defendants' Requests as exhibits. Long prior to the due date for plaintiffs' responses to the Request for Admissions (Set II), defendants provided plaintiffs with an accurate list of current third-party addresses and telephone numbers that defendants, through their investigation, had compiled in connection with the requests, cross-tabulated with the corresponding requests for admission. . .

5. Long prior to the due date for plaintiffs' responses, defendants also informed plaintiffs of their duty to make a reasonable inquiry, including contacting third parties, and cited to them a decision by the Northern District of Georgia, *Ranger Insurance Co. v. Culberson,* 49 F.R.D. 181, 183 (N.A. Ga. 1969).

---

1. The parties have resolved the other issues presented in the Expedited Motion for a Scheduling Order. *See* Joint Motion for a Scheduling Order (approved by the Court on October 30, 1990). However, Defendants recently renoticed Mr. Broad's deposition.